T0398804

STAGING THE PENINSULAR WAR

From Napoleon's invasion of Portugal in 1807 to his final defeat at Waterloo, the English theatres played a crucial role in the mediation of the Peninsular campaign. In the first in-depth study of English theatre during the Peninsular War, Susan Valladares contextualises the theatrical treatment of the war within the larger political and ideological axes of Romantic performance. Exploring the role of spectacle in the mediation of war and the links between theatrical productions and print culture, she argues that the popularity of theatre-going and the improvisation and topicality unique to dramatic performance make the theatre an ideal lens for studying the construction of the Peninsular War in the public domain. Without simplifying the complex issues involved in the study of citizenship, communal identities, and ideological investments, Valladares recovers a wartime theatre that helped celebrate military engagements, reform political sympathies, and register the public's complex relationship with Britain's military campaign in the Iberian Peninsula. From its nuanced reading of Richard Brinsley Sheridan's *Pizarro* (1799), to its accounts of wartime productions of Shakespeare, description of performances at the minor theatres, and detailed case study of dramatic culture in Bristol, Valladares's book reveals how theatrical entertainments reflected and helped shape public feeling on the Peninsular campaign.

For Pollyana and Eric,
with all my love

Staging the Peninsular War

English Theatres 1807–1815

SUSAN VALLADARES

Worcester College, University of Oxford, UK

ASHGATE

Published by
Ashgate Publishing Limited
Wey Court East
Union Road
Farnham
Surrey, GU9 7PT
England

Ashgate Publishing Company
110 Cherry Street
Suite 3-1
Burlington, VT 05401-3818
USA

www.ashgate.com

British Library Cataloguing in Publication Data
A catalogue record for this book is available from the British Library.

The Library of Congress has cataloged the printed edition as follows:
Valladares, Susan, 1985-
  Staging the Peninsular War: English theatres 1807–1815 / by Susan Valladares.
    pages cm
  Includes bibliographical references and index.
  ISBN 978-1-4724-1863-0 (hardcover) – ISBN 978-1-4724-1864-7 (ebook) – ISBN 978-1-4724-1865-4 (epub) 1. Theater–England–History–19th century. 2. Peninsular War, 1807-1814–Literature and the war. 3. English drama–19th century–History and criticism. 4. War in literature. 5. Soldiers in literature. I. Title.
  PN2594.V35 2015
  792.0941'09034--dc23

2015002613

ISBN: 9781472418630 (hbk)
ISBN: 9781472418647 (ebk – PDF)
ISBN: 9781472418654 (ebk – ePUB)

MIX
Paper from
responsible sources
FSC® C013985
www.fsc.org

Printed in the United Kingdom by Henry Ling Limited, at the Dorset Press, Dorchester, DT1 1HD

Contents

List of Figures

Acknowledgements

Thank *you* for picking up this book. I hope you enjoy reading it. The years of its making have been graced by acts of generosity and kindness far greater than I could ever have imagined.

This book began as a doctoral thesis at the University of Oxford, where I received invaluable financial assistance from the Arts and Humanities Research Council, Oriel (and subsequently Worcester) College, the English Faculty, Santander, the British Association for Romantic Studies and the Society for Theatre Research. I am grateful to the librarians, archivists and curators who welcomed me into their reading rooms; and to Eduardo Caparó, from the Biblioteca Nacional del Perú, and Jill Gage, from the Newberry Library in Chicago, who gave me 'virtual' access to their collections. Thanks to Paulo Tremoceiro for his excellent tour of the Arquivo Nacional da Torre do Tombo; Heather Romaine and her team at the University of Bristol's Theatre Collection for creating such a calm, relaxed working environment; and Jane Bradley at Bristol Central Reference Library for her kind assistance. Marcus Risdell's expert knowledge and delightful stories involving mountains and ukuleles ensured that my visits to the Garrick Club were always occasions that I eagerly looked forward to. Thanks, also, to all the staff at the Bodleian Libraries; especially Edmond Annonce, for invariably greeting me with a smile; Ernesto Gomez, for his cheerful encouragement throughout; and Colin Harris for being a dear friend.

I was first introduced to the pleasures of Romantic-period theatre by Jane Moody. She has left a legacy that is as brilliant personally as it is academically, and remains an important source of light in my life. Fiona Stafford has supported this project's development from doctoral thesis to book with a buoyancy and dedication for which I will always be grateful. Much more than a supervisor, Fiona continues to be tremendously generous with her knowledge, time and friendship. This book's strengths, Fiona, are undoubtedly yours – its weaknesses my own. Diego Saglia and Nicholas Halmi were model examiners who made the viva a truly enjoyable experience. I offer them my warmest thanks. I am also grateful to this book's readers, who responded to earlier versions with shrewd, insightful comments. *Caro* Diego, thank you for *all* your help in shaping this book; and *chevalier* Steve, thank you for always offering your support from the sidelines. Deep thanks, also, to my commissioning editor, Ann Donahue, who has overseen this book's publication with such incisiveness, kind attention and patience.

I am indebted to Stephen G. Williams, Laura Ashe and Faith Binckes for the opportunity to complete this book in the beautiful surroundings of Worcester College, where I have benefitted from the amiability, intellectual curiosity and generosity of new colleagues. Glenn Black has supported me throughout my academic career with steady encouragement – and the perfect 'master plan'. I am grateful to Marjory Szurko, for her always affectionate support; Paulina Kewes and Andrew McNeillie for their enthusiasm for this book; Femi Oyebode, for poems and friendship; Maria de Deus Duarte for making CETAPS such a congenial research base; James Grande, for introducing me to the Cobbett papers; Fernando Durán López for keeping in touch; and to Bob Malloy, for a generous and wholly unexpected gift as the manuscript of this book reached its final stages of preparation.

I am grateful to the members of the Anglo-Hispanic Horizons network – *queridos* Diego Saglia, Ian Haywood, Agustín Coletes Blanco, Alicia Laspra Rodríguez and Graciela Iglesias Rogers – for stimulating conversations and much solidarity. Thank you, also, to Sally Paley, Chris Sutherns, Julie Cochrane, Tricia Buckingham and Helen Gilio for their help in securing the reproduction rights for the illustrations included in this book. My special thanks to the production team at Ashgate for bringing these words to both page and screen; and to Ally Bethiaume, Patrick Smith and Nikki Selmes, especially, for supervising the entire process with such professionalism and kindness.

On an even more personal note, I am grateful to James Plumtree for his intellectual encouragement, unparalleled thoughtfulness and *carinho*; Charlotte Hobbs, 'history buddy' *extraordinaire*, for being such a true friend; Kiran Hinds, for the loving, gentle push that I needed to pursue this dream; Malihe Tabatabaie, for reminding me to be kind to both the book and myself; Natalie McDonald, for being such a good listener; Tomoe Kumojima, for her genial smile; Alice Violet, for her wonderful camaraderie; Rhea Ramnarine, for believing in me; and Meiko O'Halloran, for genuine friendship since our first acquaintance.

Thank you to my family – for everything. Mãeinha, I shall always treasure the memory of watching my first play with you at the small theatre in Catete (*começa, começa*) and the delightful afternoon that we spent together at the Real Gabinete Português de Leitura – thank you for keeping me focused on what matters the most. Tia Jô is never far from my heart. Tia Gloria, thank you for a love of books that makes the world a brighter place, and for a greatness of spirit that continues to take me by surprise. Tia Bibi, thank you for always knowing how to make me laugh and enjoy 'the lightness of being' (be it driving a *Fusca*, watching films together, or simply sharing stories). Uncle Bob, thank you, above all, for your loving patience. Tio Tadeu, thank you for the books and newspaper clippings. Vó Mita, thank you for making me feel so loved. Tio Nemézio, thank you for unconditional love (and the honour of being your *princesa*).

My mum, Pollyana, has been this book's most willing and most careful reader. To look back upon this book's trajectory is to relive precious memories of happiness shared with her and my brother, Eric. From reading those all-important e-mails at Guildford bus station, to finding 'the Fernando Pessoa bench' at Worcester College and learning to jump the waves (and swim) at Leme beach, Mum and Eric, you have nurtured this book in more ways than I can number. Thank you for your untiring confidence in me: *sem vocês eu nada sou*. I dedicate this book to you both, with all my love.

List of Abbreviations

AA	Astley's Amphitheatre
BCRL	Bristol Central Reference Library
BG	*The Bristol Gazette*
BM	*The Bristol Mirror*
BTR	Bristol Theatre Royal
CC	*The Collected Works of Samuel Taylor Coleridge*, edited by Kathleen Coburn *et al*. 16 vols. Princeton: Princeton University Press, 1969–2001
CG	Covent Garden Theatre
DL	Drury Lane Theatre
DW	*The Dramatic Works of Richard Brinsley Sheridan*, edited by Cecil Price. 2 vols. Oxford: Clarendon Press, 1973
EOT	*Essays On His Own Times in 'The Morning Post' and 'The Courier'*, edited by David V. Erdman. 3 vols. Princeton: Princeton University Press, 1978
ER	*The Edinburgh Review*
FFBJ	*Felix Farley's Bristol Journal*
KB/ 4/4	'Theatre Royal References (September 1805–August 1814)', Kathleen Barker Archive, University of Bristol Theatre Collection
KB/ 21/1	'Regency Theatre', Kathleen Barker Archive, University of Bristol Theatre Collection
LMA	London Metropolitan Archives
MC	*The Morning Chronicle*
MM	*The Monthly Mirror: Reflecting Men and Manners*
MP	*The Morning Post*
MR	*The Monthly Review; or, Literary Journal*
PH	*The Parliamentary History of England, from the Earliest Period to the Year 1803*, edited by T.C. Hansard. 36 vols. London, 1806–1820
SP	Sans Pareil Theatre
TB	*The True Briton*
TE	*The Theatrical Examiner*
V&A	Victoria & Albert Theatre Museum Collection

Introduction

On Saturday, 23 January 1813, London's winter patent theatres were both staging new plays. Drury Lane had been advertising Samuel Taylor Coleridge's *Remorse* for the past week. Its characters were to consist of 'Spaniards' and 'Moors', there would be 'An Invocation by Mr Bland' in Act 3, and the delivery of a prologue and epilogue on the first night, as was customary for new pieces.[1] Not to be outdone, Covent Garden announced that its new play, Robert Jameson's *The Students of Salamanca*, would bring together the company's main comic talents (including Richard Jones, John Fawcett, William Abbot and Charles Mathews) and display new scenery, costumes and decorations.[2] The competition was fierce and, as it turned out, there could only be one winner. In spite of best efforts to compress and revive *The Students of Salamanca* as a one-act piece (*The Delusion*) Covent Garden's comedy proved a failure. *Remorse*, on the other hand, received mixed critical reviews but was warmly applauded. It would become one of the most successful new tragedies on the Romantic stage – second only to Richard Brinsley Sheridan's *Pizarro* (1799).[3] But if *Remorse* and *The Students of Salamanca* looked to different genres and made disparate claims to literary quality, they did share one important attribute (also characteristic of *Pizarro*): a Spanish theme.

The *British Review* recognised that in 1813 this interest in Spain was no coincidence:

> At the present moment … any thing relating to the Peninsula is an object of interest; together with our victorious dispatches we have Spanish buttons, chocolate, mantles, fans, feathers, and bolderos [*sic*]; was it then to be supposed that the zeal of managers, shouldering each other in the eager discharge of a new office, should forget to provide us with a new Spanish play? Undoubtedly not.[4]

The 'victorious dispatches' that feature at the head of this jumbled list of Spanish items point unmistakably to Britain's involvement in the Peninsular War (1808–1814) – known in Portugal as the period of the 'French Invasions', in Spain as 'the War of Independence' and by Napoleon, famously, as his 'Spanish Ulcer'. As David Chandler explains, 'what began in 1807 as an opportunistic invasion of a practically defenceless Portugal rapidly expanded into a major struggle

---

[1] DL Playbill, 23 January 1813 (Garrick Club).
[2] CG Playbill, 23 January 1813 (Garrick Club).
[3] J.C.C. Mays, Introduction to *Remorse* (Stage) *CC: Poetical Works: Plays III.2*, 1041.
[4] *British Review*, May 1813, 361.

involving whole populations as well as armies'.[5] It also resulted, significantly, in an unexpected Anglo-Spanish alliance. This book offers the first in-depth study of the role played by the English theatres in mediating the Peninsular War and its related debates. As a popular, lively, often boisterous public space – patronised by mixed-sex audiences of different social classes and age groups – the theatre offers an ideal lens for studying the reception of a conflict that initially garnered almost unanimous support but soon after became troublesomely partisan.

Portugal and England had enjoyed good trading relations since the Middle Ages, but Spain had long been considered a national enemy. In the eighteenth century alone, England and Spain were on opposing sides during the War of the Spanish Succession (1702–1714), the War of the Quadruple Alliance (1718–1720), the War of Jenkins' Ear (1739–1748) and the American War of Independence (1775–1783). Unsurprisingly, this ensured that Spain's place in the cultural imagination remained firmly associated with the Spanish Armada of 1588 and the notorious 'Black Legend' that defined the Spanish colonial system as 'fanatical, tyrannical, and grievously inhumane'.[6] To revise these age-old suspicions would be no mean feat (even when faced with a common enemy as powerful as Napoleon), but could the theatre offer a platform for cultural redress? How was the Peninsular War depicted on stage? Did representations of Spain and Portugal undergo any significant change during this period? In its search for answers to these questions (and the articulation of several others), this book aims to provide a literarily and historically informed account of English dramatic culture between 1807 and 1815 – years often overlooked as a 'black hole' in the nation's theatre history.

It is only relatively recently that the Peninsular War – long the subject of an impressive historiography – began to receive considered attention from Romantic literary scholars, whose work tended to focus more prominently on the ideology of the French Revolution and the turbulent 1790s. Following Linda Colley's interdisciplinary *Britons: Forging the Nation 1707–1837* (1992), Simon Bainbridge's two monographs, *Napoleon and English Romanticism* (1995) and *British Poetry and the Revolutionary and Napoleonic Wars* (2003), proved especially important for contextualising our interest in the Revolutionary debate with a longer view of the Napoleonic Wars. The early 1990s also witnessed major advances in theatre studies, which began to contest the view that Romantic drama was more 'mental' than 'corporeal' (a view that privileged the figure of the playwright in his or her closet over the potential anarchy of bodies on stage and in the auditorium). Julie Carlson's *In the Theatre of Romanticism: Coleridge, Nationalism, Women* (1994) was one of the first studies to successfully challenge this false binary. Arguing that theatrical discourses were, in fact, central to the

[5]   David Chandler, *Dictionary of the Napoleonic Wars* (Hertfordshire: Wordsworth Editions, 1993; 1999), 331.
[6]   Rebecca Cole Heinowitz, *Spanish America and British Romanticism, 1777–1826: Rewriting Conquest* (Edinburgh: Edinburgh University Press, 2010), 7.

construction of Romantic national identities, Carlson focuses especially on Samuel Taylor Coleridge, whose tragedy *Remorse* significantly shaped his contemporary celebrity.[7]

As a poet, playwright, lecturer and political journalist (with specific interests in the Peninsular War), Coleridge also features prominently in this book. But whereas Carlson's approach is concerned with the canonical over the popular, mine aims to bring forgotten playwrights, performance venues and marginalised geographies to the centre of discussion. In Chapters 1 and 2 of this book the critical spotlight is directed at the entertainments put on at the patent theatres during the Peninsular War; but Chapter 3 focuses on London's minor theatres; Chapter 4 on the wartime audiences that attended Bristol's Theatre Royal and Regency Theatre; and the 'Afterword' on theatrical culture in Lisbon during the city's occupation by foreign troops. Throughout, I aim to capture the range of contemporary responses to the Peninsular War as registered by the period's most popular 'Spanish' play (Sheridan's *Pizarro*), revivals of Shakespeare, and the predominantly spectacular performances available at the minor theatres (with the book's final chapter on Bristol illustrating how each of these responses was replayed on the provincial stage). In doing so, I attempt to follow the footsteps of Gillian Russell, who, in *The Theatres of War: Performance, Politics and Society, 1793–1815* (1995), celebrates the 'plurality' of contemporary dramatic performances by discussing entertainments as seemingly distant from each other as were the plays in the licensed theatres from the amateur productions directed, acted and even promoted by sailors on deployment.

In place, therefore, of a model that pits the period's different kinds of theatrical experience in opposition to each other, I hope to testify to the enabling possibilities of playing across seemingly demarcated lines.[8] Although the

---

[7] Carlson seeks to challenge 'two cardinal principles of Coleridge studies: emphasis on imagination necessitates hostility to theatre; rejection of revolution implies a full-scale retreat from political action'. Julie Carlson, *In the Theatre of Romanticism: Coleridge, Nationalism, Women* (Cambridge: Cambridge University Press, 1994), 25.

[8] In addition to the studies by Carlson and Russell already mentioned, major contributions to Romantic-period theatre studies of recent date include: Misty Anderson, *Female Playwrights and Eighteenth-Century Comedy: Negotiating Marriage on the London Stage* (Basingstoke: Palgrave, 2002); Betsy Bolton, *Women, Nationalism, and the Romantic Stage. Theatre and Politics in Britain, 1780–1800* (Cambridge: Cambridge University Press, 2001); Jacky Bratton, *New Readings in Theatre History* (Cambridge: Cambridge University Press, 2003); Frederick Burwick, *Romantic Drama, Acting and Reacting* (Cambridge: Cambridge University Press, 2009) and *Playing to the Crowd: London Popular Theatre, 1780–1830* (New York: Palgrave Macmillan, 2011); Jane Moody, *Illegitimate Theatre in London 1770–1840* (Cambridge: Cambridge University Press, 2000); Daniel O'Quinn, *Staging Governance: Theatrical Imperialism in London 1770–1800* (Baltimore: Johns Hopkins University Press, 2005); Julia Swindells, *Glorious Causes: The Grand Theatre of Political Change 1789–1833* (Oxford: Oxford University Press, 2001); David Francis Taylor, *Theatres of Opposition: Empire, Revolution, & Richard Brinsley Sheridan* (Cambridge: Cambridge University Press, 2012); and David Worrall,

Licensing Act of 1737 had given the patent theatres a monopoly on spoken drama that amounted to virtual cultural hegemony, there remained, as David Francis Taylor argues, 'the potential for subversive statement and polemical activity within the supposedly controlled sites, and under the royal banner, of the patent theatres'.[9] Free from the divisions once imposed between the imaginary spaces of 'mental theatre' and the movement of bodies on stage, or of 'high' versus 'popular' cultures, this book explores the variegated theatrical fare available at the English theatres (metropolitan and provincial, patent and minor) during the Peninsular War.[10]

Since access to early nineteenth-century theatrical repertoires remains limited, this book is the first to provide 'A Calendar of Plays for Covent Garden, Drury Lane and Bristol Theatre Royal: 1807–1815'.[11] The Calendar shows that many of the plays performed on the patent stages were established favourites, enjoying a long history of re-appropriation by managers and audiences alike. While the Calendar does not provide cast lists or box office receipts (except when relevant for Bristol's Theatre Royal), it offers valuable clues, for instance, about the pairing of different plays, and managers' financial considerations when devising an evening's entertainment. As Jeffrey Cox has convincingly demonstrated, 'factors of scheduling' could have a crucial effect on a play's reception history and box office success.[12] The Calendar offers important empirical evidence for the argument that even the most topical of wartime plays needed to fit within the established repertoire.[13]

Theatric Revolution: Drama, Censorship, and Romantic Subcultures 1773–1832 (Oxford: Oxford University Press, 2006) and *Celebrity, Performance, Reception: British Georgian Theatre as Social Assemblage* (Cambridge: Cambridge University Press, 2013).

[9] Taylor, *Theatres of Opposition*, 11.

[10] As Peter Stallybrass and Allon White argue: 'The classificatory body of culture is always double, always structured in relation to its negation, its inverse'. *The Politics and Poetics of Transgression* (London: Methuen, 1986), 20.

[11] Drury Lane, Covent Garden, the Haymarket (as of 1766) and provincial Theatre Royals (thereafter) enjoyed a monopoly on spoken drama that would last until 1843. A word must be said about the Haymarket, which is excluded from this book on account of an unusual licence that confined its entertainments to the summer season (when Drury Lane and Covent Garden were closed). This meant that although it was considered a 'patent' theatre, it neither competed directly with Covent Garden and Drury Lane nor the minor theatres, which faced very different legal restrictions. For a comprehensive account of performances at the Haymarket, readers are referred to William J. Burling's *Summer Theatre in London, 1661–1820, and the Rise of the Haymarket Theatre* (London: Associated University Presses, 2000).

[12] Jeffrey N. Cox, 'Spots of Time: The Structure of the Dramatic Evening in the Theater of Romanticism', *Texas Studies in Literature and Language* 41.4, (Winter 1999), 403–425 (403).

[13] See introduction to 'A Calendar of Plays for Covent Garden, Drury Lane and Bristol Theatre Royal: 1807–1815' (henceforth 'Calendar').

Many of the plays performed in the early nineteenth century were stock pieces with a Spanish theme. This was largely in response to the fact that 'Spanish romance' had been one of the first new subgenres to appear on the Restoration stage. As the editors of *The London Stage* report: 'This kind of play, based upon a Spanish source, placed its emphasis upon a rigid code of conduct, had a plot filled with intrigue, and emphasised one or more high spirited women in the *dramatis personae*'.[14] In *The Spanish Plays of Neoclassical England* (1973) John Loftis identifies Samuel Tuke's *The Adventures of Five Hours* (1663) – an adaptation of Antonio Coello's *Los empeños de seis horas* (which, in the seventeenth century had been mistakenly attributed to Calderón) – as a prime example of the Spanish intrigue comedies that would prove popular with English audiences well into the nineteenth century. Characterised by fast-paced action, these comedies of mistaken identities and nocturnal contrivances often showcased the Spaniard's uncompromising attachment to honour. But as Spanish dominance approached its end in the 1660s there was, as Michael Duffy explains, 'a growing contempt' for such behaviour: 'Spanish pride, insolence and overbearing arrogance … understandable during Spain's greatness … were insufferable now Spain was in decline'.[15] As such, audiences were generally invited to dismiss, rather than emulate, the Spanish codes of conduct presented on stage. Did the Peninsular War challenge this interpretative norm? Could old 'Spanish' plays, with their cast of haughty dons, imposing duennas and indolent servants still secure packed auditoriums after the Anglo-Spanish alliance of 1808?

Understanding how the Peninsular War related to the longer history of the representation of Spain in the English theatres is an important aim of this book. My argument begins with a discussion of Sheridan's *Pizarro* that explains how old favourites could take on new meanings in order to keep up to date with shifting political sympathies. There is, indeed, an important distinction to be made between the plays and entertainments that were written in direct response to the Peninsular Campaign and older plays that were (often informally) adapted to cater to the demand for topical narratives, or otherwise seen to carry new meanings as a result of changes to public opinion on the war and national politics. The theatrical repertoires of the early nineteenth century were characterised by their variety and 'protean' nature, as much as familiarity. Stock plays with Spanish themes, such as John Fletcher's *Rule a Wife and Have a Wife* (1634), Susanna Centlivre's *The Busy Body* (1709), William Congreve's *The Mourning Bride* (1697), Edward Young's *The Revenge* (1721) and John O'Keeffe's comic opera *The Castle of Andalusia* (1782)

---

[14]   Emmet Avery, Charles Beecher Hogan, William Van Lennep, Arhur Hawley Scouten and George Winchester Stone, eds. *The London Stage 1660–1800: A Calendar of Plays, Entertainments & Afterpieces, together with Casts, Box-Receipts, and Contemporary Comment.* 11 vols. 'Part 1: 1660–1700' ed. William Van Lennep, with a critical introduction by Emmett L. Avery and Arthur H. Scouten (Carbondale: Southern Illinois University Press, 1960–68; 1965), 1: cxxii–xxiii.

[15]   Michael Duffy, *The Englishman and the Foreigner* (Cambridge: Chadwyck-Healey, 1986), 25.

were frequently performed in English theatres at the time of the war in Spain and Portugal.[16] These well-known plays did not, however, represent stable, unchanging texts. At the start of the conflict, they could be read against the grain, as I suggest in my analysis of *Pizarro* (Chapter 1) and Thomas Dibdin's 1803 comic opera, *The English Fleet in 1342* (Chapter 4). But as support for the war began to waver, their anti-Spanish quips and criticisms could also be taken at face value, as this book also illustrates.

Although the Anglo-Spanish alliance of 1808 made it a diplomatic and political requirement for Britons to revise their received image of Spain, attempts to rework representations of the stage Spaniard remained hampered by historical prejudice, or, at the very least, political caution. For audience members disappointed with the course of the war in Spain, the comic Spaniard (almost invariably dressed in sixteenth-century costume) seems to have embodied the reasons ascribed to Spain's demise since its celebrated 'Golden Age'. By proposing readings of the old and new, successful and unsuccessful plays and entertainments staged between 1807 and 1815, this book examines the extent to which the Peninsular Campaign helped redefine the theatre's importance as a forum for the contestation, as well as celebration, of war.

Britain's military operations in Spain and Portugal offer an especially interesting opportunity to engage with what has been labelled the 'total war' experience. After 1792, as David Bell explains, there began 'an astonishing transformation in the scope and intensity of warfare'.[17] Bell draws upon the theories proposed by the French historian Jean-Yves Guiomar to argue that it was the distinct 'fusion of politics and war that distinguishe[d] "modern total war" from earlier incidents of unrestrained or even exterminatory warfare' and 'drove [its] participants relentlessly *toward* a condition of total engagement and the abandonment of restraints'.[18] In order to sustain popular involvement in this new kind of warfare, a range of cultural forms were deployed and print, especially, became central to the daily experiences associated with total warfare. This was exemplified by the contemporary growth in newspapers, military memoirs, war poetry, and the emergence of new genres such as the historical novel. Mary Favret's penetrating examination of 'how military conflict on a global scale looked and felt to a population whose armies and navies waged war for decades, but always at a distance', underlines the importance of understanding Romantic

---

[16]   It was common practice in the eighteenth century to perform earlier plays in altered form. Elizabeth Inchbald duly notes that it was 'as altered by Garrick' that *Rule a Wife and Have a Wife* secured its place in the early nineteenth-century repertoire. *The British Theatre; or, A Collection of Plays, which are acted at the Theatres Royal, Drury-Lane, Covent Garden, and Haymarket ... with Biographical and Critical Remarks by Mrs Inchbald*. 25 vols. (London, 1808), Introduction to *Rule a Wife and Have a Wife*, 6: 4.

[17]   David A. Bell, *The First Total War: Napoleon's Europe and the Birth of Modern Warfare* (London: Bloomsbury, 2007), 7.

[18]   Bell, *Total War*, 8.

wartime as 'war mediated, brought home through a variety of instruments'.[19] In this book I foreground the theatre as a multimedia event that actively engaged with the inevitable complexities of this process of mediation. In Chapters 2 and 3 I respond, specifically, to Favret's important theorisation of wartime 'dailiness'. Whether 'legitimate' or 'illegitimate', the nation's theatres provided a space in which producers and consumers came into direct contact with each other, and affective responses to the military campaign were continually reworked.

As Gillian Russell contends, the contemporary response to war was 'played out in the streets, commons, and theatres of Britain, as much as it was in the printed media of the period'.[20] My argument remains, for the most part, confined to the various theatres studied herein, but my observations are predicated, nonetheless, upon Russell's broader interest in theatricality and the ways in which, after the declaration of war against France in 1793, British society was effectively 'militarized'.[21] Russell details how the patent and minor theatres contributed to this process by staging spectacular re-enactments of Britain's naval and land battles, for example.[22] In the chapters that follow I explain how these military entertainments continued to define the theatrical repertoires available during the Peninsular War. Indeed, it can be helpful to think in terms of continuity, since many of the dramaturgical practices set in place during the 1790s remained prominent between 1808 and 1814. Consider, for instance, the staging of the Gothic narratives, dramas and melodramas to which the French Revolution imparted particular poignancy.[23] George Taylor argues that these forms' popularity after 1789 attested to 'a genuine therapeutic need' for the representation of 'entrapment, dislocation, loss of family and the sensations of having lost voice, sight or hearing'.[24] In *Remorse*, which was an important but not drastic reworking of Coleridge's earlier, revolutionary drama *Osorio* (1797), the playwright retained many of his original Gothic trappings. This suggests that what Russell calls the 'textures of feeling' borne by the French Revolution remained both politically and commercially viable in the early nineteenth century.[25] But the years 1808 to 1814 marked a period of change, as well as continuity. Public opinion had, after all, been variously shaped and

---

[19]   Mary Favret, *War at a Distance: Romanticism and the Making of Modern Warfare* (Princeton: Princeton University Press, 2010), 9; 11.

[20]   Gillian Russell, *The Theatres of War. Performance, Politics and Society, 1793–1815* (Oxford: Clarendon Press, 1995), 18.

[21]   Russell, *Theatres of War*, 80.

[22]   Russell, *Theatres of War*, 59–78 esp.

[23]   On the relationship between romantic drama and melodrama see Jeffrey N. Cox, 'The Death of Tragedy; or, the Birth of Melodrama', in *The Performing Century: Nineteenth-Century Theatre's History*, ed. Tracy C. Davis and Peter Holland (Basingtoke: Palgrave Macmillan, 2007), 161–81.

[24]   George Taylor, *The French Revolution and the London Stage 1789–1805* (Cambridge: Cambridge University Press, 2000), 208.

[25]   Russell, *Theatres of War*, 3.

reshaped since the French Revolution, causing the questions articulated in the dramas of the 1790s to acquire new significance.

This book charts how the Peninsular War ascribed its own urgency to issues such as civilian involvement in war, patriotism and the articulation of national identities. As the conflict that constituted the British army's largest land campaign and witnessed the rise of Arthur Wellesley as a national hero, the Peninsular War revalorised the figure of the soldier. (The soldier was prominent not only in the auditorium, but also on stage, where his representation acquired additional nuance from the regular employment of soldiers as supernumeraries.) Although sailors continued to enjoy the spotlight in many of the plays and entertainments staged after 1808 – hornpipes, for instance, remained in high demand, especially in a naval city such as Bristol – this book attests to the popularity of military themes and the stage's pronounced interest in the Irish soldier in particular.

Scottish and Irish soldiers accounted for a significant proportion of the British army sent to the Peninsula (approximately 28% of which were Irish).[26] These men's political and religious sympathies often aroused the suspicions of their English peers, however: 'the ambivalent position of Irish soldiers, so many of them Roman Catholics in a Protestant army, and loyal servants of a state against which their countrymen periodically rebelled, was not lost on leaders and comrades alike', Richard Holmes expounds.[27] Notwithstanding, the Irish regiments sent to Spain and Portugal won significant acclaim. Holmes singles out the 88th Regiment of Foot (Connaught Rangers), whose fighting record in the Peninsula 'placed it amongst the bravest of the brave', and provides several examples of the Irish soldiers' recognised merits.[28] The Irishman (an already popular character in English drama) would continue to exert a comic stage presence, but during the Peninsular War attempts to reform the Irish stereotype began to be extended in a new direction. The genial Major O'Flaherty of Richard Cumberland's *The West Indian* (1771) exemplifies the strategic turn to sentimentalism by eighteenth-century playwrights eager to associate their Irish characters with sensibility and essential benevolence. But testimonials of Irish grit during the Peninsular War called for an even more pronounced emphasis on national courage and hardiness, as Chapters 1 and 3 explore.

By considering the stage Irishman as well as the Spaniard, this book chronicles the re-imagining of stereotypes deemed both proximately and more distantly 'other'. My interest in the English theatres' representations of Portugal as well as Spain strikes a conversation between Anglo-Lusitanian and Anglo-Hispanic Romanticism that aims to realise a similar expansion in methodological

---

[26]   Graciela Iglesias Rogers, 'Soldiering Abroad: The Experience of Living and Fighting among Aliens during the Napoleonic Wars', in *Britain's Soldiers: Rethinking War and Society 1715–1815*, ed. Kevin Linch and Matthew McCormack (Liverpool: Liverpool University Press, 2014), 40.

[27]   Richard Holmes, *Redcoat: The British Soldier in the Age of Horse and Musket* (London: Harper Collins, 2001; 2002), 64.

[28]   Holmes, *Redcoat*, 59 and ff.

perspectives. Diego Saglia's immensely influential monograph *Poetic Castles in Spain: British Romanticism and Figurations of Iberia* (2000) has ensured that Spain – once one of the 'most neglected' of Romantic geographies – is now the subject of important scholarship from both sides of the Atlantic.[29] But Anglo-Lusitanian studies have unfortunately failed to excite the same degree of international attention.[30] In *Poetic Castles* Saglia acknowledges that 'importantly related cultural geographies such as Portugal or Gibraltar have been only touched upon in passing', while Rebecca Cole Heinowitz's *Spanish America and British Romanticism, 1777–1826: Rewriting Conquest* (2010) excludes Portugal and Brazil altogether, as her title indicates.[31]

It is important to remember, however, that the Peninsular War transformed both Spain and Portugal into Europe's new theatre of war. This was poignantly registered a couple of months after the cementing of Britain's new alliance with Spain, when news arrived of the Anglo-French armistice known as the Convention of Cintra. Following the French army's defeat at the Battle of Vimeiro (an early success for the British expeditionary forces led by Sir Arthur Wellesley), the Convention was signed on 30 August 1808. It cleared Portugal of the invading army, but its terms were embarrassingly generous. Sir Harry Burrard and Sir Hew Dalrymple, the British generals who replaced Wellesley and took charge of the negotiations with Kellerman the Younger, failed to recognise the decisiveness of their victory over the French Commander in Chief, Général Jean Androche Junot. The Convention thus went so far as to guarantee the French army's safe conveyance (complete with their weapons and stolen treasures), and allowed the routed soldiers to re-enlist upon their return to France. When these terms were printed in the *London Gazette* (16 September 1808) they made for inflammatory reading. Burrard, Dalrymple and Wellesley were recalled to London where all three commanders faced a court of enquiry.

---

[29] Diego Saglia, *Poetic Castles in Spain: British Romanticism and Figurations of Iberia* (Atlanta: Amsterdam, 2000), 11. For a sample of Saglia's extensive contributions to Anglo-Hispanic studies, see this book's bibliography. In recent years there has also been an intensification of interest in the cultural legacies of 'la Guerra de la Independencia' within Spain itself, as exemplified by the publication of *Libertad frente a Tiranía: Poesía inglesa de la Guerra de la Independencia (1808–1814). Antología Bilingüe*, selected and translated by Agustín Coletes Blanco and Alicia Laspra Rodríguez (Madrid: Fundación Dos de Mayo – Espasa, 2013) the first bilingual anthology of Peninsular War poems. Notable studies of the theatre include: María Mercedes Romero Peña and Emilio Palacios Fernández, *El teatro en Madrid durante la Guerra de la Independencia: 1808–1814* (Madrid: Fundación Universitaria Española, 2006); María Mercedes Romero Peña, *El Teatro de la Guerra de la Independencia* (Madrid: Fundación Universitaria Española, 2007); and Ana María Freire López, *El teatro español entre la Ilustración y el Romanticismo. Madrid durante la Guerra de la Independencia* (Madrid: Iberoamericana/Vervuert, 2009).

[30] Scholarship within Portugal is nevertheless thriving. See, for instance, the research conducted by the Lisbon-based Centre for English Translation and Anglo-Portuguese Studies (CETAPS) <http://cetaps.com> [Accessed 21.07.13].

[31] Saglia, *Poetic Castles*, 18.

William Wordsworth added his voice to the furore with what we now know as his longest prose pamphlet, *Concerning the Relations of Great Britain, Spain, and Portugal, To Each Other, and to the Common Enemy, At This Crisis; And Specifically as Affected by the Convention of Cintra...* (1809). It was initially intended for publication in instalments in the *Courier*, but finally printed as a stand-alone publication on 27 May 1809.[32] By this time, however, Wordsworth had come to consider the Convention more philosophically, as only one symptom of the nation's general moral and political decline. His catalogue of grievances included the British army's forced retreat from Corunna and the scandalous details of the 'Mary Anne Clarke affair'.[33] Wordsworth's recognition of a troublesome imbrication of national and international politics also runs throughout this book, which recovers the complex ideological debates about Britain itself that took place during the first quarter of the nineteenth century. Domestic, as much as foreign, concerns are central to the recovery of English theatrical culture during the Peninsular War, as this book highlights in its discussion of the Old Price riots of 1809–1810, and the commotion that resulted from the arrest of Francis Burdett.

The 67 nights of rioting that transformed the auditorium of Covent Garden Theatre and caused its actor-manager John Philip Kemble such acute woe need little rehearsing after Marc Baer's seminal study, *Theatre and Disorder in Late Georgian London* (1992). My argument requires, nevertheless, that I underline Baer's observation that at the time of the protests, only the war with France received more media coverage.[34] The two events went hand-in-hand. Baer relates, for example, how the Old Price protestors (O.P.s) assumed the behaviour of patriotic citizens and delivered enthusiastic renditions of 'God Save the King' and 'Rule Britannia'. He also notes that they objected to the opera singer Angelica Catalani's expensive engagement with placards that read 'No Foreigners' and similar xenophobic messages.[35] Theatre-goers hissed, whistled, danced, raised banners and even sported a range of O.P. ephemera (including handkerchiefs, medals and other fashionable accessories that publicised their message).[36] As the *Theatrical Examiner* judiciously reported: 'the actors ...

[32]   On *Cintra*'s complex publication history see 'Introduction: General' to *Concerning the Convention of Cintra: A Bicentennial Critical Edition*, ed. Richard Gravil and W.J.B. Owen (Tirril: Humanities – Ebooks, 2009), 70–89.

[33]   From 1 February to 20 March 1809 the Duke of York's mistress Mary Anne Clarke was under investigation for the illicit sale of army commissions and promotions. See Gravil and Owen (eds), 'Commentary' to *Concerning the Convention*, 256.

[34]   Marc Baer, *Theatre and Disorder in Late Georgian London* (Oxford: Clarendon Press, 1992), 45.

[35]   Baer, *Theatre and Disorder*, 27.

[36]   Baer describes this kind of behaviour as the hallmark of 'activist audiences' and notes that it was 'only a variation of the normal patterns of audience participation in or reaction to the theatre'. *Theatre and Disorder*, 182.

had become the audience, and the audience the actors'.[37] Chapter 2 explores the implications of this for Kemble's subsequent repertoire at Covent Garden, while Chapter 4 examines the riots' surprising effect on the behaviour of theatre audiences in Bristol.

The *Examiner* was not, of course, the only newspaper to pounce upon the ironies that surfaced during the Old Price riots.[38] The *Morning Chronicle*, for example, turned to *Coriolanus* in order to equate Kemble's inept handling of the protestors with the war hero's contemptuous address to the plebeians of Rome. *Coriolanus* was a role that Kemble had played to acclaim in 1789 and 1806 but was (understandably) reluctant to revive until 1811, as I discuss in Chapter 2.[39] In its effective citation of Shakespeare *against* Kemble, the *Morning Chronicle* demonstrated that the bard could be applied for democratic, even radical uses, in addition to the politically conservative interpretations favoured by Kemble himself. The actor-manager's success as Rolla (from Sheridan's *Pizarro*) was also aggressively cited against him when, on 9 November 1809, the *Statesman* duly printed 'A Parody on Rolla's Address':

> *They*, by a strange frenzy driven, bawl, and call aloud for the *Old Prices; we* give them *blows*, and *threaten* them with *imprisonment* to obtain the *New*. *They* laugh at threats *they* do not fear; and *defy* all Bow-street runners, whom they hate. *We* serve JOHN BULL, whom we treat with *scorn*; and *our money* is the *god* whom we adore ... They *boast* they come to *improve* our *estate, encourage* our *talents*, and *free* us from all foreign aid. Yes; they want to impress *liberality* on *our* minds; but no, *we* are the slaves of *passion, avarice*, and *pride*.[40]

The *Statesman* here turns Rolla's speech on its head in order to expose Kemble as an avaricious conquistador in his own right. These parodies testify firstly, to the sequestration of the contemporary repertoire as a political weapon (effective, principally, because of its widespread familiarity); and secondly, to the characterisation of audiences who were not merely spectators, but informed and critically self-aware political agents.[41]

---

[37]   *TE*, 24 September 1809.

[38]   The press provided extensive coverage of the O.P. riots. 'The five papers, that have distinguished themselves by their violence on opposite sides, are by name *The British Press, Morning Post, Statesman, Morning Chronicle* and *Times*'. (The first two papers lent their support to the Managers, while *The Times* betrayed notable inconsistencies in its early coverage of events.) *The Rebellion; or, All in the Wrong. A serio-comic-hurly-burly, in scenes, as it was performed for two months at the new Theatre Royal, Covent Garden ...* (London, 1809), iv–v.

[39]   *MC*, 23 November 1809. *The Rebellion* (essentially a collation of previous issues of the *MM*) claimed that the *MC* 'preserved a consistent conduct throughout'. *The Rebellion*, v.

[40]   *The Rebellion*, 82–3.

[41]   Performances on the opening night finished at about 11 p.m. but the disturbances continued for another two hours. The account provided in *The Rebellion* describes the

The Licensing Act had, of course, been designed to keep a lid on overly 'activist audiences' by authorising the close monitoring of British drama by the Lord Chamberlain's Office.[42] The Act, which among other things, made it a statutory requirement for new play scripts to be sent to the Examiner of Plays two weeks prior to performance at a patent theatre, empowered the Examiner to do away with any references to politics or religion.[43] John Larpent, who was incumbent in the post from 1778 until his death in 1824, recommended extensive revisions to H.B. Code's *The Spanish Patriots A Thousand Years Ago* (1812).[44] Yet, of the Spanish- and Portuguese-themed plays in his extensive collection, only one obviously topical entertainment seems to have been refused a license. This was an application from Drury Lane dated 11 February 1809, requesting permission to perform a 'Monody on the Death of Sir John Moore', which I discuss in Chapter 1. Facing heavy fines and the threat of a revocation of their licence if they failed to comply with the Examiner's decisions, theatre managers usually adopted a system of in-house censorship before submitting play-scripts for formal evaluation. Sheridan's revisions to Theodore Hook's *The Siege of St Quintin* (1808), also detailed in Chapter 1, amount to a suggestive example of the practices employed.

Not even a rigid code of theatrical censorship, however, could restrict the Romantic stage to a simplistic, or one-sided view of contemporary politics. In fact, far from reducing the theatre's capacity to provide political commentary, the Licensing Act seems to have encouraged playwrights and managers to explore ever more innovative modes of delivering topical addresses. As Gillian Russell succinctly puts it, the laws 'generated the sensitivity which is the concomitant of censorship'.[45] Domestic concerns were often displaced to fictional, historicised settings and/or re-imagined in foreign, exotic locations. 'The correspondence between event and incorporation', as Jacky Bratton calls it, may sometimes have been more oblique than transparent, but allegorical readings (because always personal, provisional and essentially plural) offered an effective means of dodging censorship.[46]

O.P. protestors as having 'quitted the field, covered with *all* the glory of *conquest*, which encircles the brows of VISCOUNT TALAVERA!'. *The Rebellion*, 5.

[42]   See note 35, above; and Baer, *Theatre and Disorder*, 166–88.

[43]   The Licensing Act of 1737 made it illegal for performers to act 'for hire, gain or reward' outside of Westminster; Covent Garden and Drury Lane were effectively awarded a monopoly on spoken drama; the Lord Chamberlain was made responsible for licensing all playhouses; and it became a requirement for new play-scripts to be sent to the Examiner of Plays two weeks prior to an intended performance (with the Lord Chamberlain retaining the right to censor with no appeal). See David Thomas, 'The 1737 Licensing Act and its Impact', in *The Oxford Handbook of the Georgian Theatre 1737–1832*, ed. Julia Swindells and David Francis Taylor (Oxford: Oxford University Press, 2014), 91–106.

[44]   Larpent marked long passages from Code's play for excision. See Larpent Collection 1733.

[45]   Russell, *Theatres of War*, 16.

[46]   J.S. Bratton, 'Introduction' to *Acts of Supremacy: The British Empire and the Stage, 1790–1930*, ed. J.S. Bratton, Richard Allen Cave, Breandan Gregory, Heidi J. Holder and

Allegory also offered much more, of course. In Walter Benjamin's and Paul de Man's formulations, allegory is associated with emptiness, loss and the impossibility of arriving at a single, complete truth – an impossibility that may have reflected the disparate, alienating experiences engendered by the Napoleonic Wars.[47] Although this potential remains in the background rather than foreground of this study, I employ allegorical readings in order to look beyond a play's surface meanings, and to access what remains concealed or just beyond reach (for reasons that include but are not exclusive to censorship). As with any example of allegory, the readings I offer can only ever be suggestive. I hope, however, that readers of this book will be stimulated to provide their own interpretative extensions, qualifications and improvements to the analyses provided herein; and, in doing so, recover an important aspect of the early nineteenth-century theatrical experience. Contemporary reviews (both private and public) of the performances on offer at the wartime theatres suggest that audiences were not only very much attuned to the allegorical readings demanded of them but took pleasure in exceeding these (as powerfully evinced by the behaviour of the O.P. protestors). During this period of experimentation with generic hybrids and advances in stage technique and effect, audiences enjoyed a sense of participatory politics that appears to have been nothing short of liberating.

This book invites its readers to explore the implications of the recognised overlap between theatrical and political cultures by focusing on the Peninsular War as a period during which – to employ the words used by the *British Review* – new 'Spanish' plays wrestled with the old; 'Spanish buttons, chocolates, mantles, fans, feathers, and bolderos [*sic*]' became politicised props (especially at the minor theatres); and the playbill itself – that first token of an evening's entertainment – was read as a 'victorious dispatch' in its own right.[48] The Peninsular War proved bloodier, more expensive and ideologically divisive than anticipated. This book shows that for the war's entire duration, however, Spain and Portugal remained prominent on stage, alternately exciting and exasperating the crowded, buzzing auditoriums of England's metropolitan and provincial theatres.

Michael Pickering (Manchester: Manchester University Press, 1991), 4.

[47] 'Allegory designates primarily a distance in relation to its own origin, and, renouncing the nostalgia and desire to coincide, it establishes its language in the void of this temporal difference. In so doing, it prevents the self from an illusory identification with the non-self, which is fully, though painfully, recognised as a non-self'. Paul de Man, 'The Rhetoric of Temporality', in *Blindness and Insight: Essays in Rhetoric of Contemporary Criticism*, with an introduction by Wlad Godzich, 2nd ed., (Minneapolis: University of Minnesota, 1971; 1983), 207.

[48] On the 'militaristic' language associated with the acting profession in this period, see Russell, *Theatres of War*, 179–82.

Chapter 1
Pizarro, 'Political Proteus'

In the spring of 1799 'expectation was on tip-toe' for Richard Brinsley Sheridan's new play.[1] *Pizarro*, a spectacular five-act tragedy adapted from August von Kotzebue's *Die Spanier in Peru* (1796), boasted an all-star cast including John Philip Kemble, Sarah Siddons, William Barrymore and Dorothy Jordan; a musical score with accompanying vocal parts especially composed by Michael Kelly; and 'entirely new Scenes, Dresses and Decorations'.[2] In anticipation of 'overflowing' audiences, Drury Lane unbolted its doors as early as three o'clock in the afternoon. Managers correctly predicted that the already well-advertised play, celebrating 'the joint reputation of Sheridan and Kotzebue, and the first dramatic attempt of the former, after an interval of twenty years', would be certain to excite the eager curiosity of metropolitan audiences.[3] While the first performance pointed to the need for 'judicious' alterations and curtailments (in order to cut down the play's excessive running time), reviewers confidently identified its 'purity of moral sentiment' and 'genuine and enthusiastic bursts of heroic patriotism' as 'indisputable claims to the patronage of the Public'.[4] *Pizarro* was played consecutively for the remainder of the season, bringing in revenue that was desperately needed to replenish Drury Lane's depleted coffers.[5] By 1815 the text had already been issued in thirty different editions and *Pizarro* was secure in its status as a recognised 'favourite' of the patent theatres. It would be frequently staged at Drury Lane, Covent Garden and provincial Theatres Royal until the mid-nineteenth century.

This chapter investigates how and why Sheridan's tragedy about the Spanish conquest of Peru became one of the defining narratives of early nineteenth-century Britain. *Pizarro*'s first reviewers were quick to recognise that Sheridan recycled many of his parliamentary speeches for the play's dramatic oratory. William Pitt the Younger, for example, reportedly claimed that there was 'nothing new' in *Pizarro*; that he had 'heard it all long ago in [Sheridan's] speeches at Hastings's trial'.[6]

---

[1]   Michael Kelly, *Reminiscences*, ed. Roger Fiske (London: Oxford University Press, 1975), 253.

[2]   DL Playbill, 24 May 1799 (Garrick Club).

[3]   *The Times*, 25 May 1799.

[4]   *The Times*, 29 May 1799.

[5]   In its first season alone, *Pizarro* brought in £13, 624 9s. 6d. Avery, Hogan, et al. (eds), *London Stage 1660–1800*, 'Part 5: 1776–1800', 11: 2097.

[6]   Qtd. by John Loftis in 'Whig Oratory on Stage: Sheridan's *Pizarro*', *Eighteenth-Century Studies* 8.4, (summer 1975), 454–72 (459).

In *The Rhetoric of English India* (1992) Sara Suleri takes this as her cue to explore
Pizarro's debts to Sheridan's highly publicised involvement in the impeachment
of Warren Hastings, and to examine how Sheridan's management of theatrical
sympathies helped re-condition the imperial and humanist concerns expressed in
his parliamentary speeches.[7] Julie Carlson has since identified at least five alarms of
invasion in the focal speech delivered by the Peruvian hero, Rolla: 'those sounding
between Peru and Spain, India and England, and England and France … the literary
invasion of England by Germany in the 1790s and the perpetually immanent
invasion of Ireland by England in the same years'.[8] More recently still, David
Francis Taylor has written on *Pizarro* as a tragedy that 'recycles the tropes of both
the impeachment and 1798 rebellion-propaganda as part of an extended meditation
on the powerlessness of the orator in his attempt to inscribe accountability within
the apparatus of colonialism, and the inability of eloquence, however applauded, to
counter regimes of despotism and torture'.[9] Taylor's analysis of Sheridan's allusions
to his own complex political oratory gives due consideration to *Pizarro*'s inflections
of both Indian and Irish colonial concerns. But even these nuanced readings
interpret the play on an allegorical level prone to overlook *Pizarro*'s specifically
Spanish theme and – what is perhaps one of its most fascinating qualities – the
play's phenomenal stage success for over 60 years.[10] This chapter argues that
Pizarro needs to be contextualised both synchronically and diachronically if we are
to truly understand its evolution as a 'national' dramatic mainpiece.

---

[7]   In 1786 Edmund Burke produced 21 charges ('of high crimes and misdemeanours')
against Warren Hastings, the former governor-general of India. Sheridan, who was
responsible for making the case for the fourth charge (i.e., against Hastings's oppressive
treatment of the begams of Oudh), delivered a five-and-a-half hour speech on 7 February
1787. This speech won great acclaim and ensured that Sheridan continued to play a central
role in the impeachment proceedings. Hastings was formally impeached on 10 May 1787.
The prosecution before the House of Lords began on 13 February 1788 and concluded in
1795, when Hastings was acquitted by a large majority. See 'Hastings, Warren (1732–1818)',
P.J. Marshall in *Oxford Dictionary of National Biography*, ed. H.C.G. Matthew and Brian
Harrison (Oxford: Oxford UP, 2004); online ed., ed. Lawrence Goldman, October 2008
<http://ezproxy-prd.bodleian.ox.ac.uk:2167/view/article/12587> [Accessed 17.10.2014];
and Taylor, *Theatres of Opposition*, 67–71 esp.
[8]   Julie Carlson, 'Trying Sheridan's *Pizarro*', *Texas Studies in Literature and Language*
38 (3/4), (fall/winter 1996), 359–78 (362).
[9]   Taylor, *Theatres of Opposition*, 126.
[10]   See Myron Matlaw, 'This is Tragedy!!! The History of *Pizarro*', *The Quarterly
Journal of Speech* 43, (1957), 288–94. Matlaw provides a broad overview of the play's
reception in Britain and the United States between 1799 and its last performances (in 1866
and 1874 respectively). He insists, however, that 'a study of the later history of the play
does not reveal any relationship between times of political stress and resurgence in the
popularity of the play' (290). Matlaw notably neglects to consider how the Peninsular
War – the event most likely to challenge British perceptions of Spain – might have affected
Pizarro's reception history.

Set in sixteenth-century Peru, Sheridan's play offers a particularly interesting example of how stage geographies interacted with the sites of theatre production in late eighteenth- and early nineteenth-century England. By 1799 the Spaniard was, after all, nothing short of a bugbear in the English imagination. Lingering hostilities associated with Mary Tudor's marriage to Philip II, the Protestant purges, the Spanish Armada and Spain's 'Black Legend' (with its attendant narratives of colonial rapine, superstition and bigotry) ensured that Spain remained associated with strong feelings of political and cultural revulsion.[11] It is no coincidence, then, that the plots of Sheridan's comedies *The Duenna* (1775) and *The Critic* (1779) were also predicated upon anti-Spanish sentiment. Puff's play 'The Spanish Armada' (in *The Critic*) ends unforgettably with a '*flourish of drums*' and an orchestra playing 'Britons Strike Home' and 'Rule Britannia' as the English fleet advance and fire-ships destroy the Spanish squadron.[12] This characteristic hostility to Spain meant that when *Pizarro* premiered in 1799 it was easy for audiences to imagine the eponymous villain of the play as Napoleon Bonaparte. For most contemporary reviewers, *Pizarro*'s Gothic scenery and dramatisation of the Black Legend functioned as metaphors for the sublime and destructive figurations of a Europe beset by post-revolutionary anxieties. This chapter remains sensitive to these early responses but also draws attention to the ways in which *Pizarro*'s public valence was subsequently affected by other political events, including, notably, the Anglo-Spanish alliance of 1808.

In *The Political Proteus* (1804) – a series of ten letters addressed to Sheridan – William Cobbett underscores *Pizarro*'s shifting significance, interpreting the tragedy's extended run as a counterpart to what he considered its author's all-too slippery reputation as a Member of Parliament. Cobbett deconstructs the 'true English feeling' attached to Sheridan and his putatively patriotic drama by juxtaposing the playwright's early and well-known opposition to the war with his seemingly contradictory speeches in response to the 1797 Naval Mutinies and

---

[11]   *Pizarro* is replete with references to the Black Legend. In 1.1 Pizarro tries to prevent Davilla from killing the Peruvian cacique, Orozembo, whom, he claims, should undergo the pain of torture (1.1, *DW*, 2: 664). The Inquisition makes another grotesque appearance in Elvira's anticipation of the tortures that await her as Pizarro's prisoner (4.3, *DW*, 2: 693). Interestingly, the latter speech is marked for substitution in the Drury Lane promptbook (1799), where a marginal note [here transcribed in italics] replaces Elvira's description of torture with a lover's sentimental narrative: '*Quench these eyes, that so oft – O God! – have hung with love and homage on thy looks! Pierce this dishonour'd bosom which was once thy pillow! – I will bear it all, – for it will all be justice. – But when thou hopest that thy unshrinking ears* may at last be feasted with the music of my cries, I will not utter one shriek, nor groan …'. This rewriting suggests that the play's more violent references to the Black Legend were moderated for stage production. Garrick Club copy of the Drury Lane Promptbook of *Pizarro* (1799), 61.

[12]   Sheridan, *The Critic* (3.1), in *DW*, 2: 550

support for the Volunteer Movement after the collapse of the Peace of Amiens.[13] Cobbett's acerbic attack on Sheridan's politics and dramaturgy underscores how, during the course of the Napoleonic Wars, audiences' appreciation of *Pizarro* had been critically conditioned by changing social, economic, political and cultural factors.

The first section of this chapter considers the dangers ascribed to *Pizarro*'s phenomenal popularity and what this might suggest about the relationship between English tastes and contemporary international politics. As the best-known 'Spanish' play of the period, Sheridan's *Pizarro* testifies to the effectiveness of spectacle on a large scale, the cult of celebrity actors and the theatre's interest in the affective possibilities of history. Its success was not, however, confined to the stage. The play's popularity spawned various generically broad reworkings of its historical theme. These adaptations were available for mass consumption as competing translations, histories, chapbooks, songs and juvenile dramas. As a result, before the end of its first year of performance, critics had already begun to complain of a *Pizarro* surfeit, expressing anxiety about the play's ideological migration from the boards of the patent theatres to contemporary culture at large.

In this chapter's second section, I examine Sheridan's controversial decision in 1803 to issue Rolla's exhortation against foreign invasion as a stand-alone broadsheet. 'Sheridan's Address to the People: Our King! Our Country! And our God!' (1803) was published on the heels of Robert Emmet's failed Irish rebellion, while Britain resumed its war preparations after Amiens. Sheridan's broadsheet helped reinvigorate the topicality of his play-text. At the same time, however, by extracting Rolla's impassioned speech from its dramatic frame, Sheridan created a new context for the interpretation of the political ideology encoded in his play. Ever suspicious, Cobbett contemptuously derided 'Sheridan's Address' as 'typographical harlotry', 'stuck up on every dead wall, rotten post, and dirty corner in the metropolis'.[14] His language resonates, interestingly, with the accusations levelled against the play by its many conservative critics, who described *Pizarro*'s popularity as a 'contagion' – and whose fears that its message of popular resistance and liberation could spread indiscriminately, seemed only exacerbated by the newfound textual autonomy granted to Rolla's speech. In the second, crucial phase of the war against Napoleon, the relationship between Sheridan's Spanish-themed drama and the society in which it was performed remained troublesomely problematic.

Between 1808 and 1814, as explored in the final section of this chapter, *Pizarro* was once again invested with fresh political resonance. Napoleon's attempted invasion of Spain, the heroic resistance put up by the *madrileños* in the *dos de mayo* rebellion, the spread of revolution across the Spanish provinces, and the cementing of the Anglo-Spanish alliance meant that by June 1808, Iberian

---

[13]   William Cobbett, *The Political Proteus: A View of the Public Character and Conduct of R.B. Sheridan Esq.* (London, 1804), 68–94.

[14]   Cobbett, *Political Proteus*, 80.

politics had taken a strong hold of British sympathies.[15] Sheridan himself advocated for the Peninsular cause when he introduced the affairs of Spain to the House of Commons.[16] The Foreign Secretary, George Canning, responded favourably: recognising that 'no interest could be so purely British as Spanish success', Canning elaborated upon the need to conquer 'from France the complete integrity of the dominion of Spain in every quarter of the world'.[17] While *Pizarro*'s historicism meant that it was still possible to conflate French aggression with the ambition of the Spanish conquistadores, in the summer of 1808 it became a political imperative to revise the play's damning representation of Spanish imperial malignity. Hitherto a French ally and rival imperial power, Spain was now regarded as a nation actively resisting French expansionism by leading the crusade against Napoleonic tyranny. With Sheridan's theatrical success and political agenda once again overlapping, it is essential to unravel the extent to which his play's negative portrayal of the Spaniards was able to accommodate the turn in national political sympathies.

Pizarro's status as a dramatic stock piece on the Romantic stage provides a valuable opportunity to trace contemporary audiences' critical responses to political change, and to tap into the process by which theatre contributed to the formation of national identities during the Napoleonic Wars. *Pizarro*'s openness to interpretation permits it to be read as a palimpsestic play, whose meanings were constantly negotiated and contested by the complex performative, social and political relations that tied together the Romantic-period stage and state. By supplementing my study of Sheridan's play-text with a range of sources, – including playbills, periodicals, newspapers, popular prints, songs, biographies and literary anecdotes – this chapter situates *Pizarro* within the broader social and cultural discourses that helped define Britain during the Napoleonic Wars. Questions of nationhood, the processes of history and the link between agency and patriotic action came under intense scrutiny and revision during this period. Sheridan's *Pizarro* embodies fascinating evidence of how these issues were variously defined, reflected and refracted by the contemporary stage.

---

[15]   The 'Treaty of Peace, Friendship and Alliance between his Britannic Majesty and his Catholic Majesty, Ferdinand VII' was signed in London on 14 January 1809 by George Canning (Secretary of State for Foreign Affairs) and Juan Ruiz de Apodaca (named as envoy extraordinary and minister plenipotentiary of Ferdinand VII). *The Annual Register of a View of the History, Politics, and Literature, For the Year 1809* (London, 1811).

[16]   Hansard (House of Commons, HC), 'Parliamentary debates: Affairs of Spain', (15 June 1808), in *The Parliamentary Debates from the Year 1803 to the Present Time* (London, 1812), 11: 886.

[17]   Hansard, *Parliamentary Debates*, 11: 892.

The Initial Reception, 1799–1800

Pizarro's first reviewers expeditiously attributed the play's frenzied reception to its political appeal. Setting aside its merits on 'a dramatic point of view', the emphasis was placed, instead, on the techniques by which Sheridan had 'applied the text to the duties of this Country'.[18] For many, *Pizarro*'s Spanish theme offered a conveniently transparent allegorical rendering of the war against France, which had begun in 1793. As the *True Briton* explained:

> Though the struggle is between SPANIARDS and the PERUVIANS, the author has been impelled by a true sense of the important contest in which we are engaged.[19]

Arguing along the same lines, the *Morning Post* claimed that in *Pizarro* Sheridan was 'pleading at once the Peruvian and the British cause'.[20] The charges of cruelty levelled against Bonaparte for his Egyptian and Syrian campaigns even helped underline his biographical affinities to the upstart tyrant Pizarro.[21] Audiences' fascination for the theatre's new stage designs, Sheridan's fame as a playwright and the vogue for German dramas undoubtedly contributed to the play's box-office appeal, but the play's first reviewers nevertheless agreed that the interest excited by *Pizarro* was, above all, political and patriotic. War, the national character, and the resolution to fight for ideals would, from the outset, define the logic of *Pizarro*, both on stage and off.

The very first performances of Sheridan's Spanish tragedy made it clear, however, that the play's relation to – and command of – public space was controversial. Since its renovation in 1794, Drury Lane had been able to accommodate more than 3,000 spectators. The stampede on the opening night of *Pizarro* was, notwithstanding, quite exceptional, even by contemporary standards. Thousands of expectant theatregoers were disappointed. 'The conflict' between those who had secured seats and those turned away was 'extremely distressing':

> Ladies of the first fashion, in full dress, were fainting; some lost a shoe, others a hat; the stair-case windows were broken; the door-keepers could not resist the torrent, and many went in without paying; the outside of the doors were surrounded by hundreds who dared not enter, and many went away who had places rather than encounter the crowd.[22]

---

[18]   *TB*, 30 May 1799.

[19]   *TB*, 30 May 1799.

[20]   *MP*, 27 May 1799.

[21]   This association pre-dated the play's premiere. See, for example, the account of the Egyptian expedition published in *The London Packet or New Lloyd's Evening Post*, 10 December 1798.

[22]   *MP*, 25 May 1799.

This description from the *Morning Post* divides Drury Lane's socially hetero-geneous crowd into villains and victims, defining the scramble for admittance as a theatrical event in its own right. Yet, the scene, however animated, was ultimately pathetic rather than bathetic. The decidedly unembarrassed, who opportunistically made their entrance without paying, and the consequently dishevelled ladies of fashion, constituted nothing less than a microcosm of social chaos. With panicked crowds rendering the check of theatrical tickets wholly redundant, managers' traditional attempts at social segregation in terms of the theatre's physical space were woefully ineffectual. On its opening night, *Pizarro*'s uncontainable popularity was tinged with a *frisson* as frightening as it was exciting.

Unsurprisingly, the popular agitation surrounding *Pizarro* resulted in several attempts to control the play's public meaning(s). Consider, for instance, the contemporary newspapers that made it their cultural duty to remark on the celebrity figures who lent their patronage to Sheridan's play: readers were variously informed that the radical Horne Tooke attended an early performance on 20 June 1799, that Lord Nelson watched the play in early December the following year, and that even William Wilberforce, who had not been to the theatre for 20 years, seemed very satisfied with it.[23] Most illustrious of all *Pizarro*'s patrons was the Royal Family, who watched the play on 5 June 1799 during its first season and ordered a command performance in 1804. Reporting on the Royal Family's first attendance at Drury Lane after an absence of four years, the *Morning Post* established an explicit comparison between the royal visit and the play's opening night:

> The difficulties of entering the galleries and pit were ... excessive; the crowd was dreadful; several Ladies fainted, and one falling down near the door, was much bruised. On opening the box doors, the crowd was as great as on the first night of *Pizarro*; the railing was burst off; and the windows, which had been repaired, were again broken.[24]

On both occasions, fashionable ladies were injured by the crowds and the theatre itself damaged (through broken windows, most notably). The crucial difference was that on the evening of the Royal Family's attendance, audiences' impatience to secure the theatrical terrain could be figured as a sign of their loyalty to George III, rather than a merely voyeuristic curiosity for *Pizarro*.

The *True Briton* reported that while '*Pizarro* drew from the Audience great applause throughout' language could do scant justice to 'the rapturous bursts of loyalty and patriotism that arose on the delivery of those passages which expressed an attachment to a beloved Monarch'.[25] Sheridan, who personally escorted the Royal Family to their seats, was quick to exploit the patriotism already ascribed to

---

[23]   On Nelson's visit to the theatre see *Lloyd's Evening Post* 24–26 November 1800; for Wilberforce's reaction to *Pizarro* see *MP*, 31 May 1799.

[24]   *MP*, 6 June 1799.

[25]   *TB*, 6 June 1799.

Pizarro by the contemporary press.[26] In this climate, even the spring flowers and shrubs that had been used to decorate the royal box could be seen to strategically evoke the Peruvian kingdom's aromatic fruits and plants, relating George III to the play's celebrated rhetoric. For the reviewer from the *True Briton*, at least, the 'electric force' operating within the auditorium constituted decisive proof 'that our excellent Monarch reigns in the hearts of his People'.[27]

On the evening of the royal performance, the Drury Lane chorus, with the assistance of the Duke of York's band, performed 'God Save the King' to an ebullient, patriotically enraptured auditorium. Audiences also responded with animation to the play's celebrated second act, which saw John Philip Kemble (who played the part of the Peruvian hero, Rolla) deliver a morale-boosting speech to the native soldiers as they prepared to defend their homeland against the Spanish armies. The *True Briton* was not alone in seizing this scene as the affective climax to both the drama and the Royal Family's response. As *Lloyd's Evening Post* observed:

> His Majesty appeared peculiarly gratified with the noble and animated address of *Rolla* to the Peruvians, in support of their just rights as an independent and happy people, against the lawless encroachments and savage ambition of foreign Invaders.[28]

Most reviewers drew attention to the applause attendant upon Rolla's stirring speech on *Pizarro*'s opening night.[29] It is likely, therefore, that it was during this high point of the royal performance that 'the King wept in the second Act', as related by the *Morning Post*.[30] This observation not only underscored the king's sympathetic attachment to the stage narrative, but also effectively positioned George III within the play's framework of heroic action, allowing the monarch to be identified with Rolla, 'the first and best of heroes' (2.1, *DW*, 2: 667), as much as Ataliba, the Peruvian king.

At the end of Act 2 scene 2 Ataliba draws his sword and leads his soldiers into battle. With paternal care, he addresses them as 'my brethren, my sons, my friends' (2.2, *DW*, 2: 670), orders Alonzo and Rolla to assume their strategic positions, and takes responsibility for leading the main assault: 'strait [*sic*] forwards will I march to meet them, and fight until I see my people saved, or they behold their Monarch fall' (2.2, *DW*, 2: 671). But in the lead up to this war cry Ataliba significantly defers

---

[26]   Sheridan's ceremonious escort of the Royal Family was caricatured in many contemporary prints. See Isaac Cruikshank's *The Return from Pizarro* (5 June 1799); *Pizarro a New Play, or the Drury Lane Masquerade*, published by S.W. Fores (11 June 1799); and William Holland's *Returning from Pizarro!!* (June 1799).

[27]   *TB*, 6 June 1799.

[28]   *Lloyd's Evening Post*, 5–7 June 1799 (540).

[29]   *Evening Mail*, 24–27 May 1799; *The Morning Herald*, 25 May 1799; *The Oracle*, 25 May 1799.

[30]   *MP*, 6 June 1799.

his main address to the Peruvian warriors in order to allow Rolla to 'animate' their spirits (2.2, *DW*, 2: 669). Rolla's speech (recognised as one of Sheridan's original contributions to Kotzebue's text)[31] was a celebrated 'point' in the play, provoking wild bursts of applause and sentimental tears in the auditorium night after night.[32] As Thomas Moore observed, Kemble's success in Act 2 was further heightened by the fact that Rolla's speech was indebted to not only Sheridan's oratory during the Warren Hastings Trial, but also his response to 'The King's Message respecting the Designs of the Enemy' (20 April 1798).[33] These echoes would have permitted George III to identify in Rolla's speech Sheridan's public support for his own address to the nation at a time of possible invasion. Indeed, if the King truly 'wept in the second Act', then his response would not have been out of place: manly tears were commonplace in contemporary parliamentary culture (especially when the vindication of personal character was at stake), and would certainly have been in line with popular responses to the play from within the auditorium at large.[34]

'George III had every reason to be happy with *Pizarro*, particularly with its portrayal of kingship', writes Gillian Russell, for whom the characterisation of Ataliba is dependent upon the 'benevolent, paternalistic relationship to his people ... which George III had himself done much to promote'.[35] While I largely agree with this interpretation, I would nevertheless like to complicate Russell's reading of *Pizarro* by suggesting that the force of Rolla's key speech is likely to have encouraged George III to identify (however wishfully) with the inspirational Rolla, rather than the benign but from an early stage relatively passive Ataliba.[36] Even more decisive than the points of contact between Rolla's speech and Sheridan's response to the 'King's Message Respecting the Designs of the Enemy', is the fact that in *Pizarro* heroic action is patterned, specifically, on Rolla, the war hero. After Ataliba is injured, it is Rolla who leads the charge against the Spanish armies and wins the advantage; in Act 4 Rolla saves Alonzo from Spanish imprisonment;

---

[31] Rolla's harangue – an obvious borrowing from Sheridan's parliamentary oratory – was considered critical to the 'unique' character of his adaptation. See, for instance, [Stuart Moncrieff Thriepland], *Letters Respecting the Performances at the Theatre Royal, Edinburgh* (Edinburgh, 1800), 246.

[32] As Peter Thompson explains, 'points' were 'those passages of a play that could be enlivened by eye-catching stage business, much of it traditional, and for which the actor would be rewarded by ritually repeated rounds of applause'. See 'Acting and actors from Garrick to Kean', in Moody and O'Quinn (eds), *Cambridge Companion to British Theatre*, 12–13.

[33] Qtd. by Cecil Price, 'Introduction' to *Pizarro*, in *DW*, 2: 639.

[34] Christopher Reid, 'Debating Robert Clive: eloquence and identification in the eighteenth-century House of Commons'. Paper presented at the Romantic Realignments seminar series, University of Oxford, 25 February 2010.

[35] Russell, *Theatres of War*, 57.

[36] On George III's self-styling as king, see Linda Colley, 'The Apotheosis of George III: Loyalty, Royalty, and the British Nation 1760–1820', *Past and Present* 102.1, (1984), 94–129.

and finally, while Ataliba expresses his frustration at being unable to soothe Cora's despair, he is cut short by Rolla's arrival with Fernando (5.2, *DW*, 2: 700). At this point, Rolla appears '*bleeding*', returns Cora and Alonzo's missing child, and – in an unique invention of Sheridan's – dies on stage soon after.[37]

Rolla's heroism is powerfully reinforced by the play's stage directions, but narration also exercises a crucial role. This occurs most notably at the end of the second act, when a young boy excitedly relates Rolla's actions to his blind grandfather:

BOY	[...] [*Ascends a rock, and from thence into the tree*] O – now I see them – now –yes – and the Spaniards turning by the steep.
O.MAN	Rolla follows them?
BOY	He does – he does – he moves like an arrow! – now he waves his arm to our soldiers – [*Report of cannon heard.*] Now there is fire and smoke.
	....
O.MAN	Seest thou the King?
BOY	Yes – Rolla is near him! His sword sheds fire as he strikes!

(2.4, *DW*, 2: 674–5)

Ataliba may be present, but it is Rolla who saves the day. Indeed, even Pizarro admires Rolla's actions. In Act 5, as he orders his soldiers to pursue him, Pizarro watches Rolla's escape with fascination: 'With what fury he defends himself! – Ha! – he fells them to the ground – and now –' (5.2, *DW*, 2: 699). As in the boy's report to his grandfather, punctuation by dashes imparts the excitement inspired by Rolla's actions while simultaneously suggesting the difficulty of narrating the hero's fast, spirited exertions. Throughout the play, the Peruvian is depicted as energetic, spontaneous and triumphant. His very first line, which occurs half off stage, represents him as the leader *par excellence*, with trumpets announcing Rolla's entrance as he commands the Peruvian soldiers to assume their positions (2.1, *DW*, 2: 667). In the words of the *True Briton*, Drury Lane that night delivered 'a triumph of Loyalty'.[38] The play's characterisation and patterning of action nonetheless mutually suggest that *Pizarro*'s loyalism rested less on its depiction of kingship than on the heroic agency inspired by the nation's chosen leaders – not necessarily royal.

---

[37]   In Kotzebue's play, Rolla's death occurs off stage, narrated in a soldier's report to Pizarro (5.6). See *Pizarro; the Spaniards in Peru; or, the Death of Rolla. A Tragedy in Five Acts: by Augustus von Kotzebue*, transl. Anne Plumptre. 2nd ed. (London, 1799), 89.

[38]   *TB*, 6 June 1799.

Strong ideological investment in the mobilising power of heroic agency defined *Pizarro* as, first and foremost, a performative text. The play's readers and spectators were bound by markedly different perceptual limitations, as underscored by the anonymous 1799 publication *A Critique of the Tragedy of Pizarro*. In an attempt to underline *Pizarro*'s numerous inconsistencies, the *Critique* focuses significantly on how the play's meanings in the closet diverge from those fostered by its Drury Lane stagings: 'stripping it of the pomp of procession, the glitter of scenery and the noise of music', 'unprejudiced by the voice of the multitude' and 'unawed by the authority of a name', the author of the *Critique* deconstructs the play's performative agency.[39] This dismissal of *Pizarro*'s 'stage-worthiness' ironically identifies the very characteristics that seem to have caused the greatest anxiety about the political and institutional uses to which Sheridan's text could be put.

The contemporary concern over performativity was not, of course, exclusive to *Pizarro*. 'Porta', the author of a two-part essay for the *Monthly Mirror* entitled 'Defence of the Stage', claimed that 'in a theatre, a moral sentiment, well written and delivered, forces its way to the bosoms of an audience, which, elsewhere, would never be heard' (imagined, in fact, 'most irreligiously asleep' in a church).[40] But even this celebration of the theatre as 'one great source of public instruction' relies, notably, on the proper expression and delivery of 'moral' sentiments. These qualifications are best understood with reference to the next issue of the *Monthly Mirror*, which included a review of Joanna Baillie's *A Series of Plays in which it is attempted to delineate the Stronger Passions of the Mind. Each passion being the subject of a tragedy and comedy* (1798). Revealingly, the reviewer for the *Mirror* considered Baillie's design 'more philosophical than practical' because audiences – 'a large assembly of people, indiscriminately collected' – 'have neither time, inclination, nor capacity to enter minutely into discriminations of character'.[41] As Elaine Hadley explains, 'theatres had become the primary public location where all kinds of people could be legally heard and where they could be "dramatized" as contentious voices in public debate. In a theater, if not in a parliamentary election, these people could "vote" their pleasure'.[42] This helps explain why the author of the *Critique* – alarmed by *Pizarro*'s extreme popularity, audiences' predilection for spectacle and Sheridan's public renown – betrayed such little confidence in the discriminatory powers of theatre-goers. As the *Critique* acknowledges, inherent in every performance is the potential to dabble in deceit and mislead by seduction. This made Sheridan's political detractors understandably apprehensive about the

---

[39]   *A Critique of the Tragedy of 'Pizarro'* (London, 1799), 5

[40]   *MM*, January 1801, 11: 45. The first part of the essay was published in the December 1800 issue of the *MM*, 389–90. Gillian Perry suggests that 'Porta' may have been the pen name of the French actress Hyppolite Clarion, who was writing for the *MM* in 1800 and 1801. *Spectacular Flirtations: Viewing the Actress in British Art and Theater 1768–1820* (London: Yale University Press, 2007), 209.

[41]   *MM*, February 1801, 112–14.

[42]   Elaine Hadley, *Melodramatic Tactics: Theatricalized Dissent in the English Marketplace, 1800–1885* (Stanford, CA: Stanford University Press, 1995), 37.

statesman's capacity to influence the crowds at Drury Lane. To many of the play's conservative reviewers, *Pizarro*'s fantasy of national liberation could all too easily morph into a nightmarish image of radical interference.

The Spirit of the Public Journals for 1799 reprints a letter in which its author ('A Lover of Variety') deals with *Pizarro* as a double-edged threat. Not only does 'A Lover of Variety' acknowledge that the play could inflame the passions of its audiences but, through complaints of being 'Pizarroed', conceives of the play as a phenomenon in its own right. *Pizarro* had achieved an unimagined degree of popularity; so much so, in fact, that according to the letter, the play now threatened the permanence of the nation's greatest institutions (including the Royal Society and Houses of Parliament).[43] Frustrated with 'the reign of the monopolising Pizarro', the author vents despair at the social ubiquitousness of Sheridan's play-text, nervously tracing its progress across the private and public spheres, the metropolis and provinces, and different social classes.[44] This anxiety finds its most dramatic expression through an arresting personification of the play:

> I shall make no objection to Pizarro at Drury Lane, or in the booksellers' shops; but I do not like to meet him at the corner of every street, to see him lurking among the dishes of the table, disputing or causing disputes among the quidnuncs of the coffee-house, and following us not only to the doors, but half up the aisles of the churches.[45]

The author had earlier invested the name of Sheridan's play with verbal force (in order to describe a culture that had been '*Pizarroed*'). Here, rather than referring to the eponymous villain of Sheridan's piece, 'Pizarro' is used to signify the abstract identity of the play itself. The technique allows 'A Lover of Variety' to extend the dangers associated with the play's villain into a diatribe against *Pizarro*'s pervasive ideology and, more specifically, its infiltration into the public domain. Locating 'himself' within the radical fringes of London's geography, *Pizarro* is described as 'lurking', 'disputing' and 'following' the city dwellers. In a fit of conservative paranoia 'A Lover of Variety' personifies and dresses *Pizarro* in the garb of a dangerous revolutionary.

Memories of the French Terror and England's own movements for domestic reform remained highly topical in the late 1790s, invigorating the surveillance culture that monitored the circulation of Sheridan's play. Habeas Corpus Suspension Acts were passed in 1794, 1798 and 1799. Sheridan, an active speaker in the House of Commons during this period, described the Habeas Corpus Bill as 'the greatest insult that could be offered to the nation'.[46] By relegating *Pizarro* to the fringes

---

[43]   'Pizarro the Universal Topic!' in *The Spirit of the Public Journals for 1799* (London, 1800), 314–19 (315).

[44]   *Spirit ... 1799*, 317.

[45]   *Spirit ... 1799*, 315.

[46]   Hansard (HC), 'Debate in the Commons on the Habeas Corpus Suspension Bill' (13 February 1800), in *PH* (London, 1812), 34: 1466. See also: 'Debate in the Commons

of the metropolis, 'A Lover of Variety' thus effectively insinuates that Sheridan's radical Whig politics (seen to inform so much of his play's rhetoric) had exceeded the limits of constitutional and social propriety.[47] The author's description of *Pizarro*'s popularity as a 'general contagion' functions, unmistakably, as an appeal to authority against a public menace in urgent need of containment.[48]

Indeed, the public's fascination for Sheridan's *Pizarro* had helped promote a host of derivative texts, including a radical reworking of the play's romance that offered a happy ending for Cora and Rolla.[49] As the *Monthly Review* would succinctly put it, *Pizarro* became 'a hackneyed subject'.[50] But this did not mean that the offshoots of Sheridan's commercial success were unquestioning of their source narrative. Thomas Dutton, who marketed his translation of *Die Spanier in Peru* as the 'ORIGINAL of the NEW TRAGEDY, now performing at Drury-Lane Theatre', repeatedly claimed that *Pizarro*'s historical setting had been invalidated by Sheridan's pandering to the public predilection for spectacle.[51] Claiming that Alonzo's dress is 'better suited for a ball, or some grand festivity than for scenes of blood and carnage', Dutton's edition exposed a series of historical gaps and inconsistencies in Sheridan's drama.[52]

Peru itself, although exotic, was not entirely foreign to the public eye.[53] 'The mines of Mexico and Peru' often featured in late eighteenth-century newspaper reports as shorthand for the imperial economy. Following the loss of the American colonies, reports of native unrest in South America became prominent news items. In June 1790, for instance, *The Times* not only described Peru's 'insurgent state' but also speculated that it 'would require but little address in a British Commander to excite a general revolt'.[54] The emotive power kindled by Spain's Black Legend was explicitly recognised:

---

on the Habeas Corpus Suspension Bill', *PH*, 1798, 33: 1429.

[47]   Sheridan's biographer Fintan O'Toole pointedly notes that whereas in 1792 Sheridan had been seriously considered as a candidate for the role of prime minister, by 1794 he was regarded 'a potential felon'. *A Traitor's Kiss: The Life of Richard Brinsley Sheridan 1751–1816* (London: Granta, 1997), 286.

[48]   *Spirit ... 1799*, 316.

[49]   See *Pizarro: A Tragedy in Five Acts [...] by a North Briton* (London, 1799).

[50]   'Article 38', in *MR*, February 1800, 31: 211.

[51]   Thomas Dutton, *Pizarro in Peru, or the death of Rolla; being the original of the new tragedy now performing at the Theatre-Royal, Drury-Lane. Translated from the last German edition of Augustus von Kotzebue, with notes, &c. by Thomas Dutton* (London, 1799).

[52]   Dutton, *Pizarro in Peru*, 65.

[53]   In 1795 an impromptu gold rush in County Wicklow, Ireland, caused reporters to dub the area 'Little Peru' (*The Times*, 20 October 1795). Helen Maria Williams's poem *Peru* (1784) was well known by the time of *Pizarro*'s premiere, helping excite an interest in Peru that was both fictional and real.

[54]   *The Times*, 3 June 1790.

The cruelty of the first settlers from the Old World, will perhaps be never forgotten, but be handed down in traditionary remembrance from one generation to another, till the end of time.[55]

Sheridan's dramatisation of sixteenth-century Spanish designs for the New World drew upon his audiences' larger understanding of the Black Legend's continued, oppressive hold in contemporary South America.[56]

In *Pizarro* the priest Las Casas, the voice of 'reason and religion' (1.1, *DW*, 2: 662), launches a humanitarian appeal against Spanish violence:

> LAS-C   Do not, I implore you, Chieftains – Countrymen – Do not, I
>   implore you, renew the foul barbarities which your insatiate
>   avarice has inflicted on this wretched, unoffending race! But
>   hush, my sighs – fall not, drops of useless sorrow! – heart-
>   breaking anguish, choke not my utterance – All I entreat is, send
>   me once more to those you *call* your enemies.
>
>   (1.1, *DW*, 2: 661)

This sentimental supplication for diplomatic intercession can be seen to dramatise the real potential, acknowledged by the contemporary press, for Britain to step in as a substitute for Spain's colonial government. In contrast to representations of Spanish imperialism as rule by usurpation and localised tyranny, the British took pride in a model of 'good governance', exchanging conquest for commerce and styling themselves benevolent settlers. Yet, if British governance was put forward as an alternative to Spanish oppression, its substitutionalist qualities were implicitly destabilising.[57] In a political essay that appeared in *The Times* in 1787, the conquest of Peru was explicitly cited in order to declaim against the persistent 'evils' of British commerce, especially slavery:

> Have not the original tracts of the natives of Montezuma's empire, Peru, and the other extended countries of South America, felt severely the dreadful effects arising from the same source? and if fresh instances should be wanting, let us look to the conduct of a *Clive* and a *Hastings*, where, to borrow from the words of a celebrated oration of Mr. Sheridan's in the British House of Commons "we may see the genius of empire wielding the bloody sceptre in one hand, and picking pockets with the other".[58]

---

[55]   *The Times*, 27 August 1790.

[56]   It is worth comparing *Pizarro* to earlier theatrical representations such as William Davenant's *The Cruelty of the Spaniards in Peru* (1658).

[57]   Britain's imperial policy in the late eighteenth century was marked by what Daniel O'Quinn describes as 'a combination of almost unrestrained ambition and nagging trepidation that the British Empire would go the way of ancient Rome, sixteenth-century Spain, or seventeenth-century Holland'. O'Quinn, *Staging Governance*, 23.

[58]   *The Times*, 14 September 1787.

The essay brings together the exploitation of native people, Spanish colonialism, the Warren Hastings trial and Sheridan's celebrated speech in one narratorial frame. The parallel drawn between Spain's introduction of slavery to the New World and Britain's own investment in human trafficking in the late eighteenth century, may also explain why Wilberforce broke his 20 years of abstinence from the theatre in order to watch *Pizarro*.[59] But more significantly still, the essay distinctly identifies Sheridan in the attempt to remedy these prime examples of the moral degeneracy of empire. As Suleri and Taylor have compellingly argued, Sheridan's speeches in the Warren Hastings trial would continue to inflect the patriotic rhetoric of *Pizarro*.[60] The charges of corruption and oppression directed against the East India Company hovered below the play's emotive oratory, exposing the British interest in the subcontinent as one no less sanguinary than that of the Spanish conquistadores in the Americas.

Sheridan's ideological centrality in both playhouse and Parliament thus provided competing sites for the social redemption promised by his new play. Pitt's accusations against *Pizarro*'s originality suggest that, in his opinion, Sheridan was guilty of both manipulating the theatre for political ends and conducting politics as role-play. English theatres constituted contested spaces in which political ideas were disseminated and consumed. While the newspapers' initial response had been to laud *Pizarro*'s patriotic narrative (thereby promoting and ensuring its celebrity status as a national mainpiece), the play's broad appeal was soon regarded with decided mistrust. Conservative anxiety was particularly acute by the end of *Pizarro*'s first season. Whereas to some, *Pizarro* provided evidence of Sheridan's radical sympathies, others feared that the mass appeal of spectacle could lead to the confusion of theatrical illusion with reality, or even result in altogether senseless fits of hysteria.[61] In short, *Pizarro* existed as a phenomenon both on stage and off; its meanings available for circulation, negotiation and exchange (beyond institutional control).

Pizarro's Political Meanings, 1801–1803

Between March 1802 and May 1803, Britain and France enjoyed a brief respite from war. To celebrate the Peace of Amiens, the Union Club held a grand masquerade at its headquarters, Cumberland House. No expense had been spared and tickets sold out fast, with an additional six hundred unexpected revellers raising the total count

---

[59]   *MP*, 31 May 1799.
[60]   Sara Suleri, *The Rhetoric of English India* (Chicago: University of Chicago Press, 1992), see Chap. 3 esp.; and Taylor, *Theatres of Opposition*, Chap. 4.
[61]   See *London Packet or New Lloyd's Evening Post*, 18 December 1799, for its 'whimsical' report of a sailor's impassioned response to the play: 'Whenever *Pizarro* appeared the honest Tar grumbled forth his indignation, till his feelings were fully gratified in the fall of the Tyrant'.

of guests to approximately 2,000.[62] In the area surrounding the house, the attendees were invited to stroll through an avenue illuminated by a large transparency that represented '*War* subdued by Peace'. Inside, distant views of London and Paris framed the Club's 'sumptuous' ballroom, while the billiard room, with its various allegorical representations of 'the return of *Commerce* through *Peace*', was reserved for the exclusive use of the evening's guest of honour, the Prince of Wales.[63] In this highly symbolic and carefully demarcated social space, Sheridan's *Pizarro* was also unmistakably present: the *Morning Chronicle* espied among the socialites 'above a dozen *Priestesses* and *Virgins* of the Sun, chiefly copied from the dresses of Pizarro [*sic*]'.[64] These fashionable ladies would undoubtedly have been admired for their beautiful, costly dresses and the noble, dignified air these imparted.[65] But were their costume choices also politically judicious?

The Priests (rather than 'Priestesses') and Virgins of the Sun first appear in Act 2 scene 2 of *Pizarro*, a scene famous for its magnificent setting in 'The Temple of the Sun' and Rolla's speech to the Peruvians preparatory to war.[66] The mood of thanksgiving with which the scene opens nevertheless gives way to one of *Pizarro*'s most politicised moments, wherein even the rituals performed by the Priests and Virgins conclude with a song of 'praise' that doubles as a passionate call to arms:

[Priests and Virgins]
[Kelly, Dignum, Mrs Crouch, Miss Decamp, Stephens, Dufour, Leak]
....

[Thanksgiving]
Give praise, give praise, the God has heard,
Our God most awfully rever'd!
The alter his own flames enwreath'd!
Then be the conquering sword unsheath'd,
And victory sit on Rolla's brow,
Our foes to crush – to overthrow!

(2.2, *DW*, 2: 670)

---

[62] A ticket costing twenty guineas would allow one member to attend with two ladies. *MP*, 9 March 1802.

[63] *MC,* 2 June 1802.

[64] This included Lady Holland as a Priestess of the Sun. *MC,* 2 June 1802.

[65] See also *The Times*, 1 January 1801, on ladies' fashions and the trend for 'Pizarro feathers'.

[66] While Priestesses of the Sun do not, in fact, appear in *Pizarro*, they feature significantly in Kotzebue's *Die Sonnen-jungfrau* (1789) – for English translations and adaptations, see Anne Plumptre, *The Virgin of the Sun* (1799); Benjamin Thompson, *Rolla* (1800); and Frederick Reynolds, *The Virgin of the Sun* (1812). It is possible that either the reviewer for the *MC* conflated the two plays or that the masqueraders appropriated *Pizarro*'s dramatis personae, but the Temple of the Sun nevertheless constitutes a sacred space in both plays.

While the Peruvians might, in more general terms, be aligned with liberty, in this particular scene, they are at their most war-like, and their religious superstitions furthest from the British Protestant norm. In recognition of the play's aggressive male heroics, it is significant that none of the gentlemen who attended the ball seem to have chosen to dress as either Rolla or Alonzo. In *Pizarro*, the Peruvians' private and public spheres are very carefully differentiated. When the men go to battle, the women and children retreat among the rocks to safety (3.1, *DW*, 2: 676). Consequently, the men might be understood to fight in order to protect the sanctity of the private sphere, while the Virgins symbolise female moral influence and the virtues of domesticity. In their decision to don the robes of the Peruvian nobility and align themselves with this favourite scene of *Pizarro,* the ladies at the Union Club imparted a symbolic message of social reconciliation and regeneration. By engaging with the play's complex visual register (rich in contingency) they sought to express their political sympathies through an affirmation that the Peace they celebrated had been sanctioned as noble, ethical and principled. Reinventing the interplay between theatrical and political realities, the Union ladies' '*Pizarro* masquerading' testifies to the perceived centrality that Sheridan's play had acquired in contemporary society.

When the fragile Peace of Amiens collapsed in May 1803 it brought renewed fears of an imminent French invasion. Sheridan responded to this turn in political events by also looking to Act 2 scene 2 of *Pizarro*. It is characteristic of the play's 'protean' nature that the same scene that had been used by aristocratic ladies to celebrate the Peace of Amiens could, less than a year later, represent the urgent need for a return to arms. In 1803 the playwright extracted Rolla's speech in the Temple of the Sun and retitled it 'Sheridan's Address to the People: Our King! Our Country! And our God!'. Published as a broadsheet in London and Dublin, it was widely disseminated.

Sheridan's decision to divorce Rolla's speech from its original dramatic context was, however, loaded with political implication. In an engaging discussion of the links between radicalism and visual culture in the 1790s, John Barrell contends that 'the language of theatre advertising could function as a language that addressed both the polite and the vulgar much more effectively than the language, or rather the languages, of formal political debate'; 'the sheer ubiquitousness' and consequent familiarity of the playbill making it one of the 'most conspicuous, attention-seeking, visually enjoyable advertisements around'.[67] 'Sheridan's Address', as it came to be known more colloquially, reinforced this link between theatrical and political cultures, with the broadsheet's prominence in the cities of Dublin and London giving the play's

---

[67] John Barrell, 'Radicalism, Visual Culture, and Spectacle in the 1790s', *Romanticism on the Net* (May 2007), Numéro 46 [Accessed 01.07.2012] <http://www.erudit.org/revue/ron/2007/v/n46/016131ar.html> [DOI : 10.7202/016131ar].

rhetoric a visible presence in the propaganda campaign that sought to equip Britons for the renewed war effort.

This pitch of loyalist sentiment was variously (re)figured in satirical prints by Isaac Cruikshank, James Gillray and William Holland, whose caricatures, like theatrical performances, excited the interests of a broad urban audience, sensitive to political nuance. As Daniel O'Quinn asserts, there was a 'tight fit between theatrical performance, political life, and the print media of late eighteenth-century Britain'.[68] Visual satire circulated more widely than textual satire, and was more difficult to prosecute (however personal, and potentially libellous). In *City of Laughter: Sex and Satire in Eighteenth-Century London* (2006), Vic Gatrell explains how these satires 'operated within a shame-culture in which the public demolition of reputation was the most feared of social sanctions'.[69] The numerous satirical prints that capitalised upon Sheridan's theatrical fortunes in order to denounce his politics offer a neat exposition of this; the specific identification of Sheridan with Pizarro lending support to Fintan O'Toole's argument that '*Pizarro* was much more about Sheridan than it was about either Spaniards or Peruvians'.[70]

Gillray's *Pizarro Contemplating Over the Product of his New Peruvian Mine* (4 June 1799; Figure 1.1) depicts Sheridan, in full Spanish costume, greedily handling *Pizarro*'s box-office takings. With brilliant metonymy, Gillray uses the play's narrative of colonial adventure to denounce Sheridan's exploitation of patriotic sentiment. In the print, Drury Lane's neoclassical columns are decorated with cherubim blowing the trumpet of Fame while holding scrolls that read 'Morning Chronicle – Puff Puff Puff', 'Morning Herald – Puff Puff Puff', 'Courier – Puff Puff', and 'Times – Puff Puff'.[71] Cobbett's strictures on Sheridan in *The Political Proteus* would similarly declaim against the newspapers' eulogistic reviews of *Pizarro* as 'a natural alliance, a sort of family compact, between the press and the theatre'.[72] In the early 1800s the theatre's conflation of political and financial cultures continued to destabilise *Pizarro*'s claims to patriotism, making the loyalism of 'Sheridan's Address' highly questionable.

---

[68] O'Quinn, *Staging Governance*, 11.

[69] Vic Gatrell, *City of Laughter: Sex and Satire in Eighteenth-Century London* (London: Atlantic Books, 2006), 220.

[70] O'Toole, *Traitor's Kiss*, 345.

[71] These can also be read as allusions to Sheridan's *The Critic*. See especially 1.2 for Puff's definition of the various forms of the art, including 'THE PUFF DIRECT – the PUFF PRELIMINARY – the PUFF COLLATERAL – the PUFF COLLUSIVE, and the PUFF OBLIQUE, or PUFF by IMPLICATION – '. *DW*, 2: 514.

[72] Cobbett, *Political Proteus*, 206.

Figure 1.1   James Gillray, *Pizarro Contemplating Over the Product of his New Peruvian Mine*, 4 June 1799. © The Trustees of the British Museum.

Gillray's misspelt *Pizzarro* print (1 October 1799) for the *Anti-Jacobin Review* also denounces Sheridan's claim to the laurels of patriotism (Figure 1.2).[73] Here, Gillray depicts Sheridan, mounted upon Kemble's head, with a bag of money under his left arm and a scroll in his right hand, which reads 'Spoken before a select party of Friends':

> This season true my Principles I've sold
> To fool the world & pocket George's gold
> Prolific mine! – anglo-peruvian food
> Provok'd my taste – and Candidate I stood –
> While Kemble my support with LOYAL face
> Declares THE PEOPLE'S CHOICE with stage-trick grace.[74]

---

[73] The print appeared in *The Anti-Jacobin* (October 1799, 4: 318) alongside a review of *A Critique of the Tragedy of 'Pizarro'*. The author of *A Critique* also uses *The Critic* to undermine *Pizarro*'s spectacular appeal.

[74] The scroll can also be interpreted as an attack on the play's 'legitimacy'. Minor theatres often circumvented the ban on spoken dialogue by inscribing key lines onto scrolls

Figure 1.2   James Gillray, *Pizzarro*, etched by J. Chapman. 1 October 1799.
               Harry Beard Collection. © Victoria and Albert Museum, London.

The print's typographical enhancements elide Sheridan's distorted 'Speech' with
Rolla's address to the Peruvian warriors:

> ROL.   Be our plain answer this: The throne WE honour is the
>   PEOPLE'S CHOICE – the laws we reverence are our brave
>   Fathers' legacy – the faith we follow teaches us to live in bonds
>   of charity with all mankind, and die with hope of bliss beyond
>   the grave. Tell your invaders this, and tell them too, we seek no
>   change; and, least of all, such change as they would bring us.
>   [*Trumpets sound.*]
>   (2.2, *DW*, 2: 669)

In the popularly perceived metaphorical exchange that equated Pizarro and his
troops with Napoleon and his invading armies, Rolla's speech was seen to rebuke
the revolutionary threat by upholding instead the constitutional foundation of
the British monarchy. Gillray, however, rejects and reverses Rolla's supposedly
'plain answer'. Sheridan, dressed in Elizabethan costume (as Pizarro) is portrayed

and banners. See Moody, *Illegitimate Theatre in London*, 28–30.

instead as the consummate actor. The 'select party of Friends' whom he addresses is suggestive of the playwright's involvement with the 'Society of the Friends of the People', a radical group formed in 1792 to advocate parliamentary reform in the wake of the French Revolution. Despite appearances, Gillray insists that Sheridan retained a firm hold on his earlier, putatively seditious political beliefs.

The playwright's career as an outspoken Opposition Member of Parliament infused jarring political insinuations into *Pizarro*'s outwardly hegemonic appeal. In 'Pizzarro', Sheridan is depicted as if he were 'riding' Kemble because, according to Gillray, it was Kemble's conservative reputation that directed the play's patriotic success. As Shearer West carefully points out, in contradistinction to damning portrayals of Sheridan, *Pizarro* prints tended to emphasise Kemble as the play's dignified and justly celebrated star performer.[75] The perceived difference between Sheridan's excited opportunism and Kemble's refined 'classical' acting finds powerful expression in Gillray's print, where the artist comes short of caricaturing Kemble who is, in fact, quite flatteringly depicted with Romanised features.[76]

In his 1803 print *John Bull and the Alarmist* (1 September 1803; Figure 1.3) Gillray caricatures Sheridan as a dishevelled, self-serving bill-sticker who carries 'Loyal Bills' and the 'Sherry Andrew Address' under his arm.[77] In keeping with the personalised iconography of his earlier prints Gillray depicts Sheridan (with the drinker's tell-tale red nose) as an alcoholic 'Sherry Andrews'.[78] The pun on his name, which retains the clownish label of 'Merry Andrews', references performativity more generally: Sheridan is here depicted as an actor, whose speech to John Bull is a re-hash of Iago's warning to Brabantio in Shakespeare's *Othello*. Sheridan's ineffectual management of Drury Lane Theatre is also lampooned, with the ragged clothes and playbills peeping out of his breast pocket pointing to the well-known fact that *Pizarro*'s lucrative success had been desperately needed.[79]

---

[75]   Shearer West, *The Image of the Actor: Verbal and Visual Representations in the Age of Garrick and Kemble* (New York: St Martin's Press, 1991), 84.

[76]   Gillray emphasises the actor's roman nose, in probable recognition that 'Kemble was the dominant Shakespearean actor of the period, and Coriolanus ... Kemble's defining role'. Jonathan Sachs, *Romantic Antiquity: Rome in the British Imagination 1789–1832* (Oxford: Oxford University Press, 2009), 194.

[77]   By the mid-1790s the British government had developed a 'policy of issuing "alarms" – predictions first of treason at home, then increasingly of invasion abroad'. Mary Favret explains that by 1796 these 'alarms' were a recognised 'form of prophecy ... attributed to and practiced primarily by government supporters, both sincere and cynical'. *War at a Distance*, 85.

[78]   See James Gillray's *The Union-Club* (1801) where Sheridan is rendered immediately recognisable, in the words of Vic Gatrell, by 'his boozer's face bloated and nose bulbous and a bottle raised in his right hand' (*City of Laughter*, 289); and *Physical Aid, – or – Britannia Recover'd From a Trance; – also, Patriotic courage of Sherry Andrew, & a Peep Thro' the Fog* (March 1803). For Sheridan's heavy drinking and friendship with the Prince Regent, see O'Toole, *Traitor's Kiss*, 179.

[79]   Sheridan whispers to John Bull (George III): 'A Corsican Thief has just slipt from his quarters, And coming to Ravish your Wives & your Daughters!'

Figure 1.3   James Gillray, *John Bull and the Alarmist*, 1 September 1803.
               © The Trustees of the British Museum.

By portraying Sheridan in such shabby habiliment Gillray secures an efficacious shorthand for his two-pronged accusations against Sheridan's unreliability on personal and professional grounds. The 'pro bono publico' claim stated at the bottom of the playwright-manager's so-called 'Loyal Bill' further reinforces this narrative by exposing Sheridan's true intention of aiming for profit through the staging of putatively patriotic dramas, while the Jacobin cap, hanging from his coat pocket, points to persistent revolutionary loyalties. By such detailing Gillray insists that troubling contiguities persisted between Sheridan's politics after Amiens and his radicalism in the 1790s.[80] *John Bull and the Alarmist* denounces

---

[80]   John Bull in this print is George III (with his coronation chair in the background) holding a tankard with the royal coat of arms. John Bull's frothing tankard seems to conjure the popular anecdote that when John Thelwall blew off the head from a pot of porter, he boasted: "This is the way I would serve kings". See Michael Scrivener, 'Romanticism and the Law: The Discourse of Treason, Sedition, and Blasphemy in the Political Trials, 1794–1820', *Romantic Circles Praxis Series* <http://www.rc.umd.edu/praxis/law/ scrivener/mscrv.htm> [Accessed 11.04.14]. It is also worth comparing the papers carried by Sheridan to the scroll that he clutches in Gillray's earlier *Pizzarro* print (possibly referring to illegitimate theatre practices). Sheridan's putatively patriotic gestures (in *John Bull and the Alarmist*) is dismissed with the same disbelief and wariness implied by the deflation of Rolla's speech in *Pizzarro*.

Sheridan's famous 'Address' as nothing more than a political stratagem, while identifying the double-dealing Sheridan as the real cause for alarm.

In 1803 when Sheridan extracted Rolla's speech from his play he also drew attention to the defining moments of his political career. *Pizarro*'s humanitarian appeal and Rolla's choice simile, comparing the protection offered by the Spaniards to that of vultures to lambs, ' – covering and devouring them!' (2.2, *DW*, 2: 669), continues to be regarded as one of the play's most arresting political speeches, reverberating with Sheridan's declamation against colonial exploitation in India:

> This was British justice! this was British humanity! Mr. Hastings ensures to the allies of the company, in the strongest terms, their prosperity and protection; the former he secures by sending an army to plunder them of their wealth and to desolate their soil! His protection is fraught with a similar security, like that of a vulture to a lamb; grappling in its vitals! thirsting for its blood! scaring off each petty kite that hovers round; and then, with an insulting perversion of terms, calling sacrifice *protection*![81]

Rolla's address, like Sheridan's apostrophe on British justice and humanity, is also crucially dependent upon irony: ' – Yes – THEY will give enlightened freedom to *our* minds, who are themselves the slaves of passion, avarice, and pride' (2.2, *DW*, 2: 669). The verbal parallels liken the conquistador to the nabob, denouncing both types of colonisers as villainous, corrupt and dehumanised by their greed. By the early nineteenth century, the focal point of Sheridan's play resounded with political and aesthetic valences that were inextricably associated with the playwright's well-publicised career as a Member of Parliament.

There is evidence to suggest, however, that after the opening night, when Sheridan reworked his play into a more manageable performance piece, significant changes were made to Rolla's harangue. Intriguingly, this resulted in the excision of the famous vulture and lamb imagery from the 1799 and 1807 Drury Lane promptbooks for *Pizarro*.[82] Kemble, renowned for his conservative politics, is likely to have felt uncomfortable with the passage's famous allusiveness to Sheridan's political oratory, and thus removed the potential for contention altogether. If so, his decision would suggest that while memories of the Warren Hastings Trial may have helped coalesce the play's humanitarian sympathies, its colonial nuances were not limited

---

[81]   'The Trial of Warren Hastings' (13 June 1788), in *The Speeches of the Right Honourable Richard Brinsley Sheridan. With a Sketch of his Life*, edited by a Constitutional Friend. 3 vols. (London, 1842), 1. 413. David Taylor's work on Sheridan's oratory points, however, to a 'second, even more flagrant (indeed verbatim) instance of self-quotation'; Rolla's plea to Pizarro for the safety of Alonzo and Cora's child effectively being a rehash of Sheridan description of Major Naylor's testimony during the Hastings trial. *Theatres of Opposition*, 130–31.

[82]   The *Pizarro* promptbooks for 1799 and 1807 are respectively housed in the Garrick Club in London and Newberry Library in Chicago. In 2.2 of the Newberry Library's copy, the reference to 'vultures and lambs' is also cut, although emendations by another hand suggest that it was recovered for later nineteenth-century productions.

to the subcontinent. The exclusion of these key lines from the play's later production serves as an important reminder of the interpretative differences occasioned by reading the play compared to seeing it in performance (differences that will also have a significant bearing upon this book's later discussion of Shakespeare and the Spanish-themed spectacles staged at the minor theatres).

In her investigation of Romantic representations of American Indians, Astrid Wind points out that in 1781, the year after Sheridan's election to the House of Commons, there was an indigenous uprising in Peru.[83] Tupac Amaru II led the revolt, claiming to be the descendant of the last indigenous leader of the nation. His rebellion, although unsuccessful, was the first uprising against the Spanish colonists in nearly two centuries, drawing a direct line between *Pizarro* and the international news bulletins of 1781. If Amaru's revolt provided an exemplary moment of the empire 'writing back' by asserting itself against the mother country, then Sheridan's play was equally concerned with offering alternative insights into human consciousness. *Pizarro*'s narrative of invasion, although most immediately concerned with the French wars and British imperialism in India, cultivated the nation's historical mindset at its widest geographical expanse.

Simply put, *Pizarro* was a play that set out to make Britain seem less familiar. In Rolla's key speech the use of the signifiers 'they' and 'we' becomes increasingly mobile. While rhetorical coherence requires the hero's comparison between the Spaniards ('they') and Peruvians ('we/our') to draw upon points of dissimilarity between Peruvian honour and Spanish criminality, this linguistic distinction proves decidedly unstable:

> ROL   Your generous spirit has compared as mine has, the motives,
> which, in a war like this, can animate *their* minds, and OURS.
>
> (2.2, *DW*, 2: 669)

The fluctuation between second, third and first person pronouns threatens the speech's all-important ironic turn, which requires the stress to be placed on a rigidly differential us/them dynamic. While the speech inspires audiences to 'feel' its truth, as a written text it demands a degree of labour from the 'thinking' reader. The published play-text implicitly concedes this, relying upon typographical emphasis to avoid any ambiguities. The 1803 broadsheet also made distinctive use of italicisation or, as Cobbett deridingly called it, 'typographical harlotry'.[84] Particular and determinate, the use of 'we' necessarily reinforces a sense of community that excludes the distant 'they' from the space shared by the addressee and his intended audience. Sheridan's broadsheet sought to capture the performative, interactive elements of Rolla's speech and its power to induce social co-operation at a time of national stress and uncertainty.

---

[83]   Astrid Wind, 'American Indians in National Contexts: The Politics of Literary Encounter', (unpublished doctoral thesis, University of Oxford, 2002), 102.

[84]   Cobbett, *Political Proteus*, 80.

The notorious difficulty of attempting to define the political other points to *Pizarro*'s socio-cultural framing during a time of constitutional indeterminacy. Fiona Stafford neatly describes how the 1802 political debates exposed 'a new sense of Britain', forged through the war with France but 'wrought into an unfamiliar form by the Union with Ireland'.[85] Sheridan's play found a pertinent outlet in the political climate of 1801–1803, which saw the historically tense Anglo-Irish rapport make its contributions to a new sense of British identity in the making. In London, 'Sheridan's Address' was printed by the loyalist publisher James Asperne, who charged six shillings for one hundred copies of the broadsheet: in Dublin, it was available at almost half this price, costing 'Three Shilling and Three Pence per Hundred'.[86] The higher cost of living in London most probably accounts for this pricing disparity, but the cheaper (and potentially more inflammatory) Irish 'version' of Sheridan's broadsheet should not go unnoticed.

The broadsheet's parallel geographies of production and dissemination open up constructive new readings of *Pizarro*'s famous rhetorical set-piece. Sheridan's Irish patriotism had amounted, since the 1780s, to 'an innate aspect of his fame'.[87] David Francis Taylor describes the condition of Ireland as 'a political obsession' for Sheridan.[88] From his speeches denouncing the ministry's colonialist attempts to control Ireland, to his precariously close ties with the Irish rebels Edward Fitzgerald and Arthur O'Connor, Sheridan's 'Irishness' provided an alternative dimension to the politics of *Pizarro*.[89] This was especially true in relation to the play's definitions of treachery – an accusation as topical during the Peace of Amiens as it had been during the 1790s and would be again during the Peninsular War.

In the opening scene of the play, Pizarro introduces Alonzo's deflection to the Peruvian way of life as an act of betrayal both to Spain and, more personally, to Pizarro himself:

> PIZ   Alonzo! the traitor! How I once loved that man! His noble
>   mother entrusted him, a boy, to my protection. At my table did
>   he feast – in my tent did he repose. I had marked his early
>   genius, and the valorous spirit that grew with it.
>
>   (1.1, *DW*, 2: 659)

---

[85]   Fiona Stafford, '*The Edinburgh Review* and the Representation of Scotland', in *British Romanticism and the* Edinburgh Review*: Bicentenary Essays*, ed. Massimiliano Demata and Duncan Wu (Basingstoke: Palgrave Macmillan, 2002), 38.

[86]   'Sheridan's Address to the People: Our King! our Country! And our God!' (London and Dublin, 1803). Compare Shuttleworth copies 145 (1) and (2). The Bodleian Libraries, The University of Oxford.

[87]   O'Toole, *Traitor's Kiss*, 319.

[88]   Taylor, *Theatres of Opposition*, 127.

[89]   For a more detailed discussion of *Pizarro*'s Irish dimension see Astrid Wind, 'Irish Legislative Independence and the Politics of Staging American Indians in the 1790s', *Symbiosis: A Journal of Anglo-American Literary Relations*, 5 (2011), 1–16.

The intimacy implied by the emotional and physical enclosures of 'protection', 'table' and 'tent' testify to Pizarro's private affections for his one-time friend. By no coincidence, Alonzo's first appearance in the play is also associated with domestic attachments. Audiences are first introduced to Alonzo in Act 2 as a proud father and devoted husband to Cora. Many of the play's early reviewers commented on the profound ways in which playgoers appeared to have been moved by Cora's maternal affections in this scene.[90] Aware that Alonzo had recently been sleepless, nervous and overcome with 'struggling sighs', Cora anxiously inquires after his happiness. In response to her queries, Alonzo poignantly asks: 'Must not I fight against my country, against my brethren?' (2.1, *DW*, 2: 666). It is left to Cora to assuage his restlessness by arguing against the arbitrariness of national ties: 'Do they not seek our destruction, and are not all men brethren?' (2.1, *DW*, 2: 666), she asks, employing language that poignantly echoes the motto adopted by campaigners for the abolition of slavery.

When confronted by Pizarro, it is, therefore, all the more impressive that the hitherto self-tormented Alonzo should succeed in passionately defending his Spanish identity:

> AL   No! Deserter I am none! I was not born among robbers! pirates!
>   murderers! – When those legions, lured by the abhorred lust
>   of gold, and by thy foul ambition urged, forgot the honour of
>   Castilians, and forsook the duties of humanity, THEY deserted
>   ME. I have not warred against my native land, but against those
>   who have usurped its power.
>
>   (3.3, *DW*, 2: 681)

Alonzo's speech portrays the Spanish conquest of Peru as the enterprise of a selfish minority who advance corrupt claims of bringing a national project to fruition. It is tempting to construe *Pizarro*'s retelling of sixteenth-century Spanish imperialism as Sheridan's way of re-imagining his own, very personal stake in Anglo-Irish political tensions. While dramatising important reasons for the Irish Rebellion, Sheridan could feel secure enough to stand his own ground against charges of treason. In July 1803 Sheridan spoke in the Commons on 'The King's Message Relative to the Rebellion in Ireland' with a 'sincere and heartfelt love of my country'.[91] Sheridan's use of the possessive 'my' seems to originate from an attachment comparable to that which allows Alonzo to continue to refer to Spain as 'my native land', despite his naturalisation into Peruvian society.

Alonzo's speech on identity highlights the anarchic ways by which nationhood might impinge on the concepts of history and agency. During the Peninsular War, this would make the distance between the deictic markers 'we' and 'they' (so clearly italicised in 'Sheridan's Address') irreducibly vexed. By removing it from both the

---

[90]   See, for example, *Star*, 25 May 1799.
[91]   Hansard (HC), 'The King's Message Relative to the Rebellion in Ireland' (28 July 1803), in *PH,* 36: 1677.

playhouse and its originally English metropolitan audiences, the Irish publication of 'Sheridan's Address' realised a double-displacement of Rolla's set speech. In Dublin, resistance to the Union implicated the distant 'they' with the same political aggression that English audiences of *Pizarro* identified with French enmity.

In London, by contrast, 'Sheridan's Address' had all the visible signs of promoting the strength of the home guard. William Holland's *The Ghost of Queen Elizabeth!!* (20 July 1803; Figure 1.4) parodies the frequency with which sixteenth-century Spain featured in the propaganda efforts of 1803. The print depicts the spectre of the great Tudor queen threatening Napoleon with a picture of the defeat of the Spanish Armada. Elizabeth's reign, credited with successful overseas expansion and relative internal stability, provided a favourable benchmark for nineteenth-century Britain, as underlined in 1803 by the broadsheet publication of Queen Elizabeth's speech to the troops at Tilsbury (Figure 1.5). This meant that *Pizarro*'s anti-Spanish inflections coincided fortuitously with the renewed war effort, enabling 'Sheridan's Address' to retain its original dramatic purpose of inciting resistance to foreign invaders.

With Sheridan's broadsheet on display across the metropolis, *Pizarro* played to a Drury Lane auditorium packed with Volunteers. In an effort to underline the play's loyalist import, the profits from the Drury Lane performances collected at the end of the season were donated to Lloyd's Patriotic Fund, established in July 1803 to provide charitable support and reward for those wounded or killed

Figure 1.4   William Holland, *The Ghost of Queen Elizabeth!!*, 20 July 1803.
© The Trustees of the British Museum.

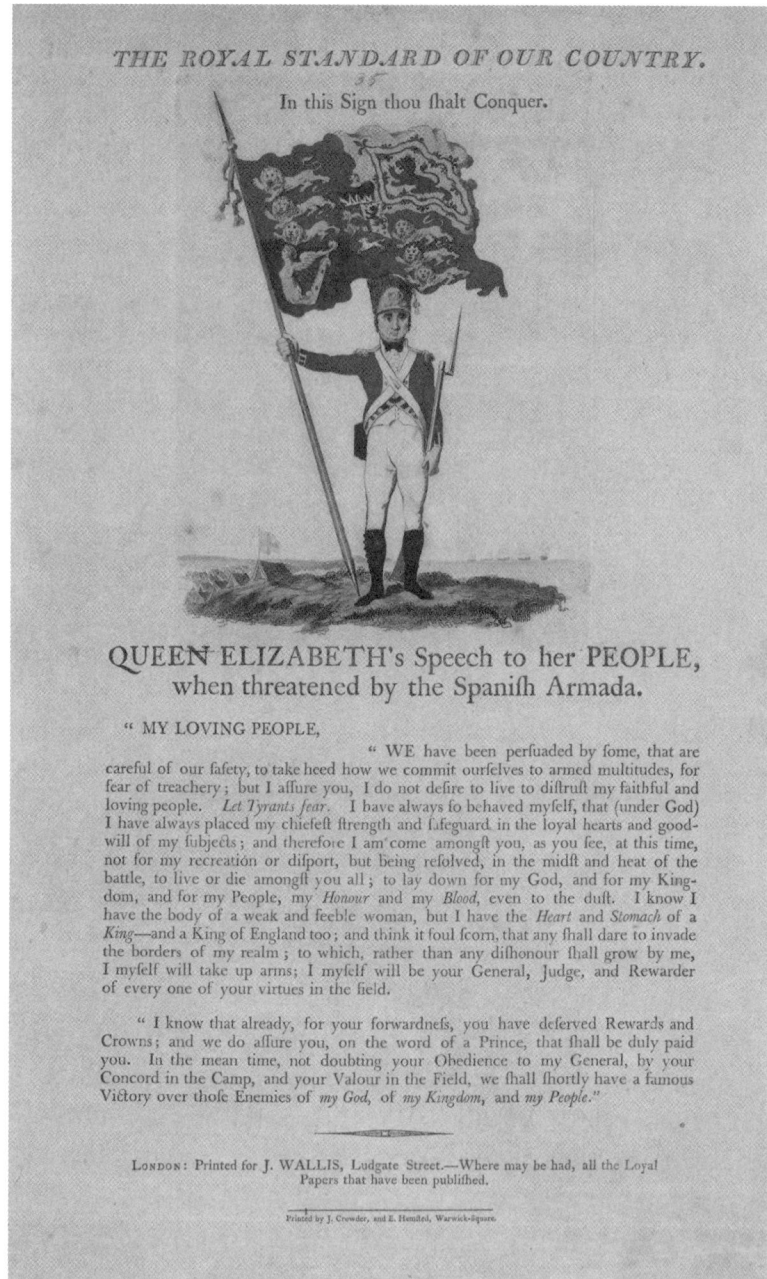

Figure 1.5   The Royal standard of our country (with) Queen Elizabeth's speech
               to her people, when threatened by the Spanish Armada, 1803. © The
               Bodleian Libraries, The University of Oxford. Curzon b. 12 (6).

in action.[92] According to O'Toole, 'by making himself champion of the Volunteer Corps, Sheridan was trying simultaneously to be true to radical principles and to wrap himself in the flag'.[93] This was bound to be tricky, but proved even more so in 1804 when, after the recession of the French invasion threat, fears of an increasingly plebeian Volunteer Movement caused the government to begin to disband its national militia.[94]

Sheridan's decision to retitle Rolla's polemic 'Sheridan's Address' and publish the speech outside its original dramatic frame was, perhaps, ideologically more costly than lucrative. Although the 1803 broadsheet found a ready market in the loyalist press and propaganda efforts to rally Volunteers, its patriotic fervour remained attached to a long and recriminatory history heightened by Sheridan's Irish loyalties and the government's later disbanding of the Volunteers. The Address's potentially radical meanings in Ireland, added to the suspicious loyalist turn taken in Sheridan's English politics, seemed to only further expose *Pizarro*'s essentially porous discourse. At the turn of the nineteenth century, the instability associated with the play's central speech strongly suggested that Sheridan's *Pizarro* was, in effect, more a process than an event *per se*. The play's authority, which had been continually questioned and pointedly reinvented since its first run, continued to generate heated political debate.

Historical Contiguities, 1808–1815

During the summer of 1807 Napoleon was at the apex of his political fortunes: having conquered or secured alliances with virtually all of the European powers, only Sweden, Britain and Portugal remained opposed to the French regime.[95] Determined to subdue Britain, 'this nation of shopkeepers', by interfering in the Iberian economy (both political and commercial), Napoleon's actions triggered a brutal war in the Peninsula. Known locally as 'La Guerra de la Independencia' (the War of Independence) the Spanish conflict was characterised by guerilla movements and generally staunch local resistance. The British were quick to espouse the cause of their Spanish compatriots. Almost any news (and indeed even absence of news) from the Peninsula attracted headline notice in the national press. Topical addresses and plays were staged at the theatres, and numerous satirical prints published on the subject of the Anglo-Spanish alliance. The transformation of the Iberian Peninsula into Britain's new focal point for military intervention meant that *Pizarro*'s narrative of imperial encroachment and patriotic agency acquired renewed relevance.

---

92 This proved a source of anxiety for Cobbett. See *Political Proteus*, 76.
93 O'Toole, *Traitor's Kiss*, 375.
94 On the Volunteer movement, see Russell, *Theatres of War*, 13.
95 Gregory Fremont-Barnes, *The Napoleonic Wars: The Peninsular Wars 1807–1814* (Oxford: Osprey Publishing, 2002), 25.

The Spaniards' fight for what Samuel Whitbread termed 'their liberty as a people, and the assertion of their independence as a nation' seemed well represented by the plight of the Peruvians in Sheridan's drama.[96] With the British nation united in support of Spain, the Peninsular Campaign was seized as a chance for 'persons who, at the beginning, blamed the principle of resisting the French revolution; to wish well to the cause of the Spaniards ... and to modify their desires of peace, in order to make it subservient to the cause of Spain'.[97] In this section, I explore how Sheridan's *Pizarro* participated in this rewriting of history in an endeavour that, once again, was both personal and public.

British support for the Peninsular War meant that by the summer of 1808 the sensationalist tendency to associate Spain with the horrors of the Black Legend was no longer viable. In the wake of the new political alliance between the two nations, it was much more convenient for British writers to evoke Spain's spirit of ancient chivalry than to propagate the grotesque narratives associated with Spanish imperial history. Sheridan's characterisation of Alonzo's equivocal 'Spanishness' reveals an especially interesting dimension to *Pizarro*'s revisionist potential. Since 1799 playbills had consistently listed Alonzo as one of the 'Spaniards', despite his attachment to Peruvian society. In Act 3 scene 3 Alonzo distinguishes himself from Pizarro and his army by insisting on a polarised demarcation between 'THEY' and 'ME'. His speech forcefully recalls Rolla's earlier patriotic address to the Peruvian army, which had also made enabling use of an 'us/them' distinction. Pizarro and Alonzo, as markedly different Spaniards, suggested that internal differences could be as important a call to action as external threats. This helped reaffirm, in short, that not all the Spaniards of Sheridan's play were villains.

The casting of Alonzo alongside other 'Spanish' characters, such as Pizarro and his corrupt generals, pointed, instead, to the use of 'national labels' as an empty rhetorical gesture. This allows Alonzo to be the epitome of Spain's uncorrupted martial spirit, as well as the character that comes closest to resembling the Peruvian hero Rolla. In 1808 Sheridan's underlying rhetoric about the fluidity of national identities could help revise monolithic preconceptions of the Spaniard as imperial villain. In order to stake a successful claim to Peninsular politics, it was clear that *Pizarro* and other stock plays in the repertoire would need to redress the lingering hostilities that had earlier allowed Sheridan and his audiences to conflate 'Spanishness' with general unworthiness.

It appears that theatre-goers were up to the challenge. In September 1812 *The Times* reviewed *Pizarro* as a play that, however haphazardly, chimed with those events of 'the great stage of real life':

> The celebrated author little thought, when writing this play, in which he pourtrays [*sic*], in the blackest colours, the worst offices of Old Spain, that in a few short years, all the eloquence, patriotism, and *energy* which he infused into

---

[96]   Hansard (HC), 'Affairs of Spain' (4 July 1808), in *Parliamentary Debates from the Year 1803 to the Present Time* (London, 1812), 11: 1142.
[97]   'Article 11', *ER*, July 1808, 12: 437.

his Peruvians, would be found inspiring the tongues, swelling the hearts, and animating the exertions of the Spanish nation, in a cause equally sacred, against an invader as foul, treacherous, and insatiable, as ever history, or the drama, have pictured out *Pizarro*.[98]

Napoleon's persistent aggression permitted Sheridan's narrative to remain topical and ideologically pertinent. This meant that during the Peninsular War, as in 1799, the horrors of the Black Legend could continue to be deflected onto the French Emperor. As a common enemy to both Britain and Spain, Napoleon became a 'double' enemy, receiving the brunt of all the odious connotations of cruelty and superstition earlier associated with the play's eighteenth-century anti-Spanish propaganda. To Robert Southey – England's most prominent Hispanist at the time – Spain's imperial history could also, interestingly, be cited as proof of the righteousness of the Spaniards' current struggle against Napoleon and his armies. In a letter to Walter Savage Landor, dated 1809, the poet accepts that 'doubtless, [the Spaniards] have much to endure; no nation owes so heavy a debt to Divine vengeance. There is retribution to be exacted for the Jews, for the American Indians, for the Dutch'.[99] Likening the Spaniards' struggle to the last stages of a penitent's redemption, Southey imagines modern Spaniards as the ironic victims of the imperial cruelties committed by their sixteenth-century counterparts. Amongst the Peninsular War's most important influences on allegorical readings of *Pizarro* was that the Peruvians had come to symbolise the Spanish, as well as British, determination to resist the Napoleonic yoke.

The Times was, of course, correct in stating that Sheridan could not have anticipated how contemporary politics would effectively rewrite the dynamics of his play's patriotic appeal, but he seems nevertheless to have closely followed the progress of the Spanish Campaign.[100] Evidence for this can be found in the extensive corrections made by Sheridan and his son, Tom, to Theodore Hook's

---

[98] *The Times*, 21 September 1812. In 1812 Wellington executed a series of successful attacks that culminated in the Battle of Salamanca and the British army's official entrance into Madrid in August 1812. These triumphs helped turn opinion at home, and may explain why *The Times* chose to make the link between *Pizarro* and Spanish patriotism at such a relatively late stage in the war. On the progress of the Peninsular War in 1812, see Rory Muir, *Britain and the Defeat of Napoleon 1807–1815* (London: Yale University Press, 1996), 193–220.

[99] The letter continues to argue that '[the Spaniards] are now passing through their purgatory, but it will purify them, and the Spaniards will come out like gold from the furnace'. Robert Southey to W.S. Landor (started before and continued on 30 September 1809), in *The Collected Letters of Robert Southey*, ed. Carol Bolton and Tim Fulford, 'Part 3: 1804–1809': Letter 1687. <http://www.rc.umd.edu/editions/southey_letters/Part_Three/HTML/letterEEd.26.1687.html> [Accessed 06.10.14].

[100] See, for instance, Sheridan's letter to Lady Bessborough (22 January 1809) in *The Letters of Richard Brinsley Sheridan*, ed. Cecil Price. 3 vols (Oxford: Clarendon Press: 1966), 3: 48–9.

manuscript for *The Siege of St Quintin* (Drury Lane, 10 November 1808).[101] Upon
receiving Hook's submission Sheridan was quick to rebuke the playwright's ill-
timed attempt to imitate *The Duenna*'s pastiche of Roman Catholicism, explaining
that 'the Public sentiment is generally making head against the no Popery cry,
and half the Patriotic enthusiasm in Spain is created and led by their Priests'.[102]
It is significant that in *Pizarro* itself, Sheridan curtailed the Catholic dimension
of Kotzebue's play as much as possible. Having described the problems in
Ireland as a struggle 'not of local discontent and partial disaffection' but, rather,
'a contest between the people and the government', it makes sense that he would
not have wished to associate the Irish populace (predominantly Catholic) with
the religious bigotry that Kotzebue's text ascribes to Spanish Catholicism.[103]

The movement for parliamentary reform on Catholic Emancipation – a hotly
debated issue – was active throughout the years of *Pizarro*'s greatest success.
The main reason for Pitt's resignation as Prime Minister in 1801 had, after all,
been George III's refusal to grant any concessions to the Catholics after the Act
of Union. In 1799 Sheridan had handled his play script with knowing dexterity.
Anne Plumptre's translation of Kotzebue's *Die Spanier in Peru*, which appears to
have been Sheridan's source text for *Pizarro*, included several damning references
to the close relationship between the Spanish church and state.[104] In Act 1 scene
4 of Plumptre's text, Las Casas shrinks at the thought that Pizarro's soldiers
hanged thirteen Indians as vengeance for the deaths of Christ and his Apostles.[105]
Sheridan's *Pizarro*, by contrast, makes no allusion to this.

Describing *The Siege of St Quintin* as 'a translation by Mr. HOOK, retouched
by Mr. SHERIDAN', the *Morning Chronicle* identified in Hook's play, 'the
same motive which gave rise to the production of Mr. Sheridan's *Pizarro*'.[106]

---

[101]   On Richard and Tom Sheridan's annotations to Hook's play script, see Tom
Lockwood, 'The Sheridans at Work: A Recovered Drury Lane Revisal of 1808', *The Review
of English Studies* 55.221, (September 2004), 487–97; and 'The Sheridans at Work Again:
The Wallace Manuscript of *The Siege of St Quintin*', *The Review of English Studies*, 58.233,
(February 2007), 89–93.

[102]   Qtd. in 'Postscript: *The Siege of St Quintin*', in *DW*, 2: 841. Sheridan's comments
point to the changing climate on Catholic Emancipation, which was a key concern for
Anglo-Irish relations. See also Sheridan's letter to S. Jernyngham (25 November 1811), in
Price (ed.), *Letters*, 135–6.

[103]   Hansard (HC), 'Debate on the King's Message respecting the Offers of the Militia
Regiments to go to Ireland' (19 June 1798), in *PH*, 33: 1503.

[104]   Sheridan seems to have written *Pizarro* after receiving a translation of *Die Spanier
in Peru*. While the manuscript is anonymous, the Drury Lane Account Book records two
payments of £25 to Anne Plumptre, who was requested to withhold publication of her
translation of the play until *Pizarro*'s opening performance. As Cecil Price proposes, 'the
evidence appears sufficient for us to conclude that Sheridan made use of Anne Plumptre's
translation'. *DW*, 2: 646.

[105]   Plumptre, *Pizarro* (1.4), 12.

[106]   *MC*, 11 November 1808. N.B. Hook's play was an adaptation of R.C. Pixérécourt's
Les Mines de Pologne. See Price, *DW*, 2: 792.

This motive, as the *Oracle of Fashion* explained to its readers, was 'merely to introduce Sentiments of Patriotism'.[107] As such, *The Siege of St Quintin* was generally accepted as a play devoid of any real literary merit, making it all the more significant that *Pizarro* should have provided the all-important point of comparison for Hook's Spanish play on 'the popular feelings of the present day'.[108] It suggests that in 1808 new meanings to *Pizarro* had been grafted onto its old ones, and Sheridan's play reinfused with the nationalist charge that had made it the decided favourite of 1799. The money, soldiers and ammunitions sent by Britain to aid Spain's national defense against the French invaders had remodelled *Pizarro* into a paradigmatic play about the patriotic spirit.

It is worthwhile, then, to consider how Hook's play compares to Sheridan's, and what this might suggest about the 'patriotic' label that reviewers had attached to both authors by the end of 1808. In contrast to Hook's first draft, the final version of the play, worked up by the two Sheridans prior to its submission to John Larpent (the Examiner of Plays), treats Spanish religious zeal with considerable care. It opens with the Spanish troops preparing for the Duke of Savoy's arrival to lead the assault against the French forces. The hero Egmont anticipates the signal for attack, alerting 'each true Spaniard that the day has come, which grants him the glorious lot to save his injured Country, or perish with its fall'. On St Lawrence's day, he affirms, 'a nation's gratitude shall mingle with religious zeal'.[109] Hook treats the representation of 'religious zeal' with significant judiciousness. As Sheridan had taken pains to explain, during the Peninsular War priests and bishops helped marshal the local resistance effort (allowing convents and monasteries to be opened up to the Allied armies).[110] This afforded Hook an opportunity to develop an effective historical parallelism. During the Franco-Habsburg War, on 10 August 1557 (the feast day of St Lawrence) the Spaniards, with the support of the English, had gained an important victory over the French King Henry II at the northern French town of St Quentin. To commemorate their success and pay homage to the martyred saint, Philip II of Spain built the illustrious Escorial Palace in the Sierra de Guadarrama. Following Sheridan's recommendations, it was prudent

---

[107] *The Oracle of Fashion*, 11 November 1808. Clipping from 'Dramatic Annals: Critiques on Plays and Performers, 1807 to 1815', collected by John Nixon (Garrick Club, London), 107 (item 105).

[108] *MC*, 11 November 1808.

[109] Theodore Hook, *The Siege of St Quintin* (1808), Larpent collection 1599. British Library Microfiche F254/700. See 1.1 [n.p.]. Further references are given after quotations in the text.

[110] On the role played by Spain's religious orders, see, for example, James Gillray's *Spanish-Patriots attacking the French-Banditti – Loyal Britons lending a lift* (15 August 1808). At the forefront of the print a Catholic monk prepares to charge a cannon while nuns wield bloody daggers at French soldiers. The arrival of another monk on horseback, blowing a trumpet to herald the arrival of a bishop (carrying both crozier and sword), seems to parody the traditional religious procession.

of Hook to align the religious and patriotic themes of his play. In *The Siege* religion provides the spur to heroic action, a rallying cry to inspire courage and conviction in the righteousness of the Spanish cause.[111]

As such, the final version of Hook's play sources its comedy not in religious pastiche but in the interplay between the Spaniards and the motley assembly of British soldiers. Scottish and Irish recruits deployed to the Peninsula between 1808 and 1814 made vital contributions to the war effort, and helped determine a new understanding of the British 'nation' at arms.[112] In *The Siege*, as in *Pizarro*, this raises questions about the different methods available to communicate national identities and allegiances. In Hook's play, the affable Irishman, Sir Leinster Kildare makes a memorable (if bemusing) first appearance. He arrives at the Spanish camp in the capacity of a messenger, proudly stating that as an Irishman by birth he has the added honour of being Alvaro's countryman. Alvaro attempts to correct him: 'You are mistaken sir, I am a Spaniard' – but Kildare, with cool confidence, insists 'So am I' (1.1, [n.p.]). In a long digression explaining how the Spaniards and Irish 'share the same root', Kildare relates that the ancient King Miletus first set foot on Ireland after his trip to Carthage.[113] He proceeds to offer physical proof of this by stating that the first six generations of the Kildare family were born with Spanish whiskers.[114] In deference to Kildare's enthusiasm – and recognition of his need for the Irishman's assistance – Alvaro, although unwilling to consent to the argument, welcomes the colonel, 'for your own nation's sake as well as ours' (1.1, [n.p.]).

---

[111]   The theme of religious zeal in *Pizarro* could also be linked to the Peninsular War, although this was problematic considering the play's generally villainous representation of Spanish characters. When Rolla is first reunited with Alonzo in the Spanish dungeon he explains: ' – this disguise I tore from the dead body of a Friar, as I pass'd our field of battle – it has gain'd me entrance to thy dungeon – now take it thou, and fly' (4.1, *DW*, 2: 688). Rolla here describes the corpse of a political enemy, but during the Peninsular War, this reference could have been seen to underscore the readiness of Spain's religious orders to engage in military conflict and sacrifice.

[112]   Between 1795 and 1810, 42% of artillery recruits came from Ireland, and 21% from Scotland. Holmes, *Redcoat*, 55–9.

[113]   From as early as the sixth century, Isidore of Seville claimed that Hibernia (the ancient name for Ireland) derived from (H)Iberia (the Latin name for the Spanish and Portuguese Peninsula). The *History of the Britons* (C9th) and *Lebor Gabála* (a treatise on Irish origins composed in the C11th) both describe the story of the sons of the Spanish soldier Mils Hispaniae/Mil Espáine who invaded Ireland. For a helpful summary of the myth's origin and claims to authenticity, see John Carey, 'Did the Irish come from Spain? The Legend of the Milesians', *History of Ireland* 9.3 (autumn 2001), 9–11. < http://www.historyireland.com/pre-history-archaeology/did-the-irish-come-from-spain/> [Accessed 06.06.2014].

[114]   It was not uncommon to portray Spanish men with inordinately large moustaches (or whiskers): consider, for example, the character of Don Ferolo Whiskerandos (the son of the Spanish Admiral) in Puff's play in *The Critic* (2.2), in *DW*, 2: 534–50.

Later in Act 2, in his attempt to convince the Scottish Captain to show more tolerance when dealing with the soldiers, Kildare once again indulges in a confused discourse on the subject of national identity:

SIR LEINSTER   However partial I may have been formerly to my own
                countrymen – by my honour I feel nothing of that
                exclusive prejudice now – I wish to encourage no
                rivalry but the emulation of who shall be forwardest
                and boldest against the Common Enemy. & whether
                I'm an Irishman, an Englishman, a Scotchman, a
                Welshman, a Swede or a Spaniard, upon my
                conscience I won't wish to recollect. Let them divide
                me equally, & take the six quarters of me between
                them – & they will make little more of me than half
                the man I wish to be to each of the remaining five.
                                                    (2.1, [n.p.])

Kildare may be somewhat inept at mathematics, but his declaration does not fail to persuade. So fervent and sincere is his disquisition that the Scottish Captain concedes: 'My heart goes w'e ye in the sentiment – tho' I'm thinking you're a wee confused with the expression o't' (2.1, [n.p]). The success of Britain's armies in Spain and Portugal was dependant upon co-operation and trust. Ambivalences needed to be redressed with regard not only to the Spanish and Portuguese, but also within the British regiments. The review published in the *Oracle of Fashion* clearly stated that '[*The Siege of St Quintin*] literally consists of nothing but invectives against the French, and fulsome Panegyrics upon the Spaniards, English, Scotch, Irish, and Welsh'.[115] The play's theme of seeing beyond the duty to one's birthplace in order to conceive of a larger sense of national commitment was an important manifestation of Hook's patriotic intent. A comparable, much more nuanced, example is provided by Sheridan's characterisation of Alonzo in *Pizarro*, and his lessons on the plurality and essential instability of national labels.

Despite competition from new, obviously topical Spanish-themed plays, *Pizarro* thus continued to retain the necessary urgency associated with its patriotic narrative. Yet, during the 1808–1809 season, when audiences were most absorbed by the war in Spain and Portugal, this book's Calendar lists only four performances of Sheridan's play at the London patent theatres.[116] This was the result of an unfortunate, if ironic, intersection between Sheridan's professional fortunes as playwright-manager and politician. On 24 February 1809, as Canning addressed the Commons on the role of Britain in the Peninsula, news arrived that

---

[115]   *The Oracle of Fashion*, 11 November 1808.

[116]   On the limited availability of playbills for this period, see Introduction to Calendar, note 3. This does not necessarily reflect the frequency with which the play was performed in the provinces. Frederick Burwick, for instance, notes that *Pizarro* was played for a 'Committee Night performance in Newcastle, after a sighting in 1809 of a French ship off the English coast'. *Romantic Drama*, 159.

Drury Lane was on fire. At the time, Covent Garden was still under reconstruction, following its own destruction by fire in September 1808. Although Covent Garden reopened the following September, it would take more than three years to rebuild Drury Lane Theatre. Sheridan, 'realising that no one would invest in a new theatre under his control' was effectively forced to resign from the Drury Lane Committee.[117] Another important consequence of the fire was that the Drury Lane dramatic company had to be temporarily relocated. At first, the actors moved to the Haymarket. Then, in April 1809, and on a more stable arrangement, they took over the much smaller Lyceum Theatre. In this new playspace the capacity for spectacular entertainments was significantly restricted, helping explain the relative absence of *Pizarro* from the company's repertoire during the first years of the Peninsular War.[118] The surviving playbills for the period 1809 to 1812 record only one (benefit) performance of *Pizarro* by the Drury Lane dramatic company (on 23 May 1809).[119]

On the face of it, a narrative dramatising Spanish plunder in Peru might not appear to have been an immediate choice for the 1809 repertoire. On the other hand, between 1801 and 1803, *Pizarro* had already proven itself capable of flexible application to changing political circumstances, of successfully striking the difficult balance between principle and pragmatism. The allegorical readings of *Pizarro* that I have already outlined suggest that during the Peninsular War, Sheridan's play would have continued to hold its own in the dramatic repertoire. A cursory look at the patents' wartime calendar testifies to the popularity of Spanish-themed plays between 1808 and 1814. The 'New Comic Ballet' of *Don Quichotte [sic]* was staged five times during the company's short stay at the King's Theatre, Haymarket in the spring of 1809.[120] John Braham's profitable engagement during the 1811 season and the acclaim he enjoyed for his impersonation of Don Alphonso in John O'Keeffe's *The Castle of Andalusia* also ensured that stage depictions of Spain remained in the spotlight. A year later, the 'very favourable' reception given to H.B. Code's *The Spanish Patriots: A Thousand Years Ago* (1812) was, according to *The Times*, largely the result of the play's well-chosen title, 'sufficiently promising to attract a tolerable auditory, because it announced something to which every British heart vibrates – the patriotism of Spain'.[121] Even

---

[117]   O'Toole, *Traitor's Kiss*, 431.

[118]   On the Lyceum's limited capacity for spectacle, see *The Times*' review (14 March 1810) of *The Maniac; or, The Swiss Banditti*: 'The scenery deserves particular commendation, and we have seldom seen on so small a scale, as that which the Lyceum admits, a finer specimen of the art …'.

[119]   *Pizarro* was played as the mainpiece to celebrate the benefit of Henry Siddons and his wife, Harriet, on 23 May 1809. During the interlude, there were songs and sketches including 'Bill Jones; or, the Ship Spectre' and 'Sylvester Daggerwood'. The afterpiece was *Ella Rosenberg*. See 'Calendar': Part B.

[120]   *Don Quichotte* was performed on 16, 23 March; 3, 6, and 10 April 1809. See 'Calendar': Part B.

[121]   *The Times*, 23 September 1812.

a quick study of the playbills suggests, therefore, that Spanish topicality would have only amplified the demand for Sheridan's play.

Once it had recovered from its own fire, the new Covent Garden Theatre testified to *Pizarro*'s enduring appeal through frequent revivals of Sheridan's tragedy.[122] The six performances of *Pizarro* staged there during the 1811–1812 season were supplemented, after 31 January 1812, with Frederick Reynolds's operatic drama *The Virgin of the Sun*. Reynolds's play was also a translation of Kotzebue, dramatising the love triangle between Rolla, Cora and Alonzo as a prequel to *Die Spanier in Peru*. The *Examiner* helpfully defined the play 'a sort of companion to *Pizarro*', containing 'the early part' of Rolla's history.[123] *The Virgin of the Sun* proved a popular hit, securing twenty-seven performances by 13 April 1812. Its success was as dependent upon Reynolds's penchant for spectacle as it was on the existing fascination for *Pizarro*.[124] *The Times*, for instance, described how 'on the rising of the curtain, which displayed the *Temple of the Sun*, the whole audience gave a shout of admiration'.[125] The opinion that the Temple was among *Pizarro*'s most magnificent scenes had been almost unanimous.[126] The enthusiasm extended to Reynolds's scenic splendour was significantly heightened by audiences' recognition of the ideological terrain already mapped out by Sheridan.

The intertheatricality that united *Pizarro* and *The Virgin of the Sun* can be compared to Covent Garden's coupling of *Pizarro* (on 30 May 1812) with another Spanish-themed play, Charles Kemble's often-performed farce *The Portrait of Cervantes; or, The Plotting Lovers* (1808).[127] The playbills for Covent Garden's 1813–1814 season provide further intriguing evidence of the strategic arrangements made to the theatre's repertoire. *Pizarro* was played once as the mainpiece to Isaac Pocock's successful melodrama *The Miller and His Men*, and twice before the pantomime of *Harlequin and the Swans; or, The Bath of Beauty.*[128] The arrangement suggests that although repeated less frequently, Sheridan's tragedy was still considered high enough in public esteem to promote the theatre's new melodramas and pantomimes. The arrangements made by John Philip

---

[122]   For example, *Pizarro* was chosen for William Claremont and Thomas Shaw's joint benefit on 9 July 1812. Songs performed that night included 'The Four Saints, or the Union' and 'The Death of Abercrombie'. See 'Calendar': Part A.

[123]   *TE*, 9 February 1812.

[124]   Reynolds's production included 'The destruction of the Temple of the Sun by an *earthquake*' in Act 1. See *The Life and Times of Frederick Reynolds, Written By Himself*, 2 vols. (London, 1826), 2: 391.

[125]   *The Times*, 3 February 1812.

[126]   See, for instance, *Morning Herald*, 25 May 1799: 'The scenery is enchanting throughout, and that of the *Temple of the Sun* superlatively magnificent'.

[127]   This farce – published under the title *Plot and Counterplot; or, The Portrait of Michael Cervantes* – was an adaptation of Michel Dieulafoy's comedy *Le Portrait de Michel Cervantes*. See Warwick Digital Collections <http://contentdm.warwick.ac.uk/cdm/ref/collection/empire/id/19402> [Accessed 18.10.14].

[128]   'Calendar': Part A: 1 December 1813; 30 December 1813; 7 January 1814.

Kemble (then manager of Covent Garden) as he structured the various elements of an evening's entertainment were as important as the choice of mainpiece itself.

In September 1809 the Drury Lane company inaugurated its new season at the Lyceum with *The Duenna*, which, if the playbills are to be trusted, was sanctioned for frequent repetition 'in consequence of the uncommon applause' it received. The frequent staging of the play during the Peninsular War may seem hard to account for, especially after Sheridan's censorious approach to Hook's manuscript play and his careful textual editing of *The Siege*'s ridicule of Roman Catholicism.[129] A good example of *The Duenna*'s religious humour occurs in Act 3 scene 5. The Spanish friars sit around a table in the priory, drinking, singing and making lecherous toasts to the abbess of St Ursuline and 'the blue-ey'd [*sic*] nun of St Catherine's'; their benefactions have been spent on wine, and their professions of abstinence exposed as excuses for private indulgence in sensual gratification.[130] Complete with glee and chorus, it is not surprising that Hook should have been drawn to this lively scene of religious hypocrisy. Although Sheridan cannot easily be cleared of a jealous motivation to defend *The Duenna*'s cultural playfulness against Hook's potential literary theft, any charges of hypocrisy against Sheridan can be mitigated by the timing of his play's new stage run. In 1808 when Hook submitted *The Siege* to the Office of the Lord Chamberlain, the British nation was gripped with avid enthusiasm for the Spanish cause: by the end of 1809 the public mood was much more circumspect.

The historian Godfrey Davies explains that although 'all Whigs were united in their detestation of the invasion of Spain, there was from the very commencement of the struggle, the widest division of opinion as to the probable success or failure of the patriots'.[131] As the conflict was prolonged and the fissures in the Spanish government made ever more visible, many Whigs retracted their support for the war. Frustrated at the inefficiency of the Cortes, the Whigs came to realise that the Spanish revolution was, at heart, fiercely conservative. The Spaniards were not so much fighting for constitutional liberty, as for the conservative pairing of 'King and Church' (associated with reactionary government in Spain). British commanders in the Peninsula complained of Spanish incompetence, while private letters sent home (and officers' memoirs, published not long afterwards) recounted stories of mutual antipathy between Spanish and British soldiers, unaccustomed, largely, to each other's religious beliefs and cultural traditions. The publication of parliamentary papers on the war further contributed to the nation's disillusionment, making many Britons resentful that their efforts had been hampered by Spanish

---

[129]   It is possible that by staging revivals of his earlier anti-Spanish comedies Sheridan was trying to compensate for the notable absence of his 'other' Spanish drama, *Pizarro* (whose demanding scene changes would have been too elaborate for the smaller Lyceum stage).

[130]   Sheridan, *The Duenna* (2.5), in *DW,* 1: 273–5 (274).

[131]   Godfrey Davies, 'The Whigs and the Peninsular Wars', *Transactions of the Royal Historical Society*, 4th series, 2 (1919), 113–31 (116).

provincial jealousies and poor co-operation.[132] The image of the Spanish patriot mobilised for action against all odds was denounced as an essentially mythical construct. Britons' early, popular and perhaps naïve support for the war in Spain became liable to serious qualification as a result.

In this politically revisionist climate, there was much uncertainty regarding what constituted a legitimately sanctioned 'Spanish' narrative. In *The Censorship of English Drama 1737–1824* (1976) Leonard Conolly relates Spencer Perceval's surprise that Drury Lane had been ordered to stop reciting a monody to the memory of Sir John Moore.[133] In February 1809 the mention of Sir John Moore was certain to excite debate. Moore had been the British Commander-in-Chief in Spain who, subject to miscommunication and poor intelligence, was unaware that Napoleon had entered Madrid in early December 1808.[134] When news arrived that Napoleon had 80,000 men at his disposal and that a superior French army was chasing the British, Moore led a desperate retreat to Corunna. When he reached Northern Spain, the military leader's brilliant defensive strategies allowed for an ultimately successful retreat of the British troops, but this, in itself, was cause for humiliation. Not even Moore's death in battle could deflect from the serious damage that the retreat inflicted on the already fragile Anglo-Spanish alliance. To make matters worse, when Moore's soldiers finally returned home, their tales of starvation, exposure to the elements, poor internal discipline and Spanish hostility horrified the nation. Readers were then invited to participate in a pamphlet war between Moore's supporters and detractors, wrestling to take control of the Commander's reputation.[135] John Larpent and Spencer Perceval – two prominent cultural arbiters whose public role was to promote the hegemonic ideal – thus found themselves, understandably, at odds on how to respond to Drury Lane's request for a Monody on the death of Sir John Moore.[136] The division in public sentiment is likely to

---

[132]   See 'Article 16', *ER*, April 1809, 14: 251. The article refers readers to John Moore's letter from Salamanca and a letter intercepted from a French officer at Vitoria, used as evidence in the House of Commons Papers. Such accusations of inertia undermined the popular image of Spanish patriotism.

[133]   L.W. Conolly, *The Censorship of English Drama 1737–1824* (San Marino: The Huntington Library, 1976), 95.

[134]   Moore's letters, published by his brother shortly after his death, rapidly went into new editions. See James Moore, *A Narrative of the Campaign of the British Army in Spain Commanded by his Excellency Lieutenant-General Sir John Moore, &c &c &c. Authenticated by Official Papers and Original Letters* (London, 1809).

[135]   See [An Officer], *Letters from Portugal and Spain: Written During the March of the British Troops Under Sir John Moore* (London, 1809); [An Officer of Staff], *Operations of the British Army in Spain: Involving Broad Hints to the Commissariat, and Board of Transports: with Anecdotes Illustrative of the Spanish Character* (London, 1809); and Adam Neale's *Letters from Portugal and Spain: An Account of the Operations of the Armies Under Sir Arthur Wellesley and Sir John Moore from the Landing of the Troops in Mondego Bay to the Battle at Corunna* (London, 1809).

[136]   'Monody on the Death of Sir John Moore', Larpent Collection 1568. BL Microfiche F254/235.

have informed Larpent's ultimate decision to reject the Drury Lane Monody. With the final verdict on Corunna still unresolved, the Examiner of Plays seems to have been unwilling to re-direct the question to the theatre's auditorium.[137]

As the Peninsular War became divested of its initial nationalist glamour, *Pizarro*'s Spanish theme, although still popular, became ever more controversial. In 1811 the reviewer for *The Times* explained that the play's first performances had been 'happily timed'. In 1799 'to hear words of courage and comfort from the stage was new'.[138] But more than a decade later, audiences suffering from the hardships of war, troubled Anglo-Spanish relations and political uncertainty at home, struggled to believe that they could still preserve 'their fortunes and their freedom'. In the words of the theatrical reviewer, 'all this now seems to have been singularly absurd'.[139]

The seeds of discord can once again be traced to that fateful year for the campaign: 1809. In his appraisal of Charles Vaughan's eulogistic narrative *The Siege of Zaragoza* (1809), Henry Brougham, writing for the *Edinburgh Review*, was quick to correct its author's 'partiality for his Saragossan friends'.[140] Instead, he wrote a forceful critique of British hopes for Spain and the military operations therein. Brougham claimed that British diplomacy bore all the ridicule associated with theatrical foppery: 'a pompous embassy' indulging 'in gaudiness and parade, and in the trappings of the East'.[141] This derision of spectacle recalls early responses to *Pizarro*, with the reference to effeminate Eastern luxury conjuring disturbing suggestions of a degenerate British empire. Brougham develops these hints into an insistence that 'No Scicily [*sic*] – no Ceuta – no Sugar islands – no cruizes in the Cattegat' should have influenced the government's Spanish Campaign.[142] The intrusion of commercial interests upon contemporary political ideology had marked consequences for both real and fictional depictions of Spain. By the 1810s Britain's mercantile interests and the global implications of Napoleon's Peninsular Campaign would seriously limit *Pizarro*'s 1808 reading as a play supporting the Spanish cause.

The war in Spain and its repercussions for the Spanish colonies excited contemporary interest, not least because it finally opened South American markets to the speculation of British merchants and traders. Gillray's 1799 satires of a money-grubbing Sheridan came full circle with the British government's very real, if ideologically dubious, financial projects for South America. Rebecca Cole Heinowitz concludes her study of Romantic-period British writings about Spanish America with the arresting anecdote of a ruined speculator whose letter to the

---

[137]   On 10 January 1812, John Philip Kemble was granted permission to deliver 'A Melologue' on the subject of Spanish victories at CG. By then, the military campaign was, significantly, on a much stronger footing.

[138]   *The Times*, 7 October 1811.

[139]   *The Times*, 7 October 1811.

[140]   'Article 16', *ER*, April 1809, 14: 245.

[141]   'Article 16', *ER*, April 1809, 14: 255–6.

[142]   'Article 16', *ER*, April 1809, 14: 258.

Morning Chronicle (dated 10 January 1826) was simply signed 'Pizarro'.[143] British commercial interests across the Atlantic had, nevertheless, hinted towards tragedy even prior to the stock market crash of 1825. Britain's political investments in South America had threatened, from as early as the 1810s, to align Ministerial policy all too closely with *Pizarro*'s characterisations of mercenary Spanish imperialism.

The insurrections in Spanish America were, nevertheless, of ideological value. In the 1790s the Venezuelan Franscisco de Miranda had come to London to seek the assistance of the British government. Many other Spanish-controlled states continued to consult the British on their plans for independence from Spain. Leigh Hunt wrote passionately about their cause, using language reminiscent of *Pizarro* in order to inform his readers of Peru's resolution to throw off Spanish rule and erect an independent state:

> May that land, which was the cradle of Spanish degeneracy, prove its grave, and a new race of men spring up in South America, to whom defeated pride may have taught reason; defeated indolence, industry; and defeated oppression, the indispensable blessing of liberty.[144]

This defence of indigenous rights against unlawful oppression chimes closely with *Pizarro*'s dramatisation of the Spanish conquest of Peru in the sixteenth century. After the disappointing convocation of the Spanish Cortes in 1810 and its failure to grant equal participation to the Creole representatives, the movement for independence from Spain gained rapid momentum. Yet, while the British government remained committed to the Peninsular Campaign, it could not afford to sponsor the independence of Spanish America, despite its financial temptations. In this climate, *Pizarro,* which had always sparked political doubts as to its putative loyalism, found itself hard-pressed – betrayed by the difficulty of speaking at once to the Spaniards and the South American Creoles.

Towards the end of Sheridan's play, Pizarro confesses to Rolla: 'I cannot but admire thee, Rolla; I wou'd we might be friends' (4.3, *DW*, 2: 694). He does so in the full knowledge that his wish will most probably be rejected. Pizarro here employs the two modal verbs, 'wou'd' and 'might', in close proximity, as if to provide a defensive anchor for his gesture. Rolla's answer, 'Become the friend of virtue – and thou wilt be mine' (4.3, *DW*, 2: 694), is, of course, alien to the Conquistador's greedy designs. It prompts Pizarro, when alone, to question the actions that his ambition have driven him to commit. He returns to the construction 'I would' in order to express his sense of personal limitation: 'I would I cou'd retrace my steps – I cannot – Would I could evade my own reflections! – No! – thought and memory are my Hell' (4.3, *DW*, 2: 694). Nevertheless, such is his fascination with Rolla that when the Spanish soldiers mistake him for a spy and bring him back to Pizarro, the Spaniard concludes his apology by asking, 'May not Rolla and Pizarro cease to be foes?' (5.2, *DW*, 2: 698). But even this

---

[143]   Heinowitz, *Spanish America*, 209.
[144]   *Examiner*, 18 February 1810.

more measured request – in search of something less than, but not divorced from, friendship – is rejected. Humiliated, and suspicious of Pizarro's role in his arrest, Rolla responds: 'When the sea divides us; yes!' (5.2, *DW*, 2: 698). This inability to bridge the distance between Old and New Spain testifies to the competing claims of *Pizarro*'s investment in justified revolt. The Creole Rebellion of Huánuco (1812) and the Rebellion of Cuzco (1814–1816) in Peru meant that during the latter part of the Peninsular War, *Pizarro*'s setting became dangerously imbricated with the movements for independence that swept Spanish America. In the 1810s, the romanticised landscape of Peru was no longer geographically and culturally remote, but troublesomely topical. The task of directing audiences' moral and political responsibilities had, it seems, finally exceeded the scope of Sheridan's play.

————————

The inherently 'protean' character of Sheridan's tragedy spoke, from the outset, to political uncertainties at home and abroad. By focusing on the play's premiere in 1799 and its performances at the time of the Peace of Amiens and Peninsular Campaign, this chapter has considered *Pizarro*'s changing relation to Romantic-period society.

The earliest reviews of *Pizarro* seized upon the physicality of actors and audience members as proof of the theatre's seemingly magical (if also dangerous) capacity to set human passions into motion. Rolla's celebrated speech constituted the emblematic focal point of this psychologically absorbing moment of spectatorship. It was published as a broadsheet after the collapse of the Peace of Amiens, at a time when *Pizarro*'s perceived capacity to transform spectatorship into participation could be used to disseminate ideals of patriotic citizenship and encourage the nation to take up arms against the invader. Five years later, during the first flush of enthusiasm for the Peninsular War, the play's rhetoric was reinfused with patriotic spark. Intriguingly, however, because the war soon found almost as many detractors as supporters, *Pizarro*'s reductive portrayal of sixteenth-century Spain was also relevant to those who protested against British involvement in the Peninsula (caricaturing the Spaniards as dreamers of a mythical golden age).[145]

Sheridan's recourse to the Black Legend meant that *Pizarro* was curiously up-to-date for opponents of the war, while those who supported the Peninsular Campaign were at liberty to continue to revise the play's literal plot (imagining nineteenth-century Spaniards in place of the righteous Peruvians and, as was customary, Pizarro and his soldiers as Napoleon and his armies). Contrary to initial

————————

[145]   In eighteenth- and early nineteenth-century satirical prints, 'the Spaniard was invariably portrayed in late sixteenth- or early seventeenth-century dress with feathered hat, slashed doublet and pantaloons or breeches, cloak and ruff…'. Duffy, *Englishman and the Foreigner*, 26. See Charles Williams, *John Bull among the Spaniards; or, Boney decently provided for* (July 1808); and Isaac Cruikshank, *The noble Spaniards; or, Britannia assisting the cause of freedom all over the world, whither friend or foe!* (20 July 1808).

predictions, the Peninsular War developed into a complex, partisan conflict. This imbued the representation of Spanish themes on stage with political controversy, and partly explains why, after 1809, Sheridan's *Pizarro* was not as popular as it might have been. But other factors, such as the fire at Drury Lane, also seem to have influenced the frequency of the play's metropolitan performances.

Pizarro's fluidity, however enabling, had its limits. When the South American question could no longer be avoided, the play's potential allegories struggled to compete with the real implications of its plot. From Venezuela to Argentina and Peru, the native people of South America were rising against the forces of Spanish imperialism – making proclamations of their liberty and independence that theatre-goers would have been quick to associate with the Peruvians of Sheridan's play. Peruvian independence was declared in 1821 and finally secured in 1824. It is no coincidence that the decreasing frequency with which *Pizarro* was presented in the 1810s corresponded to the most active years in the movement for Spanish American independence. These were also years that marked the decline of Sheridan's celebrity. He was practically forced out of the management of Drury Lane after its destruction by fire and lost his seat in the House of Commons in 1812.[146] Sheridan's reputation had always been problematically connected to the play's politics, tying together the private and the public, the fictional and the real. By the 1810s, however, the fortunes of a war with obviously global consequences determined that Sheridan's *Pizarro*, whose patriotism had always been 'debated property', could no longer be allocated a definite place in the theatrical repertoire.[147]

---

[146]   Taylor, *Theatres of Opposition*, 6.

[147]   During this period, the Viceroyalty of Peru banned performances of *Pizarro* and promoted 'loyal Spanish-American dramas' instead. The play-text itself, however, may have been read clandestinely, alongside other banned texts smuggled into the country, such as those of the French Enlightenment. Juan García del Rio (Peruvian Plenipotentiary in England and Secretary for the Liberation government of Peru) published his translation of *Pizarro* in 1844. I am indebted to the research assistance of Eduardo Caparó, Director General CSBE, BNP (Biblioteca Nacional del Perú/The National Library of Peru) for this information.

Chapter 2
Performing Shakespeare

Much has been written about the reception of Shakespeare – both on page and stage – during the Romantic period. In the introduction to his important anthology *The Romantics on Shakespeare* (1992) Jonathan Bate attests to the consequentiality of Shakespeare's celebrity not only to England but also to Germany, where the bard served as a counterweight to the 'hegemonic tendencies of French neo-classical culture' and politics.[1] With the aim of further nuancing our understanding of Shakespeare's status in the early nineteenth century, this chapter investigates how his plays were used to (re)figure concerns about British military action in the Iberian Peninsula specifically, and domestic politics more generally. It reveals how Shakespeare was recruited for both sides of the thorny political debates that took place in the English theatres and press between the Anglo-Spanish alliance of 1808 and the restoration of peace in Europe in 1815.

Widespread familiarity with Shakespeare's plays made it easy for theatre-goers to engage imaginatively with his storylines. Proof of this is readily found in early nineteenth-century reviewing culture, wherein multiple allusions are made to the political relevance of the bard's plays as suggested to – or, just as importantly, perceived by – contemporary audiences. Charged references to the Shakespearean canon often travelled across different media. A few weeks after the *Examiner* first proposed that 'The words of SHAKESPEARE may be most appropriately applied to King JOSEPH: — "That *from* the shelf the precious diadem stole, | And put it in his pocket"',[2] Thomas Rowlandson used the embedded quotation from *Hamlet* as the main conceit for his satirical print, *King Joe and Co. Making the Most of their Time Previous to Quitting Madrid* (25 September 1808; Figure 2.1). The print depicts Joseph Bonaparte and his troops – who fled to Burgos after hearing news of the French army's defeat at Bailén (16–19 July 1808) – plundering the Treasury and Royal Palaces in the course of their hasty escape from Madrid.[3]

---

[1] Jonathan Bate, *The Romantics on Shakespeare* (London: Penguin Books, 1992), 'Introduction', 9–15 esp. (9).

[2] *Examiner*, 21 August 1808.

[3] As Rory Muir explains, Joseph's escape to the Ebro only further exacerbated the French army's defeat at Bailén: 'This foolish action, as much as Bailen itself, gave the Spanish uprising credibility and damaged Napoleon's prestige throughout Europe.' *The Defeat of Napoleon*, 34.

Figure 2.1   Thomas Rowlandson, *King Joe and Co. Making the Most of their Time Previous to Quitting Madrid*, 25 September 1808. © The Trustees of the British Museum.

Rowlandson places Joseph (who had been crowned King of Spain in June 1808) at the centre of the print, reaching up to an open cupboard from which he takes the Spanish crown, while eagerly grasping a sceptre in his left hand. Joseph's 'company' consists of eight French officers and soldiers (who fill deep chests with bags of money, silver and gold plate) and one other man (not in uniform; most likely, a local *afrancesado*).[4] A crucifix, bishop's hat and staff lie on the floor as symbols of Spain's religious wealth. An officer takes from the wall a picture of the Madonna and Child (presumably to add to their loot, although another officer's raising of a mallet also engenders the possibility that this will be destroyed).[5] Rowlandson's choice of Shakespearean text thus offers a literally perfect fit for the Spanish saying that 'because Joseph could not put the crown on his head, he had put it in his pocket'.[6]

---

[4]   *Afrancesado* was the name given to the Spaniards who lent their support to French ideas, and especially Joseph Bonaparte, during the Peninsular War.

[5]   Beside the Madonna there is a picture of a nude woman (exposed by the tearing down of the curtains), which allows the print to serve not only as a denunciation of French misconduct but also as a damning attack on the hypocrisy of religious censure in Bourbon Spain.

[6]   For the saying, see, for example, C.H. Gifford, *History of the Wars Occasioned by the French Revolution*. 2 vols. (London, 1817), 1: 617. Dorothy George identifies an earlier

The Shakespearean quotation also activates its own dramatic context however. The lines occur in the closet scene shortly after Hamlet, having stabbed Polonius (hiding behind the arras), confronts his mother with the enormity of her crimes. Gertrude, begging for mercy, asks that Hamlet cease speaking: 'Thou turn'st mine eyes into my very soul; | And there I see such black and grained spot | As will not leave their tinct'.[7] Yet Hamlet persists, using the lines quoted by Rowlandson in order to denounce his uncle as an usurper to the royal throne. It is immediately after this exposure that the Ghost of Hamlet's father makes an entrance, although seen by Hamlet only. Extracting political capital from the Shakespearean quotation, Rowlandson underscores the themes of usurpation and embarrassed discovery that were as applicable to Joseph and his army as to *Hamlet*.

Rowlandson's portrayal of unruly soldiers looting to their hearts' content could also have reminded the print's viewers of *Henry V*. The artist's attack on Joseph's inordinate concern for the trappings of power resonates eloquently with the play's theme of military justice and Henry's famous soliloquy on what it truly means to be a king. This Shakespearean multivalency helps define *King Joe and Co.* as a theatrical tableau in its own right. The velvet curtains framing the image not only conjure the tapestry of the arras crucial to the setting of Act 3 scene 4 of *Hamlet* but also evoke the drop curtains characteristic of Romantic-period playhouses. In this scheme, even the disorder created by the soldiers (who throw religious relics and bags of gold and silver to the floor) permits the space to be reimagined as a storeroom for theatrical props. Scholarship on Romantic-period culture has repeatedly emphasised how theatre and politics were variously bound up with each other. As this example of the transposition of Shakespeare (from the theatre to political journalism and visual culture) forcefully insists, contemporary performances of Shakespeare were always more than just 'theatrical'.

Shakespeare's popularity during the Peninsular War can be traced back to the consolidation of his status during the mid-eighteenth century as realised most notably by David Garrick. But although influential, Garrick was not solely responsible for the cementing of Shakespeare's Romantic-period celebrity. As Robert Shaughnessy underlines:

---

print (published during the 1788 Regency crisis) that uses the same quotation and a similar visual setting. Print 7388: *King Pitt A Cut Purse of the Empire and the Rule that from a Shelf the Precious Diadem Stole, And Put in His Pocket, 'Hamlet'* (29 December 1788). *Catalogue of Political and Personal Satires Preserved in the Department of Prints and Drawings in the British Museum*. 11 vols. Volume 6: *1784–1792* (London: Printed by Order of the Trustees, 1938), 6: 534–5.

[7] *Shakespeare's Hamlet, Prince of Denmark; A Tragedy. Revised by J.P. Kemble* (London: Printed for J Ridgway, 1804), in *John Philip Kemble Promptbooks*, ed. Charles H. Shattuck, 11 vols (Charlottesville: Published for the Folger Shakespeare Library, 1974), 2: 53 (3.4).

> ...it is now recognized not only that a wide range of metropolitan and regional agents and agencies contributed to the increasing presence and diversity of Shakespeare within the cultures of performance of eighteenth-century England, but also that larger cultural and ideological forces were at work in the shaping of Shakespeare as a literary, theatrical and national icon.[8]

These forces (which, as Shaughnessy identifies, were not restricted to the stage) secured for Shakespeare's plays both cultural prestige and flexibility for political application. The latter was enhanced by the fact that because Shakespeare's plays enjoyed a pre-established place in the dramatic repertoire, they did not have to be licensed by the Examiner of Plays prior to representation at a patent theatre. The Licensing Act of 1737 required the submission of all *new* or *amended* play-texts. This meant that Shakespeare's plays (best known in their adapted Restoration forms) could escape such censorship. But the plays were subject, nevertheless, to other kinds of regulation, since only the patent theatres were permitted to stage spoken drama, as I explore in more detail in Chapter 3. Early nineteenth-century managers, actors and influential patrons cleverly exploited the loopholes in the Licensing Act when selecting Shakespeare's plays for representation. This chapter's detailing of their enterprising stratagems aims to pinpoint how political commentary – both positive and negative – could (sometimes ironically) be asserted from the very cultural platforms that received their endorsement from the Office of the Lord Chamberlain.

I begin by focusing on Coleridge, a prominent figure throughout this book, who, during the Peninsular War, delivered two series of Shakespearean lectures, freely alluded to Shakespeare in his journalistic writings and wrote a Spanish-themed tragedy, *Remorse* (1813), which, as I argue below, reverberates with Shakespearean echoes.[9] From its explicit discussion of Coleridge, the chapter then develops into a detailed account of Shakespeare in performance, which interrogates why and how the contemporary stage turned to the bard in order to reflect upon the 'Spanish cause' and its attendant social and political questions.

This chapter's key sources of evidence include John Philip Kemble's Shakespearean promptbooks and the 'Calendar of Playbills for Covent Garden and Drury Lane: 1807–1815' printed at the end of this book. The plays put on by

---

[8]   Robert Shaughnessy, 'Shakespeare and the London Stage', in *Shakespeare in the Eighteenth Century*, ed. Fiona Ritchie and Peter Sabor (Cambridge: Cambridge University Press, 2012), 161–84 (163).

[9]   For allusions to Shakespeare in Peninsular War journalism, see, for example: Coleridge, 'The War XI – Battle of Albuera 2', 5 June 1811, (which includes an allusion to *Henry IV (1)*), in *CC: EOT*, 2: 186. See also *FFBJ*, 24 September 1808 (which attacks the Convention of Cintra by quoting from *The Merry Wives of Windsor*); *BG*, 11 January 1809 (uses *Richard III* to comment on Bonaparte's retreat from Spain); *FFBJ*, 19 August 1809 (celebrates the victory at Talavera by quoting Henry's St Crispin's Day speech); and *FFBJ*, 18 September 1813 (on 'the extraordinary coincidence' between Thomas Graham's dispatches from St Sebastian and the Duke of York's description of his sons' heroic actions in *Henry VI (3)*).

Kemble with such éclat at Covent Garden were generally considered authoritative, and his published acting versions used by theatre managers across Britain. Kemble's promptbooks therefore provide a relatively reliable intimation of Shakespearean performance practices not only on the patent stages of London, but also at the nation's increasingly successful Theatre Royals. This chapter thus anticipates the specifically provincial focus of Chapter 4, while contributing, in its own right, to this book's larger argument about *English* theatre during the Peninsular War. As the first section begins to explain, between 1808 and 1815 performances of Shakespeare provided a productive (if precarious) means by which to unmask but also, significantly, repair the social, cultural and political fractures occasioned by the war against Napoleonic France.

Coleridge's Shakespeare

Coleridge's first series of Shakespearean lectures were given in 1808 at the Royal Institution in London. He would continue to lecture on the principles of poetry and, more specifically, Shakespeare and Milton – whom he regarded as the supreme representatives of English literature – until 1819.[10] During this period Coleridge was also writing political journalism, which provided him with a space in which to at once test and advocate his complex opinions about Britain's military involvement in the Iberian Peninsula. Indeed, in June 1808, when his first lecture series came to an end, Coleridge retreated to Grasmere. From the rural seclusion of the Lake District he busied himself for the next two years with preparations for his periodical *The Friend*, and his first contributions to the *Courier* (then under the editorship of Daniel Stuart). During this time, 'Coleridge's growing disillusion with the politics of opposition' was beginning to manifest itself as 'a growing admiration for the bracing effects of international war', as Philip Shaw argues.[11] His *Letters on the Spaniards* (1809–1810), written in celebration of the Anglo-Spanish alliance as a new epoch in both nations' histories, offer a prime example of this.

Coleridge's *Letters* were published serially in the *Courier* between 7 December 1809 and 20 January 1810.[12] Coleridge's belief that 'the historic muse' appears in her loftiest character as the nurse of HOPE' permitted, nevertheless, some

---

[10]   On Milton's reception in the Romantic period see: Lucy Newlyn, *Paradise Lost and the Romantic Reader* (Oxford: Clarendon Press, 1992); Nicola Trott, 'Milton and the Romantics' in *A Companion to Romanticism*, ed. Duncan Wu (Oxford: Blackwell, 1998), 520–34; and Joseph Wittreich, 'Miltonic Romanticism' in *The Oxford Handbook of Milton*, ed. Nicholas McDowell and Nigel Smith (Oxford: Oxford University Press, 2009), 687–704.

[11]   Philip Shaw (ed.), 'Introduction' to *Romantic Wars: Studies in Culture and Conflict 1793–1822* (Hampshire: Ashgate Publishing, 2000), 6.

[12]   See Samuel Taylor Coleridge to Daniel Stuart (27 September 1809), in *Collected Letters of Samuel Taylor Coleridge*, ed. Earl Leslie Griggs, 6 vols. (Oxford: Clarendon Press, 1956–71), 3: 225–7.

intriguing paradoxes to shape his text.[13] This included, most notably, the use of a single framework within which to discuss the Spaniards of the sixteenth century and their contemporary counterparts. The former are described as 'butchers of mankind' on account of the atrocities committed during the Duke of Alva's Dutch campaign, while the latter are praised as heroic resistors to the imposition of French tyranny. In order to make sense of these differences between Spain past and present, Coleridge's readers were required to examine the importance attached to British heroism in both instances.[14] As Diego Saglia insightfully explains, the poet's argument in the *Letters* rests upon the recognition that the British government, which had committed itself to the Dutch cause in the sixteenth century, would once again act as political guardians (this time, to the oppressed people of Spain).[15] To Coleridge, the recent sieges of Zaragoza and Gerona bore uncanny resemblance to Philip II's siege of Harlem (1572–1573).[16] As Saglia expounds:

> Revolution in Coleridge's reflections is rather a return to a condition that had been temporarily lost or suspended, as well as the completion of a romance in which something essential is won back. In view of this conception of revolution, the importance of the Peninsular War resides in the idea that it returns something invaluable to the English and the British nation at large…[17]

With Coleridge's mind still energised by his recent re-reading of Shakespeare, this 'return' was as much literary as it was political, as evinced by the differences between his first and second series of lectures on Shakespeare. Whereas in 1808 Coleridge's main concern had been to save the bard from the attacks of French criticism (by offering a defence based on the unity of Shakespeare's plays), his lectures three years later would be animated by a much more pronounced interest in the escalating debate about British military involvement in Spain and Portugal.

---

[13]   Coleridge, *Letters on the Spaniards*, CC*: EOT*, 2: 53 (Letter 3).
[14]   A comparable parallelism occurs in the penultimate verse of Robert Southey's *Carmen Triumphale* (1814) which apostrophises the Count of Egmont, Count of Horn (Philip de Montmorency) and 'William the Deliverer' (leader of the 1568 Dutch revolt against Spanish rule), notwithstanding the poem's overt aim to celebrate contemporary Spanish resistance. The withdrawal of French troops from the Netherlands in December 1813 allows Southey to conclude with a historical realignment whereby 'All hearts are now in one good cause combined' (l. 246). Robert Southey, *Carmen Triumphale, for the Commencement of the Year 1814*, ed. Lynda Pratt, Daniel E. White, Ian Packer, Tim Fulford and Carol Bolton, *Robert Southey: Later Poetical Works 1811–1838*, ed. Tim Fulford and Lynda Pratt, 4 vols. (London: Pickering & Chatto, 2012), 3: 36–7.
[15]   Diego Saglia, 'War Romances, Historical Analogies and Coleridge's *Letters on the Spaniards*', in Shaw (ed.), *Romantic Wars*, 138–60 (146–54).
[16]   See Ronald Fraser, *Napoleon's Cursed War: Popular Resistance in the Spanish Peninsular War* (London: Verso, 2008), 164–72 (on the sieges of Zaragoza); 297–300 (on Gerona).
[17]   Saglia, 'War Romances', in Shaw (ed.), *Romantic Wars*, 153.

Addressing audiences at the London Philosophical Society on 5 December 1811, Coleridge directed his auditors towards the related issues of education and Shakespeare's language.[18] This entailed an involved progression of ideas from Shakespeare's conceits and witticisms to an intriguing comparison of Elizabethan times with the 'age of Republicanism'. He had already used similar historical paralleling to good effect in *The Friend*, whose seventeenth number (14 December 1809) challenged its readers 'to weigh, honestly and thoughtfully, the moral worth and intellectual power of the Age in which we live' by looking back to Shakespeare, Milton and Bacon.[19] Coleridge refigured this only slightly for his lecture in order to establish a comparison between England during the reign of Elizabeth I and England during the reigns of Charles I and Charles II:

> Compare this Revolution with that of a later age where the bubling [*sic*] up and overflowing had been produced by dregs, where there was a total want of all principle and which had raised from the bottom those dregs to the top & founded a monarchy to be the poison and bane of the rest of mankind – [20]

As in his *Letters on the Spaniards*, past and present are here troublesomely intertwined. 'This Revolution' cedes, after all, only too readily to the 'later age' of the lecture itself, when the terms 'bubling up', 'overflowing', and 'total want of principle' provided an apt characterisation of Coleridge's disillusionment with the tragic turn taken by the French Revolution and *its* republican ideology. This historical comparison nevertheless constitutes a spirited political aside from which the lecturer emerged to affirm that Milton and Shakespeare were chosen as subjects illustrative of 'general truths', capable of aiding the judgement 'of all writers of all countries'.[21] In this context, Coleridge clearly equates the 'general truths' represented by Milton and Shakespeare with the nation's public affairs and ultimate standing in the international community. He was working, in short, on the empowering argument that Shakespeare's plays could bring political enlightenment at home and abroad.

In his 1811–1812 lecture series Coleridge developed this alignment of literature and politics by investigating the morality of Shakespeare's heroes and villains in much more detail. In his twelfth lecture, the commitment to a politicised Shakespeare centres specifically on the link between character and

---

[18] On Coleridge as 'a teacher of moral wisdom', see Letter 6, *Letters on the Spaniards*, *CC*: *EOT*, 2: 72.

[19] Coleridge, 'Appendix A: No 17. December 14, 1809', in *CC: The Friend*, ed. Barbara E. Rooke, 2 vols (London: Routledge & Kegan Paul, 1969), 2: 230.

[20] '1811–1812 Lectures on Shakespeare and Milton in Illustration of the Principles of Poetry' (London Philosophical Society), Lecture 6 (5 December 1811), *CC*: *Lectures 1808–1819 on Literature*, ed. R.A. Foakes, 2 vols (London: Routledge & Kegan Paul, 1987), 1: 288.

[21] Lecture 6 (5 December 1811), *CC*: *Lectures*, 1: 290.

action.[22] Exploring his fascination for the psychological depths of Shakespeare's characters, Coleridge praises *Richard II* for 'contain[ing] the most magnificent and the truest eulogium on our native country which the English language could boast and which could be found in any other not excepting the proud claims of Greece & Rome'.[23] At the heart of Shakespeare's history play is King Richard himself, who intrigues Coleridge by his 'most rapid transitions from insolence to despair, from the heights of love to the agonies of resentment & from pretended resignation to the bitterest reproaches'.[24] Shakespeare's play about Richard's struggle to come to terms with the immortal and mortal aspects of his being (the phenomenon of the king's two bodies) impressed Coleridge, first and foremost, for its strength of characterisation. He claimed, in fact, that in *Richard II* Shakespeare had reached 'the summit {of excellence} in the ~~admirable~~ preservation of character'.[25]

Coleridge's notes for this lecture do not survive, but John Payne Collier, who attended and produced a comprehensive synopsis, offers a good account of Coleridge's exegesis of that play.[26] From his description it appears that Coleridge's discussion of characterisation and morality of action in *Richard II* developed quite cogently into a consideration of political ethics during the war against Napoleon. The lecture seems to have rested firmly upon Coleridge's belief that England's safety during this period depended primarily upon its own exercise of good morality. At the same time, however, Coleridge conceded, somewhat edgily, that 'while we were proudly preeminent in morals our enemy only maintained his station by superiority in mechanical means'.[27] It was at this point that Coleridge made explicit his reading of *Richard II* as a political play that enforced a triangular relation between character, morality and nationalism.[28] To help moderate the fear of French conquest, Coleridge proceeded to quote from John of Gaunt's famous speech beginning 'This royal throne of kings, this sceptre'd isle' (Act 2 scene 1).

---

22   While I argue here for an interest in characterisation that was, above all, politically determined, I recognise that Coleridge's focus was also bound to be popular in an age that exploited the dizzying heights of theatrical celebrity. On the concept of fame in the Romantic period see *Romanticism and Celebrity Culture, 1750–1850*, ed. Tom Mole (Cambridge: Cambridge University Press, 2009).

23   Lecture 12 (2 January 1812), *CC: Lectures*, 1: 378.

24   *CC: Lectures*, 1: 382.

25   *CC: Lectures*, 1: 385.

26   Coleridge's literary lectures were never intended for publication. We are therefore dependent upon a collage of his marginalia, notes taken by audience members, and reports preserved in public newspapers, journals, private letters and diaries. The great advantage of this is that it permits us to see Coleridge through the eyes of his audience. See, for example, Joseph Cottle, *Reminiscences of Samuel Taylor Coleridge and Robert Southey* (London, 1847), 355.

27   Lecture 12 (2 January 1812), *CC: Lectures*, 1: 378.

28   Political readings of *Richard II* complicated the play's reception history. Nahum Tate's 1680 adaptation, *The Sicilian Usurper*, was banned after only two performances. Jonathan Bate, *Shakespearean Constitutions: Politics, Theatre, Criticism, 1730–1830* (Oxford: Clarendon Press, 1989), 62; 70.

Gaunt's speech, celebrating England as an island naturally fortified against invasion and blessed with royal kings, 'renowned for their deeds … (For Christian service, and true chivalry)' was an apt choice.[29] Its morale-raising rhetoric clearly met the needs of patriotism and was as serviceable to Coleridge in 1811 as it would be to other writers during later wars. But significantly, the speech was not quoted in full. Coleridge took care, instead, to omit Gaunt's final lines, which re-imagine the protection afforded to a land 'bound in with the triumphant sea' as containment 'bound in with shame'.

Audiences familiar with Shakespeare's play would have known that Gaunt – old, wise, and infirm – actually concludes his speech with apprehensions of national and personal defeat. Corrupted by 'inky blots, and rotten parchment bonds', Gaunt laments 'That England, that was wont to conquer others, | Hath made a shameful conquest of itself'. As such, his final plea, 'O, would the scandal vanish with my life, | How happy then were my ensuing death!', resonates more convincingly as the expression of a macabre wish than a realistic prognosis.[30] These dying words of dire warning would have been especially unsettling for audiences in 1811, who were prone to recognise disturbing similarities between an enfeebled Gaunt and the ageing, blind and mentally unstable George III. Coleridge's politicised reading of the play thus hinges upon a curtailed quotation of Gaunt's speech which, in its celebration of England's moral reputation but omission of the nation's vulnerability to domestic tyranny, permitted the speaker to retain his focus on the external threat posed by Napoleonic France.

At this point, it is worth remembering that Coleridge was an atypical reader of Shakespeare, who approached the bard's writings with exceptional care. Most subscribers to his lectures would have enjoyed a less complete understanding of Shakespeare's canon, their knowledge gathered from readings of selected plays, literary anthologies or dramatic performances that would have made Coleridge's editorial interferences less obvious.[31] Vicesimus Knox's *Elegant Extracts* (1784) is a good example of the 'truncated' Shakespeare available in the early nineteenth century. When issued as a miniature library in 1810 consisting of twelve volumes (six for poetry, six for prose), the *Elegant Extracts* claimed to offer its readers 'a copious selection of instructive, moral, and entertaining

---

[29]   William Shakespeare, *King Richard II*, in *The Plays of William Shakspeare* [*sic*]. *In fifteen volumes. With the corrections and illustrations of various commentators. To which are added, notes by Samuel Johnson and George Steevens*. 4th ed. Revised and augmented (with a glossarial index) by the editor of Dodsley's collection of Old Plays. 15 vols. (London, 1793), 8: 230 (2.1).

[30]   Shakespeare, *King Richard II*, 8: 231 (2.1).

[31]   As Tiffany Stern explains, in the eighteenth and early nineteenth centuries, '[Shakespeare's] plays as a whole were relegated; only particular word-conscious "literary" productions staged Shakespeare's plays in full at all.' Stern, 'Shakespeare in Drama', in Ritchie and Sabor (eds), *Shakespeare in the Eighteenth Century*, 141–60 (141).

passages' from the nation's 'most eminent' writers.[32] The fourth volume of poetry, labelled 'Dramatic', is devoted almost entirely to Shakespeare. Therein, *Hamlet*, the most popular play by Shakespeare on the Romantic stage, is the most frequently quoted (thirteen times). *Henry IV (1)* and *The Merchant of Venice*, often performed in the theatres, also feature prominently. But the selection ultimately intended to honour Shakespeare in the closet, rather than on stage. This is suggested, for instance, by the inclusion of quotations from *Henry VI (2)* and *Troilus and Cressida*, neither of which were publicly acted during this period.[33] The volume also overlooks contemporary staging practices, as exemplified by the inclusion of the King's soliloquy during the closet scene in *Hamlet* (despite its omission from contemporary commercial productions).[34] Coleridge's selective appropriation of John of Gaunt's speech at once contributed to and depended upon this tradition of being able to divorce Shakespeare's lines from their larger dramatic framework.

The importance that Coleridge ascribed to *Richard II* is confirmed by the fact that the play remained central to his lecturing in Bristol two years later. Speaking of the history plays, and *Richard II* especially, Coleridge began his fifth lecture (11 November 1813) by differentiating drama from epic.[35] This distinction would be further elucidated in his 1818–1819 lectures, in which Coleridge would explain how in epic a pre-determined fate gradually employs the will whereas in drama the fate and will appear in opposition.[36] In the contest between human action and man's predetermined destiny the historic drama presented a transitory state uniquely endowed with the merit of 'familiarizing the men to the great names of the Country, and exciting Patriotism'.[37] Coleridge proved this point to his Bristolian audiences of 1813 by again quoting Gaunt's speech. This time, he justified his use of the quotation by observing:

> An historic play requires more excitement than a tragic, thus Shakespeare never loses an opportunity of awakening a patriotic feeling; for this purpose Old *Gaunt* accuses Richard of having "*farmed* out the island".[38]

---

[32]   Vicesimus Knox, *Elegant Extracts: Being a Copious Selection of Instructive, Moral, and Entertaining Passages from the Most Eminent British Poets*, 6 vols, (London, 1810), Title page. See Books VII and VIII esp.

[33]   Knox, *Elegant Extracts*, Book VII, 4: 22; Book VII, 4: 206 and 246.

[34]   Knox, *Elegant Extracts*, Book VIII, 4: 172.

[35]   '1813 Lectures on Shakespeare and Education' (White Lion, Bristol), Lecture 5 (11 November 1813) *CC: Lectures,* 1: 559.

[36]   'Works: Copy D', *CC: Marginalia*, ed. H.J. Jackson and George Whalley, 6 vols (London: Routledge & Kegan Paul, 1998), 4: 794. Compare '1818–1819 Lectures on Shakespeare' (Alternating with Philosophical Lectures, Crown and Anchor, Strand), 'Lecture 2' (31 December 1818) *CC: Lectures,* 2: 283.

[37]   *CC: Lectures*, 1: 559.

[38]   CC: Lectures, 1: 563.

The *Bristol Gazette* took this up most dutifully by explaining to its readers that 'Shakespear [*sic*], in blending the Epic with the Tragic, has given the impression of the Drama to the history of his country'.[39] The reviewer for the *Gazette* seems to have recognised that Coleridge's application of history was, first and foremost, politically expedient.

Coleridge also took pains to remind his audiences that Shakespeare should not be read as a literal historian. His surviving notes make it clear that he perceived in *Richard II* 'the introduction of *Accidents*' that made this particular play '*Drama* not History'.[40] In the flyleaf to his annotated copy of *Richard II* Coleridge observed:

> The distinction does not depend on the quantity of historical events compared with the fictions, for there is as much *History* in Macbeth as in Richard, but in relation of the History to the Plot – in the purely historical plays the History *dir informs* the plot, in the mixt [*sic*] it *directs* it – in the rest, as Macbeth, Hamlet, Cymbeline, Lear, it subserves it.[41]

Meaning was centred, then, on 'the relation of the History to the Plot', which signified that *Richard II*, as '*Drama* not History', relied upon a sense of the past that would 'direct' rather than 'inform' its scheme of action. Dependent upon his auditors' ability to recognise the familiar, factual narrative that 'direct[s]' the plot of *Richard II*, Coleridge considered the affirmation of national identity the play's central 'drama'. To him, one of Shakespeare's greatest objects in *Richard II* had been 'to make his countrymen more patriotic; to make Englishmen proud of being Englishmen'.[42] Provided that Gaunt's speech be 'properly repeated', Coleridge felt confident that 'every man would retire from the theatre secure in his country if secure in his own virtue'.[43] *Richard II* was, for Coleridge, a play in which 'the Spirit of patriotic reminiscence' was 'all-permeating'.[44] The liberation of Spain in 1813 and Wellington's march into France that same year would have offered Coleridge's audiences a fortuitous taste of his conviction that greater moral and political unity were still very much within reach.

---

[39]   *CC: Lectures*, 1: 562. R.A. Foakes notes that the reporter for the *BG* was not always an accurate synthesiser, however, as Coleridge's letter to Mary Morgan confirms (17 November 1813; in Griggs (ed.), *Letters*, 456). *CC: Lectures*, 1: lxxxv–lxxxvi.

[40]   *CC: Lectures*, 1: 561. For *Richard II* as Shakespeare's 'purest Historic Play', see 'Works: Copy D', *CC: Marginalia*, 4: 797. Coleridge's source text was *The Works of Shakespeare: In Seven Volumes. Collated with the Oldest Copies, and Corrected; with Notes, Explanatory, and Critical*, ed. Lewis Theobald, 7 vols. (London, 1733).

[41]   'Works: Copy A', *CC: Marginalia*, 4: 712.

[42]   *Bristol Gazette* report (18 November 1813) of Lecture 5 (11 November 1813): *CC: Lectures*, 1: 563.

[43]   Lecture 12 (2 January 1812), *CC: Lectures*, 1: 378.

[44]   Coleridge, 'Works Copy D', *CC: Marginalia*, 4: 795.

From Closet to Stage

It is important to note that *Richard II* was 'not much acted' during the Romantic period. But when discussing Shakespeare's play, Coleridge was clearly thinking of *Richard II* in openly abstract terms – of the play's *potential* for political and dramatic effect, if not necessarily any specific performances. In an illuminating exposition of Coleridge's fascination for *Richard II* Julie Carlson affirms that 'Shakespeare's power, particularly the power of his drama to evoke nationalist sentiment, depends on its production on stage'.[45] In this section I respond to Carlson's invitation to reconsider the relationship between closet and stage performances by interrogating to what extent Coleridge's closeness to *Richard II* affected his transformation of the rejected revolutionary drama *Osorio* (1797) into *Remorse* (1813), a successful play with a Spanish setting that made important gestures towards Peninsular politics.

The first hint of Shakespeare's significance to the plot of *Remorse* appears in Coleridge's annotated copy of Joseph Rann's edition of *The Dramatic Works of Shakespeare* (1786–1791). Coleridge's marginalia attests to a specific interest in *Macbeth*'s early response to the witches' prophecies. Identifying the protagonist's 'First Struggl[e] of Conscience[,] his disobedien[ce] to which is to destroy him b[y] the very pang[s] of Compuncti[on]', Coleridge jotted down '"Remorse"' – the double quotation marks alluding to his own play of that name.[46] The note to *Macbeth* serves as a timely reminder that as he returned to playwriting, Coleridge was also busily preparing for his politically nuanced lectures on Shakespearean drama. It is no coincidence, then, that while revising *Osorio*, Coleridge should have chosen to draw upon *Richard II* (one of the most prominent plays in his lecture series), and that the decision to do so seems to have been responsible for some notable differences between his dramas of 1797 and 1813.

In *Osorio* the hero Albert loiters in Spain for nearly a month before finally resolving to take action. In *Remorse*, by contrast, the return to the homeland proves wholly decisive. The 1813 text opens with an apostrophe to the Spanish nation that echoes Richard II's speech upon his return from Ireland. In Shakespeare's play, the king 'weep[s] for joy' and falling to his hands, salutes his homeland. Flushed with confidence in his role as divine representative, he declares:

> RICHARD   This earth shall have a feeling, and these stones
> Prove armed soldiers, ere her native king
> Shall falter under foul rebellion's arms.[47]

---

[45]   Carlson, *Theatre of Romanticism*, 51.
[46]   'Works: Copy C', *CC: Marginalia*, 4: 770.
[47]   Shakespeare, *King Richard II*, 8: 271 (3.2).

The speech arguably captures Richard at his most magnificent and kingly. It is poignantly echoed in *Remorse*, wherein Alvar's return to Granada also serves as a call to action:

> ALVAR   If aught on earth demand an unmix'd feeling,
> 'Tis surely this – after long years of exile,
> To step forth on firm land, and gazing round us,
> To hail at once our country, and our birth place.
> Hail, Spain! Granada, hail! once more I press
> Thy sands with filial awe, land of my fathers![48]

Coleridge's intention here is less to approximate the characters of Richard and Alvar, than to establish verbal and visual parallels between his play and Shakespeare's. The new opening underscores the extent to which *Remorse*, like *Richard II*, is crucially preoccupied with the consequences of expatriation.[49]

Early in Shakespeare's play, Richard cuts short the duel between Bolingbroke and Mowbray by sentencing Bolingbroke to six years of exile and admonishing Mowbray to 'never return'.[50] When Bolingbroke comes back prematurely, York has little choice but to upbraid him: 'Why have those banish'd and forbidden legs | Dar'd once to touch a dust of England's ground?'.[51] But Bolingbroke is able to justify his return as one determined by the defence of hereditary rights from an usurping power. Coleridge's Alvar cites similar motivation, and shortly after his arrival in Granada realises his first symbolic gesture of reinstatement by adopting the disguise of a Moor. This decision contributes significantly not only to the play's sixteenth-century setting, but also to the new expansion of historical perspectives that, in line with his *Letters on the Spaniards*, Coleridge was seeking to establish.

Coleridge took care to set *Remorse* precisely during 'the reign of Philip II, just at the close of the civil wars against the Moors, and during the heat of the persecution which raged against them, shortly after the edict which forbad the wearing of Moresco apparel under pain of Death'.[52] 'By donning Moorish robes at the height

---

[48] Coleridge, *Remorse* (Printed) *CC: Poetical Works: Plays III.2*, 1239 (1.1. 4–9).

[49] See *Examiner*, 17 July 1808, on the 1,600 Spanish prisoners who were permitted to sail from Plymouth to Spain following the Anglo-Spanish alliance: 'On their embarkation, many of them took up handfuls of sand from the beach, actually kissed it with reverence and affection, as a part of the earth (as they expressed it) of the Land of true Liberty, and then carefully put it into their pockets, in order to exhibit it to their countrymen!'

[50] *King Richard II*, 8: 214 (1.3).

[51] *King Richard II*, 8: 260 (2.3).

[52] *CC: Poetical Works: Plays III.2*, 1238. In Schiller's *Don Carlos* (1787) the Prince of Asturias, Don Carlos (Philip II's son), rejects his father's campaign to subjugate the Netherlands and determines to flee Spain in order to help safeguard Dutch independence. The play ends with Philip handing over his son to the Grand Inquisitor. Two separate English translations appeared in London, dated 1798. Coleridge read Schiller's play as he prepared to write *Osorio* (1797). According to Frederick Lieder, *Don Carlos*'s only

of the Moors' persecution', Julie Carlson argues, 'Alvar treats religious and ethnic oppression in a remarkably cavalier fashion'.[53] Coleridge's admiration for Richard II and specific writing of this scene for *Remorse* points, however, to a much more nuanced interest in Alvar's choice of disguise. Whereas *Osorio*'s hero, Albert, makes his first appearance '(diguis'd as a Morescoe, and in Moorish garments)', in *Remorse*'s new Shakespearean-inflected opening, Alvar first appears 'wrapt in a Boat Cloak', which ensures that his later determination to 'linger here | In the disguise of a Morescoe chieftain' is actively dramatised as part of the play's main action.[54] As I argue elsewhere, this deliberate staging of Alvar's Moorish identity not only constitutes Coleridge's intention 'to underline the independence of character and the rebellious, defiant nature of Alvar's gesture', but ultimately 'represents so successful an attempt to incorporate otherness that Ordonio mistakes Alvar for being entirely "other"'.[55] In Act 2 scene 2 the villain Ordonio thus fails to distinguish between the disguised Spaniard and his Morisco servant, Zulimez.[56] At this point, it is worth noting that Zulimez's nationality also marks an instance of significant rewriting since his earlier counterpart, Maurice (in *Osorio*), was envisaged as a German (and in yet earlier draft versions as an Englishman named Warville).[57] This preoccupation with Moorish identity helps define Coleridge's 1813 play-text as one that responds to Peninsular politics by recognising that the war in Spain had given new relevance to that country's persecution of the Moors during the sixteenth century. At a time when 'anything relating to the Peninsula [was] an object of interest', the *British Review* was certainly right to claim that with its 'scene ... laid in Spain ... [and] Dons and Donnas for the chief agents' *Remorse* was 'exactly what the managers wanted'.[58] Coleridge's detailed treatment of his Moorish theme nevertheless insists that, for him, *Remorse* was much more than merely a wartime sop.

In his *Biographia Literaria* (1817) Coleridge renders explicit the connection between his literary lectures and subsequent celebrity as a playwright:

> I can conscientiously declare, that the complete success of the REMORSE on the first night of its representation did not give me as great or as heart-felt a pleasure, as the observation that the pit and boxes were crowded with faces

English-language performance at this time was in New York (6 May 1799). Lieder, 'Bayard Taylor's Adaptation of Schiller's *Don Carlos*', *The Journal of English and Germanic Philology* 16.1 (January 1917), 27–52.

[53]   Carlson, *Theatre of Romanticism*, 110.

[54]   Coleridge, *Osorio: A Tragedy*, *CC: Poetical Works: Plays III.1*, 73. Compare *Remorse* (Stage), *CC: Poetical Works: Plays III.2*, 1075, 1077 (1.1.77–8).

[55]   Susan Valladares, '"He that can bring the dead to life again": Resurrecting the Spanish setting of Coleridge's *Osorio* (1797) and *Remorse* (1813)', in *Romanticism and the Anglo-Hispanic Imaginary*, ed. Joselyn M. Almeida (Amsterdam: Rodopi, 2010), 133–55 (147).

[56]   Remorse (Stage), *CC: Poetical Works: Plays III.2*, 1096 (2.2.45–6)

[57]   Samuel Taylor Coleridge to William Lisle Bowles (16 October 1797), in Griggs (ed.), *Letters*, 1: 355–6.

[58]   *British Review*, May 1813; 361–70 (361–2).

familiar to me, though of individuals whose names I did not know, and of whom I knew nothing, but that they had attended one or other of my courses of lectures.[59]

Whether or not paying audiences would have been as quick to discern the affinity between Coleridge's romanticised historical play and his earlier readings of Shakespearean drama is a matter of speculation. But a Notebook entry dated 1809–1810, which sees Coleridge align his dramatic plans to Shakespeare's history plays, suggests that he sincerely hoped so.[60] For Coleridge, *Remorse*'s success was measured not only by the realisation of its audience-pleasing, money-making potential but its relationship to the themes of history, morality, agency and affect – themes that also characterised his political journalism and literary lectures.

The entry in the *Biographia Literaria* provides a useful reminder that whereas Coleridge could only imagine how readers might respond to the wartime articles published in *The Friend* and the *Courier*, he could directly witness the effects of his lectures and drama. His fascination for audience response figures in *Remorse* as a desire to discover the extent to which the stage itself might function as a psychological arena. The pivotal expression of this occurs in the conjuring scene at the end of Act 3; a scene that was always prominently advertised in the playbills (see Figure 2.2), and hinges upon Ordonio's unknowing contract of Alvar to play the part of wizard in order to persuade Teresa of his own death.[61] In thus testing the limits of performativity, Coleridge was also, by extension, denouncing the theatrical illusions that sustain political witchery. Ordonio's scheming gives literal form to the dubious mechanisms by which Napoleon had secured his power in Europe and, in so doing, fulfils the analogy between drama and politics integral to the discussion of character in Coleridge's Shakespearean lectures.[62]

The prominence given to the conjuring scene suggests, furthermore, that despite Coleridge's reservations about contemporary acting conditions, the materiality of performance was not entirely incompatible with the imaginative licence ascribed to reading.[63] The playwright's engagement with the busy, dirty

---

[59]   *CC: BL*, 1: 221.

[60]   *The Notebooks of Samuel Taylor Coleridge*, ed. Kathleen Coburn, 5 vols. in 10 (Princeton, NJ: Princeton University Press, 1957–2002), 3: Text, entry 3654 (18.18).

[61]   *TE*, 31 January 1813, described Ordonio as 'a Hamlet corrupted by bad passions'.

[62]   On *Romorse* as a play that responds to 'the prevailing rivalry between the aesthetics and mechanics of illusion', see Frederick Burwick, *Illusion and the Drama: Critical Theory of the Enlightenment and the Romantic Era* (Pennsylvania: Pennsylvania State University Press, 1991), 268–79 (268). On Ordonio as a Napoleonic 'mad Realizer of mad Dreams' see 'Essay XVI', *CC: The Friend*, 1: 124.

[63]   Coleridge famously claimed that he 'never saw any of Shakespear's [*sic*] plays performed, but with a degree of pain, disgust, and indignation'. As the *BG* summarised: 'He had seen Mrs. Siddons as *Lady*, and Kemble as *Macbeth* – these might be the Macbeths of the Kembles, but they were not the Macbeths of Shakespear; he was therefore not grieved at the enormous size and monopoly of the theatres, which naturally produced many bad and but few good actors; and which drove Shakespear from the stage, to find his proper

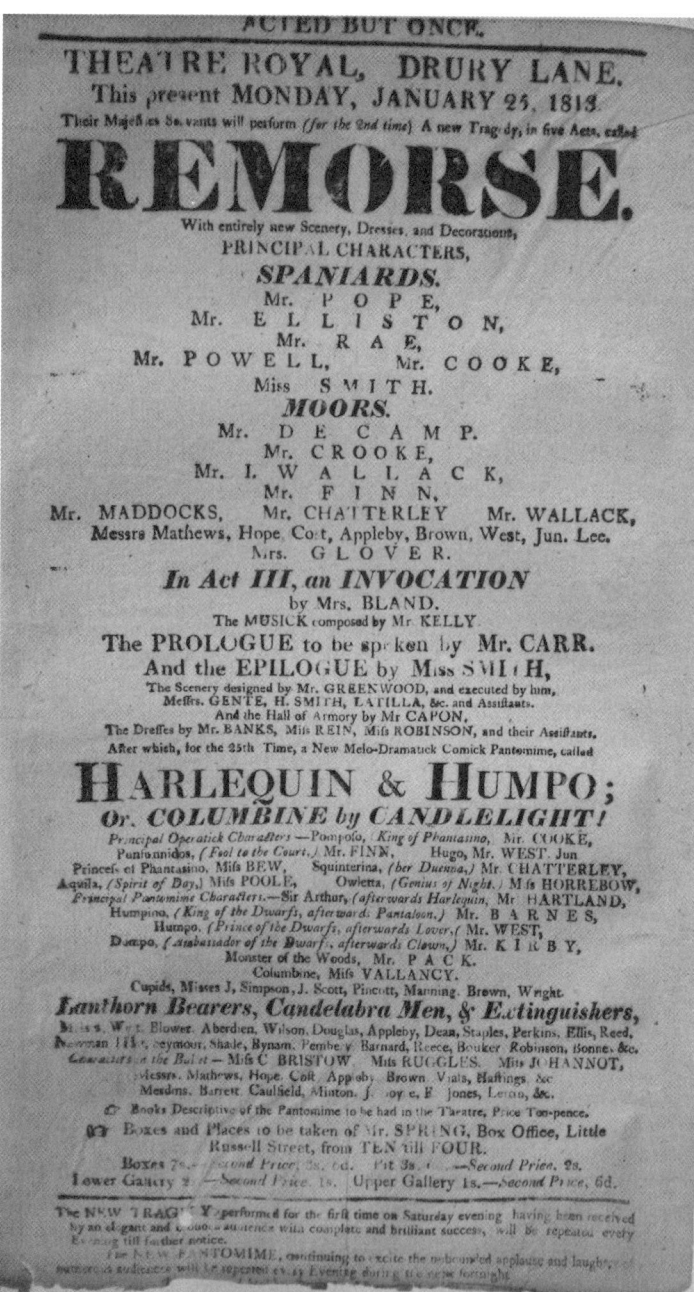

Figure 2.2   Playbill advertising *Remorse* and *Harlequin & Humpo; or,*
Columbine by Candleight! at Drury Lane Theatre, 25 January
1813. © The Art Archive/Garrick Club.

world of early nineteenth-century politics ensured that an awareness of real bodies was never far from his creative consciousness. From the cavernous playhouses of Drury Lane and Covent Garden, to the Theatre Royals (in Bristol, for instance, where *Remorse* would be performed in 1813), Coleridge recognised that dramatic performances had the power to familiarise both literate and illiterate audiences with important politicised narratives. *Remorse* celebrates the capacity of drama to provide audiences with the vicarious experiences that Coleridge deemed critical for their political and moral education; experiences, it must be added, that were characterised by careful shaping and emotional depth.

Kemble's Shakespeare, 1808–1815

Since assuming management of Covent Garden in 1803, John Philip Kemble had invested in grand Shakespearean revivals that took place every theatrical season and were renowned for their lavish display and majestic effects. As a committed antiquarian scholar Kemble generally focused his efforts on restoring historical accuracy to Shakespeare's plays.[64] Audiences agreed, for the most part, that Kemble's productions of Shakespeare were expert and accomplished. It was, nevertheless, a well-known fact that his Shakespearean productions were as dependent upon revisions by Cibber, Tate, Sheridan, Thomson, Garrick or Hull, as they were upon the bard himself. This interplay between cultural tradition and translation defined Shakespeare's place in the Romantic literary canon. As Michael Dobson explains, once the eighteenth century accepted Shakespeare as 'one of Britain's heroic forefathers, amending Shakespeare's plays became part of the vital nationalist project of rewriting the national past in order to validate the aspirations of the present'.[65] Much of this editorial energy was devoted to keeping Shakespeare's plays in line with contemporary tastes and mores. As a result, it was Nahum Tate's 1680 version of *King Lear*, rather than Shakespeare's, that held the boards until the late nineteenth century; a version that omits the Fool and rewrites

---

place, in the heart and in the closet; where he sits with Milton, enthroned on a double-headed Parnassus'. *CC: Lectures,* 1: 563. Coleridge was not, however, averse to the theatre per se. The explicit pairing of his lectures on drama with his interest in education (in the 1811 1812 and 1813 series) suggests that Coleridge, like many contemporary proponents of the theatre, ascribed a valuable didactic function to dramatic performances.

[64] The acting texts for *Julius Caesar* (which exist, significantly, in two versions – the 1811 copy released in advance of the Covent Garden production, and the 1812 version, revised and re-issued after the play's first performances) testify to Kemble's diligent study of historians and classical writers. Cicero, Livius, Seneca, Plinius, Plutarch and Appian appear in an impressive catalogue of sources. See the opening flyleaves to *Julius Caesar*, written in Kemble's hand (with transcriptions from Latin and Greek sources). Shattuck (ed.), *Promptbooks,* Vol. 4.

[65] Michael Dobson, *The Making of the National Poet: Shakespeare, Adaptation and Authorship 1660–1769* (Oxford: Clarendon Press, 1992), 187.

the conclusion, in order to provide a happy ending in which Cordelia is united with Edgar and Lear restored to the throne.[66] Indeed, even *Othello*, which did not undergo any major rewriting, was markedly different from Shakespeare's original. In keeping with older eighteenth-century versions of the play, Act 4 of Kemble's production was pruned so as to omit Othello's epileptic fit, Desdemona's Willow song and her conversation with Emilia on the topic of adultery.[67] Like Coleridge, Kemble was sensitive to questions of morality and, as a self-perceived cultural key-holder, seems to have felt that Shakespeare's plays ought to avoid offending the sensibilities of modern audiences.

Consequently, for all his antiquarian enthusiasm, Kemble never fully abandoned the popular changes made to Shakespeare's texts by earlier generations of managers and actors. Intrinsically related to Kemble's artistic and ideological appreciation of the bard was his overall desire to establish Shakespeare in an ever more commercialised theatrical market. As a savvy manager, Kemble knew that he could profit from Shakespeare but exercised caution, in order to ensure that his productions conformed to the moral and political expectations of Covent Garden's socially heterogeneous – and, as the Old Price riots proved, volatile – mix of playgoers.[68] To achieve this, he continuously invested in modernised revivals of Shakespeare's plays and the publication of his own acting versions.

Between 1789 and 1812, Kemble brought out 26 acting editions of Shakespeare's plays; publishing and republishing these as many as six times for any one play.[69] By imparting the impression that Shakespeare contributed to the nation's growing self-confidence during challenging times, Kemble's Shakespearean revivals were not stock pieces with fixed meanings and styles for delivery but open scripts that could be adapted to particular ends, often with dazzling effects.

The most popular Shakespearean plays on the early nineteenth-century stage were those that succeeded in re-creating intricate on-stage pageantry. Accordingly, one of Kemble's most elaborate exteriors was reserved for *Henry V*, '*Before the Gates of Harfleur*'.[70] In this scene, the Governor and citizens, having descended from the walls, kneel as the English enter in procession. Kemble recorded the scene in fastidious detail:

---

[66]   *Shakespeare's King Lear (With Nahum Tate's alterations), A Tragedy*, revised by J.P. Kemble (London, 1808), in Shattuck (ed.), *Promptbooks*, 5: 71–2 (5.5).

[67]   *Shakespeare's Othello, The Moor of Venice, A Tragedy*, revised by J.P. Kemble (London, 1804). Shattuck (ed.), *Promptbooks*, 7: 57–67 (Act 4).

[68]   Shakespeare continued to be performed during the disruptive O.P. riots. See 'Calendar': Part A, and *TE*, 3 June 1810: 'Mr. KEMBLE continues to draw from SHAKESPEARE a kind of stock play for the season, which is performed regularly once a week.'

[69]   Charles H. Shattuck (ed.), 'General Introduction', *Promptbooks*, 1: xiv.

[70]   *Shakespeare's King Henry the Fifth, A Historical Play*, revised by J.P. Kemble (London, 1806), in Shattuck (ed.), *Promptbooks*, 3: 27 (3.1).

*When the Gates are opened, a Bridge is discovered – The 12 French soldiers
and their Captain, drawn up on it, salute as the King crosses it.*

– The Governour [sic] and 2 Citizens come out of the Town, and kneel. – L.

Exeter takes the key from the Governour.

> *Exeunt into Harfleur –*
> *Exeter.*
> *The King.*
> *Bedford & Gloster.*
> *Westmoreland.*
> *Fluellen & Gower.*
> *Governour and Citizens.*
> *2 Lords.*
> *2 Lords.*
> *2 Heralds.*
> *Captain*
> *Soldiers, two and two.*
>
> *xxx March – <u>Orchestra</u>.*
> *Great chorus.*[71]

By Kemble's careful stage-management the characters in the procession are thus
introduced according to their rank. It is a scene that realises a symbolic grading
effect; the audience's attention directed, initially, to the gates and bridge revealed
centre-stage, before being introduced to the more elaborate human spectacle of the
entrance into Harfleur. With the Orchestra, rather than 'Great chorus', emphasising
to audiences the symbolic import of this unfolding spectacle, Kemble's *Henry V*
underlined the need to observe hierarchy and preserve good models of decorum,
both in the playhouse and outside it.

Henry V was consistently produced during the eighteenth and nineteenth
centuries, complementing regular productions of *Henry IV (1)*. While Jacky
Bratton rightly reminds us that *Henry V* is a play 'full of people voicing objections
to Henry's wars', its pairing with *Henry IV (1)* helped qualify this.[72] Together, the
plays present a dramatic narrative of patriotic achievement that charts the progress
of the once rebellious Prince of Wales into the heroic king who would lead the
English troops to victory at Agincourt. Perceived until this day as a play that seems
indomitably 'British', *Henry V*'s political topicality was further emphasised by its
early nineteenth-century subtitle, 'The Conquest of France'. This captured what
Elizabeth Inchbald described as Shakespeare's determination 'in this drama, to

---

[71]   *Henry the Fifth*, in Shattuck (ed.), *Promptbooks*, 3: 29 (3.1). I have used italics to
transcribe Kemble's handwritten description of this scene.
[72]   Jacky Bratton, 'Introduction' to Bratton, Cave et al. (eds), *Acts of Supremacy*, 11.

expose every vanity of the Gallic foe to British ridicule' and ensured that *Henry V* remained a popular play throughout the Napoleonic Wars.[73]

Kemble's annotations to the 1806 promptbook give some indication of the political significance that *Henry V* would acquire after 1808. Audiences were introduced, for example, to a new speech by Henry at the conclusion of Act 3:

> HENRY   *Were the French twice the number that they are,*
> *We would cut a passage through them to our home,*
> *Or tear the Lions out of England's coat.*
> *Forward – March. –* [74]

This morale-raising insert replaces Henry's otherwise prosaic order to set up camp and prepare the troops for their march the following day.[75] In Kemble's version, it is the 'here and now' that takes centre stage, not the 'tomorrow' of the original. This new climax brings with it much more impressive dramatic effect, enforced by a cue for the Orchestra to play 'Britons Strike Home' as the characters clear the stage in military formation. Secure in the knowledge that the plot's conclusion would be entirely in their favour, wartime audiences are likely to have taken an active part in the performance by also singing along. Kemble's production thus drew upon a historical parallelism less nuanced but not altogether divorced from that employed by Coleridge in his *Letters on the Spaniards*. His staging of *Henry V* during the Peninsular War imparted the hope that as the British spirit had prevailed in France, so too would it succeed in driving the French out of the Peninsula.

Henry V was judiciously chosen for performance at Covent Garden in November and December 1813, marking the end of a pinnacle year in the war against Napoleon.[76] After years of strategic defence Wellington had finally found himself in a position to initiate the offensive. In June 1813 the Allied armies won the prestigious town of Vitoria and secured an Austrian alliance that made Napoleon's position in Germany all the more precarious. This, in turn, enabled Wellington to begin his advance into Bayonne by crossing the Franco-Spanish border in October 1813. *The Times* noted:

---

[73]   *The British Theatre; or, A Collection of Plays, which are acted at the Theatres Royal, Drury-Lane, Covent Garden, and Haymarket ... with Biographical and Critical Remarks by Mrs. Inchbald*. 25 vols. (London, 1808), Introduction to Henry V, 2: 5.

[74]   *Henry the Fifth*, in Shattuck (ed.), *Promptbooks*, 3: 36 (3.3).

[75]   The promptbook reads: 'On to the bridge, ~~it now draws toward night: –~~
~~Beyond the river we'll encamp ourselves;~~
~~And on to-morrow bid them march away.~~'
Henry the Fifth, in Shattuck (ed.), *Promptbooks*, 3: 36 (3.3).

[76]   *Henry V* was performed at CG on 1, 8, 10 and 25 November, and 10 December 1813. 'Calendar': Part A.

Few, indeed are the periods, since the original production of this martial play, when it could have been performed with the remarkable coincidence of an event, similar to that on which its story is founded – the Invasion of France.[77]

By 1813 Wellington's pursuit of Napoleon's troops could be celebrated in the same breath as Henry V's historic victory of 1415.[78]

The Times' review of *Henry V* recognises that Kemble's success as a manager derived significantly from his ability to activate audiences' patriotic feelings. There was no guarantee, however, that Shakespeare's plays would be interpreted in the vein that Kemble intended. Take, for instance, the barbarities of warfare, dramatised by Shakespeare to such poignant effect. Henry's threat of reprisals against the citizens of Harfleur, his order to kill the French prisoners on the battlefield, and Bardolph's execution for stealing were all retained in Kemble's acting text. These violent episodes may have enhanced the victory at Agincourt by making chilling contributions to the play's 'realism', but at the time of the Peninsular War they could also double as moments wherein to contest military action.

Elizabeth Inchbald's introduction to *Henry V* for *The British Theatre* (1808) lingers unexpectedly on the observation that the English army's success at Agincourt did not bring an end to the violence. Her celebration of the victorious English army swiftly gives way to the reflection that:

> The consequences of this glorious victory were yet most horrible to the humane Britons; for the number of their prisoners amounting to more than their own triumphant army, they were commanded, even when the heat of contest had subsided, to put every Frenchman to death.[79]

Although Inchbald concedes that historians have offered various interpretations for the numbers involved ('fifteen thousand of the English only, *it is said*, defeated fifty-two thousand of the French'), she insists that 'the French army were more than twice the number of the English, and that the English slew their prisoners'.[80] She then attempts to neutralise the contentiousness implied by this repetition by directing her readers to Shakespeare's portrayal of 'the frivolous anxiety of the surviving [French] nobility' – as embodied by their herald, Montjoy, who arrives at the English camp to distinguish the corpses of French nobles from those of 'vulgar', 'common men'.[81] This damning depiction of French 'vanity' allows Inchbald to underplay the horrors of the massacre and realign her remarks with the triumphalism of Kemble's production of *Henry V*. But the fact that the Revolutionary Wars saw Britain effectively side with the French nobles makes

---

[77] *The Times*, 2 November 1813.
[78] See *Examiner* (1 August 1813) on the link between Vitoria and Agincourt.
[79] Inchbald, *British Theatre*, Introduction to *Henry V*, 2: 4–5.
[80] Inchbald, *Henry V*, 2: 4; 5, [my emphasis].
[81] *Henry the Fifth*, in Shattuck (ed.), *Promptbooks*, 3: 51 (4.7).

even this attempt at conformity somewhat suspect. Elizabeth Inchbald may have been careful to disguise any liberal views of her own when writing her 'Remarks' for Bell's *British Theatre*,[82] yet her introduction to *Henry V* seems curiously intent on exposing the distance between the lived experience of war and its representation on stage.[83] Kemble worked assiduously to define Covent Garden as a site for wartime patriotism, but not even his best efforts could keep a check on the criticisms to which 'war' itself was subject.

Re-thinking Characterisation

For the duration of the British army's engagements in Spain and Portugal, theatre managers frequently made use of occasional addresses and songs to publicise the latest military bulletins. As an importantly mixed forum, the theatre auditorium provided a space in which playgoers of all social classes were not only invited to spectate, but also reflect. Gillian Russell argues powerfully for the ways in which late eighteenth- and early nineteenth-century theatres were transformed into political arenas for re-staging the Napoleonic Wars. She explains how a relocation of time and place (as explored in my earlier analysis of *Pizarro*) could effectively circumvent contemporary censorship laws and enable playwrights, managers, actors and audiences to entertain nuanced responses to the political events of the day.[84] The referential range of critical commentaries on Sheridan's play and its changing significance during the Napoleonic Wars proves that audiences were well versed in the strategies needed for allegorical interpretations of the contemporary repertoire.

Events in the Peninsula weighed heavily upon the political consciousness of playgoers. Consider, for example, John Waldie's theatre diary for 14 August 1809, documenting a visit to the Royal Circus in Brighton:

> Mr Clarke came on to say — that he had it in command to state to the audience from his Royal Highness at the Pavilion, that he had just received dispatches from London to inform him of a glorious victory gained by Sir Arthur Wellesley & Cuesta with a very inferior force over Victor & Sebastiani — the French force is stated at 44,000, the English & Spanish at 28,000: our troops were

---

[82]   Inchbald's social circle strongly suggests that her personal political views were liberal. But she was careful to present a more conservative persona in public, as implied by her decision to publish under the respectable title of 'Mrs Inchbald'. On her contributions to *The British Theatre*, see Ben P. Robertson, *Elizabeth Inchbald's Reputation: A Publishing and Reception History* (London: Pickering & Chatto, 2013), 147–64.

[83]   See also [An Officer of the Staff], *Operations of the British Army in Spain: Including Broad Hints to the Commissariat and Board of Transport: with anecdotes illustrative of the Spanish Character* (London, 1809) – a work that challenges the received view of the Peninsular War by contrasting official bulletins and news reports with eyewitness reports (from unnamed officers).

[84]   See Chapter 1 and Russell, *Theatres of War*, 16; 54 esp.

victorious — & the enemy lost 10,000 — but we have lost above 5,000 — which may be reckoned at 7,000: General Mackenzie & General Langwerth are killed: — besides many others.[85]

This news of the Allied army's success at Talavera 'was received with cheers & God Save the King played: audience standing'.[86] Waldie's personal response to the announcement was, nevertheless, characterised by thoughtfulness, as much as jubilance. This is made evident in his oscillation between recording Clarke's address and offering his own commentary upon it, with a reflection that the estimated death toll of 5,000 British soldiers might more accurately be reckoned at 7,000.[87] As Mary Favret explains, the 'new scientific methods for calculating war fatalities and casualties' employed during this period were often met with hostility.[88] The difficult abstractions engendered by such quantifications of human experience were only heightened by the disconcerting time lag inherent to all reports of the war: 'As the newspapers made manifest, by the time a crucial victory has been reported in England, the British navy or army could, in the meantime, have suffered shattering defeat'.[89] It is this sense of living 'in the meantime', 'in constant anticipation and dread; while simultaneously living belatedly', as Favret describes it, that Waldie succeeds in capturing when he inflates the government's casualty estimates by an astounding forty per cent.[90] With feeling, he contemplates:

> Many are the acquaintances that I have there — but Lluellyn I reckon my first friend — & he, I think, must have been in the action. Heaven protect him. He is, I hope, safe — but it is a most awful idea to think how many are lost, & what anxiety & suspence [*sic*] must prevail at home.[91]

---

[85]   *The Journal of John Waldie: Theatre Commentaries, 1799–1830*, ed. Frederick Burwick, 44 vols. [http://repositories.cdlib.org/uclalib/dsc/waldie/], e-Scholarship Repository, California Digital Library [Accessed 25.03.2014]. See entry for 14 August 1809, 20: 215.

[86]   Waldie, *Journal*, 20: 215.

[87]   The Battle of Talavera (celebrated as a national victory) proved to be one of the bloodiest battles in the Peninsular Campaign and of only questionable advantage to the Allies. See Hunt's criticisms in the *Examiner*, 20 August; 27 August 1809; and *BG*, 26 October 1809.

[88]   Favret, *War at a Distance*, 36.

[89]   Favret, *War at a Distance*, 73.

[90]   Waldie's response was not atypical. In a letter to her uncle Frederick Reid (William Cobbett's brother in-law who, in 1811, was still serving under the British army in the Peninsula), Anne Cobbett writes: 'If you ever have opportunities of seeing our newspapers, it must, I think, be very galling to you, to see your situation thus falsely represented'. Anne Cobbett to Frederick Reid, 27 September 1811, MSS. Cobbett [Nuffield College Library, University of Oxford] XXIX/52/1.

[91]   Waldie, *Journal*, 20: 216.

Clarke's positive account of the British victory is thus powerfully modulated by Waldie's awareness of the qualitative costs of war; the diarist's 'anxiety & suspence' for his friends overshadowing the magic otherwise associated with the Circus performance and the collective celebration of a hard-won victory.

Waldie's response to the theatre's military broadcast also sheds light on his diary entry for the following night (recording a performance of *Macbeth* at the Theatre Royal). The entry praises Sarah Siddons's 'perfection' in Lady Macbeth's sleepwalking scene, but damns William Barrymore's stiffness and repeated blunders in the lead role. Waldie particularly derides the actor's choice of costume, noting:

> His dress was ridiculous — his action stalking & unnatural — his second dress, a Spanish habit & trunk breeches — he had not sword, but used a foil. He gave the words in an unvaried monotonous rant.[92]

Barrymore's decision to wear a 'Spanish habit', and thereby forego the tradition of playing Macbeth in Scottish dress, was most certainly inspired by the preceding night's celebration of the British victory. While the leading actor no doubt intended the costume change to signal his support for the Peninsular Campaign, Waldie's comments suggest impatience with Barrymore's overt political gesture. This impatience was, however, less a mark of political aversion *per se*, than a shrinking away from the utterly unconvincing manner in which the actor performed what should have been a noble part.[93] By Waldie's account, Barrymore's delivery of his lines was 'monotonous' and 'unnatural' – deprived of any 'spark of feeling' – while the actor's use of a cheap foil instead of a sword undermined any claims to verisimilitude.[94] Waldie's diary entry suggests that not only was he underwhelmed by Barrymore's performance, but consequently offended by the topical inflections that the actor attributed to Shakespeare's play. This disappointment was rendered all the more acute because Waldie had been at the Circus when the Allied victory was first announced, and because he had thought immediately of his friends serving in the Peninsula and probably taking part in that very engagement.

The question of realistic representation was a thorny one, especially when applied to the Shakespearean canon. The difficulties of staging *Othello*, for instance, were further compounded by its hero's race. Neither Coleridge nor Charles Lamb accepted the tradition of playing the role of Othello in blackface. 'On the Tragedies of Shakespeare, Considered with reference to their Fitness for Stage Representation' (1811), Lamb's main objection to the staging of Shakespeare's plays centres on the immediacy of live performance, wherein 'it is not what the

---

[92]   Waldie, *Journal*, 20: 226.
[93]   Macbeth was generally presented on the Romantic stage as a brave and sympathetic character. For a good overview of Romantic portrayals of Macbeth, see Carol Jones Carlisle, *Shakespeare from the Greenroom: Actors' Criticisms from Four Major Tragedies* (Chapel Hill: University of North Carolina Press, 1969), 365–73.
[94]   Waldie, *Journal*, 20: 226.

character is, but how he looks; not what he says, but how he speaks it' that matters.[95] As such, he argues that on stage, Othello's courtship of Desdemona can only come across as 'extremely revolting': although Desdemona may see 'Othello's colour in his mind', the tradition of playing Othello in blackface 'sink[s] Othello's mind in his colour'.[96] In his Bristol lecture of 9 November 1813 Coleridge also spoke out against the idea of portraying Othello as 'a negro'. According to Coleridge, Othello was 'a gallant Moor, of royal blood, combining a high sense of Spanish and Italian feeling' – a man, in short, of 'noble nature'.[97] What most interests me here is that when read side by side, Lamb's and Coleridge's aversions to a black Othello seem expressive of a mutual desire to ultimately subvert, rather than accept, racial stereotypes.

Lamb was cautious of the use of blackface, lest popular prejudice against Othello's blackness limit audiences' sympathies for his motivations. In 1813 Coleridge went a step further by recommending that Othello be represented as a Moor.[98] Unwilling to accept that the Moor might be confused for a 'negro', Coleridge underlines the fact that 'non-British' did not translate into monolithic 'otherness'. It is important to remember that Coleridge had been actively involved in the abolition movement, choosing Bristol – one of the country's chief slaving ports – as the symbolic location for his lectures of 1795, as well as this argument.[99] By the time the slave trade was abolished in 1807, the public at large was better informed and more sensitive to issues of race. Coleridge's 1813 suggestions about Othello's skin colour thus add an interesting dimension to the race question, bringing together the abolition movement with support for the Peninsular Campaign (and the accompanying fascination for Moorish history).[100]

---

[95] Charles Lamb, 'On The Tragedies of Shakespeare, Considered with Reference to their Fitness for Stage Representation' (1811), in *English Critical Essays: Nineteenth Century*, ed. Edmund D. Jones (Oxford: Oxford University Press, 1916), 113.

[96] Lamb, 'Tragedies of Shakespeare', 87.

[97] '1813 Lectures on Shakespeare and Education' (White Lion, Bristol), Lecture 4 (9 November 1813), *CC: Lectures*, 1: 555.

[98] There were also many practical considerations against the representation of a black Othello. In *The Road to the Stage* – essentially a manual for early nineteenth-century actors – Leman Rede explains that the tradition of playing Othello in blackface was already an obsolete custom by the 1820s. '[B]eing destructive of the effect of the face, and preventing the possibility of the expression being observable', Othello's blackface came to be replaced by 'a tawny tinge'. Rede recommended 'Spanish brown' as the ideal skin-tone. He also prescribed this for the character of Rolla, Sheridan's great hero, whose 'otherness' was likewise a key aspect of the play. Leman Rede, *The Road to the Stage* (London, 1827; 1836), 34.

[99] In his Bristol lectures of 1795 Coleridge alluded to *Macbeth* and *Hamlet* when speaking on slavery. Bate, *Shakespearean Constitutions*, 120.

[100] Leigh Hunt who, unlike Coleridge, was an opponent of the British military campaign in the Peninsula, nevertheless agreed with the poet on the virtues of Spain's Moorish heritage. In February 1808 Hunt suggested that the Moors were responsible for the profusion of romances brought into Spain (*TE*, 14 February 1808). On 22 May

In *Remorse*, as outlined above, Coleridge had already offered an importantly sympathetic representation of the Spanish Moors. Alhadra, the only character whose name did not change during the process of *Osorio*'s rewriting, had always been a favourite of the playwright's. In a letter to John Thelwall dated October 1797, Coleridge explained that he had projected his own feelings of spiritual uncertainty unto Alhadra – the character to whom he affectionately refers as 'my Moorish woman'.[101] This sympathetic feeling brings Coleridge's characterisation of the Moor in direct opposition to Iago's racist dislike of Othello. In contrast to the xenophobia of Othello's lieutenant, Coleridge's thoughts on race were inflected by true considerations of equality and brotherhood; thoughts conditioned by his involvement in the abolition movement and rewriting of *Remorse* to make it a play about the Peninsular War.[102] By the same token, Coleridge seems to argue in his 1813 lectures that by emphasising Othello's Moorish identity, theatre managers could offer an even more convincing (and, notably, topical) representation of the positive characteristics that Shakespeare intended for his military hero.

Nationalist Feeling

Spain's Moorish history helped define a country that originated in diversity. The emergence of the Spanish nation as a fusion of different local loyalties and cultures also provided a useful model for British authors exploring their own, often fractured, sense of national identity. Contemporary adaptations of Shakespeare's history plays offer a case in point. As already suggested by my discussion of *Henry V*, during the Napoleonic Wars the bard's dramatisations of the lives of the English monarchs could be profitably packaged as representations of the very sequence of events leading to the modern-day 'British' nation. As Marc Baer succinctly states, 'by the late eighteenth century Shakespeare had become the nation's history teacher'.[103] During the Peninsular War, moreover, Shakespeare's plays about the kings and queens of England helped transform national history into a subject worthy of great theatre.

Elizabeth Inchbald lent strong support to the didactic quality of Shakespeare's history plays by stating in her introduction to *Richard III* that 'Shakespeare's historical plays are particularly valuable, wherein faithful history is combined with

---

1808 (by which time the *Examiner* had already reported on the presence of French troops in Spain and the country's submission to Napoleon), the paper claimed that the Moors had been 'almost the only industrious subjects, because they had no share in American plunder'. As late as 10 October 1813, the *Examiner* continued to praise 'the good-natured friendship, the affectionate gentleness, the soul-subduing sorrows, the fiery revenge, the lofty magnanimity, which in succession mark the noble Moor...'.

[101] Samuel Taylor Coleridge to John Thelwall (14 October 1797), in Griggs (ed.), *Letters*, 1: 350.

[102] On the language of brotherhood in relation to the Peninsular Campaign, see, for example, claims that the Spanish Patriots could be 'identified with Englishmen' – 'we feel for them as our own brethren and our friends'. *BG*, 22 December 1808.

[103] Baer, *Theatre and Disorder*, 197.

transcendant [*sic*] poetry'.[104] The 'faithfulness' of this history was not, of course, to be taken literally. The plays were, after all, riddled with anachronisms and other historical errors. Like Coleridge, Inchbald was less interested in Shakespeare's 'fidelity' to history, than in his ability to successfully render the historical poetical. Fictionalised narratives had a key role to play in propping theatre-goers' historical understanding. Shakespeare's poetry, because 'transcend[e]nt', carries, for Inchbald, the added benefit of timelessness, resulting in plays that were as informative of the past as they were of the present. In the age of Napoleon, the magnetic pull between Richard III's deformities and seductive power of mind could be easily reapplied to the French Emperor who, although derided by the caricaturists for his short stature, was also recognisably charismatic.[105] The invitation to make such comparisons was implicit but clear.

Throughout her introductions for the *British Theatre*, Inchbald encourages readers to locate their play-going experience on a continuous spectrum of history. Her remarks on *Richard III* circumscribe 14 years to the period covered by the play. This permits her to explain how, during the reign of William and Mary, the first act was often omitted in order to dissuade audiences from associating Henry VI with James II, then living in exile across the Channel.[106] By informing readers of the play's performance history, as well as the chronology depicted within the play itself, Inchbald places the Shakespearean canon within an ever-expanding historical axis.

Henry VIII was among the most popular of Shakespeare's history plays in the early nineteenth-century repertoire. Unlike *Henry V*, *King John* and *Richard III*, however, the play did not feature any battle scenes, or even a particularly sympathetic portrayal of kingship. The role of Henry VIII may have been much coveted, but the play's more interesting scenes are given to the king's religious and political counsellors (causing Henry himself to merely preside over most of the events at court). In Kemble's productions of *Henry VIII*, the ceremonial style associated with the king's court offered an additional means for informing audience sympathy. This was indicated by the playbills' prominent advertisement of 'The Cardinal's Banquet' (Act 1), 'The Trial of Queen Katharine' (Act 2), and 'The Procession to the Christening of Princess Elizabeth' (Act 5) as the drama's main attractions.

On 20 October 1810 Covent Garden proudly publicised a performance of *Henry VIII* that would include the singing of the national anthem. That night, ceremony was indeed everything and, as so often the case with Kemble's productions, part of a strategically considered programme. In September 1810 Alllèd troops had enjoyed success at the Battle of Bussaco. The battle resulted

---

[104] Inchbald, *British Theatre*, Introduction to *Richard III*, 1: 3.

[105] On Gillray's 'Little Boney', see A. Franklin, 'John Bull in a Dream: Fear and Fantasy in the Visual Satires of 1803', in *Resisting Napoleon: The British Response to the Threat of Invasion, 1797–1815*, ed. Mark Philp (Aldershot: Ashgate, 2006), 125–40 (131).

[106] Inchbald, *British Theatre*, Introduction to *Richard III*, 1: 4.

in the repulse of the French forces led by André Masséna, and offered valuable testimony to the steadiness of William Beresford's re-modelled Anglo-Portuguese army.[107] Growing antagonism between the Anglo-Spanish allies made Bussaco especially welcome news when it was finally reported in the English press on 13 October. But towards the end of October that year George III fell seriously ill, ushering in an acute period of domestic uncertainty. Speculation about the Prince of Wales's likely change of ministry upon his appointment as Regent meant that Perceval's government 'hung in the balance', at least until the Prince's official assumption of power in February 1811.[108] When *Henry VIII* was again performed in December 1810 Britain's political future thus remained tantalisingly uncertain, with disquietude about the Prince's new government only exacerbated by the subsequent discovery that the army's success in Bussaco had not resulted in the decisive victory anticipated by Wellington. But in many ways, this only made Kemble's Shakespearean revival all the more timely.[109] By making use of spectacle and cleverly determined characterisation (as in the representation of the Spanish Queen, Katharine [*sic*], for instance), Covent Garden's 1810–1811 performances of *Henry VIII* helped affirm the importance of good government, and promoted the nation's commitment to just political action at home and abroad at a time when such assurances were most needed.

Emotionally charged spectacle defined Kemble's *Henry VIII* from its very first scene, in which Cardinal Wolsey, with only three lines of dialogue to deliver, appears on stage with a train of 24 followers:

> L. xxx *Trumpets sound.* – Enter 2 Footmen, – ~~Guards~~ – 2 Gentlemen, *1ˢᵗ.* *Herald* – one Gentleman bearing the broad seal, – another, the Cardinal's hat, – two Gentlemen with silver pillars, – two Priests with silver crosses, ~~[xxxxxxxx]~~ – two Gentlemen-ushers bareheaded with wands, – Cardinal WOLSEY, – two Pages bearing his train, – CROMWELL with despatches, two Secretaries with bags of papers, – *2* Chaplains, *Crosiers*, – *2* Gentlemen, – *2* Footmen, – ~~Guards~~. *R xxx Trumpets.*[110]

As in the promptbook for *Henry V*, the use of italics here indicates Kemble's annotations to his acting copy. On the facing page he provides further handwritten instructions pertaining to the exact order in which the different persons in Wolsey's train should make their entrance. This required dividing the cast into 14 different groups and providing an exit cue immediately after the Cardinal's brief speech. The procession itself thus absorbed the audience's attention for what

[107]   On Beresford's reorganisation of the Portuguese army, see Bell, *Total War*, 254. Beresford was awarded the Order of the Bath, in recognition of his success. Muir, *The Defeat of Napoleon*, 135.

[108]   David Gates, *The Spanish Ulcer: A History of the Peninsular* War (Cambridge, MA: Da Capo Press, 1986), 305.

[109]   Following its representation on 20 October, *Henry VIII* was staged at CG on 1, 8 and 22 December 1810; 18 and 25 May 1811, and 3 July 1811. 'Calendar': Part A.

[110]   *Henry the Eighth*, in Shattuck (ed.), *Promptbooks*, 4: 6 (1.1).

would otherwise have been a short scene. In Kemble's production of *Henry VIII* his own appearance as Wolsey was intended to signify nothing less than the stage's impressive materiality and its capacity for advantageous displays of power.

For the Cardinal's banquet scene and the masquerade dance that takes place therein, Kemble called for '*Musick* [*sic*] *in Orchestra*' and filled the stage with actors.[111] Dressed as a shepherd, it is in this scene that Henry meets and falls in love with Anne Bullen [*sic*]. But if Henry and Anne are here associated with the formality of the courtly-love tradition, Katharine, by contrast, is associated with a different sort of spectacle. Whereas visual display defines Henry's character, it more accurately complements, rather than supplements, Katharine's. As advertised by the playbills, the queen's trial was one of the play's main attractions. In order to better understand this much-anticipated scene, however, it is necessary to consider Katharine's earlier appearance as a spokesperson in the Council Chamber meeting:

> L. *Enter Guildford with a Cushion, then the Queen. Guildford places the cushion, and the Queen kneels. The King rises, takes her up, and places her by him at his L. at "take your place by us". Guildford removes the cushion to the side of the Queen's chair, and remains there.*[112]

These are the stage directions provided in Kemble's handwriting. His additions are significant for the ways in which they mirror the opening of the trial scene wherein Katharine kneels, and remains kneeling, before Henry. In Act 1 scene 2, when raised by the king and told to take her place 'by us', Katharine directly addresses Henry and his council on behalf of the suffering populace.[113] Afflicted by severe grievances, the king's subjects have vented potentially rebellious reproaches against Cardinal Wolsey, and even Henry himself. The king's response proves, however, that he is ignorant of the taxation levied in his name. Katharine evinces her political awareness by explaining that one-sixth of his subjects' substance had been raised for the war against France. By persuading Henry to pardon those who had denied the terms of the tax commission, it is Katharine who deserves the merit of averting rebellion. Although she enjoys less success in her efforts to raise Buckingham's suit, Katharine's attempt further confirms the sympathetic, principled nature of her character.

In the first two acts, Katharine's presence underlines important themes in the play's narrative. In Act 1 she speaks of domestic unrest and the more localised fissures of court life represented by the case against Buckingham. In the second, her appeals to 'friends in Spain' and the authority of the Pope help set the scene for the religious changes that would accompany Henry's new choice of queen (Anne being 'A spleeny Lutheran', as Wolsey calls her).[114] The play's compassionate characterisation of Katharine included underlining her Spanish birth, Catholic

---

[111]   *Henry the Eighth*, in Shattuck (ed.), *Promptbooks*, 4: 18 (1.4).
[112]   *Henry the Eighth*, 4: 10 (1.2).
[113]   *Henry the Eighth*, 4: 11 (1.2).
[114]   *Henry the Eighth*, 4: 38 (3.1).

Figure 2.3   William Sharp, *Mrs Siddons as Queen Catherine* (depicting Sarah
               Siddons as Catherine of Aragon in *Henry VIII*), from the original
               drawing by John Hayter, published by J. Dickinson, June 1829.
               Harry Beard Collection. © Victoria and Albert Museum, London.

creed and good political counsel.[115] In late 1810 when the play was staged at Covent Garden and the national anthem sung, it would have helped audiences replace an image of Spain tainted by anti-Papist prejudices and more generalised xenophobic mistrust, for one of heroism and honour.

In this carefully planned production of *Henry VIII* Kemble may have also intended to counter the unexpected radical inflections that the play had acquired towards the end of the 1809–1810 theatrical season. In April 1810, a month before *Henry VIII*'s first performance that season (Covent Garden, 5 May 1810), the House of Commons had issued a warrant for the arrest of Francis Burdett (Figure 2.4). A self-acclaimed 'Man of the People', Burdett was an outspoken opponent of electoral corruption, the imprisonment of Gale Jones (a popular radical), and the government's recent military campaigns. His speeches had been widely reported in the press and a letter of his to the Westminster electors – attacking the exclusion of reporters from debates on the Walcheren expedition – published in Cobbett's *Political Register*. When the Commons responded with a warrant for Burdett's confinement in the Tower, the parliamentarian challenged the arrest and refused to leave his home. Burdett's charisma won him widespread support, and resulted in clashes between government troops and the crowds that gathered outside his house. This tense climate lasted for three days: on 9 April Burdett was finally seized for imprisonment until the end of the Parliamentary session that summer.[116]

According to the *Examiner*, Burdett's arrest contributed several new resonances to *Henry VIII*.[117] Notwithstanding the fact that many of these seemingly passed 'unnoticed', audiences were particularly sensitive to King Henry's lines 'I had thought I had men of some understanding | And wisdom of my council, but I find none':

> These words were received with a burst of acclamation, which interrupted the performance; and several other passages of a similar nature were afterwards greeted in like manner.[118]

---

[115] Kemble's own Catholic faith often made him the butt of attack, as exemplified by Isaac Cruikshank's series of prints *The Stroller's Progress* (1809). Heather McPherson, 'Siddons Rediviva: Death, Memory, and Theatrical Afterlife', in *Romanticism and Celebrity Culture*, 120–40 (128).

[116] Marc Baer, 'Burdett, Sir Francis, fifth baronet (1770–1844)', in *Oxford Dictionary of National Biography*, ed. H.C.G. Matthew and Brian Harrison (Oxford: OUP, 2004); online edn, ed. Lawrence Goldman, May 2009 <http://www.oxforddnb.com/view/article/3962> [Accessed 14.04.14].

[117] Francis Burdett also alluded to Shakespeare in his speeches, as represented in Thomas Rowlandson's satirical print *The Borough mongers strangled in the tower* (26 April 1810; with lines from *Richard II*); and Charles Williams's *The patriot puzzled – or, the trusty Scot producing his vouchers* (August 1811; with lines from *Coriolanus*).

[118] *Examiner*, 13 May 1810.

Figure 2.4   Isaac Cruikshank, *The Arrest of Sir Fs Burdett, M.P.*, frontispiece
from *Walker's Full Account of the Arrest of Sir Francis Burdett*
[1810]. © The Trustees of the British Museum.

After Burdett's arrest, the Council Chamber scene (Act 5 scene 3) offered
a valuable opportunity for audience engagement with the play's newfound
topicality. The scene, which opens with Norfolk's accusations that Cranmer
has inspired the nation with dangerous ideas, dramatises Gardiner's ruling that
Cranmer be taken to the Tower. Offering apparently full confirmation of Daniel
O'Quinn's pronouncement that by the late eighteenth century 'the press is the
key link between the theatre of politics and politics of theatre',[119] the *Monthly
Mirror* for May 1810 explained that the play's depiction of 'unjust judges' had
meant 'every thing was construed with a bearing on the case of Sir FRANCIS
BURDETT'.[120] Recounting the Commons' mistreatment of the politician,
the *Monthly Mirror* explained that popular support for Burdett had been re-
enacted during the play's performance with alternate hisses and applauses from
the audience. Gardiner's line 'Receive him, and see him safe to the *Tower*' is
said to have prompted increased hisses, for example. By contrast, Cranmer

---

[119]   O'Quinn, *Staging Governance*, 22.
[120]   The reviewer adds a footnote stating that 'by virtue of the Speaker's warrant,
[Burdett was] forcibly taken from his house, and sent to the Tower'. *MM*, May 1810, 389.

(Burdett's obvious counterpart in the play) was given loud applause throughout the scene; his loyalty to Henry and the king's appreciative support of his counsellor lending a new emotive climax to Shakespeare's play.

The reviewer for the *Monthly Mirror* drew specific attention to Henry's challenge to Cranmer's accusers: 'By all that's holy, he had better starve, | Than but once *think this place becomes thee not*'.[121] By italicising the play's key phrases, the reviewer identifies the performative 'points' seized by audiences railing against Burdett's imprisonment for having denounced corrupt placeholders. At the end of the scene, Henry leaves the court in no doubt of his appreciation of Cranmer: he invites him to be Elizabeth's godfather and orders Gardiner to makes gestures of reconciliation. Burdett's supporters in the audience undoubtedly hoped that at the end of his ordeal Burdett would also be restored to his rightful place in government.

The *Monthly Mirror*'s review of *Henry VIII* was matched by its critique of another Shakespearean production at Covent Garden, *King John*. This play's anti-French rhetoric contributed significantly to its potential as a wartime favourite. According to the *Monthly Mirror*, Burdett's arrest also meant, however, that the play's nationalist appeal was newly politicised by domestic commotions. The defining moment for audience response is said to have occurred after King John's claim that 'It is the curse of kings to be attended | By slaves that take their humours for a warrant –'.[122] Burdett's recent resistance to the Speaker's order of arrest allowed audiences to place literal weight on the mention of 'a warrant'. In this excitable political climate the king's frustrations in the play doubled as a prompt for protest against Burdett's imprisonment. In the words of the *Monthly Mirror*, the lines 'produced peals of applause, indicative of the people's disapprobation of the act'.[123]

Kemble would undoubtedly have felt uneasy about the radical support evinced for Burdett within his theatre. Not only were the Old Price protests not yet fully resolved, but the beginning of the year 1810 had proven trying for the nation at large. In February and March there was a House of Commons inquiry into the failed Walcheren Expedition; difficulties in Spain caused Wellington to retreat to Portugal and assume the defensive; and Napoleon's tightening of the Continental Blockade resulted in even more economic hardship at home. Yet, despite *King John*'s openness to new radical meanings, Kemble is likely to have felt some sense of reassurance, at least, in Faulconbridge's final speech:

FAULCONBRIDGE   This England never did, nor never shall,
                    Lie at the proud foot of a conqueror,
                    But when it first did help to wound itself.[124]

---

[121] *MM*, May 1810, 389.
[122] *MM*, May 1810, 391.
[123] *MM*, May 1810, 391.
[124] *Shakespeare's King John, A Historical Play*, revised by J.P. Kemble (London, 1804), in Shattuck (ed.), *Promptbooks*, 5: 61 (5.7).

By the fall of the curtain audiences were encouraged to recognise that England's safety depended, first and foremost, on its domestic tranquillity.

In response to renewed movements for political reform, Kemble's decision to produce *King John* amounted to an insistence that Britain must remain united: internal division, as the play registered, could be as much a menace to national interests as a French invasion. But Kemble could not, of course, be sure that audiences would follow his cue. Theatre is, after all, a notoriously unpredictable enterprise that places audience response beyond the control of even the most diligent of managers. As Marvin Carlson explains:

> ... the pressure of audience response can coerce individual members to structure and interpret their experience in a way which might well not have occurred to them as solitary readers and, further, which might not have been within the interpretative boundaries planned by the creators of the performance text.[125]

The complex interaction of spectacle and characterisation central to Kemble's best productions clearly sought to bring together an empowering narrative of on stage performance and off stage nationalist feeling. But Covent Garden's actor-manager was nevertheless acutely aware that his interpretations (however carefully devised) were ultimately vulnerable to audience caprice. The impassioned response to Burdett's arrest was exemplary of the volatility of theatre-going, which, in the early nineteenth century, ascribed pleasures to both the acceptance and resistance of intended meanings.

Two Roman Plays

It was not until 1812 that Kemble first ventured to produce *Julius Caesar* – a play long absent from the patent stages.[126] His decision is likely to have been predominantly pragmatic – a competitive response, in short, to the opening of the new Drury Lane Theatre in October 1812. After the fire of 1809, Drury Lane's actors had been relocated to the King's Theatre in Haymarket and the Lyceum, where smaller stages afforded a more intimate environment for Shakespearean performances. But, interestingly, the dramatic company did not rise to the challenge and relied, instead, on only a handful of Shakespeare's comedies, produced without any new attractions.[127] It was only at the start of the 1812–1813 season, when Drury Lane could finally vie for the kind of visual splendour characteristic of the Shakespearean plays put on at Covent Garden, that Robert Elliston appeared in the role of Hamlet. With spectacle established as an integral staple of the theatrical diet, it is likely that Kemble's revival of *Julius Caesar* was largely driven by the

---

[125]   Marvin Carlson, 'Theatre Audiences and the Reading of Performance', in *Interpreting the Theatrical Past: Essays in the Historiography of Performance*, ed. Thomas Postlewait and Bruce A. McConachie (Iowa City: University of Iowa Press, 1989), 82–98 (85).

[126]   Inchbald, *British Theatre*, Introduction to *Julius Caesar*, 4: 3.

[127]   See 'Calendar': Part B.

desire to outshine the new Drury Lane Theatre by offering a novel addition to his own, already distinguished, Shakespearean repertoire.[128]

The fact that *Coriolanus* had been revived to great acclaim the previous year also meant, conveniently, that several scenes from that play could be recycled for Kemble's most recent addition to his Roman repertoire.[129] It is not, however, surprising that *Julius Caesar* was not Kemble's first choice. The *Theatrical Examiner* argued that Caesar's death at the end of Act 3 made Brutus the real 'hero' of the play, 'the arbiter of all that succeeds, and the predominant spirit to the last'.[130] For similar reasons, Elizabeth Inchbald confidently described the play as a drama designed to represent not the life, 'but solely the death of Julius Caesar'.[131] Schlegel, likewise, considered not Caesar the hero of the piece, 'but Brutus'.[132] *Julius Caesar* is, perhaps, best understood as a play that leaves open the possibility that the death of its eponymous character does not constitute a political tragedy (or, at least, not in absolute terms).

As a result, Kemble's 1812 production notably sought to recover Caesar from the margins of the play-text. He achieved this not by assuming the role of Caesar (which was played by Daniel Egerton in 1812), but that of Brutus. This allowed Kemble to better compensate for Caesar's absence from the stage by reminding audiences of the Roman leader's greatness, even after his death. His efforts were not, it seems, lost on his reviewers. *The Times*, for example, remarked that Kemble's delivery of Brutus's 'brief reflections on his early friendship for the man whom he had slain, [were] expressed with a tenderness and interest which deserved all the applause that they received'.[133] Kemble's political task was, nevertheless, an intensely challenging one. In a play that makes extreme allusions to both monarchical and republican allegiances, Shakespeare's equivocal characterisation of Julius Caesar presented obvious difficulties. Even Brutus (whose intentions, as Octavius recognises, were characterised by 'general honest thought') had been convinced that Caesar's death was in Rome's best

---

[128]   The competition between the two patent theatres (or, 'rival theatres'; *TE* 25 July 1813) only intensified in 1814 when the farce of *Jean de Paris*, playing at DL, was brought out at CG as *John of Paris*. *TE*, 6 November 1814.

[129]   Shattuck notes that *Coriolanus*'s 18 scenes were played in 12 or 13 sets that conjured the 'splendours of Augustan Rome, rather than the historically accurate mud and brick Rome of the fifth century'. He suggests that several of these sets may also have served for *Julius Caesar*. 'Introduction' to *Promptbooks*, 1: iii.

[130]   *TE*, 29 March 1812, offers a critique of the play in abstract, deferring its review of the performance to the next issue.

[131]   Inchbald, *British Theatre*, Introduction to *Julius Caesar*, 4: 5.

[132]   August Wilhelm von Schlegel, *Vorlesungen über dramatische Kunst und Literatur* (Lectures delivered in Vienna in 1808, published in an expanded version, 1809–1811), transl. John Black as *A Course of Lectures on Dramatic Art and Literature* (London, 1815; rev. A.J.W. Morrison 1846). Rptd in Bate, *Romantics*, 374.

[133]   *The Times*, 2 March 1812.

interest.[134] Could Kemble count on his audiences to recognise what a staunch monarchist like himself would have considered the play's true tragedy?

Identifying some of *Julius Caesar*'s most explosive moments of textual ambivalence can help offer insight into the measured strategies that characterised Kemble's 1812 re-staging of Shakespeare's Roman play. *Julius Caesar*'s relation to Peninsular politics may have been less direct than that exemplified by the history plays discussed in the earlier part of this chapter, but this did not detract from its openness to topical readings. Coleridge, for instance, pinned an urgently political interpretation to Brutus's lines '... what, shall one of us, | That struck the foremost man of all this world, | But for supporting robbers; shall we now | Contaminate our fingers with base bribes?' (Act 4 scene 3):

> This seemingly strange Assertion of Brutus is unhappily verified in the present Day. What are an immense Army, in whom the Lust of Plunder has quenched all the duties of the Citizen, other than Robbers, or differenced only as Fiends are from reprobate men? – Caesar supported & was supported by, those – even as Napoleon in our days.[135]

Coleridge made this annotation to Lewis Theobald's edition of *The Works of Shakespeare* (1773) – most likely, as he prepared for his lectures of 1808–1812, although he stops short of exploring the full implications of these recognised similarities between the armies that supported Caesar and Napoleon.[136] Kemble is likely to have identified even more points of contact between a revival of *Julius Caesar* and events in recent history, which included the Old Price riots of 1809 and contemporaneous reports of popular violence in Portugal and Spain.

Although the news items of 1809 may have lost much of their urgency by 1812, they were not forgotten. The 1809 riots added to the anxieties provoked by the French Revolution, and seem to have exerted considerable pressure on Kemble's already circumspect staging of crowd scenes.[137] The representation of the populace constitutes a troublesome aspect of *Julius Caesar*, as exemplified in Act 1 scene 2, wherein Casca offer a passionately enacted account of the public response to Caesar's swooning:

---

[134]   *Julius Caesar* (1812), in Shattuck (ed.), *Promptbooks*, 4: 71 (5.5).

[135]   Coleridge, 'Works: Copy A', *CC: Marginalia*, 4: 735.

[136]   On the slender connection between Coleridge's annotations to Theobald's edition of the *Works of Shakespeare* and his subsequent lectures, see *CC: Lectures 1808–1819*, 2: 430.

[137]   The representation of crowd scenes had long posed a challenge for playwrights and managers, especially in times of political crisis. See, for example: Paulina Kewes, 'Dryden and the staging of popular politics', in *John Dryden: Tercentenary Essays*, ed. Paul Hammond and David Hopkins (Oxford: Oxford University Press, 2000), 57–91 (on the Exclusion Crisis); and George Taylor, *The French Revolution and the London Stage 1789–1805* (Cambridge: Cambridge University Press, 2000), 164 esp. (for the pressures exerted by the French Revolution).

CASCA   ...the rabblement hooted, and clapp'd their chopp'd hands, and threw up their sweaty night-caps, and utter'd such a deal of stinking breath because Caesar refus'd the crown, that it had almost choak'd Caesar; for he swoon'd, and fell down at it: And, for mine own part, I durst not laugh, for fear of opening my lips, and receiving the bad air.[138]

This grotesque depiction of the crowd's infectious presence supplements Casca's derisive observation (at the start of the play) that those who once celebrated Pompey now cheer for Caesar, who 'comes in triumph over Pompey's blood'.[139] Mary Fairclough's contention that 'during the Romantic period, sympathy was understood as a disruptive social phenomenon which functioned to spread disorder and unrest between individuals and even across nations like a "contagion"' goes some way towards identifying the contemporary force exerted by Casca's choice of metaphor.[140] It also recognises, of course, that there was potential for anarchy in the collective spectatorship of this very scene.

To Kemble, Casca's warnings of a dangerously capricious, mob-like populace would certainly have felt more compelling after 1809 – the year that marked not only the actor-manager's difficulties with the Old Price rioters, but also reports of civilian assassinations in Portugal and Spain.[141] Since the latter potentially threatened to sway public opinion on the British campaign, they may help explain why Kemble did not revive the play sooner. Indeed, as late as 1812, the actor-manager would still struggle to fully exorcise the ghosts of these events from his production of *Julius Caesar*. The first two cantos of Byron's phenomenally successful *Childe Harold's Pilgrimage* (1812–1818) were published on 29 February, shortly after the play's revival. In these cantos, Byron describes Portugal as a land scarred by violence: 'this purple land, where law secures not life'.[142] The poet's accompanying Notes deliberate upon this line as an allusion to the 'well-known fact, that in the year 1809, the assassinations on the streets of Lisbon and its vicinity, were not confined by the Portuguese to their countrymen; but that Englishmen were daily butchered'.[143] In 1812 these Notes provided a reminder of

---

[138]   *Julius Caesar* (1812), in Shattuck (ed.), *Promptbooks*, 4: 14 (1.2).

[139]   *Julius Caesar* (1812), 4: 6 (1.1).

[140]   Mary Fairclough, *The Romantic Crowd: Sympathy, Controversy and Print Culture* (Cambridge: Cambridge University Press, 2013), 1.

[141]   On the 'many different murderous forms' experienced during the Peninsular War, see Bell, *Total War*, 280.

[142]   After its initial representation, *Julius Caesar* was repeated 18 times until the end of the season. 'Calendar': Part A, 1811–1812.

[143]   Lord Byron, *Childe Harold's Pilgrimage*, in *The Complete Poetical Works*, ed. Jerome J. McGann, 7 vols (Oxford: Clarendon Press, 1980), 2: 18: Canto 1, stanza 21, l. 269: and Notes (for l. 269), 187–8. Stories of popular violence featured prominently in the British press (see *Examiner*, 24 July 1808, on the gruesome fate of the French consul and a merchant at Malaga; 'murdered by the populace', 'hewn piecemeal and the fragments thrown into flames').

the disorder that could all too easily be unleashed by the crowd scenes in *Julius Caesar*. Notwithstanding, therefore, the 'scenic splendour, and classical costume' shown off in the play to such advantage, the reviewer from *The Times* lamented that on its opening night, the presence of the crowd on stage had been far from convincing: 'the populace were noisy, but certainly not numerous enough to give an idea, even with all stage allowances, of that turbulent and overwhelming concourse that would have poured round the rostrum where a Brutus was to vindicate the death of a Caesar'.[144] While Kemble was adept at commanding large numbers on stage, his energies were reserved for organised processions (as realised to such acclaim in *Henry V* and *Coriolanus*). The actor-manager seems to have had little inclination for the choreography of anonymous, potentially anarchic plebeian bodies.

Figure 2.5   Isaac Cruikshank, *King John's First Appearance at the New Theatre Covent Garden*, November 1809. © Victoria and Albert Museum, London.

---

[144]   *The Times*, 2 March 1812.

But if the Old Price riots and reports of civilian unrest in Portugal had left Kemble fearful of unruly crowds, he also recognised the need to look beyond Casca's derogatory remarks. Marc Antony's eloquent address to the populace, who subsequently choose to defend the memory of Caesar, rather than the decadent republic headed by the conspirators, provided an obvious opportunity for controlling the crowds on stage. In Act 3 scene 4 Marc Antony speaks movingly of Caesar's mantle, re-creating the moment when the traitors, and Brutus specifically, stabbed Caesar. The plebeians respond to him by crying out in angry sorrow:

1 PLE	O piteous spectacle!
2 PLE	O noble Caesar!
3 PLE	O woful day!
4 PLE	O traitors, villains!
5 PLE	We will be reveng'd: revenge; about, – seek, – burn, – fire, – kill, – slay! – let not a traitor live.[145]

Their rebellion is contagious and degenerative: cries of pity result in an impassioned string of imperatives that end with a final call for indiscriminate vengeance against all putative traitors. Uncontrolled, this is the kind of crowd scene that Kemble might have feared most acutely but, critically, Marc Antony (played by Charles Kemble) succeeds in staying the crowd's immediate impulse for retribution:

ANT	Here is the will, and under Caesar's seal. To every Roman citizen he gives, To every several man, seventy-five drachmas.
2 PLE	Most noble Caesar! – we'll revenge his death.
ANT	Hear me with patience.
ALL THE PLE	Peace, ho!
ANT	Moreover, he hath left you all his walks, His private arbours, and new-planted orchards, On this side Tyber; he hath left them you, And to your heirs for ever, To walk abroad, and recreate yourselves. Here was a Caesar: When comes such another?

---

[145] *Julius Caesar* (1812), in Shattuck (ed.), *Promptbooks*, 4: 48 (3.4).

2 PLE   Never, never: – Come, away, away:
                                         We'll burn his body in the holy place,
                                         And, with the brands, fire the traitors' houses.
                                         Take up the body.[146]

Purposefully detaining the plebeians by adumbrating on the different articles of Caesar's will, Marc Antony's final rhetorical question – 'When comes such another?' – convinces his auditors of Caesar's paternal care for his subjects. Stirred by Marc Antony's emotive oratory, the plebeians raise the hearse with Caesar's body and exit the scene, creating great tumult and noise as they prepare for civil war against Brutus's leadership.

Act 3 scene 4 testifies to the ways in which Shakespeare's Marc Antony, as *The Times* saw him, was 'less the character of history, than one which the dramatist, with his knowledge of human feelings, sketched to himself as the natural instrument for stirring up the feelings of men'.[147] His effectiveness as an orator allows, moreover, for the crowd's change of direction to be attributed not to their capriciousness (as Casca had accused), but to Marc Antony's own leadership ('Now let it work: – Mischief, thou art afoot, | Take thou what course thou wilt!').[148] Marc Antony's speeches thus contribute to the ways in which Caesar's legacy is used to direct the course of the entire play, lending particular gratification, for example, to the moment when Cassius runs into his sword exclaiming: 'Caesar, thou art reveng'd | Even with the sword that kill'd thee'.[149] Kemble could thus boast both figuratively and literally (when Caesar's ghost haunts Brutus in his tent)[150] that it was the memory of Caesar that finally destroyed the conspirators' shaky republic.

This section has so far focused on the extent to which Kemble's 1812 revival of *Julius Caesar* was affected by events that occurred as early as 1809. In so doing, it has hinted towards an early nineteenth-century repertoire whose silent history (of missed opportunities and self-imposed censorship) exerted considerable pressure on the stage representations that were subsequently offered. I now turn my attention to Kemble's 1811 production of *Coriolanus*, which was similarly affected by recent events in theatrical and political history. Considered a play of 'dangerous tendency' in consequence of the social unrest and poor harvests of the 1790s, *Coriolanus* had been removed from the repertoire during Pitt's premiership.[151] This allowed Elizabeth Inchbald to celebrate the play's revival in 1806 as 'joyful evidence – that the multitude at present are content in their various stations; and can therefore, in this little dramatic history, amuse themselves with beholding,

[146]   *Julius Caesar* (1812), in Shattuck (ed.), *Promptbooks*, 4: 49 (3.4).
[147]   *The Times*, 2 March 1812.
[148]   *Julius Caesar* (1812), in Shattuck (ed.), *Promptbooks*, 4: 50 (3.4).
[149]   *Julius Caesar* (1812), 4: 67 (5.2).
[150]   *Julius Caesar* (1812), 4: 61 (4.2).
[151]   Inchbald, *British Theatre*, Introduction to *Coriolanus*, 5: 5.

free from anger and resentment, that vainglory, which presumes to despise them'.[152] But Kemble seems to have been less confident. After the fire that destroyed Covent Garden in September 1808 audiences would have to wait until 1811 in order to see the play again. This delay may have been partly justified by the expenses entailed by a production as technically exigent as *Coriolanus*. The play's omission from the 1809–1810 and 1810–1811 seasons can also be explained, however, by the inflammatory coincidence of the Old Price riots.

After 67 nights of protest, when Covent Garden re-opened on 10 September 1810 Kemble was still afflicted with dissent over the number of private boxes. But if between 1809 and late 1810 the riots rendered *Coriolanus* an unviable choice, by 1811 Kemble was acutely aware that he needed a new box office hit. He clearly hoped that Sarah Siddons's Volumnia – a success with Drury Lane audiences in 1789 – would attract full houses once again. Both *Coriolanus* and *Julius Caesar* were political plays, open to various interpretations. But while *Coriolanus* included the staging of potentially dangerous examples of class conflict, it also dramatised an external war against the Volscians that could be useful for enticing patriotic patronage. By placing strong emphasis on martial music and ceremonial processions, Kemble sought to make this conflict immediately applicable to the Napoleonic Wars.

Military display constituted the chief attraction of Kemble's 1811 revival of *Coriolanus*, building upon the history of grand ceremonials the play already enjoyed. In Drury Lane's 1789 production, 164 supernumeraries had passed through the stage in the Ovation procession. In his eagerness to re-capture this aura of majestic ceremony, Kemble recruited an additional 76 supernumeraries for his Ovation scene (increasing the total number of actors on stage to 240). He recognised that in the enlarged Covent Garden Theatre greater stage presence would be crucial for the successful re-creation – and, as he must have hoped, supersession – of the impression of power imparted by the earlier production at Drury Lane. The degree of planning necessary for marshalling such large numbers on and off the stage is clearly indicated by Kemble's promptbook annotations. Returning to the kind of stage-management that had been adopted to such good effect in order to depict the entry into Harfleur (in *Henry V*), the Ovation scene featured real soldiers, standard bearers and military musicians. The supernumeraries were organised into four divisions: three shouts were given after each division had assembled on stage, with choristers singing George Frideric Handel's 'See the Conquering Hero' as more soldiers made their entrance. Handel's theme from *Judas Maccabaeus* (a favourite with the Royal Family, often performed during the Easter Oratorios) lent emotive force to the scene's approaching climax. By the end of the Ovation scene, the senators, roman matrons, Menenius, and Coriolanus with the 'Chief Eagle' had made grand entrances, while the supernumeraries were instructed to remain on stage until the very end, their military flags swaying in the background. Kemble's precise choreography of this scene made it one of the most magnificent in his

---

[152]   Inchbald, *British Theatre*, Introduction to *Coriolanus*, 5: 5.

entire repertoire. In 1811 it helped boost morale by reviving the military splendour of imperial Rome.[153] The scene also aimed to enforce an important lesson about public order and decorum to the theatre-goers who, two years earlier, had wreaked havoc in Covent Garden's auditorium.

Kemble's *Coriolanus* (based on both James Thomson's and Thomas Sheridan's revisions to Shakespeare's text) was as reliant on careful rewriting as it was on spectacle. Shakespeare's Act 1 opens with Coriolanus addressing angry plebeians who protest that while they starve, the patricians have packed their storehouses with grain. In 1811 – a year of bad harvests – this suggestion was entirely absent. As early as 1806 Kemble's production had opened, instead, with Menenius' explanation that the plebeians have risen in rebellion because they want 'corn at their own rates'.[154] This emphasis on commercial self-interest rather than basic needs does not excuse Coriolanus's contemptuous, scornful attitude, but it does make him appear less antipathetic than Shakespeare would have him. *The Times'* review of the play's performance on 14 December 1811 attested to Kemble's success. Responding to the interest excited by the play's action, and characterisation especially, the reviewer expressed his delight with the opposition between 'the haughty mind of a hero nobly born, who had served and saved his country' and 'the contracted, selfish, cowardly species of public spirit, which characterises an assembly of venal, and ungrateful, and self-conceited electors'.[155] Applauding Kemble for his treatment of class conflict within *Coriolanus*, the reviewer concluded that 'there is, perhaps, no part for which Mr. KEMBLE is more fitted than this Roman hero'. Kemble's decision to take his leave from the stage in the role of Coriolanus (23 June 1817) testifies to his own self-perceived success.

Coriolanus's bold, forthright disposition required that his antagonistic relationship with the citizens receive direct representation. To Kemble, the main advantage of this mode of characterisation was that it rendered Coriolanus's conduct open to the audience's judgement.[156] Jonathan Sachs, exploring the ways in which Kemble's revival of *Coriolanus* allows us to see how 'the legacy of ancient Rome was contested on the Romantic stage in relation to contemporary political disputes', describes the actor-manager's impersonation of Coriolanus as

---

[153]   At the end of 1811 Britain 'remained formally at war with all the Continental Powers' despite a series of promising, if ultimately unsuccessful attempts, by the British government to influence the policy of Russia, Austria, Prussia and Sweden. Muir, *The Defeat of Napoleon*, 176–92 (191).

[154]   *Shakespeare's Coriolanus; or, The Roman Matron, A Historical Play, adapted to the Stage, with additions from Thomson*, by J.P. Kemble (London, 1806), in Shattuck (ed.), Promptbooks, 2: 6 (1.1).

[155]   *The Times*, 16 December 1811. See also letter 'To the Editor of The Times' (*The Times*, 19 December 1811), signed 'Publicola', which takes direct issue with this review.

[156]   Compare Coriolanus's invectives to the crowd (1.1) with Menenius' address to the Romans after Coriolanus's deflection to the Volscian camp (4.5). *Coriolanus*, in Shattuck (ed.), *Promptbooks*, 2: 6; 2: 51–2 respectively.

a portrayal of 'the rightness of patrician rule in a time of popular unrest'.[157] But it was also more than that. By drawing his audiences' attention to Coriolanus's commanding gestures and statuesque poses, Kemble attempted to reclaim the play's eponymous hero as nothing less than a Romantic visionary. In Kemble's version of the play, Coriolanus is loath to address the public in order to confer his appointment, not so much because he is proud, but because he is averse to making political rhetoric out of his soldier's wounds.[158] The war hero imagines that the very concepts of truth and masculinity would be compromised if he agreed to pander to the crowds' eager curiosity, or flatter what he considers their vanity.

One of Kemble's most important departures from Shakespeare's text occurs in the fifth act, wherein Coriolanus's family visit the Volscian camp to entreat his loyalty to Rome. In Shakespeare's play, Coriolanus is finally moved by his mother's pleas. Choosing to rely, instead, on James Thomson's eighteenth-century reworking of the play, in Kemble's finale to *Coriolanus*, rhetorical power gives way to the threat of physical violence.[159] Volumnia, drawing forth a dagger with which to kill herself, causes Coriolanus to seize her hand and order the Volscians to raise the siege. *The Times*' review of the play's performance in May 1814 placed appropriate emphasis on this last act, underlining 'the most triumphant impression' produced by Coriolanus's 'final defence of his motives and conduct, before the Volscian army'.[160] The reviewer's sympathetic response to Coriolanus's character and overall commendation of the concluding act give larger social significance to the observation that 'the plaudits towards the close of the play were incessant, and the curtain fell in the midst of general acclamation'.[161] In a cavernous theatre that made rhetorical effect extremely difficult, Thomson's finale provided audiences with a powerful visual tableau that helped define Coriolanus's intervention as an act of self-sacrifice. 'Rome by thy aid is sav'd, – but thy son lost!', Coriolanus exclaimed (to those who could hear him).[162] The dramatic prop of the dagger fixed this turning point in the imagination, encouraging audiences to reappraise the hero who, earlier, seemed aloof and wholly unmoved by the entreaties of his family.

Thomas Barnes, writing for the *Examiner* in December 1813, declared himself unconvinced by this modernisation of Shakespeare's text. He dismisses Volumnia's dagger as nothing more than 'a despicable stage-expedient', and makes no attempt to disguise his contempt for Kemble's aristocratic politics.[163] Instead, Barnes extols the virtues of the citizens so damningly portrayed in Kemble's version of Shakespeare's play. Attacking Coriolanus's behaviour as proof of 'the unnatural and more hateful haughtiness of the social aristocrat', Barnes ridicules the Roman's petty, almost womanish abhorrence of his social inferiors:

---

[157] Sachs, *Romantic Antiquity*, 183.
[158] *Coriolanus*, in Shattuck (ed.), *Promptbooks*, 2: 39 (3.2).
[159] See James Thomson, *Coriolanus: A Tragedy* (1749).
[160] *The Times*, 19 May 1814.
[161] *The Times*, 19 May 1814.
[162] *Coriolanus*, in Shattuck (ed.), *Promptbooks*, 2: 60 (5.1).
[163] *TE*, 19 December 1813.

Too ignorant to know that the awl of the cobbler is as respectable an instrument as the sword of the general (perhaps more so, as it frequently exhibits more skill in its guidance,) too stupid to feel a kindly sensation towards a being worse dressed than himself, he was a nuisance to his country …[164]

Barnes here exploits the *Examiner*'s forthright opposition to the ministerial (mis) management of the Peninsular Campaign. To undermine Kemble's privileging of *Coriolanus*'s martial theme, he claims that during the Napoleonic Wars the 'sword of the general' had been all-too often brandished with insufficient skill, and armies inadequately led.[165] Kemble had critically relied on Coriolanus's military character and Thomson's dramatic finale to redefine audience sympathies. In an attack that was at once aesthetic and political, Barnes purposefully draws upon these very modifications to damn the actor-manager's aims.[166] Barnes and the reviewer for *The Times* both agreed that Kemble's extensive alterations had transformed the overall experience of watching *Coriolanus*: but their differences suggest that the production's success or failure was ultimately more contingent on the political, rather than artistic, implications of these changes.

In his series of literary lectures that took place in London (1811–1812) and Bristol (1813) during the Peninsular War, Coleridge turned to Shakespeare to explore how a nation's literary tastes could be used to bolster its political self-awareness. During a time of unrest at home and abroad, Shakespeare's most popular plays were those that centred on the themes of nation, history and identity. *The Merry Wives of Windsor* – the only comedy in the Shakespearean canon wherein the action is set entirely in England – was performed at the patent theatres every season between 1807 and 1815.[167] While the play features the popular character of Sir John Falstaff, it is his outwitting by the moral English wives that arguably represents the greatest draw. During the Peninsular War (when images of home and hearth circulated widely) audiences seem to have readily lent their support to Mrs Page's closing injunction, 'let us every one go home, | And laugh this sport o'er by a country fire'.[168] The success enjoyed by *The Merry Wives of Windsor* also serves as a reminder that Shakespeare's political application, although perhaps most immediately felt in the

[164]   *TE*, 19 December 1813.

[165]   The *Examiner* was quick to adopt a hard-line editorial policy on the British campaign in Spain, as exemplified by its issues for 17 September; 11 and 25 December 1808.

[166]   Jane Moody productively suggests that Hazlitt's well-known essay on *Coriolanus* for his *Characters of Shakespeare's Plays* (1817) might be read as an extension of Thomas Barnes's 1813 review. See *Illegitimate Theatre*, 126–7.

[167]   *The Merry Wives of Windsor* was regularly staged at CG and DL. See 'Calendar'.

[168]   *Shakespeare's Merry Wives of Windsor; A Comedy*, revised by J.P. Kemble (London, 1804), in Shattuck (ed.), *Promptbooks*, 6: 72 (5.3).

history plays, was by no means genre-specific, and that much more work remains to be done on the political import of the Shakespearean comedies.

The tradition of 'emending' Shakespeare was already well established by the early nineteenth century.[169] Kemble's decision to curtail Act 4 of *Othello* in order to render it a more 'polite' drama is symptomatic of the other significant modifications that were made to help keep Shakespeare's plays abreast of changing times.[170] The textual interventions, pageantry and wardrobe choices discussed in this chapter point to the variegated ways in which actors and managers sought to update the canon in order to provide an almost tangible 're-telling' of contemporary politics. Most audience members seem to have been prepared and willing to accept popular emendations to Shakespeare's plays. But theatre-goers could also judge harshly if they felt managers or actors went too far awry in their creative enterprise (as illustrated by Waldie's negative response to Barrymore's Macbeth). Another check on potential excess was provided by professional theatre criticism, which flourished in the form of journalistic reviews and collected editions of the nation's drama.

Shakespeare's plays were endowed with a perceived flexibility and essential openness to interpretation that, according to Coleridge, permitted the bard to belong to a process of history in the making: 'he writes not for past ages, but for that in which he lives, and that which is to follow'.[171] In May 1810 this allowed Francis Burdett's supporters to offer interpretations of *Henry VIII* that were predicated upon the Parliamentarian's arrest. At the same time, it required no great stretch of the imagination for audiences to picture the overweight and licentious Prince of Wales (the future George IV) as Shakespeare's Henry VIII, whose spurned wife, Princess Caroline, could stand in for Katharine of Aragon.[172] The royal couple's marital difficulties were widely reported in the press, and would surely have influenced audiences' interpretations of the play.

International politics were also close to hand. Kemble's sympathetic characterisation of the Spanish queen, as outlined above, allowed *Henry VIII* to be read as a study of the imbroglios of court politics and the opportunities available for strong women to assert their role in history. In the lead-up to the French invasion of Spain, the Queen Consort, Maria Luisa, had been placed under public scrutiny for her extramarital relationship with the unpopular prime minister, Manuel de Godoy. Although Ferdinand VII's title of 'el deseado' owed much to the detested Godoy faction, this domestic instability was exploited by Napoleon in order to place Joseph Bonaparte on the Spanish throne. Where Maria Luisa failed, Shakespeare's Katharine of Aragon provided an alternative model of female

---

[169]   *TE*, 22 May 1808: 'almost every fine play of SHAKESPEARE has its genealogy of emendation'.

[170]   On earlier modifications to *Othello* see Gefen Bar-On Santor, 'Shakespeare in the Georgian Theatre', in *Oxford Handbook ... Georgian Theatre*, ed. Swindells and Taylor, 213–28 (220).

[171]   Lecture 1 (28 October 1813), *CC: Lectures*, 1: 516.

[172]   On the Prince of Wales as Henry VIII in contemporary satirical prints, see Bate, *Shakespearean Constitutions*, 80.

constancy and devotion. However, in keeping with the Anglo-centric emphasis of the wartime narrative, the baptism of Princess Elizabeth in Act 5 would have functioned as a reminder that the greater tolerance inspired by Katharine's story belonged to the dawn of a specifically English, Protestant Golden Age.[173] In line with various other examples in this book, the Shakespearean dramatic repertoire confirmed that, at the very least, the Peninsular Campaign was driven as much by British political interests and values as by the desire to help the Spaniards fight the French yoke.

Theatre and politics operated as valuable counters of exchange. William Hazlitt's interest in Elizabethan literature helps contextualise the ways in which contemporary writers established comparisons between the sixteenth and early nineteenth centuries. In his lecture series, Hazlitt describes the 'Age of Elizabeth' as a period distinguished by great men, whose achievements 'had the mark of their age and country upon it'.[174] In this scheme Shakespeare 'was not something sacred and aloof from the vulgar herd of men', as some of Hazlitt's contemporaries claimed, but one who 'shook hands with nature and the circumstances of the time': 'His age was necessary to him'.[175]

The age of Elizabeth saw England overcome the Spanish Armada and establish itself against the competing claims of Spanish imperialism. The call to arms in 1803, as discussed in Chapter 1, resulted in a propaganda effort that united Sheridan's broadsheet with imprints of Queen Elizabeth's speech to the troops at Tilsbury (Figure 1.5). As the war against Napoleon developed, the difficulty of distinguishing sixteenth-century dress from Spanish stage costume would only have heightened the apparently topical pertinence of the Elizabethan plays staged between 1808 and 1814.

This chapter has focused on how Shakespeare was used to broadcast patriotic feeling during the Peninsular War. From the bulletins delivered during performances of his plays, to likenesses between Napoleon and the villains Richard III and Macbeth, Shakespeare was frequently used to keep audiences informed about the war in Spain and Portugal. In October 1813, as Wellington's forces crossed the frontier from Spain into France, Coleridge was in Bristol, delivering his third lecture on Shakespeare's plays.[176] Invigorated with political enthusiasm, he used his literary material in order to commemorate the positive turn in the war. Comparing the characters of Macbeth to Bonaparte – 'both tyrants, both indifferent to means, however barbarous, to attain their ends' – Coleridge ventured to hope that 'the fate of the latter would be like the former, in sailing

---

[173]   Schlegel saw Katherine as 'the heroine of the piece', which allowed him to argue that Shakespeare's 'true conclusion' was not represented by Elizabeth's christening, but by the Spanish Queen's death. Rptd in Bate, *Romantics*, 370–71.

[174]   William Hazlitt, *Lectures on the Dramatic Literature of the Age of Elizabeth*, 2nd ed. (London, 1821), 2.

[175]   Hazlitt, *Lectures*, 12–13.

[176]   *BG*, 11 November 1813. This report of the lecture was printed alongside a column on Napoleon's defeat.

amidst a host of foes, which his cruelty and injustice had roused against him'.[177] In conclusion, and memorable affirmation of his argument, he pointed to the Allies' recent success. Praising his nation for the lead taken in the war and good example set abroad, Coleridge celebrated that 'England, justly proud, as she had right to be, of a Shakespear [*sic*], a Milton, a Bacon, and a Newton, could also boast of a Nelson and a Wellington'.[178] By aligning the liberation of Spain with the triumphs of the Elizabethan 'Golden Age', Coleridge promoted Shakespeare as an emblem of the military glory and cultural achievements to which audiences needed to aspire in order to overcome Napoleonic France – and, to an extent, even the superficial displays and empty bombast of contemporary theatre. The fact that in his review of Kemble's *Coriolanus* Thomas Barnes was able, with a sleight of hand, to significantly qualify this kind of triumphalist narrative, only further confirms Shakespeare's centrality to a wartime dramatic repertoire that remained, above all else, politically plural.

---

[177]   Lecture 3 (4 November 1813), *CC: Lectures*, 1: 545–6.
[178]   *CC: Lectures*, 1: 546.

Chapter 3
Spectacular Stages

The ban on spoken drama outside the patent playhouses effectively limited the repertories at London's minor theatres to song, dance and spectacle. The Indian-themed horse spectacle in two acts *Baghvan-Ho; or, The Tartar Tartar'd* (Olympic New Pavilion, 1812) offers a fairy typical example of the action-packed, impressively technical entertainments put on at these venues. Playbills for *Baghvan-Ho* promised not only a magnificent re-enactment of an attack on the usurper's castle fought 'man to man, and horse to horse', but also a unique cameo by putatively 'the largest most sagacious elephant' in the kingdom.[1] In her seminal study *Illegitimate Theatre in London, 1770–1840* (2000) Jane Moody identifies 'physical peril, visual spectacle and ideological confrontation' as the key attractions of such 'illegitimate' dramaturgy.[2] This chapter at once testifies to and examines the popularity that these entertainments enjoyed during the Peninsular War.

In order to better understand the ideological purchase of the non-dramatic repertoires available between 1808 and 1814, this chapter begins by providing an overview of the reputations enjoyed by the different minor theatres. This is followed by a more detailed consideration of how managers and scriptwriters represented key events in the Peninsular Campaign, and the inter-theatrical competition that affected the strategies they pursued. As I show below, once the re-enactment of a British victory in the Peninsula had received its first example of audience approval, the event was variously re-played across the illegitimate stages of the metropolis.

Frederick Burwick estimates that between 1780 and 1830 there were in London 'two dozen' minor theatres catering to local audiences.[3] Several of these were significantly active at the time of the Peninsular War, including Sadler's Wells, the Royal Circus (renamed the Surrey Theatre in 1810), Astley's Amphitheatre, the Sans Pareil, the Olympic Pavilion, the Royalty and the Regency.[4] With the exception of the newer Olympic Pavilion and Sans Pareil Theatre these venues were located on the fringes of the theatrical city, at a distance symbolic of their

---

[1] Olympic Playbill, 5 July 1812, V&A.
[2] Moody, *Illegitimate Theatre*, 10.
[3] Burwick, *Playing to the Crowd*, 1.
[4] The Regency Theatre experienced a chequered history during this period and is consequently eclipsed in this chapter by its more established rivals. See Richard Lorenzen, *The History of the Prince of Wales's Theatre 1771–1903* (Hatfield: University of Hertfordshire Press, 2014), 23–35.

perceived social and cultural marginality.[5] But this sense of 'otherness' was not, in fact, wholly inopportune. As Moody explains, because it was assumed that 'the public entertainments offered at Sadler's Wells and other unlicensed theatres within a 15-mile radius of Westminster represented a non-dramatic sphere of bodily performance utterly distinct from the drama staged at Drury Lane and Covent Garden', '[n]o provision was made for the textual scrutiny of these entertainments'.[6] This allowed the managers of the minor theatres to enjoy a freedom of expression, which, albeit largely non-verbal, was unavailable at the patent houses, and would prove to be of considerable advantage in the cutthroat competition to stage the latest topical entertainment.

Indeed, the wartime repertoires discussed in this chapter offer interesting points of comparison to those of Covent Garden and Drury Lane.[7] In spite of the operational differences that distinguished London's minor and patent establishments, the cultural split was far from absolute. As Moody argues:

> To some extent, certainly, we can define the illegitimate in terms of a set of genres (melodrama, burlesque, extravaganza), a group of London playhouses … and the conventions of gesture and expression associated with those dramatic forms and institutions. In many ways, however, patent and minor cultures also represented overlapping and interconnected domains.[8]

Performers regularly migrated from one kind of venue to the other, and generic experimentations took place across the capital, resulting, for instance, in the staging of melodramas at Covent Garden and Drury Lane, and adaptations of Shakespeare at the Surrey Theatre. During the Peninsular War managers of London's minor and patent theatres were thus engaged in competition not only for potential patrons but also for actors, related stage personnel and even the kinds of production on offer.[9] Good examples of this cross-over can be found in the careers of the popular stage clown, Joseph Grimaldi, who was contracted to appear in pantomimes at both Covent Garden and Sadler's Wells; and Thomas

---

[5]   Philip Astley's Olympic Pavilion opened on 8 September 1806. The Sans Pareil Theatre opened on 17 November 1806.

[6]   Moody, *Illegitimate Theatre*, 18.

[7]   It can also be productive to compare these entertainments to contemporary satirical prints, which, as Charles Dibdin the Younger suggests, were similarly 'allusive to the reigning follies of the Day'. *Memoirs of Charles Dibdin the Younger*, ed. George Speaight (London: Society for Theatre Research, 1956), 102.

[8]   Moody, *Illegitimate Theatre*, 6.

[9]   When Covent Garden was destroyed by fire in September 1808 and Drury Lane, likewise, in February 1809, their loss of expensive scenery, props and promptbooks permitted the minor theatres to enjoy a temporary monopoly on the production of spectacular wartime entertainments.

Dibdin, who worked as prompter for the new Drury Lane Theatre, scriptwriter for Covent Garden and manager of the Surrey Theatre.[10]

In 1807 the minor theatres were the first to respond to – and, arguably, shape – interest in the Portuguese Royal Family's emigration to Brazil, with entertainments produced by John Philip Astley at Astley's Amphitheatre and Charles Dibdin the Younger at Sadler's Wells. Yet, if the conflict in the Peninsula made for lucrative stage business, the subject of Spanish politics, more specifically, did not. This is suggested, for instance, by Jane Scott's *Eccentricities; or, Mistakes at Madrid*, a play staged after Ferdinand VII's return to Spain in the spring of 1814 but that seems to deliberately avoid engagement with the political imbroglios of the restored regime. Throughout, this chapter interrogates how Spain was 'viewed' and 're-viewed' on the boards of London's illegitimate stages. It draws attention to the various techniques employed by theatre managers to capitalise upon the Peninsular War's box office appeal, and identifies the ways in which London's minor theatres were able to exercise significant moral, political and social power, notwithstanding the limitations imposed by the Licensing Act.

Reputations

By 1807 London's minor theatres were highly individualised venues where theatrical programmes were determined by factors ranging from managerial egos and the specific talents of the resident company, to local audience demographics and other convenient geographical determinants. Take, for example, Astley's Amphitheatre, which was located near Westminster Bridge and built in the form of a circus ring with adjoining stage.[11] The Amphitheatre was renowned for its mechanically ambitious equestrian entertainments. During the Peninsular War this included the horse and water spectacle *The Blood-Red Knights* (1810), which brought an impressive sum of £18,000 to its box office.[12] Sadler's Wells, by comparison, was the city's oldest minor theatre. Its reputation was effectively revamped in 1804 when Charles Dibdin the Younger (its manager since 1800), took advantage of the theatre's situation near the New River in order to install a water tank on stage. The first piece to benefit from this novel feature was *The Siege of Gibraltar* (1804) – an entertainment with special effects that culminated

---

[10]   On the difficulties of juggling these different roles, see Thomas Dibdin, *The Reminiscences of Thomas Dibdin* (London, 1834), 2: 1–25.

[11]   The Amphitheatre's founder was Philip Astley who retired as a sergeant major from the British army in 1766 and became a showman of renown across Britain, Ireland and the Continent. *A Biographical Dictionary of Actors, Actresses, Musicians, Dancers, Managers, and Other Stage Personnel in London, 1660–1800*, ed. Philip H. Highfill Jr, Kalman A. Burnim, and Edward A. Langhans. 16 vols. (Carbondale: Southern Illinois University Press, 1973), 1: 146–51. After 1784 Philip Astley began to entrust the management of the Amphitheatre in Lambeth to his son John Philip Conway Astley. Ibid., 143.

[12]   Moody, *Illegitimate Theatre*, 69.

in a spectacular destruction of the Spanish fleet. Complete with models built to scale by the Dockyard's shipwrights, it proved nothing short of a blockbuster sensation. In fact, not only was *The Siege of Gibraltar* a success with the regular frequenters of Sadler's Wells – which, as Jacky Bratton notes, included 'all ranks of seamen' – but it helped create a taste for Dibdin the Younger's aqua-dramas that also appealed to fashionable society (Figure 3.1).[13] It was not, therefore, unusual for residents from London's West End to negotiate the long journey to Sadler's Wells, despite its dangerous location by the toll pass, on the outskirts of the city.

Charles Dibdin the Younger's and John Astley's managerial careers depended, critically, upon the creation of specialist reputations for their theatres; reputations that were at once exclusive to specific stage conditions but also in competition with other minor and, to an extent, even patent venues. In order to continue to entice audiences from central London, Sadler's Wells invested in better lighting andthe provision of guides for the safe return of its patrons to their homes. Meanwhile, the Sans Pareil and Olympic Pavilion made the most of their central

Figure 3.1   Thomas Rowlandson, *Sadler's Wells Theatre*, 1 June 1809. Harry Beard Collection. © Victoria and Albert Museum, London.

---

[13]   J.S. Bratton, 'British Heroism and the structure of Melodrama', in Bratton, Cave, et al. (eds), *Acts of Supremacy*, 43.

location. Jane Scott, the Sans Pareil's manager and in-house dramatic talent, proudly advertised her venue as the 'Sans Pareil Theatre, Strand'.[14] By using her published songbooks and playbills to define a space for 'illegitimate' dramatic entertainments within the heart of the city, Scott effectively tested the stereotype of what an early nineteenth-century minor theatre not only *should* but, more provocatively, *could* be. When Robert Elliston became proprietor of the Olympic Pavilion in 1813 he also challenged popular assumptions about illegitimate drama by re-branding his new playhouse 'Little Drury Lane'. Elliston's experiment was, however, short-lived. 'Little Drury Lane's' proximity to the newly re-built Drury Lane Theatre unsettled the patent committee, and under mounting pressure, the Lord Chamberlain informed Elliston that having infringed the terms of his performance licence his theatre would consequently have to close. As a result, there were no performances from May to December 1813, and Elliston was only allowed to reopen the following year upon the conditions that he confine his programme to burletta performances and that the theatre revert to its original name. The ways in which the Sans Pareil and Olympic Pavilion exploited their central location help render literal the extent to which, during the Peninsular War, the minor theatres represented a dynamic and creative 'underground' culture rapidly encroaching upon patent terrain (albeit with mixed success).

Elliston had started his campaign as early as 1809, when he became manager of the then Royal Circus. He immediately announced a series of improvements, including the embellishment of the theatre's interior and the construction of additional private boxes.[15] A year later, further changes would entail the conversion of the amphitheatre into a spacious pit. This modification transformed the Royal Circus into the Surrey Theatre, a much more stage-oriented performance venue (Figure 3.2).

Robert Elliston was a cunning, if sometimes overly ambitious, entrepreneur who made a name for himself as an actor-manager (in)famous for the re-staging

---

[14]   Jane Scott was manager, writer and main actress at the Sans Pareil between 1806 and 1819. During this time, she wrote over fifty plays. Her father, John Scott (a wealthy entrepreneur, famous for the clothes and ink dye, 'Old True Blue') bought the theatre for his daughter in recognition of her talent at mounting amateur theatricals. In 1806 the theatre was a small house with no gallery. It was licensed for performance between October and March. Jane Scott wrote most of the plays performed — many of which were a financial success – and the theatre rapidly became known as a venue for burletta, pantomime and ballet. See: 'The 1806–1807 Season', *The Adelphi Theatre 1806–1900; A Calendar of Performances*. General Editors Alfred L. Nelson and Gilbert B. Cross <http://www.umass.edu/AdelphiTheatreCalendar/m06d.htm#Label009> [Accessed 09.04.14] and Jacky Bratton, 'Jane Scott the writer-manager', in *Women and Playwriting in Nineteenth-Century Britain*, ed. Tracy C. Davis and Ellen Donkin (Cambridge: Cambridge University Press, 1999), 77–98.

[15]   Advertisement dated 23 March 1809, qtd. by George Raymond in *The Life and Enterprises of R.W. Elliston, Comedian*, illustrated by George Cruikshank and 'Phiz' (London, 1857), 161.

Figure 3.2   Robert Wilkinson, *North East View of the Surrey Theatre, formerly the Royal Circus, near the Obelisk, Great Surrey Street*, 1 May 1814. © Victoria and Albert Museum, London.

of patent texts in forms suitable for the minor theatres.[16] In June 1809 he made his first appearance on stage at the then Royal Circus as the highwayman Captain Macheath in a burletta-melodrama version of John Gay's *The Beggar's Opera* (1728). A few months later, Shakespeare's *Macbeth* was performed under similar conditions.[17] Elliston's success with both these adaptations speaks suggestively to

[16]   In full testament to the crossover between legitimate and illegitimate cultures, Elliston would later become a lessee of Drury Lane. Under his management *Coriolanus* was revived and George IV's coronation celebrated in spectacular fashion. Moody, *Illegitimate Theatre*, 127–9.

[17]   In November 1809 Elliston submitted an application to 'Third Theatre Committee' for the transformation of the Surrey into an additional patent theatre. The movement for a third patent collapsed and the monopoly system was preserved. Elliston, however, continued to test the limits of his license. In August 1810, following the re-modelling of his theatre and Thomas Dibdin's recent engagement as the Surrey's artistic director, he staged an elaborate adaptation of Garrick's Shakespearean Jubilee. The playbills advertised seventeen scenes from Shakespeare's plays, and offered a full description and cast list. As

the ways in which he conceptualised his theatre's socio-political standing. Both plays were crucially implicated in an examination of state authority; *Macbeth* as a play about regicide, and *The Beggar's Opera* as a 'low-life' parody of Italian opera (that concludes not with Macheath's expected execution but an absurd dance). Elliston's re-invention of *The Beggar's Opera* and *Macbeth* as illegitimate dramas posed a challenge to the patent monopoly that was rendered all the more threatening by his obvious ability to command a successful theatrical repertoire.[18] The popular demand for both burlettas ensured that the culturally and politically symbolic dimensions of Elliston's transgressions packed a heavy punch.

Macbeth was first performed at the Royal Circus on 31 August 1809 with Elliston, in the lead role, delivering an opening address that underlined his commitment to a new mode of representation:

> Though not indulg'd with fullest pow'rs of speech
> The poet's object we aspire to reach;
> The emphatic gesture, eloquence of eye,
> Scenes, music, every energy we try,
> …………………………………
> And what we must not *say*, resolve to *do*;[19]

Although, as Elliston here claims, the impetus was on action, the written word and gestural ballet went hand in hand towards defining an experience of communitarian spectatorship. This version of *Macbeth* relied on the sparing use of scrolls and banners to relate important information to the audience. For lower-class audiences who may well have been semi-literate or illiterate, the onus was on the Circus's better-educated patrons to read the written messages aloud.[20] Such performances gave audiences the opportunity to envisage the stage's creation of meaning as an activity at once plural and active.

The kind of knowing, generic coyness illustrated by Elliston's burletta successes was symptomatic of the minor theatres' larger wartime repertoires. Constrained by the inability to disclose their subject matter 'with full pow'rs

---

with the Circus's *Macbeth*, this entailed a representation of the different scenes as ballets of action. See Christopher Murray, 'Elliston's Productions of Shakespeare', *Theatre Survey*, 11.2 (November 1970), 99–123.

[18] In 1809 J.C. Cross (stage manager for the Royal Circus) published *Circusiana, Or A Collection of the Most Famous Ballets, Spectacles, Melo-Drames, &c Performed at the Royal Circus, St George's Fields*, in two volumes. As A.C. Sprague notes, this included 'a very spectacular' *Cora; or, The Virgin of the Sun* (in Vol. 1). Sprague, 'A *Macbeth* of Few Words', in *All These to Teach: Essays in Honor of C.A. Robertson*, ed. Robert A. Bryan, Alton C. Morris, et al. (Gainesville: University of Florida Press, 1965), 81.

[19] '"Occasional Address" to *The History, Murders, Life, and Death of Macbeth…*' rptd. in Bryan, Morris, et al. (eds), *All These to Teach*, 86.

[20] On the use of scrolls and their notoriously 'idiosyncratic' spelling, see Moody, *Illegitimate Theatre*, 28–30.

of speech', illegitimate representations of Spain and Portugal depended upon a visual economy of recognisable Iberian objects and mannerisms. Boleros, castanet dances, patriotic songs and other types of symbolic shorthand (such as allusions to cape and sword drama) made frequent appearances in the topical productions staged at the minor theatres during the Peninsular War. By effective arrangement, these referents could provide audiences with narratives as politically pointed and ambitious as Elliston's controversial yet popularly acclaimed adaptations of *The Beggar's Opera* and *Macbeth*. An unfortunate result of this, however, is that the largely non-verbal productions put on at the minor theatres are extremely difficult to reconstruct, even with the aid of surviving songbooks and performance texts (when available). Where so much was dependent on the dancing and vocal abilities of the main actors, the contemporary possibilities inherent in cues for a '*pas seul*' or the singing of a favourite ballad, for instance, are notoriously difficult to recover. The songbook for Charles Dibdin the Younger's *The Wild Man* (1809) – one of Sadler's Wells greatest hits during the Peninsular War – is a case in point. The description for the fifth scene merely reads: 'Scene V – Interior of the Wild Man's Cave – Power of Music over the Savage Mind'.[21] The label hardly does justice to the fact that this was one of *The Wild Man*'s most celebrated scenes, commonly reproduced 'on Benefit nights, at almost every Theatre in Town, and many in the Country'.[22]

Dibdin the Younger's play, which is set on an exotic volcanic island, dramatises the attempts of Muley, the island's Moorish Viceregent, to subvert the legitimate line of succession during Prince Artuff's temporary absence. He attempts to poison Fadallah (the Prince's wife) and orders the murder of their young son, Adolphus. But when Rufus (Muley's henchman) retreats to a cave in order to kill Adolphus, he is distracted by the unexpected entrance of a wild boar. This causes Rufus to make a hasty escape and results in the boy's discovery by the play's eponymous Wild Man, whose savagery is confirmed by his exit in chase of the boar and re-appearance brandishing the animal's leg. The Wild Man's impressive strength proves finally heroic when he saves Adolphus from Muley's later attempt to drown him, and thereby secures the government of the island for Prince Artuff and his heir.

Jane Moody focuses her interpretation of *The Wild Man* on its 'imperial preoccupations', and offers a shrewd reading of Dibdin the Younger's much-admired fifth scene. Here, Moody argues, the 'subduing' effects of Artuff's silver flute seem to provide a correlative for 'the making of empire as a process of benevolent domination' that sees 'the savage monster consen[t] to the reasoned

---

[21]   Charles Isaac M. Dibdin, *Songs and other Vocal Compositions ... in the New Aquatic Romance, called 'The Wild Man; or, Water Pageant'* (London, 1809), 18. The play was such a success that it was revived in 1814.

[22]   Dibdin (the Younger), *Memoirs*, 102. *The Wild Man* was performed twice in Bristol to celebrate Grimaldi's engagement in November 1814. See 'Calendar': Part C.

moral superiority of the imperial state'.[23] Her analysis then moves from a consideration of Dibdin the Younger's the Wild Man to the character type of the wild man more generally, and the attributes he shares with the sailor, in particular: 'a figure of remarkable physical strength, sudden violence and gentle tenderness, the stage tar resembles the wild man in his cultural position in the periphery of civilisation'.[24] With the auditorium at Sadler's Wells dependent upon a large contingency of sailors and shipyard workers, Moody's reading invites us to consider how opportunities for self-reflection might have shaped the commercial success enjoyed by Dibdin the Younger's play. I would like to add to this by suggesting that contemporary audiences would also have understood *The Wild Man* to be an entertainment very much conversant with the Peninsular War. *The Wild Man* includes, after all, the comic characters of Don Quixote and Sancho Panca [*sic*] who, although overlooked by most of the play's scholars, are likely to have struck a chord with contemporary audiences whose interests in Spanish culture were, by this time, strongly politicised.[25]

The Wild Man's Don Quixote is immediately recognisable as a version of Cervantes's famous romantic idealist. He arrives ashore labouring under the absurd belief that his boat is an enchanted one and brags to the peasants:

> QUIXOTE   I am of the ancient order of Knights Errant who fight giants,
> destroy enchantments, redress wrongs, and never put up with
> insults, nor would I with the present; but *ye* are beneath my
> knightly resentment…[26]

This serves as the prompt for the other characters on stage – and indeed the auditorium at large – to laugh at the swaggering Don. As the peasants ridicule him, '*Quixote attacks them*'; but to the end result that '*they conquer, tie him, and carry him off in ludicrous procession, singing*'.[27] The character of Sancho Panca acts, expectedly, as Quixote's more cynical foil. He initially introduces himself as the faithful squire to 'the most redoubtable Knight-errant, Signor Don Quixote de la Mancha', and parrots his companion's claim that they have arrived 'upon this island in an enchanted boat to redress grievances, right wrongs, kill giants, and smother sorcerers'. But Sancho immediately qualifies this bombast with a prosaic translation of their quest:

---

[23]   Moody, *Illegitimate Theatre*, 92, 93.

[24]   Moody, *Illegitimate Theatre*, 97. On the sailor as a figure of paradox, see Geoff Quilley, 'Duty and Mutiny: the aesthetics of loyalty and the representation of the British sailor c.1789–1800' in Shaw (ed.), *Romantic Wars*, 80–109.

[25]   Moody's analysis of *The Wild Man* does not make any mention of these characters; while in his discussion of monstrosity in the play, Louis James dismisses the introduction of Don Quixote and Sancha Panca as 'a curious intrusion'. Louis James, 'Frankenstein's Monster in Two Traditions' in *Frankenstein, Creation and Monstrosity*, ed. Stephen Bann (London: Reaktion Books, 1994), 77–94 (86).

[26]   Dibdin (the Younger), *Wild Man*, 9 (Scene 1).

[27]   Dibdin (the Younger), *Wild Man*, 10 (Scene 1).

SANCHO   That is, to meddle with other people's business instead of our
          own, run our heads against stone walls, … and though we very
          seldom see a bed, get very often tossed in a blanket.[28]

In his 'Outline of the Plot', Dibdin the Younger claims that Quixote and Sancho
were intended 'to relieve the serious parts of the piece'.[29] What he could not assert
quite so readily, of course, is that the pair brought to the play important topical
inflections, as well as comic relief.

Dibdin the Younger, who in his *Memoirs* recognises that Sadler's Wells enjoyed
its greatest prosperity in wartime, is likely to have been keen to ensure that *The
Wild Man* remained sensitive to current political issues.[30] In 1809 this included,
of course, the recent fall in support for the Peninsular Campaign. As I discuss in
Chapter 1, after the retreat at Corunna, British operations in Spain and Portugal
came under increasing attack from members of the Opposition, who began to
raise difficult questions about the viability of further involvement in the Iberian
Peninsula. The possibility that Dibdin the Younger's juxtaposition of Don Quixote
and Sancho provided not only a springboard for much of the play's humour (as he
claimed) but also for its politics, seems supported by the play's conclusion, which
features a grand fête in honour of Don Quixote. This takes place in the Palace
Garden, by a 'lake of real water' with '*jets d'eau*':

ORLUFF   …to please the madman Quixote, with whom our Prince is
          delighted, as he is always talking of enchantments, a grand
          entertainment is to take place on the great lake, in the Prince's
          garden, when every thing is to appear as if done by magic;
          and to conclude with the supposed liberation of the Knight's
          Dulcinea from enchantment, whom he supposes in the power of
          some Sorcerer.[31]

The events here described duly occur at the end of the scene, but the symbolic
theme of 'liberation' comes to acquire much greater urgency than Lord Orluff could
have predicted. When the mock sorcerer Broganthan 'appears on an aquatic hydra'
he is, as expected, 'attacked and overcome by the joint efforts of Don Quixote
and Sancho'. But this performance results in a surprising turn from the comic to
the potentially tragic when the pardoned Muley, overcome by 'desperation' and
'disappointed ambition', seizes Adolphus and attempts to drown him – leaving it
to the play's eponymous Wild Man to save the prince and oversee Muley's death.[32]

The Wild Man's final scene was thus loaded with political implication. The
heathen Moor, unable to control his political ambitions, could be easily re-imagined
as a Napoleonic villain. By the same token, audiences are likely to have claimed the

28   Dibdin (the Younger), *Wild Man*, 12 (Scene 2).
29   Dibdin (the Younger), *Wild Man*, 4.
30   Dibdin (the Younger), *Memoirs*, 119.
31   Dibdin (the Younger), *Wild Man*, 27 (Scene 13).
32   Dibdin (the Younger), *Wild Man*, 30–31 (Scene the last).

Wild Man – impersonated by Grimaldi, the popular Clown of English pantomime – as a national hero of their own, and Don Quixote and Sancho, by extension, as his Spanish allies. In a finale that took full advantage of Sadler's Wells' aquatic tanks, the Wild Man's successful ousting of the tyrannical Moor would have made for thrilling spectatorship; providing just the kind of visual grandeur needed to support Britain's continued involvement in the Iberian Peninsula. But if *The Wild Man* ultimately affirms that modern chivalric ideals are a cause worth fighting for, it also treats the Anglo-Spanish alliance with considerable circumspection. Dibdin the Younger notably looks to the Wild Man, rather than Don Quixote and Sancho, for truly effective heroic agency.

With its fast paced scene-changes and potentially wonder-inducing special effects, the pantomimic action that defined entertainments such as *The Wild Man* could provide an effective means for reimagining contemporary political events. Leigh Hunt's essays on pantomime for the *Theatrical Examiner* celebrate the genre's 'bustle', 'variety' and 'sudden changes'.[33] 'There is', Hunt claims, 'something *real* in Pantomime: there is animal spirit in it'.[34] Defining the genre as the perfect vehicle for satire and its reformatory aims, Hunt explains how in the absence of dialogue the spectators are left 'to their several powers, to imagine what supplement they please to the mute caricature before them'.[35] The pantomimic action that characterises *The Wild Man* suggests that the ban on spoken drama at the minor theatres paradoxically enhanced, rather than reduced, these theatres' capacity to create symbolic, politically engaging narratives. During the Peninsular War, the managers and scriptwriters of the minor theatres would actively exploit this potential when devising new entertainments.

Fact or Fiction

If popular support for the war in Spain and Portugal was beginning to waver by 1809, then it is worth remembering that the government's response to the evolving Iberian crisis had been contested from the very outset. In 1807 the British government had been distracted by fears that the Danes would give in to French pressure and form an alliance against Britain. These fears resulted in the investment of Copenhagen, an operation that although ultimately successful, was hotly debated on account of its questionable morality and lambasted in Parliament by the Opposition.[36] In December 1807 the *Morning Chronicle*, wearing its political colours on its sleeves, blamed the Danish expedition for the British government's failure to act more decisively in the lead up to Napoleon's invasion

---

[33]   *TE*, 26 January 1817.

[34]   *TE*, 5 January 1817.

[35]   *TE*, 26 January 1817.

[36]   On the Danish expedition of 1807, see Rory Muir, *Britain and the Defeat of Napoleon 1807–1815* (London: Yale University Press, 1996), 23–5.

of Portugal.[37] It was only by chance, the paper claimed, that the 'ancient' Anglo-Portuguese alliance had been salvaged, and a possible invasion of Ireland averted.[38] But if the British government had been slow to act it was not, of course, indifferent to the political situation in Portugal. By 29 November 1807, the Portuguese Royal Family and 10,000 members of its court were on board ships heading to Brazil, under the protection of the British navy.[39] Lord Strangford's account of this last-minute evacuation became public knowledge in the *London Gazette* for December 1807, which immediately kindled an interest in the geography, commerce, politics and cultural life of Brazil. It also encouraged both Astley's Amphitheatre and Sadler's Wells to invest in entertainments with a Brazilian setting. To the already politicised theatre-goer, these entertainments promised visually stunning analogues for the global, as well as European, implications of Napoleon's interference in the Iberian Peninsula.

On 16 May 1808 *The Honest Criminal; or, False Evidence* was performed for the first time at Astley's Amphitheatre. 'An entirely new Grand Spectacle, some months in preparation, invented and written by Mr. Astley Jun', *The Honest Criminal* promised to delineate 'the Manners and Customs of the Portuguese in that Part of South America, called, The Brazils'.[40] With the allure of 17 new scenes, John Philip Astley promised a veritable 'Microcosm of that Country'. This new entertainment was an instant hit and gained additional appeal the following month when the British government vouchsafed its military commitment to assist the Spanish patriots. By 25 July 1808 *The Honest Criminal* had been produced 61 times and received several positive reviews.[41]

The *Morning Chronicle*, for example, praised *The Honest Criminal* for its 'truly interesting and impressive effects' and the strength of its actors, reserving particular commendation for Hannah Astley (in the character of Zara), John Crossman (who played the role of Pedro Alvares, Zara's fiancé) and Thomas Rose (as 'the truly brave British Sailor').[42] *The Honest Criminal*'s play-run was also significantly bolstered by the public's recognition that John Astley's Brazilian setting symbolised more than just a tropical travelscape: 'the Bay and City of Rio de Janeiro, as represented in this production, is certainly most beautiful, and the landing of the Prince Regent of Portugal in the Brazils, is a scene of the most pleasing and lively nature', the *Morning Chronicle* added.[43] As the new seat of the Portuguese monarchy, Brazil provided the latest refuge from the despotism of

---

[37]   *MC*, 31 December 1807. Compare *MC* 2 February 1808, wherein proposals for Lord Strangford's promotion are interpreted as proof of the 'cowardly and, crooked and puffing policy of the day'.

[38]   *MC*, 31 December 1807.

[39]   Neil Macaulay, *Dom Pedro: The Struggle for Liberty in Brazil and Portugal 1798–1834* (Durham: Duke University Press, 1986), 18.

[40]   AA Playbill, 7 June 1808. V&A.

[41]   *MC*, 25 July 1808.

[42]   *MC*, 24 May 1808.

[43]   *MC*, 24 May 1808.

Figure 3.3   Henri L'Evêque, *His R.H. the Prince Regent of Portugal and all the Royal Family, embarking at Belem quay for Brazil the 27th November 1807*, engraved by F. Bartolozzi. [1813]. © The Trustees of the British Museum.

Napoleonic France. But the very journey to Brazil also constituted an important part of the entertainment's appeal. In *The Honest Criminal* John Astley seems to have been driven by a desire to celebrate the British tar's heroic agency and redeem him, perhaps specifically, from the moral criticisms that had been levelled against the government's deployment of the Royal Navy in the summer of 1807.[44]

The spectacle opens with Hannah Astley (John Astley's wife) in the character of Zara de Almeida (the daughter of the Governor of Rio de Janeiro), returning from Lisbon with both her female attendant and fiancé, a high-ranking Portuguese Officer. In recognition of the thematic and especially topical importance of this voyage from the Old World to the New, Zara and her party are shipwrecked near Santa Cruz but fortuitously saved by 'the intrepidity of a British Sailor ... at the hazard of his own Life'.[45] The playbills explain that as a reward for his heroism, Zara's father presents the sailor with a diamond ring. In awe of its beauty, the sailor decides to travel to the interior of the country in search of Brazil's famous gold mines. During this excursion he finds himself prey to the jealous machinations of Perez (the husband of Zara's attendant) and his group of friends. In an act of self-defence the sailor kills his antagonist, thereby earning the ironic epithet of

---

[44]   See *MC*, 31 December 1807.
[45]   AA Playbill, 7 June 1808. V&A.

the 'Honest Criminal'. The plot, however, continues at full pace, with the sailor disguising himself in the dead man's clothes in order to pass as a volunteer for one of the annual expeditions to the gold mines. In the interests of dramatic suspense, the playbill's skeletal narrative concludes as Perez's friends arrive to accuse the sailor of murder and robbery. Although it is not revealed how the sailor ultimately acquits these charges, audiences were nevertheless assured that the 'total overthrow of False Evidence' would secure a happy ending for its hero.[46]

The subject of Brazil's mineral wealth would have been a familiar, if still intriguing, one for the play's viewers. On 30 December 1807 the *Morning Post* defined Rio de Janeiro as the recognised 'emporium and principal staple of the rich produce of the Brasils [*sic*]'; the country's chief city, as the *Morning Chronicle* had explained to its readers, 'owing to the gold and diamond mines in its neighbourhood'.[47] The Braganzas' relocation from Lisbon to Rio de Janeiro was seen to bring with it a host of financial and governmental benefits, including, of course, the opening of the South American markets to British trade. Indeed, the *Morning Post* attested that so 'closely connected' were the political and commercial advantages of Portugal's new seat of empire 'that it [was] difficult to separate them'.[48]

While the expedition to the mines enables *The Honest Criminal* to tap into Britons' commercial fascination for Brazil, the entertainment's many supporting roles (which included 'Mulattoes, Portuguese, Slaves, Free Negroes, Guards of the Mines, Troops of the Line, [and] Native Infantry') helped underline its political themes.[49] It was, however, the British sailor's rescue of the Portuguese party that carried the entertainment's greatest political weight. This moment of heroic fulfilment, so important to the spectacle's opening, colours the entire plot and is revived at the entertainment's conclusion, which re-creates the fête and illuminations given by the Governor of Rio De Janeiro (Zara's father in the play) to welcome the Prince Regent of Portugal.

Contemporaneous with Astley's popular Brazilian entertainment was Sadler's Wells' 'New Grand Aquatic Melo-Dramatic Spectacle', *The White Witch; or The Cataract of Amazonia* (1808).[50] With new music and specially designed scenery, the piece attempted a revolution in staging technique. The stage was split in two in order to create a dry stage at the front and a wet stage at the back, to simulate the effects of a real waterfall. But unfortunately for the theatre's proprietors, it

[46]   AA Playbill, 7 June 1808. V&A. The threat of impressment and 'false accusation of crime' were, as Jacky Bratton explains, familiar topoi of nautical melodramas. Bratton, Cave, et al. (eds), *Acts of Supremacy*, 39.
[47]   *MP*, 30 December 1807; 'The Brazils', in *MC*, 28 December 1807.
[48]   *MP*, 28 December 1807. Once British traders were given access to the Brazilian market, they also benefitted from a contraband trade that encompassed Spanish America and provided ready compensation for the loss of direct trade with Portugal. Muir, *The Defeat of Napoleon*, 30.
[49]   AA Playbill, 7 June 1808. V&A.
[50]   Sadler's Wells Playbill, 16 May 1808. LMA.

turned out that the 'waterfall', so '*magnificent*' during the day rehearsals, was '*deficient*' by lamplight, when performances were made before a paying public.[51] This contributed significantly to the entertainment's failure at the box office.

The White Witch flirts with the themes of empire, exoticism, gender and religion stimulated by audiences' newly inflected interests in South America. Like many newspaper accounts of Brazil, the published Advertisement to the play opens with a description of the geographical situation of the Amazon River. But Dibdin the Younger is quick to replace factual detailing with a much more speculative account:

> There are no European Settlements there, and very little is said to be known of the place to which implicit credit can be given. Indeed the existence of the *Amazons* is a subject of much doubt, but there are many Authors that have asserted, that there are *Amazons* about the foot of Mount Cacassus, in Arabia, as well as in South America, who assist the Men in War and undergo equally the same Hardships; heading the Troops jointly with the *Caciques*; and some that even expel the Male sex from their communities, except at stated periods, and either destroy the *Male* Children, produced by this temporary cohabitation … preserving a few to bring up as Slaves.[52]

In contrast to *The Honest Criminal*, *The White Witch* imagines a Brazilian setting culturally, as well as geographically, distant from the then capital city of Rio de Janeiro. Notice, for instance, how the Advertisement takes care to underscore the lack of any European settlement in the region, and refers, instead, to the cruel customs ascribed to the Amazonian women as proof of their primitivism. This frees Dibdin the Younger from the demands for verisimilitude associated with John Astley's Brazilian melodrama. While reports of the royal evacuation from Lisbon had validated Rio de Janeiro as a subject for popular speculation, the Amazon was only of interest by extension. The fact that the Amazon could remain a largely mythical location allowed Dibdin the Younger to easefully sidestep the ideological considerations that would have affected audiences' interests in – and responses to – Astley's depiction of the Brazilian capital.

In the Advertisement to *The White Witch* Dibdin the Younger clearly defines his setting as a '*Fiction*', a region still associated with 'much doubt' and 'very little … to which implicit credit can be given'. This is compounded by the entertainment itself, which depicts an Amazonian settlement reimagined as a community composed of 'Men and Women equally trained to Martial Exercises'.[53] Dibdin the Younger's decision to cast the pantomime actor Richard Norman in the role of Garagantua (the 'Principal Amazon' listed as one of the 'Women') signals,

---

[51]   Dibdin (the Younger), *Memoirs*, 99.

[52]   Charles Isaac M. Dibdin, *Songs, Duets, Recitatives, Chorusses, &c ... in the New Grand Aquatic Melo-Dramatic Spectacle, called 'The White Witch; or, The Cataract of Amazonia', with the argument of the piece* (London, 1808), 'Advertisement', 3.

[53]   Dibdin (the Younger), *White Witch*, 'Advertisement', 3.

furthermore, that contrary to the gender politics suggested by his Advertisement, *The White Witch* will divest the Amazons of their famed combination of female sensuality and prowess.[54] While the women in *The White Witch* may be given the visual emblems of power, the entertainment ultimately deconstructs their authority by exposing the critical influence of otherwise secondary male characters. This is borne out in the plot by the character of Pedagogue, for example, who teaches the eponymous 'White Witch' (his cousin, an Englishwoman, with whom he has been shipwrecked) to impose upon the natives' superstitious beliefs by successfully passing as a sorceress.[55]

It seems that in writing *The White Witch*, Dibdin the Younger was seeking, first and foremost, to take advantage of his theatre's potential for scenic effects. He thus ignores several opportunities for fostering cultural and political dialogue. The spectacular finale – which Dibdin the Younger would apply to such patriotic ends in *The Wild Man* – exerts limited political pressure on *The White Witch*'s plotline. Set in an immense cataract of real water, the final scene of the entertainment dramatises a battle of the good and bad spirits, resulting in the rescue of the White Witch while the villain, Jongbongee, falls prey to a crocodile. The spirit of the dead Amazon queen, Pulkawulka, appears at this climatic moment with personifications of Allegory and Truth to impress the moral that *"Virtue is Heaven's peculiar Care!"*.[56] It may be tempting to read this conclusion as a normalisation of the Amazons' superstitious belief in supernatural agency by reference to a Christian Heaven that rewards the good and punishes the wicked; but Dibdin the Younger ultimately refuses to fully bridge the gulf separating his local audiences from the entertainment's larger-than-life characters.

There is, then, very little in *The White Witch* to confidently raise it above an attempt to gain cheap laughs by showcasing the Amazon as an incommensurably mysterious foreign land. Notwithstanding, had the stage waterfall produced its desired visual effect, then Dibdin the Younger's aqua-drama would almost certainly have provided his theatre with a financial success for the 1808 season. *The White Witch* boasted, after all, an accomplished cast, an exotic setting, an obviously moralistic design and straightforward (if one-dimensional) comic appeal. Yet, although similar, at least in kind, to *The Honest Criminal*, Dibdin the Younger's fanciful '*Fiction*' should not be confused with John Astley's attempt to politicise the cityscape of Rio de Janeiro. Both managers were keen to sell tickets and fill seats, but their South American entertainments made disparate claims to topicality. In 1808 the staging of Spanish-, Portuguese- or South American-themed plays spoke to the public's acute interest in the early stages of the Peninsular War. The Brazilian spectacles at Astley's Amphitheatre and Sadler's Wells powerfully

---

[54] Dibdin (the Younger), *White Witch*, 2.
[55] The role of the White Witch was played by Charles Isaac M. Dibdin's wife, Mary. *The White Witch*, 'Principal Characters', 2.
[56] Dibdin (the Younger), *White Witch*, 20 (Scene 12).

illustrate that there was, nevertheless, an important distinction to be made between more politically alert productions, such as *The Honest Criminal* (which responded specifically to the Portuguese Royal Family's emigration), and the kind of unashamedly commercial entertainments exemplified by Dibdin the Younger's *The White Witch*. [57]

Song and Dance

Naval battles of any great significance were few and far between during the Peninsular War. When the Battle of Basque Roads (11–14 April 1809) was reported in the British press it thus provided a particularly exciting opportunity for the invention of new patriotic entertainments. The Royal Navy had successfully destroyed the French fleet that had been stationed at anchor in Biscay (blocking access to British ships) and Lord Cochrane, who commanded the attack, was celebrated as a hero. [58] The *Morning Chronicle*, which considered the naval battle 'a grand and brilliant achievement' (news 'seasonably' received after the 'disasters of the last campaign'), looked forward to Cochrane's future career; while the *Morning Post*, lauding 'the irresistible valour of the naval heroes of Britain', hesitated to pronounce 'whether the Admiralty, who planned, or the Officers, who executed the enterprize [*sic*], are most entitled to praise'. [59] A few days after the victory was made public in the *London Gazette* (22 April 1809) Astley's Amphitheatre offered its own commemoration of the battle. [60] This took the form of a nautical piece (complete with recitative, duets, choruses and glees) advertised

---

[57] After the Anglo-Spanish alliance of June 1808, Astley's Amphitheatre would build upon the success of *The Honest Criminal* with another topical production called *The Spanish Patriots*. Although this was not as popular as the earlier piece, it secured at least 38 representations by September 1808 (unidentified clipping, dated September 1808 in Astley's (1770–1827) box, V&A). *The Spanish Patriots* included the song 'Brother Joe and the Spaniards', reprinted in *Smeeton's Selection of the Most Approved Songs for 1809 …* (London, 1809).

[58] Cochrane was awarded the Order of the Bath for his services. See *The Life of Thomas, Lord Cochrane, Tenth Earl of Dundonald* by Thomas, Eleventh Earl of Dundonald, and H.R. Fox Bourne 2 vols (London, 1869), 1: 392.

[59] *MC*, 22 April 1809; *MP* 22 April 1809. The *Examiner*, 23 April 1809, drew attention to the naval victory's political significance: 'The entrustment of the service to LORD COCHRANE, whose political freedom is well known, does much honour to the Lord Commissioners: Lord NELSON, who differed materially with Mr PITT, fought the battles of that Minister with a thousand times greater glory than any *creature* could have done. The same fine spirit of thinking that makes a true Briton incorruptible upon shore makes him invincible on the waves'.

[60] AA prided itself on being 'at all times among the first to display any great national event'. See *MP*, 26 April 1809.

as 'a true and lively Portraiture of the late Proceedings and glorious Event in the Destruction of the FRENCH FLEET, in Basque Roads'.[61]

At Sadler's Wells, meanwhile, Dibdin the Younger introduced audiences to 'Basque Roads', a new song performed by Rees Jr in the character of a sailor.[62] Notable for its use of sailors' colloquialisms, 'Basque Roads' oscillated between sung and spoken dialogue. Its lyrics were clearly instructive, functioning not only as a newscast but a commentary on the battle itself:

> *Spoken*
> The fire ships led the way and forc'd Monsieur to cut and
> Run ashore under his own batteries, but that Kunouvre
> Wou'dn't do, for you know
>> Hearts of oak are our ships,
>> Hearts of oak are our men,
> And we'll fight and we'll conquer again and again.
>> With a chip chow, &c[63]

'Basque Roads' describes the launching of the fire-rockets, the British deflection of the French attack and the navy's ultimate success in washing the enemy fleet ashore. In complement to the dramatic narrative of the musical verse, the spoken parts of the song provide a lively, informative resumé of the course of the battle.

The tonal nuances in 'Basque Roads' that occur between song and speech also lend weight to the associative qualities of the popular music employed. This is exemplified by the recurrent allusions to 'hearts of oak', which would have encouraged audiences to make an immediate connection to Garrick's well-known song of that name:

> Hearts of oak are our ships, hearts of oak are our men
>> We always are ready
>> Steddy [*sic*], boys, steddy
> We'll fight and we'll conquer again and again.[64]

---

[61]   *MC*, 28 April 1809.

[62]   In his *Memoirs* Dibdin the Youger refers to the mimic and pantomime artist Thomas David Rees as 'Mr Rees Senr'. See Highfill, Burnim, and Langhans (eds), *Biographical Dictionary*, 12: 294–5.

[63]   *Recitatives, Duets, Trios, Chorusses &c with a description of the scenery and other decorations, also the fables and arguments of the Various pieces now performing at the Aquatic Theatre, Sadler's Wells* (London, 1809), 'The popular new song called "Basque Roads"', 1.

[64]   David Garrick, 'Hearts of Oak' (Edinburgh, 1776), *Eighteenth Century Collections Online*, Gale. University of Oxford <http://find.galegroup.com/ecco/infomark.do?&conte ntSet=ECCOArticles&type=multipage&tabID=T001&prodId=ECCO&docId=CW1131 37829&source=gale&userGroupName=oxford&version=1.0&docLevel=FASCIMILE> [Accessed 09.04.14].

Performances of 'Hearts of Oak' were popular in theatres during the Peninsular War, where its familiar lyrics were frequently sung with enthusiasm by actors and spectators alike. Dibdin the Younger's several references to 'hearts of oak' amounted to an unembarrassed attempt to re-create the patriotic, self-confident communal spirit already equated with Garrick's song.

'Basque Roads' also provides an ironic description of how Cochrane made his advance to the tune of 'Britons Strike Home'. According to the song's lyrics, British music was so irresistible in its charms that even the French '*Mounsieurs* all danc'd' to 'Rule Britannia'. By 1809 'Rule Britannia' (first performed in 1741) was already well established as an emblem of British imperial power.[65] It was also a favourite at the patent theatres, where it had become a sort of anthem among playgoers. In order to effect an even more emotive conclusion, the final lines of Dibdin the Younger's song reverberated with allusions to 'God Save the King' (to 'Send Him victorious, happy and glorious | Long to reign over us').[66] By a clever interlacing of the recent naval victory with the titles and lyrics of popular patriotic songs, Dibdin the Younger helped reinvigorate the spirits of an increasingly weary and disillusioned public. 'Basque Roads' created the opportunity for theatre-goers to forget their anxieties and, by the moving experience of an entire auditorium in song, come together as a national community.

At the Sans Pareil Theatre, Jane Scott also looked to the Battle of Basque Roads for her wartime repertoire. On 6 July 1809 she introduced audiences to a new military and naval burletta spectacle, *The Double Defeat; or British Tars and Austrian Troops*. The Franco-Austrian War (which began in April 1809 with the Austrian army's invasion of Bavaria) had resulted in a host of speculations about the fate of Europe.[67] The main scene of *The Double Defeat* – with its depiction of the naval engagement in Basque Roads as well as the 'Achievements of the Austrians on the Banks of the Danube' – made important claims to both the Peninsula and central Europe as active fronts in the war against Napoleonic expansionism.[68] This scene, which was proudly advertised in the playbills, functions as a useful reminder that Britain's war effort between 1808 and 1814 was not limited to the Iberian Peninsula. Following *The Double Defeat*, audiences were introduced to a new dance called 'Britons Strike Home; or, Which of the Three' – an interlude rendered all the more attractive by the engagement of 'Miss Twamley', from the Opera House, who performed the new *pas deux* with Goodwin (the theatre's resident ballet master). An Occasional Address was then delivered in-between the 'new Grand serious spectacle' of *Female Courage; or, The Banditti of the Rock* and the comic pantomime of *Harlequin Cottager, or, The Wandering Fairy*.

---

[65] In 1815 the Sadler's Wells pantomime *Harlequin Brilliant* depicted the launching of 'the good ship Britannia' to the tune of 'Rule Britannia' (sung by the entire company). Dibdin (the Younger), *Memoirs*, 112–13.

[66] Dibdin (the Younger), 'Basque Roads', 2.

[67] See, for example, *Examiner* 7 May 1809.

[68] SP Playbill, 6 June 1809. V&A.

As a final gesture in celebration of Cochrane's successful attack on the French fleet, the performances that night concluded with a hornpipe in the character of a British sailor.

The surviving performance records suggest, nevertheless, that Scott's selection of entertainments that evening did not attract much notice. There were no further representations of *The Double Defeat* or *Female Courage*, and neither play-text was published. The Amphitheatre's special effects and Rees Jr's singing at Sadler's Wells may simply have been bigger draws, but the mainpiece's relatively late production date is likely to have been the biggest factor contributing to its box office failure. On 22 May a court martial was held on board the *Gladiator* (off Portsmouth) to investigate Rear Admiral Eliab Harvey's allegedly insubordinate addresses to Admiral Gambier. Gambier had been the commander of the fleet at Basque Roads, despite the fact that responsibility for the actual attack was given to Cochrane. Harvey's alleged pronouncement that Gambier was 'a man unfit to command the fleet' was, significantly, partly echoed by Cochrane himself, when he refused to consent to the ministry's proposed Vote of Thanks for Gambier's services.[69] Cochrane argued that Gambier had unnecessarily delayed the expedition of the line-of-battle ships required for the attack at Basque Roads, and justified his dissent on account of his position as a Parliamentarian. But this provoked Gambier to demand another court martial in order to clear his name. Cochrane's trial would only start on 26 July (ending with Gambier's unanimous acquittal on 4 August), but as early as 7 June both the *Morning Chronicle* and *Morning Post* had announced a likely court martial 'in consequence of some of the opinions that have been given relative to the operations in Basque Roads'.[70] Cochrane's opposition to the Vote of Thanks was also publicly reported, and gleefully seized upon by William Cobbett as an opportunity to pit the "Jacobin" Scottish Lord against 'a cabinet of great big ministers and statesmen'.[71]

When Jane Scott's representation of the Battle of Basque Roads premiered at the Sans Pareil it thus referred to an event not only more involved than imagined three months previously (at the time of Astley's celebrations), but of still uncertain

---

[69] *The Scots Magazine and Edinburgh Literary Miscellany* (July 1809), 71: 553–5 (554). The press published full accounts of Harvey's court martial. See *MC* 24 May 1809; *Morning Post* 24 May1809; *Examiner* 28 May 1809; *Flower's Political Review and Monthly Register* (May 1809), 355.

[70] *MC* 7 June 1809. The degree of public curiosity is captured by the *MP*'s report of the 'vast crowds' that gathered at Portsmouth 'in anxious expectation of hearing the proceedings of the Court Martial called for by Admiral Lord GAMBIER ... demanded in consequence of the reports that were propagated relative to the occurrences, and his conduct in Basque Roads as Commander in Chief of the Channel Fleet'. On this occasion, however, the shot of gunfire from the *Gladiator* (the customary signal for a court martial) announced 'nothing more than a trial of two private seamen on a charge of desertion'. *MP* 21 June 1809.

[71] *MP* 9 June 1809; *Cobbett's Weekly Political Register*, 10 June 1809.

political outcome.[72] More problematically still, the second highlight of the entertainment – the 'Achievements of the Austrians on the Banks of the Danube' – was effectively invalidated on its opening night by the Battle of Wagram (5–6 July 1809). (Napoleon's second crossing of the Danube took the Austrians by surprise and resulted in a decisive (if costly) French military victory that irrevocably turned Scott's promises for a 'double defeat' against her.[73]) During the Peninsular War, ticket sales at the minor theatres were, for the most part, boosted by new military and naval entertainments. The failure of *The Double Defeat* suggests, however, that the inherently volatile combination of political and theatrical fortunes carried as many risks as rewards.

In order to remain competitive theatre managers therefore needed to be on a continuous search for the distinctive sense of novelty that would place their venue at a cut above the rest. They often achieved this by investing in impressive new scenery, mechanical contrivances and the engagement of star actors. The Sans Pareil's success with *The Bashaw; or, The Midnight Adventures of Three Spaniards*, which was staged 59 times between 23 January and 22 April 1809, offers a good example of the kind of programme on demand.[74] Scott, whose artistic vision and skills as an actress were equally celebrated, wrote the script and played the part of Clara, 'a Spanish Lady, Disguised as the Bashaw'.[75] The *Morning Chronicle* identified her acting as one of the chief attractions of the piece.[76] The *Times* followed suit, in a suspiciously puff-like review that asserted:

> It is truly the most elegant thing of the kind we have ever witnessed. The music is fascinating to a degree; so is the Dance in the first Act. The torch light business in the Second Act has a novel and pleasing effect. Miss SCOTT plays and sings the female Bashaw to admiration; nor does she look the worse for the assumed mustachios.[77]

Cross-dressing roles had acquired immense popularity since the Restoration, when women were first allowed to perform on the British stage. (Peter Thomson

---

[72]   On 5 July 1809 the *MC* anxiously looked forward to the conclusion of the court martial ('an unpleasant business'). It is tempting to think that Jane Scott's relatively late celebration of Cochrane's exploits at the Battle of Basque Roads might communicate her sympathies for the radical Scottish Lord.

[73]   Chandler, *Dictionary*, 471–6. I am grateful to Nicholas Rodger for drawing my attention to the significance of this battle.

[74]   A Calendar of Plays for the Sans Pareil is available online and is the main source for the statistical data provided in this chapter. See *The Adelphi Theatre 1806–1900: A Calendar of Performances*. General Editors Alfred L. Nelson and Gilbert B. Cross <http:// www.umass.edu/AdelphiTheatreCalendar/hist.htm> [Accessed 09.04.14].

[75]   Jane Scott, *Songs, Chorusses, Duetts, Trios, &c in The Bashaw; or, 'Midnight Adventures of Three Spaniards'. From a Spanish Tale. A Melodramatic Spectacle* (London, 1809).

[76]   *MC*, 26 January 1809.

[77]   *The Times*, 31 January 1809.

notes that 'close to one quarter of the plays staged between 1660 and 1700 called for an actress (or two) to expose normally concealed parts of the body in male costume'.[78]) This constituted a distinctive aspect of *The Bashaw*'s visual appeal. Less immediate, but no less important, were the ways in which Scott's impersonation of the Bashaw gestured towards contemporary politics.

Scott's decision to specifically market her play as the adaptation of a 'Spanish Tale' functions as the first clue to the conflation of images of East and West that are likely to have structured her entertainment more generally.[79] With British soldiers struggling to gain ground in the Peninsula, *The Bashaw* re-directed attention to the possibilities attendant upon the recent peace concluded between Britain and Turkey (5 January 1809). This peace, which ruptured relations between Turkey and Russia (a French ally), was seen to put pressure on enemy lines.[80] The future of Europe hung in the balance. Letters received from the Admiralty-office suggested that:

> If Bonaparte stations a large army still in Spain, that will operate in a favourable manner for Austria – if on the contrary he withdraws his army from Spain, and directs his whole attention towards Austria, Spain will have time to recruit strength, to raise new levies, and to combine her resources.[81]

Scott's sensuality as the cross-dressing Clara spoke to distant political desires, as well as more immediately physical ones.[82]

Interestingly, the terms used by the *Morning Chronicle* to review *The Bashaw* after its initial performances were not dissimilar to those used by the first reviewers of Richard Brinsley Sheridan's phenomenally popular *Pizarro*:

> Have you seen the Bashaw at the Sans Pareil Theatre, is the first question in every fashionable circle at the West end of the Town? [*sic*] Have you seen the Bashaw? – the first question in every Coffee and Counting House in the City. Nor can we wonder at the estimation in which the Public hold it. The Patriotic

---

78   Peter Thomson, *Cambridge Introduction to English Theatre, 1660–1900* (Cambridge: Cambridge University Press, 2006), 54. For an earlier example of a woman playing the role of the Bashaw, see Charles Dibdin the Elder, *The Seraglio; A Comic Opera* (1776).

79   The role of Clara is not listed under the female parts but at the head of the male cast list. Unfortunately, the only copy of the songbook that I have been able to locate is incomplete. Jane Scott, *Songs, choruses, duets, trios, &c. in 'The Bashaw; or, Midnight Adventures of Three Spaniards'. A melo-dramatic spectacle.* London, 1809. The Bodleian Libraries, The University of Oxford, shelfmark reference: Harding D 1950–1964.

80   Russia had entered into an alliance with France under the terms of the Treaty of Tilsit (1807).

81   *The Lancaster Gazette and General Advertiser, for Lancashire, Westmoreland, &c.*, 11 March 1809 ('London, Saturday, March 4').

82   In 1809 Scott's performance is likely to have received additional charge from the public scandal surrounding Frederick, Duke of York, and his mistress Mary Anne Clarke. See *Examiner* 26 March 1809.

Lines at the conclusion, independent of its other merits, render it worthy every unbounded patronage it has already received. Every English heart must feel and hand approve them. – The other entertainments at this beautiful Theatre, though each excellent in their kind, must all give way. The reigning favourite of the day is the Bashaw.[83]

The Bashaw's 'patriotic lines' are significantly recognised for their ability to bring together an approving audience. From the West End of London to the city's financial core, *The Bashaw*'s 'unbounded patronage' knew no geographic – or, by implication, social – limits. 'The reigning favourite of the day', *The Bashaw* (and indeed, Scott as Clara/the Bashaw) benefitted from the engagement of skilled actors; John Isaacs, Mrs James F. Pyne and Abraham Slader all assuming leading parts. These actors, who had come from Covent Garden Theatre after the fire of September 1808, helped make *The Bashaw* the highlight of the 1809 season.

The Bashaw's success ensured its revival the following year, when it was played 12 times between 22 January and 3 April 1810.[84] Scott's *Disappointments; or, Love in Castile* premiered at the Sans Pareil not long afterwards, on 3 December 1810. It was the first play of the winter calendar, with an Opening Address written and delivered by Jane Scott. The Address conformed to the custom among women playwrights to affably satirise female agency. Introducing *Disappointments* with its new scenery, costumes and decorations, Scott curried audience sympathy by revealing the company's anxieties for the play's success. To this end, it makes a spectacle of its author: 'Then there's Miss, the *Authoress*, a little conceited thing – aye, 'tis true, | Do you know, she fancies that she is a *favourite* with you'.[85] The objectifying distance implied by the use of the third person is rendered ironic here because spoken by the authoress herself. With a repertoire that included the entertainments of *Ulthona, The Red Robber, The Magistrate, The Two Misers of Smyrna, The Bashaw,* and *Mary the Maid of the Inn,* as well as the comic pantomimes of *Mother White Cap, The Necromancer* and *The Magic Pipe,* Scott's positive expectations were fully justified. Indeed, as Jacky Bratton explains, 'in a period where authors' names are given little publicity', the Sans Pareil playbills stand out for their bold, proud announcement that "the whole of the entertainments [were] written by Miss Scott".[86] Taking advantage of this celebrity, the Address shifts from Scott's self-representation as a conceited author, to an amiable, if scatter-brained, first person speaker who places her audiences' pleasures at a premium:

---

[83]   *MC*, 3 February 1809. Compare 'Pizarro the Universal Topic!' in *Spirit ... 1799*, 314–9.

[84]   <http://www.umass.edu/AdelphiTheatreCalendar/m09d.htm> [Accessed 07.05.14].

[85]   Jane Scott, *Songs, Duets, and Chorusses* [*sic*] *in the New Serio-Comic Burletta, entitled* Disappointments; or, Love in Castile (London, 1810), 'Opening Address', 4.

[86]   Bratton, 'Jane Scott the writer-manager', in Davis and Donkin (eds), *Women and Playwriting*, 81.

'I'm prating at a random rate, | When in due form I ought to *supplicate*'.[87] Shortly afterwards, the prompt bell rings, blurring the delivery of the Address with the mainpiece itself:

> Lud, don't ring yet, I know I'm running on,
> But have a little Patience, Sir, and I'll be gone;
> Bless my soul, when talking is the plan,
> And *Women* have to *speechify* – stop their tongues who can.[88]

Playing up to the period's reductive gender norms, Scott quickly concludes with an urbane address to the gentlemen in her audience. Her comic tone, I would like to suggest, is directly related to the ensuing performance; Scott's correlation of female authorship and audience expectation possibly amounting to an acknowledgement of the ideological hedging that characterises the mainpiece itself.

Due to the Sans Pareil's central location within Westminster, the theatre's burletta scripts were submitted to the Examiner of Plays.[89] John Larpent, as already mentioned, was renowned for his intolerance to any allusions that might provoke political or religious dissent. While Scott's main decision to publish *Disappointment*'s songbook was probably financial, it also raises intriguing questions about the differences between print and performance (complicated, to some degree, by the fact that songbooks were often purchased inside the theatre). In this case, the play's readers (whether at home, or with songbook in hand in the auditorium) seem to have enjoyed a much more rounded interpretative experience than that offered by the performance alone. It is, after all, only the published songbook that provides any clear indication of Scott's political interests.

In 'The Plot preceding the opening of the Piece' – defined as an attempt to 'open the mind to the situation of the Characters at the rise of the curtain' – Scott takes considerable pains to explain the circumstances of her play's leading male characters.[90] Therein, she relates that Don Alvares, a disgraced Portuguese nobleman, has fallen victim to the 'private machinations of his enemies'. Following his resignation as Prime Minister, Alvares escapes with his son, Foliano, 'in disgust from the Court'. The father and son end up in Spain after Foliano falls in love with a young lady travelling there.[91] By leaving open the possibility that Alvares' plight might be mirrored by that of Seberto (a Portuguese gentleman disguised as a peasant), whose own experiences of political foulplay took place during Alvares' period of government, Scott begins to describe a Portuguese court falling apart through inner dissension. In making her readers

---

[87]   Scott, *Disappointments*, 4.
[88]   Scott, *Disappointments*, 4.
[89]   The Olympic did so likewise. See *Catalogue of Larpent Plays in the Huntington Library*, compiled by Dougald MacMillan (San Marino; California: San Pasqual Press, 1939).
[90]   Scott, *Disappointments*, 5–6 (6).
[91]   Scott, *Disappointments*, 5.

privy to this intriguing political backdrop, Scott introduces the obstacles likely
to frustrate the younger generation's hopes for romantic fulfilment in the main
plot. The play's spectators, by contrast, received a very different first impression
of its action. As a performance, *Disappointments* opens with a dance and choral
lay by the peasant community, but at no point does the musical action on stage
directly address the politicised ante-plot to which Scott alerts her readers.[92]
The main plot of *Disappointments* functions, instead, by drawing attention
to the worn-out, familiar stereotypes of Spanish peasants, love intrigues and
religious hypocrisy.[93]

Why, then, does Scott take care to 'open the mind to the situation of the
Characters at the rise of the curtain', if only to overlook that mindset during the
course of the play itself? As I have already suggested, the Opening Address (also
published as part of her songbook) may provide an answer. In the Address, Scott
portrays herself as a proud author before playfully retreating as a ditsy woman.
Similarly, *Disappointments* teases its audiences with the interests of an anterior
political plot that its songs subsequently fail to develop. Scott knew that to fill
seats in her playhouse, she had to meet certain expectations. Engagement with
hard politics risked censure not only from Larpent but also from her theatre's
patrons, more likely to privilege stagecraft over statecraft. Scott's burletta thus
deliberately, and successfully, avoids the intricacies of Peninsular politics by
complying to a superficial Spanish theme. Produced 56 times between December
1810 and March 1811, the piece boasted Spanish dances by Goodwin, and included
a mock bolero (in character) danced on its opening night.[94] It appears, nevertheless,
that Scott could not resist testing the ideological potential of her Spanish setting,
however under-developed. By including in her published songbook a synopsis
of the preceding plot, Scott encouraged her literate audiences to supplement
their memories of the Sans Pareil performance with a politicised narrative that
added depth and substance to *Disappointment*'s arguably skittish action. The
joint publication of the 'Opening Address' and 'Plot preceding the opening of the
Piece' suggests that the theatrical economy posed its own threats to scriptwriters'
creative ambitions. But if Jane Scott's talents were at times curtailed by financial
imperatives, then her publication of *Disappointments*' songbook evinces a marked
reluctance to allow the measurement of her success to be limited exclusively to the
Sans Pareil's box office takings.

Battlefields

In their determination to transform generic limitations into decided advantages,
managers of London's minor theatres concentrated on the production of grand,
visually arresting narratives about the British campaign in Spain and Portugal.

---

[92] Scott, *Disappointments*, 7 (1.1).
[93] Scott, *Disappointments*, 11–12 (2.2).
[94] SP Playbill, 3 December 1810. V&A.

John Philip Astley and Robert Elliston were quick to discover that much profit could be gained by literally transposing the Peninsular battlefields onto their stages.[95] Between 1810 and 1811, a succession of British victories in Portugal made this a particularly attractive prospect. The Battle of Bussaco (27 September 1810) and the battles of Fuentes de Oñoro (3–5 May 1811) and Albuera (near Badajoz, Spain, 16 May 1811) played a crucial role in facilitating Wellington's expulsion of the French army from Portuguese territory. By the end of April 1811 the townspeople of Elvas were lauding Wellington the heroic 'Restorer of the Kingdom of Portugal' – a gesture that spoke to the symbolic, as well as strategic, significance of the recent victories.[96] Although the war was far from over, the myth of French invincibility had finally been shattered and important progress made in the Peninsula by the Allied army.

This proved an auspicious time for the production of a new military piece at Astley's Amphitheatre – *Lisbon; or, 'Ruse De Guerre' on the Banks of the Tagus* (1811). As a prelude to the main entertainment and pantomime, *Lisbon* would run consecutively from 10 June to 5 August 1811 in support of 'the popular grand naval, military, equestrian and pedestrian Spectacle', *The Tyrant Saracen and Noble Moor*; and the pantomimes *Harlequin's Amour; or, Jupiter and Europa* (until 8 July), and *The Mandarin; or, Harlequin in China* (thereafter).[97] Newspaper advertisements promised that *Lisbon* would include 'a Sketch of Massena's quick

---

[95]   The minors' policy of 'bringing the war home' was, to some extent, complemented by their frequent engagement of international performers. The Olympic Pavilion, for example, hired a ropedancer from Lisbon (*MC*, 24 January1809); while for its 1811–1812 season, the SP engaged 'Signor Montignani "from [the] Lisbon Opera"' (Frank McHugh, 'The 1811–1812 Season': Theatre History Summary <http://www.umass.edu/AdelphiTheatreCalendar/m11d.htm> [Accessed 09.04.14]). Montignani had first been contracted by DL, where he appeared in the comic ballet *The Village Doctor* (May 1810) but received poor reviews (*MM*, May 1810, 392). At Scott's theatre, he was active as a composer, choreographer and performer. London's growing community of Spanish and Portuguese political exiles ranged from the well-educated circle at Holland House to the prisoners of war liberated after the Anglo-Spanish alliance of 1808. On the latter, see Old Bailey Proceedings Online, <http://www.oldbaileyonline.org> [Accessed 09.04.14]: September 1808, trial of Joze Kertein [t18080914–119]. Stranded sailors often found lodgings in the Wapping neighbourhood of East London – home to many other sailors, boat-builders and instrument-makers of the naval trade. They are likely to have attended the theatres as second-price gallery spectators. For an example of the cultural activities of London's upper class Spanish émigrés, see *MC*'s advertisement, 10 April 1812, for a masquerade at the Argyle-Street Rooms.

[96]   The contributions made by Spanish soldiers at Albuera helped improve otherwise strained Anglo-Spanish military relations. The two countries remained locked in political disputes, however. In 1811 the fate of the South American colonies constituted yet another point of grievance – as suggested by the performance history of *Pizarro* (see Chapter 1). Muir, *The Defeat of Napoleon*, 155–6.

[97]   *MC*, 10 June 1811. The piece was later advertised as *Lisbon, Or the Cunning of War on the Banks of the Tagus* (*MC*, 16 July 1811).

retreat from Portugal, and the spirited pursuit and attack by the British Army, &c. commanded by the Gallant Lord Wellington'. To this would be added the 'Battle and Defeat of the French Army under Marshal Soult, by part of the Allied army by Marshal Beresford, at Albuera, on the 16th of May, in the former's furious attempt to relieve Badajoz in Spain'.[98] Albuera may have been a bloodbath, and Fuentes de Oñoro 'probably the least convincing of all Wellington's victories' (according to Rory Muir, who points to a rare strategic mistake by Wellington), but Astley's entertainment was clearly aimed at final results (the re-capture of Almeida, Massena's retirement south to Andalusia, and Albuera as the event that paved the road to Badajoz).[99] In short, *Lisbon* aimed to offer audiences a clarity of military design that, however illusory to the combatants themselves, was deemed essential for raising public morale.

Verisimilitude at Astley's Amphitheatre seems, then, to have hinged less on the promise of a realistic depiction of the latest battle than on a dramatisation of its *reported* significance. This entailed a privileging of 'event' that focused quite literally on the outcome or consequences of the British army's operations in Spain and Portugal. *Lisbon*'s success derived in large part from the military display that already constituted one of the chief attractions of the mainpiece *The Tyrant Saracen and Noble Moor* and the ideological confrontation encoded in the latter's title.[100] In the midsummer of 1811, with operations in Spain and Portugal temporarily suspended due to soaring temperatures, audiences in London continued to celebrate the results of the earlier battles of Fuentes de Oñoro and Albuera. *Lisbon* aimed to keep patriotic feeling high by retaining the focus on end results and, in doing so, offered much needed 'justification' for a military campaign that had been significantly maligned since 1809.

'The spirited pursuit and attack by the British army' integral to *Lisbon*'s action also proved prophetic of a new turn in military strategy that would see Wellington assume a much more aggressive front. In 1812 an Anglo-Portuguese offensive took Ciudad Rodrigo and Badajoz by storm. With the fall of Ciudad Rodrigo (19–20 January 1812) and capitulation of Badajoz (on 6 April 1812, after the two failed sieges of 1811) the Allies succeeded in opening up two of the main routes into Spain.[101] At the Surrey, Elliston responded to the war bulletins with a '*petite* Melo-Dramatic Spectacle' called *The Siege of Ciudad Rodrigo*. Boasting 'incidents and situations similar and appropriate to the recent gallant and glorious achievement of our victorious Army in the Peninsula', *The Siege* included a large,

---

[98]   *MC*, 10 June 1811.

[99]   Muir, *The Defeat of Napoleon*, 150.

[100]   *The Tyrant Saracen and Noble Moor*, which required the engagement of 20 specially trained horses, premiered on 15 April 1811. *The Times*, 13 April 1811.

[101]   Wellington had already made two unsuccessful attempts to capture Badajoz in 1811. See David Gates, *The Spanish Ulcer: A History of the Peninsular War* (Cambridge, MA: Da Capo Press, 1986), 252–6 (first siege); 270–76 (second siege) and 334–9 (on the successful third siege).

illuminated transparency of Wellington – the hero of the day.[102] In his assessment of this entertainment, Frederick Burwick stresses that 'the battleground is historical Spain' but what it predominantly offers is 'a celebration of Wellington as Britain's national hero'.[103] By ascribing to Wellington what was, in fact, a triumphant result for the Anglo-Portuguese forces, *The Siege* adopted a form of symbolic shorthand reminiscent of *Lisbon*.

The Amphitheatre also looked to recent events in Spain in order to provide what was effectively a sequel to its summertime military prelude. *The Siege and Capture of Badajoz* was staged in May 1812, only a month after the successful breach. Although military entertainments were always conditioned by a necessary time lag between a Peninsular battle and its report, Astley's speed in mounting the spectacle was once again impressive. He swiftly promoted his new entertainment as:

> An Accurate stage representation in Fourteen Scenes, of the glorious and unparalleled SIEGE, STORMING and TAKING, at the point of the Sword and Bayonet, the strong OUTWORK and CITY of BADAJOZ, by the brave and gallant Allied Army, commanded by Field Marshal the Most Noble Lord Wellington – Characters (Besieged and Besiegers) are inserted in the Bills of the Day.[104]

As with *Lisbon*, an identification of 'event' was key, with the siege, storming and taking constituting the entertainment's principal structural points.[105]

The siege, as I consider at greater length in Chapter 4, proved an especially popular subject in contemporary literature. In his exploration of Byron's decision to write about sieges, Simon Bainbridge explains:

> As a form of warfare, the siege can be seen as particularly suited to literary representation, offering a series of dramatic set piece actions (trenching, cannonade, assault) that had become particularly formalized during the seventeenth and eighteenth centuries (following the manuals of the French military architect Vaub[a]n) and that contributed to a single, decisive action – the taking of a fortress and the annihilation or total surrender of the enemy.[106]

His comments apply with equal force to the theatrical representations discussed in this section. As Astley's advertisement suggests, the appeal of *The Siege and Capture of Badajoz* exceeded the 'accurate' re-enactment of the British soldiers'

---

[102]   Christopher Murray, *Robert William Elliston: Manager* (London: Society for Theatre Research, 1975), 45.

[103]   Burwick, *Playing to the Crowd*, 128.

[104]   *MC*, 7 May 1812.

[105]   On the night of its first representation, *The Siege and Capture of Badajoz* was presented alongside the spectacle of *The Brave Cossack* – a pairing that again testified to the pan-European scale of the Napoleonic Wars.

[106]   Simon Bainbridge, '"Of war and taking towns": Byron's siege poems', in Shaw (ed), *Romantic Wars*, 161–84 (164).

skilled manoeuvres with the sword and bayonet. Although military display was undoubtedly an important element, the entertainment's success ultimately rested upon its creation of a narrative punctuated with dramatic stage tableaux (of the 'siege' and 'storming') and a spectacular conclusion ('the taking').

The 14 different scenes of Astley's military spectacle demanded costly but necessary investment. Audiences would, after all, carefully scrutinise the entertainment's various sets. Many theatre-goers were likely to have been familiar with the plans of battleworks printed in the *London Gazette* and subsequently used as the basis of the Badajoz panorama in Leicester Square.[107] Information about the fall of Badajoz was readily available. On 28 April 1812 the *Morning Chronicle* printed a letter from a British officer in Spain detailing the difficulties of the horrific nocturnal assault. The paper reported how after scaling the fortress walls at Badajoz, British soldiers jumped to the other side, only to fall on a '*cheveaux de frize*, formed of old swords ground to the utmost sharpness'.[108] Badajoz embodied, in short, the inhumanity of total warfare. Its high death count would have lent painful poignancy to Astley's observation that the list of Besieged and Besiegers would be added to 'the Bills of the day'. By conflating the lists of fictional and real casualties, Astley ensured that his playbills doubled as an important form of commemoration for the families of the wounded and the dead; and, by giving individual recognition to the supernumeraries engaged each night, also fulfilled their primary purpose of introducing audiences to the various soldiers who worked casually for the Amphitheatre while awaiting their own deployment to the Peninsula.

In the summer of 1812, the Allied victory at Salamanca provided the Surrey with an opportunity to add lustre to its own representation of Badajoz:

> The splendid VICTORY OF SALAMANCA and the FALL OF BADAJOZ; the piece produced at this Theatre under the latter Title, and which was constantly received with the most flattering applause, will by particular desire, be reproduced on this occasion.[109]

Knowingly competing against Astley's carefully planned spectacle, Elliston ascribed similar urgency to his theatre's use of set design – this time, locating patriotic significance not only in the fidelity of his scenography, but in the geographical pattern presented. In the lead-up to the triumphant storming of Badajoz, the Surrey offered a representation of a Portuguese village (busy with wedding preparations), followed by the depiction of a Portuguese village plundered

---

[107] See *A Short Description of Badajoz, and the surrounding country; With Extracts from the London Gazette. Explanatory of the Picture Exhibiting in the PANORAMA, Leicester Square, Representing the Siege in 1812* (London, 1813).

[108] *MC*, 28 April 1812.

[109] *MC*, 31 August 1812. The Surrey was also competing against Astley's 'grand Military Spectacle in two acts': *The Battle of SALAMANCA! The Town Major and Spanish Heroine*.

and destroyed, and then, finally, the view before Badajoz (in Extremadura, Spain). Determined by an overall goal of charting the movement of the Allied troops from Portugal into Spain, the play not only celebrated Anglo-Portuguese success in driving away the French but introduced audiences to a new chapter in the British military campaign in the Peninsula. The Surrey's representation of the final view before Badajoz provided audiences with an horizon expanded along both literal and figurative axes. The progression of scenes was calculated for maximum effect, unfolding a sequence of events that climaxed with the storming of Badajoz and, by implication, the brilliant victory at Salamanca that this would facilitate, as inevitable rallying points for British patriotic feeling.

At Sadler's Wells, Dibdin the Younger also presented audiences with a new military entertainment called *The Battle of Salamanca*. Boasting specially commissioned music and scenery, the piece introduced a 'Bayonet Charge' modelled on the real battle. Dibdin the Younger offers a detailed description of it in his *Memoirs*:

> My readers will probably recollect, that the English and French charged each other, each in an immensely extended line; and that each marched up the Charge, with the utmost coolness and intrepidity; – their Bayonets were locked in each other, – an instant pause took place, the Eyes of each fixed upon his adversary; when the determined aspect of the British Soldiers, produced such an appalling effect upon the elite of the Emperor, that they suddenly and simultaneously,

Figure 3.4   Isaac Robert Cruikshank, *The Battle of Salamanca*. Illustration from Francis L. Clarke's *The Life of the Most Noble Arthur, Marquis and Earl of Wellington*, 1812. © The Trustees of the British Museum.

turned tail, and ran off, at speed. Doubtlessly, the high character which the English Soldiers, who are said to surpass all the troops in the known world at the *pas de charge*, bore, was most material in effecting this unprecedented panic.[110]

In his depiction of the confrontation between the two troops as a moment of silent engagement – the bayonets are locked and the soldiers' eyes fixed upon their opponents – Dibdin the Younger is, of course, more faithful to the dramatic military tableau staged at Sadler's Wells than the battle itself. He nevertheless boasted that the theatre's long stage enabled him 'to muster two very respectable *lines* of Infantry, properly armed, and accoutred, so that our *pas de charge*, in miniature, presented a very striking likeness to the full length, large as life, Portrait, from which it was copied'.[111]

Dibdin the Younger's putatively 'large as life' representation should not, however, be confused for one that was necessarily 'true to life'. Although the affective power of the bayonet scene would have been significantly heightened by the theatre's employment of real soldiers (as the manager notes, it was 'customary at all Theatres to engage bodies of the military, nightly, for such (and other) exhibitions'[112]), a first hand description of the Battle of Salamanca can provide an illuminating counter-narrative to the account recorded in Dibdin the Younger's *Memoirs*. On 22 August 1812 the *Leeds Mercury* published a letter from a local soldier serving in General Clinton's brigade. The soldier relates that once the order for the charge was given ('those heights must be carried, and we will do it with the bayonet'), the word '*Prepare*' was instantly heeded: 'all knew the meaning, and hailed the word with a shout that rent the sky; we advanced double quick and the enemy fled'.[113] He naturally makes no mention of the tense dramatic stillness to which Dibdin the Younger refers in his *Memoirs*. It is only, in fact, the act of writing itself that occasions the opportunity for reflection. This is powerfully realised by the soldier's recounting of the troops' further advance 'under a heavy fire of grape and canister, and musquetry'. When ordered to "Charge", he explains:

> Off we set, our men falling on every side in sections. – The enemy stood till the bayonets of our men's firelocks were bloodied to the sockets. By the holy snuff, (a Spanish oath) the thought makes my heart jump again, for I did not know whether my head was on or off at that time; but our fellows were not to be restrained, and it was a long time before they could be stopped. At last we collected together what was left of us.[114]

In this confrontation the bayonet is no longer merely a weapon of intimidation: its very real 'bloodied' socket mirrors, instead, the soldier's dissociative state of not knowing 'whether my head was on or off'. Such a scene of decimation resists

---

[110]   Dibdin (the Younger), *Memoirs*, 107.
[111]   Dibdin (the Younger), *Memoirs*, 107.
[112]   Dibdin (the Younger), *Memoirs*, 107.
[113]   *Leeds Mercury*, 22 August 1812 ('Victory in Spain').
[114]   *Leeds Mercury*, 22 August 1812 ('Victory in Spain').

expression (as highlighted by the writer's jarring citation of a Spanish, rather than English, oath to almost, inappropriately, comic effect). The description of the day's battle then closes with a list of casualties: 'we have no less than 81 officers killed and wounded in the division', the soldier states, noting that 'the number of rank and file we have not been able to ascertain'. His letter, like Dibdin the Younger's entertainment, celebrates the decisiveness of the victory at Salamanca, but it does not overwrite the horrific violence that was needed to secure it.[115]

In her study of the minor theatres' responses to the Napoleonic Wars, Gillian Russell compellingly argues that 'the representation of war as spectacle ... entailed a development of the symbolic relationship between stage space and the field of battle'.[116] While the appearance of reality was critical, Russell notes that the battles re-staged at the minor theatres were vulnerable to becoming – and indeed were often criticised as –'overdetermined'. She concludes that 'people attended Astley's and Sadler's Wells not because their entertainments were more or less theatrical [than those at the patent theatres] but because the theatre, like the camp and the parade ground, catered to the desire to *see* war'.[117] While *The Siege and Capture of Badajoz* and *The Battle of Salamanca* strongly attest to this curiosity for the spectacular, they also emphasise, however, the need to understand the war as a series of events that could be easily narrativised.[118]

The representations of the siege of Badajoz (at the Amphitheatre) and of the Battle of Salamanca (at Sadler's Wells) speak to the importance attached to the temporal, as well as visual, dimensions of the minors' military re-enactments. Mary Favret's discussion of 'wartime' offers a productive framework in which to understand this. 'Waiting', as Favret explains, was a crucial component of the early nineteenth-century experience of war. Drawing upon Rory Muir's scholarship on the military tactics of the Napoleonic period, Favret underlines how both Napoleon and Wellington had recognised – and invested in – 'the strategic advantage of keeping troops busily in abeyance', while 'the home front discovered its own versions of waiting in wartime and filled them with affective potency'.[119] In especially incisive readings of Jane Austen's *Persuasion* (1818) and the war diary of the sailor John Wetherell, Favret traces the anxieties occasioned by this 'meantime' of war. She explores how, by chronicling the 'everyday', writers

---

[115]   As Jerome Christensen observes: 'Wartime, as all-engrossing spectacle, does not exist for frontline soldiers mired in the intimate, blind, and chronically tactical space of the battlefield; it is concocted for those whom, in "Fears in Solitude," Coleridge calls "spectators and not combatants," those who "read of war, / The best amusement for our morning meal!"'. *Romanticism at the End of History* (Baltimore: Johns Hopkins University Press, 2000), 4.

[116]   Russell, *Theatres of War*, 70

[117]   Russell, *Theatres of War*, 74.

[118]   This narrative demands, significantly, an opportunity for retrospection otherwise illusive to the real experience 'wartime' (Compare Christensen, *Romanticism at the End of History*, 5).

[119]   Favret, *War at a Distance*, 75.

sought to escape from 'the conflicted position of a wartime that falls between expectation and belatedness'.[120]

Dibdin the Younger seems to define *The Battle of Salamanca* as a kind of wartime spectacle actively engaged in an attempt to overturn the prolonged apprehension associated with this domestic experience of the 'meantime'. For Dibdin the Younger, the climax is reached as the lines march upon the charge. But once the soldiers are face-to-face, intimidation itself proves decisive enough to forestall physical violence. With their bayonets 'locked in each other' and the 'Eyes of each fixed upon his adversary', the pressing pause that should serve as a prelude to the employment of the bayonets gives way, instead, to the flight of the enemy, who 'suddenly and simultaneously, turned tail, and ran off, at speed'. This effectively defines the 'bayonet charge' as the key event within Dibdin the Younger's representation of the larger battle (even though, as the letter to the *Leeds Mercury* explains, it was, in fact, preliminary to a violent bayonet attack later that day).

The military re-enactments staged at the minor theatres can thus be seen to have offered selective interpretations of the Allied army's successes in the Peninsula. The representations of Ciudad Rodrigo, Badajoz and Salamanca staged at Astley's Amphitheatre, the Surrey and Sadler's Wells replaced the complex human dimensions of warfare with one of geopolitical order. While melodramatic spectacles and burlettas could be variously interpreted, these military re-enactments were tightly linear. Entertainments such as *The Siege and Fall of Badajoz* and *The Battle of Salamanca* required audiences to plot military events in ways that necessarily ascribed meaning to the Peninsular War and inspired faith in the promise of its final (triumphant) resolution. Although this amounted, primarily, to a cashing-in on patriotic feeling, the minor theatres' re-enactments of the British army's successes in Spain and Portugal also offered an important release from the dreadful anticipation of waiting for the latest war news – a liberation, in short, from the oppressive confines of the 'meantime'.

Heroes

To celebrate the victory at Salamanca, Wellington was given the title of 'Marquess', and a handsome pension to support it.[121] In 1813, the year of the Battle of Vitoria, he would receive further honours. As Rory Muir details:

---

[120]   Favret, *War at a Distance*, 161–5; 77.

[121]   Muir, *The Defeat of Napoleon*, 217. See also Francis Burdett's argument that there should have been a general inquiry into the military campaign before the House of Commons was called upon to give its Vote of Thanks for Salamanca. (Burdett contested the government's response to the battle by suggestively adding it to the existing catalogue of 'boasted and overpraised victories'.) Hansard (HC), 'Parliamentary debates: Vote of Thanks to the Marquis of Wellington &c, for the Victory of Salamanca, (3 December 1812), in *Parliamentary Debates*, 24: 150–71 (162).

At the beginning of the year he had ben made Colonel of the Royal Regiment of Horse Guards (the Blues) – a post both honourable and lucrative. In March he became a Knight of the Garter on the death of the Marquess of Buckingham, whose aide-de-camp he had been at Dublin Castle in 1788–9. The Portuguese made him Duque de Victoria in April,[122] while Parliament thanked him and his army for Vitoria without dissent – Lord Holland giving a panegyric on his skill.[123]

Ministerial recommendations that Wellington be made a field marshal in the British army were also finally heeded. Although the Duke of York had previously opposed this for pragmatic reasons, the Battle of Vitoria (21 June 1813) ensured that Wellington's promotion was swiftly conferred by the Prince Regent himself. The Allied victory had, after all, struck the decisive blow to the French occupation of Spain. Vitoria allowed for the liberation of the northern provinces (with the exception of Catalonia) and prompted the French troops to make a hasty escape to France.[124]

When news of Vitoria reached England in the first week of July, it was greeted with three nights of general illuminations. Wellington's exploits were celebrated by fantastic displays at Carlton House, Somerset House, and the homes of the Spanish Ambassador and Spanish Consul. At Vauxhall, more than one thousand guests joined the Royal Family and foreign ambassadors to celebrate the Allied success. The pleasure gardens were decorated to their full magnificence: Wellington's name was projected onto the colonnades, as were 'the names of all the principal cities and towns in the Peninsula' – known as 'the scenes of British glory' – to which were added, 'on the same line, the names of the British generals who had achieved the victories'.[125] The standard of the 100th regiment of French horse (which had been taken during the battle) was put on display and Marshal Jourdan's baton visibly placed among the plate.[126]

In the summer of 1813 Vitoria seemed synonymous with victory and, once again, the minor theatres were quick to add to the roistering.[127] In his *Memoirs*,

---

[122]   The title 'Duque da Vitória' (literally meaning 'the duke of the victory') in fact predates the Spanish battle. In his account of the Battle of Vitoria Southey notes: 'It is also remarkable, that the Prince of Brazil, before the battle of Vitoria was fought, should have conferred the title of Duque da Vitoria upon Lord Wellington'. Robert Southey, *History of the Peninsular War* (London, 1832), 3: 627.

[123]   Muir, *The Defeat of Napoleon*, 265–6.

[124]   Muir, *The Defeat of Napoleon*, 265 and Chandler, *Dictionary*, 469.

[125]   Rev. Joseph Nightingale, *London and Middlesex; or, An Historical, Commercial, & Descriptive Survey of the Metropolis of Great-Britain: Including Sketches of its Environs, and a Topographical Account...* (London, 1815), 3: 73–7 (75).

[126]   Nightingale, *London and Middlesex*, 74. On Jourdan's baton, see also George Cruikshank's satirical print *The Battle of Vittoria* (7 July 1813).

[127]   The Franco-Spanish Treaty of Valençay was signed on 10 December 1813. In his eagerness to re-consolidate his position in the Rhine, Napoleon reluctantly agreed to Ferdinand VII's release from French captivity and acknowledged his restoration. Fraser, *Napoleon's Cursed War*, 467.

Figure 3.5   Unmounted fan leaf in commemoration of Wellington's successes
at Salamanca and Vitoria, published by J. Lauriere [1813]. At
the centre is a bust of the Duke of Wellintgon with two English
soldiers either side of him. On the wings are two poems of 18 lines
commemorative of the Allied victories at Salamanca and Vitoria ©
The Trustees of the British Museum.

Charles Dibdin the Younger recalls celebrating 'the Duke of Wellington's Victories
with a 'musical and military melang[e]', *Vittoria, or Wellington's Laurels*.[128] Songs
from Dibdin the Younger's *Vittoria*, which included 'Jourdan and His Marshal's
Staff' (sung to the familiar tune of 'Sir Sidney Smith') were re-printed in popular
songbooks of the period. His musical ballet of action was performed within a
week of the first London illuminations. Its full title – *Vittoria; or, Wellington's
Laurels* – emphasises Wellington's apotheosis as the nation's great hero.[129] But in
a theatre that significantly depended upon the patronage of the lower orders, the
contributions made by ordinary soldiers were also given some accolade.

In the second scene of *Vittoria* the song 'The Captain's a Bold Man' calls for a
trio of English, Irish, and Spanish soldiers to sing to the tune of 'Balinamona ora'.
By setting the song to a popular Irish tune Dibdin the Younger gives appreciative
acknowledgement to the Irish soldiers who took part in the British campaign. The
Spanish soldier, by contrast, is marginalised by the song's arrangement. In the
second verse, the Spaniard sings: 'The Spaniards and Portuguese both have agreed |

---

[128]   Dibdin (the Younger), *Memoirs*, 107.
[129]   Dibdin the Younger's celebration of Wellington extended to various plays that
season, including the 1814 aquadrama *Vive Le Roi; or, The White Cockade* (London, 1814).
See esp. Scene 11, which takes place in a tent in the Allied Camp and includes a song by a
British Officer saluting Wellington as 'Arthur, Britain's pride'. *Vive Le Roi*, 24.

To carry their point or for freedom to bleed'.[130] But his role in the song is eclipsed almost entirely by the humorous rivalry between the British soldiers. Dibdin the Younger playfully exploits contemporary Anglo-Irish animosity with soldiers who compete over their devotion to the cause, attempting to outdo each other as they issue a series of threats against the French. This play-off within the British army is realised through the song's many puns, as marked by its opening, which sees the English soldier sing in celebration of Wellington's war *tactics* while the Irishman puts up his fists to represent 'a nice pair of *tack-sticks*' against the French.[131]

Dibdin the Younger's song initially exploits but then seeks to repair local animosities by showing how the Peninsular War had helped unite an otherwise suspicious army of diverse British recruits. There was a large measure of wishful thinking in this. The war in the Peninsula had brought added urgency to the 'Irish question' and made relations between the nation states even more tense. Ireland featured repeatedly in the *Examiner*'s political and theatrical journalism. In response to popular (mis)representations of the stage Irishman, in 1808 Hunt condemned Richard Cumberland's comic opera *The Jew of Mogadore* for its placing of an Irishman in Morocco, 'merely for the sake of his brogue'.[132] 'The moment ... one sees an Irishman coming on the stage, all the blunders of the modern drama, voluntary and involuntary, rush upon one's mind', Hunt explained, when reviewing Marianne Chambers's new comedy *Ourselves* (1811). Appreciative of Chambers's talents but disappointed with her characterisation of the Irish Mr O'Shanaghan, Hunt concludes his review with the recommendation that the playwright excise her 'occasional pruriency of imagination'.[133] Although reductive stereotypes of the Irishman prevail in Dibdin the Younger's *Vittoria*, they are not gratuitous, in contrast to the examples cited by Hunt. The Irishman's propensity to violence remains comic, but his already mentioned boast of beating the French with his '*tack-sticks*' symbolises, in this instance, the attributes of a brave soldier committed to the war. Richard Allen Cave describes the 'stock Paddy' of the period as a character defined by his 'dishevelled appearance', 'shambling gait', Irish brogue, and inseparable keg and shillelagh (symbols of 'booze and violence').[134] It is all the more significant, then, that instead of his shillelagh (cudgel), Dibdin the Younger's Irishman should hold up his fists – a declaration of his preparedness for hand-to-hand combat in the fight for Spanish liberty.

In 1814 *Fairburn's Comic Constellation* reprinted several songs from Dibdin the Younger's *Vittoria*, including 'Ifs and Buts' (another trio by English, Irish

---

[130]   Charles Isaac M. Dibdin, *Vocal Compositions, &c. in the New Musical Ballet of Action, called 'Vittoria, or Wellington's Laurels'*... (London, 1813), 3–5 (4) (Scene 2).

[131]   Dibdin (the Younger), *Vittoria, or Wellington's Laurels*, 3.

[132]   *TE*, 8 May 1808.

[133]   *TE*, 10 March 1811.

[134]   Richard Allen Cave, 'Staging the Irishman', in Bratton, Cave, et al. (eds), *Acts of Supremacy*, 63.

and Spanish soldiers) and the eponymous 'Wellington's Laurels'.[135] The latter was delayed for the finale of Dibdin the Younger's play, which saw the stage illuminated in honour of Wellington, 'The Great Captain', and a portrait of the hero raised in full sight of the auditorium, while the company – and most likely the audience – sang in unison to his renown. With a chorus of 'Heart of Oak is our chief! hearts of oak are our men!', *Vittoria*'s finale celebrated Wellington as a saviour 'Who supports falling freedom' and 'oppression knocks down'.[136] Vitoria may have been an Allied victory, but at Sadler's Wells it was celebrated as yet another unquestionably British achievement.

Also included in *Fairburn's Comic Constellation* was 'Vittoria; or King Joseph's Last Gun', performed at Astley's Amphitheatre to the tune of 'The Bold Dragoon'. The song recounts the events that led to the engagement at Vitoria. Napoleon is caricatured as 'little Boneyparte', 'With his swagg'ring frown, | And iron crown', while the Spaniards (represented by a 'master Don') respond indignantly to Bonaparte's gift of the Spanish throne to his 'brother Joey':

> No damme if you do:
>> For one and all
>> Will stand or fall,
> To our own monarch's cause so hearty,
>> For while we're back'd by England,
> Lads, a fig for Mr. Boneyparte.
>> Whack! pull away, &c.[137]

The verse allows for a direct dramatisation of the Spanish point of view but, as with Dibdin the Younger's song, the main part belongs to a British voice. Notice how the speaker is casually referred to as an anonymous 'master Don' and the successful realisation of his resolution made to depend upon British support for the war. The fourth verse proudly asserts that as soon as British help was sought, 'in a crack, each Briton swore | He'd join 'em heart and hand'.[138] This nationalist perspective is confirmed and validated by the use of the first person plural to celebrate British ethics:

> For, 'tis well known,
> We've always shewn
>> Our friendship for each injur'd party,
>> Och! 'tis Britons have the knack
> Of thumping little Boneyparte.
>> Whack! pull away, &c.[139]

[135] *Fairburn's Comic Constellation, or Eccentric Repository for 1814, Embracing an Extensive, Eccentric, Curious, & Droll Collection of New Songs, Now singing and lately sung at the Theatres Royal, Sadler's Wells, &c...* (London, 1814).
[136] 'Wellington's Laurels' in *Fairburn*, 'The Finale and Chorus', 22.
[137] 'Vittoria ... Last Gun', in *Fairburn*, 19.
[138] 'Vittoria... Last Gun', in *Fairburn*, 19.
[139] 'Vittoria... Last Gun', in *Fairburn*, 19.

'[B]rave Wellington and British lads' save the day, chasing Napoleon's armies back to France and increasing national glory with the successes reaped by the army and navy alike. In 'Vittoria; or King Joseph's Last Gun', as in Dibdin the Younger's popular songs about the Peninsular War, pride in the British character seems fully validated by the recent military victory. But this celebration came at a cost to the native troops whose vital contributions to the Allied war effort were consequently overlooked.

By the end of 1813 Wellington's cult of adulation was in full swing: it positively thrived after Waterloo, when Sadler's Wells, for example, announced its new song 'Waterloo; or, Wellington for ever'.[140] With equal enthusiasm, on 11 September 1815, the Royal Circus (the Surrey having reverted to its original name) commemorated the Battle of Waterloo with another popular adaptation of Shakespeare, this time, of *Richard III*.[141] The Circus's production of *Richard III*, which was performed for the benefit night of its stage manager, T.P. Cooke, poignantly re-imagined the Battle of Bosworth Field as the site of Napoleon's final defeat. Playbills printed in eye-catching red and black ink commemorated the event by drawing specific attention to the appearance of Richmond, 'Accoutred in a REAL FRENCH CUIRASS, Stripped from a Cuirassier, on the Field of Battle, at Waterloo and which bears the indenture of Several Musket Shot and Sabre Cuts'.[142] By replacing stage property with real battle armour, the Circus production presented its audiences with an authentic relic from the Napoleonic Wars, all the more valuable for its 'Several Musket Shot and Sabre Cuts'. The play's dramatisation of Richmond's success in battle and his subsequent coronation as Henry VII thereby became counterparts to the new world order symbolised in 1815 by Wellington's triumph at Waterloo.

---

[140]   Advertisement: Sadler's Wells, 3 July 1815. V&A.

[141]   Robert Elliston gave up management of the Surrey in March 1814. The lease was then taken up by a triumvirate of managers (Dunn, Heywood and Branscomb), 'with a view to returning the theatre to its "Royal Circus and Equestrian" form'. William G. Knight, *A Major London 'Minor': the Surrey Theatre 1805–1865* (London: The Society for Theatre Research, 1997), 17.

[142]   Royal Circus Playbill, 11 September 1815, V&A. After Napoleon's defeat there was a boom in Waterloo tourism. Numerous visitors (Walter Scott and Robert Southey among them) returned home with relics from the battlefield, and a Waterloo Museum was established in London (Pall Mall). See Stuart Semmel, 'Reading the Tangible Past: British Tourism, Collecting, and Memory after Waterloo' in *Representations* 69 Special Issue: Grounds for Remembering (Winter 2000), 9–37.

Eccentricities and *Disappointments*

Philip Shaw reads Waterloo 'as a wound or fissure in the text of historical memory'.[143] His engaging study *Waterloo and the Romantic Imagination* (2002) examines the representational difficulties entailed by the battle's 'sublime' status and the instabilities experienced in its aftermath (including, pointedly, the threat to national identity associated with peacetime):

> The contest between Britain and France was … imagined, on one level, as a form of total war, of system against system predicated on the inevitability of a decisive outcome. But warfare unbound, whether this is imagined in the origin or in the tendency of society, was regarded by many as a principle to be resisted … for every assertion of the inherent value of violent confrontation there were many more from those who wished to transform the progress of history once and for all.[144]

Shaw thus convincingly argues that Waterloo – an event that 'exceeded the simplistic desires of the state' – resisted being reduced to 'the status of a historical object'.[145] With this in mind, I here focus on the very different but nevertheless acute representational difficulties already experienced in 1814, a year marked by Napoleon's first abdication and the return of Ferdinand VII to Spain.

British hopes had ridden high for Ferdinand's restoration, as exemplified by Astley's 1813 production of *Ferdinand of Spain; or, Ancient Chivalry*; a 'Grand Heroic, Equestrian and Pedestrian Spectacle, in Two Parts' staged during the final phases of the Peninsular Campaign. The entertainment hinged upon what might be best imagined as a spectacular scene of moral retribution. In the words of *The Times*:

> A Castle is fired, and a splendid scene of conflagration ensues: the falling beams, enveloped in masses of flame, – the explosion, – the ruinous confusion, – together with the trampling of horses, formed one of the most striking combinations that we ever witnessed.[146]

The 'blow up', as Jane Moody attests, was one of the great mainstays of the illegitimate repertoire; a marker, as she describes it, of 'that irreducible confrontation between freedom and despotism, good and evil'.[147] But, if in 1813 Ferdinand could be thus effectively romanticised as a figure of heroic agency, then the violent repression that characterised his government would quickly bring an end to such idealisations.

---

[143] Philip Shaw, *Waterloo and the Romantic Imagination* (Basingstoke: Palgrave Macmillan, 2002), 6.

[144] Shaw, *Waterloo*, 8–9.

[145] Shaw, *Waterloo*, 9; 15.

[146] *The Times*, 20 April 1813.

[147] Moody, *Illegitimate Theatre*, 28. See also 98–106.

Ferdinand VII received an enthusiastic welcome upon his return to Valencia on 16 April 1814. In fact, such was the fervour generated by his person that the townspeople unhitched the horses from his carriage in order to pull the coach for themselves.[148] But if Ferdinand had the support of the local populace, he was quick to lose the favour of the British government. Ministers had expected Ferdinand to swear an oath to uphold Spain's new civil rights and to accept certain limitations to his rule in line with the 1812 Constitution (passed by the Cortes in his absence, and guaranteeing limited religious and political freedoms to the Spanish people). Instead, Ferdinand abolished the Constitution and the Cortes' decrees, making it clear that 'anyone who advocated obedience' to either of these 'would be guilty of lese-majesty and punishable by death'.[149] Ronald Fraser explains that as a result of such measures, 'the country's educated classes were now divided into two warring camps'; 'the reformers on the one hand, the ultra-conservatives, backed by the Church, on the other'.[150] It became increasingly clear that the Allied victory in Spain had not assured political stability.

Britons' political disappointments with the restored regime were forcefully registered by the *Monthly Review*'s response to Preston Fitzgerald's *Spain Delivered; A Poem in Two Cantos* (1813), which took advantage of a late notice in December 1814 in order to measure the distance between Spain in 1813 and the present day.[151] 'Thousands of British lives have been immolated, and millions of British treasure expended', the reviewer argues, 'only to recall the most senseless and savage despotism, coupled with all the horrors of the Inquisition'.[152] Fitzgerald's poem had been written in jubilant anticipation that the battles of Salamanca and Vitoria would result in the 'liberation' of Spain, figured, significantly, as an event both physical and spiritual ('When rising freedom's radiant pow'r | Would pour the golden flood of day, | With renovate, refulgent sway').[153] Fitzgerald seems to have anticipated a political horizon similar to that envisaged by Astley at his conclusion to *Ferdinand of Spain*, but the expectations of both authors exceeded

---

[148]   Fraser, *Napoleon's Cursed War*, 467. Ferdinand VII's return to Madrid was greeted with equal ebullience. Ibid., 470.

[149]   Fraser, *Napoleon's Cursed War*, 468.

[150]   'Three nineteenth-century civil wars and the greatest of all in the twentieth, followed by forty years of Franco's dictatorship – more than a century and a half in all – would be needed before this division could be sufficiently healed in a modern constitution which permitted the free interplay of parliamentary politics under a constitutional monarchy'. Fraser, *Napoleon's Cursed War*, 470.

[151]   See 'Translator's Preliminary Remarks' to *The Inquisition Unmasked: Being an Historical and Philosophical Account of that Tremendous Tribunal*, trans. by William Walton (London, 1816); and George Cruikshank's satirical print *Twelfth Night; or, What You Will* (1814), wherein Ferdinand VII is depicted wearing a crown gruesomely adorned with hanging corpses.

[152]   'Monthly Catalogue: Article 12', *MR*, December 1814, 75: 437–9 (437).

[153]   Qtd. in *MR*, December 1814, 75: 438.

the subsequent reality. By December 1814 the reviewer for the *Monthly* could only lament that

> Alas! the Deliverance of Spain, which so recently excited all the enthusiasm of joy, is now become a subject which is overshadowed with the most melancholy reflections! … Now, the Deliverance of Spain is only the transfer of her from one despotism to another.[154]

The reviewer's repeated pun on Fitzgerald's title not only keeps the ostensible subject of the review in focus but also indexes the abortive nature of Spain's promised 'deliverance'.

Ferdinand's return posed, then, considerable representational challenges to British commentators of the Peninsular War. I would like to suggest that Jane Scott's apparent ambivalence towards post-war Spain testifies to at least some of these frustrations. The 1814–1815 season was an important one for the Sans Pareil, which had undergone several improvements in the period of its closure during the summer and autumn months. When the theatre reopened in December 1814 audiences benefitted from an enlarged playhouse with a new front and neoclassical designs that adorned the exterior and interior. The pit had been expanded to accommodate eight hundred spectators, and twelve new boxes added that allowed the house, when full, to take in £200. Other embellishments, such as a central ventilator, aimed at improving audiences' comfort and imparting the overall impression that the theatre they attended was a more refined establishment (now called the Strand Theatre).[155] In celebration of this grand reopening, Jane Scott wrote a new burletta, *Eccentricities; or, Mistakes at Madrid*, which was performed 22 times between 26 December 1814 and 16 February 1815.[156] Its title alerted audiences to a Spanish theme and implied that there would be comic results for its advertised 'eccentricities' and 'mistakes'. Four years earlier, Scott had also chosen a Spanish-themed play to inaugurate her 1810 season and showcase the alterations then made to her playhouse; *Disappointments; or, Love in Castile* receiving its premiere on 3 December 1810 (as discussed above).[157] On both occasions, Scott sought to combine her audiences' curiosity to see the theatre's improved play-space with their interests in Iberian affairs.

The four years that separated the two productions had, however, resulted in markedly different opinions about Spain and its government. If in 1810 Scott had wavered uneasily between her wish to explore Peninsular politics and satisfy audiences' received ideas about the people, religion and culture of Spain, then in

---

[154] *MR*, December 1814, 75: 437.

[155] *The Adelphi Theatre 1806–1900*: 'The 1814–1815 Season': Theatre History Summary <http://www.umass.edu/AdelphiTheatreCalendar/m14d.htm> [Accessed 09.04.14].

[156] <http://www.umass.edu/AdelphiTheatreCalendar/m14d.htm> [Accessed 09.04.14].

[157] The improvements to the theatre before the first performance of *Disappointments* were also advertised in the playbills: 'The House has been embellished, in the Audience Part' (SP Playbill, 3 December 1810, V&A).

1814, Britons' very real 'disappointments' with the Bourbon restoration placed even greater pressures on a politicised Spanish play. Once again, Scott seems to have recognised the need to tread a fine line. Despite the potentially topical resonance of its title, *Eccentricities; or, Mistakes in Madrid* centred on the themes of love, marriage and mistaken identity. There was, furthermore, nothing distinctly Spanish about the play's action or characterisation.

Eccentricities opens in a village near Madrid, with 'lads and lasses dancing around a poll decorated with flowers'.[158] The attraction of the play's foreign setting is, however, immediately qualified by Scott's unmistakably English depiction of the Mayday festivities, which sees the first scene conclude with a rendition of 'God Save the King' after the wedding announcements made by the town crier.[159] Mayday celebrations are rooted in the history of most Western European countries, and did not, therefore, require such irreducibly English signifiers. Indeed, after 1808, springtime celebrations in the free areas of Spain had become inextricably associated with the memory of Madrid's *dos de mayo* rebellion. Murat's bloody reprisal of the rebellion had transformed the rioters in Madrid from victims into political martyrs, and news of the uprising had not only fuelled the resistance effort in other Spanish provinces but played a crucial role in the securement of the Anglo-Spanish alliance. It is curious, therefore, that in the winter of 1814, Scott should have chosen to write about Mayday in Madrid, seemingly ignoring that 2 May 1808 was one the most symbolic dates in the Spanish political calendar. The version of her play submitted to Larpent reveals other irregularities. The play is given two subtitles – *Eccentricities; or, Mistakes at Madrid; or, The Village Witch* – while the character list offers two versions of the play's dramatis personae; the first, 'If Played Spanish', and the second, 'If Played English'. In this scheme, Don Fransisco, 'If Played English', becomes Sir Francis Fairthorn, the Marquis de Marmont becomes Lord St Clarville, while Donna Julia's English counterpart becomes simply Julia (in contrast to Donna Marcella, who acquires the distinctly Anglicised name of Winifred). The stage directions then describe the play's setting in 'either Madrid and a village near it or London – and Environs'.[160]

After a run of performances, playwrights would often tweak their play-scripts in reaction to popular audience response (resulting in printed texts that often differed in many points from the manuscript copies sent for licensing). But political feeling is likely to have accounted for at least some of Scott's hesitations between a Spanish or English setting. Even *Disappointments*, which provided only obscure references to Spanish politics, at least delivered on its promise of a Spanish setting, and included an intriguing account of 'The Plot preceding the opening of the Piece', which served as an important supplement to the main action. Jane Scott's apparent indifference to *Eccentricities*' Spanish inflections seems to

---

[158]   Jane Scott, *Eccentricities; or, Mistakes at Madrid; or, The Village Witch* (1814), Huntington Library Larpent Collection 1836, at the British Library, F 254/90, 1 (1.1).

[159]   Scott, *Eccentricities*, 5 (1.1).

[160]   Scott, *Eccentricities*, 1 (1.1).

point to a personal uneasiness with Ferdinand's Spain; or, at the very least, to her recognition that by December 1814, the political situation in Spain ensured that a Spanish-themed comedy carried much less commercial appeal.

─────────────

The managers of London's minor theatres operated under difficult working conditions, subject not only to legal censorship but also intense rivalry and meddling from the patent committees, possessive of their rights to legitimate drama. Under these demanding conditions, the minor theatres helped develop pantomime into what Hunt termed 'the best medium of dramatic satire'.[161] The Olympic's production of *Harlequin & Don Quixote* (January 1813) offers a good example of the ways in which contemporary pantomimes succeeded in tapping into audiences' larger wartime interests. Described as 'a New Grand, Romantic, Serio Comic-Pantomime' complete with a 'Grand Burlesque Charge of Cavalry', *Harlequin & Don Quixote* was an entertainment that clearly intended to not only amuse but instruct the Olympic's patrons.[162] The choice of Spanish characters and military action reflected Britons' new sense of optimism after Salamanca and the general anticipation that the campaign in Spain was approaching its final stages. Pantomimes like *Harlequin & Don Quixote* seem to have been particularly well suited to charting the public's changing opinions about the war without unduly alarming the political censors.

Theatre proprietors, whether minor or patent, shared the fear that over-excited audiences might degenerate into savage, unruly mobs. But audience activism at the more populist minor theatres could be particularly dangerous. On the whole, the minor theatres tended to adopt what could pass as conservative responses to the war. They staged entertainments that ridiculed Roman Catholicism, made fun of Spaniards' complicated love intrigues, and saluted the patriotism of British soldiers and sailors. Many of the entertainments discussed in this chapter are nevertheless more politically nuanced than they first appear. In addition to the alternative readings already offered, it is worth noting that several of the entertainments discussed in this chapter exhibited a fascination with the Spanish countryside and peasant life. In *The Wild Man*, Dibdin the Younger presents an assertive group of peasants who are organised and efficient enough to arrest Don Quixote shortly after his first mysterious appearance. Scott also opens her politically circumspect *Disappointments* with a group of peasants performing a dance. At the Olympic, among the several supernumeraries listed for *Harlequin & Don Quixote*, the playbills listed 'country people' whose centrality to the pantomime was underscored by the manager's recognition that 'numerous auxiliaries [were] expressly engaged for the occasion'.[163] Similarly, in August

─────────────

[161] *TE*, 26 January 1817.
[162] Olympic Playbill, 11 January 1813. LMA.
[163] Olympic Playbill, 11 January 1813. LMA.

1814 the Royalty Theatre advertised its new Spanish ballet by drawing special attention to its representation of the 'Peasants' Courtship'.[164]

Between 1808 and 1814, traditional images of the Spanish peasantry were emphatically political. Local populations had taken up arms and engaged in violent acts of retribution, as I explain in Chapter 2 when outlining Kemble's anxiety about the crowd scenes in *Julius Caesar*. But the Spanish peasants were also firmly linked to the guerrilla movement, which began, as David Chandler explains, when 'bands of defeated Spanish regular soldiery linked up with bandits, peasantry and priests'.[165] The peasants depicted in the minor theatres' wartime entertainments helped characterise this important civilian contribution to the war effort in Spain and Portugal (otherwise relegated to the margins by the predominantly nationalist emphasis placed on British sacrifice). In the minor theatres, this focus on peasant life could also serve as a reminder to popular audiences of their own political power, allowing the energetic stage presence of common men and women to be interpreted as political encouragement of a potentially radical kind.

The entertainments at the minor theatres appear to have been crucially implicated in the movement towards total war as a new form of warfare demanding mass participation; 'a war of peoples' in contrast to the familiar 'war of elites', as Russell posits.[166] In line with recent scholarship highlighting the important role played by print culture in the consolidation of such experiences, this chapter has repeatedly drawn attention to the ways in which contemporary journalism was used to formulate new entertainments, such as John Astley's Brazilian spectacle of 1808.[167] Newspapers not only provided a space in which productions were habitually advertised and reviewed, but from which managers often culled sensational plotlines or the statistical details needed for realistic re-enactments. Under the persistent pressure to provide audiences with something new, the minor theatres became adept at the production of topical repertoires, as exemplified by their re-staging of the battles of Basque Roads, Ciudad Rodrigo, Badajoz, Salamanca and Vitoria. During the Peninsular War, London's minor theatres were more than venues for popular entertainment: they disseminated 'news' in their own right; provided a forum for public opinion; and, through the re-enactment of recent battles, aimed to offer an antidote to the anxious 'meantime' of war.

Despite the ban on spoken dramas, the minor theatres responded to the Peninsular Campaign with a range of politically relevant and provocative entertainments. While the prohibition of speech and the geographical distances that characterised London's older minor theatres entailed certain disadvantages,

---

164 Royalty Theatre Playbill, 16 August 1814. LMA.
165 Chandler, *Dictionary*, 187.
166 Russell, *Theatres of War*, 33.
167 See esp. Favret, *War at a Distance*; and Neil Ramsey, *The Military Memoir and Romantic Literary Culture, 1780–1835* (Farnham: Ashgate, 2011).

the burlettas staged at the Sans Pareil and aquatic dramas at Sadler's Wells, for example, suggest that when it came to creating new wartime entertainments, the managers of the minor theatres were arguably more ambitious, experimental and innovative than their legitimate counterparts.[168]

---

[168] Dibdin the Younger even introduced local shop fronts as part of his popular pantomime scenery (a "walking advertisement" for his sponsors). *Memoirs*, 101.

Chapter 4
Playing to the Provinces

In London, playhouses were distinguished by the price, kind, and perceived quality of their entertainments. While the patent theatres offered comedies, tragedies and an annual Christmas pantomime, equestrian evolutions at Astley's Amphitheatre and water spectacles at Sadler's Wells represented the different kinds of non-dramatic performances available at the capital's minor theatres. This book has shown that during the Peninsular War London's disparate stages provided valuable opportunities for both the diversion and instruction of mass audiences. English theatre cannot, however, be confined to the cultural life of Westminster and its immediate vicinity. By the early nineteenth century theatrical activity was also flourishing in the provinces, where the nation's many Theatre Royals played a key role in promoting the related feelings of civic amelioration and patriotism.

This chapter focuses on Bristol as a case study for provincial theatre during the Peninsular War. In much the same way, however, that London cannot serve as an index for the varied theatrical fare that occurred outside it, nor can 'provincial theatre' be explained through generalisation. An analysis of the entertainments available at Barnstaple, Liverpool or York, for example, would testify to political and cultural pressures distinct from those discussed in this chapter. Each provincial playhouse enjoyed a unique identity. As the social historian Peter Clark underlines, 'the British urban system of the early nineteenth century was remarkable for its pluralism and diversity'.[1] I have selected Bristol as this chapter's case study because, as a busy port city, it brings together the discourses of war, trade and politics. Although the city has been primarily studied for its links to the slave trade, by the late eighteenth century Bristol enjoyed a vibrant theatrical culture, as this chapter attests. Bristol is also important for its symbolic association to Coleridge, who features prominently in this book in his capacities as playwright, journalist and Shakespearean critic.

During the Peninsular War, Bristol's Theatre Royal and Regency Theatre (an 'illegitimate' playhouse that was active from 1811 to 1813) provided local audiences with an exciting theatrical culture characterised by military bespeaks, an active tradition of dramatic criticism, the engagement of star actors and impressive on-stage spectacle. It is crucial, therefore, that we tackle what Loren Kruger calls the 'geographical parochialism' that for so many years limited British theatre studies to

---

[1]   Peter Clark, 'Introduction' to *The Cambridge Urban History of Britain.* 3 vols. *Volume 2: 1540–1840*, ed. Peter Clark (Cambridge: Cambridge University Press, 2000), 16.

the London stages.[2] This chapter adopts the revisionist agenda set by scholars such as Frederick Burwick, Jane Moody, Jill Sullivan and Kathleen Wilson – whose various studies of Romantic and Victorian provincial theatres have begun to successfully challenge our metropolitan-based assumptions – in order to investigate the extent to which the Peninsular War affected theatre-going in Bristol.[3] By exploring the entertainments provided by both the city's legitimate and illegitimate theatres this chapter spotlights the range of cultural projects that were locally available, and the ideological – as well as geographical – distances that distinguished English provincial and metropolitan cultures between 1807 and 1815.

The Provincial Landscape

In the late eighteenth century, the nation's provincial capitals began to undergo a series of civic improvements.[4] The introduction of street lighting, new architectural designs and provisions for polite amusement all aimed to increase standards of living in the provinces. An important result of this heightened local consciousness was the recognition that the margins, and not only London, could shape the nation's cultural hegemony. The actor and theatre manager James Winston was quick to recognise that the early nineteenth century offered a new age for entertainments outside of the metropolis. Between 1804 and 1805 he published 24 installments of *The Theatric Tourist*, a book that provided architectural plates, a short historical overview and lively anecdotes for each provincial theatre included.[5] His intention had been to publish 90 installments (this, in itself, being merely a sample from his working list of more than 280 provincial playhouses),[6] but the venture was cut short by inadequate

---

[2] Loren Kruger, 'History Plays (in) Britain: Dramas, Nations and Inventing the Present', in *Theorizing Practice: Redefining Theatre History*, ed. W.B. Worthen and Peter Holland (Hampshire: Palgrave Macmillan, 2003), 151–76 (151).

[3] See: *The Journal of John Waldie*, ed. Frederick Burwick <http://repositories. cdlib.org/uclalib/dsc/waldie/>, e-Scholarship Repository, California Digital Library; Jane Moody, 'Dictating to the Empire: Performance and Theatrical Geography in Eighteenth Century Britain', in Moody and O'Quinn (eds), *Cambridge Companion to British Theatre, 1730–1830*; Jill Sullivan, *The Politics of Pantomime: Regional Identity in the Theatre 1860–1900* (Hatfield: University of Hertfordshire Press, 2011); and Kathleen Wilson, *The Sense of the People: Politics, Culture, and Imperialism in England, 1715–1785* (Cambridge: Cambridge University Press, 1995), 21–41. See also Jan Fergus, *Provincial Readers in Eighteenth-Century England* (Oxford: Oxford University Press, 2006).

[4] See, esp., Peter Borsay, *The English Urban Renaissance: Culture and Society in the Provincial Town 1660–1770* (Oxford: Clarendon Press, 1989).

[5] James Winston, *The Theatric Tourist. A facsimile of the first and only edition of 1805 preceded by a facsimile of the original prospectus*, ed. Iain Mackintosh, with an Introduction by Marcus Risdell (London: Society for Theatre Research and The British Library, 2008).

[6] Bratton, *New Readings*, 30.

financial backing.[7] Notwithstanding, Winston's elegant and colourful book still offers an important testament to the popular and influential culture of theatre-going that existed in the English provinces by the time of the Peninsular War.

The emergence of Bristol's Theatre Royal – and, indeed, the majority of the playhouses listed in Winston's publication – was the result of a great boom in theatre building that occurred at the end of the previous century. One of the main incentives for this was the extension of letters patent to the provinces, which began after 1766 when Samuel Foote was awarded 'Theatre Royal' status for his playhouse in the Haymarket.[8] When Bristol acquired its patent status in 1778, the playhouse in King Street (active since 1766) received official permission to stage legitimate drama, boast the prestigious title of 'Theatre Royal' and display the royal coat of arms.[9] A decade later, in 1788, the Theatrical Representations Act empowered local magistrates to license 'legitimate' drama outside of London for a period of up to 60 days. These measures contributed to a growing sense of cultural independence from the capital. Whereas before, local theatre companies had to find all sorts of clever disguises by which to entice a paying audience, the granting of letters patent and Theatrical Representations Act transformed provincial theatrical careers from risqué ventures into esteemed forms of social entrepreneurship.[10]

Proliferating road networks and improved communications meant that metropolitan actors also benefited from the establishment of provincial Theatres Royal. When Drury Lane and Covent Garden closed for the summer months, star actors such as John Philip Kemble, Sarah Siddons and George Frederick Cooke found employment in theatres as distant as Dublin, York and Edinburgh. Profitable touring circuits also developed within the provinces; Henry Thornton, for example, managed the Oxford, Reading, Newbury and Windsor theatres.[11]

---

[7] Marcus Risdell, Introduction to *Theatric Tourist*, [n.p.]. On James Winston as theatre historian see Bratton, *New Readings*, 29–33.

[8] Foote's license was a form of compensation for a riding accident with the Duke of York that left him maimed. See Peter Thomson, *The Cambridge Introduction to English Theatre, 1660–1900* (Cambridge: Cambridge University Press, 2006), 127.

[9] The theatres at Bath and Norwich had been the first to acquire letters patent (in 1768). Allardyce Nicoll, *The Garrick Stage: Theatres and Audience in the Eighteenth Century* (Manchester: Manchester University Press, 1980), 64–5.

[10] In order to avoid legal action by local magistrates, dramatic companies often advertised 'tea parties' in which 'concerts of music' would be provided. Bristol's 1766 theatre was, in fact, 'illegal' until it received its patent status. Early playbills thus advertised 'A Concert of Music interspersed with specimens of Rhetorick' so that managers could not be accused of selling a dramatic performance *per se*. Kathleen Barker, *The Theatre Royal, Bristol 1766–1966: Two Centuries of Stage History* (London: The Society for Theatre Research, 1974), 14.

[11] Paul Ranger, 'A Matter of Choice: A Comparison of Locations and Repertoire in Some English Provincial Theatres', *Nineteenth-Century Theatre Research* 10.2, (winter 1982), 61–84.

This investment in local culture continued to be of ideological significance during the Peninsular War. From the arrival of the Asturian delegates in London to reports of guerrilla warfare in the Spanish mountains, the war in Iberia was presented to the British public as a conflict motivated by patriotic feelings that had been nurtured, first and foremost, by local allegiances. When writing about the war from the Lake District, William Wordsworth and Samuel Taylor Coleridge enjoyed what they both considered an ultimately advantageous distance from the centre of government.[12] Coleridge's decision to pointedly sign and date each of his *Letters on the Spaniards* (1809–1810) from 'Grassmere' [*sic*] could even be seen to underscore how contemporary concerns about the British 'nation' had been heightened by the Spaniards' localised responses to the French invasion.[13] But to what extent was the Peninsular War influential to the formation of a Bristolian's identity?

Although much has been written about Bristol's nineteenth-century history, the great majority of accounts have focused on the Abolition of the Slave Trade Act of 1807.[14] The consequent eclipsing of the Peninsular War period is surprising, not least because it offers the opportunity to investigate the immediate economic and social consequences of abolition to everyday life in Bristol. The loss of trade in the human trafficking that had linked Bristol's ports to West Africa, the West Indies and America meant that after 1807 Bristol became even more dependent on its other trading partners (which included, significantly, the Iberian Peninsula).[15] On 28 May 1808 *Felix Farley's Bristol Journal* reported that a neutral ship from Oporto had arrived with a cargo of wines; 'the first vessel that has loaded for this port since Portugal has been in the power of the French'.[16] Notices of this kind suggest that commercial concerns are likely to have complicated local theatrical representations of the war and its social consequences. Managers of Bristol's

---

[12]   This distance from London also entailed frustrations, however. It was often difficult to acquire the latest news and see works through to press. On the delays occasioned by the provincial post see, for example: Samuel Taylor Coleridge to Daniel Stuart (28 December 1808), in Griggs (ed.), *Letters*, 3: 151; and Samuel Taylor Coleridge to Basil Montagu (7 December 1809), in Griggs (ed.), *Letters*, 3: 162 (post-script).

[13]   Samuel Taylor Coleridge, *Letters on the Spaniards*, in *CC: EOT*, 2: 37–100. See also William Wordsworth's pamphlet *Concerning The Relations of Great Britain, Spain, and Portugal, to Each Other, and to the Common Enemy at this Crisis; and specifically as affected by the Convention of Cintra* (London, 1809).

[14]   In 2007 Bristol's Central Reference Library celebrated the 200th anniversary of the Bill with an exhibition called 'Bristol in 1807: A Sense of Place', resulting in the publication of *Bristol in 1807: Impressions of the City at the Time of Abolition*, ed. Anthony Beeson (Bristol: Redcliffe Press, 2009).

[15]   Iberian commodities (such as merino wool, sherry, and port) would have been a familiar sight at the city's docks. Spanish wool, which had formed 'one of the largest imports into Bristol', sold at inflated prices during the Peninsular War. John Latimer, *The Annals of Bristol in the Nineteenth-Century* (Bristol, 1887), 34.

[16]   *FFBJ*, 28 May 1808 ('Shipping News').

Theatre Royal and Regency Theatre realised that unlike their peers in other, more isolated provinces, they had to satisfy audiences with vested economic – as well as political – interests in Spain and Portugal.[17]

In national terms, Bristol was one of England's most affluent cities. Several of its citizens were very wealthy; mostly as a result of the city's history of slavery, foreign and domestic trade or booming finance industry, which included ship and fire insurance.[18] According to Edward Shiercliff's *Bristol and Hotwell Guide* (1805), dues from customs and exports exceeded 'half a million annually'.[19] The trade in raw materials also meant that Bristol was renowned for its many secondary industries, including sugarhouses, brass and iron foundries, and various manufactories for glass, cotton, china and wool. Bristol's position in the 1800s was not, however, quite as promising as it had seemed at the end of the eighteenth century. Then, Bristol had dominated the economic and social life of the West Country. During the Peninsular War, by contrast, the shortfall in credit resulted in rising unemployment, vagrancy and other related social hardships. The years 1808 and 1811 saw economic distress throughout Britain, resulting from the demands of war and the beginnings of agricultural and industrial depressions. Competition from the rival port city of Liverpool also meant that local merchants lost out on valuable trade. *Felix Farley's Bristol Journal* laid much of the blame on the Bristol Dock Company, whose plans for a floating harbour and to create what was called a 'new cut' in the river proved expensive and poorly managed. When the new dock finally opened in 1807 its exorbitant charges made Bristol one of the most expensive port cities in Britain. This coincided with the year of abolition and Bristolians' unease over its implications. On the edge of an identity crisis, early nineteenth-century Bristol was under acute pressure to re-assert its public image.

During the years of the Peninsular War the City Corporation thus initiated a series of attempts to underscore Bristol's reputation as a notable centre for economic exchange, political discourse, cultural enlightenment and sociability. This entailed a commitment to extend the existing programme of municipal reform, which had already resulted in the construction of an Assembly Room and theatre (designed by Thomas Patey on the model of Drury Lane). Both buildings aimed to enhance the city's 'respectability' and engender a new sense of pride

---

[17]   In 1814 Jere Hill was the Spanish Vice Consul for Bristol and its neighbouring ports. On 3 May 1814, to celebrate the sixth anniversary of the *dos de mayo* revolt, the city's '*Spanish and Portuguese Gentlemen*' met at the Montague Tavern for a celebratory dinner. The gathering was reported in detail by *FFBJ*, which reprinted the President's address in full. *FFBJ*, 7 May 1814.

[18]   W.E. Minchinton, 'Bristol – Metropolis of the West in the Eighteenth Century', The Alexander Prize Essay, *Transactions of the Royal Historical Society*, 5th series, Vol. 4 (December 1954), 69–89 (85–6).

[19]   Edward Shiercliff, *The Bristol and Hotwell Guide containing an Account of that Opulent City* (Bristol, 1805), rptd in Beeson, *Bristol in 1807*, 19.

among its citizens. In his study of the development of English urbanism, Philip Waller defines the townscape as

> an ideological as well as built environment, carrying iconographic and mythological significance. It is a disputed terrain, fought over from political, economic, and social causes and for metaphysical reasons.[20]

When the playhouse in King Street acquired 'Theatre Royal' status in 1778, it found itself at the heart of this 'disputed terrain'. Its location near the Green (one of Bristol's principal public walks) provided the local population with a symbolic site for civic communality, where a gender-mixed and socially heterogeneous audience could resume the day's round of political and social gossip.[21] Bristol may have been famous for its slaving ports, but its theatrical culture constituted a crucial aspect of its evolving identity.

Bristol's Theatre Royal

True to its Drury Lane blueprint, Bristol's Theatre Royal was rectangular in shape. Below the stage there was room for traps and other machinery: above, there was an attic space for the preparation of new scenery, which could be easily slid on stage with the help of the groove system. In 1766 the theatre held a total of 1,600 spectators (750 in the boxes, 320 in the pit and 530 in the gallery).[22] The auditorium was further augmented in 1800, following a series of modifications to the original gallery space by the architect James Saunders.[23] But if Bristol's Theatre Royal still remained considerably smaller than the enlarged Drury Lane Theatre, its capacity for scenic display was, nevertheless, granted comparable importance. As this book has shown, melodramas and pantomimes were fast becoming the main attractions for nineteenth-century theatre-goers. Scenes evoking foreign strangeness and splendour were, furthermore, very popular in Bristol, where a population composed of different nationalities and inclusive of many merchants, sailors and soldiers, resulted in an even more pronounced demand for recognisable representations of far away places.

London tastes were a key consideration for the Theatre Royal's managers, who invariably used their playbills to draw attention to an entertainment's favourable reception in the capital. A play's popularity in the metropolis became, in fact,

---

[20]   Philip Waller, 'Introduction: The English Urban Landscape: Yesterday, Today, and Tomorrow', in *The English Urban Landscape* ed. Philip Waller (Oxford: Oxford University Press, 2000), 11.

[21]   W. Sheppard, *The New Bristol Guide* (Bristol, 1804), rptd in Beeson, *Bristol in 1807*, 118.

[22]   Nicoll, *The Garrick Stage*, 41.

[23]   Nicoll, *The Garrick Stage*, 42; and 'Theatre Royal (Bristol)' entry in The Theatres Trust Website <http://www.theatrestrust.org.uk/resources/theatres/show/736-theatre-royal-bristol> [Accessed 20.04.14].

a relatively reliable indicator of whether or not managers from the provincial theatres would add it to their repertoires in the first place. This did not mean, however, that audiences in Bristol were content with straightforward imitations. The early nineteenth century marked a period of cultural organisation and change throughout Britain that made the provinces keen to assert their individuality. Audiences required that the quality of entertainments be at least equal to those presented in London, but this did not, of course, exclude the possibility that plays might be altered, improved, or altogether rejected by Bristolians' own good sense and critical judgment.

The well-kept roads connecting Bristol to the capital meant that popular London plays could be mounted within a matter of weeks. *Remorse* had opened at Drury Lane on 23 January 1813; it arrived in Bristol before the Theatre Royal's Easter closure. Playbills lauded *Remorse* as 'Mr. Coleridge's very popular new TRAGEDY ... now performing at the Theatre Royal, Drury-Lane, with the most distinguished Applause'.[24] The theatre's manager, William Dimond Jr, had good reason to expect a crowded auditorium: *Remorse*'s Spanish setting lent the play topical appeal; it had run in London for 20 consecutive nights; and even promised to attract a local following (Coleridge, as the *Bristol Gazette* affirmed, was, after all, 'a Gentleman well known in Bristol').[25] Yet, despite its positive reception in London by 'a full auditory', *Remorse*'s local representation seems to have been decidedly underwhelming.[26]

Coleridge's play was first performed in Bristol on 5 April 1813, after an initial performance in Bath on 27 March (as part of the respective theatres' joint circuit arrangement).[27] It then received a further local representation to mark Mrs Weston's benefit night on 1 August 1814. But these were the only two times that *Remorse* was staged in Bristol during the Peninsular War. Why then, did *Remorse*, which played continuously to full houses in London, apparently fail to impress audiences at Bristol's Theatre Royal? There is evidence to suggest that the play's political import was not a contributing factor. The reviewer from the *Bristol Gazette*, for example, was sceptical, from the outset, about the feasibility of the playwright's literary aims. He considered Coleridge's attempt to define the 'inward struggle of the soul' a rare ambition for a stage more suited to the depiction of strong passions.[28] While Coleridge 'by some has been thought to have succeeded', the reviewer nevertheless maintained that the play was better suited to the closet than

---

[24] BTR Playbill, 5 April 1813. BCRL. Intriguingly, CG's failed comedy, *The Students of Salamanca*, was performed before *Remorse*, on 8 March 1813 (although once only). See 'Calendar': Part C.

[25] *BG*, 8 April 1813. KB/ 4/4.

[26] *FFBJ*, 23 January 1813. *BG*, 4 February 1813, also emphasised that Coleridge's play had received 'great applause' in London.

[27] The Theatre Royals in Bath and Bristol operated a joint circuit and thus shared one dramatic company. The theatrical season in Bristol ran from late September to early July. Winston, 'Theatre Royal, Bath', in *Theatric Tourist*, 5.

[28] *BG*, 8 April 1813. KB/ 4/4.

the stage. The local failure of *Remorse* was specifically attributed, furthermore, to an amateur performance on its opening night: 'We never saw a Play worse represented', the reviewer claimed; singling out Henry Bengough, who played the role of Ordonio, and Mrs Weston, who impersonated Alhadra, for their inferior acting. These principal actors 'seemed to have tried their utmost to rant and out bawl each other', which may explain why, in 1814, when the play received its second performance, Coleridge agreed to involve himself directly with the company's rehearsals.[29]

Local audiences held their acting tradition in high regard and may well have shared the *Bristol Gazette*'s embarrassment over the lead actors' interpretation of Coleridge's play. If so, then the theatre's new management was at least partly to blame. William Wyatt Dimond, the actor-manager responsible for Bristol's Theatre Royal since 1787, died in 1812.[30] His duties then passed to his son, William Dimond Jr (Figure 4.1), a popular writer of melodrama who spent most of his time in London, and used the Theatre Royal to promote his own dramatic pieces, including *The Peasant Boy* and *The Foundling of the Forest.*[31] When *Remorse* made its début in Bristol the play's tragic theme consequently stood out in a theatrical repertoire that, with the exception of the Shakespearean plays performed by London actors on tour, was saturated with comedies and melodramas. On *Remorse*'s opening night, Bengough and Mrs Weston, more accustomed to acting in melodramas than serious tragedy, seem to have forgotten to re-tune the emotional pitch of their performance.

Ironically, the local failure of *Remorse* must have only bolstered Dimond Jr's determination to continue investing in the melodramas (including, notably, his own) that already defined the Theatre Royal's repertoire. Bristolian audiences' apparent indifference to *Remorse* serves, nevertheless, as a sharp reminder of the important relationship that existed between new dramas and the established repertoire. For all its local and topical appeal, Coleridge's tragedy could not offset the practical limitations that affected the stock company.

On the other hand, *Pizarro*'s spectacular scenery and what Dana Van Kooy calls its 'melodramatic theatrics' helped ensure that Sheridan's drama became a regular fixture on the local stage.[32] Frequently revived to mark the engagement of

---

[29]   *BG*, 8 April 1813. In late July 1814, Coleridge thus wrote to J.J. Morgan explaining that he would soon be meeting with two local actors (having made an appointment to read lines with Bengough, who would again play Ordonio). Samuel Taylor Coleridge to J.J. Morgan (late July 1814), in Griggs (ed.), *Letters*, 3: 520–21.

[30]   Arnold Hare, 'William Wyatt Dimond: Provincial Actor Manager', in *Scenes from Provincial Stages: Essays in Honour of Kathleen Barker*, ed. Richard Foulkes (London: The Society for Theatre Research, 1994), 55–64 (61).

[31]   Barker, *Theatre Royal*, 73. After a very successful run at DL, *The Peasant Boy* was performed in Bristol on 16 December 1811. *The Foundling of the Forest* was exported from CG to BTR on 9 November 1812. See 'Calendar': Part C.

[32]   Dana Van Kooy reads *Pizarro* as a 'proto-melodrama' that 're-presented the public with multiple and often contradictory histories of imperial power'. 'Darkness Visible: The

Figure 4.1   William M. Bennett, *William Dimond, Esq.*, published by Vernor, Hood & Sharpe, 1 January 1808. Harry Beard Collection. © Victoria and Albert Museum, London.

a star actor, *Pizarro* was performed at the Theatre Royal 14 times between 1808 and 1815. The staging of *Pizarro* on 11 January 1808 was in large part intended to promote Sarah Siddons's Elvira – a performance that had received enthusiastic reviews the previous year. According to the *Bristol Gazette*, in 1807 Siddons successfully opened up new possibilities for the role:

> When she is taken from the sight of Pizarro in the last act, instead of the disgusting rant, which we have been accustomed to hear, she exclaims with a firm and a resolute look, (a fit subject for the chisel or the pencil) 'that I have *liv'd* ignobly has been Pizarro's fault, that I shall *die* nobly shall be my own'.[33]

The actress's sympathetic role-playing was a recognisable hallmark of her best performances. In 1816, Hazlitt would remember Siddons as 'Tragedy personified': 'Power was seated on her brow, passion emanated from her breasts as from a shrine'.[34] The *Bristol Gazette* employed similar language to describe the actress's performance of Elvira in the play's 1808 production; a performance, the reviewer claimed, that made it seem as if 'Nature speaks thro' her'.[35] This fascination for Siddons also entailed a strong degree of local pride. The celebrated actress had started her career in Bath and offered regular performances on the Bristol stage. Her return to Bristol to play one of the most famous roles of the Romantic stage represented an important homecoming – the city's local darling returning to court her first audiences.

The patriotic inflections attributed to Sheridan's Spanish tragedy made it a particularly attractive choice for the Theatre Royal's wartime repertoire. Although the political did not necessarily guarantee profitability (as *Remorse*'s local failure reminds us), *Pizarro*'s status as an already established repertoire piece seems to have heightened its ideological appeal. With its perceived meanings repeatedly challenged and variously re-affirmed during the long war against Napoleonic France, *Pizarro*'s history remained open to re-writing.

In November 1808 the actor Charles Mayne Young chose the role of Rolla to mark the end of his engagement at the Theatre Royal. As the *Bristol Gazette* then reported:

> It has been remarked of the composition of Pizarro [*sic*], that it is 'English gilt on German gingerbread,' but Mr. Young's abilities are of that sterling stuff which requires nothing but its own intrinsic value to give it currency. Good sense and sound judgment pervaded his representation of Rolla, and making allowance for the setting of *claptraps*, and the hollow patriotism of an echo, (defects of the author, not the actor) the working up of the feelings, was considerable.[36]

Early Melodrama of British Imperialism and the Commodification of History in Sheridan's *Pizarro*', in *Theatre Journal* 64.2 (May 2012), 179–95 (182).

[33]   *BG*, 2 April 1807. KB/ 4/4.

[34]   William Hazlitt, 'Mrs. Siddons' (*The Examiner*, 15 June 1816), in *The Fight and Other Writings*, ed. Tom Paulin and David Chandler (London: Penguin Books, 2000), 48; 50.

[35]   *BG*, 14 January 1808. KB/ 4/4.

[36]   *BG*, 3 November 1808. KB/ 4/4.

Although the reviewer finds fault with *Pizarro*'s supposedly empty rhetoric, he relishes Young's capacity to reinvigorate contemporary audiences, presumably more tired and cynical of the war than Sheridan's admirers in 1799. He identifies a clear instance of Young's success in Act 5 scene 2, wherein Rolla pleads for Pizarro's mercy on behalf of Cora and Alonzo's missing child. Bending his knee 'with reluctance, as if his joints had refused their office, and with a countenance struggling between horror and disgust' but soon after 'forgetting his own dignity in his tenderness for Cora', Young is credited with a 'masterly performance'. In a surprising turn, however, the reviewer claims that the actor's subsequent seizure of the child occurred in a manner so 'feeble and languid' that it undermined the delivery of his final line in that scene:

> 'Then was this good sword *Heavens* [*sic*] gift, not *thine*', forms an antithesis of sense and emphasis, which should not, we presume, be spoken with the flourish of a sword and arm, as if the actor would carry the applause of the gallery, by a *coup de main*, but it should be delivered with the point of the sword extended towards his pursuers, and with the breath held hard, the sinuses strained, and the firm tone of voice that nature assumes when courage is 'wound up to the sticking place'.[37]

The reviewer's observation that Young embellished his performance with 'the flourish of a sword and arm, as if the actor would carry the applause of the gallery', aligns this performative moment with the many '*claptraps*' mentioned earlier. Although this recognisable juncture in the play attracts criticism rather than applause, the reviewer significantly tempers his reservations by offering suggestions for a new, putatively better, method of delivery. 'With the point of the sword extended', 'breath held hard' and 'firm tone of voice', he imagines Young completing the 'effect as new as it was judicious' associated with his first gesture of supplication to Pizarro. The *Bristol Gazette*'s response to Young's performance suggests that during the first year of British military action in the Iberian Peninsula, patriotic feeling could be challenged, revived and ultimately reclaimed in Bristol through the re-staging of stock plays.

The comments published in the *Bristol Gazette* also point to the fact that the appreciation of local theatrical culture was closely related to the dramatic reviews circulated in the provincial press. At the time of the Peninsular War, the main newspapers serving Bristol and its surrounding areas were *The Bristol Gazette, Bristol Mercury, Bristol Mirror* and *Felix Farley's Bristol Journal*. Theatre managers relied on these papers in order to source material for new productions, place advertisements, and, of course, for theatrical reviews (from the newspapers' editorial team and correspondents, as well as the occasional puff). By the early nineteenth century, however, the practice of puffing was already giving way to the increasingly professional standards of theatrical criticism. Local theatre reviewers' attention to detail and budding respect for critical objectivity

---

[37] *BG*, 3 November 1808. KB/ 4/4.

contributed significantly to the recognition of the Theatre Royal's centrality to Bristol's cultural evolution during the Peninsular War.

When the Theatre Royal began to privilege spectacular over more strictly dramatic entertainments, the local newspapers were therefore quick to marshal their attacks on the perceived 'debasement' of the stage. In October 1813 the *Bristol Mirror* reprinted a letter from 'A Lover of the Drama' who despaired 'to see how miserably degraded the Stage is become': 'rope-dancers, – horses – dogs – follow in quick succession'.[38] The incensed writer considers it outrageous that a stage credited with the thespian training of many London stars had come to rely so heavily on circus performances. As a self-declared 'Lover of the Drama' he is further vexed by the audacity of the theatre's managerial committee, who celebrated and advertised these non-dramatic spectacles with 'all the pomposity and glorious circumstance of some mighty affair'. Bristol's tradition of theatrical journalism offered the writer a public outlet for his frustrations, and helped foster belief in the inherent possibility that action could be taken to preserve the Theatre Royal's cultural standing.

In Bristol, theatrical news was, then, just as important as any other news. As a reader of the *Bristol Mirror* insisted to its editor in 1814:

> I regard it as much a part of your duty to keep an eye on the public amusements, as upon the news of the day. The morals of the people are greatly dependent on the state of the Stage; and if the latter be suffered to run riot, the former will be debased.[39]

In short, the theatre's perceived didacticism effectively meant that newspaper editors were duty-bound to keep an intellectual check on the range of entertainments provided. The letter to the *Bristol Mirror* serves as a useful reminder that not only did the stage refigure the latest debates in politics and society, but that what happened on stage and in the auditorium was seen to reflect upon the city's population at large.

Military Patrons

The numerous letters about the city's theatres sent to the local newspapers testify to Bristolians' active commitment to cultural advancement. In this garrison city full of troops awaiting deployment, theatre auditoriums registered a strong military presence. On 8 July 1811 Henry Bengough's benefit night at the Theatre Royal took in an impressive £179 thanks, in large part, to the patronage of the officers of the Oxford Regiment.[40] These officers formed part of the celebrated Light Division that was present during most of the conflicts in the Peninsula. In

---

[38] *BM*, 23 October 1813. KB/ 4/4.
[39] *BM*, 29 October 1814. KB/ 4/4.
[40] The theatre performances patronised by the military were among the most profitable on record. See 'Calendar': Part C.

1811 the Regiment's 2nd battalion were in Bristol awaiting installation with the main forces near Almeida. By the date of Bengough's benefit, its soldiers could boast colours won in Vimeiro, Corunna, Bussaco and Fuentes de Oñoro – battles that had received plenty of media coverage in the London and local presses.[41] It was only natural, therefore, that patriotic flourishes should characterise the Division's 'bespeak' night at the Theatre Royal.[42] The Oxford Regiment chose Shakespeare's *Coriolanus* for their mainpiece, followed by a range of musical interludes, including 'Graham & Glory, or The Battle of Barrosa' sung by Henry Gattie. Theodore Edward Hook's successful melodrama of *Tekeli* (1806) was played as an afterpiece.

In the summer of 1811 the Battle of Barrosa was fresh in the public imagination. Walter Scott's *The Vision of Don Roderick* – a poem written to raise funds for the 'Portuguese Sufferers' – had just been published (on 2 July 1811). The poem tells the story of Don Roderick (the last Visigoth king of Spain), whose descent into an enchanted cavern results in a series of visions that relate Spanish history from the time of the Moorish invasion to the Peninsular War, concluding with the Allies' anticipated expulsion of the French invaders. In both the poem's main verse and accompanying notes, Scott reserved special praise for the Scottish leader General Graham, whose small army succeeded in defeating two French divisions and capturing the British army's first regimental eagle at Barrosa (Figure 4.2). The French eagle, which its army was sworn to protect to death, was a symbolic token of pride and glory. In Bristol's Theatre Royal, an audience mainly composed of soldiers was certain to have cheered loudly at the end of *Coriolanus* and sung along to Gattie's patriotic song. That night, the Theatre Royal was at once extolling Graham's heroism and that of its influential military patrons, soon to return to the Peninsula on active duty.

'Bespeaks', such as that of the Oxford Regiment, were an important tradition for provincial theatres; they brought the house valuable receipts, and empowered influential patrons to request the programme of their choice and support their favourite actors. There were several other instances of bespeaks by the military community in Bristol's Theatre Royal during the Peninsular War. On 9 June 1813, for example, the name 'Lieutenant General Gordon Cuming' was printed at the header of the playbills, indicating that the plays performed that night were of his choosing. It was also common for the military presence to cross over from the auditorium to the stage and orchestra. On 19 July 1813 the theatre announced that

---

[41] The Oxford Regiment would continue a distinguished career of action in the Peninsula, where it would acquire a reputation as one of the most admired regiments in the British army. For a helpful introduction to the British army's regiments in Spain and Portugal (including the 52nd (Oxfordshire) Infantry), see Mike Chappell's *Wellington's Peninsula Regiments (2): The Light Infantry* (Oxford: Osprey Publishing: 2004).

[42] A 'Bespeak' meant that the plays performed that night had been especially chosen (in this case, by the officers) and a financial incentive paid to the managers (either in the form of a subsidy or through the extensive distribution of tickets). St Vincent Troubridge, *The Benefit System in the British Theatre* (London: Society for Theatre Research, 1967), 33.

Figure 4.2   J. Barton Pym, *A Study of the French Imperial Eagle taken by His Majesty's 2nd Battalion at Barrosa, 5 March 1811*, published by Anthony Cardon, April 1811. © The Trustees of the British Museum.

the band of the Longford Regiment would 'play several select pieces of music' on the Vinings' benefit night. It was no coincidence that the choice of afterpiece was *The Blood-Red Knights; or, The Chieftains of Ireland*. From July 1807 to June 1813 the Longford Regiment had been stationed in Galway, Killarney, Roscrea, Cork, Wexford and Waterford to help quell Catholic dissent.[43]

In their recent reassessment of what constituted a soldier in the Georgian period, Kevin Linch and Matthew McCormack make a case for the need to 'rethink the relationship between the military and society'. They argue that 'this should involve deeper analysis of the transformation and transfer from military to civilian identities, and the assimilation of the soldier's experience into a broader context'.[44]

---

[43]   J.E. Cookson, *The British Armed Nation, 1793–1815* (Oxford: Oxford University Press, 1997), 173.

[44]   Kevin Linch and Matthew McCormack, 'Defining Soldiers: Britain's Military, c. 1740–1815', in *War in History* 20.2 (2013), 144–59 (159).

As Linch and McCormack remind us, men tended to serve 'part-time' in the armed forces or for only specific phases of their lives. Their study puts pressure on David Bell's argument that the experience of 'total war' resulted in an effective separation of the military from society. 'The social world of the British officer', the authors contend, 'continued to be [dominated] by polite manners, gentlemanly honour codes and lavish dances'.[45] While the communal experience of theatre-going is likely to have incited behaviour of a rowdier kind from the Theatre Royal's military patrons, it qualifies as one of the 'collective experiences' that contributed to the ways in which soldiers both defined themselves and were assessed by the communities they served.[46] The presence of soldiers in the theatre, as both audience members and supernumeraries (and, in the case of the Longford Regiment, military musicians), involved an expressive blurring of their professional and civilian identities.

Local Audiences

Troop movements in and around Bristol clearly influenced the local theatrical economy. Kathleen Barker argues that so significant was this relationship that 'once the end of the Napoleonic Wars brought about the demobilisation of troops, the inadequacy of the true local following for the theatre was revealed; only the stimulus of a major star would bring a good audience'.[47] There seems, however, to have been a stronger 'local following' for Bristol's Theatre Royal than Barker allows. During the Peninsular War several entertainments in the repertoire testified to a pronounced interest in local geography. On 29 June 1808 a popular dance called 'Bristol Sailors & Savages' was introduced as an interlude on Charles Connor's benefit night. It was repeated on 19 June 1809 for Robert Gomery's benefit. The following month, on 7 July, audiences were treated to a new comic song: 'Colin Clum's Visit to Bristol with his Account of the Play-House, & Peep at The Forty Theives'. This song, mixing the recognisably Bristolian with references to the spectacular pantomime of *The Forty Thieves*, was a success with local audiences. A slightly altered version – 'Cuddy Clump's first visit to London & Bristol; or, a Peep at the Forty Thieves' – was performed after Act 4 of *A Budget of Blunders* on 13 June 1810. The following year, the Egans celebrated their benefit

[45]   Linch and McCormack, 'Defining Soldiers', 147.

[46]   Linch and McCormack identify the importance of music and signing as 'bodily, emotional experiences, both individually and collectively' that 'are as much a part of "muscular bonding" as marching or drilling, and indeed played an important role in both, keeping time and spurring "the Heart of the Soldier"'. 'Defining Soldiers', 157.

[47]   Barker, *Theatre Royal*, 78. By 1815 Bristol's theatre was already facing financial crisis and mounting moral censure from the city's influential non-conformist sectors. Under religious pressure, all the papers, except the *Bristol Gazette*, refrained from printing theatrical reviews. This deprived the Theatre Royal of valuable advertisement opportunities for new productions. Falling standards at the Theatre Royal were also largely to blame, as suggested by the letter from 'A Lover of the Drama'. *BM*, 23 October 1813. KB/ 4/4.

night with an entertainment called 'Farmer Stump; or, a Peep at Bristol Fashions'.[48]
This predilection for geographically specific songs and entertainments suggests a
significant degree of local attachment.

References to local geography could also help advertise a new production. In
March 1810, for example, the *Bristol Gazette* reserved particular praise for Robert
Elliston's impersonation of Puff in Sheridan's *The Critic*:

> With the true magic of genius, he transferred Bristol to Tilsbury, and Tilsbury
> to Bristol, and occasionally gave this with 'a local habitation and a name' by
> treating the ear with lines peculiar to the latter place, while the eye was amused
> with the scenery of the former.[49]

Elliston asserted a distinct claim to Sheridan's play, delivering his lines with a
strong West Country accent and working against the stage's pictorialism in order
to conjure a space of action directly related to local playgoers' daily experiences.[50]
His experimentation exemplifies an important aspect of the construction of urban
identities between 1807 and 1815, when adaptations of well-known plays – and
localised afterpieces and songs, especially – featured prominently in the Theatre
Royal's repertoire. While the exposure of provincial follies endowed these
entertainments with broad comic appeal, they also carried a degree of reference
more specifically aimed at Bristol's native audiences (since, presumably, only a
'true' Bristolian would be quick enough to follow the more nuanced puns and
jokes that re-imagined the local topography).

Local networks of sociability were held in high regard. This was evinced in
early 1809 when the celebrated opera singer Angelica Catalani was engaged at
the Theatre Royal. Despite some initial uncertainties about the likely popular
reception of foreign music, Catalani was well received in Bristol.[51] As the *Bristol
Gazette* reported, the real highlight of the engagement occurred when:

> After *Il Fanatico per la Musica* some of the audience called for *God Save the
> King*. Madame Catalani complied immediately with their wishes, and sang this
> national song with a distinctness of articulation truly wonderful in a foreigner.
> She was loudly and repeatedly applauded during the performance.[52]

---

[48]   See 'Calendar': Part C.
[49]   *BG*, 15 March 1810. KB/ 4/4.
[50]   Elliston's acting career started in Bath's Theatre Royal, where he played a minor role
in *Richard III* (14 April 1791). Christopher Murray, "Elliston, Robert William (1774–1831)."
Oxford Dictionary of National Biography. Online ed. Ed. Lawrence Goldman. Oxford:
Oxford University Press, <http://www.oxforddnb.com/view/article/8724> [Accessed
29.05.10]. In 1811 Elliston set up a Literary Association in John Street, Bristol, but this
proved unsuccessful. Raymond, *Life and Enterprises*, 187.
[51]   *BG*, 23 February 1809. KB/ 4/4.
[52]   *BG*, 23 February 1809.

The success of Catalani's 'God Save the King' turned the novelty of the evening's entertainment on its head.[53] 'Loudly and repeatedly applauded', Catalani's opening night would be remembered, first and foremost, for its rousing display of British feeling, and only secondly for the delights of Italian opera.

Yet if in February 1809 Catalani had sung 'God Save the King' by popular request, less than eight months later she would be branded a British traitor. On 18 November 1809, following the singer's cancellation of most of her performances in Bath and Bristol, the *Bristol Mirror* recounted a few of the 'absurd and ridiculous' reports in circulation. These claimed that her husband was 'a Member of the Legion of Honour – that he was the spy of the French government' and, moreover, that Catalani herself 'contributed annually Seven Thousand Pounds to BONAPARTE'S Exchequer, towards carrying on the war against this country!'.[54] The *Bristol Gazette* was quick to recognise that 'a still more serious occasion now notorious in London' was largely responsible for this.[55] The paper refers, of course, to the havoc at Covent Garden created by the Old Price rioters, whose many grievances included Catalani's inflated salary (of £75 per night).[56]

Marc Baer points out, however, that popular opposition to Catalani in fact pre-dated the 1809 season:

> She had been humiliated trying to sing 'God Save the King' in English at a private concert in 1807. Several of her performances had to be cancelled due to ill health, which in time was interpreted by some, rightly or wrongly, as 'affecting illness in order to indulge her caprice, and trifle with the public'. The public mood shifted most violently when Catalani turned down a request to do a benefit night for the Middlesex Hospital at the King's Theatre.[57]

Baer implies that Kemble's engagement of Catalani in 1809 therefore amounted to poor managerial judgement, but it is interesting to note that when the singer made her first appearance in Bristol (in February of that year) she seems to have escaped such criticism. This confirms the *Bristol Gazette*'s contention that in Bristol, at least, the Old Price riots were largely culpable for the turn in public sympathies. Baer notes that 'on the first night of the riots in 1809 cries from the audience had

---

[53] Elliston's biographer, George Raymond, explains that Madame Catalani had a card in which the lyrics to 'God Save the King' were written in a phonetic mix of English and Italian: 'Oh Lord avar God | Arais schaeter | Is enemis and | Mece them fol | Confond tear | Politekse frosstre | Their nevise trix | On George avar hopes | We fix God save the | Kin'. Raymond, *Life and Enterprises*, 344. Compare the O.P. song 'Ejaculations of the Great Catalani to the British Public', in which the singer is 'made to speak in an unidentifiable patois'. Baer, *Theatre and Disorder*, 203.

[54] *BM*, 18 November 1809. KB/ 4/4.

[55] *BG*, 16 November 1809. KB/ 4/4.

[56] Baer, *Theatre and Disorder*, 27.

[57] Baer, *Theatre and Disorder*, 213.

included "No Foreigners – No Catalani'".[58] This vein of protest was memorably captured by Charles Williams's satirical print, *The House that Jack Built* (28 September 1809; Figure 4.3). Published ten days after the start of disturbances at Covent Garden, Williams's print pictures an elegantly dressed and over-jewelled Catalani as 'the Cat engaged to squall'.

Figure 4.3   Charles Williams, *The House that Jack Built*, published by S.W. Fores, 28 September 1809. © Victoria and Albert Museum, London.

The *Bristol Gazette*, meanwhile, rendered its stance unequivocal:

> The public have a right to express their approbation, or disapprobation of any performer in a place of public amusement, according to their taste or feeling on the subjects; but to hunt down a foreigner and a woman, merely because she is eminent in her profession, is unworthy of the gallantry and liberality of Englishmen. Those who *discountenance* the engagement of foreigners at our place of amusement, upon principle, will do so most effectually, by *never shewing* [sic] *their faces* there.[59]

---

58   Baer, *Theatre and Disorder*, 211.
59   *BG*, 16 November 1809.

In his eagerness to promote cultural awareness, the writer for the *Bristol Gazette* publicises his respect for Catalani's susceptibilities as 'a foreigner and a woman', arguing that her very 'otherness' gave occasion for local audiences to prove 'the gallantry and liberality of Englishmen'. 'The value of theatre', as Baer reminds us, 'was seen by many in terms of what it had to teach the nation about itself'.[60] The O.P.s' determined resistance to Kemble's reforms was, according to Baer, predominantly driven by their desire to preserve 'the moral economy'.[61] The war with France rendered urgent the need to defend the stage against foreign influences and preserve the good qualities of 'Englishmen', Baer explains, outlining what he illuminatingly describes as the O.P.s' strategy of 'pragmatic nationalism'.[62] A version of this 'pragmatic nationalism' can be found in the comments published in the *Bristol Gazette* – a newspaper of characteristically Oppositional views. In contrast to the O.P. protesters, who capitalised upon xenophobic feeling in order to deride Catalani, the paper called for the expulsion from the auditorium of the local men and women who indulged in such 'un-English' behaviour. In 1809 this valorisation of 'the gallantry and liberality' of true 'Englishmen' also carried a chivalric charge that was particularly resonant for a readership invested in the Peninsular War.[63]

Spain may not have been the 'original birthplace' of romance, but, as Diego Saglia explains, 'both the literary genre and the chivalric tradition manifested themselves in peculiarly intense ways in the Spanish tradition'.[64] Indeed, what Saglia instructively calls the 'Spanish imaginary' represented 'a desirable fictional space', which could be used, as he outlines, to 'accommodate some of the topical, domestic, and international, issues of early nineteenth-century Britain'.[65] The reviewer for the *British Gazette* does not, it must be emphasised, directly refer to Spain, but nor does he need to. The O.P. riots had confirmed the 'tight linkage between social memory and contemporary history', as Baer underscores.[66] The *Bristol Gazette*'s revival of English 'gallantry and liberality' – employed to remind audiences of their national duty to rescue and protect (in this case, a maligned opera singer, from the emotional violence directed against her) – would have been understood to depart not only from an idealisation of the English character,

---

[60]   Baer, *Theatre and Disorder*, 193.

[61]   Baer, *Theatre and Disorder*, 22 ff.

[62]   On the O.P.s' defence of positive English qualities, see Baer, *Theatre and Disorder*, 204, 217–18; on 'pragmatic nationalism', 212–21.

[63]   As Samuel Taylor Coleridge put it, the Peninsular War provided 'a common focus in the cause of Spain, which made us all once more Englishmen…'. *CC: BL*, 1: 189.

[64]   Saglia, *Poetic Castles*, 54. As Saglia explains, 'Edmund Burke's elegy on "the age of chivalry" in *Reflections on the Revolution in France* (1790) was only the most conspicuous and authoritative example in a vast number of ideological uses of the romance and the institution of chivalry in the hands of Tory, Whig and radical writers trying to rationalize historical events which, after 1789, seemed to have taken a "fabulous" turn' (56).

[65]   Saglia, *Poetic Castles*, 70.

[66]   Baer, *Theatre and Disorder*, 211.

but from a chivalric context strongly associated with Edmund Burke and most urgently reinvigorated by the Peninsular War.[67]

The reviewer for the *Bristol Gazette* also imparts the intriguing impression that an appropriate response to Catalani's re-engagement could, in fact, strengthen the local community.[68] Catalani's first performance had represented a successful transgression of the borders of history, culture and tradition. In February 1809 the unexpected popularity of a foreigner singing the British anthem had provided both an act of difference available for appropriation and a thinking point for audiences trying to make sense of a pan-European war. In recognition of this, the *Bristol Gazette* called for audiences to exercise similar open-mindedness in response to Catalani's re-engagement in November 1809. The paper also implicitly argued that London should not be considered an unquestionable paradigm for imitation.

By this period, as Daniel O'Quinn emphasises, 'the entire house, and not merely the stage, operates as a performance space'.[69] O'Quinn argues, crucially, for an 'autoethnographic' theatre, whose entertainments 'turned on the recognizability of character', even when depicting foreign spaces and customs.[70] This important activity of self-reflection contributed significantly to the formation of local identities, as suggested by the *Bristol Gazette*'s angry response to the damning of Catalani. By the early nineteenth century, such 'autoethnography' would help audiences develop more sophisticated interpretations of the political narratives they encountered outside, as well as within, the theatre. As readers of the *Bristol Gazette* were effectively warned, Bristolians had a duty to control, rather than emulate, the tendencies of the capital. This was an important point to make at a time of increasingly partisan politics (both domestic and international).

The Repertoire System

Most of the plays presented in Bristol's Theatre Royal during the Peninsular War were stock pieces that dated from the eighteenth century. These included Robert Benson's musical entertainment *Britain's Glory; or, A Trip to Portsmouth* (1796), John O'Keeffe's celebrated opera *The Castle of Andalusia* (1783), Samuel Foote's farce *The Mayor of Garratt* (1764), John Philip Kemble's opera *Lodoiska* (1794) and his afterpiece *The Pannel* (1788). (The latter was an adaptation of Isaac Bickerstaff's *'Tis Well It's No Worse* – a translation of

---

[67] On chivalry, see my discussion of Charles Dibdin the Younger's *The Wild Man* (1809) in Chapter 3.

[68] Catalani was, in fact, able to recover her popularity with local audiences. By June 1814 she was singing to great acclaim at the 'Grand Musical Festival for the Benefit of the Infirmary'. *FFBJ*, 18 June 1814.

[69] O'Quinn, *Staging Governance*, 11.

[70] O'Quinn, *Staging Governance*, 11. This interest in autoethnography is developed even further in O'Quinn's study of theatrical entertainments during the American War: *Entertaining Crisis in the Atlantic Imperium 1770–1790* (Baltimore: Johns Hopkins University Press, 2011).

Calderón's *El escondido y la tapada*.[71]) It is significant that these stock pieces were able to survive the turbulent social and political changes of the early nineteenth century. Older plays, enjoying the pre-existing approval of the Lord Chamberlain's Office, were less likely to be singled out for political censorship; but this did not mean, of course, that their application to contemporary events was any less pointed (as *Pizarro*'s stage history confirms). Whereas in earlier decades, the negative representation of a Spanish theme could be taken at face value, in the self-conscious years of state-sponsored military action in Spain and Portugal, symbols of Spanish backwardness or shortcomings took on new purchase.

In a socially and culturally aspirant city such as Bristol, Spanish-themed comedies about disguise, recognition and exposure reverberated with political implications that stretched beyond their immediate comic appeal. Cross-dressing and self-conscious role-playing were common to most of these comedies and loaded with significance for audiences, who, as this chapter has argued, were themselves experimenting with new models of civic identity. In Kemble's *The Pannel* identities are as readily put on as they are taken off. The local popularity of this afterpiece largely derived from the fact that the role of Beatrice had been specifically designed to showcase the talents of Dorothy Jordan and was chosen by the actress whenever she appeared on the Bristol stage.[72]

The theme of disguise is also central to O'Keeffe's *The Castle of Andalusia* and John Tobin's *The Honey Moon* (1805), whose plots provide servants with opportunities to impersonate their masters. In O'Keeffe's comic opera, it takes Fernando a moment of deliberate reflection to recognise his servant Pedrillo *'in an elegant morning gown, cap and slippers'*.[73] Shaken by the surprise, he re-asserts his authority by enlisting Pedrillo to fulfil his duties: 'Then Sir, if you are a gentleman of such prodigious merit, be so obliging, with submission to your cap and gown, as to – pull off my boots'.[74] The grammatical dash is here suggestive of an order merely given at whim, to re-assert his superiority. Later in Act 3, Pedrillo secures his public vengeance when, richly dressed, and with an air of *'great authority'*, he rebukes Fernando (now disguised as his servant) for acting negligently. Fernando, humbled, reflects in an aside: 'If this be my picture, I blush for the original'.[75] At this comic point, the intimacy of the aside helps normalise the play's democratic politics by reminding audiences that the inversion of roles has been carefully planned, and that they too have been complicit in its execution.

---

[71]   John Philip Kemble, *The Pannel, As altered by J.P. Kemble, from Bickerstaff's translation of Calderón's El escondido y la tapada* (London, 1789), Introduction.

[72]   *The Pannel* was performed on 28 January 1811, 18 January 1813, and on 24 and 31 January 1814. Dorothy Jordan was engaged on all these dates. See 'Calendar': Part C.

[73]   John O'Keeffe, *The Castle of Andalusia: A Comic Opera in Three Acts*, in *British Theatre*, 22: 39 (2.2).

[74]   O'Keeffe, *Castle*, in *British Theatre*, 22: 39 (2.2).

[75]   O'Keeffe, *Castle*, in *British Theatre*, 22: 52 (3.1).

A parallel scene occurs in *The Honey Moon*, when the Duke of Aranza tries to play a trick on his young bride, Juliana, in order to teach her a lesson about pride. Juliana, believing that the Duke has acted as a fraud, demands justice. She is unknowingly allowed to make her suit before a mock court, presided over by Jaquez, the Duke's servant. When Jaquez, dressed as the Duke, first makes his appearance at the palace, the servants '*in vain endeavour to restrain their Laughter*'.[76] Furious, Jaquez threatens the servants: 'Am I the first great man that has been made offhand by a tailor? Show your grinders again, and I'll hang you like onions, fifty on a rope'.[77] The Duke's clothes fall unnaturally from the servant's smaller frame. Jaquez himself admits that it feels like wearing 'armour', and that the 'sword has a trick of getting between my legs, like a monkey's tail, as if it was determined to trip up my nobility – '.[78] He is determined, nevertheless, to act the part and parody his master to perfection. In his concern for appearances and social decorum, Jaquez thus threatens to 'hang' his fellow servants, warning that there will be 'transportation at least' if they give any indication of already knowing him. His allusions to crime and punishment make it clear that the role of magistrate is uppermost in his thoughts. When the real Duke appears, he is impressed by his servant's role-play. In two asides, he acknowledges that '[t]he rogue reproves me well!' and 'does it to the life!'.[79] These intimate confessions to the audience emphasise, as in *The Castle of Andalusia*, that it is the master's good humour that allows the carnivalesque to develop into a comic, rather than frightful, vision of a revised social order. It was as important to make this point during the Peninsular War, as it had been in the immediate aftermath of the French Revolution.[80]

Alone on stage, Jaquez's reflections reveal, interestingly, that his experimental role-play has been tinged with more serious ironies:

> JAQUEZ   I begin to find, by the strength of my nerves, and the steadiness of my countenance, that I was certainly intended for a great man; – for what more does it require to be a great man, than boldly to put on the appearance of it? – How many sage politicians are there, who can scarce comprehend the mystery of a mousetrap; – valiant generals, who wouldn't attack a bulrush,

---

[76]   John Tobin, *The Honey Moon; A Comedy in Five Acts*, in *British Theatre*, 25: 42 (3.2).

[77]   Tobin, *Honey Moon*, in *British Theatre*, 25: 43 (3.2).

[78]   Tobin, *Honey Moon*, in *British Theatre*, 25: 42 (3.2).

[79]   Tobin, *Honey Moon*, in *British Theatre*, 25: 43–4 (3.2).

[80]   By 1809 the Convention of Cintra, the forced resignation of the Duke of York as Commander in Chief of the British army (following 'the Mary Anne Clarke affair'), and the disastrous Walcheren expedition could be variously cited as evidence of the need for domestic reform. For an investigation into the various meanings and interpretations of 'reform' during this period, see *Re-thinking the Age of Reform: Britain 1780–1850*, ed. Arthur Burns and Joanna Innes (Cambridge: Cambridge University Press, 2003).

unless the wind were in their favour ... shining examples – that a
man will never want gold in his pocket, who carries plenty of
brass in his face![81]

Jaquez's new identity has taught him that power involves little more than a
convincing social performance – a lesson that gives satiric bite to Tobin's comedy
about an old Spanish duke who marries a beautiful young wife. As Elizabeth
Inchbald explained: '[Tobin] respected the stage as the best vehicle by which wit,
poetry, and morality, could be conveyed to the good and the bad, the wise and the
ignorant, of the community'.[82] In Bristol, where the playwright had received his
education, *The Honey Moon* was performed eleven times between 1808 and 1815.[83]
During this period, Tobin's presentation of identity as dynamic, improvised and
essentially performative carried significant political meaning.

In the quotation above, Jaquez explicitly compares his acting bravado to that
of the 'stage politician' and 'valiant general'. These comparisons may well have
reminded audiences of other opportunities for the re-invention of public and
private identities. At the time of the Peninsular War political reputations were
very much at stake; including those of the British ministers who co-ordinated the
war effort back home, as well as the military commanders (notably Moore and
Wellington) whose strategies were tested in the battlefields. Indeed, when news
of the Convention of Cintra reached England in September 1808, the terms of the
treaty so incensed the British public that the generals who signed it (including the
then Arthur Wellesley) were recalled for a court of Inquiry in November that year.
In his long prose pamphlet *Concerning The Relations of Great Britain, Spain, and
Portugal, to Each Other, and to the Common Enemy at this Crisis; and specifically
as affected by the Convention of Cintra* ... (1809), William Wordsworth argued
that the British generals in Portugal 'mistook the counters of the game for the stake
played for'.[84] The words 'seduced' and 'blind' – resonant for a comedy of intrigue
such as Tobin's *The Honey Moon* – crop up several times in Wordsworth's prose.

On 6 October 1808 the *Bristol Gazette* called for an immediate recall of the
generals who signed the Convention of Cintra. The paper's disaffection for
Wellesley was further emphasised in 1809 when, in contrast to the local Tories who
promoted his victory at Talavera as an example of tactical genius, the *Bristol Gazette*
insisted: 'Lord Wellington has exactly come up to what we expected of him – he
has expended some millions of money and some thousands of lives, and now must
return as he went'.[85] With heavy sarcasm, the editor here accentuates the problems
of discrimination and illusion explored more playfully in Tobin's play. In this period
of fierce accusations, the dramatic irony of Jaquez's soliloquy about identity could

---

[81] Tobin, *Honey Moon*, in *British Theatre*, 25: 46–7 (3.2).
[82] Tobin, *Honey Moon*, in *British Theatre*, 25: 4.
[83] Inchbald notes that Tobin was educated by 'the Reverend M. Lee, of Bristol'.
British Theatre, 25: 3.
[84] Richard Gravil and W.J.B. Owen (eds), *Concerning the Convention*, 136.
[85] *BG*, 26 October 1809.

help audiences reimagine the heated political debates that circulated in the press. In short, Tobin's comedy of intrigue was a play charged with political implication for a wartime audience whose secret knowledge of the different impersonations taking place on stage pointed to the more serious gaps between perception and reality in political affairs. During the Peninsular War, the Theatre Royal's production of the *The Pannel*, *The Castle of Andalusia*, and *The Honey Moon* – all of which were set in Spain and placed a premium on the theme of disguise – sent messages that could be interpreted as sharply topical, as well as divertingly funny.

English Heroism

When Thomas Dibdin's *The English Fleet in 1342* (1803) was staged at the Theatre Royal for the actor William Mineard Bennett's benefit night (27 June 1810) patriotic display was uppermost on the agenda.[86] Dibdin's comic opera had received its first performance at Covent Garden on 13 December 1803.[87] Written in the aftermath of the short-lived Peace of Amiens, it was intended as a morale-boosting piece for the renewed war against Napoleon. Its success in London was long lived and soon extended to the provinces. *The English Fleet*'s main themes encompassed legitimate succession, popular resistance to invasion, siege warfare, female heroic agency, British naval prowess and chivalric rescue. These themes would retain their topical appeal during the protracted war against Napoleonic expansionism and acquire notable urgency during the Peninsular War.

As its title indicates, a sense of historical perspective is crucial to the action of *The English Fleet*; so much so, in fact, that the list of dramatis personae concludes with a suggestion that 'For the historical foundation of this Opera' the reader should consult the second volume of Hume's *History of England*.[88] *The English Fleet in 1342* dramatises the conflict between the House of Blois (supported by France) and the House of Mo[u]ntfort (supported by England) during the Breton War of Succession – one of the most important events at the start of the Hundred Years War. The opera tells the story of Jane, Countess of Brittany, who, in the absence of her captured husband, carries out the defence of Rennes. After resisting the armies of Charles de Blois, the Countess retires to the castle of Hennebonne, from which she inspires the townspeople, and even endures hunger and deprivation but refuses to capitulate. In the tense timeframe of 24 hours, every minute registers her anxious hopes for the arrival of English aid.

---

[86]   Playbills stated that at the end of the play there would be a representation of 'The British Fleet at Anchor'. The *English Fleet in 1342* had already been performed on 8 January 1810 and would be performed again after Bennett's benefit on 23 July 1810, 18 May 1812 and 20 February 1815. See 'Calendar': Part C.

[87]   Allardyce Nicoll, 'Hand-List of Plays, 1800–1850', in *History of English Drama*, 4: 297.

[88]   Tomas Dibdin, *The English Fleet, in 1342*; *An Historical Comic Opera, in Three Acts* (London, 1805).

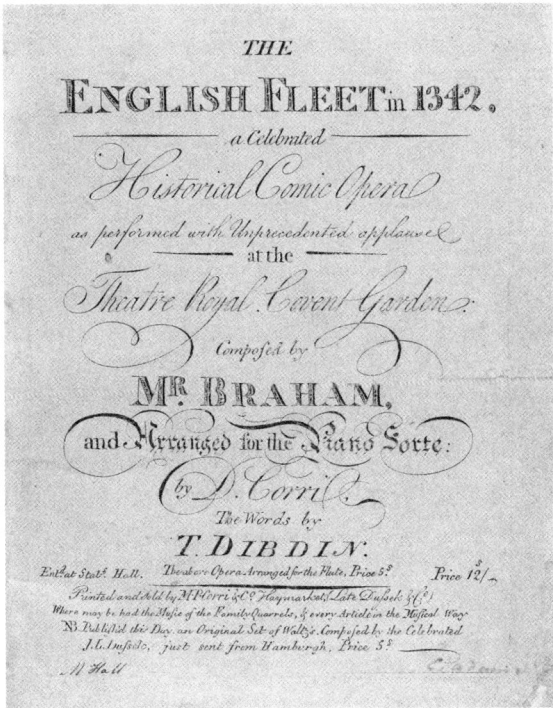

Figure 4.4   Title page of music score for *The English Fleet in 1342*.
             © National Maritime Museum, Greenwich, London.

Siege plays such as *The English Fleet* were particularly resonant for an island nation trying to resist France. As I argue in Chapter 1, ideas about British liberty and keeping out the invader became especially prevalent after 1802. The notion of a stronghold was, moreover, of literal significance during the Peninsular War, which saw a revival in siege warfare. As Kelly DeVries and Richard Holmes explain:

> By the time of the French Revolutionary wars, sieges had ceased to be the central business of warfare and the style of warfare which featured them had begun to change … Nevertheless … they remained a part of warfare.
> During the Peninsular war Wellington besieged and stormed Badajoz and Ciudad Rodrigo, and Spanish defence of Saragossa in 1808–1809 was a mark of popular resistance to France…[89]

---

[89]   Kelly DeVries and Richard Holmes: 'siege warfare' in *The Oxford Companion to Military History*. (Oxford: Oxford University Press, 2001) <http://www.oxfordreference.com/view/10.1093/acref/9780198606963.001.0001/acref-9780198606963-e-1177> [Accessed 16.04.14].

This specific identification of the siege with the British campaign in Spain is underscored by David Gates's summary observation that 'during the Napoleonic wars as a whole, sieges were almost unheard of outside the peninsula'.[90] By 1810 Bristolians would have been familiar with several examples of siege warfare. Ciudad Rodrigo was still under siege, as was Cadiz (the seat of the Spanish Junta and naval arsenal of southwest Spain), which was besieged by the French on 5 February 1810, only a few months before Bennett's benefit night performance. The popular defence of the two sieges of Zaragoza had also attracted much attention. The first siege of Zaragoza (15 June and 13 August 1808), characterised by the heroism of General Palafox and defence of the Portillo Gate (especially by Agustina Zaragoza y Domenech, the so-called 'Maid of Zaragoza'), resulted in an inspiring Spanish victory that was widely reported in the British press. In 1809 when the French succeeded in their second siege of the city (20 December 1808–20 February 1809), *Felix Farley's Bristol Journal* thus remained committed to the memory of the previous summer. The newspaper advertised Charles Vaughan's recent publication of his *Narrative of the Siege of Zaragoza* (1809) and reprinted selected extracts from it on 17 and 24 June 1809.

Vaughan's *Narrative* recounted Agustina Zaragoza's impressive courage during the French army's attempted storming of the city:

> Augustina [*sic*] rushed forward over the wounded, and slain, snatched a match from the hand of a dead artilleryman, and fired off a 26 pounder, then jumping upon the gun made a solemn vow never to quit it alive during the siege...[91]

Vaughan's description may be framed in the past tense but his rapid succession of verbs lends exciting immediacy to Agustina's actions. As the representative of a new model of (gendered) heroic agency, Agustina Zaragoza is likely to have been uppermost in at least some theatre-goers' minds as they applauded the valorous actions of the Countess of Brittany.[92]

In Dibdin's comic opera, the Countess makes her first appearance '*in brilliant armour*'.[93] She directs herself with the composure of an accomplished military leader but never relinquishes her primary responsibilities as a wife and mother:

> COUNTESS ...Before oppression called my lord from home, the household
> duties, and my boy's instruction employed my happier hours; but
> can ye wonder, when great occasion calls for great resistance, if,

---

[90]   David, Gates: 'Peninsular war', in *Oxford Companion to Military History*: <http://www.oxfordreference.com/view/10.1093/acref/9780198606963.001.0001/acref-9780198606963-e-971> [Accessed 16.04.14].

[91]   Charles Vaughan, *Narrative of the Siege of Zaragoza* (London, 1809), 15–16.

[92]   In *Childe Harold's Pilgrimage* (1812) Byron describes Agustina 'walk[ing] daily in the Prado, decorated with medals and orders, by command of the Junta'. *Childe Harold's Pilgrimage*, in McGann (ed.), *Complete Poetical Works*, 2: 189 (Note to l.584).

[93]   Dibdin, *English Fleet*, 30 (2.3).

in the cause of husband, prince, and people, I leave the milder manners of my sex, and, fearless, join amid the ranks of war?[94]

The exigencies of warfare justify the Countess's masculine comportment, while the uncertain political climate gives heightened significance to her maternal devotion. As the Countess explains in her address to the 'Warriors of Britanny [*sic*]', it is her son who inspires her to take action; 'his infancy oppressed by those who spurn at lineal right, and lineal freedom', the bonds of mother and child acquire urgent political resonance as a result of the French attack.[95]

In the French camp, Charles de Blois bitterly exclaims: '… this is the age, that female heroes thrive in! The martial Governess of yonder castle has kept us hard at bay, even while her Lord is captive in our camp'.[96] With begrudging irony, Blois concedes that the Countess has been remarkably successful in resisting the siege. Adela, his consort, reveals genuine admiration for 'the valiant Countess' and observes that the English, meanwhile, 'are proud to own a Queen, who holds the homage of her subjects, less by her rank, than by the many virtues which adorn her'.[97] Dibdin's readers, with their volume of Hume's *History* by their side, are here invited to explore the implications of examining the Countess in the same light as the English queen-consort, Philippa of Hainault. The comparison would also have been suggested to theatre-goers familiar with George Colman the Younger's *The Surrender of Calais* (1791). In this popular repertoire play Queen Philippa succeeds in convincing King Edward to free his prisoners:

> QUEEN   …Let it not dwell within your thoughts, my Liege, thus to oppress these men: and Royal Sir, since you were free to promise, in remembrance of the poor service which my weak endeavours wrought in your absence, for your realm, to grant whatever boon I begged – now, on my knee, I beg it, Sir; release these wretched men; make me the means of cheering the unhappy; and though my claim were tenfold what it is, upon your bounty, 'twould reward me nobly.[98]

The kneeling queen here exercises a supplicant role comparable to Queen Katharine's in Kemble's production of *Henry VIII* (discussed in Chapter 2). Philippa's femininity is, however, defined differently from that of Dibdin's Countess, whose more active role is determined by her inability to defer to the authority of her imprisoned husband. What Queen Philippa, Queen Katharine and the Countess of Brittany all share, nevertheless, is an association with justice. King Edward's pardon would prove, as Philippa explains, that 'mercy, valour, and

---

[94]   Dibdin, *English Fleet*, 30 (2.3).
[95]   Dibdin, *English Fleet*, 31 (2.3).
[96]   Dibdin, *English Fleet*, 45 (3.1).
[97]   Dibdin, *English Fleet*, 45 (3.1).
[98]   George Colman Jun., *The Surrender of Calais. A Play in Three Acts…* (1791; Dublin, 1792), 58 (3.2). On the role of women in the play consider the characterisation of Julia.

compassion ... characterize the Englishman'.[99] By the Countess's approximation
to Queen Philippa, Adela qualifies her lover's portrait of a 'martial governess'
to suggest that the Countess's compassion made her worthy of 'the homage of
her subjects'. Inspired by this, Adela urges that their prisoners be treated with
humanity and subsequently makes her own arrangements for refreshments to be
sent to the Count.[100]

But while the women in Dibdin's comic opera are defiant and brave, they are
ultimately unequal to the demands of war. Towards the end, even the redoubtable
Countess contemplates a ceasefire. After the Lord of Leon warns her about
Charles's ruthlessness and the desperate nature of her situation, the alarmed
mother writes to the English king, asking protection for her son. Soon after, she
hears cheers of 'Huzza' announcing the arrival of the English fleet: she runs to the
window, tears her letter, and cries out that there shall be 'No capitulation!'. The
exhausted Countess then *'faints in the arms of her Attendants'*.[101] Her physical
collapse is significant because it allows heroic agency to be unequivocally
transferred to the approaching English fleet. *'Cannon is heard, and the flashes
are seen thro' the window – The scene closes'*.[102] By this spectacular arrival,
the English fleet would have illuminated the stage with flashes of gunfire and
made it shake with the thunderous groan of their prop cannons. The Countess
has acted as necessity obliged, but the true heroism of the play is reserved for
the English.

Dibdin's comic opera sustains a continual engagement with the theme of
English heroism. The opening act, for instance, sees the cottager Jeannetta reunited
with her husband, Philip, and son, Valentine, recently returned from England.
Philip reveals that the English are preparing a fleet to provide succour for the
Bretons. This determines his homecoming toast – '"Success to the arms of the
King of England!" for his cause and ours are the same' – and the song that follows
in celebration of English values and traditions: [103]

SONG. – PHILIP.
In England I've seen the brave sons of roast beef,
Rais'd high on prosperity's wings:
Saw wealth and good humour beyond all belief;
But travellers see strange things.
Chorus   Strange things!
Strange things!
Travellers see strange things!
....

[99]   Colman, *Surrender,* 58 (3.2).
[100] Dibdin, *English Fleet*, 47 (3.1).
[101] Dibdin, *English Fleet*, 59 (3.4).
[102] Dibdin, *English Fleet*, 59 (3.4).
[103] Dibdin, *English Fleet*, 7 (1.1).

> Believe me, no falsehood I wish to advance,
> > From truth my authority springs,
> I've seen England can never be conquered by France,
> > But travellers see strange things
> *Chorus* Strange things! &c.[104]

Philip's song, with the comic refrain of 'Strange things!', envisages English liberty and prosperity as foreign luxuries. Dibdin's transparent purpose is to use Philip's song to defamiliarise cultural values and give audiences an appreciation of the true worth of English ideals. These ideological underpinnings were still important during the Peninsular War. As hereditary enemies, English and Spanish soldiers were often suspicious of each other, and the local Spanish populace equivocal about English interference. Rory Muir observes that in 1810, after Talavera, Ocaña, and the loss of Andalusia, Spain's reputation in Britain was at its lowest point.[105] This would have given particular resonance to Philip's claim that 'the British throne never deserted its allies', rendering Dibdin's nationalist emphasis on British solidarity and commitment acutely topical.[106]

In large measure, the Peninsular War renewed the political apprehensions that had inspired Dibdin to write *The English Fleet* in 1803. This is comparable to the ways in which *Pizarro* received additional charge after the collapse of Amiens and the first reports of unrest in Spain. Dibdin, like Sheridan, could not have known that historical circumstances would make his comic opera seem so apt to Bristolians during the Peninsular War. The Theatre Royal's manager, William Dimond, was quick to recognise, however, that the opportunities for heroic patriotism engendered by the war would allow *The English Fleet* to make as strong an impression in the auditorium in 1810 as it had in 1803.

On Bennett's benefit night, audiences would have understood that Spanish women of all ranks were taking an active part in their country's resistance efforts. As early as 12 May 1808, the *Bristol Gazette* had drawn attention to the 'most conspicuous part' played by women in the Madrid riots.[107] These Spanish women were praised for taking up arms in the defence of their homes. As such, they formed a striking contrast to the women of France, whose involvement with the excesses of the Terror had led to their demonisation in the English press. In his rich discussion of the distance between these two characterisations of female agency, Diego Saglia posits Vaughan's *Narrative of the Siege of Zaragoza* as an instrumental text:

> Vaughan's first-hand tale of female heroism provided other writers with the image of a woman who daringly escapes fixed schemes and invades a male field of agency yet also remains a highly sexual object.[108]

---

[104] Dibdin, *English Fleet*, 8 (1.1).
[105] Muir, *The Defeat of Napoleon*, 116.
[106] Dibdin, *English Fleet*, 18–19 (1.2).
[107] *BG*, 12 May 1808.
[108] Saglia, *Poetic Castles*, 196.

This new image of the Spanish heroine re-shaped the experience of watching *The English Fleet*. Whereas Dibdin's first audiences would have needed to define the character of the Countess *against* the models of female agency associated with the French Revolution, by 1810 the Countess could be understood as a heroine in the mould of Agustina Zaragoza. By introducing examples of feminine action that could be as readily associated with conservatism as with radicalism, the Peninsular War had contributed new inflections to *The English Fleet*'s gendered politics.

The topicality of *The English Fleet* was, indeed, manifold. Beyond its representation of female characters or the obvious heroism of an English Fleet, in 1810 the opera could also be seen to speak to domestic unrest in Spain. Educated audiences are likely to have recognised the fate of the Spanish Bourbons in the Countess's account of her husband's betrayal:

> COUNTESS ...but when 'tis known that my lov'd husband went, on public faith, to plead his cause in France's capital, sanctioned by France's ruler, when 'tis known, that, in famed Paris, spite of all promise, he was made a prisoner, and his birthright attempted in his absence, then shall future times forgive a female spirit, who throws the distaff from her hand, and, 'gainst assassins, grasps the pointed spear.[109]

At the time of the Peninsular War the Countess's description of the French court's double-dealing could be interpreted as an allusion to Ferdinand VII's similar entrapment at Bayonne. In *An Exposure of the Arts and Machinations which led to the usurpation of the Crown of Spain and the means pursued by Bonaparte to carry his views into effect* (1808) Pedro Cevallos explains that on the orders of Napoleon, Ferdinand VII journeyed to Bayonne, where the prince and his father were induced to abdicate their rights to the Spanish throne.[110] As an Opposition paper, the *Bristol Gazette* posed the question of legitimate rule in very different terms: 'What can the once proud and chivalrous Spaniards think of their Kings and Princes, when they see the son drivelling penitence before the father, and the father licking the feet of a foreign usurper ...'.[111] Regardless of political sympathies, however, was the certainty of foul play, and that from Bayonne Napoleon was 'paving the way for the introduction of foreign tyranny'.[112] The Count's imprisonment by the French

---

[109] Dibdin, *The English Fleet*, 31 (2.3).

[110] Pedro Cevallos's text was reviewed by Francis Jeffrey and Henry Brougham for the *Edinburgh Review* 'Article 14', *ER*, October 1808, 13: 215–34. Their predictions about the course of the war in Spain and reflections on the domestic reform movement proved sufficiently provocative for 25 prominent readers (including Walter Scott) to cancel their subscriptions to the periodical. See Susan Manning, 'Walter Scott, Antiquarianism and the Political Discourse of the *Edinburgh Review*, 1802–1811', in *British Romanticism and the 'Edinburgh Review': Bicentenary Essays*, ed. Massimiliano Demata and Duncan Wu (Basingstoke: Palgrave Macmillan, 2002), 102–23.

[111] *BG*, 2 June 1808.

[112] *BG*, 2 June 1808.

Charles de Blois would have made the plot of *The English Fleet* seem remarkably close to recent events in Spain.

Certain aspects of the opera were, nevertheless, intrinsically related to its date of composition. The *English Fleet* includes, for instance, a comic representation of the Spanish officer Don Carlos that, with the intention of boosting morale in 1803, takes on a predictably derisive tone. The Spaniard's characterisation is developed in Act 2 scene 1, which details the relationship between the leaders of the French, Spanish and Genoese troops. In compliance with reductive national stereotypes, Carlos takes the requisite 'siesta', is described as inordinately proud and makes pretensions to a grandiose authority that he clearly lacks. But 'Don Carlos Alonzo Alphonso Conquestador, son of the principal writing-master to the Prince of Asturias' merely amuses the French troop leader, La Valette. Responding to the Spaniard's obvious feelings of self-importance, the Frenchman cynically suggests: 'Why, the worst they could say would be, that your father *flourished* in the fourteenth century, and his son was too apt to follow his example'.[113] These comments would certainly have seemed *passé* to many of the Peninsular War's supporters, but disillusionment with the Anglo-Spanish alliance meant that even these mocking references to the Spaniard's haughtiness and misplaced sense of honour could provide theatre-goers with pointed political commentary, as well as comedy.

While the Anglo-Spanish alliance had exerted new pressures on negative portrayals of the Spanish character, the progress of cultural diplomacy proved slow, and often without consequence. Dibdin's lampooning of the Spaniard thus remained popular on the Bristol stage, with *The English Fleet*'s persistence in the repertoire between 1808 and 1814 reflecting the inconsistency of attempts to revise national stereotypes. The summer of 1808 may have been a heady time for Anglo-Spanish politics but older prejudices against Spain were never fully overturned. For detractors of the war, reports of the strained alliance must have seemed to merely confirm their inherited suspicions. Indeed, as the war progressed, even Spain's disparate army of resistance fighters – once the subject of wide praise in the British press – would have to cede its laurels. The popular war songs discussed in Chapter 3 neatly exemplify how the British army came to be seen as the Iberian Peninsula's true source of salvation from French tyranny. This development was conveniently matched by the action of *The English Fleet*, which posits the English as omniscient agents of rescue.

In Act 5 of Dibdin's comic opera, the English fleet commanded by Sir Walter Manny arrives at the crucial hour, boasting what Philip had earlier described as 'great guns, which are just invented'.[114] This representation of the 'English Fleet'

---

[113]   Dibdin, *English Fleet*, 23 (2.1).
[114]   Dibdin, *English Fleet*, 19 (1.2).

(as advertised in the Theatre Royal playbills) gave audiences an occasion to celebrate the Royal Navy as a paradigm of maritime warfare:[115]

> *The English fleet discover'd at anchor, with splendid banners flying, the decks and shrouds mann'd and arm'd in the appropriate old English style. – A grand march plays, while the English Admiral is received in all military pomp by the Count, Countess, and all the Characters of their party.*[116]

This patriotic representation would have seemed particularly well-tailored to Bristol, the launching pad for so many of the regiments sent to the Iberian Peninsula.

Between 1808 and 1814, Spain, like fourteenth-century Brittany, was engaged in a fraught war defined by siege tactics, heroic intervention by the local community, and a resolution to uphold hereditary government and religious traditions. During this period, Dibdin's comic opera was performed to highlight key dates in the Theatre Royal's calendar, including Bennett's benefit night, and the engagements of Martha Frances Dickons (8 January 1810) and Charles Incledon (18 May 1812). William Dimond recognised that *The English Fleet*'s naval theme and dramatisation of heroic action continued to exert popular appeal and accrue value.

Shakespeare in Bristol

Between 1808 and 1815 the Shakespearean productions put on at Bristol's Theatre Royal either marked a benefit night or the engagement of a London actor. This chapter has already mentioned that on 8 July 1811 *Coriolanus* was played at the Theatre Royal under the patronage of the Oxford Regiment and that several songs that night enhanced the play's martial themes, especially 'Graham & Glory, or The Battle of Barrosa'. With the British victory symbolically heightened by the capture of the French regimental eagle, the final ovation scene, in which Coriolanus enters with the 'Chief Eagle', would have been all the more momentous. The playbills for the 1812 production of *Coriolanus* also proudly announced that at the end of Act 2 there would be 'A Grand Ovation, upon the return of Caius Marcius from the Conquest of Corioli'.[117] The Theatre Royal Committee was clearly keen to capitalise upon Kemble's twofold fame as leading tragedian and manager.

The attempt to put on a local production comparable to Covent Garden's technically exigent revival of Shakespeare's Roman play would be riddled with practical difficulties. But these were mitigated, to some extent, by Bristol's

---

[115]   Bristol TR Playbill, 27 June 1810. BCRL. See also *FFBJ*, 28 September 1811 (on the Royal Navy's 'fresh generation of youthful heroes').

[116]   Dibdin, *English Fleet*, 62 (3.6).

[117]   The play was performed again in October 1813 (and the role of Coriolanus played by Charles Mayne Young). In 1814, with London audiences engrossed by the competition between Young and Edmund Kean, John Philip Kemble returned to the Bristol Theatre Royal, where he played the part of Coriolanus to popular acclaim. See 'Calendar': Part C.

garrison status, which provided the Theatre Royal with numerous soldiers and sailors who could swell the auditorium and act as supernumeraries on stage. When Kemble's grand ovation scene was replicated in Bristol, troops awaiting deployment were engaged in the play's carefully orchestrated military procession. This kind of organised participation provided a good opportunity for the army (and navy) to impress civilian audiences, as I suggest above.[118] On the four occasions during the Peninsular War when *Coriolanus* was played in Bristol, Shakespeare's play imparted direct messages of social control and public loyalism delivered by (and to) those soon to depart for the front-lines.

These local productions of Shakespeare's plays were, however, less dependent on the stock company than on star actors from London on tour. Bristol's urban development in the late eighteenth century had entailed the generation of turnpike trusts (established all over England to help create a network of well-maintained roads). As already explained, this permitted star actors from the metropolis to arrive in Bristol by mail coach and fulfil short engagements, sometimes during the London theatre season itself.[119] The engagement of star actors certainly helped enhance the theatre's appeal to wartime audiences.

By bringing renowned actors to the provinces, Bristol's Theatre Royal fostered belief in a truly national standard of Shakespearean performance. This came, nevertheless, at a cost to the leading actors of the local stock company, who were thereby prevented from assuming principal roles.[120] Although this presented a clear disadvantage to provincial actors, there were box office benefits to be enjoyed. Five performances of *King Lear* were staged at the Theatre Royal between 1808 and 1815. Four of these occurred during or after October 1810, when the London patents, in deference to George III's ill health, no longer staged the play.[121] This gave Bristol's theatre-goers the thrilling opportunity to see

---

[118] Military parading by the Volunteer forces was popular in Bristol during the wars. To celebrate their seventh anniversary, the Volunteers assembled at Queen's Square and marched to Leigh Down for inspection. The regiment of 800 men divided into two groups and enacted a sham fight. *FFBJ* praised the Volunteers for 'great steadiness and much military science', noting that the artillery '*played* with great effect' and that a number of people assembled 'to see this pleasing military spectacle'. *FFBJ*, 28 July 1810.

[119] BTR was also advantageously positioned to recruit actors making an onward journey to Dublin. See, for instance, *FFBJ*, 30 September 1809, on the engagement of Sarah Smith.

[120] 'The popularity of visiting performers with a London reputation undermined the authority and standards of the stock company'. Roswell and Anthony Jackson, *The Repertory Movement: A History of Regional Theatre in Britain* (Cambridge: Cambridge University Press, 1984), 9. See also: Barker, *Theatre Royal* 73; and Moody, 'Dictating to the Empire', 32.

[121] See 'Calendar': Part C. After years of absence from Bristol, Kemble returned to the Theatre Royal to play Lear on 7 and 21 December 1812. On 11 April 1814, he performed Lear again but it seems that although 'correct, scholar-like, and critical' Kemble's impersonation lacked the 'transcendent excellence' of his King John, Macbeth,

Kemble, one of the Romantic stage's most celebrated actors, perform the lead role in a tragedy considered 'taboo' for the times. The repertoire at Bristol's Theatre Royal amounted to a selective – and at times exclusive – response to the capital's favourites, as also suggested by the local indifference to *Remorse*.

Shakespeare's plays were fashionable commodities that distinguished the artistic cachet of the Theatre Royal's wartime repertoire. By limiting performances of Shakespeare to the engagement of a star actor or to mark a benefit night, the Theatre Royal was able to promote the cultural exclusivity associated with the national bard, and to impart the impression that Shakespeare belonged to a larger, national project, dependent upon the mobility of actors and the beneficence of the local community to support its favourite plays and players. When in 1813 Coleridge came to Bristol's White Lion Inn to deliver his series of Shakespearean lectures, his success was also interpreted as a sign of civic amelioration. The *Bristol Gazette* proudly reported that it was 'much to the credit of the literary feeling of Bristol that the room overflowed'.[122]

Advertisements for Coleridge's lecture series stated that he had come to Bristol 'at the suggestion of several Gentlemen of this city'.[123] In his choice of venue Coleridge followed the footsteps of John Thelwall, who had lectured at the White Lion Inn in September 1808 (on the topic of senatorial and popular oratory). These lectures were advertised in the local press as including 'a PHILIPPIC *against the Oppressor of Europe*, an ODE addressed to the Energies of Britain on behalf of the Spanish, and other Recitations'.[124] Nicholas Roe has argued that Thelwall's journey to the West Country in 1797 is likely to have been a symbolic one:

> For Thelwall, the excursion to Somerset was less an escape from the dangers of London than a homecoming in a provincial landscape long associated with resistance – a resistance that in the days of King Alfred had arguably led to the foundation of England itself.[125]

This landscape may have acquired new associations by 1808, but its early significance is likely to have remained, lending particular gratification, therefore, to the '*bumper*' audience that attended Thelwall's farewell lecture.[126]

---

and Richard (*BG*, 14 April 1814). Whether this was due to the demands of the role, or less frequent opportunities for its performance, it is difficult to say.

[122]   *BG*, 4 November 1813.

[123]   *FFBJ*, 23 October 1813.

[124]   *BG*, 22 September 1808. For an overview of the series see *BG*, 29 September 1808: Part 1 – literary lectures (on Alexander's Feast and John Gilpin); Part 2 – lectures on elocution 'as a social accomplishment … with an appeal to FEMALE INTELLECT and FEMALE PATRIOTISM'; Part 3 – elocution of the stage.

[125]   Nicholas Roe, 'John Thelwall and the West Country: The Road to Nether Stowey Revisited', in 'John Thelwall: Critical Reassessments', *Romantic Circles: Praxis Series* <http://www.rc.umd.edu/praxis/thelwall/HTML/praxis.2011.roe.html> [Accessed 11.04.14].

[126]   *FFBJ*, 8 October 1808.

Thewall had first delivered his 'Ode Addressed to the Energies of Britain In Behalf of the Spanish Patriots' at the Freemason's Tavern in London on 25 July 1808. It constituted a crucial part of the lectures that he offered in Bristol.[127] The speaker's interlacing of literary and political themes would, however, prove problematic. At least one correspondent of *Felix Farley's Bristol Journal* called into question Thelwall's patriotism. On 8 October 1808 the paper printed Thelwall's reply to 'H.F.', who had accused the orator of a 'sinister attempt to promote the views of the Gallic tyrant'. Thelwall retaliated by characterising the attack as 'a tissue of the grossest misrepresentation', and insisting that 'the Heroism and Energy of Britain in the Cause of National Independence in General, and of the noble struggle of Spanish Patriotism in particular' had been genuinely felt.[128]

Judging by the price of admission (7s, 6d. for the course; or 3s, 6d. per lecture) Thelwall expected a predominantly middle-class audience.[129] The criticisms levelled against him by H.F. – whom Thelwall sneeringly characterised as 'the anonymous paragraphist [of] a provincial newspaper' – incited, nevertheless, a response more passionate than mannered; a heartfelt defence that suggested, moreover, interesting contiguities between 'Citizen John', the radical orator of the 1790s, and 'Mr Thelwall', the re-invented elocutionist. Weighing his intention, honesty and feeling against the 'pretended criticism', 'grossest misrepresentation' and 'malicious writings' of his antagonist, Thelwall accepts that on the subject of Napoleon's 'powers and talents of mind, honest men may perhaps differ'.[130] While this admission rings true to the qualified praise for Napoleon that would emerge in his later political journalism for *The Champion*, the semantic redundancy of the construction 'may perhaps' betrays an uneasiness about venturing such an opinion in the first volatile years of the Peninsular Campaign.[131] Thelwall thus swiftly normalises his statement with an affirmation that the 'Gallic-Tyrant['s]' 'ambitious designs' were universally abhorred. He then concludes with a defiant promise to repeat the 'Farewell Philippic'. This represented, for Thelwall, an opportunity to re-assert his public identity. He half acknowledges this by pointing out that although it would be impossible to repeat the 'precise words' of a lecture that had been improvised and spontaneous, he could not be induced 'to change one iota of sentiment, or retract any opinion' previously expressed.[132]

---

[127] The title page to Thelwall's published Ode notes that it was 'intended to accompany the Poem and Oration on the Death of Lord Nelson' and is paginated accordingly. The Ode was published shortly after its first performance.

[128] *FFBJ*, 8 October 1808.

[129] *BG*, 22 September 1808.

[130] *FFBJ*, 8 October 1808.

[131] See *The Champion*, 30 January 1820: 'In the very vices and tyranny of Napoleon, there was a grandeur of soul, a magnificence of conception, a potency of execution, which made some atonement for his oppressions'. Qtd in Michael Scrivener's *Seditious Allegories: John Thelwall and Jacobin Writing* (Pennsylvania: The Pennsylvania State University Press, 2001), 265.

[132] *FFBJ*, 8 October 1808. See John Thelwall, 'Ode Addressed to the Energies of Britain in behalf of the Spanish Patriots'.

The excitement occasioned by Thelwall's final lecture at the White Lion Inn is likely to have been remembered by Coleridge's 1813 audiences as they gathered to hear the one-time 'Citizen Sam' offer his political readings of Shakespeare's greatest plays. Much had happened, however, in the five years that separated the two lecture series. Thelwall had visited Bristol in the aftermath of the Convention of Cintra, when public opinion about the conduct of the British campaign in the Iberian Peninsula reached its first ebb. This is likely to explain at least partly why H.F. went to such pains to challenge Thelwall's 'patriotic' commitment. In 1813, by contrast, the liberation of Portugal and advancement of British troops from Spain into France had encouraged renewed confidence in a proximate, successful outcome for the war.[133] That year, local reviews of Coleridge's lectures featured alongside notifications of the general illuminations held in celebration of French defeats.[134] As Coleridge stood at the podium delivering his third lecture, he compared Macbeth to Napoleon and alluded to recent Allied successes, effectively reclaiming the White Lion Inn as a space for the discussion of literature, politics and, of course, the changing meanings of patriotism, which had proved so contentious in 1808.[135]

Coleridge's lectures also had an obvious influence on the theatrical criticism of the *Bristol Gazette*. On 4 November 1813 the paper printed a comprehensive account of Coleridge's lecture of 2 November on the subject of *Macbeth*. In that lecture, Coleridge set himself against the 'prejudiced idea of *Lady Macbeth* as a Monster' and focused considerable energy on recovering the femininity of her character. The *Bristol Gazette* recounted Coleridge's impression that, throughout the play, she was determined 'to *bully* conscience'. Defining Lady Macbeth as 'a woman of a visionary and day-dreaming turn of mind', Coleridge explained that 'So far is the woman from being dead within her, that her sex occasionally betrays itself in the very moments of dark and bloody imagination'. Quoting Lady Macbeth's image of 'plucking her nipple from the boneless gums of her infant', Coleridge underlined the very grotesqueness of her language as evidence of the force of its appeal, concluding that the line could only achieve such startling effect because Lady Macbeth remained solemnly attached to the bonds of maternal love.[136]

Echoes of Coleridge's lecture continued to reverberate more than six months later when, in May 1814, the *Bristol Gazette* published its review of a recent production of *Macbeth* at the Theatre Royal. Significantly, the *Bristol Gazette* drew attention to the same scenes and language used by Coleridge to argue for a reassessment of Lady Macbeth's character. When the reviewer speaks of Mrs Weston's Lady Macbeth he also quotes the lines: 'I have given suck and know

---

[133]   See. *FFBJ*, 16 October; and *BG*, 21 October 1813.
[134]   See *FFBJ*, 6 November 1813.
[135]   *BG*, 11 November 1813. See Hugh Cunningham, 'The Language of Patriotism, 1750–1914', in *History Workshop* No. 12 (autumn 1981) 8–33.
[136]   *BG*, 4 November 1813.

how sweet it is &c', recognising that they have often been thought to show 'a monster savageness'.[137] 'Yet the very words themselves "I know how sweet it is" betray maternal softness', upholds the reviewer, obviously glorying in Coleridge's literary convictions.[138] His comments suggest that Coleridge's lectures attracted more than passing interest. In Bristol's social calendar these lectures belonged, instead, to a larger tradition of visiting orators, actors and celebrity-studded Shakespearean productions that were held in high regard. This ensured that the cultural and political implications of Coleridge's arguments continued to be felt long after his formal farewell.[139]

Bristol's Minor Theatre

The Theatre Royal may have been Bristol's dominant theatrical establishment, but it was not its only one. In 1811 Walter Jenkins purchased and converted the Assembly Rooms that would become Bristol's 'second' theatre, the Regency. In the past, the Assembly Rooms in Prince Street had been hired for various reasons, including balls, concerts and glamorous dinners. After 1810 the Rooms even served as a storehouse for iron.[140] As a result of Jenkins's alterations, box seats replaced the old orchestra and a new portable stage was introduced, which could be mounted and dismantled at short notice. At first, the refurbished space was used for concerts organised by the flautist Andrew Ashe (from the Bath Assembly Rooms), but in August 1812 Dennis Lawler took a lease on the building and converted it into a venue for theatrical entertainments.[141] The lack of a royal patent, meant, however, that no spoken plays could be legally performed.

Like the London minors, the Regency was limited to musical, mimic or spectacular performances. It was, nevertheless, still perceived to pose a significant threat to the proprietors of the Theatre Royal, who conspired to shut it down. In Bristol, the competition between the Regency Theatre and Theatre Royal would expose the fine line dividing the legitimate and illegitimate stages and reveal how, during the Peninsular War, Bristol's playhouses were transformed into sites for both cultural and political contestation.

---

[137]   *BG*, 5 May 1814.

[138]   Following Coleridge's lead, the reviewer also cites Lady Macbeth's response to the murder of Duncan as a turning point in her characterisation.

[139]   Coleridge returned to Bristol in 1814 to deliver four lectures on Milton, one on 'poetic taste' and another on Cervantes. Although the notes for these lectures do not survive, Coleridge's discussion of *Don Quixote* in the 1818–1819 lecture series suggests a long-standing interest in the philosophical dimension of Cervantes's writing. '1814 Lectures on Milton and Cervantes' (White Lion, Bristol), Lecture 6 (21 April 1814) *CC: Lectures*, 2: 14–15.

[140]   Beeson, *Bristol in 1807*, 26.

[141]   *BG*, 21 November 1811. KB/ 21/1.

In the summer of 1812, with the Theatre Royal still closed before the start of its new season, Lawler announced that his theatre would open with the representation of a burletta 'founded on the glorious achievements of Earl Wellington'.[142] But, according to Kathleen Barker, this entertainment never 'materialised'. Barker blames internal squabbles and notes that Lawler's management was short lived.[143] The choice of entertainment remains significant, nonetheless. By this burletta, Lawler sought to respond directly to the public interest in the Peninsular War. Designed to profit from local patriotic sentiment, it was just the kind of entertainment likely to appeal to Bristol's large community of servicemen.

From the outset, the Regency was eager to compare itself to the London minors. The theatre's first advertisements had thereby introduced the public to 'Mr Lawler (from Mr Elliston's Theatre, London)', underscoring the fact that the Regency's voguish new manager had links to the Surrey Theatre.[144] A month later, another advertisement was printed in the *Bristol Mirror*, stating that in consideration of 'their small sphere of action, the performances at [the Regency] may safely challenge comparison with those of the *little* theatres in the Metropolis'.[145] Lawler was well aware that his London connections could endow his theatre with extra prestige. This was also recognised by his successor, 'Mr Clarke', who took over the theatre's management in November 1812. Clarke created a new company for the Regency that specifically drew upon the metropolis's large pool of accomplished actors, including the equestrian turned pantomimic actor William Miller, and several others from the Surrey Theatre.[146] The capital's minor theatres provided a model and measure for Bristol's new illegitimate stage. Both of the Regency's managers recognised this: Lawler thus imported entertainments from the Surrey, while Clarke contracted many actors who had made their reputations in London. By these gestures they helped propagate the impression that the illegitimate repertoire had, like the legitimate canon, come to acquire a national character.

The question of genre was a weighty consideration for any minor theatre. Lawler deliberately drew the public's attention to this when he launched his opening season. Promising 'Grandeur, Interest and Comic Effect', he placed an advertisement in *Felix Farley's Bristol Journal* defining the kinds of performances that would be on offer:

> The more juvenile part of society will find in them that entertainment which they could not derive from the regular Drama, intended for the gratification of

---

142   *FFBJ*, 15 August 1812.

143   The theatre closed on 22 October 1812 and re-opened a month later under a new manager, 'Mr Clarke', who had worked at the theatres in Weymouth, Exeter, Cork, Limerick and Waterford. Barker, 'The Night the Statue Got Stuck!', 5. KB/ 21/1.

144   When John Cartwright Cross died in 1809, Dennis Lawler replaced him as the main scriptwriter for the Surrey Theatre. J. Decastro, *The Memoirs of J. Decastro Comedian*, ed. R. Humphreys (London, 1824), 160.

145   *BM*, 12 September 1812. KB/ 21/1.

146   *FFBJ*, 14 November 1812. KB/ 21/1.

the mature and expanded mind; yet they will be sufficiently rational to agreeably amuse the adult, and occasionally be made the humble instrument of celebrating the glorious victories of our army and navy.[147]

The manager was conscious of the snobbery that his theatre would have to overcome. In his puff Lawler takes pains, therefore, to define the Regency's entertainments as straightforward, uncomplicated pieces specifically suited to younger audiences. Their 'rationality' he claims, would not preclude the adult's enjoyment, but he concedes that such pieces might not attract the 'mature and expanded mind'. These realistic, grounded claims to simplicity were, nevertheless, somewhat qualified by Lawler's final observation that there would be a variety of entertainments 'celebrating the glorious victories of our army and navy'. By adding nationalist feeling to the Regency's educative value, the manager called for audiences of all classes and ages to lend their patronage to the Regency. The war in the Iberian Peninsula made Lawler's advertised entertainment about Wellington's victories an obvious choice for an illegitimate theatre avoiding censure and seeking to attract large audiences on its opening night. Whether or not the entertainment was, in fact, performed, pales in significance to the anticipation engendered by Lawler's publicity campaign.

For the remainder of its short but eventful existence, the Regency produced a range of spectacles that could be broadly classified as tangentially topical. In November 1812 the theatre engaged 'Signor Duharro' (billed as having performed in London, Lisbon and Madrid). Duharro offered a circus-like fare of entertainments described as 'Polanderic Exercises' of balancing chairs, ladders, sticks and hats.[148] Two nights after his first appearance, Duharro performed again. This time, he shared the stage with John Betterton (billed as 'Mr Betterton Jr'), who played the role of Don Guzman in the theatre's first representation of *Don Juan; or, The Libertine Destroyed*.[149] This pantomime ballet – hugely successful in London – was, as Moyra Haslett explains, one of the many variations of Tirso de Molina's *El burlador de Sevilla* (1630).[150] It proved especially popular in the 1810s and is likely to have had its appeal in Bristol enhanced by the engagement of an Iberian performer on the night of its premiere. *Don Juan* was, however, a difficult play to stage. When *Don Juan* was performed on 4 December 1812 the Regency's audiences were amused to discover that Don Guzman's statue was too big for the stage and could not be wheeled-in from the side rooms.[151] This book has shown

---

[147]   *FFBJ*, 15 August 1812. KB/ 21/1.

[148]   Regency Playbill, 2 December 1812. BCRL.

[149]   Regency Playbill, 4 December 1812. BRCL. Invariably billed as 'Mr Betterton Junior', John Betterton was the son of the actor Thomas William Betterton (d. 1834) and brother to the celebrated actress Mrs Julia Glover (*née* Betterton). See Highfill Jr, Burnim, and Langhans (eds), *Biographical Dictionary*, 2: 99–101.

[150]   Moyra Haslett, *Byron's Don Juan and the Don Juan Legend* (Oxford: Clarendon Press, 1997), 19.

[151]   Barker, 'The Night the Statue Got Stuck!', 6.

that much of the appeal excited by stage representations of Spain and Portugal derived from the spectacular. *Don Juan*'s notable absence from the Regency's repertoire after this first, failed attempt points to the larger implications of the theatre's scenographic shortcomings. Boasting a much better capacity for special effects, the Theatre Royal, by contrast, performed *Don Juan* seven times between 1808 and 1815 – a series of performances crowned by the visually impressive representation of a 'sea storm and shipwreck'.[152]

Most of the plays staged at the Regency were imported from London. The considerable staging difficulties that this could entail were hinted at earlier in 1812 when Clarke chose Matthew Lewis's equestrian drama *Timour the Tartar* to inaugurate his appointment as manager. He had then curtailed audiences' expectations for the Regency's first production of the play by appending to the playbills an extract from Lewis's Preface:

> 'I constructed the Drama in such a manner, that by substituting a combat on foot for one on horseback, the cavalry might be omitted without injury to the Plot, and I understand that the Piece has been acted in the Country with the above alteration and with much applause'.[153]

To this, Clarke added the observation that 'the Author's assertion has been amply justified' by the 'crowded auditories which have nightly attended the performance of TIMOUR the TARTAR at the Theatres Royal, Edinburgh, York, &c'.[154] His comments aimed to encourage popular esteem for the piece without detracting from the smaller scale of its production.

The following year, on 27 July 1813, Regency audiences were invited to a performance of *Timour the Tartar* that this time included 'the EQUESTRIAN TROOP and their Celebrated HORSES'.[155] The decision to re-stage the play in this fashion stemmed from a series of improvements to the playhouse and Clarke's greater willingness to dig into the Regency's coffers. The most notable scenes in the new production involved a procession of real horses to escort the princess Mingrella, a combat on horseback at the end of the first act, and a grand finale that called for an attack of cavalry and infantry (set against the backdrop of the fortress at moonlight). This performance of *Timour the Tartar* was not, however, provided by the stock company, but by performers on tour from London. Such one-off engagements proved that when it came to spectacular display, the Regency's managers were willing to compensate for their own inexperience by importing from the metropolitan minors. Clarke's increased investment in scenography, special effects and professional performers represented a larger long-term strategy to become a minor theatre adept at staging the metropolis's greatest illegitimate successes.

152   'Calendar': Part C, 26 June 1811.
153   Regency Playbill, 27 November 1812. BCRL.
154   Regency Playbill, 27 November 1812.
155   Regency Playbill, 27 July 1813. BRCL.

During their tenure, the Regency's managers were presented with several opportunities to devise new patriotic pieces. The year 1812 marked a turning point in the war against Napoleon. Positive predictions made in June were confirmed in September, when it was reported that following the victory at Salamanca, the army had been able to march into Madrid and liberate the Spanish capital; that the siege of Cadiz had been finally raised; and that Astorga had surrendered to the Gallician army.[156] *Felix Farley's Bristol Journal* proudly celebrated this new chapter in the British campaign and the 'powerful appeal which it makes to the public feeling and opinion in Spain'.[157] Even the *Bristol Gazette*, which had long been opposed to British involvement in the Peninsula, claimed that the only fault in the dispatch from Salamanca was its modesty, which 'hardly does justice to the brilliancy of the exploit'.[158] The Regency, in turn, prepared for the representation of a new spectacle called *The Battle of Salamanca; or, British Glory*, which premiered in November 1812.

The Battle of Salamanca was written and adapted by George Male. It boasted a rousing musical score; a cast of Spanish, French, and English characters (listed separately in the playbills); and specifically designed scenery, such as a view of Lord Wellington's tent. The list of dramatis personae included 'Lord Wellington', and 'Gabriel, (a Goatherd)' as the lead Spanish role. This suggests that, similar to the Sans Pareil production of *Disappointments; or, Love in Castile* (1810), simplifications of Spanish life dominated *The Battle of Salamanca*'s visual economy, although greater emphasis would be placed on the 'recent occurrences' that Male's production had been designed to celebrate and for which purpose supernumeraries had been expressly hired.[159]

The full title of the entertainment – *The Battle of Salamanca; or, British Glory* – allocates to its two constituent parts apparently equal importance. This reflects the larger culture of reportage on the Peninsular War, which, as already discussed, frequently attributed the victories in Spain to the British, rather than Allied, camp. On 26 November 1813 the *Bristol Gazette* thus disavowed any sense of surprise that the Spaniards had demonstrated 'sluggish indifference'. Convinced that Sir John Moore's doubts about Spanish commitment to the war had 'proved correct', the paper concluded pithily: 'In short, the tug of war in the Peninsula, is between the French and English, and the question simply is; can we drive the French out of Spain?'.[160] *The Battle of Salamanca* intended to leave audiences in no doubt about British heroism: when the play was performed on 30 December, Betterton Jr delivered 'A Patriotic Address' in the character of a British tar and danced a sailor's hornpipe.

---

[156]   See *FFBJ*, 20 June and 12 September 1812; *BG*, 20 August 1812.
[157]   *FFBJ*, 12 September 1812.
[158]   *BG*, 20 August 1812.
[159]   Regency Playbill, 30 December 1812. BCRL.
[160]   *BG*, 26 November 1813.

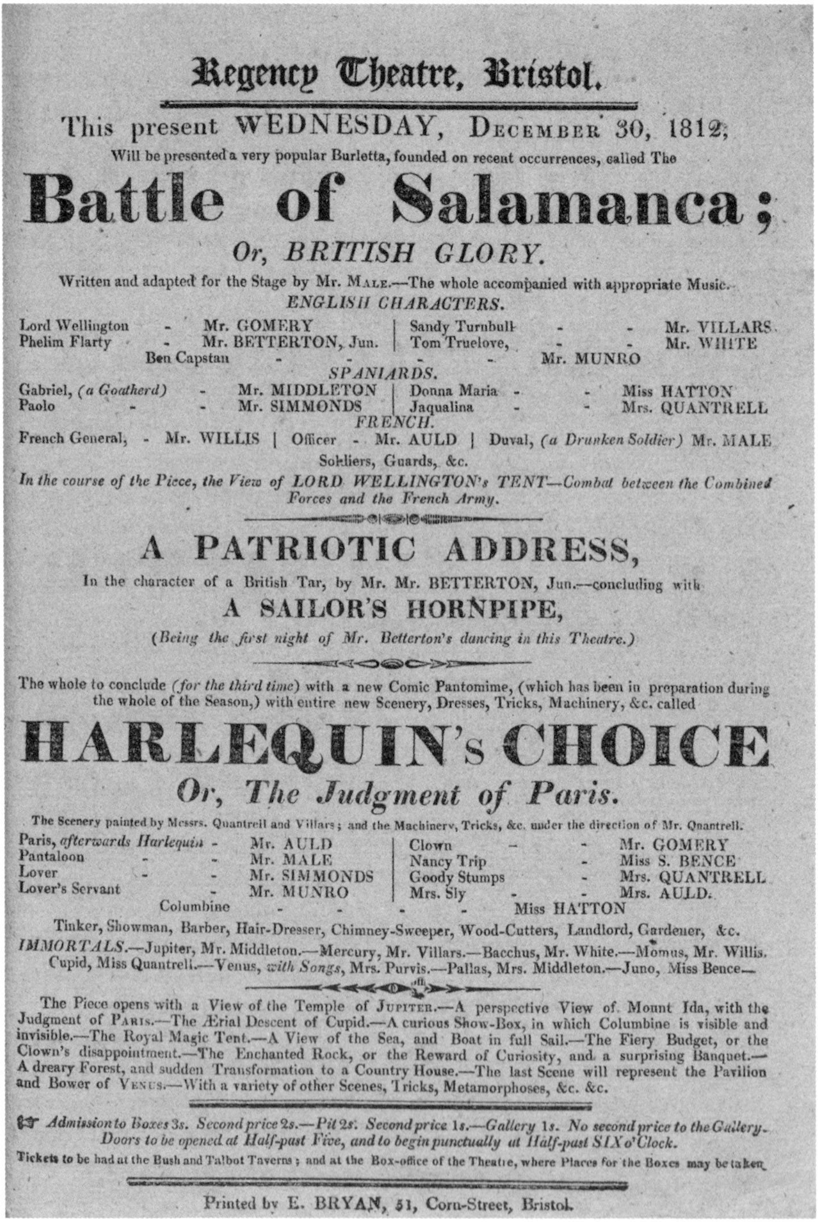

Regency Theatre, Bristol.

This present WEDNESDAY, DECEMBER 30, 1812;

Will be presented a very popular Burletta, founded on recent occurrences, called The

Battle of Salamanca;

Or, BRITISH GLORY.

Written and adapted for the Stage by Mr. MALE.—The whole accompanied with appropriate Music.

ENGLISH CHARACTERS.

Lord Wellington - Mr. GOMERY | Sandy Turnbull - - Mr. VILLARS
Phelim Flarty - Mr. BETTERTON, Jun. | Tom Truelove, - - Mr. WHITE
Ben Capstan - - - - Mr. MUNRO

SPANIARDS.

Gabriel, *(a Goatherd)* - Mr. MIDDLETON | Donna Maria - - Miss HATTON
Paolo - - Mr. SIMMONDS | Jaqualina - - Mrs. QUANTRELL

FRENCH.

French General, - Mr. WILLIS | Officer - Mr. AULD | Duval, *(a Drunken Soldier)* Mr. MALE
Soldiers, Guards, &c.

In the course of the Piece, the View of LORD WELLINGTON's TENT—Combat between the Combined Forces and the French Army.

A PATRIOTIC ADDRESS,

In the character of a British Tar, by Mr. Mr. BETTERTON, Jun.—concluding with

A SAILOR'S HORNPIPE,

(Being the first night of Mr. Betterton's dancing in this Theatre.)

The whole to conclude *(for the third time)* with a new Comic Pantomime, (which has been in preparation during the whole of the Season,) with entire new Scenery, Dresses, Tricks, Machinery, &c. called

HARLEQUIN's CHOICE

Or, The Judgment of Paris.

The Scenery painted by Messrs. Quantrell and Villars; and the Machinery, Tricks, &c. under the direction of Mr. Quantrell.

Paris, *afterwards Harlequin* - Mr. AULD | Clown - - Mr. GOMERY
Pantaloon - - Mr. MALE | Nancy Trip - Miss S. BENCE
Lover - - Mr. SIMMONDS | Goody Stumps - Mrs. QUANTRELL
Lover's Servant - Mr. MUNRO | Mrs. Sly - - Mrs. AULD.
Columbine - - - - Miss HATTON

Tinker, Showman, Barber, Hair-Dresser, Chimney-Sweeper, Wood-Cutters, Landlord, Gardener, &c.
IMMORTALS.—Jupiter, Mr. Middleton.—Mercury, Mr. Villars.—Bacchus, Mr. White.—Momus, Mr. Willis. Cupid, Miss Quantrell.—Venus, *with Songs*, Mrs. Purvis.—Pallas, Mrs. Middleton.—Juno, Miss Bence—

The Piece opens with a View of the Temple of JUPITER.—A perspective View of Mount Ida, with the Judgment of PARIS.—The Ærial Descent of Cupid.—A curious Show-Box, in which Columbine is visible and invisible.—The Royal Magic Tent.—A View of the Sea, and Boat in full Sail.—The Fiery Budget, or the Clown's disappointment.—The Enchanted Rock, or the Reward of Curiosity, and a surprising Banquet.—A dreary Forest, and sudden Transformation to a Country House.—The last Scene will represent the Pavilion and Bower of VENUS.—With a variety of other Scenes, Tricks, Metamorphoses, &c. &c.

☞ *Admission to Boxes 3s. Second price 2s.—Pit 2s. Second price 1s.—Gallery 1s. No second price to the Gallery. Doors to be opened at Half-past Five, and to begin punctually at Half-past SIX o'Clock.*

Tickets to be had at the Bush and Talbot Taverns; and at the Box-office of the Theatre, where Places for the Boxes may be taken

Printed by E. BRYAN, 51, Corn-Street, Bristol.

Figure 4.5 Playbill advertising *The Battle of Salamanca* and *Harlequin's Choice* at the Regency Theatre, Bristol, 30 December 1812. Photography by David Emeney. Bristol Museums, Galleries & Archives. Reproduced by kind permission of Bristol Reference Library.

The supernumeraries who took part in *The Battle of Salamanca* were, of course, rehearsing not only an important conflict, but anticipating an even more complete victory in the larger war, which it was expected their own deployment to Spain and France would help realise. But the high costs involved in mounting such topical and putatively accurate representations of the British army's latest actions were sufficient to impose a limit on the number of entertainments of this kind. Wary of too often exceeding their budget with large-scale spectacles, the Regency's managers tended to opt for shorter patriotic interludes instead. Topical addresses and dances thus featured prominently in the wartime repertoire, with the hornpipe proving especially popular in a naval city such as Bristol. Addresses were frequently delivered by actors 'in character' as sailors, while ballet dances similarly exploited nautical themes, as highlighted, for example, by 'The Sailor's Return', which was performed on 2 March 1813 for Clarke's benefit.[161]

Many theatre scholars have shown interest in the variety of dramatic entertainments available at Romantic-period playhouses on any given night.[162] Particular attention has been devoted to the potential points of contact between mainpiece and afterpiece, with more recent theorisations of the relationship between these two principal parts of the programme suggesting that a mix of ideological and more immediately pecuniary considerations were at stake.[163] The performances available at the Regency Theatre draw attention to this but also, significantly, to the often-overlooked interludes that commonly took place between the mainpiece and afterpiece. The fact that these *entr'acte* entertainments were frequently listed in playbills and newspaper advertisements defines them as performative highlights in their own right.

In both legitimate and illegitimate theatres, *entr'acte* divertissements could bear a direct relationship to the mainpiece and/or afterpiece; as suggested by the Theatre Royal's programme for 3 August 1808, when 'A British Sailor's Address to the Volunteers' helped accentuate the other entertainments' patriotic inflections.[164] But if the underlining of topical themes at the Theatre Royal constituted an important function of the interludes on offer, at minor theatres, such as the Regency, they were an integral part of the performance. In venues restricted by law to a repertoire based on song and dance, actors' acrobatic or vocal abilities were as much on display in the mainpiece and afterpiece as in the interludes that bridged them. The patriotic interludes presented at the minor theatres could thus be seen to have

---

[161] Regency Playbill, 2 March 1813. BCRL.

[162] See *The Stage and the Page: London's "Whole Show" in the Eighteenth Century Theatre*, ed. George Winchester Stone Jr. (Berkeley: University of California Press, 1981); Jeffrey N. Cox, 'Spots of Time: The Structure of the Dramatic Evening in the Theater of Romanticism', *Texas Studies in Literature and Language* 41.4, (winter 1999), 403–425; Daniel O'Quinn, *Staging Governance: Theatrical Imperialism in London 1770–1800* (Baltimore: Johns Hopkins University Press, 2005).

[163] O'Quinn, *Staging Governance*, 14; see also Chapter 1, for my discussion of the afterpieces to *Pizarro*.

[164] See 'Calendar': Part C.

a much more direct effect on the preceding mainpiece. This was illustrated, for instance, by the Regency's programme for 17 December 1812. The date marked the engagement of the London actress Ann Hatton (*née* Hinds) who played Fanny Bull to Betterton Jr's Captain Cleveland in the popular burletta *The Land We Live In; or, Free-Born Britons*. When she stepped forward *entr'acte* to deliver the address of a Female Volunteer and dance a military hornpipe, Ann Hatton would have helped link the evening's interludes to the nationalist sentiments advertised by the mainpiece.[165]

The energetic stage presence of an actress such as Ann Hatton is likely to have encouraged audiences to perceive a holistic design to the different parts of the theatrical bill. The ability to forge such associations was emblematic of the minor theatres' importance to the wartime economy but their success was nevertheless regarded with suspicion. Although Lawler and Clarke (unlike their London counterparts) did not have to compete with other local minors, they needed to ensure that the Regency was not considered a rival to the Theatre Royal.[166] Both managers carefully scheduled their performances to avoid clashes with the patent theatre, but the Theatre Royal's proprietors seem to have regarded the Regency as a threat to their livelihoods. Matters started to come to a head in December 1812, when Clarke issued complaints at the bottom of his advertisements that the Regency's large playbills, usually plastered across the city, had been 'invariably torn down and destroyed by some malicious and ill-disposed Persons'.[167] The identities of these offenders were never disclosed, but it is probable that the Theatre Royal Committee was in some way involved.

In 1813 such was the antagonism between the different proprietors, that the Theatre Royal contracted an informer against the Regency. This theatrical spy attended Betterton Jr's benefit night (18 January 1813) which he soon after denounced as an 'illegal' performance; the playbills having advertised a Russian spectacle that was never staged.[168] In response, the *Bristol Mirror* printed a vituperative attack against the Theatre Royal's petty proceedings, accusing the proprietors of exercising 'an Eastern policy' that 'can bear no rival near the throne'.[169] The episode offers neat confirmation of Jane Moody's argument that 'at the centre of debates about theatrical regulation in this period are a set of difficult questions about the meaning and consequences of cultural democracy'.[170] By charging the Theatre Royal with 'Eastern' despotism, the *Bristol Mirror* redirected

---

[165]   Regency Playbill, 17 December 1812. BCRL.

[166]   The Regency also faced other forms of indirect competition from visiting circuses and fairs. See Kathleen Barker, *Bristol at Play: Five Centuries of Live Entertainment* (Wiltshire: Moonraker Press, 1976), 19–23.

[167]   Regency Playbill, 2 December 1812. BCRL.

[168]   *BM*, 14 December 1812 advertised a forthcoming 'local sketch' by Mark Lonsdale; 'pourtraying [*sic*] the patriotic fervour of the brave Russians, and to celebrate the retributive vengeance which has at length overtaken the atrocities of their merciless invader'. KB/ 21/1.

[169]   *BM*, 23 January 1813. KB/ 21/1.

[170]   Moody, *Illegitimate Theatre*, 243.

the oriental excesses expected from Betterton Jr's advertised performance to the management of the Theatre Royal itself. It was a well-tried strategy that would have prompted readers to imagine the Regency, famous for its production of 'national burlettas' and spectacles, as an establishment in need of defence from a tyrannical patent monopoly.[171] The managers of the Regency had, from the start, sought to capitalise upon wartime feeling, with Lawler and Clarke making valiant efforts to push beyond the limitations associated with a provincial minor theatre. By celebrating the Regency's nationalist repertoire, the *Bristol Mirror* may not have been able to save the theatre's fortunes but it offered fitting recognition of the Regency's cultural and political importance to the city.

Faced with tenacious opposition from the Theatre Royal Committee and mounting administrative troubles of his own, Clarke was forced to close the Regency before the end of 1813. It is likely, however, that the end of the Napoleonic Wars would only have increased the difficulties of running Bristol's minor theatre. The range of military and especially naval acts at the Regency had, after all, been one of its main attractions. The fortunate coincidence between the theatre's period of activity and Wellington's greatest successes in the Peninsula meant that the Regency had been able to advertise its first entertainments as patriotic events attractive to civilian, naval and military audiences.[172] This chapter has shown that Bristol's legitimate and illegitimate theatres directly benefitted from the city's garrison status, as confirmed by the popular tradition of military bespeaks at the Theatre Royal, for example. The social comedies that were produced again and again at the Theatre Royal shared a thematic interest in role-playing that seems to have accrued additional political resonance during the Peninsular War. I have suggested that the career of Arthur Wellesley might have offered a point of reference for audiences of *The Castle of Andalusia* and *The Honey Moon*; but these plays' political inflections were not, of course, confined to this interpretation alone. As I hope to have underlined by my more detailed analysis of *The English Fleet in 1342*, the best repertoire plays were characterised by an interpretative openness that resists neat explication. During the Peninsular War, the topical appeal of a play such as *The English Fleet* rested as much on its straightforward derision of the Spanish character Don Carlos, as on the new models of female heroism enacted by the Countess of Brittany.

In Bristol dramatic performances were closely related to the political notices and commentaries circulated in the local press. The *Bristol Gazette*, *Bristol Mirror* and *Felix Farley's Bristol Journal* frequently spoke to the national and local interests served by the city's theatrical culture and related 'performances',

---

[171]   On the link between patent theatrical practice and political corruption, see Moody, *Illegitimate Theatre*, 15.

[172]   To celebrate the Spanish campaign in 1813, the Regency produced a new pantomime entertainment, *Gil Blas; or, The Fools of Fortune. BM*, 25 January 1813. KB/21/1.

including Thelwall's and Coleridge's politicised lecture series. In *Entertaining Crisis in the Atlantic Imperium 1770–1790* (2011) Daniel O'Quinn identifies and explores the fascinatingly symmetrical relationship between the strategies employed for reading a contemporary newspaper and those activated by stage performances:

> A typical paper from the period is a remarkable montage of information: advertisements sit adjacent to shipping news, political news is interspersed with social news, and everything is assembled to maximize the amount of print per page. What this means is that the logical links between items are not important to the production and layout of the page but become important in the paper's reception. Reading the paper therefore becomes all about complex acts of dispersion and collection that vary from reading event to reading event.[173]

In this identification of the overlap between political and theatrical cultures, O'Quinn offers a particularly helpful outline of the daily papers' generic mix (from shipping news to social news), and the impetus that this consequently placed on the reader to develop his or her own sequencing for the various reports provided. With nineteenth-century provincial newspapers still organised in an apparently ad-hoc manner, it is productive to extend this interpretation to the theatrical performances described in this chapter, whose meanings, as O'Quinn argues, were clearly as dependent upon the agency of the audience as the actors on stage.

By focusing on Bristol, this chapter has examined the socio-economic and political transformations that affected provincial theatre-going during the Peninsular War. In line with recent scholarship in theatre history, it has represented a move away from an exclusively metropolitan study of the Romantic stage, in order to explore how both the Theatre Royal and Regency promoted a new sense of urban consciousness, significant at local and national levels. The facts that *Remorse* was not a favourite with local audiences and that *King Lear* was performed at Bristol's Theatre Royal during the Peninsular War confirm the need for strict caution when making generalisations about British theatre based on London alone. Local managers may have tried to conform to metropolitan fashions by investing a considerable proportion of their budget in hiring star actors and importing the latest stage successes, but they also took pains to distinguish their theatrical fare and make it proudly, even exclusively, Bristolian.

Although by the time of the Peninsular War the provinces were experiencing a downturn in their so-called urban renaissance, theatre audiences in Bristol remained committed to exploring their sense of civic identity. Elliston played up to this when he performed the role of Puff with a West Country accent; as did the *Bristol Gazette*, when it rose to Catalani's defence and argued that local audiences should show more tolerance than their metropolitan counterparts. During the Peninsular War, Bristol's cultural relationship with London was ambivalent. The

---

[173]   O'Quinn, *Entertaining Crisis*, 9.

city's popular, energetic and celebrated theatrical culture proves, however, that in the early nineteenth century, a certain distance from the centre of government and policy-making could be replete with advantages.

Afterword

English theatre during the Peninsular War offered a range of patriotic, action-packed and visually impressive popular entertainments. From spoken drama at the patent playhouses to ballets and burlettas at the minors, theatre-going in both London and the provinces provided a form of Romantic-period sociability within the reach of almost everyone.[1] This book has explored the resourcefulness and creativity of British managers, playwrights, performers and their audiences, in response to the legal and other socio-political restrictions enforced against the early nineteenth-century stage. In its consideration of how interpretative strategies were applied to blockbusters such as Coleridge's *Remorse* (1813), Sheridan's *Pizarro* (1799) and the many eighteenth-century stock pieces that saturated the theatrical repertoire, this book has maintained that by clever circumvention of contemporary censorship, during the Peninsular War the nation's crowded and excitable theatre auditoriums functioned as spaces of political discovery, assertion and confrontation.

For Britons, whose battles were fought, lost, and won on foreign soil, it made sense to employ allegory to relocate their political doubts, fears, speculations and aspirations to distant lands. In Portugal and Spain, where the effects of war were much more immediate, theatre-going between 1807 and 1815 was an altogether different experience. The twin shackles of economic hardship and political censorship caused theatres to be sporadically closed, dramatic companies disbanded and auditoriums sparsely populated. In closing, I turn my attention to the Iberian experience in its own right, focusing on Portugal, where Britain's military and economic alliances were the strongest, to consider how the theatres in Lisbon responded to the Peninsular War's ideological, as well as more practical, challenges.[2]

When the French arrived in Lisbon in November 1807 they found three main theatres: the populist Salistre theatre (inaugurated in 1782), the Teatro da Rua dos Condes (which specialised in comedies and ballets), and the Real Teatro de São Carlos (famous for its Italian operas). In the attempt to normalise their military presence, French leaders made swift arrangements to establish control of these venues. Général Jean Androche Junot's 'Address to the Nation', delivered from the Palacio do Quartel-Geral de Lisboa (1 February 1808), rendered transparent the cultural aims of the new regime: 'Good administration of the public revenue will

---

[1]   On 'sociability' in this period see *Romantic Sociability: Social Networks and Literary Culture in Britain, 1770–1840*, ed. Gillian Russell and Clara Tuite (Cambridge: Cambridge University Press, 2002).

[2]   On theatre in Madrid during the Peninsular War, see Introduction, note 29.

safeguard the fruits of labour to each employee; public instruction, the mother of civilisation, will spread throughout the provinces; and the Algarve and Beira Alta will also, one day, have their Camões'.[3] The homage to Luis de Camões, author of the great epic poem *Os Lusiadas* (1572), accentuates Junot's professed desire to see the literary arts flourish in the Portuguese provinces (as well as the capital), and permits the 'Address to the Nation' to set the agenda for the French army's expansive political aims. Junot's confidence was not misplaced. French-inspired Neo-Classical culture had, since the late eighteenth century, been flourishing in Portugal; and the theatre, he realised, could be used to encourage liberal thought and other facets of French ideology.

The nineteenth-century theatre historian Francisco da Fonseca Benevidas noted that shortly after Junot assumed control of the city, a gala spectacle was produced at the Real Teatro São Carlos, the city's principal theatre, where Francisco Antonio Lodi (under the orders of a government edict from Paris) had been forced to accept the post of artistic director.[4] Surviving records of the theatre's employees during this time state that Lodi undertook his charge from 4 March until 15 September 1808; that is, the date of the French army's 'felix [*sic*] expulção', their happy expulsion.[5] Indeed, the Convention of Cintra marked a turning point in Lisbon's theatrical history. As French troops evacuated the capital, an Anglo-Portuguese army replaced them. But the British, unlike the French, had no specific cultural briefing and taking control of the São Carlos was not a high priority. Most of the accounts of Portuguese theatre written by British soldiers serving in the Peninsula confirm this in their repeated grievances about the low quality of entertainments. The English army surgeon Samuel Broughton claimed, for example, that the theatres in Lisbon were 'scarcely worthy of notice'.[6]

Broughton, writing in 1813, explains that the São Carlos was open every night of the week, but that it was 'a large, gloomy, and very badly lighted house'. He does, nevertheless, concede that 'at one period perhaps this opera was unrivalled in Europe', and even goes so far as to imagine it in its heyday, when attended by

  3   'As rendas públicas bem administradas segurarão a cada empregado o prémio do seu trabalho; a instrução pública, esta mãe da civilização dos povos, se derramará pelas Províncias; e o Algarve e Beira Alta terão também um dia o seu Camões'.'Junot's Address to the Portuguese Nation, Palacio do Quartel-Geral de Lisboa, 1 Feburary 1808', reprinted in *Bibliotheca Histórica, Política, e Diplomatica da Nação Portugueza*, ed. Joaquim Joze Ferreira de Freitas (London, 1830), 82–4 (83) [my translation].
  4   Francisco da Fonseca Benevidas, *O Real Theatro de São Carlos de Lisboa: desde a sua fundação em 1793 até a actualidade* (Lisbon, [1883]), 100.
  5   AT 1522 (992–1114), 'Nota das Pessoas que farão Emprezarios do Real Theatro de São Carlos desde a sua primeira arbetura athe [*sic*] este presente anno [*sic*] de 1816 – a Saber'. Arquivo Nacional da Torre do Tombo.
  6   Samuel Daniel Broughton, *Letters from Portugal, Spain, & France, written during the Campaigns of 1812, 1813, & 1814, Addressed to a Friend in England. Describing: The Leading Features of the Provinces Passed Through, and the State of Society, Manners, Habits &c. of the People* (London, 1815), 46.

the Portuguese Royal Family and 'when Catalani and several of the first singers were engaged, and the elder and the younger Vestris, and Angiolini were the principal supporters of the ballets'.[7] Yet, for his own part, Broughton remained distinctly unimpressed. In his *Letters from Portugal, Spain, & France, written during the Campaigns of 1812, 1813, & 1814* (1815) Broughton comments, for instance, on the appearance of the Portuguese ladies, whose sombre attire of black dress proved such a contrast to the 'the gay and lively exhibition which a well-filled row of boxes presents in an English theatre'. He also noted that the theatre had various sentries, 'at different points in the pit and lobbies, who controul [*sic*] every expression of approbation or discontent in the audience that affords the slightest interruption of what is going forward'.[8] This was certainly not the rowdy auditorium of an English theatre. Indifferent to his new surroundings, Broughton retreats nostalgically, in recollection of the 'elegance' and 'beauty' of London playhouses and their 'gay' convivial audiences.[9]

Angelica Catalani, who upon her arrival in London in 1806 proved so popular on the English stage, had earlier performed to acclaim in Lisbon, as Broughton rightly observes.[10] During the war, many of the São Carlos's greatest stars sought exile abroad. Italian opera singers – as Kemble would attempt to convince his own audiences – demanded extraordinarily high salaries but, facing financial straits, theatre managers in Lisbon had few incentives to offer their performers. The Real Teatro São Carlos could extend only paltry remuneration for the poorly attended productions that were irregularly put on.

Lisbon's principal theatre had been built for the city's elite and its entertainments were too expensive for the lower classes. Since its opening on 30 June 1793 the theatre had received frequent visits from the Portuguese Royal Court, whose members opted for the operas at the São Carlos in preference to the entertainments available at the Teatro da Rua dos Condes, the other big playhouse. At the São Carlos, as Broughton observed, there were no galleries. Instead, an impressive space was carved out for the 'tribuna real', or royal box, which was the equivalent of three regular boxes in length and another three in height. With the Royal Family in exile at the time of the war, these seats were reserved for the leaders of the Anglo-Portuguese army.

Despite working to a much less precise cultural agenda than the French, the Regency government released numerous cultural edicts after the invading troops' first exodus in September 1808. These edicts underscored that the government authorities were also keen to keep the city's theatres under regulation. The 'Avisos' sent to the

---

[7]   Broughton, *Letters*, 46; 47.

[8]   Broughton, *Letters*, 47.

[9]   Broughton, *Letters*, 47.

[10]   Angelica Catalani arrived in Lisbon in 1804, where she quickly secured her position as one of the most celebrated singers at the Real Teatro São Carlos. She also became a star attraction in London (and the provinces she toured, including Bristol). 'Biographical Sketches of Illustrious and Distinguished Characters: Madame Catalani' in *La Belle Assemblée* (August 1821), 51–2; and *The Grove Book of Opera Singers*, ed. Laura Macy (Oxford: Oxford University Press, 2008), 81.

Cultural Police (considered in more detail below) are particularly interesting insofar as they reveal a theatrical repertoire whose political content, as Broughton suggests in his account of the São Carlos, was carefully scrutinised and monitored.

As the main chapters in this book have illustrated, the English public were accustomed to associating the Spaniards with cultural backwardness, religious superstition and Inquisitorial oppression. While the 'Black Legend' grossly exaggerated these elements of the national character it is true, nevertheless, that rigorous censorship in Spain and Portugal affected the exchange of ideas and literatures that defined the European Enlightenment. Censorship had been exercised in Portugal since the Middle Ages and increased with the church's expansion in the sixteenth century. In 1768 the *Real Mesa Censoria* was created in an attempt to transfer literary censorship from the Church to the State. By 1795 control of censorship returned to Portugal's episcopal authorities, although final approval still belonged to the royal court. The general outline of this system remained in place during the Peninsular War, regulating, for instance, the transmission of foreign texts such as London and Spanish newspapers, as well as the city's theatrical repertoire.[11] The censorship records for February 1809 thus state that the theatrical entertainment *Restauração dos Algarves* (*The Restoration of the Algarves*) would be refused a license, unless changes were made to the play's portrayal of contemporary personages. In September that same year, authorities were also alerted to *Palafox em Saragoça,* a play about the first siege of Zaragoza and its successful defence by the native population. While the play was not prohibited, the Inspector advised that its representation be suspended until the political situation appeared clearer.[12] The second siege of Zaragoza had, after all, ended in a French victory and the heroic Palafox was presumed dead.[13] Three months later, however, in the interests of enhancing wartime morale, approval was given for *Os Patriotas de Aragão* (*The Patriots of Aragon*). This play is likely to have been a reworking of the earlier drama about Palafox, since its full title, when performed in July 1810, was *Os Patriotas de Aragão ou o triunfo de Palafox* (*The Patriots of Aragon; or, The Triumph of Palafox*).

In London, the theatres helped bring news of the war to local audiences, alerting them to the latest conflicts in the Peninsula and commemorating important victories. The kind of spectacular ballets that were so popular in London were, it seems, also in high demand in Lisbon. David Cranmer notes that between 1809 and 1811 a series of 'bailados belicos' (military ballets) were staged at the Real Teatro São Carlos.[14] He lists, and provides performance dates for: *A Batalha do Vimeiro*

[11]   Cx. 491, 'Index da Mesa Censoria'. Arquivo Nacional da Torre do Tombo.

[12]   ATT 1521 (Teatro 992–1113), 'Index das Ordens Mandadas expedir pelo Governo Relativas a Theatros [*sic*]'. Lo. 2o. da Policia (20 September 1809). Arquivo Nacional da Torre do Tombo.

[13]   Palafox was, in fact, taken prisoner by the French, and held at the Vincennes fortress until the end of the war. Fraser, *Napoleon's Cursed War*, 227.

[14]   David Cranmer, 'A Batalha do Bussaco: Um retrato musical', in *Coloquio: A Guerra Peninsular, perspectivas multidisciplinarias*, ed. Maria Leonor Machado de Sousa. 2 vols.

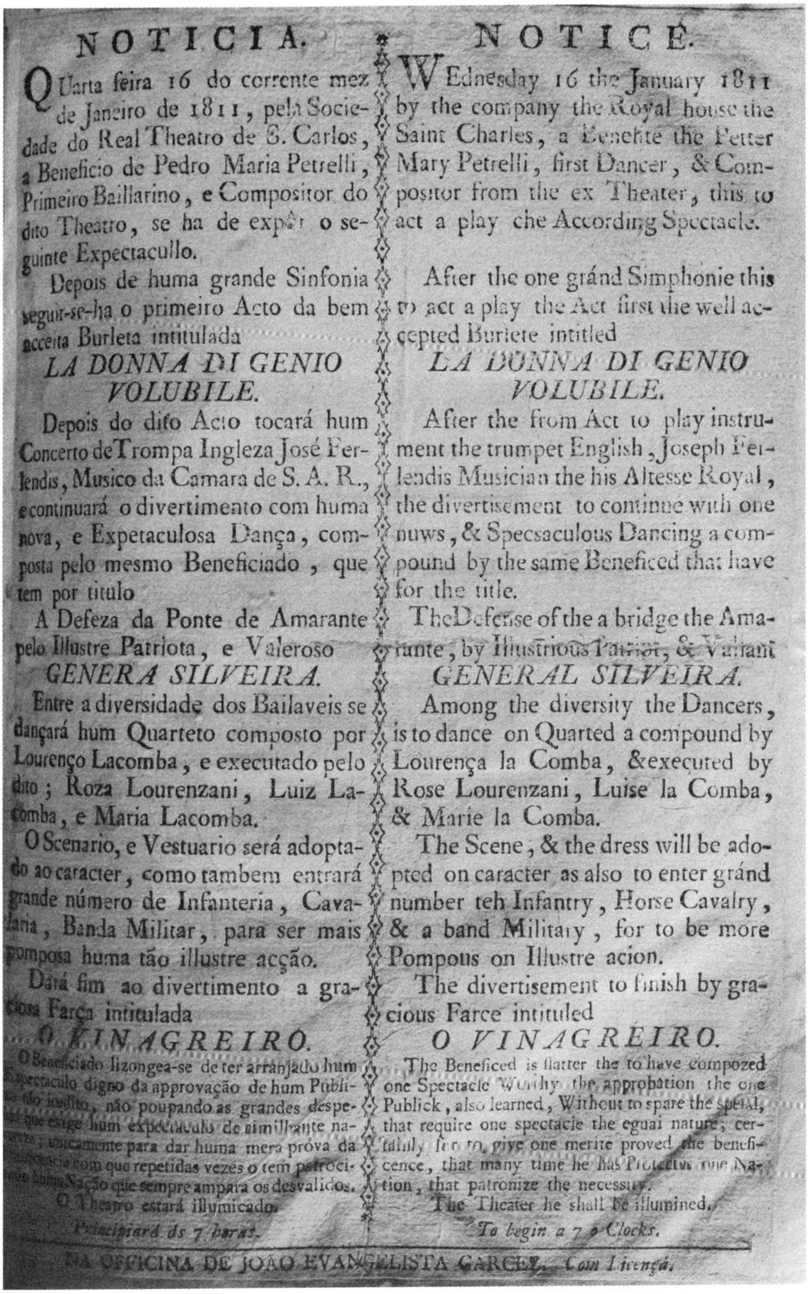

NOTICIA.

Quarta feira 16 do corrente mez de Janeiro de 1811, pela Sociedade do Real Theatro de S. Carlos, a Beneficio de Pedro Maria Petrelli, Primeiro Baillarino, e Compositor do dito Theatro, se ha de expôr o seguinte Expectacullo.

Depois de huma grande Sinfonia seguir-se-ha o primeiro Acto da bem acceita Burleta intitulada

LA DONNA DI GENIO VOLUBILE.

Depois do dito Acto tocará hum Concerto de Trompa Ingleza José Ferlendis, Musico da Camara de S. A. R., e continuará o divertimento com huma nova, e Expetaculosa Dança, composta pelo mesmo Beneficiado, que tem por titulo

A Defeza da Ponte de Amarante pelo Illustre Patriota, e Valeroso

GENERA SILVEIRA.

Entre a diversidade dos Bailaveis se dançará hum Quarteto composto por Lourenço Lacomba, e executado pelo dito; Roza Lourenzani, Luiz Lacomba, e Maria Lacomba.

O Scenario, e Vestuario será adoptado ao caracter, como tambem entrará grande número de Infanteria, Cavalaria, Banda Militar, para ser mais pomposa huma tão illustre acção.

Dará fim ao divertimento a graciosa Farça intitulada

O VINAGREIRO.

O Beneficiado lizongea-se de ter arranjado hum Espectaculo digno da approvação de hum Público tão illustre, não poupando as grandes despezas que exige hum expectaculo de simillhante natureza; unicamente para dar huma mera próva da [illegible] com que repetidas vezes o tem patrocinado huma Nação que sempre ampara os desvalidos.

O Theatro estará illumicado.

Principiará ás 7 horas.

NOTICE.

Wednesday 16 the January 1811 by the company the Royal house the Saint Charles, a Benefite the Petter Mary Petrelli, first Dancer, & Compositor from the ex Theater, this to act a play che According Spectacle.

After the one gránd Simphonie this to act a play the Act first the well accepted Burlete intitled

LA DONNA DI GENIO VOLUBILE.

After the from Act to play instrument the trumpet English, Joseph Ferlendis Musician the his Altesse Royal, the divertisement to continue with one nuws, & Specsaculous Dancing a compound by the same Beneficed that have for the title.

TheDefense of the a bridge the Amarante, by Illustrious Patriot, & Vaillant

GENERAL SILVEIRA.

Among the diversity the Dancers, is to dance on Quarted a compound by Lourença la Comba, &executed by Rose Lourenzani, Luise la Comba, & Marie la Comba.

The Scene, & the dress will be adopted on caracter as also to enter gránd number teh Infantry, Horse Cavalry, & a band Military, for to be more Pompous on Illustre acion.

The divertisement to finish by gracious Farce intituled

O VINAGREIRO.

The Beneficed is flatter the to have compozed one Spectacle Worthy the approbation the one Publick, also learned, Without to spare the spend, that require one spectacle the eguai nature; certainly for to give one merite proved the beneficence, that many time he has Protector one Nation, that patronize the necessity.

The Theater he shall be illumined.

To begin a 7 o Clocks.

NA OFFICINA DE JOÃO EVANGELISTA GARCEZ. *Com Licença.*

Figure 5.1 Bilingual Playbill advertising *A Defesa da Ponte de Amarante* at the Real Teatro São Carlos, 16 January 1811. © The Art Archive/ Garrick Club.

(25 October 1809; repeated in 1815), *Os Patriotas de Aragão* (6 July 1810), *O Triunfo da Espanha ou o redimento de Dupont* (17 August 1810), *A Restauração do Porto ou um dos triunfos do heroi Wellesley* (5 September 1810), *A Defeza* [*sic*] *da Ponte de Amarante por Silveira* (16 January 1811), and *A Batalha do Bussaco* (published in 1811).[15] Each of these entertainments was, of course, symbolically linked to the latest battles in the Peninsular Campaign.

The British generals who signed the Convention of Cintra may have underestimated Wellington's success at the Battle of Vimeiro, but at the Real Teatro São Carlos the battle was celebrated with a glorious balletic representation of the expulsion of the French invaders. In 1809 this ballet was doubly significant as a celebration of Portugal's second liberation. The start of the year had seen the French take advantage of Britain's reduced military presence after Corunna in order to make a second attempt to take Lisbon. Soult and his troops advanced fast and took possession of the town of Chaves by March 1809. Another ballet, *A Defesa da Ponte de Amarante*, was written to laud Wellington's return to Portugal and his command of the Anglo-Portuguese army. Wellington's leadership had helped the army secure the strategic bridge at Amarante and reclaim Chaves. This forced the French to retreat to Porto where, on 12 May 1809, they suffered heavy casualties and were coerced by Allied troops to retreat from Portugal once again. The title of the São Carlos ballet praised this recovery of the Portuguese town as 'one of Wellington's triumphs'. By April 1811 the liberation of Portugal called for yet more celebration; the battles of Bussaco (27 September 1810) and Sabugal (11 April 1811) having resulted in the drumming out of the French army. *A Batalha do Bussaco*, 'a military and historical piece', was written to extol the victory.

The musical score for *A Batalha do Bussaco* is indicative of the methods employed to stage these obviously patriotic pieces. Its music was published in Lisbon in 1811 and clearly intended as a commemorative artefact. The work's title page, for instance, is embellished by an ornate border that relies upon different fonts to entice the reader's interest, placing emphasis on the battle, the piece's dedication to the Anglo-Lusitanian army, and, above all, 'The Illustrious, Excellency, Lord Viscount Wellington', whose other titles of honour are also detailed.

A Batalha do Bussaco opens dramatically, with a description of the enemy troops that have assumed an advantageous position from the heights of the town. The next section describes the arrival of the 88th English Regiment commanded by Lt Colonel Wallace, the 45th Regiment under Lt Colonel Meade, and the 8th Portuguese Regiment led by Lt Colonel Douglas. A bayonet fight ensues, the French Generals Merle and Maucun are injured, and the enemy lose their

---

(Lisbon: Comissão Portuguesa de História Militar/Centro de Estudos Anglo-Portugueses, 2008), 2: 239–44 (241).

[15] The longer titles translate to: *The Triumph of Spain; or, Dupont's Surrender*, *The Restoration of Porto; or, One of the Heroic Wellesley's Triumphs*, and *Silveira's Defence of the Bridge of Amarante*.

strategic stronghold.[16] The description of the action is invariably characterised by an identification of the specific regiments employed in the successful Allied charge. Managers of the Portuguese theatres, like those of the London minors, were dependent upon official dispatches and news bulletins for their re-creation of accurate battle formation and military techniques. Targeted at an audience composed primarily of soldiers, such features would have strongly influenced judgements about the merits of the available repertoire.

It is worth noting that there could be a time lag of as much as one year between the 'ballets' performed at the São Carlos and the battles they depicted. English audiences placed a premium on novelty and newsworthiness. In Lisbon not only did it take much longer to mount these patriotic, spectacular pieces but their perceived purpose was, in any case, inflected somewhat differently. This book has shown that while English spectacles made prominent claims to the public's political sympathies, decisions about the repertoire were often made on the basis of managerial whim and inter-theatre competition. In Portugal, by contrast, wartime entertainments operated in a disparate theatrical economy that received official encouragement from the government, and had been specifically designed to raise morale and inspire confidence in the Anglo-Portuguese army.

When the São Carlos closed at the end of 1811 a concerted effort was made to help revive theatrical culture in the city. This entailed the transfer of its management to the committee of the Teatro da Rua dos Condes, who were given two months to reorganise the Italian company. In the meantime, the authorities permitted the new managers of the São Carlos to stage the Portuguese musical farces that had previously characterised the dramatic repertoire at the Rua dos Condes.[17] These remarkable concessions underscore the importance attached to theatre-going during the war. Alexandre Jose Ferreira Castello (the Portuguese Cultural Secretary in 1812) attested to this in his insistence on the potential benefits of theatrical representations for society at large. Good management of the theatre, he contended, could correct moral vices, advance civility, and improve political and social virtues.[18]

During the Peninsular War Lisbon's theatrical personnel were thus invested with a series of social responsibilities. Manoel Baptista da Paula, who became the São Carlos's new manager, was given a set of official instructions for his new post. In the 'Instrucções ou Regulamento Provisòrio do Real Theatro Nacional de

---

[16] Antonio Joze do Rego, *Batalha do Bussaco: Peça Militar, e Historica para Forte-Piano, Dedicado Ao Vallor* [sic], *e Gloria do Exercito Anglo-Luzo, e do seu chefe o Ill mo e Ex.mo Lord Visconde Wellington. Conde do Vimeiro, Cavalleiro da Ordem do Banho, Gram [sic] Cruz da Ordem da Torre, e Espada* (Lisbon, 1811). A copy can be found in the CETAPS Library, Lisbon.

[17] ATT 1521 (Teatro 992–1113), 'Index das Ordens Mandadas Expedir pelo Governo Relativas a Theatros', Lo. 39 de Avizos (20 Mar 1812). Arquivo Nacional da Torre do Tombo.

[18] ATT 1521 (Teatro 992–113), *Instrucções ou Regulamento Provisòrio do Real Theatro Nacional de S. Carlos* (Lisbon, 1812). Arquivo Nacional da Torre do Tombo.

São Carlos' the Cultural Inspector made his expectations implicit but clear. In a document that praises Paula for the 'constant proofs of patriotism' demonstrated in his programme choices, the Inspector credits the manager for his commitment to a monthly lottery that helped raise funds for the military budget and provided support for the 'Portuguese Sufferers'.[19] By the same token, he gives recognition to Paula's impressive and costly spectacles, staged to celebrate symbolic dates in the socio-political calendar. In this acknowledgement the British are described as 'our intimate allies'.[20] Such political rhetoric helped justify the strong emphasis placed on the production of occasional pieces to celebrate, for example, the birthdays of the British Royal Family. It also points, significantly, to the importance of a spectacular and musical programme designed to entertain the many British servicemen who found themselves in Lisbon but were unfamiliar with the Portuguese language. This provision for the recreational activities of British troops confirms that men such as Broughton, begrudging as they often were, are likely to have been the theatre's primary patrons.[21]

On 25 October 1809 the celebrations for George III's Jubilee extended to Lisbon, where the Envoy Extraordinary and Minister Plenipotentiary to Portugal, John Charles Villiers, hosted a sumptuous dinner and invited his guests to the Real Teatro São Carlos for a performance of *A Batalha do Vimeiro*. On this occasion, Wellington and William Beresford (the evening's guests of honour) are likely to have enjoyed seats in the theatre's imposing royal box. From the São Carlos, the company then made their way to the Teatro da Rua dos Condes, where 'God Save the King' was sung in Portuguese. This finale would have made for a stirring moment of theatrical spectatorship comparable, at least in kind, to the initial enthusiasm in Bristol for Catalani's unique renditions of 'God Save the King', as discussed in Chapter 4. In England the Jubilee, as Stuart Semmel importantly underlines, was an event

---

[19]   In England there was a nationwide subscription to raise money for the 'Relief of the Portuguese Sufferers'. Contributions were interpreted as a sign of patriotic charitableness. See *FFBJ*, 25 May 1811, on the donation of 5s. by Mary Walker, a vendor of oranges: 'her gift is as liberal and noble minded as any which we record'. Profits from the sale of Walter Scott's *The Vision of Don Roderick* (1811) also went towards the fund.

[20]   *Instrucções*, 3 ('nossos íntimos Alliados') [my translation].

[21]   Unimpressed with the theatres in the Iberian Peninsula, British soldiers often staged their own amateur theatricals. Large open spaces or abandoned farms served as sets, and the regimental band provided musical accompaniment. Antony Brett-James explains that in Fuente Guinaldo, a ruined chapel 'became the theatre for an ambitious performance of Shakespeare's *Henry IV* with scenery painted by Captain John Bell, the Deputy Adjutant-General...'. Performed on 18 November 1811, the play was attended by officers from other divisions and Captain John Kent, who played Hotspur, 'became a draw whenever he was billed to appear'. *Life in Wellington's Army* (London: Greg Allen & Unwin Ltd, 1972), 160–66 (160–61). The Garrick Club in London holds two bilingual playbills (for the Real Teatro São Carlos, dated 16 January 1811 [Figure 5.1], and for the Teatro Salistre, dated 21 January [1811]).

'constructed by contention as much as it was by consensus'.[22] In the Portuguese theatres, however, only 'loyalist devotion' seems to have been on display.

The allegorical dramas that dominated Lisbon's wartime theatrical repertoire served obvious political ends. Catering for an audience of British soldiers and officials, who were, for the most part, strangers to the language and bewildered by their host nation's social customs, managers knew that interpretative transparency was crucial. Broughton's account of an opera he saw in 1813 suggests that he had no difficulty in understanding its intended meanings and mode of execution.[23] Between 1808 and 1814 Lisbon's theatres had the official aims of re-enacting highlights of the war, extolling the Peninsula's military heroes and commemorating symbolic anniversaries, such as the birthday of the Prince Regent or George III's Jubilee.

The French had been quick to realise that a nation's culture could be the key to political advancement. When Junot and his men left Lisbon they took their projects for the theatre with them, but it did not take long for the Regency government to introduce its own measures, which included the appointment of cultural inspectors and the instigation of a series of regulations to ensure that this valuable platform for public address and instruction was not lost. During a period of dangerous instability and potential revolution, the Portuguese Theatres' Regulations Act (1812) explicitly refers to the need to 'contain the public' by implementing regulations for the enforcement of social control (as policed both within the theatres and promoted by them).[24]

Playing to an audience of both Portuguese and British patrons, allegorical and musical dramas at the Real Teatro São Carlos had the express purpose of uniting an audience whose many cultural differences were represented first and foremost by a linguistic barrier. While there does not seem to have been any real attempt to resolve the cultural prejudices that coloured many British accounts of Portugal, the stage provided a powerful transformation of the 'here and now'. In Lisbon, an audience of different nationalities and customs came together in a propagandist theatre that aimed to boost morale and encourage a sense of cosmopolitan citizenship. The physical and psychological traumas of living in a warzone meant that performances at the São Carlos were periodic and the quality of entertainments somewhat poor. But the Portuguese authorities never relinquished their belief in a theatre resplendent with social and political possibilities. The instatement of specific legal provisions and the evidence of the personal commitment needed to ensure the São Carlos's survival have left a clear legacy of the theatre's perceived importance to a nation at war.

---

[22]   Stuart Semmel, 'Radicals, Loyalists, and the Royal Jubilee of 1809', in *Journal of British Studies* 46.3 (July 2007), 543–69 (545).

[23]   Broughton, *Letters*, 55–7.

[24]   The Cultural Inspector was appointed to 'contain the populace within the limits of just liberty, and to put an end to any noise or disorder that might disturb the public order' [my translation]. *Instrucções*, 'Article X', ('…fazendo com a sua authoridade conter o Povo dentro dos limites de huma justa liberdade, e pondo termo a qualquer ruido, ou desordem que pertube o socego publico').

A Calendar of Plays for Covent Garden, Drury Lane and Bristol Theatre Royal: 1807–1815
A Short Introduction

The duration of the Peninsular War coincides with the first quarter of the nineteenth century as a period particularly under-represented in English theatre history. *The London Stage, 1660–1800: A Calendar of Plays, Entertainments & Afterpieces, Together with Casts, Box-receipts and Contemporary Comment* (11 vols, 1960–1968) provides an indispensible chronicle of the plays performed in London's patent theatres until the end of the eighteenth century, but its closest analogue for theatre post-1800 is J.P. Wearing's *The London Stage, 1890–1899: A Calendar of Plays and Players* (2 vols, 1976). While Allardyce Nicoll and William Burling have published important records of early to mid-nineteenth-century theatrical performances, a trip to the archives is still required for a full picture of the entertainments available at the time of the Peninsular War.[1] The arrangement of Nicoll's 'Hand List of Plays Produced Between 1800 and 1850' makes it difficult to gage the relationship between the different plays in the repertoire, while Burling focuses exclusively on London's summer patent theatre, the Haymarket. I here attempt to offer some redress by providing 'A Calendar of Plays for Covent Garden, Drury Lane and Bristol Theatre Royal', which spans the years 1807 to 1815 examined in this book.

This Calendar falls somewhere in-between Nicoll's 'Handlist' and the daily listings provided by *The London Stage 1660–1800*.[2] The Calendar does not include details about casting or comments about the dramatic company, but its seasonal arrangement permits the reader to trace connections between different plays and entertainments (topically themed, or to show off the engagement of a star actor, for

---

[1]   Allardyce Nicoll's still authoritative *A History of English Drama, 1660 1900*. 6 vols (Cambridge: Cambridge University Press, 1955–1959) includes a 'Hand List of Plays Produced Between 1800 and 1850'. See also William Burling's appendix to *Summer Theatre in London, 1661–1820, and the Rise of the Haymarket Theatre* (London: Associated University Presses, 2000) for performances spanning from 1801 to 1820.

[2]   Every attempt has been made to check this Calendar's accuracy but as Charles Beecher Hogan admits of his own Calendar, 'it is altogether certain that in a great many instances what I have recorded is, to put it bluntly, erroneous'. Avery, Hogan, et al. (eds), *London Stage 1660–1800*, 'Part 5: 1776–1800', 11: v.

example); compare the performances available at the patent theatres on any given night; and better understand how managers sought to offset the high costs of their more spectacular productions by promoting established favourites. Parts A and B are based on the virtually complete collection of Covent Garden and Drury Lane playbills available at the Garrick Club in London.[3] Part C derives from the theatre historian Kathleen Baker's comprehensive records for the Theatre Royal in Bristol (to which I have added details from the local playbills available at Bristol's Central Reference Library).[4]

Parts A to C of this Calendar thus rely upon the evidence provided by contemporary playbills, rather than private sources (such as diaries and letters), or newspaper reports (the other principal form of theatrical advertising). The main reason for this deferral to the playbills is that the advertisements in the newspapers did not always reflect the last-minute changes to the programme that might be occasioned by an actor's indisposition or licensing difficulties, for example. Indeed, from as early as the mid-eighteenth century, playbills were frequently reprinted on the day of performance. When collected by avid theatre-goers they were often further annotated to reflect the final programme on offer (as exemplified by several of the playbills used to create this Calendar).

Early nineteenth-century playbills presented information about the performance time and venue, the choice of entertainments (often including those that took place *entr'acte*), the roles assumed by the various members of the dramatic company, and the main scene changes for pantomimes and other spectacular productions. On occasion, the playbills also included an outline of the main plot – critical for the recovery of performances for which no play-text survives, or was ever published. 'In the playbill we have not only evidence for what was performed by whom and when', as Jacky Bratton explains, 'but also for those most difficult and evanescent aspects of theatre history – the expectations and dispositions of the audience, their personal experience of theatre'.[5]

The period's playbills need to be treated cautiously, however. They make frequent references, for example, to 'audience approbation' and the 'disappointed Ladies and Gentlemen' for whom additional performances were promised. But these notices, as contemporary reviewers insisted, were often grossly misleading. Playbills were designed to promote ticket sales and it was not unusual for managers

---

[3]   The distinct scarcity of Drury Lane playbills for the period between September 1808 and March 1809 makes the Calendar incomplete for this season. The reason generally ascribed to this is that Sheridan, in financial straits (exacerbated by the fire that destroyed Drury Lane), could not afford to pay for advertising. So severe was the shortage of playbills that John Genest reports 'even the performers could not get any'. *Some Account of the English Stage from the Restoration in 1660 to 1830.* 10 vols. (Bath, 1832), 2: 115.

[4]   Kathleen Barker's research notes and publications were bequeathed to the University of Bristol's Theatre Collection. I am grateful to the Collection's archivists for granting me free access to this invaluable resource.

[5]   Jacky Bratton, *New Readings in Theatre History* (Cambridge: Cambridge University Press, 2003), 39.

to exploit the printed word as a means of 'puffing' damned or indifferently received plays. The playbills that form the basis of this Calendar have thus been used to provide empirical evidence of 'what' was on offer at the patent houses between 1807 and 1815, and to identify the entertainments that relied upon a Spanish or Portuguese theme (highlighted herein using bold font). Parts A to C of this Calendar record the choice of mainpiece and afterpiece, and include brief descriptions of the interludes (when available and/or especially relevant to the book's argument). A few additional notes (about benefit performances, the engagement of star actors and box-office takings) have been appended to Part C in recognition of the larger recovery project entailed for the Bristol Theatre Royal.

It is no coincidence that the entertainments listed in bold font were often scheduled for performance on dates symbolically related to the Peninsular Campaign. Covent Garden's season for 1810–1811 hints at a spirited commitment to bring the sights and sounds of modern Spain to London audiences. The Christmas pantomime *Harlequin and Asmodeus; or, Cupid on Crutches* (1810) was performed 46 times between 26 December 1810 and 25 June 1811. It represented a significant coup for John Philip Kemble's wartime repertoire. As the theatre's playbills dutifully listed, the pantomime's main scenes included views of the Grand Prado at Madrid, an amphitheatre at Cadiz, a Spanish Bull Fight, the Cadiz Harbour (which had been under siege since 1810), a Spanish Hotel and Lodging House.

The Calendar's use of bold font is intended to facilitate the reader's recognition of the pantomime's Spanish setting and, by extension, its likely topical inflections. But it is important to note that this kind of 'signposting' overlooks plays in which a Spanish or Portuguese character plays only a minor role, or where merely a passing reference is made to national or cultural interests. A good example is afforded by Joseph Addison's *Cato* (1713), which was revived at Covent Garden in 1811 and played alongside *Harlequin and Asmodeus* six times that year. In the final act of Addison's play, Cato, the Roman Senator and defender of the Republic, chooses to commit suicide rather than surrender to Caesar. But shortly afterwards, Porcius brings news of a sail arriv'd | From Pompey's son:

> PORCIUS   … who through the realms of Spain
>   Calls out for vengeance on his father's death,
>   And rouses the whole nation up to arms.
>   Were Cato at their hand, once more might Rome
>   Assert her rights and claim her liberty. – [6]

By 1811 *Cato* already enjoyed a rich history of political appropriation as a play that was famously apposite to Whigs and Tories alike. Theatre-goers accompanying the progress of the Peninsular Campaign are likely to have ascribed patriotic import to Porcius' dramatic allusion to a mobilised Spanish nation – an interpretation that

---

[6] *Addison's Cato, A Tragedy*, adapted to the stage by J.P. Kemble (London, 1811), in Shattuck (ed.), *Promptbooks*, (5.1), 10: 52.

would have been all the more immediate on the occasions when *Cato* was played alongside *Harlequin and Asmodeus*. Addison's tragedy has not, however, been highlighted in the Covent Garden Calendar since, notwithstanding this potentially loaded reference to Spain, the play does not provide a direct representation of the Spanish nation or its people.

Cato serves as a useful reminder that there were many other plays, some lacking even second-hand references to Spain or Portugal, which acquired topical inflections during the Peninsular War. This Calendar has been designed as a factual supplement for the arguments advanced in Chapters 1 to 4 of this book – its use of bold font supporting but not overwriting the allegorical readings proposed. It also aims to encourage new research. *Staging the Peninsular War* looks to the evidence provided by this Calendar in order to tell *its* story of a wartime repertoire, but many other compelling narratives remain to be told.

Appendix A

Calendar of Covent Garden Playbills 1807–1808

Date (*Notes*)	Mainpiece	Interlude	Afterpiece
M. Sep 14 **1807**	Romeo and Juliet		The Poor Soldier
W. Sep 16	The Beggar's Opera		Raising the Wind
F. Sep 18	The Wheel of Fortune		The Escapes; or, The Water Carrier
M. Sep 21	Cymbeline, King of Britain		The Farmer
W. Sep 23	Wild Oats; or, The Strolling Gentlemen		The Quaker
F. Sep 25	Speed the Plough		**Paul and Virginia**
M. Sep 28	Cymbeline		Rosina
W. Sep 30	The Provoked Husband; or, A Journey to London		Lock and Key
			Songs
F. Oct 2	The School of Reform; or, How to Rule a Husband		Rosina
M. Oct 5	**King Henry the Eighth**		Tom Thumb the Great
W. Oct 7	Cymbeline		**The Padlock**
Th. Oct 8	Macbeth		Hartford Bridge
F. Oct 9	The Road to Ruin		Of Age To-morrow
M. Oct 12	**King Henry the Eighth**		The Wedding Day
W. Oct 14	The School for Prejudice		The Turnpike Gate
Th. Oct 15	**The Mourning Bride**		Tom Thumb the Great
F. Oct 16	The Road to Ruin		Of Age To-morrow
M. Oct 19	**King Henry the Eighth**		The Flitch of Bacon
T. Oct 20	Artaxerxes		The Wedding Day
W. Oct 21	The Rage		Tom Thumb the Great
Th. Oct 22	**Pizarro**		The Son in Law (*by permission of the Haymarket*)
F. Oct 23	The Beggar's Opera		Arbitration; or, Free and Easy
M. Oct 26	Coriolanus; or, The Roman Matron		The Review; or, The Wags of Windsor
T. Oct 27	George Barnwell; or, The London Merchant		Harlequin and Mother Goose; or, The Golden Egg (*with new scenes*)

Date (*Notes*)	Mainpiece	Interlude	Afterpiece
W. Oct 28 **1807**	The Poor Gentleman		Harlequin and Mother Goose
Th. Oct 29	**Isabella; or, the Fatal Marriage**		Too Friendly by Half
F. Oct 30	The Beggar's Opera		Too Friendly by Half
M. Nov 2	Coriolanus		Harlequin and Mother Goose
T. Nov 3	A Cure for the Heart-ache		Harlequin and Mother Goose
W. Nov 4	John Bull; or, An Englishman's Fireside		Harlequin and Mother Goose
Th. Nov 5	Count of Narbonne		Harlequin and Mother Goose
F. Nov 6	Romeo and Juliet		Harlequin and Mother Goose
S. Nov 7	**King Henry the Eighth**		Fortune's Frolics
M. Nov 9	Coriolanus		Harlequin and Mother Goose
T. Nov 10	The Road to Ruin		Harlequin and Mother Goose
W. Nov 11	The Winter's Tale		The Flitch of Bacon
Th. Nov 12	Speed the Plough		Harlequin and Mother Goose
F. Nov 13	The Winter's Tale		Harlequin and Mother Goose
S. Nov 14	The Heir at Law		The Turnpike Gate
M. Nov 16 *Last night of* Mother Goose	The Winter's Tale		Harlequin and Mother Goose
T. Nov 17 *Never Acted Before*	**Two Faces Under a Hood**		Mistake upon Mistake; or, Appearance is against them
W. Nov 18	**Two Faces Under a Hood**		Raising the Wind
Th. Nov 19	**Two Faces Under a Hood**		The Midnight Hour
F. Nov 20	**Two Faces Under a Hood**		Arbitration
S. Nov 21	**Two Faces Under a Hood**		Katharine and Petruchio
M. Nov 23	The Winter's Tale		Harlequin and Mother Goose
T. Nov 24	**Two Faces Under a Hood**		**The Follies of a Day**
W. Nov 25	Macbeth		Harlequin and Mother Goose
Th. Nov 26	**Two Faces Under a Hood**		Animal Magnetism
F. Nov 27	Jane Shore		Harlequin and Mother Goose
S. Nov 28	The School of Reform		Tom Thumb the Great

Date (*Notes*)	Mainpiece	Interlude	Afterpiece
M. Nov 30 **1807**	The Winter's Tale		Harlequin and Mother Goose
T. Dec 1	The Provoked Husband; or, A Journey to London		The Blind Boy
W. Dec 2	**King Henry the Eighth**		The Blind Boy
Th. Dec 3	**Two Faces Under a Hood**		The Blind Boy
S. Dec 5	**Two Faces Under a Hood**		The Blind Boy
M. Dec 7	Jane Shore		The Blind Boy
T. Dec 8	**Two Faces Under a Hood**		The Blind Boy
W. Dec 9	**King Henry the Eighth**		The Blind Boy
Th. Dec 10	**Two Faces Under a Hood**		The Blind Boy
F. Dec 11	The Winter's Tale		The Blind Boy
S. Dec 12	**Two Faces Under a Hood**		The Blind Boy
M. Dec 14	**The Revenge**		The Blind Boy
T. Dec 15	**Two Faces Under a Hood**		The Blind Boy
W. Dec 16	The Confederacy		The Blind Boy
Th. Dec 17	John Bull		The Blind Boy
S. Dec 19	Othello, The Moor of Venice		The Blind Boy
T. Dec 22	**Two Faces Under a Hood**		The Blind Boy
T. Dec 29	The Confederacy		Harlequin in his Element; or, Fire, Water, Earth and Air
Th. Dec 31	**Two Faces Under a Hood**		Harlequin in his Element
F. Jan 1 **1808**	The Dramatist		Harlequin in his Element
M. Jan 4	**The Mountaineers**		Harlequin in his Element
W. Jan 6	The Wheel of Fortune		Harlequin in his Element
M. Jan 11	**The Mountaineers**		Harlequin in his Element
W. Jan 13	The Wanderer; or, The Rights of Hospitality		Harlequin in his Element
Th. Jan 14	The Wanderer		Harlequin in his Element
F. Jan 15	The Wanderer		Harlequin in his Element
S. Jan 16	The Wanderer		Harlequin in his Element
M. Jan 18	**The Mountaineers**		Harlequin in his Element

Date (*Notes*)	Mainpiece	Interlude	Afterpiece
T. Jan 19 **1808**	The Wanderer		Harlequin in his Element
W. Jan 20	The Wanderer		Harlequin in his Element
Th. Jan 21	The Wanderer		Harlequin in his Element
F. Jan 22	The Wanderer		Harlequin in his Element
S. Jan 23	The Wanderer		Harlequin in his Element
M. Jan 25	**The Mountaineers**		Harlequin in his Element
T. Jan 26	The Wanderer		Harlequin in his Element
W. Jan 27 *By particular desire*	**Two Faces Under a Hood**		Harlequin in his Element
Th. Jan 28	The Wanderer		Harlequin in his Element
F. Jan 29	Othello		Harlequin in his Element
S. Jan 30	Oratorios – The Messiah		
M. Feb 1	**The Mountaineers**		Harlequin in his Element
T. Feb 2	The Wanderer		**Paul and Virginia**
W. Feb 3	The Woodman		Harlequin in his Element
Th. Feb 4	The Woodman		The Blind Boy
F. Feb 5	The Woodman		Harlequin in his Element
S. Feb 6	Hamlet, Prince of Denmark		'We Fly by Night'; or, Long Stories
M. Feb 8	**The Mountaineers**		Harlequin in his Element
T. Feb 9 *Never Acted Before*	Begone Dull Care; or, How Will it End		**The Padlock**
W. Feb 10	Begone Dull Care		The Blind Boy
Th. Feb 11	Begone Dull Care		Harlequin in his Element
F. Feb 12	Begone Dull Care		The Blind Boy
S. Feb 13	Begone Dull Care		The Blind Boy
M. Feb 15	Begone Dull Care		Harlequin in his Element
T. Feb 16	Begone Dull Care		The Blind Boy
W. Feb 17	Oratorios –The Messiah		
Th. Feb 18	Begone Dull Care		The Blind Boy
F. Feb 19	Begone Dull Care	Poor Jack; or, The Benevolent Tars of Old England	Lock and Key
S. Feb 20	Begone Dull Care		The Blind Boy
M. Feb 22	Hamlet		Harlequin in his Element
T. Feb 23	Begone Dull Care	Poor Jack	Tom Thumb the Great

Date (*Notes*)	Mainpiece	Interlude	Afterpiece
W. Feb 24 **1808**	Begone Dull Care	Poor Jack	'We Fly by Night'
Th. Feb 25	The Wanderer		Who Wins? Or, The Widow's Choice
F. Feb 26	Begone Dull Care		Who Wins?
S. Feb 27	The Woodman		Who Wins?
M. Feb 29	Romeo and Juliet		Harlequin in his Element
T. Mar 1	Begone Dull Care	Poor Jack	Who Wins?
Th. Mar 3	The Wanderer	The Highland Laddie	Who Wins?
F. Mar 4	Oratorios – Grand Selection of Sacred Music		
S. Mar 5	The Woodman		Who Wins?
M. Mar 7	Jane Shore		Harlequin in his Element
T. Mar 8	Begone Dull Care	The Highland Laddie	Who Wins?
W. Mar 9	Oratorios – The Messiah		
Th. Mar 10	The Man of the World	The Highland Laddie	Who Wins?
F. Mar 11	Oratorios – Acis and Galatea, with a Grand Miscellaneous Act		
S. Mar 12	The Merchant of Venice		Who Wins?
M. Mar 14	King Richard the Third		Harlequin in his Element
T. Mar 15	The Woodman		Raising the Wind
W. Mar 16	Oratorios – Grand Selection		
Th. Mar 17	The Man of the World	The Highland Laddie	The Blind Boy
F. Mar 18	Oratorios – L'Allegro Il Penseroso		
S. Mar 19	The Merchant of Venice		Love a-la Mode
M. Mar 21	King Richard the Third		Harlequin in his Element
T. Mar 22	The Travellers in Switzerland		Who Wins?
W. Mar 23	Oratorios – Grand Selection		
Th. Mar 24	The Man of the World	The Highland Laddie	Who Wins?
F. Mar 25	Oratorios – The Messiah		
S. Mar 26	The Merchant of Venice		Love a-la Mode
M. Mar 28	Othello		Harlequin in His Element
T. Mar 29	The Travellers in Switzerland		Who Wins?
W. Mar 30	Oratorios – Entire New Grand Selection		
M. Mar 31	The Man of the World		Bonifacio and Bridgetina; or, The Knight of the Hermitage; or, The Windmill Turret; or, The Spectre of the North East Gallery

Date (*Notes*)	Mainpiece	Interlude	Afterpiece
F. Apr 1 **1808**	Oratorios – Dettingen Te Deum, with two Grand Miscellaneous Acts		
S. Apr 2	The Merchant of Venice		Bonifacio and Bridgetina
M. Apr 4	Othello		Bonifacio and Bridgetina
T. Apr 5	Every Man in his Humour		Bonifacio and Bridgetina
W. Apr 6	Oratorios – The Messiah		
Th. Apr 7	The Man of the World		Bonifacio and Bridgetina
S. Apr 9 *Last night of the company's performances until the holidays. Mr Lewis's Night*	The Fashionable Lover	New songs	The Blind Boy
M. Apr 18	King Richard the Third		Harlequin and Mother Goose
T. Apr 19	**The Mountaineers**		Bonifacio and Bridgetina
W. Apr 20	The Man of the World		Harlequin and Mother Goose
Th. Apr 21	Two Gentlemen of Verona		Harlequin and Mother Goose
F. Apr 22	The Merchant of Venice		Harlequin and Mother Goose
S. Apr 23	Hamlet		Who Wins?
M. Apr 25	King Richard the Third		Harlequin and Mother Goose
T. Apr 26	Two Gentlemen of Verona		Of Age To-morrow
W. Apr 27	The Merry Wives of Windsor		Harlequin and Mother Goose
Th. Apr 28	The Man of the World	The Highland Laddie	Tom Thumb the Great
F. Apr 29	Two Gentleman of Verona		Who Wins?
S. Apr 30	The Merchant of Venice		Love a-la Mode
M. May 2	Hamlet		Harlequin and Mother Goose
T. May 3 *Mr Cooke's Night*	Bonduca: Queen of Ancient Britons		'We Fly By Night'
W. May 4	The Man of the World	The Highland Laddie	Tom Thumb the Great
Th. May 5	Bonduca		Who Wins?
F. May 6	The Tempest; or, The Enchanted Island		The Review (*by permission of the Haymarket*)
S. May 7	The Fashionable Lover		Who Wins?
M. May 9	Hamlet		Harlequin and Mother Goose

Date (*Notes*)	Mainpiece	Interlude	Afterpiece
T. May 10 **1808**	The Merry Wives of Windsor	The Highland Laddie	Tom Thumb the Great
W. May 11 *Miss Smith's Night*	Macbeth	Miss Smith will recite Collins's Ode on the Passions – accompanied by appropriate music (*by particular desire*)	Love a-la Mode
Th. May 12	King Henry the Fourth (Part One)		Who Wins?
F. May 13	The Wheel of Fortune		**The Follies of a Day**
S. May 14	The Man of the World	The Highland Laddie	Peeping Tom
M. May 16	King Richard the Third		Harlequin and Mother Goose
T. May 17 *Benefit of Mr Fawcett*	**Pizarro**	Songs	The Blind Boy
W. May 18 *Benefit of Mr C Kemble*	King Lear	The Day after the Wedding; or, A Wife's First Lesson	Raymond and Agnes
Th. May 19 *Mrs Dickons*	**Two Faces Under a Hood**	A Musical Pasticcio	Raising the Wind (*by particular desire*)
F. May 20	The Man of the World	The Highland Laddie	Tom Thumb the Great
S. May 21 *Benefit of Mr Pope*	**The Revenge**		Love a-la Mode
M. May 23	King Lear		Harlequin and Mother Goose
T. May 24 *Never Acted Before. Mrs C Kemble's night*	Match-making; or, 'Tis a wise child that knows its own father	Personation; or, Fairly taken in	The Blind Boy
W. May 25 *Mr Bellamy's Night*	**The English Fleet in 1342**	The United Methodists; or, Feast of Apollo	Irishman in London
Th. May 26	King Lear		Raymond and Agnes
F. May 27 *Mr Jones's Night*	The Way to Get Married	Songs	The Blind Boy
S. May 28 *Mr Incledon's Night*	**The Duenna**	'Harmonious Meeting' – several songs	Love a-la Mode
M. May 30	King Lear		Harlequin and Mother Goose
T. May 31 *Mr Emery's Night*	The Blind Bargain	Songs	The Review
W. Jun 1 *Mr Farley's Night*	Alexander the Great; or, The Rival Queens	Songs	Oscar and Malvina
		A Vauxhall Gala; or, A Rural Masquerade ('*with the exact representation of the gardens on a gala night*')	
		'Pas deux' from the pantomime Mother Goose	

Date (*Notes*)	Mainpiece	Interlude	Afterpiece
Th. Jun 2 **1808** *Benefit of Mr Blanchard*	Inkle and Yarico	Songs	Raymond and Agnes
F. Jun 3 *Benefit of Mr Taylor. Last night of the company's performances until the holidays*	The Man of the World	Songs The Recruiting Sergeant	The Deserter of Naples
S. Jun 4 *Mess Ashley's Night (Whitsun Eve)*	Oratorios – The Messiah		
M. Jun 6	King Lear		Oscar and Malvina
T. Jun 7 *Mrs Mattock's last Benefit*	**The Wonder; A Woman Keeps a Secret**	Garrick's 'Ode to Shakespeare' Songs	Raymond and Agnes
W. Jun 8 *Benefit of Miss Norton – Mr Cooke's last appearance in King Richard this season*	King Richard the Third	The Apprentice (*reduced to 1 Act*) Miss S Norton to dance De Caro's Hornpipe Songs	The Blind Boy
Th. Jun 9 *Benefit of the four Misses Adams*	The Road to Ruin	The Oak and the Ivy; or, The Origin of a British Tar	Oscar and Malvina
F. Jun 10 *Benefit of Mr Claremont and Mr King*	The Wanderer	The Highland Laddie Music and entertainments 'The Election; or, A Squeeze for the Hustings' (*recitation by Mr Claremont*) Songs and dance	Tom Thumb the Great
S. Jun 11	Speed the Plough	Songs	The Blind Boy
M. Jun 13 *Benefit of Mr Brandon, Box-Book and House-Keeper*	**Pizarro**	Songs	[*Farce and other entertainments 'as advertised', but not specified*]
T. Jun 14 *By particular desire. Last time of* Mother Goose*. Benefit of Mr Grimaldi and Mr Bologna Jr*	The School of Reform	Day after the Wedding	Harlequin and Mother Goose
W. Jun 15 *Benefit of Mrs Dibdin and Mr Waddy*	**The English Fleet in 1342**	Vauxhall Gala 'Pas deux' from Mother Goose	The Life of the Day

Date (*Notes*)	Mainpiece	Interlude	Afterpiece
Th. Jun 16 **1808** *Miss Bolton's Night*	Abroad and at Home	Eloisa, at the Tomb of Abelard	Tom Thumb the Great
		The Day after the Wedding	
		Music	
F. Jun 17	Begone Dull Care	The Highland Laddie	Who Wins?
S. Jun 18	The Road to Ruin	Songs	Of Age To-morrow
M. Jun 20 *Benefit of Mr Glassington, Prompter*	Hamlet	New Military Dance Broad Sword Exercise Songs	Who Wins?
T. Jun 21 *Mr Munden's Night*	Laugh When You Can	**The Portrait of Cervantes; or, The Plotting Lovers**	The Turnpike Gate
		Comic songs (*by particular desire*)	
Th. Jun 23	The Suspicious Husband	Songs	The Poor Soldier
F. Jun 24	The School of Reform	The Highland Laddie Songs	Fortune's Frolics
S. Jun 25	The Road to Ruin	Dancing – 'Pas deux'	**The Child of Nature**
M. Jun 27 *Last night of the company performaning this season*	Macbeth		**The Portrait of Cervantes**

Calendar of Covent Garden Playbills 1808–1809

Date (*Notes*)	Mainpiece	Interlude	Afterpiece
Note: After Covent Garden burnt down, the company acted at the **King's Theatre**, from 19 September to 3 December 1808. On 5 December 1808 they then moved to the **Haymarket**, where they acted until 31 May.			
M. Sep 12 **1808**	Macbeth		Raising the Wind
W. Sep 14	The Woodman		**The Portrait of Cervantes; or, The Plotting Lovers**
F. Sep 16	**Isabella; or, The Fatal Marriage**		The Escapes; or, The Water Carriers
M. Sep 19	**Pizarro**		**The Portrait of Cervantes**
M. Sep 26 **King's Theatre, Opera House, Haymarket**	Douglas		Rosina
W. Sep 28	Beggar's Opera		**The Portrait of Cervantes**
F. Sep 30	The Grecian Daughter		The Poor Soldier
M. Oct. 3	Macbeth		**The Portrait of Cervantes**
W. Oct 5	Hamlet, Prince of Denmark		The Quaker (*to conclude with a rural dance*)
F. Oct 7	The Stranger		The Forest of Hermanstadt; or, Princess and No Princess
M. Oct 10	Macbeth		The Forest of Hermanstadt
W. Oct 12	Hamlet		The Forest of Hermanstadt
Th. Oct 13	The Man of the World		The Forest of Hermanstadt
F. Oct 14	The Stranger		The Forest of Hermanstadt
M. Oct 17	Macbeth		The Forest of Hermanstadt
W. Oct 19	The Merchant of Venice		The Forest of Hermanstadt
Th. Oct 20	The Gamester		Who Wins? Or, The Widow's Choice

Date (*Notes*)	Mainpiece	Interlude	Afterpiece
F. Oct 21 **1808**	John Bull; or, An Englishman's Fireside		**The Portrait of Cervantes**
M. Oct 24	King Richard the Third		The Poor Soldier.
T. Oct 25	**The Mourning Bride**		The Flitch of Bacon
W. Oct 26	The Man of the World		'We Fly by Night'; or, Long Stories
Th. Oct 27	The Gamester		The Review; or, The Wags of Windsor (*by permission of the Haymarket*)
F. Oct 28	The Woodman		The Forest of Hermanstadt
M. Oct 31	Romeo and Juliet		The Forest of Hermanstadt
T. Nov 1	Macbeth		Who Wins?
W. Nov 2	The Merchant of Venice		The Blind Boy
Th. Nov 3	**King Henry the Eighth**		The Blind Boy
F. Nov 4 *For the Benefit of the Families of those who unfortunately suffered by the Late Fire in Covent Garden. King's Theatre, Haymarket.*	**The Mourning Bride**		The Forest of Hermanstadt
M. Nov. 7	**King Henry the Eighth**		The Blind Boy
T. Nov 8	Every Man in his Humour		Love a-la-Mode
W. Nov. 9	King Richard the Third		Tom Thumb the Great
Th. Nov. 10	The Exile		The Jew and the Doctor
F. Nov 11	The Exile		Love a-la Mode
S. Nov 12	The Exile		**The Portrait of Cervantes**
M. Nov 14	The Exile		Tom Thumb the Great
T. Nov 15	The Exile		**The Follies of a Day**
W. Nov 16	The Exile		The Village Lawyer
Th. Nov 17	The Exile		Katharine and Petruchio
F. Nov 18	The Exile		The Review
M. Nov 21 *Last week of acting at the Opera House*	The Exile		The Birth-Day
T. Nov 22	The Exile		**The Portrait of Cervantes**
W. Nov 23	The Exile		Animal Magnetism
Th. Nov 24	The Exile		Mistake upon Mistake; or, Appearance is Against Them
F. Nov 25	The Exile		Who Wins?

Date (*Notes*)	Mainpiece	Interlude	Afterpiece
S. Nov 26 **1808**	**King Henry the Eighth**		The Forest of Hermanstadt
M. Nov 28	The Exile		Tom Thumb the Great
T. Nov 29	The Exile		The Review
W. Nov 30	The Exile		**The Portrait of Cervantes**
Th. Dec 1	The Exile		Who Wins?
F. Dec 2	The Exile		The Poor Soldier
S. Dec 3 *Last night of acting at the Opera House*	Macbeth		The Forest of Hermanstadt
M. Dec 5 **Theatre Royal, Haymarket**	**The Mountaineers**		A School for Authors
T. Dec 6	The Exile		A School for Authors
W. Dec 7	The Africans; or, War, Love, and Duty (*by permission of the proprietors of the Haymarket*)		A School for Authors
Th. Dec. 8	The Exile		A School for Authors
Fri. Nov 9	The Africans		A School for Authors
S. Dec 10	The Exile		A School for Authors
M. Dec 12	Hamlet		A School for Authors
T. Dec. 13	The Exile		A School for Authors
W. Dec. 14	The Man of the World		A School for Authors
Th. Dec. 15	The Exile		A School for Authors
F. Dec. 16	Town and Country	The Double Wedding	A School for Authors
S. Dec 17	The Exile	The Double Wedding	A School for Authors
M. Dec. 19	King Richard the Third	The Double Wedding	Who Wins?
T. Dec. 20	The Exile	The Double Wedding	Raising the Wind
W. Dec. 21	Othello, The Moor of Venice	The Double Wedding	**The Portrait of Cervantes**
Th. Dec. 22	Town and Country	The Double Wedding	Arbitration; or, Free and Easy
F. Dec 23 *Last night of acting until the holidays*	Venice Preserv'd; or, A Plot Discovered	The Double Wedding	A School for Authors
M. Dec. 26	Venice Preserv'd		Harlequin and Mother Goose; or, The Golden Egg ('*Two Entire New Scenes – the first representing the Ruins of the Theatre Royal Covent-Garden, which changes to a NEW Theatre*')
T. Dec. 27	Town and Country		Harlequin and Mother Goose
W. Dec 28	The Exile		Harlequin and Mother Goose

Date (*Notes*)	Mainpiece	Interlude	Afterpiece
Th. Dec 29 **1808**	Jane Shore		Harlequin and Mother Goose
F. Dec 30	**The Busy Body**		Harlequin and Mother Goose
S. Dec 31	The Exile		Harlequin and Mother Goose
M. Jan 2 **1809**	Hamlet		Harlequin and Mother Goose
T. Jan 3	The Beaux Stratagem		Harlequin and Mother Goose
W. Jan 4	The Iron Chest		Harlequin and Mother Goose
Th. Jan 5	**The Busy Body**		Harlequin and Mother Goose
F. Jan 6	Speed the Plough		Harlequin and Mother Goose
S. Jan 7	The Poor Gentleman		Harlequin and Mother Goose (*Scene 2 – 'an exact representation of the laying of the FOUNDATION STONE as it appeared on Saturday, the 31 December last; which changes to a NEW theatre'*)
M. Jan 9	**The Revenge**		Harlequin and Mother Goose
T. Jan. 10	The Iron Chest		Harlequin and Mother Goose
W. Jan 11	Macbeth		Who Wins?
Th. Jan 12	The Man of the World		Harlequin and Mother Goose
F. Jan 13	The Gamester		Harlequin and Mother Goose
S. Jan. 14	Othello		Tom Thumb the Great
M. Jan. 16	The Merchant of Venice		Harlequin and Mother Goose
T. Jan 17	The Provoked Husband; or, A Journey to London		Harlequin and Mother Goose
W. Jan 18	Macbeth		**The Portrait of Cervantes**
Th. Jan 19	The Exile		The Prisoner at Large
F. Jan 20	The Gamester		Harlequin and Mother Goose
S. Jan 21	The Exile		Katharine and Petruchio
M. Jan 23	King Richard the Third		Harlequin and Mother Goose
T. Jan 24	King Henry the Fourth (Part One)		Harlequin and Mother Goose
W. Jan 25	Macbeth		Tom Thumb the Great
Th. Jan 26	The Exile		De La Perouse; or, The Desolate Island

Date (*Notes*)	Mainpiece	Interlude	Afterpiece
F. Jan 27 **1809**	The Gamester		De La Perouse
S. Jan 28	New Way to Pay Old Debts		De La Perouse
T. Jan 31	Hamlet		De La Perouse
W. Feb 1	The Man of the World		De La Perouse
Th. Feb. 2	Othello		De La Perouse
F. Feb 3 *Haymarket*	Every Man in his Humour		De La Perouse
S. Feb. 4	**King Henry the Eighth**		De La Perouse
M. Feb 6	Hamlet		De La Perouse
T. Feb. 7	The Gamester		Is He a Prince?
Th. Feb 9	Macbeth		Is He a Prince?
F. Feb 10	The Exile		Is He a Prince?
S. Feb 11	**King Henry the Eighth**		Is He a Prince?
M. Feb. 13	King Lear		De La Perouse
T. Feb 14	The Gamester		Is He a Prince?
Th. Feb 16	The Man of the World		De La Perouse
F. Feb 17	Macbeth		Is He a Prince?
M. Feb 20	King Lear		De La Perouse
T. Feb 21	The Gamester		Is He a Prince?
Th. Feb 23	The Exile		Is He a Prince?
S. Feb 25	Macbeth		Is He a Prince?
M. Feb 27	King Lear		De La Perouse
T. Feb 28	**King Henry the Eighth**		Is He a Prince?
Th. Mar 2	The Exile		Is He a Prince?
S. Mar 4	Macbeth		Is He a Prince?
M. Mar 6	King Lear		De La Perouse
T. Mar 7	The Exile		Who Wins?
Th. Mar 9	Independence; or, The Trustee		Is He a Prince?
S. Mar 11	Independence		The Blind Boy
M. Mar 13	Independence		De La Perouse
T. Mar 14	Independence		Tom Thumb the Great
Th. Mar 16	The Iron Chest		Is He a Prince?
S. Mar 18	The Exile		Who Wins?
M. Mar 20	King Lear		De La Perouse
T. Mar 21	Speed the Plough		The Poor Soldier
Th. Mar 23	The Wheel of Fortune		The Blind Boy
S. Mar 25	The Exile		**The Portrait of Cervantes**
M. Apr 3	King Richard the Third		De La Perouse
T. Apr 4	Macbeth		Harlequin and Mother Goose
W. Apr 5	The Man of the World		De la Perouse
Th. Apr 6	**King Henry the Eighth**		Harlequin and Mother Goose
Fr. Apr 7	The Merchant of Venice		Harlequin and Mother Goose
S. Apr 8	**The Mourning Bride**		The Blind Boy

Date (*Notes*)	Mainpiece	Interlude	Afterpiece
M. Apr 10 **1809**	Hamlet		Harlequin and Mother Goose
T. Apr 11	The Gamester		Who Wins?
W. Apr 12	The Exile		Raising the Wind
Th. Apr 13	The Wheel of Fortune		The Review
F. Apr 14	The Merry Wives of Windsor		Tom Thumb the Great
S. Apr 15	**King Henry the Eighth**		The Quaker
M. Apr 17	King Richard the Third		Harlequin and Mother Goose
T. Apr 18	Macbeth		Love a-la Mode
W. Apr 19	The Exile		De La Perouse
Th. Apr 20	John Bull		Tom Thumb the Great
F. Apr 21	The Man of the World		The Blind Boy
S. Apr 22	The Stranger		Who Wins?
M. Apr 24	Othello		Harlequin and Mother Goose
T. Apr 25	Every Man in his Humour		Rosina
W. Apr 26	The Exile		De La Perouse
Th. Apr 27	The Merchant of Venice		Love a-la Mode
Fr. Apr 28	The Iron Chest		The Blind Boy
S. Apr 29	Macbeth		Arbitration; or, Free and Easy
M. May 1 *For the Benefit of Mr Cooke*	New Way to Pay Old Debts	'Waltz en trois'	The King and the Miller of Mansfield
T. May 2 *For the Benefit of Mr Young*	**Pizarro**		Tom Thumb the Great
W. May 3 *Benefit of Mr Munden*	**The English Fleet in 1342**	The Rival Soldiers	Lock and Key
Th. May 4 *Benefit of Mr Fawcett*	The Exile	Blue Devils Songs	De La Perouse
F. May 5 *By particular desire*	Venice Preserv'd	Personation; or, Fairly Taken In	**Plot and Counterplot** *(for that night only, by permission of the proprietors of the Haymarket)*
S. May 6	King Henry the Fourth (Part One)		Raising the Wind
M. May 8	Hamlet		Harlequin and Mother Goose
T. May 9 *For the Benefit of Mr and Mrs C Kemble*	**The Wonder; A Woman Keeps a Secret**	Personation	The Blind Boy

Date (*Notes*)	Mainpiece	Interlude	Afterpiece
W. May 10 **1809** *Benefit of Mr Jones*	Lovers' Vows	Blue Devils Songs	**The Critic; or, A Tragedy Rehearsed** (*to conclude with a Grand Sea Fight, and 'Rule Britannia'*)
Th. May 11 *Benefit of Mr Blanchard*	The Exile	Songs	**The Portrait of Cervantes**
F. May 12 *Benefit of Mr Emery*	The Heir at Law	Comic songs	Love Laughs at Locksmiths
S. May 13	The Merry Wives of Windsor		The Quaker
M. May 15 *Benefit of Mr Farley*	The Dramatist	'Pantodesichorea' (an entertainment of singing and dancing…[*by particular desire and for that night only*]) Songs	Valentine and Orson
T. May 16 *Benefit of Mr Taylor*	The School for Reform	**'English Tars and Lord Cochrane'**, by Mr Taylor Imitations of several well-known London performers Songs	No Song, No Supper (*by permission of the proprietors of the late Theatre Royal, Drury Lane*)
W. May 17 *Benefit of Mr and Mrs Liston*	**The Mountaineers** Previous to the play, an Occasional Address by Mr Liston	Doctor Last's Examination (*a comic sketch taken from Foote's 'The Devil on Two Sticks'*) Blue Devils Songs	Tom Thumb the Great (*by particular desire*)
Th. May 18 *Benefit of Miss Norton*	Laugh When You Can	The Rival Soldiers Favourite song – **'The Hero of Corunna'** (*commemorative of the Death of General Sir John Moore*) – sung by Mr Bellamy 'Pas seul' by Miss Adams	The Blind Boy
Fri May 19 *Last night of performances until the holidays. Benefit of Messrs Waddy and Field*	The Castle Spectre	Personation A new Turkish Divertissement in which will be introduced 'A Grand Shawl Dance' Songs	Love a-la Mode
M. May 22	Othello		Valentine and Orson

Date (*Notes*)	Mainpiece	Interlude	Afterpiece
T. May 23 **1809** *Benefit of Mr* *Grimaldi*	**The Busy Body**	New song – 'Margery Muggins; or Looney Lump's Lamentation' New dance – The Sisters	Harlequin and Mother Goose (*'With three entire new scenes representing the Ruins, Foundation Stone, New Theatre'*)
W. May 24 *Benefit of Mr* *Brandon-Box-Book,* *and House-Keeper*	A Cure for the Heart-ache	Songs – **'English Tars, and Lord Cochrane'**, 'The Old Commodore', 'John Bull in Town, or British Wool for ever', 'Each has a lover but me'	**The Critic** (*to conclude with a Grand Sea Fight and 'Rule Britannia'*)
Th. May 25 *Benefit of Mr* *Claremont and Mr* *King*	The Man of the World	Songs Military Hornpipe and Manual Exercise by Miss Adams	De La Perouse
F. May 26	The Poor Gentleman	'Pas seul' and a Sailor's Hornpipe Songs	**The Padlock**
S. May 29	**The English Fleet in 1342**		Katharine and Petruchio
M. May 29 *Benefit of Mr Lewis* *and the last time of* *his ever appearing* *on any stage*	**Rule a Wife and Have a Wife** (*Mr Lewis will attempt to take a last leave of the Public*)	The Ghost (*an entertainment in 1 Act, previous to the play*)	Valentine and Orson
T. May 30 *Benefit of Mr* *Glassington,* *Prompter* *Last Night*	**Pizarro**	Songs and dance Personation	Tom Thumb the Great

Calendar of Covent Garden Playbills 1809–1810

Date (*Notes*)	Mainpiece	Interlude	Afterpiece
M. Sep 18 **1809**	Macbeth		The Quaker
New Theatre Royal, Covent Garden			
Note: New Prices introduced			
T. Sep 19	The Beggar's Opera		Is He a Prince?
W. Sep 20	King Richard the Third		The Poor Soldier
Th. Sep 21	Love in a Village		Who Wins? Or, The Widow's Choice
F. Sep 22	John Bull; or, An Englishman's Fireside		The Quaker
S. Sep 23	The Woodman		Raising the Wind
M. Oct 9	King Richard the Third		Raising the Wind
T. Oct 10	The Woodman		The Village Lawyer (*by permission of the proprietors of the Haymarket*)
W. Oct 11	The Heir at Law		**The Padlock**
Th. Oct 12	Love in a Village		Animal Magnetism
F. Oct 13	Speed the Plough		Rosina
S. Oct 14	The Poor Gentleman		The Flitch of Bacon
M. Oct 16	King Richard the Third		The Farmer
T. Oct 17	The Road to Ruin		Peeping Tom (*by permission of the Haymarket*)
W. Oct 18	Wild Oats; or, The Strolling Gentlemen		Lock and Key
Th. Oct 19	The Merchant of Venice		Who Wins?
F. Oct 20	**The Duenna**		All the World's a Stage
S. Oct 21	Othello, The Moor of Venice		Is He a Prince?
M. Oct 23	The Woodman		Oscar and Malvina; or, The Hall of Fingal
T. Oct 24	The Iron Chest		Oscar and Malvina
W. Oct 25 *For the Benefit of the Fund of The Society for the Discharge and Relief Of Persons Imprisoned for Small Debts*	The Man of the World		The Jubilee
Th. Oct 26	Laugh When You Can	The Jubilee	Oscar and Malvina
F. Oct 27	The Jubilee	The Beaux Stratagem	Oscar and Malvina
S. Oct 28	The Jubilee	The School of Reform	Raising the Wind
M. Oct 29	The Jubilee	The Grecian Daughter	The Flitch of Bacon
T. Oct 31	The Exile		**The Portrait of Cervantes; or, The Plotting Lovers**
W. Nov 1	Every Man in his Humour		Oscar and Malvina

Date (*Notes*)	Mainpiece	Interlude	Afterpiece
Th. Nov 2 **1809**	The Grecian Daughter		The Turnpike Gate
F. Nov 3	A Cure for the Heart-ache		Oscar and Malvina
S. Nov 4	The Grecian Daughter		The Review; or, The Wags of Windsor (*by permission of the Haymarket*)
M. Nov 6	Othello		The Blind Boy
T. Nov 7	The Exile		The Jew and the Doctor
W. Nov 8	Inkle and Yarico		The Miser
Th. Nov 9	Romeo and Juliet		The Poor Soldier
F. Nov 10	The Man of the World		Oscar and Malvina
S. Nov 11	Love in a Village		Animal Magnetism
M. Nov 13	King Richard the Third		The Quaker
T. Nov 14	**The Busy Body**		**The Portrait of Cervantes**
W. Nov 15	Speed the Plough		The Blind Boy
Th. Nov 16	Romeo and Juliet		Hartford Bridge
Fr. Nov 17	The Woodman		'We Fly By Night'; or, Long Stories
S. Nov 18	The Cabinet		**The Child of Nature**
M. Nov 20	King Richard the Third		**Don Juan; or, The Libertine Destroyed**
T. Nov 21	The Suspicious Husband		**Don Juan**
W. Nov 22	The Exile		**Don Juan**
Th. Nov 23	Every Man in His Humour		**Don Juan**
F. Nov 24	The Way to Get Married		**Don Juan**
S. Nov 25	**The English Fleet in 1342**		Raising the Wind
M. Nov 27	The Roman Father		**Don Juan**
T. Nov 28	The School for Prejudice		**Don Juan**
W. Nov 29	The Exile		Is He a Prince?
Th. Nov 30	The Roman Father		**Don Juan**
F. Dec 1	A Cure for the Heart-ache		The Jubilee ('*To conclude with an appropriate scene representing the Attack and Destruction of the French Convoy in the Bay of Rosas*')
S. Dec 2	**The English Fleet in 1342**		Who Wins?
M. Dec 4	Othello		**Don Juan**
T. Dec 5	The Beggar's Opera		The Blind Boy
W. Dec 6	The Man of the World		Oscar and Malvina
Th. Dec 7	The Woodman		**Don Juan**
F. Dec 8	The Merchant of Venice		Tom Thumb the Great
S. Dec 9	The Exile		**The Portrait of Cervantes**

Date (*Notes*)	Mainpiece	Interlude	Afterpiece
M. Dec 11 **1809**	The Woodman		**Don Juan**
T. Dec 12	John Bull		The Farmer
W. Dec 13	Every Man in his Humour		Oscar and Malvina
Th. Dec 14	The Provoked Husband; or, A Journey to London		Tom Thumb the Great
F. Dec 15	The Wheel of Fortune		The Blind Boy
S. Dec 16	The Exile		All the World's a Stage
M. Dec 18	Hamlet		**Don Juan**
T. Dec 19	The Merchant of Venice		The Poor Soldier
W. Dec 20	Hamlet		Is He a Prince?
Th. Dec 21	The Man of the World		'We Fly By Night'
F. Dec 22	King Lear		The Waterman
S. Dec 23	The Exile		Tom Thumb the Great
T. Dec 26	The Roman Father		Harlequin Pedlar; or, The Haunted Well
W. Dec 27	The Wheel of Fortune		Harlequin Pedlar
Th. Dec 28	The Merchant of Venice		Harlequin Pedlar
F. Dec 29	King Lear		Harlequin Pedlar
S. Dec 30	The Iron Chest		Harlequin Pedlar
M. Jan 1 **1810**	Romeo and Juliet		Harlequin Pedlar
T. Jan 2	The Poor Gentleman		Harlequin Pedlar
W. Jan 3	**The Revenge**		Harlequin Pedlar
Th. Jan 4	The School of Reform		Harlequin Pedlar
F. Jan 5	King Lear		Harlequin Pedlar
S. Jan 6	The Provoked Husband		Harlequin Pedlar
M. Jan 8	King Richard the Third		Harlequin Pedlar
T. Jan 9	Speed the Plough		Harlequin Pedlar
W. Jan 10	**The Revenge**		Harlequin Pedlar
Th. Jan 11	The Man of the World		Harlequin Pedlar
F. Jan 12	King Lear		Harlequin Pedlar
S. Jan 13	The Merchant of Venice		Harlequin Pedlar
M. Jan 15	Hamlet		Harlequin Pedlar
T. Jan 16	**The Conscious Lovers**		Harlequin Pedlar
W. Jan 17	**The Revenge**		Harlequin Pedlar
Th. Jan 18	The Man of the World		Harlequin Pedlar
F. Jan 19	King Lear		Harlequin Pedlar
S. Jan 20	The Merchant of Venice		Harlequin Pedlar
M. Jan 22	Othello		Harlequin Pedlar
T. Jan 23	**The Conscious Lovers**		Harlequin Pedlar
W. Jan 24	**The Revenge**		Harlequin Pedlar
Th. Jan 25	The Man of the World		Harlequin Pedlar
F. Jan 26	The Exile		Harlequin Pedlar
S. Jan 27	The Merchant of Venice		Harlequin Pedlar
M. Jan 29	King Richard the Third		Harlequin Pedlar
W. Jan 31	The Jealous Wife		Harlequin Pedlar
Th. Feb 1	The Man of the World		Harlequin Pedlar
F. Feb 2	The Exile		Harlequin Pedlar
S. Feb 3	The Merchant of Venice		Love a-la Mode
M. Feb 5	Othello		Harlequin Pedlar
T. Feb 6	The Jealous Wife		Harlequin Pedlar
W. Feb 7	The Man of the World		Harlequin Pedlar

Date (*Notes*)	Mainpiece	Interlude	Afterpiece
Th. Feb 8 **1810** *Never Acted Before*	The Free Knights; or, The Edict of Charlemagne		Raising the Wind
F. Feb 9	The Free Knights		All the World's a Stage
S. Feb 10	The Free Knights		Is He a Prince?
M. Feb 12	The Free Knights		Harlequin Pedlar
T. Feb 13	The Free Knights		'We Fly By Night'
W. Feb 14	The Free Knights		Harlequin Pedlar
Th. Feb 15	The Free Knights		Harlequin Pedlar
F. Feb 16	The Free Knights		A Budget of Blunders
S. Feb 17	The Free Knights		A Budget of Blunders
M. Feb 19	The Free Knights		A Budget of Blunders
T. Feb 20	The Free Knights		A Budget of Blunders
W. Feb 21	The Free Knights		A Budget of Blunders
Th. Feb 22	The Free Knights		A Budget of Blunders
F. Feb 23	The Free Knights		A Budget of Blunders
S. Feb 24	The Free Knights		A Budget of Blunders
M. Feb 26	King Lear		Harlequin Pedlar
T. Feb 27	The Free Knights		Who Wins?
Th. Mar 1	The Jealous Wife		A Budget of Blunders
F. Mar 2	**The Revenge**		Honest Thieves
S. Mar 3	The Free Knights		Oscar and Malvina
M. Mar 5	King Lear		Harlequin Pedlar
T. Mar 6	Every Man in his Humour		A Budget of Blunders
Th. Mar 8	The Man of the World		The Farmer
S. Mar 10	**The Castle of Andalusia**		**Don Juan**
M. Mar 12	King Lear		Harlequin Pedlar
T. Mar 13	New Way to Pay Old Debts		Honest Thieves
Th. Mar 15	King Henry the Fourth (Part One)		Tom Thumb the Great
S. Mar 17	The Man of the World		The Blind Boy
M. Mar 19	King Lear		Harlequin Pedlar
T. Mar 20 *By particular desire*	The Exile		Raising the Wind
Th. Mar 22	King Henry the Fourth (Part One)		**Paul and Virginia**
S. Mar 24	Othello		Tom Thumb the Great
M. Mar 26	King Lear		Harlequin Pedlar
T. Mar 27	The Free Knights		The Irishman in London
Th. Mar 29	How to Tease, and How to Please		The Quaker
S. Mar 31	How to Tease, and How to Please		Rosina
M. Apr 2	How to Tease, and How to Please		Harlequin Pedlar
T. Apr 3	**The Castle of Andalusia**		Honest Thieves
Th. Apr 5	King Henry the Fourth (Part One)		**Paul and Virginia**

Date (*Notes*)	Mainpiece	Interlude	Afterpiece
S. Apr 7 **1810**	The Jealous Wife		The Review
M. Apr 9	Hamlet		The Waterman
T. Apr 10	The Confederacy		Tom Thumb the Great
Th. Apr 12	Speed the Plough		Hartford Bridge
S. Apr 14	King Henry the Fourth		**Paul and Virginia**
Last night of	(Part One)		
performing until the			
holidays			
M. Apr 23	King Richard the Third		Harlequin Pedlar
T. Apr 24	Macbeth		**Don Juan**
W. Apr 25	The Wheel of Fortune		Harlequin Pedlar
Th. Apr 26	The Grecian Daughter		Oscar and Malvina
F. Apr 27	King Henry the Fourth		**Paul and Virginia**
	(Part One)		
S. Apr 28	The Gamester		Who Wins?
M. Apr 30	Macbeth		'We Fly By Night'
T. May 1	All in the Wrong		The Blind Boy
W. May 2	Douglas		Lock and Key
Under the Patronage			
of His Royal			
Highness the Prince			
of Wales. For the			
Benefit of the Fund			
for the Relief of Aged			
and Infirm Actors,			
and the Widows and			
Children of Actors			
Deceased			
Th. May 3	The Gamester		Tom Thumb the Great
F. May 4	**The Castle of**		**The Child of Nature**
	Andalusia		
S. May 5	**King Henry the**		The Waterman
	Eighth		
M. May 7	Hamlet		Harlequin Pedlar
T. May 8	Macbeth		The Flitch of Bacon
W. May 9	King Henry the Fourth		The Poor Soldier
	(Part One)		
Th. May 10	**King Henry the**		The Farmer
	Eighth		
F. May 11	The Merchant of Venice		Love a-la Mode
S. May 12	King John		The Birth Day
M. May 14	Macbeth		Harlequin Pedlar
T. May 15	Love in a Village	Feast of Apollo	Raising the Wind
Mr Incledon's Night		Songs	
W. May 16	The Man of the World	'Black Eye'd Susan' (*by particular desire*)	Oscar and Malvina
Th. May 17	King John		**Paul and Virginia**
F. May 18	Othello	The Rival Soldiers	No Song No Supper
Mr Young's Night			
S. May 19	**King Henry the**		Is He a Prince?
	Eighth		
M. May 21	Hamlet		Harlequin Pedlar

Date (*Notes*)	Mainpiece	Interlude	Afterpiece
T. May 22 **1810** *Mr Munden's Night*	Every One Has His Fault	Songs In the course of the evening, Collins's Ode on the Passions	The Turnpike Gate
W. May 23	King Lear	High Life Below Stairs	The Deserter of Naples
Th. May 24	King John		Tom Thumb the Great
F. May 25	Macbeth	Personation; or, Fairly Taken In	Love a-la Mode
S. May 26	**King Henry the Eighth**		The Escapes; or, The Water Carrier
M. May 28	King John		Harlequin Pedlar
T. May 29 *Mrs Dickons's Night*	**The English Fleet in 1342**	Songs	The Blind Boy
W. May 30 *Mr and Mrs C Kemble's Night*	The School for Scandal	Personation	The Devil to Pay
Th. May 31	**Isabella; or, The Fatal Marriage**	High Life Below Stairs	The Deserter of Naples
F. Jun 1 *Mr Bellamy's Night*	The Cabinet	The Glorious First of June; or, British Sailor's Jubilee	Tom Thumb the Great
S Jun 2 *Mr Jones's Night*	Fontainebleau	Songs The Day after the Wedding; or, A Wife's First Lesson	Love a-la Mode
M. Jun 4 *In Honour of His Majesty's Birthday*	Macbeth	The Jubilee	The Deserter of Naples
T. Jun 5 *Mr Blanchard's Night*	King Henry the Fourth (Part One)	Songs and dancing	No Song, No Supper
W. Jun 6 *Mrs H Johnston's Night*	The School of Reform; or, How to Rule a Husband	'Pas deux' from Harlequin and Mother Goose; or, The Golden Egg Songs	High Life Below Stairs
Th. Jun 7	The Widow's Only Son		The Escapes
F. Jun 8 *Mr and Mrs Liston's Night*	The Foundling of the Forest (*by permission of the proprietors of the Haymarket*)	Blue Devils Songs	Killing No Murder (*by permission of the Haymarket*)
M. Jun 11	King John		Harlequin Pedlar
T. Jun 12	Hamlet	Songs	Harlequin and Mother Goose
W. Jun 13 *Mr Emery's Night*	Speed the Plough	Songs	The Escapes
Th. Jun 14 *Benefit of Mr Brandon, Box, Book, and House-Keeper*	King Lear	Description of 'A Storm' with appropriate scenery	The Turnpike Gate
F. Jun 15	The Road to Ruin	Imitations, 'chiefly of the old school'	Rosina

Date (*Notes*)	Mainpiece	Interlude	Afterpiece
S. Jun 16 **1810**	**Isabella**		Harlequin and Mother Goose
M. Jun 18	Macbeth		Harlequin and Mother Goose
T. Jun 19 *Mr Taylor's Night*	Maid of the Mill	Songs	The Prisoner at Large
		Description of 'A Storm'	
W. Jun 20 *Miss Norton's Night*	The Exile	Songs	Tom Thumb the Great
Th. Jun 21	King John		Harlequin and Mother Goose
F. Jun 22 *Mrs Clarke's Night*	The Merchant of Venice	Songs	Lock and Key
S. Jun 23	Love in a Village	Songs (*by particular desire*)	Raising the Wind
M. Jun 25	King John		The Taming of the Shrew
T. Jun 26 *Mr Grimaldi's Night*	Every One Has His Faults	'The Bold Sergeant; or, Fairly Taken in' (*new dance*)	Harlequin and Mother Goose
		Songs	
W. Jun 27 *Miss Bolton's Night*	Abroad and at Home ('*Between the acts: A new Grand Spanish Bolero, by Miss Adams and Miss S Adams*')	Songs and dancing	Harlequin and Mother Goose
		Blue Devils	
Th. Jun 28 *Benefit of Mr Glassington, Prompter*	King Lear	Songs	The Blind Boy
F. Jun 29 *Mr Waddy and Mr Claremont's Night*	The Poor Gentleman	Songs	**Don Juan**
S. Jun 30	John Bull	Songs	The Poor Soldier
		A Double Hornpipe	
M. Jul 2	King John		The Taming of the Shrew
T. Jul 3 *Mr Webb and Mr Ware, Leader of the Band*	The Beggar's Opera	Song and Dancing	Honest Thieves
		Overture to Lodoiska	
W. Jul 4	Macbeth		The Farmer
Th. Jul 5	The Beaux Stratagem		The Quaker
F. Jul 6 *Last Night*	Hamlet		The Waterman
S. Jul 7 *Under The Patronage of His Royal Highness the Prince of Wales*	Subscription Concert		

Calendar of Covent Garden Playbills 1810–1811

Date (*Notes*)	Mainpiece	Interlude	Afterpiece
M. Sep 10 **1810**	The Beggar's Opera		Raising the Wind
W. Sep 12	The Wheel of Fortune		The Escapes; or, The Water Carrier
F. Sep 14	Love in a Village		**The Child of Nature**
M. Sep 17	The Suspicious Husband		Harlequin and Mother Goose; or, The Golden Egg
M. Sep 24	The Exile		Harlequin and Mother Goose
W. Sep 26	**The English Fleet in 1342**		The Irishman in London
Th. Sep 27	The School for Reform		Who Wins? Or, The Widow's Choice
F. Sep 28	All in the Wrong		The Turnpike Gate
M. Oct 1	Romeo and Juliet		Harlequin and Mother Goose
T. Oct 2	Speed the Plough		The Blind Boy
W. Oct 3	The Beggar's Opera		Raising the Wind
Th. Oct 4	John Bull; or, An Englishman's Fireside		**Paul and Virginia**
F. Oct 5	Fontainebleau		Animal Magnetism
M. Oct 8	Hamlet, Prince of Denmark		Oscar and Malvina
T. Oct 9	**The Conscious Lovers**		Of Age To-morrow
W. Oct 10	**Abroad and at Home**		High Life Below Stairs
Th. Oct 11	The Exile		Peeping Tom
F. Oct 12	**The English Fleet in 1342**		Oscar and Malvina
S. Oct 13	King Lear		The Waterman
M. Oct 15	Romeo and Juliet		Harlequin and Mother Goose
T. Oct 16	The Heir at Law		The Bridal Ring
W. Oct 17	Macbeth		The Bridal Ring
Th. Oct 18	The Beaux Stratagem		The Bridal Ring
F. Oct 19	The Iron Chest		The Bridal Ring
S. Oct 20	**King Henry the Eighth** (*Anthem to be sung*)		**The Padlock**
M. Oct 22	**The Revenge**		Harlequin and Mother Goose
T. Oct 23	The Gamester		**The Child of Nature**
W. Oct 24	Inkle and Yarico		Oscar and Malvina

Date (*Notes*)	Mainpiece	Interlude	Afterpiece
Th. Oct 25 **1810**	**The Mountaineers** (*End of the Play 'God save the King', verse and chorus, by the performers*)		The Escapes
F. Oct 26	The Woodman		The Blind Boy
S. Oct 27	King John		Tom Thumb
M. Oct 29	King Lear		Harlequin and Mother Goose
T. Oct 30	**Isabella; or, The Fatal Marriage**		Poor Soldier
W. Oct 31	A Cure for the Heart-Ache		**Paul and Virginia**
Th. Nov 1	King Henry the Fourth (Part One)		High Life Below Stairs
F. Nov 2	Every Man in His Humour		Rosina
W. Nov 14	The Wheel of Fortune		La Perouse; or the Desolate Island
Th. Nov 15	Macbeth		The Village Lawyer
F. Nov 16	The Woodman		La Perouse
S. Nov 17	King John		The Agreeable Surprise
M. Nov 19	**The Mountaineers**		La Perouse
T. Nov 20	The Gamester		'We Fly By Night'; or, Long Stories
W. Nov 21	The Provoked Husband; or, A Journey to London		La Perouse
Th. Nov 22	As You Like It		The Blind Boy
F. Nov 23	The Exile		**The Child of Nature**
S. Nov 24	King John		The Agreeable Surprise
M. Nov 26	**The Mountaineers**		La Perouse
T. Nov 27	The Gamester		**The Child of Nature**
W. Nov 28	As You Like It		La Perouse
Th. Nov 29 *Never Acted Before*	Gustavus Vasa		The Spoil'd Child
F. Nov 30	Gustavus Vasa		**The Child of Nature**
S. Dec 1	**King Henry the Eighth**		The Spoil'd Child
M. Dec 3	Gustavus Vasa		Tom Thumb the Great
T. Dec 4	The Gamester		La Perouse
W. Dec 5	Gustavus Vasa		All the World's a Stage
Th. Dec 6	Othello, The Moor of Venice		The Spoil'd Child
F. Dec 7	Gustavus Vasa		**The Child of Nature**

Date (*Notes*)	Mainpiece	Interlude	Afterpiece
S. Dec 8 **1810**	**King Henry the Eighth**		All The World's a Stage
M. Dec 10	King Henry the Fourth (Part One)		La Perouse
T. Dec 11	**Isabella**		XYZ
Th. Dec13	The Merchant of Venice		The Spoil'd Child
F. Dec 14	Gustavus Vasa		**The Child of Nature**
S Dec 15	King John		All the World's a Stage
M. Dec 17	**The Mountaineers**		La Perouse
T. Dec 18	Macbeth		Miss Lucy; or, The Virgin Unmask'd
W. Dec 19	Gustavus Vasa		The Spoil'd Child
Th. Dec 20	The Merchant of Venice		Miss Lucy
F. Dec 21	The Exile		All the World's a Stage
S. Dec 22	**King Henry the Eighth**		The Spoil'd Child
W Dec 26	Every Man in His Humour		**Harlequin and Asmodeus; or, Cupid on Crutches**
Th. Dec 27	As You Like It		**Harlequin and Asmodeus**
F. Dec 28	Every One Has His Fault		**Harlequin and Asmodeus**
S. Dec 29	New Way to Pay Old Debts		**Harlequin and Asmodeus**
M. Dec 31	Romeo and Juliet		**Harlequin and Asmodeus**
T. Jan 1 **1811**	The Provoked Husband		**Harlequin and Asmodeus**
W. Jan 2	The Wheel of Fortune		**Harlequin and Asmodeus**
Th. Jan 3	**The English Fleet in 1342**		**Harlequin and Asmodeus**
F. Jan 4	New Way to Pay Old Debts		**Harlequin and Asmodeus**
S. Jan 5	The Twelfth Night; or, What You Will		**Harlequin and Asmodeus**
M. Jan 7	King Richard the Third		**Harlequin and Asmodeus**
T. Jan 8	The Jealous Wife		**Harlequin and Asmodeus**
W. Jan 9	Othello		**Harlequin and Asmodeus**
Th. Jan 10	Gustavus Vasa		**Harlequin and Asmodeus**
F. Jan 11	The Twelfth Night		**Harlequin and Asmodeus**
S. Jan 12	**Much Ado About Nothing**		**Harlequin and Asmodeus**

Date (*Notes*)	Mainpiece	Interlude	Afterpiece
M. Jan 14 **1811**	Gustavus Vasa		**Harlequin and Asmodeus**
T. Jan 15	All in the Wrong		**Harlequin and Asmodeus**
W. Jan 16	The Merry Wives of Windsor		**Harlequin and Asmodeus**
Th. Jan 17	Gustavus Vasa		**Harlequin and Asmodeus**
F. Jan 18	The Inconstant; or, The Way to Win Him		**Harlequin and Asmodeus**
S. Jan 19	The Twelfth Night		**Harlequin and Asmodeus**
M. Jan 21	Othello		**Harlequin and Asmodeus**
T. Jan 22	The Confederacy		**Harlequin and Asmodeus**
W. Jan 23	Gustavus Vasa		**Harlequin and Asmodeus**
Th. Jan 24	The Merry Wives of Windsor		**Harlequin and Asmodeus**
F. Jan 25	The Twelfth Night		**Harlequin and Asmodeus**
S. Jan 26	Cato		**Harlequin and Asmodeus**
M. Jan 28	Cato		**Harlequin and Asmodeus**
T. Jan 29	Gustavus Vasa		**Harlequin and Asmodeus**
Th. Jan 31	Cato		**Harlequin and Asmodeus**
F. Feb 1	The Twelfth Night		**Harlequin and Asmodeus**
S. Feb 2	Cato		**Harlequin and Asmodeus**
M. Feb 4	Cato		**Harlequin and Asmodeus**
T. Feb 5	The Knight of Snowdoun		Animal Magnetism
W. Feb 6	The Knight of Snowdoun		**Harlequin and Asmodeus**
Th. Feb 7	The Knight of Snowdoun		**Harlequin and Asmodeus**
F. Feb 8	The Knight of Snowdoun		**Harlequin and Asmodeus**
S. Feb 9	The Knight of Snowdoun		**Harlequin and Asmodeus**
M. Feb 11	The Knight of Snowdoun		**Harlequin and Asmodeus**
T. Feb 12	The Knight of Snowdoun		**Harlequin and Asmodeus**
W. Feb 13	The Knight of Snowdoun		**Harlequin and Asmodeus**

Date (*Notes*)	Mainpiece	Interlude	Afterpiece
Th. Feb 14 **1811**	The Knight of Snowdoun		**Harlequin and Asmodeus**
F. Feb 15	The Knight of Snowdoun		The Spoil'd Child
S. Feb 16	Cato		Tom Thumb the Great
M. Feb 18	Every Man in His Humour		Blue Beard; or, Female Curiosity
T. Feb 19	The Twelfth Night		Blue Beard
W. Feb 20	The Knight of Snowdoun		Blue Beard
Th. Feb 21	New Way to Pay Old Debts		Blue Beard
F. Feb 22	The Knight of Snowdoun		Blue Beard
S. Feb 23	Cato		Blue Beard
M. Feb 25	Romeo and Juliet		Blue Beard
T. Feb 26	The Knight of Snowdoun		Blue Beard
W. Feb 28	The Knight of Snowdoun		Blue Beard
S. Mar 2	Cato		Blue Beard
T. Mar 5	The Knight of Snowdoun		Blue Beard
Th. Mar 7	The Knight of Snowdoun		Blue Beard
S. Mar 9	Cato		Blue Beard
M. Mar 11	King Henry the Fifth; or, The Conquest of France		Blue Beard
T. Mar 12	Gustavus Vasa		Blue Beard
Th. Mar 14	The Knight of Snowdoun		Blue Beard
S. Mar 15	Cato		Blue Beard
M. Mar 18	King Henry the Fifth		Blue Beard
T. Mar 19	As You Like It		Blue Beard
Th. Mar 21	The Knight of Snowdoun		Blue Beard
S. Mar 23	Cato		Blue Beard
M. Mar 25	King Henry the Fifth		Blue Beard
T. Mar 26	The Rivals		Blue Beard
Th. Mar 28	The Knight of Snowdoun		Blue Beard
S. Mar 30	Hamlet		Blue Beard
M. Apr 1	King Richard the Third		Blue Beard
T. Apr 2	The Rivals		Blue Beard
Th. Apr 4	The Knight of Snowdoun		Blue Beard
S. Apr 6	Hamlet		Blue Beard
M. Apr 8	Romeo and Juliet		Blue Beard
T. Apr 9	The Knight of Snowdoun		Blue Beard
W. Apr 17	The Comedy of Errors		Blue Beard

Date (*Notes*)	Mainpiece	Interlude	Afterpiece
Th. Apr 18 **1811**	Cato		Blue Beard
F. Apr 19	Othello		Blue Beard
S. Apr 20	Hamlet		Blue Beard
M. Apr 22	Macbeth		Blue Beard
T. Apr 23	The Gazette		Blue Beard
Never Acted Before	Extraordinary		
W. Apr 24	Gazette Extraordinary		Blue Beard
Th. Apr 25	Gazette Extraordinary		Blue Beard
F. Apr 26	Gazette Extraordinary		Blue Beard
S. Apr 27	The Gamester		The Spoil'd Child
M. Apr 29	The Comedy of Errors		Timour the Tartar
			(*First Time*)
T. Apr 30	Gazette Extraordinary		Timour the Tartar
W. May 1	Douglas		Timour the Tartar
Th. May 2	Gazette Extraordinary		Timour the Tartar
F. May 3	Gazette Extraordinary		Timour the Tartar
S. May 4	King John		Timour the Tartar
M. May 6	Cato		Timour the Tartar
T. May 7	Gazette Extraordinary		Timour the Tartar
W. May 8	Knight of Snowdoun		Timour the Tartar
Th. May 9	Gazette Extraordinary		Timour the Tartar
F. May 10	**The Mountaineers**		Timour the Tartar
S. May 11	The Country Girl		Timour the Tartar
M. May 13	King Richard the Third		Timour the Tartar
T. May 14	Gazette Extraordinary		Timour the Tartar
W. May 15	Macbeth		Timour the Tartar
Th. May 16	The Twelfth Night		Timour the Tartar
F. May 17	The Wheel of Fortune		Timour the Tartar
S. May 18	**King Henry the Eighth**		Timour the Tartar
M. May 20	Cato		Timour the Tartar
T. May 21	Macbeth		Timour the Tartar
W. May 22	Gazette Extraordinary		Timour the Tartar
Th. May 23	New Way to Pay Old Debts		Timour the Tartar
F. May 24	All's Well that Ends Well		Timour the Tartar
S. May 25	**King Henry the Eighth**		Timour the Tartar
M. May 27	King Richard the Third		Timour the Tartar
T. May 28	Macbeth		Timour the Tartar
W. May 29	**The English Fleet in 1342**	Songs	Tom Thumb the Great
Mr Incledon's Night	(*to conclude with 'Rule Britannia'*)	Description of 'A Storm' (*in character, by Mr Incledon*)	
Th. May 30	Hamlet	Songs	La Perouse
Mr Young's Night			
F. May 31	The Poor Gentleman	Songs	The Farmer
Mr Munden's Night			

Date (*Notes*)	Mainpiece	Interlude	Afterpiece
M. Jun 3 **1811**	Cato		**Harlequin and Asmodeus**
T. Jun 4 *Mr Fawcett's Night*	King Henry the Fourth (Part One)	Songs (*including 'When Britons Strike Home' and 'God Save the King', verse and chorus*)	Harlequin and Mother Goose
W. Jun 5	Macbeth		La Perouse
Th. Jun 6 *Mrs Dickons's Night*	The Exile	Songs Description of 'A Storm' (*in character, by Mr Incledon*)	Oscar and Malvina
F. Jun 7 *For the Benefit of Mr and Mrs Kemble*	**Much Ado About Nothing**	Blue Devils	Harlequin and Mother Goose
S. Jun 8	**Pizarro**		The Farmer
M. Jun 10	**Pizarro**		**Harlequin and Asmodeus**
T. Jun 11 *Mrs Jordan's only appearance in London for these three years past. Mr Jones's Night*	The Country Girl	Fashion! Or, A Peep at the Exhibition Songs	Who Wins?
W. Jun 12 *Mr H Johnston's Night*	**Rule a Wife and Have a Wife**	Songs	**Harlequin and Asmodeus**
Th. Jun 13 *For the Benefit of Mr Blanchard*	The Knight of Snowdoun	Songs	'We Fly By Night'
F. Jun 14 *Mr and Mrs Liston's Night*	The Young Quaker	Songs **The Portrait of Cervantes; or, The Plotting Lovers**	Bombastes Furioso
S. Jun 15	The Poor Gentleman	'A Favourite new Hornpipe'	The Turnpike Gate
M. Jun 17	**Pizarro**		Harlequin and Mother Goose
T. Jun 18	Cato	Popular 'pas deux' from Mother Goose	Valentine and Orson
W. Jun 19 *Mr Emery's Night*	The School of Reform	Songs	The Blind Boy
Th. Jun 20 *For the Benefit of Mr Brandon, Box, Book and House-Keeper*	**The Mountaineers**	Songs	Valentine and Orson

Date (*Notes*)	Mainpiece	Interlude	Afterpiece
F. Jun 21 **1811** *Mr Taylor's Night*	The Beggar's Opera	Songs Imitations of well known London performers, by Mr Taylor Hob in the Well (musical piece *not acted these 15 years*)	Bombastes Furioso
S. Jun 22	All's Well that Ends Well	Songs	**The Child of Nature**
M. Jun 24	**Pizarro**		Harlequin and Mother Goose
T. Jun 25 *Mr Grimaldi's Night*	The Rivals	Songs, including 'Typitywitchet', by Grimaldi	**Harlequin and Asmodeus**
W. Jun 26 *Miss Bolton's Night*	The Exile	Songs Description of 'A Storm' (*in character, by Mr Incledon*)	The Escapes
Th. Jun 27 *Miss S Booth's Night*	Romeo and Juliet	Songs Collins's Ode on the Passions	The Romp; or, A Cure for the Spleen
F. Jun 28 *Mr Ware, Leader of the Band and Mr Claremont's Night*	**The English Fleet in 1342**	Songs	Valentine and Orson
S. Jun 29	The School of Reform		The Waterman
M. Jul 1	Hamlet		Timour the Tartar
T. Jul 2	The Soldier's Daughter		Timour the Tartar
W. Jul 3	**King Henry the Eighth**		Timour the Tartar
Th. Jul 4	King Richard the Third		Timour the Tartar
F. Jul 5	**The Wonder; A Woman Keeps a Secret**		Timour the Tartar
S. Jul 6	All in the Wrong		Timour the Tartar
M. Jul 8	The Country Girl		Timour the Tartar
T. Jul 9	A Cure for the Heart-ache	Songs	Timour the Tartar
W. Jul 10	Speed the Plough	'Pas deux'	**The Padlock**
Th. Jul 11	The Way to Keep Him		Blue Beard
F. Jul 12	School for Scandal		Blue Beard
S. Jul 13	A Trip to Scarborough		Blue Beard
M. Jul 15	Macbeth		Timour the Tartar
T. Jul 16	The Country Girl		Timour the Tartar
W. Jul 17	**Pizarro**		Timour the Tartar
Th. Jul 18	School for Scandal		Timour the Tartar
F. Jul 19	Othello		Timour the Tartar

Date (*Notes*)	Mainpiece	Interlude	Afterpiece
S. Jul 20 **1811** *Last night of Mrs Jordan's performing*	The Soldier's Daughter		Timour the Tartar
M. Jul 22	Macbeth		Timour the Tartar
T. Jul 23	**Pizarro**		Timour the Tartar
W. Jul 24	The Exile	Mr Taylor's Imitations of several principal performers Grimaldi's 'Tipity-witchet'	Timour the Tartar (*last night of the Equestrian Company*)
Th. Jul 25 *Last Night* *Benefit for the Relief of the British Prisoners in France*	Hamlet (*At the end of the play:* 'God Save the King', *verse and chorus by Madame Catalani and other performers*)	Grand Scene and Aria from Semiramide and the favourite ballad of 'Cease your funning' by Madame Catalani	Timour the Tartar

Calendar of Covent Garden Playbills 1811–1812

Date (*Notes*)	Mainpiece	Interlude	Afterpiece
M. Sep 9 **1811**	Romeo and Juliet		**Harlequin and Asmodeus; or, Cupid on Crutches**
W. Sep 11	The Wheel of Fortune		La Perouse: or, The Desolate Island
F. Sep 13	Othello, The Moor of Venice		All the World's a Stage
M. Sep 16	King Richard the Third		**Harlequin and Asmodeus**
T. Sep 17	Speed the Plough		The Quaker
W. Sep 18	Macbeth		The Spoil'd Child
Th. Sep 19	The Provoked Husband; or, A Journey to London		La Perouse
F. Sep 20	**The Duenna**		Valentine and Orson
S. Sep 21	The Gamester		The Devil to Pay; or, The Wives Metamorphosed
M. Sep 23	Hamlet, Prince of Denmark		Harlequin and Mother Goose; or, The Golden Egg
T. Sep 24	**The Duenna**		High Life Below Stairs
W. Sep 25	King John		The Blind Boy
Th. Sep 26	The Cabinet		Valentine and Orson
F. Sep 27	The Merry Wives of Windsor		**Harlequin and Asmodeus**
S. Sep 28	**Isabella; or, The Fatal Marriage**		The Review; or, The Wags of Windsor
M. Sep 30	King Henry the Fourth (Part One)		Raymond and Agnes; or, The Castle of Lindenbergh
T. Oct 1	The Exile		Raymond and Agnes
W. Oct 2	Macbeth		Raymond and Agnes
Th. Oct 3	The Cabinet		Raymond and Agnes
F. Oct 4	The Woodman		Raymond and Agnes
S. Oct 5	**Pizarro**		The Quaker
M. Oct 7	**The Mountaineers**		Oscar and Malvina
T. Oct 8	The Cabinet		Tom Thumb the Great
W. Oct 9	Macbeth		**The Child of Nature**
Th. Oct 10	The Woodman		Raymond and Agnes
F. Oct 11	The Twelfth Night; or, What you Will		La Perouse
S. Oct 12	The Grecian Daughter		Raymond and Agnes
M. Oct 14	Othello		**Harlequin and Asmodeus**
T. Oct 15	**Pizarro**		The Romp
W. Oct 16 *Never Acted Before*	Kamtchatka; or, The Slave's Tribute		High Life Below Stairs
Th. Oct 17	Kamtchatka		The Miser
F. Oct 18	Kamtchatka		Tom Thumb the Great
S. Oct 19	**King Henry the Eighth**		Of Age To-morrow

Date (*Notes*)	Mainpiece	Interlude	Afterpiece
M. Oct 21 **1811**	Kamtchatka		Valentine and Orson
T. Oct 22	The Woodman		The Romp
W. Oct 23	Macbeth		**The Follies of a Day**
Th. Oct 24	The Cabinet		Animal Magnetism
F. Oct 25	The Cabinet		Raymond and Agnes
S. Oct 26	**King Henry the Eighth**		Is He a Prince?
M. Oct 28	Cato		**Harlequin and Asmodeus**
T. Oct 29	**The English Fleet in 1342**		Raising the Wind
W. Oct 30	Measure for Measure		The Blind Boy
Th. Oct 31	The Woodman		**The Follies of a Day**
F. Nov 1	**The English Fleet in 1342**		Raymond and Agnes
S. Nov 2	Macbeth		The Spoil'd Child
M. Nov 4	Romeo and Juliet		La Perouse
T. Nov 5	Measure for Measure		All the World's a Stage
W. Nov 6 *Never Acted Before*	Up to Town		**The Child of Nature**
Th. Nov 7	The Twelfth Night		Tom Thumb the Great
F. Nov 8	Venice Preserv'd		**The Portrait of Cervantes**
S. Nov 9	Othello		Valentine and Orson
M. Nov 11	Up to Town		**The Child of Nature**
T. Nov 12	Up to Town		The Birth-Day
W. Nov 13	Measure for Measure		The Wedding Day
Th. Nov 14	Up to Town		**The Portrait of Cervantes**
F. Nov 15	The Cabinet		Raymond and Agnes
S. Nov 16	Venice Preserv'd		The Midnight Hour
M. Nov 18	Romeo and Juliet		La Perouse
T. Nov 19	Macbeth		Is He a Prince?
W. Nov 20	**The English Fleet in 1342**		The Birth-Day
Th. Nov 21	Measure for Measure		**Paul and Virginia**
F. Nov 22	Love in a Village		Raymond and Agnes
S. Nov 23	Venice Preserv'd		The Wedding Day
M. Nov 25	The Knight of Snowdoun		A Tale of Mystery
T. Nov 26	The Gamester		**Paul and Virginia**
W Nov 27	The Woodman (*by particular desire*)		A Tale of Mystery
Th. Nov 28	The Winter's Tale		**The Follies of a Day**
F. Nov 29	The Wheel of Fortune		Rosina
S. Nov 30	Measure for Measure		Tom Thumb the Great
M. Dec 2	Othello		**Paul and Virginia**
T. Dec 3	Venice Preserv'd		The Blind Boy
W. Dec 4	**The Honey Moon**		The Poor Soldier
Th. Dec 5 *Last fortnight of Mrs Siddons's acting until after Easter*	The Winter's Tale		The Review

Date (*Notes*)	Mainpiece	Interlude	Afterpiece
F. Dec 6 **1811**	The Man of the World		Rosina
S. Dec 7	**Pizarro**		The Poor Soldier
M. Dec 9	Romeo and Juliet		La Perouse
T. Dec 10	**King Henry the Eighth**		Animal Magnetism
W. Dec 11	The Iron Chest		**The Portrait of Cervantes**
Th. Dec 12	Macbeth		**Paul and Virginia**
F. Dec 13	**The Honey Moon**		The Poor Soldier
S. Dec 14	Coriolanus; or, The Roman Matron		The Spoil'd Child
M. Dec 16	**The English Fleet in 1342**		A Tale of Mystery
T. Dec 17 *Last week of Mrs Siddons's acting until after Easter*	Coriolanus		Of Age To-morrow
W. Dec 18	The Rivals		The Highland Reel
Th. Dec 19	Coriolanus		**The Portrait of Cervantes**
F. Dec 20	The Winter's Tale		Highland Reel
S. Dec 21	Coriolanus		**The Follies of a Day**
M. Dec 23 *The last time of performances until the holidays. The last night of Mrs Siddons's acting until after Easter*	Coriolanus		**Paul and Virginia**
T. Dec 26	George Barnwell; or, The London Merchant		Harlequin and Padmanaba; or, The Golden Fish
F. Dec 27	The Merry Wives of Windsor		Harlequin and Padmanaba
S. Dec 28	Venice Preserv'd		Harlequin and Padmanaba
M. Dec 30	The Knight of Snowdoun		Harlequin and Padmanaba
T. Dec 31	Jane Shore		Harlequin and Padmanaba
W. Jan 1 **1812**	The Cabinet		Harlequin and Padmanaba
Th. Jan 2	Hamlet		Harlequin and Padmanaba
F. Jan 3	Venice Preserv'd		Harlequin and Padmanaba
S. Jan 4	The Wheel of Fortune		Harlequin and Padmanaba
M. Jan 6	King Richard the Third		Harlequin and Padmanaba
T. Jan 7	Percy		Harlequin and Padmanaba

Date (*Notes*)	Mainpiece	Interlude	Afterpiece
W. Jan 8 **1812**	The Comedy of Errors		Harlequin and Padmanaba
Th. Jan 9	Cato		Harlequin and Padmanaba
F. Jan 10	Jane Shore		Harlequin and Padmanaba
S. Jan 11	The Foundling of the Forest		Harlequin and Padmanaba
M. Jan 13	King Richard the Third		Harlequin and Padmanaba
T. Jan 14	The Foundling of the Forest		Harlequin and Padmanaba
W. Jan 15	King Henry the Fourth (Part One)		Harlequin and Padmanaba
Th. Jan 16	Comedy of Errors		Harlequin and Padmanaba
F. Jan 17	New Way to Pay Old Debts		Harlequin and Padmanaba
S. Jan 18	The Foundling of the Forest	'At the end of the play, Miss Smith will recite a melologue upon National Music. Original Air of Greece, Switzerland, **Spain**, Ireland, England &c &c'	Harlequin and Padmanaba
M. Jan 20	Cato		Harlequin and Padmanaba
T. Jan 21	The Knight of Snowdoun		Harlequin and Padmanaba
W. Jan 22	**The Revenge**		Harlequin and Padmanaba
Th. Jan 23	**The Revenge**		Harlequin and Padmanaba
F. Jan 24	Comedy of Errors		Harlequin and Padmanaba
S. Jan 25	The Twelfth Night		Harlequin and Padmanaba
M. Jan 27	**The Revenge**		Harlequin and Padmanaba
T. Jan 28	Comedy of Errors		Harlequin and Padmanaba
W. Jan 29	Hamlet		Harlequin and Padmanaba
F. Jan 31 *Never Acted Before*	**The Virgin of the Sun**		Raising the Wind
S. Feb 1	**The Virgin of the Sun**		Harlequin and Padmanaba
M. Feb 3	**The Virgin of the Sun**		Harlequin and Padmanaba
T. Feb 4	**The Virgin of the Sun**		Harlequin and Padmanaba
Th. Feb 6	**The Virgin of the Sun**		Harlequin and Padmanaba

Date (*Notes*)	Mainpiece	Interlude	Afterpiece
F. Feb 7 **1812**	**The Virgin of the Sun**		Harlequin and Padmanaba
S. Feb 8	**The Virgin of the Sun**		Harlequin and Padmanaba
M. Feb 10	**The Virgin of the Sun**		Harlequin and Padmanaba
T. Feb 11	**The Virgin of the Sun**		Harlequin and Padmanaba
Th. Feb 13	**The Virgin of the Sun**		Harlequin and Padmanaba
S. Feb 15	**The Virgin of the Sun**		Harlequin and Padmanaba
M. Feb 17	**The Virgin of the Sun**		Harlequin and Padmanaba
T. Feb 18	**The Virgin of the Sun**		Harlequin and Padmanaba
Th. Feb 20	**The Virgin of the Sun**		Harlequin and Padmanaba
S. Feb 22	**The Virgin of the Sun**		Tom Thumb the Great (*by particular desire*)
M. Feb 24	**The Virgin of the Sun**		Harlequin and Padmanaba
T. Feb 25	**The Virgin of the Sun**		Frost and Thaw
Th. Feb 27	**The Virgin of the Sun**		Frost and Thaw
S. Feb 29	Julius Caesar		Frost and Thaw
M. Mar 2	**The Virgin of the Sun**		Harlequin and Padmanaba
T. Mar 3	Julius Caesar		The Spoil'd Child
Th. Mar 5	**The Virgin of the Sun**		Harlequin and Padmanaba
S. Mar 7	Julius Caesar		The Romp
M. Mar 9	**The Virgin of the Sun**		Harlequin and Padmanaba
T. Mar 10	Julius Caesar		**The Follies of a Day**
Th. Mar 12	**The Virgin of the Sun**		La Perouse
S. Mar 14	Julius Caesar		**The Portrait of Cervantes**
M. Mar 16	**The Virgin of the Sun**		Harlequin and Padmanaba
T. Mar 17	Julius Caesar		Is He a Prince?
Th. Mar 19 *Miss Smith's Night*	**Isabella**	Songs Collins's Ode on the Passions (*with appropriate music*)	The Blind Boy
S. Mar 21 *Last night of performances until the holidays*	Julius Caesar		The Midnight Hour
M. Mar 30	Romeo and Juliet		Timour the Tartar
T. Mar 31	**The Virgin of the Sun**		Timour the Tartar
W. Apr 1	Julius Caesar		Tom Thumb the Great
Th. Apr 2	The Wheel of Fortune		Timour the Tartar

Date (*Notes*)	Mainpiece	Interlude	Afterpiece
F. Apr 3 **1812**	**The Virgin of the Sun**		Timour the Tartar
S. Apr 4	Julius Caesar		**Paul and Virginia**
M. Apr 6	King Richard the Third		Timour the Tartar
T. Apr 7	**The Virgin of the Sun**		Timour the Tartar
W. Apr 8	Julius Caesar		Timour the Tartar
Th. Apr 9	The Winter's Tale		The Blind Boy
F. Apr 10	Othello		Timour the Tartar
S. Apr 11	Macbeth		**The Portrait of Cervantes**
M. Apr 13 *Last week of* Timour the Tartar	**The Virgin of the Sun**		Timour the Tartar
T. Apr 14	Coriolanus		Is He a Prince?
W. Apr 15	As You Like It		Timour the Tartar
Th. Apr 16	Julius Caesar		Timour the Tartar
F. Apr 17	The Exile		Timour the Tartar
S. Apr 18	King John		**Paul and Virginia**
M. Apr 20	Julius Caesar		Timour the Tartar
T. Apr 21	The Gamester		**The Child of Nature**
W. Apr 22	**The Virgin of the Sun**		**The Follies of a Day**
Th. Apr 23	**The Mountaineers**		The Birth-Day
F. Apr 24	Comedy of Errors		The Secret Mine
S. Apr 25	**King Henry the Eighth**		The Spoil'd Child
M. Apr 27	**The Revenge**		The Secret Mine
T. Apr 28	Measure for Measure		**Paul and Virginia**
W. Apr 29	The Cabinet		The Secret Mine
Th. Apr 30	Julius Caesar		The Secret Mine
F. May 1	Rule a Wife and Have a Wife		The Secret Mine
S. May 2	The Grecian Daughter		The Secret Mine
M. May 4	King Richard the Third		The Secret Mine
T. May 5	Coriolanus		**The Follies of a Day**
W. May 6	**The Virgin of the Sun**		The Secret Mine
Th. May 7	Julius Caesar		The Secret Mine
Fr. May 8	**Rule a Wife and Have a Wife**		The Secret Mine
S. May 9	The Gamester		The Secret Mine
M. May 11	Cato		The Secret Mine
T. May 12	Venice Preserv'd		The Secret Mine
W. May 13	**The Virgin of the Sun**		The Secret Mine
Th. May 14	Julius Caesar		The Secret Mine
F. May 15	King John		The Secret Mine
M. May 18	King Richard the Third		The Secret Mine
T. May 19	**King Henry the Eighth**		The Secret Mine
W. May 20	**The Virgin of the Sun**		The Secret Mine
Th. May 21	Julius Caesar		The Secret Mine
F. May 22	The Rivals		The Secret Mine
S. May 23	Coriolanus		All the World's A Stage
M. May 25	Hamlet		Timour the Tartar
T. May 26	Macbeth		The Spoil'd Child
W. May 27	**The Virgin of the Sun**		Timour the Tartar

Date (*Notes*)	Mainpiece	Interlude	Afterpiece
Th. May 28 **1812**	Julius Caesar		Timour the Tartar
F. May 29	The Knight of Snowdoun		Timour the Tartar
S. May 30	**Pizarro**		**The Portrait of Cervantes**
M. Jun 1	Hamlet		Timour the Tartar
T. Jun 2	**Isabella**		Timour the Tartar
W. Jun 3 *Benefit Night*	Cymbeline, King of Britain	Songs	La Perouse
Th. Jun 4 *Mr Fawcett's Night*	Julius Caesar	Songs	The Secret Mine
F. Jun 5 *Mr C Kemble's Night*	King Richard the Third		Comus
S. Jun 6	Douglas		Timour the Tartar
M. Jun 8	King John		Timour the Tartar
T. Jun 9 *Mr Jones's Night*	Cymbeline	Songs	The Liar
W. Jun 10 *Miss Feron's Night –* *Under the Patronage* *of His Royal* *Highness the Duke of* *Cumberland*	The Cabinet	Songs The Sultana; or, A Peep into the Seraglio	The Poor Soldier
Th. Jun 11 *Last night but Seven* *of Mrs Siddons's* *acting. Mrs H* *Johnston's Night*	The Stranger		Blue Beard; or, Female Curiosity (*last performance of the Equestrian Troops*)
F. Jun 12 *Mr Blanchard's Night*	Julius Caesar	Songs, including popular Irish ballads	Valentine and Orson
S. Jun 13 *Last night but six of* *Mrs Siddons's acting*	The Gamester		Blue Beard
M. Jun 15	**Pizarro**		Blue Beard
T. Jun 16 *Benefit Night*	Romeo and Juliet	Songs Bombastes Furioso	High Life Below Stairs (*including a mock minuet*)
W. Jun 17 *Mr Emery's Night*	**The English Fleet in 1342**	Songs	**The Portrait of Cervantes**
Th. Jun 18 *Mr Farley's Night*	The Stranger	Songs	Harlequin and Padmanaba
F. Jun 19 *Mr Taylor's Night*	The Exile	Imitations of several well- known London performers Songs	The Escapes; or, The Water Carrier
S. Jun 20	**King Henry the Eighth**		The Liar
M. Jun 22	Coriolanus		La Perouse
T. Jun 23 *For the Benefit of Mr* *Brandon, Box, Book* *and House-Keeper*	King Henry the Fourth (Part One)	Bombastes Furioso Songs	Oscar and Malvina

Date (*Notes*)	Mainpiece	Interlude	Afterpiece
W. Jun 24 **1812** *Mr Grimaldi's Night*	Cato	Songs	Harlequin and Padmanaba
			'Pas deux' from Harlequin and Mother Goose; or, The Golden Egg
Th. Jun 25	The Winter's Tale		Tom Thumb the Great
F. Jun 26 *Benefit of Mr* *Glassington,* *Prompter*	Measure for Measure	Songs	The Escapes
S. Jun 27 *Last night but one of* *Mrs Siddons's acting*	Venice Preserv'd		**Paul and Virginia**
M. Jun 29 *Last time of Mrs* *Siddons's acting*	Macbeth		All the World's a Stage
T. Jun 30	The Cabinet	Songs and dancing	The Spoil'd Child
W. Jul 1 *Miss Bolton's Night*	The Foundling of the Forest	Bombastes Furioso Songs (*several by* *particular desire*)	La Perouse
Th. Jul 2 *Miss S Booth's Night*	The Castle Spectre	Moore's Melologue on National Music Songs	Trick for trick; or, The Admiral's Daughter ('*during which Miss S* *Booth will introduce the* *Broad Sword Hornpipe* *and a New **Castanet*** ***Dancing Song***')
F. Jul 3 *Mrs Powell's Night*	**The Virgin of the Sun**	Hornpipe Songs	Three and the Deuce
S. Jul 4	The Knight of Snowdoun		**The Portrait of** **Cervantes**
M. Jul 6 *Never Acted Before*	A Touch at the Times		Trick for Trick (*Broad Sword Hornpipe* *by Miss S Booth*)
T. Jul 7	A Touch at the Times		Trick for Trick (*Broad Sword Hornpipe* *by Miss S Booth*)
W. Jul 8 *Mr Bologna Jun's* *Night*	**The Honey Moon** (*with* *a dance incidental to* *the piece*)	The Treacherous Baron; or, Albert and Emma Songs during the course of the evening	Harlequin and Padmanaba (*with a* '*Pas deux' from Mother* *Goose*)
Th. Jul 9 *Mess Claremont and* *Shaw's Night*	**Pizarro**	Songs	Oscar and Malvina
F. Jul 10	Speed the Plough		The Quaker
S. Jul 11	The Twelfth Night	Various Hornpipes and Songs	Animal Magnetism
M. Jul 13	**Isabella**		Valentine and Orson

Date (*Notes*)	Mainpiece	Interlude	Afterpiece
T. Jul 14 **1812** *Benefit of Mr Broadhurst, Mr Ware, Leader of the Band*	Fontainebleau *(Previous to which, Mozart's celebrated overture to Zauberflote)*	Songs Bombastes Furioso	Harlequin and Padmanaba
W. Jul 15 *Last Night*	Hamlet		Tom Thumb the Great

Calendar of Covent Garden Playbills 1812–1813

Date (*Notes*)	Mainpiece	Interlude	Afterpiece
M. Sep 7 **1812**	Romeo and Juliet		Harlequin and Padmanaba; or, The Golden Fish
W. Sep 9	The Beggar's Opera (*including a hornpipe in fetters*)		Trick for Trick; or, The Admiral's Daughter ('*Miss S Booth will introduce the Broad Sword Hornpipe*')
F. Sep 11	The Foundling of the Forest	Dancing	The Escapes; or, The Water Carrier
T. Sep 15	The Beggar's Opera		**The Portrait of Cervantes; or, The Plotting Lovers**
W. Sep 16	The Merry Wives of Windsor		The Taming of the Shrew
Th. Sep 17	The School of Reform		Midas
F. Sep 18	The Foundling of the Forest		Midas
S. Sep 19	**Pizarro**		Midas
M. Sep 21	King Richard the Third		Midas
T. Sep 22	**English Fleet in 1342**		Midas
W. Sep 23	**The Virgin of the Sun**		Midas
Th. Sep 24	Venice Preserv'd		Midas
F. Sep 25	Love for Love		Midas
S. Sep 26	Pizarro		Midas
M. Sep 28	Othello, The Moor of Venice		Midas
T. Sep 29	**The English Fleet in 1342**		Midas
W. Sep 30	The Exile		Midas
Th. Oct 1	Macbeth		Midas
F. Oct 2	The Cabinet ('*Mr Incledon, in the character of Lorenzo, will introduce Shield's celebrated Battle Song*')		Midas
S. Oct 3	King Henry the Fourth (Part One)		**Paul and Virginia**
M. Oct 5	Romeo and Juliet		Midas
T. Oct 6 *Never Acted Before*	The Aethiop; or, The Child of the Desert		Raising the Wind
W. Oct 7	The Aethiop		Midas
Th. Oct 8	The Aethiop		The Quaker
F. Oct 9	The Aethiop		Midas
S. Oct 10	The Aethiop		Midas
M. Oct 12	The Aethiop		Killing No Murder
T. Oct 13	The Aethiop		Midas
W. Oct 14	**Pizarro**		Killing No Murder
Th. Oct 15	Comedy of Errors		Midas
F. Oct 16	**The Virgin of the Sun**		Schniederkins
S. Oct 17	**The Revenge**		Schniederkins

Date (*Notes*)	Mainpiece	Interlude	Afterpiece
M. Oct 19 **1812**	Hamlet, Prince of Denmark		Harlequin and Padmanaba (*by particular desire and for the last time*)
T. Oct 20	The Merry Wives of Windsor		Schniederkins
W. Oct 21	The Beggar's Opera		La Perouse; or, The Desolate Island
Th. Oct 22	Macbeth		Schniederkins
F. Oct 23	Love for Love		Midas
S. Oct 24	The Lord of the Manor		Schniederkins
M. Oct 26	The Tempest; or, The Enchanted Island		The Escapes
T. Oct 27	The Lord of the Manor		Killing no Murder
W. Oct 28	The Tempest		The Farmer
Th. Oct 29	The Lord of the Manor		The Taming of the Shrew
F. Oct 30	**The Virgin of the Sun**		Midas
S. Oct 31	The Tempest		Love Laughs at Locksmiths
M. Nov 2	The Lord of the Manor		Valentine and Orson
T. Nov 3	Barbarossa		**Paul and Virginia**
W. Nov 4	The Lord of the Manor		Tom Thumb the Great
Th. Nov 5	Barbarossa		Midas
F. Nov 6	The Lord of the Manor		The Cheats of Scapin
S. Nov 7	Zara		Love Laughs at Locksmiths
M. Nov 9	The Tempest		Oscar and Malvina
T. Nov 10	Earl of Essex		The Farmer
W. Nov 11	The Lord of the Manor	Bombastes Furioso	Raymond and Agnes; or, The Castle of Lindenberg
Th. Nov 12	Douglas		Killing no Murder
F. Nov 13	The Recruiting Officer		Midas
S. Nov 14	Douglas		The Turnpike Gate
M. Nov 16	The Tempest	Bombastes Furioso	The Quaker
T. Nov 17	Alexander the Great		**The Portrait of Cervantes**
W. Nov 18	The Recruiting Officer		Hit or Miss (*never before acted at this theatre*)
Th. Nov 19	Douglas		The Turnpike Gate
F. Nov 20	The Lord of the Manor		Love, Law and Physick
S. Nov 21	Alexander the Great		Love, Law and Physick
M. Nov 23	**Pizarro**		Love, Law and Physick
T. Nov 24	Alexander the Great		Love, Law and Physick
W. Nov 25	The Tempest		Love, Law and Physick
Th. Nov 26	Tancred and Sigismunda		Love, Law and Physick
F. Nov 27	The Lord of the Manor		Love, Law and Physick
S. Nov 28	Alexander the Great		Love, Law and Physick
M. Nov 30	King Richard the Third		Love, Law and Physick
T. Dec 1	Alexander the Great		Love, Law and Physick

Date (*Notes*)	Mainpiece	Interlude	Afterpiece
W. Dec 2 **1812** *Never Acted Before*	**The Renegade**		The Spoil'd Child
Th. Dec 3	**The Renegade**		Love, Law and Physick
F. Dec 4	Alexander the Great	Bombastes Furioso (*by particular desire*)	Midas
S. Dec 5	**The Renegade**		Love, Law and Physick
M. Dec 7	**The Renegade**		Oscar and Malvina
T. Dec 8	Alexander the Great	Bombastes Furioso	Midas
W. Dec 9	**The Renegade**		Love, Law and Physick
Th. Dec 10	**The Renegade**		Love, Law and Physick
F. Dec 11	**The Renegade**		Love, Law and Physick
S. Dec 12	The Earl of Warwick		The Farmer
M. Dec 14 *By particular desire*	Macbeth		Love, Law and Physick
T. Dec 15 *The last night but two of Mr Betty's performances*	Alexander the Great	Bombastes Furioso	Midas
W. Dec 16	**The Renegade**		Love, Law and Physick
Th. Dec 17	The Lord of the Manor		The Escapes
F. Dec 18	**The Renegade**		Love, Law and Physick
S. Dec 19	Alexander the Great		Killing No Murder
M. Dec 21	Venice Preserv'd		Hit or Miss
T. Dec 22 *Last night of Mr Betty's performances*	The Siege of Damascus		Love, Law and Physick
W. Dec 23 *Last night of performances until the holidays*	**The Renegade**	Bombastes Furioso	Midas
S. Dec 26	George Barnwell		Harlequin and the Red Dwarf; or, The Adamant Rock
M. Dec 28	The Earl of Essex		Harlequin and the Red Dwarf
T. Dec 29	Comedy of Errors		Harlequin and the Red Dwarf
W. Dec 30	**Much Ado About Nothing**		Harlequin and the Red Dwarf
Th. Dec 31	The Merry Wives of Windsor		Harlequin and the Red Dwarf
F. Jan 1 **1813**	The Lord of the Manor		Harlequin and the Red Dwarf
S. Jan 2	**The Renegade**		Harlequin and the Red Dwarf
M. Jan 4	**The Mountaineers**		Harlequin and the Red Dwarf
T. Jan 5	The Rivals		Harlequin and the Red Dwarf
W. Jan 6	**The Renegade**		Harlequin and the Red Dwarf
Th. Jan 7	The Jealous Wife		Harlequin and the Red Dwarf

Date (*Notes*)	Mainpiece	Interlude	Afterpiece
F. Jan 8 **1813**	The Lord of the Manor		Harlequin and the Red Dwarf
S. Jan 9	**The Renegade**		Harlequin and the Red Dwarf
M. Jan 11	Haroun Alraschild [*Altered from* The Aethiop]		Harlequin and the Red Dwarf
T. Jan 12	**The Renegade**		Harlequin and the Red Dwarf
W. Jan 13	Midas	Love, Law and Physick	Harlequin and the Red Dwarf
Th. Jan 14 *By particular desire*	Comedy of Errors	Bombastes Furioso	Harlequin and the Red Dwarf
F. Jan 15	The Lord of the Manor		Harlequin and the Red Dwarf
S. Jan 16	**The Renegade**		Harlequin and the Red Dwarf
M. Jan 18	The Tempest		Harlequin and the Red Dwarf
T. Jan 19	Midas	Love, Law, and Physick	Harlequin and the Red Dwarf
W. Jan 20	**The Renegade**		Harlequin and the Red Dwarf
Th. Jan 21	The Lord of the Manor		Harlequin and the Red Dwarf
F. Jan 22 *'The only time these pieces can be acted together'*	Midas	Love, Law, and Physick	Harlequin and the Red Dwarf
S. Jan 23 *Never Acted Before*	**The Students of Salamanca**		Harlequin and the Red Dwarf
M. Jan 25	**The Students of Salamanca**		Harlequin and the Red Dwarf
T. Jan 26	**The Students of Salamanca**		Harlequin and the Red Dwarf
W. Jan 27	**The Students of Salamanca**		Harlequin and the Red Dwarf
Th. Jan 28	Midas	Love, Law and Physick	Harlequin and the Red Dwarf
F. Jan 29	**The Students of Salamanca**		Harlequin and the Red Dwarf
M. Feb 1	**Pizarro**		Harlequin and the Red Dwarf
T. Feb 2	**The Students of Salamanca**	Bombastes Furioso	The Waterman Songs
W. Feb 3	Midas	Love, Law and Physick	Harlequin and the Red Dwarf
Th. Feb 4	**The Renegade**		Harlequin and the Red Dwarf
F. Feb 5	The Lord of the Manor		Harlequin and the Red Dwarf

Date (*Notes*)	Mainpiece	Interlude	Afterpiece
S. Feb 6 **1813**	Midas	Love, Law, and Physick	Harlequin and the Red Dwarf
M. Feb 8	Jane Shore	Poor Vulcan	Mount Ida
T. Feb 9	The Iron Chest	Poor Vulcan	Mount Ida
W. Feb 10	**The Wonder; A Woman Keeps a Secret**	Poor Vulcan	Mount Ida
Th. Feb 11	**The Renegade**	Poor Vulcan	Mount Ida
F. Feb 12	Midas	Love, Law and Physick	Harlequin and the Red Dwarf (*with new scenes*)
S. Feb 13	The Soldier's Daughter	Poor Vulcan	Mount Ida
M. Feb 15	**Pizarro**		Harlequin and the Red Dwarf
T. Feb 16	**The Wonder**	Poor Vulcan	Mount Ida
W. Feb 17	Love for Love		The Devil to Pay; or, The Wives Metamorphosed Songs
Th. Feb 18	Midas	Love, Law, and Physick	Harlequin and the Red Dwarf
F. Feb 19	The Country Girl		The Turnpike Gate
S. Feb 20	**Isabella; or, The Fatal Marriage**	The Vulcan	Mount Ida
M. Feb 22	As You Like It		Harlequin and the Red Dwarf
T. Feb 23	**Isabella**		La Perouse
W. Feb 24	Love for Love		The Devil to Pay
Th. Feb 25 *Never Acted Before*	At Home (*with music and dancing*)	Midas	Love, Law, and Physick
F. Feb 26	At Home	Midas	Love, Law and Physick
S. Feb 27	The Country Girl		At Home
M. Mar 1	As You Like It		At Home
T. Mar 2 *By particular request*	At Home	Midas	Love, Law and Physick
W. Mar 3	At Home	**The Delusion** [*altered from* The Students of Salamanca]	Love, Law, and Physick
Th. Mar 4	At Home	**The Delusion**	Love, Law and Physick
M. Mar 8	As You Like It		At Home
T. Mar 9	At Home	Midas	Love, Law and Physick
Th. Mar 11 *By particular desire*	The Lord of the Manor		At Home
S. Mar 13	As You Like It		At Home
M. Mar 15	At Home	Midas	Love, Law and Physick
T. Mar 16	The Country Girl		At Home
W. Mar 17	Oratorios – 'Acis and Galatea', with a Grand Miscellaneous Act		
Th. Mar 18	Love for Love		The Devil to Pay
F. Mar 19 *Oratorios*	Oratorios – The Messiah (*by particular desire*)		

Date (*Notes*)	Mainpiece	Interlude	Afterpiece
S. Mar 20 **1813**	A Trip to Scarborough	Bombastes Furioso (*by particular desire*)	At Home
M. Mar 22	At Home	Midas	Love, Law and Physick
T. Mar 23	The School for Scandal		At Home
W. Mar 24 *Oratorios*	Oratorios – A Grand Selection (*to conclude with Madame Catalani singing 'God Save the King'*)		
Th. Apr 1	The School for Scandal		Midas (*'by the particular request of numerous families'*)
F. Apr 2 *Last night but two of Oratorios*	Oratorios – A Grand Selection		
S. Apr 3	A Trip to Scarborough	Bombastes Furioso	At Home
M. Apr 5	At Home	Midas	Love, Law and Physick
T. Apr 6	The School for Scandal		At Home
W. Apr 7	Oratorios – A Grand Selection (*'Rule Britannia', at the end of Part One, by particular desire*)		
Th. Apr 8	At Home	**The Pannel**	Midas (*'by particular request of the numerous Parties who have been disappointed of Boxes'*)
F. Apr 9 *Last night of Oratorios*	A Grand Selection, from the Compositions of the most favourite authors (*At the end of Part One, by particular desire, Madame Catalani to sing 'Rule Britannia'*)		
S. Apr 10 *Last night of performances until the holidays*	Midas	**The Pannel**	Love, Law and Physick
M. Apr 19	Douglas		Aladdin; or, The Wonderful Lamp (*first time*)
T. Apr 20	The Country Girl		Aladdin
W. Apr 21	Alexander the Great		Aladdin
Th. Apr 22	As You Like It		Aladdin
F. Apr 23	At Home	**The Pannel**	Aladdin
S. Apr 24	At Home	The Devil to Pay	Aladdin
M. Apr 26	Alexander the Great		Aladdin
T. Apr 27 *Never Acted Before*	Education		Aladdin
W. Apr 28	Education		Aladdin
Th. Apr 29	Education		Aladdin

Date (*Notes*)	Mainpiece	Interlude	Afterpiece
F. Apr 30 **1813**	Education		Aladdin
S. May 1	Education		Aladdin
M. May 3	Education		Aladdin
T. May 4	Education		Aladdin
W. May 5	Education		Aladdin
Th. May 6	Education		Aladdin
F. May 7	Education		Aladdin
S. May 8	Education		Three Weeks After Marriage (*by particular desire*)
M. May 10	Alexander the Great		Aladdin
T. May 11	Education		Aladdin
W. May 12	Education		Aladdin
Th. May 13	Education		Aladdin
F. May 14	Education		Aladdin
S. May 15	Education		Aladdin
M. May 17	Education		Aladdin
T. May 18	Education		Aladdin
W. May 19	Education		Aladdin
Th. May 20	At Home	**The Pannel**	Aladdin
F. May 21	Education		Aladdin
S. May 22 *Last time this season*	As You Like It		Midas
M. May 24 *By particular desire*	**Pizarro**	Bomabstes Furioso	Midas
T. May 25 *Triennial Benefit for the aged and infirm actors and actresses and the widows and children of such as have belonged to the Theatre Royal, Covent Garden. Mrs Siddons's and Mrs Jordan's participation*	The Gamester		The Devil to Pay
W. May 26	Education		Aladdin
Th. May 27	At Home	Midas	Love, Law, and Physick
F. May 28	Education		Aladdin
S. May 29 *Never Acted Before*	The Brazen Bust	**The Pannel**	Midas
M. May 31 *Last night but one of Mr Betty's performing this season*	Alexander the Great		The Brazen Bust
T. Jun 1 *Mrs Jordan's Night*	Way to Keep Him		The Devil to Pay
W. Jun 2 *For the Benefit of Mr Young*	Coriolanus; or, The Roman Matron		Love, Law and Physick

Date (*Notes*)	Mainpiece	Interlude	Afterpiece
Th. Jun 3 **1813** *Benefit of Mrs C Kemble*	Julius Caesar	Personation (*for this night only*)	Brazen Bust
F. Jun 4	Education		Aladdin
S. Jun 5 *Benefit of Mess Ashleys*	A Grand Selection of Music (*At the end of Part One: 'Rule Britannia'*)		
M. Jun 7	Coriolanus	Bombastes Furioso	At Home (*Act 1 – Shawl Dance by Miss Booth*)
T. Jun 8 *For the Benefit Mr Incledon*	The Lord of the Manor	Songs Description of 'A Storm' (*in character*)	Killing No Murder
W. Jun 9 *For the Benefit Mr Mathews*	The Bee Hive	'Mr Mathews will recite The Hobbies in the manner of An Amateur' The Sleep Walker The Mail Coach Songs	**The Critic; or, A Tragedy Rehearsed**
Th. Jun 10 *For the Benefit of Mr Jones. Mrs Jordan's last night of performing this season*	A Trip to Scarborough	Darkness Visible	Aladdin
F. Jun 11 *Mrs Siddons's offer to act for the Benefit of Mr C Kemble*	Macbeth		The Brazen Bust
S. Jun 12 *Mr Betty's Night – his last performance this season*	King Richard the Third		The Weathercock
M. Jun 14 *By particular desire*	Education		Harlequin and the Red Dwarf (*'with the additional scenes of the watchman and vegetable figure'*)
T. Jun 15 *For one night only*	Midas	'At the end of Midas, Mr Mathews to recite the Hobbies in the manner of an amateur of fashion' Love, Law and Physick	Blue Beard (*'Grand Equestrian troop to perform wonderful elocutions'*)
W. Jun 16 *For the Benefit of Mr Emery*	The School of Reform; or, How to Rule a Husband	Bombastes Furioso Songs	Hit or Miss (*with songs*)
Th. Jun 17 *For the Benefit of Mr and Mrs Liston*	Africans; or, War, Love, and Duty	The Rival Soldiers Songs	Hamlet Travestie (*in 2 Acts, by particular request*)

Date (*Notes*)	Mainpiece	Interlude	Afterpiece
F. Jun 18 **1813** *Madame Catalani, for the Benefit of Mrs Gibbs*	'Hope told a flattering tale' and 'Rule Britannia' (*verse and chorus*), by Madame Catalani	Songs	Aladdin The Sleep Walker
	Five Miles Off; or, The Finger Post		
S. Jun 19 *Last time this season*	Education		Hit or Miss Songs
M. Jun 21	Coriolanus		Aladdin
T. Jun 22 *For the Benefit of Mr Blanchard*	At Home (*Act 1- A Shawl Dance by Miss Booth*)	The Bee Hive	Love, Law, and Physick
W. Jun 23 *Benefit of Mr Taylor*	**The English Fleet in 1342**	Songs Blue Devils Mr Taylor's Imitations of several well-known London Performers	The Rival Soldiers
Th. Jun 24 *First and only time this season of* Timour the Tartar	Midas Songs	Songs The Sleep Walker	Timour the Tartar ('*and by consent of Mess Astley, Davis and Park, the Equestrian troop will perform wonderful evolutions*')
F. Jun 25 *Miss S Booth's Night*	Douglas (*by desire, and for the first time in London, Miss S Booth will play the part of Young Norval*)	Miss Booth will recite Collins's Ode on the Passions Bombastes Furioso	The Romp
S. Jun 26	John Bull; or, An Englishman's Fireside	Songs	The Farmer
M. Jun 28	Hamlet		Tom Thumb the Great
T. Jun 29 *Benefit of Mr Brandon, Box, Book and House- Keeper*	The Castle Spectre	Bombastes Furioso Songs	The Sleep Walker
W Jun 30 *Benefit of Mr Sinclair*	The Lord of the Manor	Songs	Hit or Miss Midas
Th. Jul 1 *Benefit of Mr Grimaldi*	Five Miles Off	Love, Law and Physick Songs, including 'Typitywitchet' by Grimaldi	Harlequin and the Red Dwarf
F. Jul 2 *Benefit of Mr and Mrs Bishop. New Burletta and first appearance at this theatre of the Principal dancers and corps de ballet from the Opera House*	The Rival Soldiers	**The Troubador** ('*A Grand Spanish Ballet*', *by the principal dancers of the Opera House*)	Harry le Roy! ('*Rural divertissement incidental to the opera*') Killing No Murder

Date (*Notes*)	Mainpiece	Interlude	Afterpiece
S. Jul 3 **1813**	The Jealous Wife	'Four and twenty Lord Mayor's Shows', by Mr Mathews (*by particular desire*)	The Turnpike Gate
M. Jul 5	Harry le Roy	The Sleep Walker	Midas
T. Jul 6 *Benefit of Miss Bolton and her last appearance on the stage*	The Tempest	Songs including 'Battle of La Hogue' by Mr Incledon The Bee Hive The Mail Coach	Harry le Roy!
W. Jul 7 *Benefit of Mr Abbott*	**Pizarro**	Songs Personation (*by particular desire and last time this season*)	Killing No Murder
Th. Jul 8 *Benefit of Mr Bologna Jr*	Love, Law and Physick (*with songs*)	Aladdin Songs	Harlequin and the Red Dwarf (*in 1 Short Act*) Robinson Crusoe and His Man Friday (Part 1)
F. Jul 9 *For the Benefit of Mr Broadhurst and Mrs Sterling*	Love in a Village	Harry le Roy Songs from Moore's celebrated Irish Melodies	At Home
S. Jul 10	The School of Reform	Scotch 'pas deux' Hornpipe by Miss Godfrey ('*7 years old, pupil of Mr Jackson*')	The Quaker
M. Jul 12	Foundling of the Forest	The Waterman	The Spoil'd Child
T. Jul 13 *Benefit of Mr Glassington, Prompter*	Education	Love, Law, and Physick	Robinson Crusoe and his Man Friday
W. Jul 14 *Benefit of Mr Ware, leader of the band*	**The Critic**	The Sleep Walker Songs Overture to Zaira 'Pas deux' from Harlequin and Mother Goose; or, The Golden Egg, by Grimaldi and Bologna Jr	Aladdin
Th. Jul 15 *Benefit of Mess Claremont, Slader, and Mrs Davies* *Last Night*	The Castle Spectre	Songs Bombastes Furioso	Killing No Murder

Calendar of Covent Garden Playbills 1813–1814

Date (*Notes*)	Mainpiece	Interlude	Afterpiece
M. 6 Sep **1813** *The Theatre will open, having undergone various alterations and the whole of the interior being entirely newly decorated*	John Bull; or, An Englishman's Fireside		Killing No Murder
T. Sep 7	The Tempest; or, The Enchanted Island		Love, Law, and Physick
W. Sep 8	**Rule a Wife and Have a Wife**		Midas
Th. Sep 9	The Exile		Rosina
F. Sep 10	The Castle Spectre		Rosina
M. Sep 13	The Stranger		Aladdin; or, The Wonderful Lamp (*Scenes include Aladdin's Flying Palace, Aladdin's grand procession, the descent of Aladdin's palace*)
W. Sep 15	Clandestine Marriage		Midas
Th. Sep 16	Poor Gentleman	Bombastes Furioso	Rosina
M. Sep 20	The Stranger		Aladdin
W. Sep 22	The Lord of the Manor		The Sleep Walker
Th. Sep 23	Artaxerxes	The Wedding Day	Love, Law, and Physick
F. Sep 24	The Road to Ruin		Midas
M. Sep 27	The Stranger		Aladdin
T. Sep 28	Artaxerxes	At Home	Tom Thumb the Great
W. Sep 29	The Lord of the Manor		The Sleepwalker
Th. Sep 30	Artaxerxes	Bombastes Furioso	Aladdin
F. Oct 1	The Merry Wives of Windsor		**Paul and Virginia**
M. Oct 4	Alexander the Great		Harlequin and the Red Dwarf; or, The Adamant Rock
T. Oct 5	The Nondescript	Selima and Azor (*in 2 Acts*)	The Sleep Walker
W. Oct 6	Artaxerxes	All the World's a Stage	Aladdin
Th. Oct 7	Othello, The Moor of Venice		Selima and Azor
F. Oct 8	The Merchant of Venice		Selima and Azor
S. Oct 9	Artaxerxes	At Home (*Act 1 – A shawl dance by Miss Booth*)	The Sleep Walker
M. Oct 11	Alexander the Great	Bombastes Furioso	Midas
T. Oct 12	Artaxerxes	Animal Magnetism	Aladdin
W. Oct 13	Othello		Rosina

Date (*Notes*)	Mainpiece	Interlude	Afterpiece
Th. Oct 14 **1813**	Artaxerxes	**The Portrait of Cervantes; or, The Plotting Lovers**	The Bee Hive
F. Oct 15	Education		Selima and Azor
S. Oct 16	Artaxerxes	Bombastes Furioso	Love, Law, and Physick
M. Oct 18	**Pizarro**		Midas (*by particular desire*)
T. Oct 19	Artaxerxes	At Home (*Act 1 – Shawl Dance*)	The Sleep Walker
W. Oct 20	The Lord of the Manor		Aladdin
Th. Oct 21	Venice Preserv'd		The Miller and His Men
F. Oct 22	The Beggar's Opera		The Miller and His Men
S. Oct 23	Artaxerxes (*compressed into 2 Acts*)	The Miller and His Men	The Sleep Walker
M. Oct 25	Romeo and Juliet		The Miller and His Men
T. Oct 26	Artaxerxes (*compressed*)	The Miller and His Men	The Sleep Walker
W. Oct 27	The Beggar's Opera		The Miller and His Men
Th. Oct 28	Venice Preserv'd		The Miller and His Men
F. Oct 29	The Beggar's Opera		The Miller and His Men
S. Oct 30	Artaxerxes	The Miller and His Men	The Sleep Walker
M. Nov 1	King Henry the Fifth; or, The Conquest of France		The Miller and His Men
T. Nov 2	Artaxerxes	The Miller and His Men	The Sleep Walker
W. Nov 3	The Beggar's Opera		The Miller and His Men
Th. Nov 4	Hamlet, Prince of Denmark		The Miller and His Men
F. Nov 5	Artaxerxes	The Miller and His Men	Killing No Murder
S. Nov 6	The Beggar's Opera		Aladdin
M. Nov 8	King Henry the Fifth		The Miller and His Men
T. Nov 9	Midas	The Sleep Walker	The Miller and His Men
W. Nov 10	King Henry the Fifth		The Invisible Bridegroom
Th. Nov. 11	The Lord of the Manor		The Miller and His Men
F. Nov 12	**The Duenna**		Love, Law, and Physick
S. Nov 13	Artaxerxes	The Invisible Bridegroom	The Miller and His Men
M. Nov 15	Antony and Cleopatra (*with alterations and additions by Dryden*)		The Invisible Bridegroom
T. Nov 16	**The Duenna**		The Miller and His Men
W. Nov 17	Antony and Cleopatra		Midas
Th. Nov 18	Artaxerxes	At Home	The Miller and His Men
F. Nov 19	Antony and Cleopatra		The Bee Hive
S. Nov 20	**The Duenna**		The Miller and His Men
M. Nov 22	Antony and Cleopatra		Aladdin
T. Nov 23	Artaxerxes	The Sleep Walker	The Miller and His Men
W. Nov 24	The Beggar's Opera		The Miller and His Men
Th. Nov 25	King Henry the Fifth		The Deserter
F. Nov 26	The Lord of the Manor		The Miller and His Men

Date (*Notes*)	Mainpiece	Interlude	Afterpiece
S. Nov 27 **1813**	Midas	Folly as it Flies (*reduced into 3 Acts*)	The Miller and His Men
M. Nov 29	Antony and Cleopatra		Aladdin
T. Nov 30	**The Duenna**		The Sleep Walker
W. Dec 1	**Pizarro**		The Miller and His Men
Th. Dec 2	Artaxerxes	Folly as it Flies	Bombastes Furioso
F. Dec 3	Coriolanus; or, The Roman Matron		At Home – Romeo Rantall ('*by most particular desire*')
S. Dec 4	**The Duenna**		The Miller and His Men
M. Dec 6	Antony and Cleopatra		Aladdin
T. Dec 7	Love in a Village		At Home (*Mr Mathews as Romeo Rantall, 'by most particular desire'*)
W. Dec 8	King Richard the Third		Midas
Th. Dec 9	The Beggar's Opera	Mrs Wiggins (*1 Act*)	Aladdin
F. Dec 10	King Henry the Fifth		The Miller and His Men
S. Dec 11	Love in a Village		Love, Law, and Physick
M. Dec 13	Coriolanus		Aladdin
T. Dec14	Love in a Village		The Miller and His Men
W. Dec 15 *Never Acted Before*	For England, Ho!	The Sleep Walker	Bombastes Furioso
Th. Dec 16	Artaxerxes	Mrs Wiggins	For England, Ho!
F. Dec 17	For England, Ho!	The Sleep Walker	The Miller and His Men
S. Dec 18	Love in a Village		For England, Ho!
M. Dec 20	The Beggar's Opera	Mrs Wiggins	For England, Ho!
T. Dec 21	For England, Ho!	Fair Game	Aladdin
W. Dec 22	Love in a Village		For England, Ho!
Th. Dec 23	Love in a Village		For England, Ho!
M. Dec 27	Douglas		Harlequin and the Swans; or, The Bath of Beauty (*Among key scenes – 'The Pillar of Europe', by Pugh*)
T. Dec 28	The Stranger		Harlequin and the Swans
W. Dec 29	For England, Ho!	At Home	Harlequin and the Swans
Th. Dec 30	**Pizarro**		Harlequin and the Swans
F. Dec 31	For England, Ho!	The Sleep Walker	Harlequin and the Swans
S. Jan 1 **1814**	The Miller and His Men (*interspersed with songs*)	Midas	Harlequin and the Swans
M. Jan 3	Alexander the Great		Harlequin and the Swans
T. Jan 4	Antony and Cleopatra		Harlequin and the Swans
W. Jan 5	Artaxerxes	Mrs Wiggins	Harlequin and the Swans

Date (*Notes*)	Mainpiece	Interlude	Afterpiece
Th. Jan 6 **1814**	Love in a Village		Harlequin and the Swans
F. Jan 7	**Pizarro**		Harlequin and the Swans
S. Jan 8	**The Duenna**		Harlequin and the Swans
M. Jan 10	The Miller and His Men	Midas	Harlequin and the Swans
T. Jan 11	Artaxerxes	Bombastes Furioso	Harlequin and the Swans
W. Jan 12	Love in a Village		Harlequin and the Swans
Th. Jan 13	Antony and Cleopatra		Harlequin and the Swans
F. Jan 14	**The Duenna**		Harlequin and the Swans
S. Jan 15	Coriolanus		Love, Law, and Physick
M. Jan 17	Midas	The Miller and His Men Bombastes Furioso	Harlequin and the Swans
T. Jan 18	Macbeth		Harlequin and the Swans
W. Jan 19	Love in a Village		Harlequin and the Swans
Th. Jan 20	Cato		Harlequin and the Swans
F. Jan 21	**The Duenna**		Harlequin and the Swans
S. Jan 22	Coriolanus		Harlequin and the Swans
M. Jan 24	Midas	The Miller and His Men Bombastes Furioso	Harlequin and the Swans
T. Jan 25	Macbeth		Harlequin and the Swans
W. Jan 26 *Never Acted Before*	The Farmer's Wife		Harlequin and the Swans
Th. Jan 27	Hamlet		Harlequin and the Swans
F. Jan 28	Artaxerxes	The Miller and His Men	Harlequin and the Swans
S. Jan 29	**Pizarro**		The Sleep Walker
M. Jan 31	King Richard the Third		Harlequin and the Swans
T. Feb 1	The Farmer's Wife		All the World's a Stage
W. Feb 2	Coriolanus		Midas
Th. Feb 3	The Farmer's Wife		Harlequin and the Swans
F. Feb 4	Julius Caesar		The Bee Hive
S. Feb 5	The Farmer's Wife		The Miller and His Men
M. Feb 7	**King Henry the Eighth**		Harlequin and the Swans
T. Feb 8	The Farmer's Wife		Katharine and Petruchio
W. Feb 9	Julius Caesar		The Spoil'd Child

Date (*Notes*)	Mainpiece	Interlude	Afterpiece
Th. Feb 10 **1814**	The Farmer's Wife		Harlequin and the Swans
F. Feb 11	Hamlet		Katharine and Petruchio
S. Feb 12	The Farmer's Wife		Aladdin
M. Feb 14	Coriolanus		The Miller and His Men
T. Feb 15	The Farmer's Wife		Harlequin and the Swans
W. Feb 16	Julius Caesar		Rosina
Th. Feb 17	The Farmer's Wife		Harlequin and the Swans
F. Feb 18	Cato		The Sleep Walker
S. Feb 19	The Farmer's Wife		Aladdin
M. Feb 21	As You Like It		Harlequin and the Swans
T. Feb 22	The Farmer's Wife		Harlequin and the Swans
Th. Feb 24	Country Girl		The Wandering Boys; or, The Castle of Olival (*first time*)
F. Feb 25	Oratorios – The Messiah (*New orchestra*)		
S. Feb 26	Love in a Village		The Wandering Boys
M. Feb 28	Artaxerxes	The Devil to Pay; or, The Wives Metamorphosed	The Wandering Boys
T. Mar 1	Midas	The Wandering Boys	The Miller and His Men
W. Mar 2	Oratorios – First Act of The Creation, and Two Grand Miscellaneous Acts		
Th. Mar 3	**The Wonder; A Woman Keeps a Secret**		The Wandering Boys
F. Mar 4	Oratorios – Grand Selection. 'At the commencement of the Second Act (*by particular desire*) will be repeated Cherubini's celebrated Overture to Anacreon'		
S. Mar 5	The Farmer's Wife		The Wandering Boys
M. Mar 7	Artaxerxes	The Devil to Pay	Harlequin and the Swans
T. Mar 8	The Farmer's Wife		The Wandering Boys
W. Mar 9	Oratorios – Acis and Galatea, with A Grand Miscellaneous Act		
Th. Mar 10	A Trip to Scarborough	The Sleep Walker	The Miller and His Men

Date (*Notes*)	Mainpiece	Interlude	Afterpiece
F. Mar 11 **1814**	Oratorios – A Grand Selection. *Songs by Catalani including 'God Save the King', and 'Nelson' by Mr Braham*		
S. Mar 12	The Beggar's Opera	**The Pannel**	The Wandering Boys
M. Mar 14	King Richard the Third		Aladdin
T. Mar 15	The Farmer's Wife		Harlequin and the Swans
W. Mar 16	Oratorios – The Messiah		
Th. Mar 17	Artaxerxes	Love, Law, and Physick	The Miller and His Men
F. Mar 18	Oratorios – First Act of the Creation, with Two Grand Miscellaneous Acts		
S. Mar 19	King Richard the Third		Midas
M. Mar 21	Hamlet		Harlequin and the Swans
T .Mar 22	Love in a Village		Aladdin
W. Mar 23	Oratorios – A Grand Selection		
Th. Mar 24	The Farmer's Wife		The Miller and His Men
F. Mar 25	Oratorios – A Grand Selection		
S. Mar 26	Hamlet		The Sleep Walker
M. Mar 28	King Richard the Third		Harlequin and the Swans
T. Mar 29	**Pizarro**		The Escapes; or, The Water Carrier
W. Mar 30	Oratorios – A Grand Selection		
Th. Mar 31	The Woodman		The Miller and His Men
F. Apr 1	Oratorios – First Act of the Creation, Second Act selected from The Messiah, and A Grand Miscelleanous Act		
S. Apr 2	Hamlet		The Miller and His Men ('*by particular desire and positively for the last time*')
M. Apr 11 *First Time*	King Henry the Fifth		Sadak and Kalasrade; or, The Waters of Oblivion
T. Apr 12	**The Revenge**		Sadak and Kalasrade
W. Apr 13	The Stranger		Sadak and Kalasrade
Th. Apr 14	As You Like It		Sadak and Kalasrade

Date (*Notes*)	Mainpiece	Interlude	Afterpiece
F. Apr 15 **1814**	A Trip to Scarborough	Bombastes Furioso	Sadak and Kalasrade
S. Apr 16	Hamlet		Sadak and Kalasrade
M. Apr 18	King Richard the Third		Sadak and Kalasrade
T. Apr 19	The Woodman		Sadak and Kalasrade
W. Apr 20	Debtor and Creditor		Sadak and Kalasrade
Th. Apr 21	Debtor and Creditor		Sadak and Kalasrade
F. Apr 22	Debtor and Creditor		Sadak and Kalasrade
S. Apr 23	Debtor and Creditor		Sadak and Kalasrade
M. Apr 25	Debtor and Creditor		Sadak and Kalasrade (*'Monsieur Soissons, Principal dancer from the Theatre at Bordeaux will make his first appearance in a grand "pas Seul"'*)
T. Apr 26	Debtor and Creditor		Sadak and Kalasrade
W. Apr 27	Love in a Village		Sadak and Kalasrade
Th. Apr 28	Antony and Cleopatra		Sadak and Kalasrade
F. Apr 29	Artaxerxes	The Sleep Walker	Sadak and Kalasrade
S. Apr 30	The Woodman		Sadak and Kalasrade
M. May 2	Hamlet		Sadak and Kalasrade
T. May 3	Lionel and Clarissa (*with songs*)		Sadak and Kalasrade
W. May 4	Debtor and Creditor		Sadak and Kalasrade
Th. May 5	The Farmer's Wife		The Miller and His Men
F. May 6	Othello		[*None stated*]
S. May 7	**The Jew**	The Devil to Pay	Sadak and Kalasrade
M. May 9	The Beggar's Opera	The Sleep Walker	Timour the Tartar
T. May 10	Lionel and Clarissa		Timour the Tartar
W. May 11	Debtor and Creditor		Timour the Tartar
Th. May 12	Love in a Village		Timour the Tartar
F. May 13	Othello		Timour the Tartar
S. May 14	**The Jew**	**The Pannel**	Timour the Tartar
M. May 16	Artaxerxes	The Devil to Pay	Blue Beard; or, Female Curiosity
T. May 17	Lionel and Clarissa		Blue Beard
W. May 18	Coriolanus		The Miller and His Men
Th. May 19	Love in a Village		Timour the Tartar
F. May 20	A Trip to Scarborough	Harry le Roy! (*to conclude with a rural divertissement incidental to the burletta*)	Timour the Tartar
S. May 21	Hamlet		Timour the Tartar
M. May 23	**Pizarro**		Sadak and Kalasrade
T. May 24	Richard Coeur de Lion	The Devil to Pay	The Miller and His Men
W. May 25	Julius Caesar		Sadak and Kalasrade
Th. May 26	Richard Coeur de Lion	Tricking's Fair in Love	**The Child of Nature**
F. May 27	Macbeth		Richard Coeur De Lion

Date (*Notes*)	Mainpiece	Interlude	Afterpiece
S. May 28 **1814** *Annual Benefit Whitsun Eve*	A Grand Selection from the compositions of the most favourite authors, Ancient and Modern		
M. May 30	**King Henry the Eighth**		Aladdin
T. May 31 *Benefit of Mr Young*	Othello		Richard Coeur de Lion
W. Jun 1	The School for Scandal		The Miller and His Men
Th. Jun 2	Artaxerxes	The Sleep Walker	Sadak and Kalasrade
F. Jun 3	Love in a Village		Sadak and Kalasrade
S. Jun 4	The Stranger	Bombastes Furioso	Richard Coeur de Lion
M. Jun 6	Othello		Richard Coeur de Lion
T. Jun 7 *Benefit of Mr Incledon*	**The Castle of Andalusia**	Description of 'A Storm' (*in character, with appropriate scenery*) Songs, Duets, and Glees (*to conclude with 'God Save the King' and 'Rule Britannia'*)	Love, Law, and Physick
W. Jun 8 *Benefit of Mr Mathews*	Love a-la Mode	Catch Him Who Can Mathews's Imitations	Dead Alive (*by permission of the Haymarket*) Favourite comic songs
F. Jun 10 *Mr Emery's Benefit*	The School for Prejudice; or, The Jew and Yorkshireman	Songs	The Bee Hive
M. Jun 13	**The Grand Alliance** (*'in compliment to our **Illustrious Visitors**, an allegorical festival'*)	Richard Coeur de Lion Dead Alive	Sadak and Kalasrade
T. Jun 14 *Benefit of Miss Stephens*	The Cabinet	**The Grand Alliance** The Storm, by Incledon	Katharine and Petruchio
W. Jun 15 *Benefit of Mr and Mrs Liston*	Broad But Not Too Long; or, How to Damn a New Piece	Who Wants a Guinea?	Catch Him Who Can
Th. Jun 16 *For the Benefit of Mr Blanchard*	The Exile	**The Grand Alliance**	The Miller and His Men
F. Jun 17 *'In consequence of the Illustrious strangers attending this evening, Mr Taylor's Benefit is obliged to be postponed until Monday next'*	Hamlet	**The Grand Alliance**	Sadak and Kalasrade
S. Jun 18	The Cabinet	**The Grand Alliance**	The Miller and His Men

Date (*Notes*)	Mainpiece	Interlude	Afterpiece
M. Jun 20 **1814** T. Jun 21 *By the Desire of His Excellency the Hetman of the Cossacks, Count Platoff. For the Benefit of Mr Farley*	The Woodman Fontainebleau, or Our Way in France (*2 Acts*)	**The Grand Alliance** Harlequin and Mother Goose; or, The Golden Egg ('*in the pantomime will be introduced* **The Bull Fight**, *and the favourite scene of the Dog Cart, and the Oyster Duet*') Mr Mathews, with songs	Sadak and Kalasrade Blue Beard (*in which, by consent of Messrs Astley, Davies, and Parker 'the Grand Equestrian Troop will perform their Wonderful evolutions*')
W. Jun 22 *By the Desire of Prince, Marshal Blucher*	Fontainebleau	Bombastes Furioso **The Grand Alliance**	Harlequin and Mother Goose ('*in the pantomime will be introduced* **The Bull Fight**, *and the favourite scene of the Dog Cart, and the Oyster Duet*')
Th. Jun 23	The Miller and His Men	Harlequin and Mother Goose	Sadak and Kalasrade
F. Jun 24 *For the Benefit of Miss S Booth*	Romeo and Juliet	Songs The Rival Soldiers	The Spoil'd Child
S. Jun 25	Road to Ruin	'A pas de trois'	**Paul and Virginia**
M. Jun 27 *For the Benefit of Mr Sinclair*	**The Castle of Andalusia**	Songs Mrs Wiggins	Midas
T. Jun 28 *For the Benefit of Mr Brandon, Box, Book and House-Keeper*	The Woodman	**The Grand Alliance**	The Sleep Walker
W. Jun 29 *For the Benefit of Mess. Bologna Jun. and Grimaldi*	Fontainebleau	For England Ho!	Harlequin and Mother Goose ('*including* **The Bull Fight**, *and the favourite scene of the Dog Cart, and the Oyster Duet*')
Th. Jun 30 *By particular desire*	**Pizarro**		Harlequin and Mother Goose ('*including* **The Bull Fight**, *and the favourite scene of the Dog Cart, and the Oyster Duet*')
F. Jul 1 *Benefit of Mrs McGibbon*	Macbeth	A Day After the Wedding; or, A Wife's First Lesson Songs	Catch Him Who Can
S. Jul 2	The Lord of the Manor (*with some alterations to introduce new songs*)		**The Portrait of Cervantes**

Date (*Notes*)	Mainpiece	Interlude	Afterpiece
M. Jul 4 **1814**	**The Castle of Andalusia**	Mrs Wiggins	Midas
T. Jul 5 *For the Benefit of Mrs Sterling, Mrs Faucit and Mr Vining*	The Foundling of the Forest	Songs The Rival Soldiers	La Perouse; or, The Desolate Island
W. Jul 6 *Benefit of Mr Broadhurst*	Lionel and Clarissa	Songs Bruce's Address to His Army: 'Scots wha ha'e wi' Wallace bled' (words by Robert Burns), by Mr Broadhurst	Killing No Murder
Th. Jul 7	Richard Coeur de Lion	'Grand pas seul', by Madame Caroline Pavie Bombastes Furioso **The Grand Alliance**	Sadak and Kalasrade
F. Jul 8 *For the Benefit of Mess. Claremont Porteus*	King Henry the Fourth (Part One)	The Rival Soldiers	Love a-la Mode
S. Jul 9	Clandestine Marriage		Midas
M. Jul 11 *For the Benefit of Mr Glassington, Prompter*	Artaxerxes	The Miller and His Men	Aladdin
T. Jul 12 *By Desire of His Excellency the Prince Platoff, Hetman of the Cossacks. For the Benefit of Mr Ware, Leader of the Band*	The Lord of the Manor	The Bee Hive	Robinson Crusoe, and his man Friday (Part One)
W. Jul 13 *By Desire, and under the immediate patronage of the Most Noble His Grace the Duke of Wellington, who will this evening honour the theatre with His presence*	The Farmer's Wife	**The Grand Alliance**	Sadak and Kalasrade
Th. Jul 14 *By Desire of His Excellency the Prince Platoff, Hetman of the Cossacks*	The Exile	Songs	Harlequin and Mother Goose
F. Jul 15 *Last Night*	The Stranger	'The Old Commodore' 'A pas de trois' Hornpipe in character	**Paul and Virginia**

Calendar of Covent Garden Playbills 1814–1815

Date (*Notes*)	Mainpiece	Interlude	Afterpiece
M. Sep 12 **1814**	**Pizarro**		The Miller and His Men
T. Sep 13	Lord of the Manor		Timour the Tartar
W. Sep 14	Midas	**The Child of Nature**	Timour the Tartar
		The Grand Alliance	
Th. Sep 15	Hamlet, Prince of Denmark		Timour the Tartar
F. Sep 16	The Exile		Timour the Tartar
S. Sep 17	King Henry the Fourth (Part One)		Aladdin; or, The Wonderful Lamp
M. Sep 19	The Beggar's Opera	The Miller and His Men	Harlequin and Mother Goose; or, The Golden Egg
W. Sep 21	Love in a Village		Aladdin
F. Sep 23	Artaxerxes	Bombastes Furioso	The Miller and His Men
M. Sep 26	Alexander the Great	**Doctor Sangrado**	Richard Coeur de Lion (*A grand 'pas deux' introduced*)
W. Sep 28	The Woodman	**Doctor Sangrado**	Aladdin
F. Sep 30	Artaxerxes		The Forest of Bondy; or The Dogs of Montargis (*In Act 1, a pastoral 'pas deux'*)
M. Oct 3	**Pizarro**		The Forest of Bondy
W. Oct 5	Lord of the Manor		The Forest of Bondy
Th. Oct 6	Romeo and Juliet		The Forest of Bondy
F. Oct 7	Romeo and Juliet		The Forest of Bondy
M. Oct 10	Romeo and Juliet		The Forest of Bondy
T. Oct 11	Love in a Village		The Forest of Bondy
W. Oct 12	The Cabinet		The Forest of Bondy
Th. Oct 13	Venice Preserv'd		The Forest of Bondy
F. Oct 14	Venice Preserv'd		The Forest of Bondy
M. Oct 17	Romeo and Juliet		The Forest of Bondy
T. Oct 18	The Maid of the Mill		Forest of Bondy
W. Oct 19	Venice Preserv'd		Midas
Th. Oct 20	The Maid of the Mill		The Forest of Bondy
F. Oct 21	Venice Preserv'd		The Forest of Bondy
S. Oct 22	Coriolanus; or, The Roman Matron		The Miller and His Men
M. Oct 24	Romeo and Juliet		The Forest of Bondy
T. Oct 25	Cato		The Forest of Bondy
W. Oct 26	Venice Preserv'd		Richard Coeur de Lion (*Act 3 – A dance incidental to the piece. A grand 'pas deux'*)
Th. Oct 27	Hamlet		The Forest of Bondy
F. Oct 28	Venice Preserv'd		The Forest of Bondy
S. Oct 29	Julius Caesar		**The Portrait of Cervantes; or, The Plotting Lovers**

Date (*Notes*)	Mainpiece	Interlude	Afterpiece
M. Oct 31 **1814**	Romeo and Juliet		The Miller and His Men
T. Nov 1	The Wheel of Fortune		Rosina
W. Nov 2	Venice Preserv'd		The Forest of Bondy
Th. Nov 3	**Pizarro**		Rosina
F. Nov 4	**Isabella; or, The Fatal Marriage**		The Spoil'd Child
S. Nov 5	Julius Caesar		Midas
M. Nov 7	Romeo and Juliet		Blue Beard; or, Female Curiosity
T. Nov 8	The Wheel of Fortune		Blue Beard
W. Nov 9	Venice Preserv'd		The Forest of Bondy
Th. Nov 10	**The Mountaineers**		Timour the Tartar
F. Nov 11	**Isabella**		The Forest of Bondy
S. Nov 12 *First Time*	John of Paris	A Day after the Wedding; or, A Wife's First Lesson	Timour the Tartar
M. Nov 14	Romeo and Juliet		John of Paris
T. Nov 15	A New Way to Pay Old Debts		John of Paris
W. Nov 16	Venice Preserv'd		John of Paris
Th. Nov 17	**The Revenge**		John of Paris
F. Nov 18	**Isabella**		John of Paris
S. Nov 19	Artaxerxes	The Mayor of Garratt	Timour the Tartar
M. Nov 21	Romeo and Juliet		Timour the Tartar
T. Nov 22	Coriolanus		The Miller and His Men
W. Nov 23	Venice Preserv'd		Rosina
Th. Nov 24	**King Henry the Eighth**		The Forest of Bondy
F. Nov 25	**Isabella**		Agreeable Surprise
S. Nov 26	The Maid of the Mill		Timour the Tartar
M. Nov 28	**Isabella**		Timour the Tartar
T. Nov 29	King Richard the Third		The Forest of Bondy
W. Nov 30	Venice Preserv'd		Rosina
Th. Dec 1	Julius Caesar		The Miller and His Men
F. Dec 2	Love in a Village		Timour the Tartar
S. Dec 3	Artaxerxes	**The Child of Nature**	Timour the Tartar
M. Dec 5	Romeo and Juliet		Blue Beard
T. Dec 6	**The Mountaineers**		The King and the Duke; or, Which is Which?
W. Dec 7	Venice Preserv'd		The King and the Duke
Th. Dec 8	King John		The King and the Duke
F. Dec 9	**Isabella**		The King and the Duke
S. Dec 10	John of Paris	The King and the Duke	Aladdin
M. Dec 12	Venice Preserv'd		Timour the Tartar
T. Dec 13	Julius Caesar		The King and the Duke
W. Dec 14	The Gamester		The King and the Duke
Th. Dec 15	Coriolanus		The Forest of Bondy
F. Dec 16	**Isabella**		The King and the Duke
S. Dec 17	John of Paris	The King and the Duke	Aladdin
M. Dec 19	Romeo and Juliet		Timour the Tartar
T. Dec 20 *The last night of Mr Kemble's performing*	Macbeth		The King and the Duke; or, Which is Which?

Date (*Notes*)	Mainpiece	Interlude	Afterpiece
W. Dec 21 **1814**	Venice Preserv'd		John of Paris
Th. Dec22	The Gamester		The Forest of Bondy
F. Dec 23	**Isabella**		Aladdin
The last night of performing before the holidays			
M. Dec 26	George Barnwell		Harlequin Whittington, Lord Mayor of London (*to conclude with a grand display of fireworks*)
T. Dec 27	Lord of the Manor		Harlequin Whittington
W. Dec 28	Venice Preserv'd		Harlequin Whittington
Th. Dec 29	The Forest of Bondy	Midas	Harlequin Whittington
F. Dec 30	**Isabella**		Harlequin Whittington
S. Dec 31	The Gamester		Harlequin Whittington
M. Jan 2 **1815**	The Tempest; or, The Enchanted Island		Harlequin Whittington
T. Jan 3	Venice Preserv'd		Harlequin Whittington
W. Jan 4	Love in a Village		Harlequin Whittington
Th. Jan 5	**Isabella**		Harlequin Whittington
F. Jan 6	The Forest of Bondy	John of Paris	Harlequin Whittington
S. Jan 7	The Gamester		Harlequin Whittington
M. Jan 9	Romeo and Juliet		Harlequin Whittington
T. Jan 10	The Tempest		Harlequin Whittington
W. Jan 11	**Isabella**		Harlequin Whittington
Th. Jan 12	The Miller and His Men	The King and the Duke	Harlequin Whittington
F. Jan 13	The Gamester		Harlequin Whittington
S. Jan 14	The Forest of Bondy	Rosina	Harlequin Whittington
M. Jan 16	The Beggar's Opera	Katharine and Petruchio	Harlequin Whittington
T. Jan 17	Venice Preserv'd		Harlequin Whittington
W. Jan 18	The Tempest		Harlequin Whittington
Th. Jan 19	**Isabella**		Harlequin Whittington
F. Jan 20	The Forest of Bondy	John of Paris	Harlequin Whittington
S. Jan 21	The Gamester		Harlequin Whittington
M. Jan 23	Romeo and Juliet		Harlequin Whittington
T. Jan 24	Artaxerxes		Harlequin Whittington **The Portrait of Cervantes**
W. Jan 25	Venice Preserv'd		Harlequin Whittington
Th. Jan 26	**Pizarro**		Harlequin Whittington
F. Jan 27	The Gamester		Harlequin Whittington
S. Jan 28	The Forest of Bondy	John of Paris	Harlequin Whittington
M. Jan 30	Oratorios – Handel's Messiah		
T. Jan 31	**Isabella**		Harlequin Whittington
W. Feb 1	**Brother and Sister**	Raising the Wind	Harlequin Whittington
Th. Feb 2	The Gamester		**Brother and Sister**
F. Feb 3	**Brother and Sister**	Killing No Murder	Harlequin Whittington
S. Feb 4	The Stranger		**Brother and Sister**
M. Feb 6	**Brother and Sister**	Love, Law and Physick	Harlequin Whittington
T. Feb 7	Romeo and Juliet		**Brother and Sister**
Th. Feb 9	The Stranger		Hit or Miss!

Date (*Notes*)	Mainpiece	Interlude	Afterpiece
F. Feb 10 **1815**	Oratorios – First Act of the Creation Two Grand Miscellaneous Acts		
S. Feb 11	The Stranger		**Brother and Sister**
M. Feb 13	**Brother and Sister**	Love, Law and Physick	Harlequin Whittington
T. Feb 14	**Isabella**		**Brother and Sister**
W. Feb 15	Oratorios – A Grand Selection The Messiah		
Th. Feb 16	The Stranger		Hit or Miss!
F. Feb 17	Oratorios – The Messiah		
S. Feb 18	The Stranger		Rosina
M. Feb 20	The Beggar's Opera	The Sleep Walker	Harlequin Whittington (*introducing the pyrotechnic art of The Salamander; or, Living Serpent of Fire, by Signor Rugieri*)
T. Feb 21	The Gamester		**Brother and Sister**
W. Feb 22	Oratorios – A Grand Selection. Haydn's Grand Military Movement		
Th. Feb 23	Venice Preserv'd		The Forest of Bondy
F. Feb 24	Oratorios – A Grand Selection Mozart's Celebrated overture to Zauberflote		
S. Feb 25	The Stranger		Love Laughs at Locksmiths
M. Feb 27	Artaxerxes	The Sleep Walker	Harlequin Whittington
T. Feb 28	Romeo and Juliet		Love Laughs at Locksmiths
W. Mar 1	Oratorios – A Grand Selection, including the Overture to Atlanta		
Th. Mar 2	**Isabella**		The Miller and His Men
F. Mar 3	Oratorios– A Grand Selection. Haydn's Military Movement		
S. Mar 4	The Stranger		The Sleep Walker
M. Mar 6	**The Virgin of the Sun**		Aladdin
T. Mar 7	The Gamester		The Forest of Bondy
W. Mar 8	Oratorios – A Grand Selection		
Th. Mar 9 (*Miss O'Neill's indisposition having resulted in a change of intended performances*)	Love in a Village		Love, Law and Physick

Date (*Notes*)	Mainpiece	Interlude	Afterpiece
F. Mar 10 **1815**	Oratorios – The Messiah		
S. Mar 11	The Farmer's Wife		The Sleep Walker
M. Mar 13	**The Virgin of the Sun**		Harlequin Whittington
T. Mar 14	The Stranger		Love Laughs at Locksmiths
W. Mar 15	Oratorios – Grand Selection 'Viva Enrico' Haydn's Military March		
Th. Mar 16 *'Miss O'Neill's indisposition – cannot appear this evening'*	The Tempest		The Miller and His Men
F. Mar 17	Oratorios – A Grand Selection The Messiah		
S. Mar 18 *Miss O'Neill's only performance before Easter*	The Stranger		The Forest of Bondy
M. Mar 27	Zembuca; or, The Net-Maker and his Wife (*to conclude with 'the bombardment, storming and conflagration of the fortress'*)	The Sleep Walker	Harlequin Whittington
T. Mar 28	King Henry the Fourth (Part One)		Zembuca
W. Mar 29	John of Paris	Love Laughs at Locksmiths	Zembuca
Th. Mar 30	Romeo and Juliet		Zembuca
F. Mar 31	Artaxerxes	**Love in Limbo**	Zembuca
S. Apr 1	**Isabella**		**Love in Limbo**
M. Apr 3	King Henry the Fourth (Part One)		Zembuca
T. Apr 4	The Gamester		Zembuca
W. Apr 5	**Brother and Sister**	Love, Law and Physick	Zembuca
Th. Apr 6	Venice Preserv'd		Zembuca
F. Apr 7 *Never Acted Before*	**The Noble Outlaw**		Hit or Miss!
S. Apr 8	The Stranger		Zembuca
M. Apr 9	**The Noble Outlaw**		Zembuca
T. Apr 11	**Isabella**		Zembuca
W. Apr 12	**The Noble Outlaw**		Zembuca
Th. Apr 13	Venice Preserv'd		Zembuca
F. Apr 14 *By particular desire*	John of Paris	The Sleep Walker	Zembuca
S. Apr 15	The Stranger		Love, Law and Physick
M. Apr 17	Julius Caesar		Zembuca
T. Apr 18	The Gamester		The Forest of Bondy
W. Apr 19	Macbeth		Zembuca

Date (*Notes*)	Mainpiece	Interlude	Afterpiece
Th. Apr 20 **1815**	Romeo and Juliet		Zembuca
F. Apr 21	The Beggar's Opera	Bombastes Furioso	Zembuca
S. Apr 22	The Stranger		The Escapes; or, The Water Carrier
M. Apr 24	**Pizarro**		Zembuca
T. Apr 25	**Isabella**		**Brother and Sister**
W. Apr 26	The Wheel of Fortune	Bombastes Furioso	Zembuca
Th. Apr 27	The Stranger		John of Paris
F. Apr 28	Comus	The Bee Hive	Zembuca
S. Apr 29 *Miss O'Neill's Night*	The Grecian Daughter		Comus
M. May 1	Coriolanus		Comus
T. May 2	The Grecian Daughter		**Brother and Sister**
W. May 3	Comus	Mrs Wiggins	Zembuca
Th. May 4	The Stranger		John of Paris
F. May 5	Comus	Bombastes Furioso	Zembuca
S. May 6	The Grecian Daughter		Love, Law and Physick
M. May 8	Romeo and Juliet		Comus
T. May 9	The Wheel of Fortune		Comus
W. May 10	The Stranger		**Brother and Sister**
Th. May 11	Artaxerxes	Love, Law and Physick	Zembuca
F. May 12	Venice Preserv'd		The Forest of Bondy
S. May 13 *Mess Ashleys' and S. Wesley's Annual Benefit*	A Grand Selection of Melodies – Ancient and Modern favourites. 'Mr S Wesley to perform an organ concerto'		
M. May 15	Coriolanus		Harlequin Whittington
T. May 16	Romeo and Juliet		Zembuca
W. May 17	Comus	The Fortune of War!	The Miller and His Men
Th. May 18	**Isabella**		The Fortune of War!
F. May 19	The Beggar's Opera	The Fortune of War!	The Miller and His Men
S. May 20	Venice Preserv'd		The Fortune of War!
M. May 22	Alexander the Great	The Fortune of War!	Midas
T. May 23	The Grecian Daughter		The Fortune of War!
W. May 24	Comus	The Fortune of War!	Zembuca
Th. May 25	The Stranger		The Fortune of War!
F. May 26	Comus	The Fortune of War!	The Forest of Bondy
S. May 27	Venice Preserv'd		The Fortune of War!
M. May 29	The Gamester		The Fortune of War!
T. May 30 *Mr Incledon's Night*	Lord of the Manor	Feast of Anacreon Popular songs Description of 'A Storm' (*in the character of a seaman*)	Killing No Murder
W. May 31 *Benefit of Mr Mathews*	Mail Coach Adventures	Imitations Fontainebleau; or, Our Way in France	Crumpy the Hunchback: or, Frolicks in Bag[h]dad
Th. Jun 1	The Stranger		The Fortune of War!

Date (*Notes*)	Mainpiece	Interlude	Afterpiece
F. Jun 2 **1815** *Dramas and a* *masquerade for the* *Benefit of Mr Jones*	Love and Gout; or, Arrivals and Marriages	**Brother and Sister**	Masquerade to the performers of all the London Theatres (*Songs, duets,* *choruses. 'A balloon* *will ascend over the pit,* *and burst and distribute* *smaller balloons, with* *a shower of mottos* *among the spectators.* *"God Save the King",* *in full chorus, with the* *characters unmasked'*)
S. Jun 3 *Last night but one of* Isabella	**Isabella**		The Fortune of War!
M. Jun 5	The Grecian Daughter		Comus
T. Jun 6 *Benefit of Miss* *Foote. Mr Betty* *solicited*	Alexander the Great	'Death of Nelson', by Mr Sinclair The Sultan	Aladdin
W. Jun 7 *For the Benefit of* *Miss Stephens*	Telemachus	Crumpy the Hunchback	The Forest of Bondy
Th. Jun 8	The Stranger		The Fortune of War!
F. Jun 9 *Mr Emery's Night*	Education	Songs	Love, Law and Physick
S. Jun 10 *Last Night but one of* Venice Preserv'd *this* *season*	Venice Preserv'd		John of Paris
M. Jun 12	Romeo and Juliet		Zembuca
T. Jun 13 *Mr Young's Night*	The Beggar's Opera	A Tale of Mystery	Comus
W. Jun 14 *Mr and Mrs Liston's* *Night*	Inkle and Yarico	Music Mad! (*a* *dramatic sketch*) Songs	Ali Baba; or, The Forty Thieves
Th. Jun 15 *Last night of* The Gamester	The Gamester		The Fortune of War!
F. Jun 16 *Mr Farley's Night*	Timour the Tartar (*equestrian troops*)	Mail Coach Adventures Songs Imitations	**Brother and Sister** Mr Farley's Masquerade to the performers of all the London Theatres –Fireworks and a Balloon (*to* *conclude with 'God* *Save the King' in full* *chorus, the characters* *unmasked*)
S. Jun 17	The Stranger		The Fortune of War!

Date (*Notes*)	Mainpiece	Interlude	Afterpiece
M. Jun 19 **1815** *Last night of* The Grecian Daughter *this season*	The Grecian Daughter		The Forty Thieves
T. Jun 20	Love in a Village	Bombastes Furioso	The Sleep Walker
W. Jun 21 *Benefit of Mrs Gibbs*	Mail Coach Adventures Imitations	Manual exercise (*by Simon Paap, of Holland*) Asiatic Divertissement (*'composed by the ballet master of the Opera House'*)	Fountainebleau Masquerade to the performers of all the Lonson Theatres (*'God Save the King', in full chorus, by the characters unmasked*)
Th. Jun 22 *Last night of* Isabella	**Isabella**		Hit or Miss!
F. Jun 23 *For the Benefit of Mr Taylor*	**Castle of Andalusia**	New songs	Blind Boy
S. Jun 24 *Miss O'Neill's recovery*	The Stranger		Love Laughs at Locksmiths
M. Jun 26 *Last night of* Romeo and Juliet	Romeo and Juliet		Comus
T. Jun 27 *Mr Sinclair's Night*	Lord of the Manor	The Rival Soldiers	Oscar and Malvina
W. Jun 28 *Miss S Booth's Night*	The Will (*first time*)	Reformation	The Forty Thieves
Th. Jun 29	Jane Shore		**Brother and Sister**
F. Jun 30 *For the Benefit of Mr Brandon, Box, Book and House-Keeper*	**The Duenna**	Songs Description of 'A Storm' The Rival Soldiers	Blind Boy
S. Jul 2	Jane Shore		Two Doctor Hobbs's
M. Jul 3	Jane Shore		Comus
T. Jul 4 *Miss Matthews and Mr Grimaldi's Night*	Lord of the Manor	Valentine and Orson	Harlequin Whittington
W. Jul 5 *Last night but one of Miss O'Neill's performances this season*	Venice Preserv'd		The Sleep Walker
Th. Jul 6 *Benefit of Mr Abbott*	The Exile	**La Belle Alliance** (*'in commemoration of the great events now passing' – In the course of the piece – 'The Battle of Waterloo'*)	**The Critic; or, A Tragedy Rehearsed**
F. Jul 7 *Last night of Miss O'Neill's performances*	Jane Shore		Hit or Miss!

Date (*Notes*)	Mainpiece	Interlude	Afterpiece
S. Jul 8 **1815**	The Clandestine Marriage	Comic Songs	**Paul and Virginia**
M. Jul 10 *Benefit of Mr Glassington, Prompter*	The Tempest	Valentine and Orson Manual Exercises (*by Simon Paap*) Comic Songs	Harlequin Whittington
T. Jul 11 *Benefit of Mr and Mrs Bishop*	The Siege of Belgrade	Songs Description of 'A Storm' Bombastes Furioso	Tekeli (*including 'a grand battle, the springing of a mine and the Castle of Montgatz blown up'*)
W. Jul 12 *Benefit of Mr Broadhurst*	The Maid of the Mill	Melange of Songs 'The Bee Proffers Honey' (*by particular desire*)	**The Critic** (*to conclude with a grand sea fight and the destruction of the Spanish Armada*)
Th. Jul 13 *Benefit of Mr Bologna Jun*	Comus	Tekeli Dances Grand Race by Real Ponies	Oscar and Malvina
F. Jul 14	Love in a Village	Waltz	Love Laughs at Locksmiths
S. Jul 15	The Poor Gentleman		**Paul and Virginia**
M. Jul 17 *Benefit of Mr Ware, Leader of the Band*	Steibelt's favourite overture to Romeo and Juliet Point of Honour (*Act 3 – ceremony of shooting a deserter*)	The Zauberflote (*by particular desire*) The Sleep Walker Imitations	The Forest of Bondy
T. Jul 18	The Lord of the Manor	The Miller and His Men 'Mr Ellar, for the night only, will fly from the back of the gallery'	Robinson Crusoe and His Man Friday
W. Jul 19 *For the Benefit of Mr Claremont and Master Williams*	**Brother and Sister**	Songs and duets Fontainebleau	A Tale of Mystery
Th. Jul 21 *Last night of the company performing this season*	The Woodman	Songs	Raising the Wind

Appendix B

Calendar of Drury Lane Playbills 1807–1808

Date (*Notes*)	Mainpiece	Interlude	Afterpiece
Th. Sep 17 **1807**	The Country Girl		The Weathercock
S. Sep 19	The West Indian		No Song, No Supper
T. Sep 22	**The Wonder; A Woman Keeps a Secret**		The Poor Soldier
Th. Sep 24	Adelgitha; or, The Fruits of a Single Error		The Poor Soldier
S. Sep 26	Love for Love		The Doctor and the Apothecary
T. Sep 29	**Pizarro**		The Poor Soldier
Th. Oct 1	The School for Scandal		A House to be Sold
S. Oct 3	**The Honey Moon**		The Deserter
M. Oct 5	**Pizarro**		The Devil to Pay
T. Oct 6	Percy		Poor Soldier
Th. Oct 8	The Soldier's Daughter		The Forty Thieves
S. Oct 10	Love in a Village		The Wedding Day
M. Oct 12	George Barnwell		The Forty Thieves
T. Oct 13	Love in a Village		The Liar
Th. Oct 15	The Provoked Husband; or, A Journey to London		The Forty Thieves
S. Oct 17	Love in a Village		The Mock Doctor
M. Oct 19	Romeo and Juliet		The Forty Thieves
T. Oct 20	All in the Wrong		The Poor Soldier
W. Oct 21	Love in a Village		The Irishman in London
Th. Oct 22	The School for Friends		The Forty Thieves
S. Oct 24	**The Honey Moon**		Three Weeks After Marriage
M. Oct 26	The West Indian		The Forty Thieves
T. Oct 27 *Never Acted Before*	Time's a Tell-Tale		Fortune's Frolics
W. Oct 28	Time's a Tell-Tale		No Song, No Supper
Th. Oct 29	The Travellers; or, Music's Fascination		The Lying Valet
S. Oct 31	Time's a Tell-Tale		Rosina
M. Nov 2	Time's a Tell-Tale		The Forty Thieves
T. Nov 3	Time's a Tell-Tale		Rosina
W. Nov 4	**The Duenna**		The Divorce
Th. Nov 5	Time's a Tell-Tale		Rosina
F. Nov 6	Love for Love		The Divorce
S. Nov 7	Time's a Tell-Tale		Matrimony
W. Nov 11	Time's a Tell-Tale		Rosina
Th. Nov 12	The Travellers		Bon Ton

Date (*Notes*)	Mainpiece	Interlude	Afterpiece
F. Nov 13 **1807**	Time's a Tell-Tale		The Wood Daemon; or, 'The Clock Has Struck'
S. Nov 14	**Much Ado About Nothing**		The Divorce
M. Nov 16	The Jealous Wife		The Wood Daemon
T. Nov 17	The Cabinet		Three Weeks After Marriage
W. Nov 18	Time's a Tell-Tale		The Wood Daemon
Th. Nov 19	All in the Wrong		Ella Rosenberg
F. Nov 20	Love in a Village		Ella Rosenberg
S. Nov 21	A Trip to Scarborough		Ella Rosenberg
M. Nov 23	The Country Girl		Ella Rosenberg
T. Nov 24	The Cabinet		Ella Rosenberg
W. Nov 25	Time's a Tell-Tale		Ella Rosenberg
Th. Nov 26	**The Wonder**		Ella Rosenberg
F. Nov 27	The Haunted Tower		Ella Rosenberg
S. Nov 28	The Inconstant		Ella Rosenberg
M. Nov 30	The Siege of Belgrade		Ella Rosenberg
T. Dec 1	As You Like It		Ella Rosenberg
W. Dec 2	Time's a Tell-Tale		Ella Rosenberg
Th. Dec 3	False Alarms; or, My Cousin		Ella Rosenberg
S. Dec 5	The Cabinet		Ella Rosenberg
M. Dec 7	The Way to Keep Him		The Wood Daemon
T. Dec 8	The Travellers		The Citizen
W. Dec 9	Time's a Tell-Tale		Tekeli; or, The Siege of Montgatz
Th. Dec 10	**The Honey Moon**		Ella Rosenberg
F. Dec 11	The Inconstant		Tekeli
S. Dec 12	Lionel and Clarissa		Ella Rosenberg
M. Dec 14	Love for Love		Tekeli
T. Dec 15	Lionel and Clarissa		Ella Rosenberg
W. Dec 16	Faulkner		The Weathercock
Th. Dec 17	Faulkner		Tekeli
S. Dec 19	The Cabinet		Matrimony
T. Dec 22	The Belle's Stratagem		Ella Rosenberg
T. Dec 29	A Bold Stroke for a Wife		Furibond; or, Harlequin Negro
Th. Dec 31	She Stoops to Conquer; or, The Mistakes of a Night		Furibond
F. Jan 1 **1808**	Beaux Stratagem		Furibond
M. Jan 4	Romeo and Juliet		Furibond
W. Jan 6	Earl of Warwick		Furibond
M. Jan 11	**Pizarro**		Furibond
W. Jan 13	**Much Ado About Nothing**		Furibond
Th. Jan 14	**The Duenna**		Furibond
F. Jan 15	**The Busy Body**		Furibond
S. Jan 16	All in the Wrong		Furibond
M. Jan 18	The Castle Spectre		Furibond
T. Jan 19	A Trip to Scarborough		Furibond

Date (*Notes*)	Mainpiece	Interlude	Afterpiece
W. Jan 20 **1808**	The Cabinet		Furibond
Th. Jan 21	**The Honey Moon**		Furibond
F. Jan 22	Something to Do		Furibond
S. Jan 23	The Siege of Belgrade	Songs	Furibond
M. Jan 25	Romeo and Juliet		Furibond
T. Jan 26	The Cabinet		Ella Rosenberg
W. Jan 27	The Rivals		Matrimony
Th. Jan 28	Love for Love		Furibond
F. Jan 29	The Travellers		Ella Rosenberg
M. Feb 1	**Pizarro**		Furibond
T. Feb 2	The Cabinet		The Mayor of Garratt
W. Feb 3	The School for Scandal		Ella Rosenberg
Th. Feb 4	The Suspicious Husband		The Devil to Pay
F. Feb 5	False Alarms		Ella Rosenberg
S. Feb 6	**The Chances**		The Weathercock
M. Feb 8	The Castle Spectre		Furibond
T. Feb 9	**The Chances**		Ella Rosenberg
W. Feb 10	**She Wou'd and She Wou'd Not**		Matrimony
Th. Feb 11 *Never Acted Before*	Kais; or, Love in the Deserts		The Virgin Unmask'd
F. Feb 12	Kais		The Mayor of Garratt
S. Feb 13	Kais		The Irishman in London
M. Feb 15	Kais		The Mayor of Garratt
T. Feb 16	Kais		The Citizen
Th. Feb 18	Kais		Three Weeks after Marriage
F. Feb 19	Kais		Ella Rosenberg
S. Feb 20	Kais		Ways and Means
M. Feb 22	Kais		The Mayor of Garratt
T. Feb 23	Kais		The Devil to Pay
W. Feb 24	Kais		Ella Rosenberg
Th. Feb 25	Kais		Ways and Means
F. Feb 26	Kais		The Divorce
S. Feb 27	Kais		Matrimony
M. Feb 29	**Pizarro**		Ella Rosenberg
T. Mar 1	**The Chances**		In and Out of Tune
Th. Mar 3	Kais		The Mayor of Garratt
S. Mar 5	The Inconstant		In and Out of Tune
M. Mar 7	**Pizarro**		In and Out of Tune
T. Mar 8	Kais		Ella Rosenberg
Th. Mar 10	**The Wonder**		In and Out of Tune
S. Mar 12	Kais		The Mayor of Garratt
M. Mar 14	The West Indian		Rosina
T. Mar 15	All in the Wrong		The Poor Soldier
Th. Mar 17	The Cabinet		Three Weeks after Marriage
S. Mar 19	**The Chances**		The Prize
M. Mar 21	The Country Girl		Tekeli
T. Mar 22	The Haunted Tower		The Mayor of Garratt
Th. Mar 24	The Belle's Stratagem		Ella Rosenberg

Date (*Notes*)	Mainpiece	Interlude	Afterpiece
S. Mar 26 **1808**	Kais		The Devil to Pay
M. Mar 28	**Pizarro**		The Citizen
T. Mar 29	**The Honey Moon** (*including a dance incidental to the piece*)		Tekeli
Th. Mar 31 *Never Acted Before*	The World		Rosina
S. Apr 2	The World		The Deserter (*Act 2 – Military manoeuvres – Dead march and the ceremony used in shooting a deserter*)
M. Apr 4	The World		Tekeli
T. Apr 5	The World		Ella Rosenberg
Th. Apr 7	The World		The Mayor of Garratt
S. Apr 9	The World		Ways and Means
M. Apr 18	The World		Tekeli
T. Apr 19	The World		The Mayor of Garratt
W. Apr 20	The World		Ella Rosenberg
Th. Apr 21	The World		Three Weeks After Marriage
F. Apr 22	The World		Caractacus
S. Apr 23	The World		Caractacus
M. Apr 25	The World		Caractacus
T. Apr 26	The World		Caractacus
W. Apr 27	The World		Caractacus
Th. Apr 28	The World		Caractacus
F. Apr 29	The World		Caractacus
S. Apr 30	The World		No Song, No Supper
M. May 2 *For the Benefit of Mr Bannister*	The Heir at Law (*first time at this theatre by permission of the Royal Haymarket*)	Sylvester Daggerwood, with a new comic song: 'The Tragedy of Othello; or, Fine Fleecy Hoisery!' Songs and dancing	The Minor
T. May 3 *Never Acted Before*	The Jew of Mogadore		Fortune's Frolics
W. May 4	The Jew of Mogadore		Caractacus
Th. May 5	The Jew of Mogadore		Caractacus
F. May 6	The World		Caractacus
S. May 7	The Jew of Mogadore		Caractacus
M. May 9 *Mr Braham's Night*	The Wife of Two Husbands	An Harmonic Meeting Duets and Airs	The Hunter of the Alps (*by permission of the Proprietors of the Theatre Royal Haymarket*) Celebrated duet of 'Vive le Roi', by Signora Storace and Mr Braham
T. May 10	The Jew of Mogadore		The Devil to Pay

Date (*Notes*)	Mainpiece	Interlude	Afterpiece
W. May 11 **1808** *'For the Benefit of Mr D'Egville – Madame Catalani has kindly offered her services (by permission of the proprietors of the King's Theatre)'*	**The Honey Moon** (*End of Act 2: Madame Catalani will perform for that night only: 'A new grand scena, a la pompa', in recitative and aria*)	La Fête Chinoise; or, The Chinese Festival (*by the King's Theatre dance corps*) Shawl Dance	Caractacus
Th. May 12 *Never Acted Before at this theatre. For the Benefit of Miss Duncan*	Which is the Man?	The New Actress Songs and Hornpipe The Purse	The Highland Reel
F. May 13	The World		Caractacus
S. May 14	The Jew of Mogadore		Three Weeks after Marriage
M. May 16 *For the Benefit of Mr Elliston*	**Much Ado About Nothing**	Edgar and Emmeline Dances and songs, including a duet by Mr Braham and Signora Storace	Tekeli
T. May 17	The World		Caractacus
W. May 18 *By particular desire. For the Benefit of Mrs Mountain*	The Travellers	Jamie and Anna (*Scotch pastoral New music with a Caledonian Overture*) New songs and a dance	Blue Devils (*by permission of the proprietors of the Theatre Royal, Haymarket*)
Th. May 19	The World		Ella Rosenberg
F. May 20	Kais		Caractacus
S. May 21	The Inconstant		The Mayor of Garratt
M. May 23 *Mr Johnstone's Night*	False Alarms	Sylvester Daggerwood, with new comic song 'The Tragedy of Othello, or Fine Fleecy Hoisery!' (*by particular desire and for that night only*)	The Irishman in Italy 'A favourite shawl dance, new allemande and waltz' Grand Masquerade
T. May 24 *Last night of the new comedy* The World	The World		Ella Rosenberg
W. May 25 *Benefit of Mr Palmer and Mr Welsh*	The Wife of Two Husbands	Blue Devils	The Devil to Pay
Th. May 26 *Miss Pope's last Benefit and last appearance on the stage*	The Heir at Law	Songs Farewell Address Edgar and Emmeline (*compressed into 1 Act*)	Caractacus

Date (*Notes*)	Mainpiece	Interlude	Afterpiece
F. May 27 **1808** *For the Benefit of Mr Spring, Box, Book, and House-Keeper*	First Love	The Millers Mrs Wiggins	Peeping Tom (*by permission of the proprietors of the Theatre Royal, Haymarket*)
S. May 28	The Haunted Tower	The Millers	The Weathercock
M. May 30 *Signora Storace's last night and last appearance on the stage. Signor Naldi's first and only appearance this season*	The Cabinet	Italian Cantata, 'in which Signor Naldi, Signora Storace, and Mr Braham will perform songs from the opera of Kais' Dancing Farewell address in music by Signora Storace	Love Laughs at Locksmiths (*by permission of the proprietors of the Theatre Royal, Haymarket*)
T. May 31 *Benefit of Mr Mathews*	The School of Shakespeare ('*The inimitable scenes of the Poet, selected for the purpose, and digested into five acts, will exemplify in the strongest colours of our immortal bard, AMBITION, VANITY, REVENGE, COWARDICE, AND SLANDER*')	Sylvester Daggerwood – 'The Tragedy of Othello; or, Fine Fleecy Hoisery!' Songs, including two new comic songs by Mr Mathews	The Agreeable Surprise (*by permission of the proprietors of the Theatre Royal, Haymarket*)
W. Jun 1 *Never Acted Before. For the Benefit of Mr Russell and Mr Gibbon*	The Mysterious Bride (*with dances incidental to the piece*)	Edgar and Emmeline A new song 'written Expressly' for the occasion and composed by M.P. King called 'The Glorious First of June'	The Mayor of Garratt
Th. Jun 2	The West Indian	Blue Devils	Ella Rosenberg
F. Jun 3 *Benefit of Miss Lyon*	**The Duenna**	Songs	The Sultan
M. Jun 6 *Mr Johnston's Benefit (Machinist and Decorator)*	The Mysterious Bride	Songs	Caractacus
T. Jun 7 *Benefit of Mr Wewitzer, Mr Eyre, and Mr Cooke*	John Bull; or, An Englishman's Fireside	Songs	Tekeli

Date (*Notes*)	Mainpiece	Interlude	Afterpiece
W. Jun 8 **1808** *For the Benefit of* *Mrs Harlowe, Miss* *Ray, and Mr Fisher*	Deaf and Dumb; or, The Orphan Protected	Lovers' Quarrels 'Mail Coach', by Mr Mathews Dancing	Ella Rosenberg
Th. Jun 9 *For the Benefit of Mr* *Dignum*	The Soldier's Daughter	Mrs Wiggins (*by* *permission of* *the proprietors* *of the Theatre* *Royal, Haymarket*)	The Poor Soldier
F. Jun 10 *Last time this season*	The Country Girl	Songs Sylvester Daggerwood – 'The Tragedy of Othello; or Fine Fleecy Hoisery!' Comic songs Shawl dance and Del Caro's hornpipe Allemande, by D'Egville's pupils	The Shipwreck
S. Jun 11	**The Mountaineers**		The Weathercock
M. Jun 13 *Benefit of Mr Kelly*	Ways and Means Madame Catalani (*by* *permission of the King's* *Theatre*) 'will perform for the first and only time on an English stage, the celebrated Ghost scene from the serious opera of SERAMIDE'	The Irishman in London Popular air by Madame Catalani 'Hope told a flattering tale'	The Secret Marriage (*as* *performed at the King's* *Theatre*)
T. Jun 14	The Mysterious Bride	Sylvester Daggerwood	Ella Rosenberg
W. Jun 15	A Bold Stroke for a Wife	Songs Description of 'A Storm' and a favourite hornpipe	Rosina
Th. Jun 16	Love in a Village	Allemande Shawl dance and favourite hornpipe (*in the character of a* *sailor*)	The Mayor of Garratt
F. Jun 17	The Belle's Stratagem	Allemande Shawl dance	No Song, No Supper
S. Jun 18 *Benefit of Mr Lacy* *Last night of the* *company performing* *this season*	A Trip to Scarborough	Del Caro's hornpipe and a 'pas seul' The Purse	Rosina Imitations

Calendar of Drury Lane Playbills 1808–1809

Date (*Notes*)	Mainpiece	Interlude	Afterpiece
Note: On 24 February Drury 1809 Lane burnt down. The theatrical company moved first to the **King's Theatre in Haymarket**, then the **Lyceum**. The company returned to the **King's Theatre** for the final performance of the season.			
S. Sep 17 **1808**	**The Honey Moon**		Rosina
T. Sep 20	Hamlet		The Irishman in London
Th. Sep 22	Love in a Village		The Citizen
S. Sep 24	Country Girl		Ella Rosenberg
Th. Mar 16 **1809** **King's Theatre, Haymarket**	Man and Wife; or, More Secrets than One	Sylvester Daggerwood	**Don Quichotte**
M. Mar 20	**The Honey Moon**	Les Jeux Floraux	The Mock Doctor
Th. Mar 23	Country Girl	**Don Quichotte**	The Irishman in London
M. Apr 3	Douglas	**Don Quichotte**	The Weathercock
Th. Apr 6	All in the Wrong	**Don Quichotte**	The Mayor of Garratt
M. Apr 10 *'Madame Catalani has kindly and voluntarily given her Services on this particular Occasion for this night only'. King's Theatre, Haymarket*	Three and the Deuce (*Mr Mathews to introduce the favourite song of 'The Mail Coach'*)	La Semiramide	**Don Quichotte**
T. Apr 11 **Lyceum Theatre**	John Bull; or, An Englishman's Fireside		The Prize; or, 2,5,3,8
W. Apr 12	The Rivals		The Citizen
Th. Apr 13	The Soldier's Daughter		Rosina
F. Apr 14	The West Indian		Of Age To-morrow
S. Apr 15	The Cabinet (*In the course of the opera, the favourite air of '**The Sprightly Castanet**' by Mrs Mountain*)		The Anatomist
M. Apr 17	**The Honey Moon**		No Song, No Supper
T. Apr 18	Man and Wife		The Weathercock
W. Apr 19	The Cabinet (*In the course of the opera, the favourite air of '**The Sprightly Castanet**' by Mrs Mountain*)	Love in a Tub	The Virgin Unmask'd

Date (*Notes*)	Mainpiece	Interlude	Afterpiece
Th. Apr 20 **1809**	Heir at Law		Three Weeks after Marriage
F. Apr 21	Grieving's a Folly		Rosina
S. Apr 22	Grieving's a Folly		Three and the Deuce
M. Apr 24	Grieving's a Folly	Love in a Tub	The Mayor of Garratt
T. Apr 25	Grieving's a Folly		The Wedding Day
W. Apr 26	Grieving's a Folly	Love in a Tub	Of Age To-morrow
Th. Apr 27	Grieving's a Folly		Three and the Deuce
F. Apr 28	Grieving's a Folly	Love in a Tub	The Devil to Pay
S. Apr 29	The Cabinet		The Mock Doctor
M. May 1	Grieving's a Folly	Duet of 'All's Well'	**Temper; or, The Domestic Tyrant**
T. May 2	Grieving's a Folly	Duet of 'All's Well'	**Temper**
W. May 3	Grieving's a Folly	Love in a Tub	**Temper**
Th. May 4	Grieving's a Folly	Love in a Tub	**Temper**
Fri. May 5	Grieving's a Folly	Love in a Tub	**Temper**
S. May 6	The Haunted Tower		**Temper**
M. May 8	Grieving's a Folly		Three and the Deuce
T. May 9	Grieving's a Folly	Duet of 'All's Well'	The Wedding Day
W. May 10	The Cabinet		**Temper**
Th. May 11	Grieving's a Folly	Duet of 'All's Well'	The Mayor of Garratt
F. May 12	Grieving's a Folly	Love in a Tub	**Temper**
S. May 13	The Cabinet		Three and the Deuce
M. May 15 *Benefit of Mr Bannister*	The Poor Gentleman	Sharp Set; or, The Village Hotel New comic songs	The Weathercock
T. May 16	John Bull	Mrs Wiggins	Ella Rosenberg
W. May 17 *For the Benefit of Miss Duncan*	**The Honey Moon**	Interlude taken from Harlequin's Invasion Love in a Tub	The Devil to Pay
Th. May 18 *For the Benefit of Mr Dowton*	Grieving's a Folly	Blue Devils Songs by Mr Braham Love in a Tub	The Jew and the Doctor
F. May 19	The Heir at Law	Duet of 'All's Well' Sylvester Daggerwood Songs by Mr Braham	Matrimony
M. May 22 *For the Benefit of Mr Elliston*	Three and the Deuce	Songs **The Critic; or, A Tragedy Rehearsed** (*in 3 Acts*)	The Irishman in London
T. May 23 *For the Benefit of Mr and Mrs H Siddons*	**Pizarro**	Songs Recitation of 'Bill Jones; or, The Ship Spectre' Sylvester Daggerwood	Ella Rosenberg

Date (*Notes*)	Mainpiece	Interlude	Afterpiece
W. May 24 **1809**	**The Critic**	Songs	Three and the Deuce
Th. May 25 *Mr Palmer's Benefit*	The School for Scandal	My Grandmother The Manager in Distress (*previous to the mainpiece*)	Three and the Deuce
F. May 26 *For the Benefit of Mrs Bishop (late Miss Lyon)*	Love in a Village	Blue Devils Songs Love in a Tub	The Mayor of Garratt
S. May 27	Grieving's a Folly (*at the end of Act 2: Hornpipe from Robinson Crusoe, and 'A New Scotch Pastoral Dance'*)	Songs	**The Critic**
M. May 29 *Benefit of Mr Johnstone*	The West Indian	Love in a Tub	The Irishman in Italy Songs, including 'The Bold Dragoon'
T. May 30 *Mr Braham's Night*	The Cabinet	Songs	The Prize
W. May 31	The Jealous Wife	'Grand Scena from Semiramide'	Love in a Tub Three and the Deuce
Th. Jun 1	**The Honey Moon**	Blue Devils	The Mayor of Garratt
F. Jun 2 *For the Benefit of Mr Eyre and Miss Ray*	Man and Wife	Love in a Tub	The Deserter
S. Jun 3	**The Critic**	Songs	The Devil to Pay Three and the Deuce
M. Jun 5 *Benefit of Mr Johnston (Machinist and Decorator) and Miss Boyce*	Grieving's a Folly	'The Mail Coach', by Mr Mathews Blue Devils	The Blind Boy
T. Jun 6 *Benefit of Mr Dignum*	The School for Scandal ('*in Act 2, Mr Dignum will sing the celebrated Song called* **'The Hero Of Corunna'** *Commemorative of the death of General MOORE*')	Blue Devils Songs	The Weathercock
W. Jun 7	Grieving's a Folly		**The Critic**
Th. Jun 8	She Stoops to Conquer; or, The Mistakes of a Night		Rosina
F. Jun 9	**The Honey Moon**	Love in a Tub	The Prize
S. Jun 10	Heir at Law	Blue Devils	The Mayor of Garratt
M. Jun 12 *Benefit of Mr Raymond*	The Stranger	High Life Below Stairs	The Prize

Date (*Notes*)	Mainpiece	Interlude	Afterpiece
M. Jun 12 **1809** **King's Theatre** *For the Benefit of Mr Spring, Box, Book, and House-Keeper* *Last Night*	John Bull	Sylvester Daggerwood Love in a Tub	The Three and the Deuce (*including song of 'The Mail Coach'*)

Calendar of Drury Lane Playbills 1809–1810

Date (*Notes*)	Mainpiece	Interlude	Afterpiece
M. Sep 25 **1809**	**The Duenna**		The Mayor of Garratt
Lyceum Theatre			
T. Sep 26	John Bull; or, An Englishman's Fireside		Rosina
W. Sep 27	**The Duenna**		Fortune's Frolics
Th. Sep 28	She Stoops to Conquer; or, The Mistakes of a Night		No Song, No Supper
F. Sep 29	John Bull		The Devil to Pay
S. Sep 30	The Haunted Tower		The Irishman in London
M. Oct 2	The Jealous Wife		The Deserter (*in Act 2: Military manoeuvres, The Dead March, and ceremony used in shooting a deserter*)
T. Oct 3	The Heir at Law		Rosina
Th. Oct 5	The Haunted Tower		The Mayor of Garratt
S. Oct 7	The West Indian		The Weathercock
M. Oct 9	The Jealous Wife		The Deserter
T. Oct 10	The West Indian		The Weathercock
W. Oct 11	The Haunted Tower		The Mayor of Garratt
Th. Oct 12	The Heir at Law		The Deserter
F. Oct 13	Love in a Village		Three and the Deuce
			Mr Mathews with the favourite song of 'The Mail Coach'
S. Oct 14	The Soldier's Daughter		Fortune's Frolics
M. Oct 16	The Stranger		Three and the Deuce
			'The Mail Coach'
T. Oct 17	The Soldier's Daughter		Fortune's Frolics
W. Oct 18	The Cabinet (*with additional songs*)		Honest Thieves
			Songs
Th. Oct 19	**The Wonder; A Woman Keeps a Secret**		No Song, No Supper
F. Oct 20	Grieving's a Folly		The Prize; or, 2, 5, 3, 8
S. Oct 21	The Will		Three Weeks after Marriage
M. Oct 23	The Beaux Stratagem		Three and the Deuce
			Songs
T. Oct 24	The Cabinet		Honest Thieves
W. Oct 25	Sylvester Daggerwood	Britain's Jubilee	Three and the Deuce
Th. Oct 26	**The Busy Body**		Britain's Jubilee
F. Oct 27	The Poor Gentleman		Britain's Jubilee
S. Oct 28	The Jew		Britain's Jubilee
M. Oct 30	The Wheel of Fortune		Britain's Jubilee
T. Oct 31	The Cabinet (*with songs, as before*)		Britain's Jubilee

Date (*Notes*)	Mainpiece	Interlude	Afterpiece
W. Nov 1 **1809**	The Rivals		Britain's Jubilee
Th. Nov 2	The Dramatist		No Song, No Supper
F. Nov 3	Love in a Village		Britain's Jubilee
S. Nov 4	The Suspicious Husband		Britain's Jubilee
M. Nov 6	**Much Ado About Nothing**		Britain's Jubilee
T. Nov 7	**The Duenna**		The Honest Thieves
W. Nov 8	The School for Scandal	Britain's Jubilee	The Irishman in London
Th. Nov 9	George Barnwell	Britain's Jubilee (*compressed into 1 Act*)	The Prize
F. Nov 10	The Beggar's Opera		The Weathercock
S. Nov 11	The Will	Britain's Jubilee	The Midnight Hour
M. Nov 13	Man and Wife; or, More Secrets than One	Britain's Jubilee	Three Weeks after Marriage
T. Nov 14	The Suspicious Husband	Britain's Jubilee	Matrimony
W. Nov 15	The Belle's Stratagem		My Grandmother
Th. Nov 16	**The Duenna**		The Midnight Hour
F. Nov 17	**Much Ado About Nothing**		The Honest Thieves
S. Nov 18	The School for Scandal		Matrimony
M. Nov 20	Man and Wife		Not at Home!
T. Nov 21	The Beggar's Opera		Not at Home!
W. Nov 22	**The Busy Body**		Not at Home!
Th. Nov 23	A Bold Stroke for a Wife		Not at Home!
F. Nov 24	The Poor Gentleman		Not at Home!
S. Nov 25	The Cabinet		Not at Home!
M. Nov 27	Man and Wife		My Grandmother (*by particular desire*)
T. Nov 28	The Inconstant; or, The Way to Win Him		Not at Home!
W. Nov 29	The Haunted Tower		Not at Home!
Th. Nov 30	Heir at Law		Not at Home!
F. Dec 1	**The Honey Moon**		No Song, No Supper
S. Dec 2	**The Duenna**		The Honest Thieves (*by particular desire*)
M. Dec 4	The Soldier's Daughter		Rosina
T. Dec 5	The Merry Wives of Windsor		Three and the Deuce
W. Dec 6	Love in a Village		The Midnight Hour
Th. Dec 7	The Castle Spectre		Of Age To-morrow
F. Dec 8	The Inconstant		No Song, No Supper
S. Dec 9	The Dramatist		Matrimony
M. Dec 11	**The Honey Moon**		The Prize
T. Dec 12	**The Duenna**	Not at Home! (*compressed into 1 Act*)	Three Weeks after Marriage
W. Dec 13	Man and Wife		Of Age To-morrow
Th. Dec 14	The Castle Spectre		The Mayor of Garratt
F. Dec 15	The Merry Wives of Windsor		Matrimony
S. Dec 16	The School for Scandal		My Grandmother

Date (*Notes*)	Mainpiece	Interlude	Afterpiece
M. Dec 18 **1809**	The Jealous Wife		Three and the Deuce
T. Dec 19	Sudden Arrivals; or,		Rosina
Never Acted Before	Too Busy by Half		
W. Dec 20	Sudden Arrivals		The Devil to Pay
Th. Dec 21	Sudden Arrivals		No Song, No Supper
F. Dec 22	Sudden Arrivals		The Weathercock
S. Dec 23	Sudden Arrivals		The Midnight Hour
T. Dec 26	George Barnwell		Cinderella; or, The Little Glass Slipper
W. Dec 27	Sudden Arrivals		Cinderella
Th. Dec 28	The Castle Spectre		Cinderella
F. Dec 29	**The Duenna**		Cinderella
S. Dec 30	The Merry Wives of Windsor		Cinderella
M. Jan 1 **1810**	**The Honey Moon** (*with a dance incidental to the piece*)		Cinderella
T. Jan 2	The Cabinet		Cinderella
W. Jan 3	John Bull		Cinderella
Th. Jan 4	As You Like It		Cinderella
F. Jan 5	The Haunted Tower ('*in the course of the Opera, the favourite song of the "The Sprightly Castanets", by Mrs Mountain, accompanied on the castanets by herself*')		Cinderella
S. Jan 6	**The Child of Nature**	The Honest Thieves	Cinderella
M. Jan 8	Adelgitha; or, The Fruits of a Single Error		Cinderella
T. Jan 9	Love in a Village		Cinderella
W. Jan 10	John Bull		Cinderella
Th. Jan 11	The Rivals		Cinderella
F. Jan 12	The Confederacy		Cinderella
S. Jan 13	The Beggar's Opera		Cinderella
M. Jan 15	As You Like It		Cinderella
T. Jan 16	**The Mountaineers**		Cinderella
W. Jan 17	Sudden Arrivals		Cinderella
Th. Jan 18	The Confederacy		Cinderella
F. Jan 19	The Cabinet		Cinderella
S. Jan 20	Ways and Means	The Honest Thieves	Cinderella
M. Jan 22	Up All Night; or, The Smuggler's Cave		Mayor of Garratt
T. Jan 23	The Hypocrite		Cinderella
W. Jan 24	The Confederacy		The Irishman in London
Th. Jan 25	**Much Ado About Nothing**		No Song, No Supper
F. Jan 26	The Merry Wives of Windsor		Honest Thieves
S. Jan 27	Man and Wife		Midnight Hour
M. Jan 29	Up All Night		Three and the Deuce
W. Jan 31	The Hypocrite		The Mayor of Garratt

Date (*Notes*)	Mainpiece	Interlude	Afterpiece
Th. Feb 1 **1810**	Up All Night		Who's the Dupe?
F. Feb 2	John Bull		Ella Rosenberg
S. Feb 3	Riches! Or, The Wife and Brother		Of Age To-morrow
M. Feb 5	Riches!		Honest Thieves
T. Feb 6	Riches!		Matrimony
W. Feb 7	Riches!		Ella Rosenberg
Th. Feb 8	Riches!		The Mayor of Garratt
F. Feb 9	Riches!		Midnight Hour
S. Feb 10	Riches!		The Review; or, The Wags of Windsor
M. Feb 12	Riches!		My Grandmother
T. Feb 13	Up All Night		Ella Rosenberg
W. Feb 14	Hypocrite		The Review
Th. Feb 15	Riches!		**The Critic; or, A Tragedy Rehearsed**
F. Feb 16	The Confederacy		The Honest Thieves
S. Feb 17	John Bull		Ella Rosenberg
M. Feb 19	Riches!		The Review
T. Feb 20	The Hypocrite		The Mayor of Garratt
W. Feb 21	Which is the Man?		**The Critic**
Th. Feb 22	**The Duenna**		Who's the Dupe?
F. Feb 23	Ways and Means	Ella Rosenberg	High Life Below Stairs
S. Feb 24	The Merry Wives of Windsor		The Review
M. Feb 26	Riches!		Hit or Miss!
T. Feb 27	The Hypocrite		Hit or Miss!
Th. Mar 1	A Trip to Scarborough		Hit or Miss!
F. Mar 2	The School for Scandal		Hit or Miss!
S. Mar 3	Which is the Man?		Hit or Miss!
M. Mar 5	Riches!		Hit or Miss!
T. Mar 6	**Much Ado About Nothing**		Hit or Miss!
Th. Mar 8	**The Honey Moon**		Hit or Miss!
S. Mar 10	Hypocrite		Hit or Miss!
M. Mar 12	Riches!		Hit or Miss!
T. Mar 13	The Maniac; or, The Swiss Banditti		The Weathercock
Th. Mar 15	The Maniac		Hit or Miss!
S. Mar 17	The Maniac		Hit or Miss!
M. Mar 19	The Maniac		Hit or Miss!
T. Mar 20	The Maniac		Hit or Miss!
Th. Mar 22	The Maniac		Hit or Miss!
S. Mar 24	The Maniac		Hit or Miss!
M. Mar 26	The Maniac		Hit or Miss!
T. Mar 27	The Maniac		Hit or Miss!
Th. Mar 29	The Maniac		Hit or Miss!
S. Mar 31	The Maniac		Hit or Miss!
M. Apr 2	The Maniac		Hit or Miss!
T. Apr 3	The Maniac		Hit or Miss!
Th. Apr 5	The Maniac		Hit or Miss!
S. Apr 7	The Maniac		Hit or Miss!

Date (*Notes*)	Mainpiece	Interlude	Afterpiece
M. Apr 9 **1810**	The Maniac		Hit or Miss!
T. Apr 10	The Maniac		Hit or Miss!
Th. Apr 12	The Maniac		Hit or Miss!
S. Apr 14	The Maniac		Hit or Miss!
M. Apr 23	George Barnwell; or, The London Merchant	The Village Doctor (*'Composed by Monsieur Francesco Antonio Montigiani. A Celebrated Mime and Principal Grotesque Dancer, from the Theatre at* **Lisbon**, *and in which he will make his first appearance in England'*)	The Midnight Hour
T. Apr 24	The Confederacy	The Village Doctor	The Weathercock
W. Apr 25	The Cabinet	The Village Doctor	The Mayor of Garratt
Th. Apr 26	Riches!	The Village Doctor	No Song, No Supper
F. Apr 27	**The Honey Moon**	The Village Doctor	Of Age To-morrow
S. Apr 28	The School for Scandal	The Village Doctor	My Grandmother
M. Apr 30	The Maniac		Hit or Miss!
T. May 1	The Inconstant		Hit or Miss!
W. May 2	Hypocrite	Croaking; or, 'Heaven send we may be all alive this day three months!' (*taken and altered from Goldsmith's* Good Natured Man, *compressed into 1 Act*)	The Honest Thieves
Th. May 3 *Benefit of Miss Duncan*	Know Your Own Mind	Songs	The Citizen
F. May 4 *Benefit of Mr Philipps*	**The Duenna**	Songs, including the celebrated dialogue of 'Vive le Roi' from the opera of The English Fleet Sylvester Daggerwood (*in 1 Act*)	Love Laughs at Locksmiths Songs
S. May 5	The Maniac		Hit or Miss!
M. May 7 *Mr Johnstone's Benefit*	John Bull		The Review
T. May 8	The Maniac		Hit or Miss!
W. May 9 *Mrs Edwin's Benefit*	Hypocrite	'The favourite air of **"The Sprightly Castanets"**, by Mrs Mountain Accompanied on the Spanish castanets, by herself (*by particular desire*) and other songs'	Ella Rosenberg

Date (*Notes*)	Mainpiece	Interlude	Afterpiece
Th. May 10 **1810** *Mr De Camp's Benefit*	**The Critic**	Three and the Deuce	The Review
F. May 11	The Maniac		Hit or Miss!
S. May 12	The Maniac		Hit or Miss!
M. May 14 *Mr Mathews' Benefit*	The Clandestine Marriage	Songs	Killing No Murder (*by permission of the proprietors of the Theatre Royal, Covent Garden*)
T. May 15 *Benefit of Mr Palmer*	The Confederacy	Songs	The Review
W. May 16 *Mrs Mountain's Benefit*	False Alarms (*Songs interspersed throughout the play, including* **'We Merry Little Spanish Girls'**, *accompanied on the castanets. End Act 2 – by desire, a favourite new glee for three voices, 'O never say that I was false at heart'*)		The Midnight Hour
Th. May 17	John Bull	Hornpipe	The Mayor of Garratt
		Songs	
F. May 18	The Maniac		Three Weeks after Marriage
S. May 19 *Mr Smith's Benefit*	Up All Night (*by permission of the Proprietors of the English Opera*)	Songs	The Review
M. May 21	The Clandestine Marriage	Songs	Three and the Deuce (*by particular desire*)
T. May 22 *Mr Melvin's Benefit*	The West Indian Songs	Songs	The Adopted Child (*by particular desire*)
W. May 23	The Hypocrite (*by particular desire*)	Songs ('*In the course of the Evening* **Miss Kelly will sing a New Castanet Song,** *composed and accompanied on the Harp by Mr Weippert*')	The Honest Thieves
Th. May 24 *Mr Horn's Benefit*	**The Duenna**	Songs (*by particular desire*)	**The Critic**
F. May 25	The School for Scandal		Rosina
S. May 26	Hypocrite (*by particular desire*)	'Favourite hornpipe by Miss Wells from the Opera House'	Ella Rosenberg
		Sylvester Daggerwood	

Date (*Notes*)	Mainpiece	Interlude	Afterpiece
M. May 28 **1810** *Benefit of Mr Sprig, Box, Book and House-keeper*	The Clandestine Marriage (*by particular desire*)	Musical Medley (*including* **'We Merry Little Spanish Girls'** *by Mrs Mountain, accompanied by herself on the castanets. Composed by Mr Reeve*)	The Poor Soldier
T. May 29	The Inconstant	Merit and Fortune Songs	The Midnight Hour
W. May 30	The Cabinet		The Citizen
Th. May 31	Know Your Own Mind	Songs	The Weathercock
F. Jun 1 *Last Night*	As You Like It	Songs	Of Age To-morrow

Calendar of Drury Lane Playbills 1810–1811

Date (*Notes*)	Mainpiece	Interlude	Afterpiece
Th. Sep 20 **1810**	The Hypocrite		The Mayor of Garratt
Theatre Royal, Lyceum			
F. Sep 21	The Soldier's Daughter		The Honest Thieves
S. Sep 22	As You Like It		Matrimony
T. Sep 25	Man and Wife; or, More Secrets than One		No Song, No Supper
F. Sep 28	The Jealous Wife		The Devil to Pay
S. Sep 29	The Heir at Law		The Mayor of Garratt
T. Oct 2	The Stranger		Ella Rosenberg
W. Oct 3	The Clandestine Marriage		The Midnight Hour
Th. Oct 4	The School for Scandal		Of Age To-morrow
S. Oct 6	The Jealous Wife		The Weathercock
M. Oct 8	The Clandestine Marriage		Hit or Miss!
W. Oct 10	The Way to Keep Him		Hit or Miss!
Th. Oct 11	The Beaux Stratagem		Rosina
S. Oct 13	The Castle Spectre		Hit or Miss!
M. Oct 15	The Clandestine Marriage		Hit or Miss!
T. Oct 16	The Way to Keep Him		Hit or Miss!
W. Oct 17	**Much Ado About Nothing**		Hit or Miss!
Th. Oct 18	John Bull; or, An Englishman's Fireside		The Quaker
S. Oct 20	**The Busy Body**		Hit or Miss!
M. Oct 22	The Clandestine Marriage		Hit or Miss!
T. Oct 23	The Belle's Stratagem		The Review; or, The Wags of Windsor
W. Oct 24	The Cabinet		Hit or Miss!
Th. Oct 25	The West Indian		Three and the Deuce
S. Oct 27	All in the Wrong		Hit or Miss!
M. Oct 29	The Clandestine Marriage		Hit or Miss!
T. Oct 30	The Heir at Law		The Devil to Pay
W. Oct 31	**The Mountaineers**		The Midnight Hour
Th. Nov 1	Love in a Village		Hit or Miss!
F. Nov 2	John Bull		No Song, No Supper
W. Nov 14	The Clandestine Marriage		Hit or Miss!
Th. Nov 15	The Hypocrite		The Review
F. Nov 16	John Bull		The Mayor of Garratt
S. Nov 17	The Confederacy		Hit or Miss!
M. Nov 19	A Trip to Scarborough		Hit or Miss!
T. Nov 20	All in the Wrong		Matrimony
W. Nov 21	False Alarms; or, My Cousin	Songs	Ella Rosenberg

Date (*Notes*)	Mainpiece	Interlude	Afterpiece
Th. Nov 22 **1810**	The Clandestine Marriage		The Irishman in London
F. Nov 23	The Hypocrite		Hit or Miss!
S. Nov 24	Up All Night; or, The Smuggler's Cave		**Two Strings to Your Bow**
M. Nov 26	The Country Girl		Hit or Miss!
T. Nov 27	The Confederacy		The Review
W. Nov 28	The Cabinet		**Two Strings to Your Bow**
Th. Nov 29	All in the Wrong		The Mayor of Garratt
F. Nov 30	The Country Girl		Transformation; or, Love and Law
S. Dec 1	The Hypocrite		Transformation
M. Dec 3	The Merry Wives of Windsor		Transformation
T. Dec 4	**The Duenna** (*Mr Philipps, in the character of Carlos, will introduce a new cavatina, called 'Love's Holiday'*)		Transformation
W. Dec 5	Deaf and Dumb		Transformation
Th. Dec 6	The Clandestine Marriage		Transformation
F. Dec 7	The Rivals		Transformation
S. Dec 8	The Hypocrite		Transformation
M. Dec 10	Riches! Or, the Wife and Brother		Transformation
T. Dec 11	The Way to Keep Him		Hit or Miss!
Th. Dec 13	Deaf and Dumb		Transformation
F. Dec 14	The Confederacy		Transformation
S. Dec 15	Hypocrite		Hit or Miss!
M. Dec 17	Man and Wife		Transformation
T. Dec 18	John Bull		Hit or Miss!
W. Dec 19	The Castle Spectre		Transformation
Th. Dec 20	The School for Scandal		Hit or Miss!
F. Dec 21	Up All Night		The Honest Thieves
S. Dec 22	The Hypocrite		Hit or Miss!
W. Dec 26	George Barnwell		The Magic Bride
Th. Dec 27	False Alarms	'Favourite duet by Mr Philipps and Mrs Mountain'	The Magic Bride
F. Dec 28	**The Honey Moon** (*with a dance incidental to the piece*)		The Magic Bride
S. Dec 29	The Hypocrite		The Magic Bride
M. Dec 31	John Bull		The Magic Bride
T. Jan 1 **1811**	The Clandestine Marriage		The Magic Bride
W. Jan 2 *Never Performed Before*	Lost and Found		The Magic Bride

Date (*Notes*)	Mainpiece	Interlude	Afterpiece
Th. Jan 3 **1811**	Lost and Found		The Magic Bride
F. Jan 4	Lost and Found		The Magic Bride
S. Jan 5	Lost and Found		The Magic Bride
M. Jan 7	Lost and Found		Hit or Miss!
T. Jan 8	Lost and Found		The Magic Bride
W. Jan 9	Lost and Found		Transformation
Th. Jan 10	Lost and Found		The Magic Bride
F. Jan 11	Lost and Found		The Review
S. Jan 12	The Hypocrite		Hit or Miss!
M. Jan 14	Lost and Found		The Honest Thieves
T. Jan 15	The School for Scandal		The Mayor of Garratt
W. Jan 16	The Merry Wives of Windsor		Three and the Deuce
Th. Jan 17	**The Honey Moon**		Hit or Miss!
F. Jan 18	The Hypocrite		Raising the Wind
S. Jan 19	The Stranger		The Bee Hive
M. Jan 21	Lost and Found		The Bee Hive
T. Jan 22	The Country Girl		The Bee Hive
W. Jan 23	Man and Wife		The Bee Hive
Th. Jan 24	The Rivals		The Bee Hive
F. Jan 25	The Hypocrite		The Bee Hive
S. Jan 26	The Clandestine Marriage		The Bee Hive
M. Jan 28	John Bull		The Bee Hive
T. Jan 29	**The Honey Moon**		The Bee Hive
Th. Jan 31 *Never Performed Before*	The Peasant Boy		The Mayor of Garratt
F. Feb 1	The Peasant Boy		Hit or Miss!
S. Feb 2	The Peasant Boy		The Honest Thieves
M. Feb 4	The Peasant Boy		The Bee Hive
T. Feb 5	The Peasant Boy		The Bee Hive
W. Feb 6	The Peasant Boy		The Bee Hive
Th. Feb 7	The Peasant Boy		The Bee Hive
F. Feb 8	The Peasant Boy		The Bee Hive
S. Feb 9	The Peasant Boy		The Bee Hive
M. Feb 11	The Peasant Boy		The Bee Hive
T. Feb 12	The Peasant Boy		The Bee Hive
W. Feb 13	John Bull		The Bee Hive
Th. Feb 14	The Peasant Boy		Hit or Miss!
F. Feb 15	The Hypocrite		The Bee Hive
S. Feb 16	The Peasant Boy		The Bee Hive
M. Feb 18	The Peasant Boy		The Bee Hive
T. Feb 19	The School for Friends		The Bee Hive
W. Feb 20	The Peasant Boy		Hit or Miss!
Th. Feb 21	The Clandestine Marriage		The Bee Hive
F. Feb 22	The Peasant Boy		The Bee Hive
S. Feb 23	The Hypocrite		Hit or Miss!
M. Feb 25	The Peasant Boy		The Bee Hive
T. Feb 26	The Peasant Boy		Hit or Miss!
Th. Feb 28	The Peasant Boy		Mayor of Garratt

Date (*Notes*)	Mainpiece	Interlude	Afterpiece
S. Mar 2 **1811** *Never Performed Before*	Ourselves		No Song, No Supper
M. Mar 4	Ourselves		The Bee Hive
T. Mar 5	Ourselves		Hit or Miss!
Th. Mar 7	Ourselves		The Bee Hive
S. Mar 9	Ourselves		The Bee Hive
M. Mar 11	Ourselves		The Bee Hive
T. Mar 12	Ourselves		Hit or Miss!
Th. Mar 14	Ourselves		The Bee Hive
F. Mar 15	Ourselves		The Bee Hive
M. Mar 18	Ourselves		The Bee Hive
T. Mar 19 *First Night of Mr Braham's Engagement*	The Haunted Tower ('*in the course of the opera, the favourite song "***The Sprightly Castanets"***, by Mrs Mountain, accompanied to the castanets, by herself'*)		The Mayor of Garratt
Th. Mar 21	Ourselves		The Bee Hive
S. Mar 23	False Alarms	Songs	Raising the Wind
M. Mar 25	Ourselves		The Bee Hive
T. Mar 26	The Cabinet		Three and the Deuce
Th. Mar 28	The Peasant Boy		Hit or Miss!
S. Mar 30	The Siege of Belgrade		The Weathercock
M. Apr 1	Ourselves		The Bee Hive
T. Apr 2	The Siege of Belgrade		The Midnight Hour
Th. Apr 4	The Peasant Boy		Hit or Miss!
S. Apr 6	The Cabinet		The Review
M. Apr 15	George Barnwell	Sylvester Daggerwood	The Bee Hive
T. Apr 16	The Peasant Boy		Hit or Miss!
W. Apr 17	**The Castle of Andalusia**	Songs	Three and the Deuce
Th. Apr 18	Ourselves		The Bee Hive
F. Apr 19	**The Castle of Andalusia**		The Honest Thieves
S. Apr 20	The Hypocrite		Hit or Miss!
M. Apr 22	Ourselves		The Bee Hive
T. Apr 23	**The Castle of Andalusia**		Raising the Wind
W. Apr 24	The Peasant Boy		Hit or Miss!
Th. Apr 25	**The Castle of Andalusia**		The Midnight Hour
F. Apr 26	The Rivals		The Bee Hive
S. Apr 27 *Never Performed Before*	The Americans		**Two Strings to Your Bow**
M. Apr 29	Ourselves		The Bee Hive
T. Apr 30	The Americans		The Mayor of Garratt
W. May 1	The Americans		Raising the Wind
Th. May 2	The Americans		The Weathercock
F. May 3	The Americans		Three Weeks after Marriage

Date (*Notes*)	Mainpiece	Interlude	Afterpiece
S. May 4 **1811**	The Americans		The Midnight Hour
M. May 6	The Americans		The Bee Hive
T. May 7	The Americans		Raising the Wind
W. May 8	The Clandestine Marriage		Hit or Miss!
Th. May 9	The Americans		The Bee Hive
F. May 10	**The Honey Moon**		The Honest Thieves
S. May 11	The Americans		Of Age To-morrow
M. May 13	The Americans		Three and the Deuce
T. May 14	The Americans		Hit or Miss!
W. May 15	The Hypocrite		The Review
Th. May 16	The Americans		The Bee Hive
F. May 17	The Country Girl		No Song, No Supper
S. May 18 *Last night of Mr Braham's Engagement*	The Americans		Hit or Miss!
M. May 20	Where to Find a Friend		The Mayor of Garratt
T. May 21	The Confederacy		The Bee Hive
W. May 22 *Never Acted Before at this Theatre. For the Benefit of Mrs Mountain*	Inkle and Yarico	Songs (*including 'The Death of Abercrombie'*)	The Agreeable Surprise
Th. May 23 *Mr Braham's Night and Last Performance this Season*	**The Castle of Andalusia**	Songs	The Midnight Hour
F. May 24 *Mr Bishop's Benefit*	**The Duenna**	A Grand Musical Pasticcio	Hit or Miss!
S. May 25	The Hypocrite		The Bee Hive
M. May 27	The West Indian Songs	The Horse and the Widow	Hit or Miss!
T. May 28 *For the Benefit of Mrs Powell*	The Peasant Boy	Sylvester Daggerwood 'A MONODY will be spoken by Mrs Powell, dressed as a British Officer'	The Honest Thieves
W. May 29	The School for Scandal		The Bee Hive
Th. May 30	**The Honey Moon**		The Irishman in London
F. May 31 *For the Benefit of Mr Raymond (with the assistance of Mr Braham and Mr Incledon)*	The Cabinet	Description of 'A Storm' by Mr Incledon The Morning Post and Morning Herald	Twenty Years Ago
M. Jun 3 *For the Benefit of Mr Mathews*	Inkle and Yarico	Songs	**The Critic; or, A Tragedy Rehearsed**
T. Jun 4 *For the Benefit of Mr Dignum*	The Clandestine Marriage	Songs	Hit or Miss!

Date (*Notes*)	Mainpiece	Interlude	Afterpiece
W. Jun 5 **1811** *For the Benefit of Mr Melvin*	The Suspicious Husband	Blue Devils	The Review
Th. Jun 6 *For the Benefit of Mr Smith and Miss Kelly*	Plots! Or, the North Tower (*by permission of the proprietors of the English Opera*)	Songs Description of 'A Storm'	Modern Antiques; or, The Merry Mourners
F. Jun 7 *For the Benefit of Mr Palmer*	The Jealous Wife	Songs	Hit or Miss!
S. Jun 8 *For the Benefit of Mr and Mrs Horn*	**The Castle of Andalusia**	Songs	The Bee Hive
M. Jun 10 *For the Benefit or Mr Spring, Box, Book and House-Keeper*	Inkle and Yarico	Songs The Horse and the Widow	**The Critic**
T. Jun 11	The Soldier's Daughter		The Bee Hive
W. Jun 12	The Way to Keep Him	Poor Vulcan (*by particular desire, Act 1*)	Hit or Miss!
Th. Jun 13	**The Castle of Andalusia**	'Richard and Betty at Hickleton Fair' ('*a Yorkshire Tale founded on Facts*') Songs and dancing Description of 'A Storm'	The Review
F. Jun 14	The Rivals		The Weathercock
S. Jun 15	Man and Wife		**Two Strings to Your Bow**
M. Jun 17	**The Duenna**		The Midnight Hour
T. Jun 18 *Last Night*	The Clandestine Marriage		Of Age To-morrow

Calendar of Drury Lane Playbills 1811–1812

Date (*Notes*)	Mainpiece	Interlude	Afterpiece
M. Sep 23 **1811** **Theatre Royal, Lyceum**	The Clandestine Marriage		The Irishman in London
T. Sep 24	John Bull; or, An Englishman's Fireside		The Mayor of Garratt
W. Sep 25	The Cabinet		Honest Thieves
Th. Sep 26	**Much Ado About Nothing**		Of Age To-morrow
F. Sep 27	As You Like It		Matrimony
S. Sep 28	The Confederacy		The Weathercock
M. Sep 30	M.P. or, The Bluestocking!		The Mayor of Garratt
T. Oct 1	M.P. or, The Bluestocking!		The Honest Thieves
W. Oct 2	M.P. or, The Bluestocking!		The Midnight Hour
Th. Oct 3	The Inconstant; or, The Way to Win Him		The Review; or, The Wags of Windsor
F. Oct 4	M.P. or, The Bluestocking!		The Weathercock
S. Oct 5	M.P. or, The Bluestocking!		The Bee Hive
M. Oct 7	M.P. or, The Bluestocking!		The Bee Hive
T. Oct 8	M.P. or, The Bluestocking!		The Review; or, The Wags of Windsor
W. Oct 9	M.P. or, The Bluestocking!		The Bee Hive
Th. Oct 10	Man and Wife; or, More Secrets than One		The Midnight Hour
F. Oct 11	John Bull		Of Age To-morrow
S. Oct 12	**The Honey Moon**		The Honest Thieves
M. Oct 14	The Country Girl		The Green-Eyed Monster; or, How to get your money!
T. Oct 15	M.P. or, The Bluestocking!		The Green-Eyed Monster
W. Oct 16	The Confederacy		The Green-Eyed Monster
Th. Oct 17	M.P. or, The Bluestocking!		The Green-Eyed Monster
F. Oct 18	The Way to Get Married		The Green-Eyed Monster
S. Oct 19	M.P. or, The Bluestocking!		The Green-Eyed Monster
M. Oct 21	The Way to Get Married		Raising the Wind
T. Oct 22	**The Duenna**		The Bee Hive
W. Oct 23	M.P. or, The Bluestocking!		**Don Juan; or, The Libertine Destroyed**

Date (*Notes*)	Mainpiece	Interlude	Afterpiece
Th. Oct 24 **1811**	A Trip to Scarborough		**Don Juan**
F. Oct 25	The Beggar's Opera		**Don Juan**
S. Oct 26	The Beaux Stratagem		**Don Juan**
M. Oct 28	The Clandestine Marriage		**Don Juan**
T. Oct 29	M.P. or, The Bluestocking!		Raising the Wind
W. Oct 30	The Jealous Wife		**Don Juan**
Th. Oct 31	**The Kiss!**		**Don Juan**
F. Nov 1	**The Kiss!**		The Green-Eyed Monster
S. Nov 2	**The Kiss!**		**Don Juan**
M. Nov 4	**The Kiss!**		**Don Juan**
T. Nov 5	**The Kiss!**		Raising the Wind
W. Nov 6	**The Kiss!**		**Don Juan**
Th. Nov 7	**This Kiss!**	Sylvester Daggerwood	The Green-Eyed Monster
F. Nov 8	**The Kiss!**	The Virgin Unmask'd	The Bee Hive
S. Nov 9	George Barnwell	The Green-Eyed Monster (*compressed into 1 Act*)	**Don Juan**
M. Nov 11	**The Kiss!**		Hit or Miss!
T. Nov 12	Up All Night; or, The Smuggler's Cave		Honest Thieves
W. Nov 13	The Hypocrite		Hit or Miss!
Th. Nov 14	Lionel and Clarissa		The Irishman in London
F. Nov 15	**The Kiss!**	Lovers' Quarrels	Hit or Miss!
S. Nov 16	Lionel and Clarissa		Midnight Hour
M. Nov 18	The Hypocrite	The Green-Eyed Monster	**Don Juan; or, The Libertine Destroyed**
T. Nov 19	The Siege of Belgrade		The Mayor of Garratt
W. Nov 20	The West Indian		Rejection; or, Every-Body's Business
Th. Nov 21	Lionel and Clarissa		Rejection
F. Nov 22	Lionel and Clarissa		Hit or Miss!
S. Nov 23	**The Castle of Andalusia**		The Devil to Pay
M. Nov 25	John Bull		The Weathercock
T. Nov 26	The Cabinet		Honest Thieves
W. Nov 27	The Rivals		The Bee Hive
Th. Nov 28	**The Castle of Andalusia**		Modern Antiques
F. Nov 29	Lionel and Clarissa		Midnight Hour
S. Nov 30	The Siege of Belgrade		Who's the Dupe
M. Dec 2	False Alarms; or, My Cousin	Songs	**Don Juan**
T. Dec 3	The Rivals		Love Laughs at Locksmiths
W. Dec 4	The Cabinet		Three Weeks after Marriage
Th. Dec 5	The Hypocrite		The Review
F. Dec 6	Lionel and Clarissa		The Citizen

Date (*Notes*)	Mainpiece	Interlude	Afterpiece
S. Dec 7 **1811**	The Maniac; or, The Swiss Banditti		Who's the Dupe?
M. Dec 9	The Way to Get Married		Hit or Miss!
T. Dec 10	Siege of Belgrade		Ways and Means
W. Dec 11	The Rivals		Love Laughs at Locksmiths
Th. Dec12	The Maniac		High Life Below Stairs
F. Dec 13	Lionel and Clarissa		The Irishman in London
S. Dec 14	**The Castle of Andalusia**		Honest Thieves
M. Dec 16	All in the Wrong		The Bee Hive
T. Dec 17	The Americans	Songs	Modern Antiques
		An Harmonic Meeting by some votaries of Apollo	
W. Dec 18	The Heir at Law		The Poor Soldier
Th. Dec 19	The Maniac		Ways and Means
F. Dec 20	Lionel and Clarissa		High Life Below Stairs
S. Dec 21 *Last night of Mr Braham's Engagement*	The Americans		The Citizen
M. Dec 23	The Stranger		The White Cat; or, Harlequin in Fairy Wood (*scenes include a 'splendid subaqueous transluscent temple'*)
Th. Dec 26	George Barnwell		The White Cat
F. Dec 27	Lionel and Clarissa		The White Cat
S. Dec 28	The Jew		The White Cat
M. Dec 30	The Inconstant		The White Cat
T. Dec 31	Up All Night		The White Cat
W. Jan 1 **1812**	John Bull		The White Cat
Th. Jan 2 *Never Performed Before*	Right and Wrong		The White Cat
F. Jan 3	Right and Wrong		The White Cat
S. Jan 4	Right and Wrong		The White Cat
M. Jan 6	Right and Wrong	Sylvester Daggerwood	The White Cat
T. Jan 7	Right and Wrong	Lovers' Quarrels	The White Cat
W. Jan 8	Right and Wrong	The Green-Eyed Monster	The White Cat
Th. Jan 9	Lionel and Clarissa		The White Cat
F. Jan 10	The Rivals		The White Cat
S. Jan 11	The Peasant Boy		The White Cat
M. Jan 13	**She Wou'd and She Wou'd Not**		The White Cat
T. Jan 14	Up All Night		The White Cat
W. Jan 15	The Castle Spectre		The White Cat
Th. Jan 16	The Peasant Boy		The White Cat

Date (*Notes*)	Mainpiece	Interlude	Afterpiece
F. Jan 17 **1812**	**She Wou'd and She Wou'd Not**		The White Cat
S. Jun 18	The Cabinet		The White Cat
M. Jan 20	Man and Wife		The White Cat
T. Jan 21	M.P. or, The Bluestocking!		The White Cat
W. Jan 22	**She Wou'd and She Wou'd Not**		The White Cat
Th. Jan 23	The Peasant Boy		The White Cat
F. Jan 24	The Dramatist	The Purse; or, The Benevolent Tar	The White Cat
S. Jan 25	M.P. or, The Bluestocking!		The White Cat
M. Jan 27	**She Wou'd and She Wou'd Not**		The White Cat
T. Jan 28	Lionel and Clarissa		The White Cat
W. Jan 29	**She Wou'd and She Wou'd Not**		The White Cat
F. Jan 31	M.P. or, The Bluestocking!		The White Cat
S. Feb 1	**She Wou'd and She Wou'd Not**		The White Cat
M. Feb 3	The Peasant Boy		The White Cat
T. Feb 4	M.P. or, The Bluestocking!		The White Cat
Th. Feb 6	**She Wou'd and She Wou'd Not**		The White Cat
F. Feb 7	The Maid of the Mill		The White Cat
S. Feb 8	Lionel and Clarissa		The White Cat
M. Feb 10	**She Wou'd and She Wou'd Not**		Hit or Miss!
T. Feb 11	The Maid of the Mill		The White Cat
Th. Feb 13	The Clandestine Marriage		The Bee Hive
S. Feb 15	The Maid of the Mill		The White Cat
M. Feb 17	The Peasant Boy		The White Cat
T. Feb 18	**She Wou'd and She Wou'd Not**		The Review
Th. Feb 20	M.P. or, The Bluestocking!		The White Cat
S. Feb 22	Maid of the Mill		The Honest Thieves
M. Feb 24	The Rivals		The White Cat
T. Feb 25	M.P. or, The Bluestocking!		Hit or Miss!
Th. Feb 27 *First night of the new drama*	The House of Morville		Raising the Wind
S. Feb 29	The House of Morville		The White Cat
M. Mar 2	The House of Morville		The White Cat
T. Mar 3	The House of Morville		The White Cat
Th. Mar 5	The House of Morville		The White Cat

Date (*Notes*)	Mainpiece	Interlude	Afterpiece
S. Mar 7 **1812** *First time of the new* *farce*	The House of Morville		Turn Out!
M. Mar 9	The House of Morville		Turn Out!
T. Mar 10	The House of Morville		Turn Out!
Th. Mar 12	The Hypocrite		Turn Out!
S. Mar 14	The West Indian		Turn Out!
M. Mar 16	The House of Morville		Turn Out!
T. Mar 17	The Rivals		Turn Out!
Th. Mar 19	The Hypocrite		Turn Out!
S. Mar 21	**The Honey Moon**		Turn Out!
M. Mar 30	The House of Morville		The White Cat
T. Mar 31	Maid of the Mill		The White Cat
W. Apr 1	**She Wou'd and She Wou'd Not**		The White Cat
Th. Apr 2	Man and Wife		Turn Out!
F. Apr 3	The Clandestine Marriage		Turn Out!
S. Apr 4	Lionel and Clarissa		Turn Out!
M. Apr 6	**The Honey Moon**		Turn Out!
T. Apr 7	**The Castle of Andalusia**		Turn Out!
W. Apr 8	The Hypocrite		Turn Out!
Th. Apr 9	The Jealous Wife		Turn Out!
F. Apr 10	The Maid of the Mill		Quadrupeds; or, The Manager's Last Kick (*for the first time by this company and with permission of the proprietors of the English Opera*)
S. Apr 11 *Never Performed* *Before*	Prejudice; or, Modern Sentiment		The Bee Hive
M. Apr 13	Sons of Erin; or, Modern Sentiment		Quadrupeds
T. Apr 14	Sons of Erin		Turn Out!
W. Apr 15	Sons of Erin		Quadrupeds
Th. Apr 16	Sons of Erin		Turn Out!
F. Apr 17	Sons of Erin		Quadrupeds
S. Apr 18	Sons of Erin		Turn Out!
M. Apr 20	Sons of Erin		Quadrupeds
T. Apr 21	Sons of Erin		Turn Out!
W. Apr 22	Sons of Erin		Quadrupeds
Th. Apr 23	Sons of Erin		Turn Out!
F. Apr 24	Sons of Erin		The Castle of Sorrento
S. Apr 25	Sons of Erin		Turn Out!
M. Apr 27	King Henry the Fourth (Part One)		Three and the Deuce
T. Apr 28	Sons of Erin		Quadrupeds; or, The Manager's Last Kick

Date (*Notes*)	Mainpiece	Interlude	Afterpiece
W. Apr 29 **1812**	The Country Girl	Songs	Matrimony
For the Benefit of			
Miss Duncan			
Th. Apr 30	Sons of Erin		Turn Out!
F. May 1	Sons of Erin		Love Laughs at
			Locksmiths
S. May 2	Sons of Erin		Quadrupeds
M. May 4	The Rivals	Songs	False and True; or, The
For the Benefit of Mr	(*by particular desire*)		Irishman in Italy
Johnstone			
T. May 5	Sons of Erin		Quadrupeds
W. May 6	The Devil's Bridge		Raising the Wind
Never Performed			
Before			
Th. May 7	The Devil's Bridge		Turn Out!
F. May 8	The Devil's Bridge		The Midnight Hour
S. May 9	Lionel and Clarissa	Songs (*by Mr Braham*)	The Irishman in London
For the Benefit of			
Mrs Dickons			
M. May 11	The Devil's Bridge		The Honest Thieves
T. May 12	The Devil's Bridge		High Life Below Stairs
W. May 13	The Devil's Bridge		Turn Out!
Th. May 14	The Devil's Bridge		The Mayor of Garratt
F. May 15	The Devil's Bridge		Hit or Miss!
Last nigt of			
performing until the			
holidays			
M. May 18	Sons or Erin		Turn Out!
T. May 19	The Americans	Songs (*by Mr Braham*)	**The Critic; or, A**
For the Benefit of Mr			**Tragedy Rehearsed**
De Camp		Favourite 'pas deux'	
		from The Forty Thieves	
W. May 20	The Devil's Bridge		The Review
Th. May 21	The Wife of Two		How to Die for Love!
For the Benefit of	Husbands		(*first time*)
Miss Kelly			
F. May 22	The Cabinet		How to Die for Love!
S. May 23	The Devil's Bridge		How to Die for Love!
M. May 25	Sons of Erin	Songs	How to Die for Love!
For the Benefit of Mr			
Raymond			
T. May 26	The Wife of Two		How to Die for Love!
	Husbands		
W. May 27	**The Castle of**		How to Die for Love!
	Andalusia		
Th. May 28	Sons of Erin		How to Die for Love!
F. May 29	Sons of Erin		How to Die for Love!
S. May 30	The Devil's Bridge		How to Die for Love!
M. Jun 1	The Devil's Bridge		How to Die For Love!

Date (*Notes*)	Mainpiece	Interlude	Afterpiece
T. Jun 2 **1812** *For the Benefit of Mr Palmer*	**The Duenna**	'Mr Palmer will deliver a selection of his celebrated Portraits from the living and the dead' Songs	The Honest Thieves
W. Jun 3	The Devil's Bridge		How to Die for Love!
Th. Jun 4 *For the Benefit of Mr Dignum*	The Maid of the Mill	Songs (*by Mr Dignum*)	**The Critic**
F. Jun 5	**She Wou'd and She Wou'd Not**		Hit or Miss!
S. Jun 6 *Last night of Mr Braham's Engagement*	The Devil's Bridge		How to Die for Love!
M. Jun 8 *Mr Braham's Night and last appearance this season*	The Maniac	Songs An Harmonic Meeting by some votaries of Apollo	How to Die for Love!
T. Jun 9	Sons of Erin		How to Die for Love!
W. Jun 10 *For the Benefit of Mr Spring, Box, Book and House-Keeper*	**The Honey Moon** (*with a dance incidental to the piece*)	Songs Blue Devils	Turn Out!
Th. Jun 11	Sons of Erin	The Virgin Unmask'd	Turn Out!
F. Jun 12	Sons of Erin	'A pas seul', by Miss Bristow Songs	How to Die for Live!
S. Jun 13	Sons of Erin		How to Die for Love!
M. Jun 15	Sons of Erin	Blue Devils	How to Die for Love!
T. Jun 16	The Rivals		How to Die for Love!
W. Jun 17	The Hypocrite	Songs	How to Die for Love!
Th. Jun 18 *Last Night*	John Bull	Sylvester Daggerwood Songs (*including 'God Save the King'*)	How to Die for Love!
For the Benefit of the British Prisoners in France			

Calendar of Drury Lane Playbills 1812–1813

Date (*Notes*)	Mainpiece	Interlude	Afterpiece
S. Oct 10 **1812** **Opening of Theatre Royal, Drury Lane, with an Occasional Address by Mr Elliston**	Hamlet, Prince of Denmark		The Devil to Pay; or, The Wives Metamorphosed
M. Oct 12	Occasional Address by Elliston		The Irishman in London
T. Oct 13	**The Duenna** Occasional Address		The Review; or, The Wags of Windsor
W. Oct 14	**Much Ado About Nothing** Occasional Address		The Bee Hive
Th. Oct 15	The Hypocrite Occasional Address		Turn Out!
F. Oct 16	The Rivals Occasional Address		The Midnight Hour
S. Oct 17	Lionel and Clarissa Occasional Address		No Song, No Supper
M. Oct 19	Hamlet, Prince of Denmark Occasional Address		Of Age To-Morrow
T. Oct 20	As You Like It Occasional Address		Turn Out!
W. Oct 21	All in the Wrong Up All Night; or, The Smuggler's Cave		How to Die for Love!
Th. Oct 22	**The Wonder; A Woman Keeps a Secret**		The Weathercock
F. Oct 23	The Merry Wives of Windsor		High Life Below Stairs
S. Oct 24	**The Honey Moon**		The Poor Soldier
M. Oct 26	The Maid of the Mill		The Irishman in London
T. Oct 27	**Much Ado About Nothing**		Three and the Deuce
W. Oct 28	Sons of Erin; or, Modern Sentiment		The Prize; or, 2, 5, 3, 8
Th. Oct 29	The Beaux Stratagem		Turn Out!
F. Oct 30	**The Castle of Andalusia**		How to Die for Love!
S. Oct 31	The Rivals		Of Age To-morrow
M. Nov 2	As You Like It		The Review; or, The Wags of Windsor
T. Nov 3	**The Honey Moon**		Three and the Deuce
W. Nov 4	Lionel and Clarissa		Who's the Dupe?

Date (*Notes*)	Mainpiece	Interlude	Afterpiece
Th. Nov 5 **1812**	All in the Wrong		The Weathercock
F. Nov 6	**She Wou'd and She Wou'd Not**		No Song, No Supper
S. Nov 7	King Henry the Fourth (Part One)		Matrimony
M. Nov 9	**The Castle of Andalusia**		The Citizen
T. Nov 10	The Beaux Stratagem		How to Die for Love!
W. Nov 11	The Maid of the Mill		**The Pannel**
Th. Nov 12	**The Honey Moon**		Turn Out!
F. Nov 13	The Inconstant; or, The Way to Win Him		The Bee Hive
S. Nov 14	Hamlet		Hit or Miss!
M. Nov 16	King Henry the Fourth (Part One)		**The Pannel**
T. Nov 17	**Rule a Wife and Have a Wife**		Matrimony
W. Nov 18	Hamlet		The Prize
Th. Nov 19	Lionel and Clarissa		The Mock Doctor
F. Nov 20	Sons of Erin		My Grandmother
S. Nov 21	**The Honey Moon**		Netley Abbey
M. Nov 23	The Confederacy		Raising the Wind
T. Nov 24	The Inconstant		Hit or Miss!
W. Nov 25	Hamlet		The Mayor of Garratt
Th. Nov 26	The West Indian		The Quaker
F. Nov 27	Up All Night		The Honest Thieves
S. Nov 28	The Provoked Husband; or, A Journey to London		Netley Abbey
M. Nov 30	**The Honey Moon**		Three and the Deuce

'The original explanatory address by Mr Elliston' |
T. Dec 1	**Isabella; or, The Fatal Marriage**		Raising the Wind
W. Dec 2	The Rivals		The Quaker
Th. Dec 3	The West Indian (*with 'The Sprig of Shelelagh and Shamrock So Green' introduced by Mr Johnstone, in the character of Major O'Flaherty*)		Turn Out!
F. Dec 4	The Hypocrite		How to Die for Love!
S. Dec 5	**Isabella**		The Review
M. Dec 7	The Provoked Husband		High Life Below Stairs
T. Dec 8	Douglas		Matrimony
W. Dec 9	**Rule a Wife and Have a Wife**		My Grandmother
Th. Dec 10	The Clandestine Marriage		The Irishman in London
F. Dec 11	The Suspicious Husband		Three and the Deuce

Date (*Notes*)	Mainpiece	Interlude	Afterpiece
S. Dec 12 **1812**	Isabella		**The Assignation; or, Right at Last**
M. Dec 14	The Jealous Wife		The Mayor of Garratt
T. Dec 15	Douglas		The Irishman in London
W. Dec 16	**The Honey Moon**		Turn Out!
Th. Dec 17	**The Castle of Andalusia** (with new songs)		How to Die for Love!
F. Dec 18	All in the Wrong		The Review
S. Dec 19	Romeo and Juliet		The Quaker
M. Dec 21	**The Castle of Andalusia**		The Honest Thieves
T. Dec 22	Isabella		Hit or Miss!
W. Dec 23	The Cabinet		The Midnight Hour
S. Dec 26	George Barnwell		**Harlequin and Humpo; or, Columbine by Candlelight**
M. Dec 28	Man and Wife; or, More Secrets than One		**Harlequin and Humpo**
T. Dec 29	Romeo and Juliet		**Harlequin and Humpo**
W. Dec 30	John Bull; or, An Englishman's Fireside		**Harlequin and Humpo**
Th. Dec 31	Douglas		**Harlequin and Humpo**
F. Jan 1 **1813**	The Rivals		**Harlequin and Humpo**
S. Jan 2	Romeo and Juliet		**Harlequin and Humpo**
M. Jan 4	**The Castle of Andalusia**		**Harlequin and Humpo**
T. Jan 5	**The Honey Moon**		**Harlequin and Humpo**
W. Jan 6	The Twelfth Night; or, What You Will		**Harlequin and Humpo**
Th. Jan 7	King Henry the Fourth (Part One)		**Harlequin and Humpo**
F. Jan 8	Jane Shore		**Harlequin and Humpo**
S. Jan 9	False Alarms; or My Cousin (*with additional songs*)		**Harlequin and Humpo**
M. Jan 11	John Bull		**Harlequin and Humpo**
T. Jan 12	**The Castle of Andalusia**		**Harlequin and Humpo**
W. Jan 13	Romeo and Juliet		**Harlequin and Humpo**
Th. Jan 14	False Alarms		**Harlequin and Humpo**
F. Jan 15	Jane Shore		**Harlequin and Humpo**
S. Jan 16	**The Castle of Andalusia**		**Harlequin and Humpo**
M. Jan 18	**The Honey Moon**		**Harlequin and Humpo**
T. Jan 19	The West Indian		**Harlequin and Humpo**
W. Jan 20	John Bull		**Harlequin and Humpo**
Th. Jan 21	Sons of Erin		**Harlequin and Humpo**
F. Jan 22	Lionel and Clarissa		**Harlequin and Humpo**
S. Jan 23	**Remorse**		Raising the Wind
Never Acted Before			
M. Jan 25	**Remorse**		**Harlequin and Humpo**

Date (*Notes*)	Mainpiece	Interlude	Afterpiece
T. Jan 26 **1813**	**Remorse**		**Harlequin and Humpo**
W. Jan 27	**Remorse**		**Harlequin and Humpo**
Th. Jan 28	**Remorse**		**Harlequin and Humpo**
F. Jan 29	**Remorse**		**Harlequin and Humpo**
S. Jan 30	Sacred Oratorio – The Messiah ('*for which occasion, a new and splendid Gothick Orchestra*')		
M. Feb 1	**Remorse**		**Harlequin and Humpo**
T. Feb 2	**Remorse**		**Harlequin and Humpo**
W. Feb 3	**Remorse**		**Harlequin and Humpo**
Th. Feb 4	**Remorse**		**Harlequin and Humpo**
F. Feb 5	**Remorse**		**Harlequin and Humpo**
S. Feb 6	**She Wou'd and She Wou'd Not**		**Harlequin and Humpo**
M. Feb 8	**Remorse**		**Harlequin and Humpo**
T. Feb 9	**The Castle of Andalusia**		**Harlequin and Humpo**
W. Feb 10	**Remorse**		The Absent Apothecary
Th. Feb 11	The Clandestine Marriage		The Absent Apothecary
F. Feb 12	**Remorse**		Hit or Miss!
S. Feb 13	False Alarms (*In Act 3 – The last words of Marmion, as written by Walter Scott*)		How to Die for Love!
M. Feb 15	**Remorse**		**Harlequin and Humpo**
T. Feb 16	**The Castle of Andalusia**		The Irishman in London
W. Feb 17	Jane Shore		The Review
Th. Feb 18	The Way to Keep Him		The Quaker
F. Feb 19	**Remorse**		**Harlequin and Humpo**
S. Feb 20	The Devil's Bridge		The Honest Thieves
M. Feb 22	**The Honey Moon**		**Harlequin and Humpo**
T. Feb 23	The Devil's Bridge		The Mayor of Garratt
W. Feb 24	**Remorse**		**Harlequin and Humpo**
Th. Feb 25	The Devil's Bridge		The Birth-Day
F. Feb 26	**Remorse**		**Harlequin and Humpo**
S. Feb 27	The Devil's Bridge		Turn Out!
M. Mar 1	Love for Love		**Harlequin and Humpo**
T. Mar 2	Romeo and Juliet		The Irishman in London
Th. Mar 4	The Devil's Bridge		**Harlequin and Humpo**
F. Mar 5	Sacred Oratorio – The Messiah (*with 'Gothick Orchestra*')		
S. Mar 6	The Devil's Bridge		Ways and Means; or, A Trip to Dover
M. Mar 8	The School for Scandal		The Review
T. Mar 9	John Bull		The Birth-Day (*by particular desire*)
W. Mar 10	The Rivals		Three and the Deuce

Date (*Notes*)	Mainpiece	Interlude	Afterpiece
F. Mar 12 **1813**	Sacred Oratorio – Redemption, 'being a grand selection from the favourite works of Handel, as performed at his commemoration in Westminster Abbey' (*with 'Gothick Orchestra'*)		
S. Mar 13	Robin Hood; or, Sherwood Forest		Ways and Means
M. Mar 15	The School for Scandal		**Harlequin and Humpo**
T. Mar 16	Robin Hood		The Irishman in London
W. Mar 17	Sacred Oratorio – The Creation, 'interspersed with select and appropriate readings' (*with 'Gothick Orchestra'*)		
Th. Mar 18	The Devil's Bridge		The Children in the Wood (*first time at this theatre, by permission of the proprietors of the Theatre Royal, Haymarket*)
F. Mar 19	Sacred Oratorio – The Creation		
	Readings from Milton's Paradise Lost by Miss Smith		
S. Mar 20	The Gamester		The Prize
M. Mar 22	**Remorse**		**Harlequin and Humpo** (*by particular desire*)
T. Mar 23	Robin Hood		Ways and Means
W. Mar 24	Grand Selection from the Works of Handel and Haydn		
	Readings by Miss Smith chiefly from Milton and Dryden		
Th. Apr 1	The Devil's Bridge		The Children in the Wood
F. Apr 2	Grand Selection from Handel, Haydn, and Mozart		
	Readings by Miss Smith		
S. Apr 3	The School for Scandal		The Review
M. Apr 5	The Merry Wives of Windsor		**Harlequin and Humpo**
T. Apr 6	**The Honey Moon**		The Irishman in London

Date (*Notes*)	Mainpiece	Interlude	Afterpiece
W. Apr 7 **1813**	Oratorios – A Grand Selection from the works of Handel, Mozart, and the Most Admired Authors, with appropriate readings by Miss Smith		
Th. Apr 8	Othello, The Moor of Venice		The Children in the Wood
F. Apr 9	Oratorios – of sacred music from the works of Handel, Haydn, Jomelli etc. with readings by Miss Smith		
S. Apr 10 *For the Benefit of Mr Raymond*	The Devil's Bridge	Songs The Celebrated Amateur of Fashion will recite 'Bucks Have at Ye All!'	The Honest Thieves
M. Apr 19	The Beaux Stratagem		Lodoiska
T. Apr 20	The Rivals		Lodoiska
W. Apr 21	Othello		Lodoiska
Th. Apr 22	Recrimination; or, A Curtain Lecture		Lodoiska
F. Apr 23	The Jealous Wife		Lodoiska
S. Apr 24	**She Wou'd and She Wou'd Not**		Lodoiska
M. Apr 26 *For the Benefit of Mr Dowton*	The School for Wives	Reconciliation; or, Hearts of Oak! (*in 1 Act*) Songs	The Mayor of Garratt
T. Apr 27	The Clandestine Marriage		Lodoiska
W. Apr 28	**The Honey Moon**		Lodoiska
Th. Apr 29	The Hypocrite		Lodoiska
F. Apr 30	Hamlet		The Irishman in London
S. May 1	**Rule a Wife and Have a Wife**		Lodoiska
M. May 3 *For the Benefit of Miss Smith*	The Grecian Daughter	Song by Mr Lovegrove Miss Smith will recite Mr Collins's Ode on the Passions (*by particular desire*)	Three Weeks After Marriage
T. May 4	The School for Wives		Lodoiska
W. May 5	The Devil's Bridge		Lodoiska
Th. May 6	The Rivals		Lodoiska
F. May 7	Hamlet		Lodoiska
S. May 8	The Heir at Law		Lodoiska

Date (*Notes*)	Mainpiece	Interlude	Afterpiece
M. May 10 **1813**	**The Wonder**	'Rule Britannia!' by Madame Catalani	Ella Rosenberg
Madame Catalani's First and Only Appearance for the Benefit of Mr Elliston		Blue Devils	
T. May 11	**Remorse**		Lodoiska
W. May 12	The Peasant Boy	Apollo's Festival	The Review
Mr Braham's Night		Songs	
Th. May 13	The Russian	Mayor of Garratt	Lodoiska
Never Acted Before			
F. May 14	The Russian	Turn Out!	Lodoiska
S. May 15	The Russian	Raising the Wind	Lodoiska
M. May 17	The Devil's Bridge	Bannister's Budget	The Children in the
For the Benefit of Mr Bannister		(*with songs, including 'London Newspapers'*)	Wood
T. May 18	The Russian	The Prize	Lodoiska
W. May 19	The Russian	The Bee Hive	Lodoiska
Th. May 20	The Russian	How to Die for Love!	Lodoiska
F. May 21	The Russian	Ways and Means	Lodoiska
S. May 22	The Russian	Turn Out!	Lodoiska
M. May 24	The Russian	The Citizen	Lodoiska
T. May 25	The Devil's Bridge		The Russian
W. May 26	Sons of Erin	Songs	Three and The Deuce
For the Benefit of Mrs Davison		The Purse	
Th. May 27	The Russian	The Mock Doctor	Lodoiska
F. May 28	**The Castle of Andalusia**		The Russian
S. May 29	Venice Preserv'd		The Irishman in London
M. May 31	False Alarms (*with songs by Braham, and last words of* Marmion)	Songs	The Irishman in Italy (*with additional songs, in character, by Mr Johnstone*)
For the Benefit of Mr Johnstone		An Anti-Gallican Planxty call'd 'Beau Napperty' (*by particular desire*)	
T. Jun 1	Overture to Mozart's La Clemenza di Tito	Songs	The Children in the Wood
For the Benefit of Mr Philipps			
	Fontainebleau (*songs interspersed, with a harp performance at the end of Act 2*)		
W. Jun 2	The Haunted Tower		Rosalie et Donzival; ou, L'heureuse Ruse
For the Benefit of Mrs Dickons			
			In the course of the ballet, 'a **Spanish Dance called** *Tripoli*, by Miss Smith'
Th. Jun 3	**The Mountaineers**	Songs (*by Mr Braham*)	Three and the Deuce
For the Benefit of Mr Rae			
F. Jun 4	Douglas		Lodoiska

Date (*Notes*)	Mainpiece	Interlude	Afterpiece
S. Jun 5 **1813**	Grand Selection of Ancient and Modern Music in three parts – with readings by Miss Smith		
M. Jun 7	The Devil's Bridge		The Honest Thieves
T. Jun 8 *For the Benefit of Mrs Mountain*	The Peasant Boy	Songs, including '**The popular Castanet Song accompanied on the Spanish Castanets** and a new Polacca Duet'	Peeping Tom (*by permission of the proprietors of the Theatre Royal, Haymarket*)
		Grand Piano Forte	
		The Blue Devils	
W. Jun 9	Venice Preserv'd		Lodoiska
Th. Jun 10	The Maniac; or, The Swiss Banditti	Songs	The Russian
F. Jun 11 *Never Acted Before*	Lose No Time	Sylvester Daggerwood	Lionel and Clarissa
		Songs	
S. Jun 12 *For the Benefit of Mr Lovegrove*	Overture to Mozart's La Clemenza di Tito	Songs	Overture to Mozert's Zauberflote
		Orchestra music	
	Fontainebleau		Ella Rosenberg
M. Jun 14	Douglas		Lose No Time
T. Dec 15 *For the Benefit of Mr T Dibdin*	The Peasant Boy	Collins's Ode on the Passions, recited by Mr Elliston	The Irishman in Italy
		Songs	
W. Jun 16 *Only night of the Corps de Ballet from the Opera House*	Polly; A Sequel to the Beggar's Opera	Songs	The Children in the Wood (*by permission of the proprietors of the Theatre Royal, Haymarket*)
		Grand Russian Fete	
Th. Jun 17 *For the Benefit of Mr Knight and Mr Pyne*	Inkle and Yarico	Songs	Ella Rosenberg
		Hyde Park in an Uproar, or the Don Cossack in London	
		'London Newspapers' (*sung by Mr Bannister, in character*)	
F. Jun 18	**The Mountaineers**	Songs	Lose No Time
		An Harmonic Meeting	
		'A Variety of Imitations of several performers who have appeared on the London boards, in the Characters of Macbeth, Richard the Third, Old Rapid, and Romeo!!!'	

Date (*Notes*)	Mainpiece	Interlude	Afterpiece
S. Jun 19 **1813**	Romeo and Juliet		The Irishman in London
M. Jun 21	Polly	Songs (*by Mr Braham*)	The Honest Thieves
T. Jun 22	Douglas		**The Pannel**
The Only Night			
of Mrs Siddons's			
appearance at			
this Theatre. For			
the Benefit of the			
Theatrical Fund (for			
the relief of actors			
and actresses, who			
from age or infirmity,			
are no longer able			
to follow their			
professional duties)			
W. Jun 23	Rich and Poor	Killing No Murder	The Hole in the Wall
For the Benefit of		Songs (*by Mr Mathews*	
Miss Kelly		*and Mr Braham*)	
Th. Jun 24	The Maniac		The Hole in the Wall
F. Jun 25	False Alarms	Garrick's 'Ode to	The Hole in the Wall
		Shakespeare' (*by*	
		particular desire)	
S. Jun 26	**The Castle of**	Songs	The Hole in the Wall
For the Benefit of Mr	**Andalusia**		
Spring, Box, Book		Collins's Ode on	
and House-Keeper		the Passions	
		Seeing is Believing	
M. Jun 28	The Rivals	Seeing is Believing	The Hole in the Wall
T. Jun 29	Sons of Erin	Blue Devils	The Hole in the Wall
W. Jun 30	Fontainebleau		Overture to
			Mozart's Zauberflote
			Ella Rosenberg
Th. Jul 1	John Bull	Songs	The Hole in the Wall
		'An entire new	
		Guarrocha by Miss C	
		Bristow'	
F. Jul 2	The Hypocrite	Songs, including	No Song, No Supper
For the Benefit of Mr	(*at the end of Act 4 –*	'The Army and Navy	
Dignum	*ballad of 'The Girl that*	for Ever!'	
	loves a Sailor')	Sylvester Daggerwood	
S. Jul 3	**The Castle**	Songs	The Hole in the Wall
	of Andalusia		
M. Jul 5	The School for Scandal	Blue Devils	The Hole in the Wall
T. Jul 6	The	Songs, including 'The	The Hole in the Wall
Last Night	Clandestine Marriage	Death of Nelson' and	
	(*at the end of the play:*	'The Bay of Biscay'	
For the Benefit of the	*'God Save the King'*		
British Prisoners in	*and chorus*)	'The celebrated Mr	
France		Ries, late from St	
		Petersburg, will perform	
		a Russian Rondo on the	
		Piano Forte'	

Calendar of Drury Lane Playbills 1813–1814

Date (*Notes*)	Mainpiece	Interlude	Afterpiece
S. Sep 11 **1813**	The School for Scandal		The Review; or, The Wags of Windsor
T. Sep 14	The Rivals		The Children in the Wood
Th. Sep 16	**Rule a Wife and Have a Wife**		Of Age To-morrow
S. Sep 18	John Bull; or, An Englishman's Fireside		Three and the Deuce
M. Sep 20	The Jealous Wife		No Song, No Supper
T. Sep 21	**Much Ado About Nothing**		Matrimony
Th. Sep 23	As You Like It		The Weathercock
S. Sep 25	**The Honey Moon**		Lodoiska
M. Sep 27	King Henry the Fourth (Part One)		Honest Thieves
T. Sep 28	The Way to Keep Him		Lodoiska
W. Sep 29	Lionel and Clarissa		The Irishman in London
Th. Sep 30	The Merry Wives of Windsor		The Review
S. Oct 2	**The Honey Moon**		Lodoiska
M. Oct 4	Speed the Plough		The Children in the Wood
T. Oct 5	The Merchant of Venice		Lodoiska
W. Oct 6	A Cure for the Heart-ache		**Two Strings to Your Bow**
Th. Oct 7	King Henry the Fourth (Part One)		Matrimony
F. Oct 8	Speed the Plough		Ella Rosenberg
S. Oct 9	The Merry Wives of Windsor		Three and the Deuce
M. Oct 11	The Merchant of Venice		Children in the Wood
T. Oct 12	Gondolphin, The Lion of the North!		Raising the Wind
W. Oct 13	Gondolphin		Of Age To-morrow
Th. Oct 14	Gondolphin		The Mayor of Garratt
F. Oct 15	**The Honey Moon**		The Irishman in London
S. Oct 16	A Cure for the Heart-ache		**Two Strings to Your Bow**
M. Oct 18	**Remorse**		Three and the Deuce
T. Oct 19	The Way to Get Married		Honest Thieves
W. Oct 20	**The Wonder; A Woman Keeps a Secret**		How to Die for Love!
Th. Oct 21	The School for Authors	Lodoiska	The Hole in the Wall
F. Oct 22	The Heir at Law		The School for Authors
S. Oct 23	The Maid of the Mill		The Mock Doctor
M. Oct 25	A Bold Stroke for a Wife		The School for Authors
T. Oct 26	A Cure for the Heart-ache		**Two Strings to Your Bow**

Date (*Notes*)	Mainpiece	Interlude	Afterpiece
W. Oct 27 **1813**	The Way to Get Married		The Review
Th. Oct 28	**The Duenna**		The Citizen
F. Oct 29	A Bold Stroke for a Wife		Matrimony
S. Oct 30 *Never Acted Before*	First Impressions; or, Traders in the West		The Weathercock
M. Nov 1	First Impressions		Ella Rosenberg
T. Nov 2	First Impressions		The Bee Hive
W. Nov 3	First Impressions		High Life Below Stairs
Th. Nov 4	First Impressions		My Grandmother
F. Nov 5	First Impressions		Modern Antiques; or, The Merry Mourners
S. Nov 6	First Impressions		Turn Out!
M. Nov 8	First Impressions		Three and the Deuce
T. Nov 9	First Impressions		The Review
W. Nov 10	First Impressions		Turnpike Gate
Th. Nov 11	First Impressions		Modern Antiques
F. Nov 12	First Impressions		Turn Out!
S. Nov 13	The Devil's Bridge		**Two Strings to Your Bow**
M. Nov 15	First Impressions		Turnpike Gate
T. Nov 16	**The Castle of Andalusia**		The Honest Thieves
W. Nov 17	First Impressions		Modern Antiques
Th. Nov 18	Romeo and Juliet		Three and the Deuce
F. Nov 19	A Cure for the Heart-ache		The Turnpike Gate
S. Nov 20	The Devil's Bridge		High Life Below Stairs
M. Nov 22	Romeo and Juliet		Who's to Have Her?
T. Nov 23	**The Castle of Andalusia**		Who's To Have Her?
W. Nov 24	The School for Scandal		Who's To Have Her?
Th. Nov 25 *Never Acted Before*	Illusion; or, The Trances of Nourjahad	The School for Authors	Who's To Have Her?
F. Nov 26	Illusion	Who's To Have Her?	The Honest Thieves
S. Nov 27	Illusion	Who's To Have Her?	The Citizen
M. Nov 29	Illusion	Who's to Have Her?	The Mayor of Garratt
T. Nov 30	Illusion	Who's To Have Her?	The Mock Doctor
W. Dec 1	Illusion	Who's the Dupe?	Turn Out!
Th. Dec 2	Illusion	Who's To Have Her?	The Irishman in London
F. Dec 3	Illusion	Sylvester Daggerwood	The Children in the Wood
S. Dec 4	Illusion	Who's to Have Her?	Raising the Wind
M. Dec 6	Illusion		First Impressions
T. Dec 7	Illusion	Who's to Have Her?	Modern Antiques
W. Dec 8	Occasional Address by Mrs Edwin	Illusion	High Life Below Stairs
	Orange Boven; or, More Good News		
Th. Dec 9	Illusion	Who's to Have Her?	The Midnight Hour

Date (*Notes*)	Mainpiece	Interlude	Afterpiece
F. Dec 10 **1813**	An Occasional Address by Mrs Edwin	Illusion	**Two Strings to Your Bow**
	Orange Boven (Dances include **Spanish Dance, 'La Zapatedo** [*sic*]')		
S. Dec 11	Occasional Address	Illusion	The Deuce is in Him
	Orange Boven, with dances		
M. Dec 13	Occasional Address	Illusion	Crotchet Lodge
	Orange Boven, with dances		
T. Dec 14	Occasional Address	Illusion	Who's To Have Her?
	Orange Boven, with dances		
W. Dec 15	Occasional Address	Illusion	The Turnpike Gate
	Orange Boven, with dances		
Th. Dec 16	Occasional Address	Illusion	The Deuce is in Him
	Orange Boven, with dances		
F. Dec 17	Occasional Address	Crotchet Lodge	Illusion
	Orange Boven, with dances		
S. Dec 18	Occasional Address	Fortune's Frolics	Illusion
	Orange Boven, with dances		
M. Dec 20	Man of the World		Illusion
T. Dec 21	Ways and Means	**Orange Boven**, with dances	Illusion
W. Dec 22	The Devil's Bridge		Illusion
Th. Dec 23	Three and the Deuce	**Orange Boven**, with dances	Illusion
M. Dec 27	George Barnwell		Harlequin Harper; or, A Jump from Japan!
T. Dec 28	A Bold Stroke for A Wife		Harlequin Harper
W. Dec 29	The Merchant of Venice		Harlequin Harper
Th. Dec 30	She Stoops to Conquer; or, The Mistakes of a Night		Harlequin Harper
F. Dec 31	Romeo and Juliet		Harlequin Harper
S. Jan 1 **1814**	A Cure for the Heart-ache		Harlequin Harper
M. Jan 3	Othello, The Moor of Venice		Harlequin Harper
T. Jan 4	**Orange Boven**, with dances	The Children in the Wood	Harlequin Harper
W. Jan 5	Venice Preserv'd		Harlequin Harper

Date (*Notes*)	Mainpiece	Interlude	Afterpiece
Th. Jan 6 **1814**	Ways and Means	**Orange Boven**, with dances	Harlequin Harper
F. Jan 7	**The Honey Moon**		Harlequin Harper
S. Jan 8	The Devil's Bridge		Harlequin Harper
M. Jan 10	John Bull		Harlequin Harper
T. Jan 11 *Never Acted Before*	Narensky; or, The Road to Yaroslaf		Harlequin Harper
W. Jan 12	Narensky		Harlequin Harper
Th. Jan 13	Narensky		Harlequin Harper
F. Jan 14	Narensky		Harlequin Harper
S. Jan 15	Narensky		Harlequin Harper
M. Jan 17	Narensky		Harlequin Harper
T. Jan 18	Narensky		Harlequin Harper
W. Jan 19	Narensky		Harlequin Harper
Th. Jan 20	Speed the Plough		Harlequin Harper
F. Jan 21	Narensky		Harlequin Harper
S. Jan 22	The Heir at Law		Harlequin Harper
M. Jan 24	Othello		Harlequin Harper
T. Jan 25	**The Castle of Andalusia**		Honest Thieves
W. Jan 26 *Kean's first appearance at this theatre*	The Merchant of Venice		The Apprentice
Th. Jan 27	Narensky		Illusion
F. Jan 28	**She Wou'd and She Wou'd Not**		Harlequin Harper
S. Jan 29	The Devil's Bridge		Illusion
M. Jan 31	Wild Oats		Harlequin Harper
T. Feb 1	The Merchant of Venice		Illusion
W. Feb 2	**The Castle of Andalusia**		The Apprentice
Th. Feb 3	The Merchant of Venice		The Irishman in London
F. Feb 4	Wild Oats		The Children in the Wood
S. Feb 5 *New Farce*	The Merchant of Venice		Rogues All; or, Three Generations
M. Feb 7	The Devil's Bridge		Illusion
T. Feb 8	The Merchant of Venice		Harlequin Harper
W. Feb 9	Wild Oats		The Turnpike Gate
Th. Feb 10	The Merchant of Venice		The Apprentice
F. Feb 11	Fontainebleau; or, Our Way in France		Illusion
S. Feb 12	King Richard the Third		Turn Out!
M. Feb 14	The Devil's Bridge		Illusion
T. Feb 15	The School for Scandal		Love in a Camp; or, Patrick in Prussia
W. Feb 16	Wild Oats	**Leander and Leonora** (*'A new ballet dance from the favourite farce of* The Padlock, *with the corps de ballet'*)	Modern Antiques
Th. Feb 17	John Bull	**Leander and Leonora**	Love in a Camp

Date (*Notes*)	Mainpiece	Interlude	Afterpiece
F. Feb 18 **1814**	Wild Oats	**Leander and Leonora**	Deuce is in Him
S. Feb 19	King Richard the Third	Sylvester Daggerwood	**Leander and Leonora**
M. Feb 21	King Richard the Third		Harlequin Harper
T. Feb 22	The Devil's Bridge		Illusion
Th. Feb 24	King Richard the Third	Blue Devils	**Leander and Leonora**
F. Feb 25	Oratorios – The Messiah, The Mount of Olives and A Grand Miscellaneous Act		
S. Feb 26	The Merchant of Venice	**Leander and Leonora**	Love in a Camp
M. Feb 28	King Richard the Third		Harlequin Harper
T. Mar 1	Wild Oats	**Leander and Leonora**	Deuce is in Him
W. Mar 2	Oratorios – The Creation, Mount of Olives, A Grand Miscellaneous Act		
Th. Mar 3	King Richard the Third	**Leander and Leonora**	The Mayor of Garratt
F. Mar 4	Oratorios – Grand Selection, with readings of Paradise Lost by Miss Smith		
S. Mar 5	The Merchant of Venice		Illusion
M. Mar 7	King Richard the Third		Turn Out!
T. Mar 8	The Siege of Belgrade (*with songs*)	**Leander and Leonora**	The Apprentice
W. Mar 9	Oratorios – Mount of Olives, A Grand Miscellaneous Act, The Creation. With readings from Paradise Lost by Miss Smith		
Th. Mar 10	King Richard the Third		**Two Strings to Your Bow**
F. Mar 11	Oratorios – Acis and Galatea, Mount of Olives. With readings by Miss Smith		
S. Mar 12	Hamlet, Prince of Denmark		The Prize; or, 2, 5, 3, 8
M. Mar 14	King Richard the Third		Three and the Deuce
T. Mar 15	The Siege of Belgrade		The Irishman in London
W. Mar 16	Oratorios – A Grand Miscelleanous Act, Requiem by Mozart, Mount of Olives. With readings by Miss Smith		
Th. Mar 17	The Merchant of Venice		The Children in the Wood
F. Mar 18	Oratorios – A Grand Miscellaneous Act, Requiem by Mozart, Mount of Olives. With readings by Misss Smith		

Date (*Notes*)	Mainpiece	Interlude	Afterpiece
S. Mar 19 **1814**	Hamlet		My Grandmother
M. Mar 21	King Richard the Third		Love in a Camp
T. Mar 22	Wild Oats		Lodoiska
W. Mar 23	Oratorios – A Grand Miscellaneous Act, Mount of Olives, **A New Song in Honour of Wellington**, with a melologue on National Music recited by Miss Smith		
Th. Mar 24	The Merchant of Venice		Illusion
F. Mar 25	Oratorios – Overture from Zauberflote, A Grand Miscellaneous Act, Creation, with a melologue on National Music (by T Moore) recited by Miss Smith		
S. Mar 26	Hamlet		The Deuce is in Him
M. Mar 28	King Richard the Third		The Mock Doctor
T. Mar 29	The Merchant of Venice		Illusion
W. Mar 30	Oratorios – Requiem by Mozart, songs including '**In Honour of Wellington**' and 'Britons Strike Home', and Overture to Zauberflote		
Th. Mar 31	Hamlet		The Honest Thieves
F. Apr 1	Oratorios – Mount of Olives, Overture to Zauberflote, Creation. With appropriate readings by Miss Smith		
S. Apr 2 *For the Benefit of Mr Raymond*	Every One Has His Fault	'The Nelson of the Day' (*ballad*)	Lodoiska
M. Apr 11	George Barnwell		Illusion
T. Apr 12 *Never Acted Before*	The Woodman's Hut	The Mayor of Garratt	The Children in the Wood
W. Apr 13	The Woodman's Hut	Narensky	Modern Antiques
Th. Apr 14	The Woodman's Hut	Blue Devils	The Deuce is in Him
F. Apr 15	Wild Oats		The Woodman's Hut
S. Apr 16	Narensky	The Midnight Hour	The Woodman's Hut
M. Apr 18	King Richard the Third		The Citizen
T. Apr 19	Three and the Deuce	The Woodman's Hut	Turn Out
W. Apr 20	Every One Has His Fault		The Woodman's Hut
Th. Apr 21	The Merchant of Venice		The Woodman's Hut
F. Apr 22	**The Honey Moon**		The Woodman's Hut
S. Apr 23	Hamlet		Matrimony

Date (*Notes*)	Mainpiece	Interlude	Afterpiece
M. Apr 25 **1814**	King Richard the Third		**Two Strings to Your Bow**
T. Apr 26	Narensky	Intrigue	The Woodman's Hut
W. Apr 27	Illusion	Intrigue	The Woodman's Hut
Th. Apr 28	The Merchant of Venice		The Woodman's Hut
F. Apr 29	The Twelfth Night	Intrigue	The Woodman's Hut
S. Apr 30	Hamlet		The Citizen
M. May 2 *Benefit of Mr Elliston*	Wild Oats		Lodoiska
T. May 3	King Richard the Third		The Apprentice
W. May 4	Lionel and Clarissa		The Woodman's Hut
Th. May 5	Othello	Intrigue	**Leander and Leonora**
F. May 6	Illusion	Intrigue	The Woodman's Hut
S. May 7	Othello		The Woodman's Hut
M. May 9	Venice Preserv'd	Collins's Ode on the Passions accompanied by appropriate music	The Turnpike Gate
T. May 10	King Richard the Third	Intrigue	The Purse; or, The Benevolent Tar
W. May 11 *Mrs Davison's Night*	The Belle's Stratagem	Scotch and Irish songs	The Irish Widow
		Leander and Leonora	
Th. May 12	Othello	Intrigue	Blue Devils
F. May 13	Fontainebleau		The Woodman's Hut
S. May 14	Othello		The Review
M. May 16	King Richard the Third	Intrigue	**Leander and Leonora**
T. May 17	The School for Wives	Songs	The Farmer
W. May 18 *Mr Braham's Night*	False Alarms; or, My Cousin (*including the new song of 'PEACE, or Vivant les Bourbons'*)	Seeing is Believing Apollo's Festival Songs 'God Save the King', 'The Prince and Old England For Ever', and 'The Death of Abercrombie' (*by Mr Braham*)	How to Die for Love!
Th. May 19	Othello		The Farmer
F. May 20	Illusion	Intrigue	The Woodman's Hut
S. May 21	Othello		Raising the Wind
M. May 23	King Richard the Third	Intrigue	**Leander and Leonora**
T. May 24	**The Castle of Andalusia**		The Woodman's Hut
W. May 25 *Benefit of Mr Kean*	Riches! Or, The Wife and Brother		The Turnpike Gate
Th. May 26	Othello		The Farmer
F. May 27	Riches!		The Woodman's Hut

Date (*Notes*)	Mainpiece	Interlude	Afterpiece
S. May 28 **1814** *Whitsun Eve* *Engagement of* *Madame Marconi* *from the Imperial* *Theatre of Vienna*	Grand Selection – including Mount of Olives Ode on the Fate of Tyranny, recited by Miss Smith	'PEACE; or, Vivant les Bourbons', by Mr Braham 'Triumph of England!' (*the words taken from* *an ode written by* *A. Donovan Esq on* *the Allied Sovereigns'* *expected arrival in* *London*)	[Performances will conclude with the national air: 'Rule Britannia!']
M. May 30 *Benefit of Mr* *Bannister*	The Surrender of Calais	Bannister's Budget Songs	Lodoiska
T. May 31	King Richard the Third	Intrigue	Seeing is Believing
W. Jun 1	Riches!		The Woodman's Hut
Th. Jun 2	Othello		The Woodman's Hut
F. Jun 3	False Alarms	Auld Robin Gray	Intrigue
S. Jun 4	Othello		The Woodman's Hut
M. Jun 6 *Benefit of Mr* *Johnstone*	Sons of Erin	Songs **Leander and Leonora**	Matrimony
T. Jun 7	King Richard the Third		The Farmer
W. Jun 8	The Iron Chest	**Leander and Leonora**	The Turnpike Gate
Th. Jun 9			
Theatre closed- **Illuminations**			
M. Jun 13	King Richard the Third	Auld Robin Gray	Seeing is Believing
T. Jun 14 *For the Benefit of* *Miss Kelly*	Inkle and Yarico	Songs by Mr Mathews, who will also perform Hamlet's Advice to the Players, in imitation of several celebrated performers (*by permission of* *the proprietors of* *the Theatre Royal,* *Covent Garden*) The Beggar on Horseback (*compressed* *into 1 Act*)	The Highland Reel
W. Jun 15	Overture to Mozart's Zauberflote The Iron Chest	Russian Pas de Deux Songs	Fair Cheating; or, The Wise-ones outwitted
Th. Jun 16	Othello		The Woodman's Hut
F. Jun 17	The Surrender of Calais	**Leander and Leonora** (*introducing, by* *particular desire, the* *favourite Pas Russe*) Mr De Camp to sing the Italian bravura 'Maestro was an Opera Singer"	Ella Rosenberg

Date (*Notes*)	Mainpiece	Interlude	Afterpiece
S. Jun 18 **1814**	Othello		The Woodman's Hut
M. Jun 20	King Richard the Third		Fair Cheating
T. Jun 21	**The Revenge**	Seeing is Believing	The Citizen
W. Jun 22 *Benefit of Mr Palmer and Mr Bellamy*	The Twelfth Night	Russian Pas Deux	Flitch of Bacon
Th. Jun 23	Othello		Fair Cheating
F. Jun 24	Riches!		Illusion
S. Jun 25	Othello		Flitch of Bacon
M. Jun 27	King Richard the Third		High Life Below Stairs
T. Jun 28 *Benefit of Mr T Dibdin and Mr Oxberry*	The School for Prejudice; or, The Jew and the Yorkshireman	'Farmer Stump's Peep at the London Fashions' (*sung by Mr Knight*)	Illusion
W. Jun 29	Hamlet		Turn Out
Th. Jun 30	Othello		The Woodman's Hut
F. Jul 1	Speed the Plough	The Purse	Ella Rosenberg
S. Jul 2	Othello		The Woodman's Hut
M. Jul 4	King Richard the Third		Flitch of Bacon
T. Jul 5 *For the Benefit of Mr J Smith*	Love in a Village (*including the song* **'Valiant Wellington, the Hero of England'**, *by Mr Smith*)	Songs	The Farmer
W. Jul 6	The Merchant of Venice		The Turnpike Gate
Th. Jul 7	Othello		The Woodman's Hut
F. Jul 8 *Benefit of Mr Spring, Box, Book and House-Keeper*	The West Indian	Rival Soldiers Songs	Lock and Key
S. Jul 9 *Mr Kean's last appearance as Iago this season*	Othello		Woodman's Hut
M. Jul 11 *Mr Kean's last appearance this season in* King Richard the Third	King Richard the Third		Lock and Key
T. Jul 12	The School for Prejudice	Songs, including a grand National Air in Honour of Peace called 'England the Anchor and Hope of the World'	The Farmer
W. Jul 13 *Mr Kean's last appearance this season in* Hamlet	Hamlet		Modern Antiques
Th. Jul 14 *Mr Kean's last appearance this season in* Othello	Othello		The Deuce is in Him

Date (*Notes*)	Mainpiece	Interlude	Afterpiece
F. Jul 15 **1814** *For the Benefit of Mr Dignum*	A Cure for the Heart-ache (*with songs. At the end of Act 4 – 'The Army and Navy for ever'*)	Seeing is Believing	The Turnpike Gate
S. Jul 16 *Last Night*	King Richard the Third		The Mock Doctor

Calendar of Drury Lane Playbills 1814–1815

Date (*Notes*)	Mainpiece	Interlude	Afterpiece
T. Sep 20 **1814** **Theatre to open after several alterations and new embellishments**	Occasional Address by Mrs Edwin The Rivals		The Bee Hive
Th. Sep 22	Occasional Address by Mrs Edwin Wild Oats; or, The Strolling Gentlemen		The Review; or, The Wags of Windsor
S. Sep 24	Occasional Address by Mrs Edwin The Hypocrite		The Turnpike Gate
T. Sep 27	Occasional Address by Mrs Edwin The West Indian		The Three and the Deuce
Th. Sep 29	Occasional Address by Mrs Edwin **The Honey Moon**		The Woodman's Hut
S. Oct 1	Occasional Address by Mrs Edwin The School for Scandal		The Prize; or, 2, 5, 3, 8
M. Oct 3	Occasional Address by Mrs Edwin King Richard the Third		Lock and Key
T. Oct 4	Occasional Address by Mrs Edwin Man and Wife; or, More Secrets than One		The Children in the Wood (*by permission of the proprietors of the Theatre Royal, Haymarket*)
Th. Oct 6	Occasional Address by Mrs Edwin Othello, The Moor of Venice		The Honest Thieves
S. Oct 8	**Rule a Wife and Have a Wife**		The Irishman in London
M. Oct 10	King Richard the Third		The Weathercock
T. Oct 11	The Rivals		The Woodman's Hut
W. Oct 12	John Bull; or, An Englishman's Fireside		Illusion; or, The Trances of Nourjahad
Th. Oct 13	Hamlet, Prince of Denmark		Turn Out!
S. Oct 15 *Never Acted Before*	Policy; or, Thus Runs the World Away		The Woodman's Hut
M. Oct 17	King Richard the Third		Of Age To-morrow
T. Oct 18	Policy	Sylvester Daggerwood	The Review
W. Oct 19	Policy	Blue Devils	Matrimony

Date (*Notes*)	Mainpiece	Interlude	Afterpiece
Th. Oct 20 **1814**	Othello		Illusion
F. Oct 21	Policy	The Purse; or the Benevolent Tar	The Woodman's Hut
S. Oct 22	Othello		The Three and the Deuce
M. Oct 24	King Richard the Third		The Irishman in London
T. Oct 25	Policy	My Grandmother	The Honest Thieves
W. Oct 26	Lionel and Clarissa		Ways and Means; or, A Trip to Dover
Th. Oct 27	Hamlet		The Woodman's Hut
F. Oct 28	Policy	Intrigue	Illusion
S. Oct 29	The Merchant of Venice		Ella Rosenberg
M. Oct 31	King Richard the Third		The Mayor of Garratt
T. Nov 1 *Never Acted Before*	Jean de Paris	The Children in the Wood	Policy
W. Nov 2	Jean de Paris	The Bee Hive	The Woodman's Hut
Th. Nov 3	Riches! Or, The Wife and Brother		Jean de Paris
F. Nov 4	Illusion	The Purse; or, The Benevolent Tar	Jean de Paris
S. Nov 5	Macbeth (*with new scenes*)		The Mock Doctor
M. Nov 7	King Richard the Third		Jean de Paris
T. Nov 8	Macbeth		Jean de Paris
W. Nov 9	The Devil's Bridge		Jean de Paris
Th. Nov 10	Macbeth		Jean de Paris
F. Nov 11	**The Castle of Andalusia**		Jean de Paris
S. Nov 12	Macbeth		Jean de Paris
M. Nov 14	King Richard the Third		Jean de Paris
T. Nov 15	The Fair Penitent		Jean de Paris
W. Nov 16	The Devil's Bridge		Jean de Paris
Th. Nov 17	Macbeth		Jean de Paris
F. Nov 18	The Fair Penitent		Jean de Paris
S. Nov 19	Macbeth		Fortune's Frolics
M. Nov 21	King Richard the Third		Jean de Paris
T. Nov 22	The Belle's Stratagem		Jean de Paris
W. Nov 23	**The Castle of Andalusia**		Midnight Hour
Th. Nov 24	Macbeth		Jean de Paris
F. Nov 25	The Belle's Stratagem		The Woodman's Hut
S. Nov 26	Macbeth		Jean de Paris
M. Nov 28	King Richard the Third		Jean de Paris
T. Nov 29 *Never Acted Before*	Hypocrite		The Ninth Statue; or, The Irishman in Bagdad
W. Nov 30	The Devil's Bridge (*by permission of the proprietors of the English Opera*)		The Ninth Statue
Th. Dec 1	Macbeth		The Ninth Statue

Date (*Notes*)	Mainpiece	Interlude	Afterpiece
F. Dec 2 **1814**	All in the Wrong		The Ninth Statue
S. Dec 3	Macbeth		The Ninth Statue
M. Dec 5	King Richard the Third		The Ninth Statue
T. Dec 6	**Rule a Wife and Have a Wife**		The Ninth Statue
W. Dec 7	Fontainebleau; or, Our Way in France		The Ninth Statue
Th. Dec 8	Macbeth		The Ninth Statue
F. Dec 9	The School for Scandal		The Ninth Statue
S. Dec 10	Macbeth		The Ninth Statue
M. Dec 12	King Richard the Third		The Ninth Statue
T. Dec 13	The Devil's Bridge		The Ninth Statue
W. Dec 14	The Merchant of Venice		The Ninth Statue
Th. Dec 15	Macbeth		The Ninth Statue
F. Dec 16	The Belle's Stratagem		The Ninth Statue
S. Dec 17	Othello		The Ninth Statue
M. Dec 19	King Richard the Third		The Ninth Statue
T. Dec 20	A Cure for the Heart-ache		The Ninth Statue
W. Dec 21	The Belle's Stratagem		The Ninth Statue
Th. Dec 22	Macbeth		The Ninth Statue
F. Dec 23 *Last night of performing before the holidays*	Jane Shore		The Ninth Statue
M. Dec 26	George Barnwell		The Valley of Diamonds; or, Harlequin Sinbad (*including the scene of 'the splendidly illuminated Palace of Pantomime'*)
T. Dec 27	King Richard the Third		The Valley of Diamonds
W. Dec 28	The Belle's Stratagem		The Valley of Diamonds
Th. Dec 29	Macbeth		The Valley of Diamonds
F. Dec 30	Jane Shore		The Valley of Diamonds
S. Dec 31	Hamlet		The Valley of Diamonds
M. Jan 2 **1815**	Romeo and Juliet		The Valley of Diamonds
T. Jan 3	The Ninth Statue	Policy	The Valley of Diamonds
W. Jan 4	The School for Scandal		The Valley of Diamonds
Th. Jan 5	Macbeth		The Valley of Diamonds
F. Jan 6	Jane Shore		The Valley of Diamonds

Date (*Notes*)	Mainpiece	Interlude	Afterpiece
S. Jan 7 **1815**	Romeo and Juliet		The Valley of Diamonds
M. Jan 9	King Richard the Third		The Valley of Diamonds
T. Jan 10	Romeo and Juliet		The Valley of Diamonds
W. Jan 11	The School for Scandal		The Valley of Diamonds
Th. Jan 12- (*Kean with cold – replaced by Mr Elliston in the part of Macbeth*)	Macbeth		The Valley of Diamonds
F. Jan 13	The Belle's Stratagem		The Valley of Diamonds
S. Jan 14	Romeo and Juliet		The Valley of Diamonds
M. Jan 16	Jean de Paris	Ways and Means	The Valley of Diamonds
T. Jan 17	The Birth-Day	Fortune's Frolics	The Valley of Diamonds
W. Jan 18	The School for Scandal		The Valley of Diamonds
Th. Jan 19	Macbeth		The Valley of Diamonds
F. Jan 20	All in the Wrong		The Valley of Diamonds
S. Jan 21	Romeo and Juliet		The Valley of Diamonds
M. Jan 23	King Richard the Third		The Valley of Diamonds
T. Jan 24	Romeo and Juliet		The Valley of Diamonds
W. Jan 25	The School for Scandal		The Valley of Diamonds
Th. Jan 26	Jean de Paris	The Birth-Day	The Valley of Diamonds
F. Jan 27	All in the Wrong		The Valley of Diamonds
S. Jan 28	Romeo and Juliet		The Valley of Diamonds
M. Jan 30	Oratorios – Handel's The Messiah, Mount of Olives, 'God Save the King', and A Grand Miscellaneous Act		
T. Jan 31	Romeo and Juliet		The Valley of Diamonds
W. Feb 1	As You Like It		The Valley of Diamonds
Th. Feb 2	Macbeth		The Ninth Statue
F. Feb 3	The Provoked Husband; or, A Journey to London		The Valley of Diamonds

Date (*Notes*)	Mainpiece	Interlude	Afterpiece
S. Feb 4 **1815**	Hamlet		The Ninth Statue
M. Feb 6	King Richard the Third		The Valley of Diamonds
T. Feb 7	As You Like It		The Ninth Statue
Th. Feb 9	Macbeth		Jean de Paris
F. Feb 10	Oratorios – Two Grand Miscellaneous Acts, **The Grand Battle Sinfonia** composed by Beethoven, The Creation		
S. Feb 11	Hamlet		The Valley of Diamonds
M. Feb 13	Town and Country		The Ninth Statue
T. Feb 14 *Last night of Miss Walstein's Engagement*	The Provoked Husband		Jean de Paris
W. Feb 15	Oratorios–TheMessiah, Acis and Galatea Part III – **The Grand Battle Sinfonia**		
Th. Feb 16	Macbeth		The Valley of Diamonds
F. Feb 17	Oratorios – Mount of Olives, **The Grand Battle Sinfonia**, The Creation, A Grand Selection		
S. Feb 18	Town and Country		The Woodman's Hut
M. Feb 20	King Richard the Third	Indian Nuptials	Blue Devils
T. Feb 21	Town and Country		Jean de Paris
W. Feb 22	Oratorios – Requiem by Mozart, A Grand Selection, **The Grand Battle Sinfonia**		
Th. Feb 23	Town and Country	Indian Nuptials	**Two Strings to Your Bow**
F. Feb 24	Oratorios – A Grand Selection, A Selection from Mozart's Zauberflote, and **The Grand Battle Sinfonia**		
S. Feb 25	Hamlet		Poor Relations
M. Feb 27	Town and Country	Indian Nuptials	The Citizen
T. Feb 28	Douglas		The Ninth Statue
W. Mar 1	Oratorios – Acis and Galatea, The Creation, A Grand Selection, **The Grand Battle Sinfonia**		
Th. Mar 2	Town and Country		Jean de Paris

Date (*Notes*)	Mainpiece	Interlude	Afterpiece
F. Mar 3 **1815**	Oratorios – A Grand Selection, The Mount of Olives, Elijah raising the Widow's Son, and **The Grand Battle Sinfonia**		
S. Mar 4	Romeo and Juliet		Fortune's Frolics
M. Mar 6 *First Time*	King Richard the Second (*'with considerable alterations and additions'*)		The Turnpike Gate
T. Mar 7	The West Indian		The Children in the Wood
W. Mar 8	Oratorios – Requiem by Mozart, Elijah raising the Widow's Son, A Grand Selection, and **The Grand Battle Sinfonia**		
Th. Mar 9 *First Time*	King Richard the Second (*'with considerable alterations and additions'*)		The Midnight Hour
F. Mar 10	Oratorios – Elijah raising the Widow's Son, A Grand Selection, Selections from Mozart's Zauberflote, and **The Grand Battle Sinfonia**		
S. Mar 11	King Richard the Second		Past Ten O'Clock, and a Rainy Night
M. Mar 13	King Richard the Second		Past Ten O'Clock, and a Rainy Night
T. Mar 14	King Richard the Second		Past Ten O'Clock, and a Rainy Night
W. Mar 15	Oratorios – Elijah raising the Widow's Son, A Grand Selection, A Grand Military Act, Songs (*'Britons! Strike Home!'*, *in honour of* **Wellington**, *by Mr Pyne and Mrs Dickons, with full chorus*), and **The Grand Battle Sinfonia**		
Th. Mar 16	King Richard the Second		Past Ten O'Clock, and a Rainy Night

Date (*Notes*)	Mainpiece	Interlude	Afterpiece
F. Mar 17 **1815** *Last night of Oratorios*	Oratorios – A Grand Selection, The First, Second and Third Hymns, The Mount of Olives, and **The Grand Battle Sinfonia**		
S. Mar 18 *Last night of performing before the holidays. For the Benefit of Mr Raymond*	The Siege of Belgrade	Songs	Past Ten O'Clock, and a Rainy Night
M. Mar 27	Jean de Paris	Past Ten O'Clock, and a Rainy Night	The Valley of Diamonds
T. Mar 28	Illusion	Past Ten O'Clock, and a Rainy Night	The Ninth Statue
W. Mar 29 *First Time*	The Unknown Guest		Past Ten O'Clock, and a Rainy Night
Th. Mar 30	The Unknown Guest		Past Ten O'Clock, and a Rainy Night
F. Mar 31	The Unknown Guest		Past Ten O'Clock, and a Rainy Night
S. Apr 1	The Unknown Guest		Past Ten O'Clock, and a Rainy Night
M. Apr 3	The Unknown Guest		Past Ten O'Clock, and a Rainy Night
T. Apr 4	The Unknown Guest		Past Ten O'Clock, and a Rainy Night
W. Apr 5	The Unknown Guest		Past Ten O'Clock, and a Rainy Night
Th. Apr 6	The Unknown Guest		Past Ten O'Clock, and a Rainy Night
F. Apr 7	Wild Oats		The Irishman in London
S. Apr 8	King Richard the Second		Past Ten O'Clock, and a Rainy Night
M. Apr 10	King Richard the Second		Past Ten O'Clock, and a Rainy Night
T. Apr 11	The Unknown Guest		The Honest Thieves
W. Apr 12	King Henry the Fourth (Part One)		Past Ten O'Clock, and a Rainy Night
Th. Apr 13	King Richard the Second		Past Ten O'Clock, and a Rainy Night
F. Apr 14	King Henry the Fourth (Part One)		Jean de Paris
S. Apr 15	Macbeth		Past Ten O'Clock, and a Rainy Night
M. Apr 17	King Richard the Third		The Ninth Statue; or, The Irishman in Bagdad
T. Apr 18	King Richard the Second		Fortune's Frolics
W. Apr 19	The Unknown Guest		The Woodman's Hut

Date (*Notes*)	Mainpiece	Interlude	Afterpiece
Th. Apr 20 **1815**	Othello		Rosina
F. Apr 21	King Henry the Fourth (Part One)		The Adopted Child
S. Apr 22 *First Time*	Ina		**Two Strings to Your Bow**
M. Apr 24	King Richard the Third		The Ninth Statue
T. Apr 25	King Henry the Fourth (Part One)		The Adopted Child
W. Apr 26	Town and Country		Rosina
Th. Apr 27	The Unknown Guest		Ways and Means
F. Apr 28	King Richard the Second		The Three and the Deuce
S. Apr 29 *First Time at this Theatre*	Wheel of Fortune		Ways and Means
M. May 1	King Richard the Third		Jean de Paris
T. May 2	John Bull		The Flitch of Bacon
W. May 3	Macbeth		The Ninth Statue
Th. May 4	Wheel of Fortune		Ways and Means
F. May 5	**The Honey Moon**		Rosina
S. May 6	Wheel of Fortune		The Flitch of Bacon
M. May 8	King Richard the Second		The Woodman's Hut
T. May 9	King Henry the Fourth (Part One)		Ella Rosenberg
W. May 10 *Mr Braham's Night*	The Devil's Bridge	Songs The Festival of Apollo (*to conclude with 'God Save the King'*)	Three Weeks After Marriage
Th. May 11	The Wheel of Fortune		Lodoiska
F. May 12	Town and Country		Lodoiska
S. May 13	Oratorios – Part I – Beethoven's Mount of Olives. Part II – A Grand Selection The Liberation of Germany 'To conclude with Beethoven's **Grand Battle Sinfonia, Descriptive of the Battle and Victory at Vittoria, gained by the armies under the command of Field-Marshal His Grace The Duke of Wellington'**		
M. May 15	King Richard the Third		Lodoiska

Date (*Notes*)	Mainpiece	Interlude	Afterpiece
T. May 16 **1815**	The Devil's Bridge	Drive Love out at the Door, He'll get in at the Window	The Adopted Child
W. May 17	The Merry Wives of Windsor		Lodoiska
Th. May 18	The Wheel of Fortune	Drive Love out at the Door, He'll get in at the Window	Past Ten O'Clock, and a Rainy Night
F. May 19	Wild Oats	Drive Love out at the Door, He'll get in at the Window	Fortune's Frolics
S. May 20	The Merchant of Venice		Lodoiska
M. May 22 *For the Benefit of Mr Elliston*	The Jew	**Leander and Leonora** Three Weeks after Marriage (*by particular desire*)	The Woodman's Hut
T. May 23	The Wheel of Fortune	Drive Love out at the Door, He'll get in at the Window	The Prize
W. May 24 *Mr Kean's Night*	**The Revenge**		The Tobacconist (*first time at this theatre*)
Th. May 25	King Richard the Second		Lodoiska
F. May 26	**The Revenge**		Of Age To-morrow
S. May 27 *Mrs Davison's Night*	**A Bold Stroke for a Husband**	Songs Blue Devils	The Highland Reel (*to conclude with a Highland Fling*)
M. May 29 *Never Acted Before here.* *Mr Bartley's Benefit*	The Family Legend	Collins's Ode on the Passions, accompanied by appropriate music	The Adopted Child (*by particular desire*)
T. May 30	**The Revenge**		The Weathercock
W. May 31 *Mr Munden's Benefit*	The Road to Ruin	Songs	Honesty's The Best Policy
Th. Jun 1 *Mr Bannister's Benefit Night, and last appearance*	The World	Songs	The Children in the Wood (*by permission of the Haymarket*) The Rival Soldiers
F. Jun 2	**The Revenge**	Drive Love out at the Door, He'll get in at the Window	Honesty's the Best Policy
S. Jun 3	Macbeth		Honesty's the Best Policy
M. Jun 5	King Richard the Third		Honesty's the Best Policy
T. Jun 6 *Benefit of Mrs Dickons*	Artaxerxes	The Irishman in London Songs (*with the participation of Mr Naldi*)	Ella Rosenberg
W. Jun 7	**The Revenge**		Lodoiska

Date (*Notes*)	Mainpiece	Interlude	Afterpiece
Th. Jun 8 **1815** *Mr T Dibdin and Mr Philipps*	**The English Fleet in 1342**	'A splendid Egeirophadron: or, Polyscenic Pasticcio' (*comprising a cento of variety*)	Past Ten O'Clock, and a Rainy Night
F. Jun 9	Hamlet		Jean de Paris
S. Jun 10 *For the Benefit of Mr Rae*	The Foundling of the Forest (*Act 2 – 'a ballet incidental to the piece, in which Miss Smith will dance the celebrated* **Guarachia** *[sic] and a grand 'pas deux' with Mr D'Egville'*)	Songs The Rival Soldiers	The Honest Thieves
M. Jun 12 *Mr Johnstone's Benefit Night*	The Rivals	Songs Drive Love out at the Door, He'll get in at the Window	The London Hermit; or, Rambles in Dorsetshire
T. Jun 13	Othello		Past Ten O'Clock, and a Rainy Night
W. Jun 14	**The Revenge**		The Woodman's Hut
Th. Jun 15 *Miss Kelly's Benefit*	Charles the Bold; or, The Siege of Nantz	Midas	Harlequin Hoax; or, A Pantomime Proposed (*by permission of the proprietors of the Theatre Royal, Lyceum. To conclude with a grand display of Fireworks*)
F. Jun 16 *Last night this season of Mr Kean's Iago*	Othello		Charles the Bold
S. Jun 17 *Last night this season of Mr Kean's Shylock*	The Merchant of Venice		Charles the Bold
M. Jun 19 *Last night this season of Mr Kean's King Richard the Second*	King Richard the Second		Charles the Bold
T. Jun 20	**Rule a Wife and Have a Wife**		Charles the Bold
W. Jun 21 *Mr Lovegrove's Benefit*	The School for Scandal	Gallimaufry Songs, including 'The Death of Nelson' by Braham (*by particular desire*), and 'the favourite **Guarachia** [*sic*] by Miss Smith'	The Woodman's Hut
Th. Jun 22	**Rule a Wife and Have a Wife**		Charles the Bold

Date (*Notes*)	Mainpiece	Interlude	Afterpiece
F. Jun 23 **1815**	Sons of Erin (*by particular desire, with songs inserted*)	Hornpipe and songs Intrigue	**The Critic; or, A Tragedy Rehearsed**
S. Jun 24	**Rule a Wife and Have a Wife**		Charles the Bold
M. Jun 25 *Last night this season of Mr Kean's Romeo*	Romeo and Juliet		Ella Rosenberg (*by particular desire*)
T. Jun 27	**Rule a Wife and Have a Wife**		Charles the Bold
W. Jun 28 *Last night this season of Mr Kean's Luke*	Riches!		Charles the Bold
Th. Jun 29 *Last time this season of Mr Kean's Leon and the new melodrame*	**Rule a Wife and Have a Wife**		Charles the Bold
F. Jun 30	The Peasant Boy (*with songs*)	Chrononhotonthologos (*in 1 Act, 'the most tragical tragedy that ever was tragedized by a company of tragedians'*)	The Woodman's Hut Songs
S. Jul 1 *For the Benefit of Mr Knight and My Pyne*	Wild Oats 'Last time this season that Miss Smith will dance the celebrated **Guarachia'**	A Comic Miscellany, consisting of several songs	Past Ten O'Clock, and a Rainy Night
M. Jul 3	King Richard the Third	An Address by Mrs Edwin, in honour of 'the **Immortal Wellington**', at the conclusion of which 'God Save the King' will be sung by the whole of the vocal company	Past Ten O'Clock, and a Rainy Night
T. Jul 4 *For the Benefit of Theatrical Fund (founded in 1766 by David Garrick)*	'An address written expressly for the occasion, delivered by Mr S Penley' **The Mountaineers**	Address spoken by Mrs Edwin, in honour of 'the **Immortal Wellington**', at the conclusion of which 'God Save the King'	Charles the Bold
W. Jul 5 *Benefit of Mr Spring, Box, Book and House-Keeper*	The Way to Get Married (*by particular desire*)	**Leander and Leonora** A Day after the Wedding 'Death of Abercrombie' (by Mr Braham)	Bon Ton: or, High Life Below Stairs

Date (*Notes*)	Mainpiece	Interlude	Afterpiece
Th. Jul 6 **1815** *No Performances this* *Evening on account* *of the death of Samuel* *Whitbread, Esq*	**[The Mountaineers]**	[Address by Mrs Edwin: **Immortal** **Wellington**, 'God Save the King']	[The Tobacconist]
F. Jul 7 *Last night of Mr Kean's* *performances*	**The Mountaineers**	Address by Mrs Edwin in honour of 'the **Immortal** **Wellington**', at the conclusion of which 'God Save the King'	The Tobacconist
S. Jul 8	The Way to Get married (by particular desire)	Rival Soldiers Songs	**The Critic**
M. Jul 10 *For the Benefit of* *Mr Bellamy and Mr* *Palmer*	The World	Address by Mrs Edwin in honour of 'the **Immortal** **Wellington**', at the conclusion of which 'God Save the King' Songs The Quaker	Past Ten O'Clock, and a Rainy Night
T. Jul 11	The Peasant Boy	Bon Ton	Tom Thumb the Great
W. Jul 12	M.P. Or, the Blue- Stocking! (*with songs introduced,* *by permission of the* *English Opera*)	Address by Mrs Edwin in honour of 'the **Immortal** **Wellington**', at the conclusion of which 'God Save the King'	The Turnpike Gate
Th. Jul 13 *Last night of the* *company performing* *this season*	Charles the Bold	Address by Mrs Edwin in honour of 'the **Immortal** **Wellington**', at the conclusion of which 'God Save the King'	Past Ten O'Clock, and a Rainy Night The Ninth Statue

Appendix C

Calendar of Bristol Theatre Royal Playbills 1807–1815

Date	Mainpiece	Interlude	Afterpiece	Engagement / **Benefit** (House receipts/*Notes*)
M. Sep 28 1807 [Start of 1807–1808 season]	Hamlet, Prince of Denmark		The Agreeable Surprise	Young
W. Sep 30	The Stranger		The Quaker	Young
F. Oct 2	The Provoked Husband; or, A Journey to London		Robin Hood; or, Sherwood Forest	Young
M. Oct 5	**The Mountaineers**	Personation; or, Fairly Taken In	Katharine and Petruchio	Young
T. Oct 6	The Heir at Law		Catch Him Who Can	Young (*Extra night because of Prince of Wales' visit to Bristol*)
W. Oct 7	Venice Preserv'd		'We Fly By Night'; or, Long Stories	Young
F. Oct 9	**Rule a Wife and Have a Wife**		The Review; or, The Wags of Windsor	Young
M. Oct 12	**Much Ado About Nothing**	The Gretna Blacksmith	Love and Folly	Young
		Youth		
W. Oct 14	Othello, the Moor of Venice		Tekeli; or, The Siege of Montgatz	Young
F. Oct 16	The Suspicious Husband		Tekeli	
M. Oct 19	Macbeth		The Hunter of the Alps	Young
W. Oct 21	The Curfew		Tekeli	
F. Oct 23				(*Preparations for Pantomime*)
M. Oct 26	The Earl of Warwick		Harlequin and Mother Goose; or, The Golden Egg	
W. Oct 28	Adrian and Orilla		Harlequin and Mother Goose	
F. Oct 30	The Wheel of Fortune		Harlequin and Mother Goose	
M. Nov 2	The Haunted Tower		Harlequin and Mother Goose	
W. Nov 4	Town and Country		Harlequin and Mother Goose	
Th. Nov 5	George Barnwell		Harlequin and Mother Goose	
F. Nov 6	Lovers' Vows		Harlequin and Mother Goose	

350

Date	Mainpiece		Afterpiece	Notes
	...y and County		Harlequin and Mother Goose	
M. Nov 16	Laugh When You Can	The Jovial Millers	The Adopted Child	
M. Nov 23	The Dramatist		No Song, No Supper	
M. Nov 30	The Duenna		Raising the Wind	
M. Dec 7	Time's a Tell-Tale		Rosina	
M. Dec 14	Time's a Tell-Tale		The Young Hussar	
M. Dec 21	Adelgitha		The Young Hussar	
M. Dec 28	The Honey Moon		The Forty Thieves	
W. Dec 30	Adelgitha		The Forty Thieves	
M. Jan 4 1808	The Castle of Andalusia		The Forty Thieves	
M. Jan 11	Pizarro		The Children in the Wood	Mrs Siddons
M. Jan 18	The Gamester		Tekeli	Mrs Siddons
M. Jan 25	Macbeth		The Young Hussar	Mrs Siddons
M. Feb 1	The Grecian Daughter		Tekeli	Mrs Siddons
M. Feb 8	King Henry the Eighth; or, The Fall of Cardinal Wolsey		The Old Maid	Mrs Siddons
M. Feb 15	Mary Queen of Scots		The Review	
M. Feb 22	Acrian and Orilla		Ella Rosenberg	*(MS alteration to the playbill, which originally advertised The Siege of Belgrade. This was changed due to 'Mrs Windsor's indisposition')*
M. Feb 29	Time's a Tell-Tale		Ella Rosenberg	
M. Mar 7	The Wanderer		The Blind Boy	
M. Mar 14	The Wanderer		The Blind Boy	
M. Mar 21	Adelgitha		Harlequin and Mother Goose	
M. Mar 28	Begone Dull Care; or, How Will it End		Ella Rosenberg	
M. Apr 4	Love Makes a Man		Who's The Dupe?	
M. Apr 11				*(No performances: Holy Week)*
M. Apr 18	The Wanderer		Harlequin and Mother Goose	
M. Apr 25	Barbarossa		The Young Hussar	Master Betty
M. May 2	Tancred and Sigismunda		Ella Rosenberg	Master Betty
M. May 9	Mahomet		The Weathercock	Master Betty
M. May 16	The Revenge	The Brave and the Fair (*a dance*)	The Hunter of the Alps	Master Betty

351

Date	Mainpiece	Interlude	Afterpiece	Engagement / Benefit (House receipts/*Notes*)
M. May 23 **1808**	The World		The Blind Boy	
M. May 30	The World		The Two Misers	
W. Jun 8	The Siege of Belgrade		The Blind Boy	Mrs Windsor
W. Jun 15	The Man of the World		The Young Hussar	Cooke
M. Jun 20	The Merchant of Venice		Love a-la Mode	Cooke
M. Jun 22	King Richard the Third		The Sultan	Cooke
F. Jun 24	New Way to Pay Old Debts		Ella Rosenberg	Cooke
M. Jun 27	A Cure for the Heart-ache	The Scotch Laddies	Harlequin and Mother Goose	Gomery (£50 in the house)
W. Jun 29	The West Indian	Bristol Sailors	A Tale of Mystery	Connor
F. Jul 1	**The Wonder; A Woman Keeps a Secret**	'Buo-napar-te', sung by Mr Herbert	Love and Folly	Sanders (Box-Book Keeper) ('Under the Patronage of the different Lodges of Free and Accepted Masons, of this City and Province', £67 in the house)
		The Gretna Blacksmith		
		Youth		
M. Jul 4	Fontainebleau	The Mayor of Garratt (*in 1 Act*)	The Black Forest; or, The Natural Song	Egerton (MS note to playbill: £80 in the house)
		Dances		
		'A British Sailor's Address to the Volunteers, with his Welsh, Irish, and Scotch Messmates' Remarks, "in character" by Mr Egerton'		
W. Jul 6	The Voice of Nature	Little Bob and Little Ben	Too Many Cooks	Miss Mills and Mrs Grove (£54)
F. Jul 8	Wives as they were and Maids as they are		Love Laughs at Locksmiths	Part of Office-keepers (Tickets from Dunn) (£86 in the house)
M. Jul 11	Tamerlane the Great	The Purse	The Drummer	Miss Marriot (£64)

W. Jul 13 1808	The Cabinet	An Address to the Volunteers by Mr Egerton	Serena and Azor	Bennett (£60 in the house)
F. Jul 15	The World		'We Fly By Night'	Part of Office-keepers (Tickets from Underwood) (£77)
M. Jul 18	Cymbeline	[Poetical address]	Hunt the Slipper	Miss Jameson (*Cymbeline, by desire of Major Evans and the Officers of the Royal Carmarthen Fusiliers*) (£85 in the house)
W. Jul 20	George Barnwell		**Whistle for it; or, The Spanish Patriots** 'Death of Nelson' 'A Patriot's Address by Miss Fisher, in the Character of The Genius of Britain; and "Rule Britannia" in Full Chorus'	Mr and Mrs Sedley (*Whistle for It; or, The Spanish Patriots* – 'New drama in one act by the Hon. G. Lamb. *In the course of which will be displayed the Celebrated NAVAL PILLAR, Inscribed with the names of our DEPARTED HEROES, and decorated with a PROFUSION of VARIE-GATED LAMPS, and other brilliant Illuminations and Devices*' c. £58–£67 taken)
F. Jul 22	The Honey Moon	Dances	Lock and Key	Part of Office-keepers (£86)

353

Date	Mainpiece	Interlude	Afterpiece	Engagement / Benefit (House receipts/*Notes*)
M. Jul 25 1808	The Surrender of Calais	Divertissement 'To Celebrate the Glorious Intelligence Daily arriving of **SPANISH HEROISM!** In the course of which will be displayed the Celebrated NAVAL PILLAR, Inscribed with the names of our DEPARTED HEROES, and decorated with a PROFUSION of VARIEGATED LAMPS, and other brilliant Illuminations and Devices, BRITANNIA attended by her LION, BRITISH FLEET, etc.'	Animal Magnetism	Miss Fisher (£58 in the house)
W. Jul 27	The Siege of Belgrade		The Blind Boy	Charlton (£80)
F. Jul 29	Every One Has His Fault		The Hunter of the Alps	Gallie, Sims, Cushing, Smith, Lodge and Miss Summers (£112)
M. Aug 1	The Iron Chest	The Blue Devils	Who Wins	Lovegrove (£160)
W. Aug 3	The Days of Yore; or, England's King Preserv'd	**Whistle for it; or, The Spanish Patriots** (*to conclude with 'Rule Britannia' in full chorus*)	Fortune's Frolics; or, A True born Englishman	Mallinson (£95)
F. Aug 5	Adrian and Orilla	'A British Sailor's Address to the Volunteers' Dances	Ella Rosenberg	Smith (the Treasurer)
M. Aug 8 1808 [End of 1807–1808 season]	The Inconstant	The Jovial Millers	The Prize; or, 2, 5, 3, 8	Mr and Mrs C. Kemble
M. Oct 3 1808 [Start of 1808–1809 season]	**The Revenge**	The Jovial Millers	'We Fly by Night'	Young
W. Oct 5	The Suspicious Husband		Ella Rosenberg	Young
F. Oct 7	Macbeth		The Review	Young
M. Oct 10	Hamlet		My Grandmother	Young

Date	Mainpiece		Afterpiece	Performer
W. Oct 12 1808	Love in a Village		The Blind Boy	Young
F. Oct 14	Much Ado About Nothing		Harlequin and Mother Goose	Young
M. Oct 17	Rule a Wife and Have a Wife	Watkin and Winney; or, Taffy's Disaster	Katharine and Petruchio	
W. Oct 19	The Siege of Belgrade		Catch him who can	Young
F. Oct 21	Othello	Watkin and Winney	The Weathercock	Young
M. Oct 24	The Iron Chest		Of Age To-morrow	Young
W. Oct 26	The Stranger	Watkin and Winney	The Devil to Pay	Young
F. Oct 28	The Mountaineers	Watkin and Winney	Ella Rosenberg	Young
M. Oct 31	Pizarro		A Tale of Mystery	Young
M. Nov 7	The Honey Moon		The Blind Boy	
M. Nov 14	The World		Harlequin and Mother Goose	Blissett
M. Nov 21	She Stoops to Conquer; or, The Mistakes of a Night		Plot and Counterplot: or, The Portrait of Cervantes	
M. Nov 28	The Man of the World		Plot and Counterplot	Cooke
M. Dec 5	King Lear		Love Laughs at Locksmiths	Cooke
M. Dec 12	Every Man in his Humour		Plot and Counterplot	Cooke
M. Dec 19	The Provoked Husband		Inkle and Yarico	Blissett
M. Dec 26	Adrian and Orilla	Gretna Blacksmith	The Blind Boy	
M. Jan 2 1809	Love in a Village		Ella Rosenberg	Mrs Dickons
M. Jan 9	Lionel and Clarissa		No Song, No Supper	Mrs Dickons
M. Jan 16	Artaxerxes		The Weathercock	Mrs Dickons
M. Jan 23	The Hero of the North		The School for Authors	(Performances cancelled owing to illness and weather)
W. Feb 1	The Exile		The School for Authors	
M. Feb 6	The Exile			
M. Feb 13	Semiramide	Gretna Blacksmith	Paul and Virginia	
M. Feb 20	La Didone	The Jovial Millers	Il Fanatico per la Musica	Mme Catalani
M. Feb 27	Man and Wife		Il Furbo contra Il Furbo	Mme Catalani
M. Mar 6	Man and Wife		Tom Thumb the Great	
M. Mar 13	The Exile		Harlequin and Mother Goose	
M. Mar 20				
M. Mar 27	The Duenna		Is He a Prince?	(Holy Week)
M. Apr 3	The Country Girl		Harlequin and Mother Goose	Mrs Dickons
M. Apr 10	The Belle's Stratagem		Is He a Prince?	Mrs Jordan
M. Apr 17			The Poor Soldier	Mrs Jordan

355

Date	Mainpiece	Interlude	Afterpiece	Engagement / Benefit (House receipts/Notes)
M. Apr 24 **1809**	Man and Wife	The Jovial Millers	The Sultan	Mrs Jordan
W. Apr 27	Adrian and Orilla		The Forty Thieves	
M. May 1	The Way to Keep Him		The Devil to Pay	Mrs Jordan
M. May 8	The Exile		Robin Hood	Mrs Windsor
M. May 15	The Hero of the North		Tom Thumb the Great	
M. May 22	Alexander the Great		Inkle and Yarico	
M. May 29	Grieving's a Folly		**Paul and Virginia**	
W. Jun 7	The Rivals		The Turnpike Gate	Munden
M. Jun 12	The Birth-Day	Blue Devils	The Farmer	Munden
M. Jun 19	Grieving's a Folly	Bristol Sailors and Savages (*ballet dance*)	**Don Juan** (*including the admired dance from Mother Goose, in wooden shoes*)	Gomery (*his last Benefit*) (£77.15.0)
W. Jun 21	Man and Wife		Is He a Prince?	Part of Office-keepers
F. Jun 23	Othello		The Midnight Hour	Part of Office-keepers
M. Jun 26	The English Merchant	Tars on Shore (*with a view of the British Fleet riding at anchor*) The Musical Fanatic (*after which Mr Egerton will give a description [for the last time] of 'A Naval Engagement between an English and French Frigate in the Chops of the Channel'*)	Death of General Wolfe; or, The Night before the Battle (*last scene will form a representation of West's celebrated Picture of the General's Death*)	Egerton (*Farewell Benefit*)
W. Jun 28	The Stranger	Blue Devils	Robin Hood	Sanders (Box-Book Keeper)
F. Jun 30	The Poor Gentleman	Dryden's Ode on 'Alexander's Feast' recited by Master Weeks	Ella Rosenberg	Part of Office-keepers
M. Jul 3	**Pizarro**	'Laughing and Crying Philosophers' (*comic duet*)	The Jew and the Doctor	Miss Marriott (£70)

356

Date				Bengough and Cunningham
W. Jul 5 **1809**	Henry II, or; The Fall of Fair Rosamund	Songs (*including a new comic song* by Mr Gattie (*in the character of a British Tar*) *'recounting the Brilliant Exploits of Lord Cochrane in Basque Roads'*)	Love in a Camp; or, Patrick in Germany	
F. Jul 7	Romeo and Juliet	The Rival Soldiers / New Comic Song—'Colin Clum's Visit to Bristol with his Account of the Play-House and Peep at The Forty Thieves', by Mr Mallinson	Chrononhontanthologos; King of Queerummania!	Abbott and Mrs Grove (£59.13)
M. Jul 10	Deaf and Dumb; or, The Orphan Protected	The Cooper (*musical interlude*)	The Citizen	Miss Jameson (c. £70–£80)
W. Jul 12	The Soldier's Daughter	Little Red Riding Hood / 'Dowland will dance a hornpipe and go through the Six Divisions of the Austrian Broad Sword Exercise'	The Blind Boy	Dowland (£60)
F. Jul 14	The Wife of Two Husbands; or The Mysterious Robber	The Day of Victory (*to open with a view of the British Fleet at anchor*) / 'Rule Britannia' and Patriotic address in the character of Britannia by Miss Jameson / Songs (*including 'A New Song recounting the exploits of Lord Cochrane in Basque Roads' by Mr Gattie*)	The Quaker	Bennett (c. £45)
M. Jul 17	The Castle Spectre	'God Save the King' in chorus / The Day after the Wedding; or, A Wife's First Lesson / Songs	The Maid of the Oaks	Miss Fisher

Date	Mainpiece	Interlude	Afterpiece	Engagement / **Benefit** (House receipts/*Notes*)
W. Jul 19 **1809**	King Charles I; or, The Royal Martyr	Military hornpipe by Dowland and Austrian Broad Sword Exercise	Tekeli	<u>Charlton</u> (£90)
		'A New Song recounting the exploits of Lord Cochrane in Basque Roads (*by Mr Gattie*) in the character of a British tar'		
F. Jul 21	Town and Country		Inkle and Yarico	<u>T. Gattie, Webber, Sims, Dickenson, Smith, Loge, Miss Summers, Miss Martin</u> (£119)
M. Jul 24	The Clandestine Marriage	'A British Sailor's Address'	False and True; or, The Irishman in Italy	<u>Lovegrove</u> (£116)
W. Jul 26	Fatal Curiosity	Hob in the Well The Castle of FitzAllen; or, The True-born English Sailor	Modern Antiques; or, The Merry Mourners	<u>Mallinson</u> (£160)
F. Jul 28	Alexander the Great		Matrimony	
M. Jul 31 1809 [End of 1808–1809 season]	**Much Ado About Nothing**		Of Age To-morrow	Mr and Mrs C. Kemble
M. Oct 2 1809 [Start of 1809–1810 season]	Venice Preserv'd		Rosina	Miss Smith
W. Oct 4	The Soldier's Daughter		Is He a Prince?	Miss Smith
F. Oct 6	Douglas	Personation	My Grandmother	Miss Smith
M. Oct 9	Adrian and Orilla		The Blind Boy	Miss Smith
W. Oct 11	**The Honey Moon**		The Weathercock	Miss Smith
F. Oct 13	Othello		Tekeli	Miss Smith
M. Oct 16	The Jealous Wife		We Fly by Night	Miss Smith
W. Oct 18	Love in a Village		The Flitch of Bacon	Miss Smith
F. Oct 20	Hamlet		The Midnight Hour	
M. Oct 23	Tancred and Sigismunda		The Blind Boy	Miss Smith
W. Oct 25	The Stranger	Loyal and Patriotic Songs and Glees (*to conclude with 'Rule Britannia' in full chorus*)	The Agreeable Surprise	Miss Smith

Date	Mainpiece	Afterpiece / Additional	Performer
F. Oct 27 1809	**Isabella; or, The Fatal Marriage**		The Quaker	Miss Smith
M. Oct 30	The Grecian Daughter	Collins's 'Ode on the Passions'; Lock and Key	Miss Smith
W. Nov 1	Man and Wife	Killing No Murder	
F. Nov 3	Adelgitha; or, The Fruits of a Single Error	La Provençal (*dance*); Killing no Murder	The Giroux
M. Nov 6	The Clandestine Marriage	Dancing; The Young Hussar	The Giroux
W. Nov 8	**Pizarro**	The Rival Milk Maids (*dance*); The Devil to Pay	The Giroux
F. Nov 10	George Barnwell	**The Happy Disguise; or, Love in Spain** (*'new serio-comic ballet dance'*); Killing No Murder	The Giroux
M. Nov 13	The Dramatist; or, Stop Him Who Can!	La Provençal; A Tale of Mystery	The Giroux
W. Nov 15	The West Indian	Dancing; Of Age To-morrow	The Giroux
F. Nov 17	Percy	**The Happy Disguise; or Love in Spain**; The Rival Soldiers	The Giroux
M. Nov 20	**The Honey Moon**	Rival Milk Maids (*dance*); Of Age To-morrow	The Giroux and Elliston
M. Nov 27	The Suspicious Husband	Dancing; The Hunter of the Alps	The Giroux and Elliston
W. Nov 29	The Three and the Deuce	**The Happy Disguise; or Love in Spain**; The Deaf Lover	The Giroux and Elliston
M. Dec 4	**A Bold Stroke for a Wife**	The Prize	Bannister
M. Dec 11	The Jew	Peeping Tom of Coventry	Bannister
M. Dec 18	The City Wives' Confederacy	Bannister's Imitation of Beggars and Ballad Singers; Ways and Means; or, A Trip to Dover	Bannister
Th. Dec 21	Bannister's Second Budget (*divertissement*)		Bannister
W. Dec 27	The Exile	Killing No Murder	
M. Jan 1 **1810**	Love in a Village	The Children in the Wood	Mrs Dickons
M. Jan 8	**The English Fleet in 1342**	Tom Thumb the Great	Mrs Dickons
M. Jan 15	The Maid of the Mill	No Song, No Supper	Mrs Dickons
M. Jan 22	The Foundling of the Forest	Rosina	
M. Jan 29	The Foundling of the Forest	Raymond and Agnes	
M. Feb 5	The Siege of Belgrade	The Midnight Hour	Braham
M. Feb 12	The Haunted Tower	Who's the Dupe?	Braham

Date	Mainpiece	Interlude	Afterpiece	Engagement / Benefit (House receipts/Notes)
M. Feb 19 **1810**	The Cabinet	Songs	Raising the Wind	Braham
M. Feb 26	Venoni		The Paragraph	
M. Mar 5	**The Wonder**		The Three and the Deuce	Elliston
M. Mar 12	**The Mountaineers**		**The Critic; or, A Tragedy Rehearsed**	Elliston
M. Mar 19	The Beaux Stratagem		The Critic	Elliston
M. Mar 26	The Foundling of the Forest		Raymond and Agnes	
M. Apr 2	King Henry the Fourth; or, The Humours of Sir John Falstaff		Raymond and Agnes	Blissett
M. Apr 9	Adrian and Orilla		**Don Juan**	
M. Apr 16				(Holy Week)
M. Apr 23	The Foundling of the Forest		Oscar and Malvina	
M. Apr 30	The Tempest		Oscar and Malvina	
M. May 7	Jane Shore		Valentine and Orson	Mrs Litchfield
M. May 14	The Earl of Essex		A Budget of Blunders	
M. May 21	Speed the Plough		A Budget of Blunders	
M. May 28	The Deserted Daughter		Lock and Key	
T. Jun 5	The Exile		Poor Vulcan	Miss Matthews (£89)
W. Jun 6	**The Honey Moon**		Catch Him Who Can	Part of Office-keepers
F. Jun 8	The Chapter of Accidents		Killing No Murder	Part of Office-keepers
M. Jun 11	Hero of the North	Personation	No Song, No Supper	Mrs Windsor
W. Jun 13	**King Henry the Eighth**	Songs	A Budget of Blunders (After Act 4: 'Cuddy Clump's First Visit to London and Bristol; or a Peep at the Forty Thieves')	Mr and Mrs Sedley (Retiring Benefit) (£51)
F. Jun 15	The Jealous Wife	A Day after the Wedding (by particular desire)	Love Laughs at Locksmiths	Cozens
M. Jun 18	The Castle Spectre		A Tale of Terror; or, A Castle Without a Spectre	Miss Marriot (last Benefit Miss Marriot's Farewell Speech) (£78)
W. Jun 20	George Barnwell	Songs The Mayor of Garratt	**Paul and Virginia**	Evans (£92)

Date	Mainpiece		Afterpiece	Part of Office-keepers
	The West Indian		Ella Rosenberg	Miss Jameson (£103)
F. Jun 22 1810				
M. Jun 25	Oroonoko; or, The Royal Slave	Edgar and Emmeline	Katharine and Petruchio	
W. Jun 27	**The English Fleet in 1342** (*to conclude with a representation of The British Fleet at Anchor*)	The Day after the Wedding	The Prisoner at Large; or, The Haunted Chamber	Bennett (£75.14.6)
F. Jun 29	The School for Friends	The Rival Soldiers	A Budget of Blunders (*by particular desire*)	(Various Tickets)
	'Dibdin's popular song "Naval Victories", by a Gentleman of this city' (*first appearance*)			
M. Jul 2	King John: or, England Preserv'd	The King and the Miller of Mansfield	High Life Below Stairs	Bengough (£87)
W. Jul 4	**Pizarro**		The Forty Thieves	Charlton (*Acting Manager*) (£151)
F. Jul 6	The Poor Gentleman	Not at Home	Tom Thumb	Cunningham and Webber
M. Jul 9	The Blind Bargain	**The Critic**	The Iron Mask	Lovegrove
W. Jul 11	Secrets Worth Knowing	Comic Songs 'English Hearts of Oak'	The Black Forest	Mallinson
F. Jul 13	John Bull; or, An Englishman's Fireside	Songs	The Forty Thieves	Mrs Grove
M. Jul 16	The Beggar's Opera		A Budget of Blunders	Incledon
W. Jul 18	Love in a Village		The Quaker	Incledon
F. Jul 20	**The Castle of Andalusia**		Lock and Key	Incledon
M. Jul 23 1810 [End of 1809–1810 season]	**The English Fleet in 1342**		The Waterman	Incledon
M. Oct 1 1810 [Start of 1810–1811 season]	Raising the Wind [*Not played?*]			Johnstone
W. Oct 3	The West Indian		The Irishman in London	Johnstone
F. Oct 5	The Rivals		The Review	Johnstone
M. Oct 8	John Bull		A Budget of Blunders	Johnstone
W. Oct 10	The West Indian		Honest Thieves	Johnstone
F. Oct 12	False and True		The Irishman in London	Johnstone
M. Oct 15	Othello		A Tale of Mystery	Pope

Date	Mainpiece	Interlude	Afterpiece	Engagement / **Benefit** (House receipts/*Notes*)
W. Oct 17 1810	The Jealous Wife		**Don Juan**	Pope
F. Oct 19	**The Mountaineers**	The Weathercock	The Black Forest	Pope
M. Oct 22	**Pizarro**		No Song, No Supper	
W. Oct 24	**Rule a Wife and Have a Wife**		A Tale of Mystery	
F. Oct 26	The Provoked Husband		**Don Juan**	Pope
M. Oct 29	King Lear		The Blind Boy	Pope
W. Oct 31	The Point of Honour		La Perouse; or, The Desolate Island	
F. Nov 2	The Chapter of Accidents		La Perouse	*(No performances this week because of the death of Her Royal Highness Princess Amelia)*
M. Nov 5				
M. Nov 12	The Foundling of the Forest		La Perouse	
W. Nov 14	The Clandestine Marriage		La Perouse	
Th. Nov 15	George Barnwell		La Perouse	
F. Nov 16	**The Honey Moon**		Hit or Miss	
M. Nov 19	The Jew		La Perouse	Bannister
M. Nov 26	The Heir at Law	Dermot and Kathleen	Peeping Tom of Coventry	Bannister
M. Dec 3	The World		Ella Rosenberg	Bannister
M. Dec 10	A Cure for the Heart-ache		The Jew and the Doctor	Elliston
M. Dec 17	The Dramatist		The Three and the Deuce	Elliston
F. Dec 21	**The Honey Moon**		Of Age To-morrow	Elliston
W. Dec 26	The Castle Spectre		Valentine and Orson	
M. Dec 31	**The Doubtful Son**		Valentine and Orson	
M. Jan 7 1811	The Curfew		La Perouse	
M. Jan 14	**The Doubtful Son**		La Perouse	
M. Jan 21	The School for Scandal		The Sultan	Mrs Jordan
M. Jan 28	The Soldier's Daughter		**The Pannel**	Mrs Jordan
M. Feb 4	All in the Wrong		The Devil to Pay	Mrs Jordan
M. Feb 11	A Trip to Scarborough		The Wedding Day	Mrs Jordan
M. Feb 18	Hamlet		Rosina	Elliston

362

Date	Mainpiece	Additional pieces	Afterpiece	Benefit / Notes
	Pizarro		The Doctor and The Apothecary	Elliston
M. Mar 4	**The Doubtful Son**		La Perouse	
M. Mar 11	Speed the Plough		The Blind Boy	
M. Mar 18	The Maniac		The Prisoner at Large	
M. Mar 25	The Foundling of the Forest		The Forty Thieves	
M. Apr 1	Know Your Own Mind		Inkle and Yarico	
M. Apr 8				(*Holy Week*)
M. Apr 15	The Beggar's Opera		The Forty Thieves	Incledon
M. Apr 22	**The Castle of Andalusia**		The Quaker	Incledon
M. Apr 29	Columbus		Out of Place	
M. May 6	Ourselves		Oscar and Malvina	
M. May 13	Columbus		The Bee Hive	
M. May 20	The Foundling of the Forest		The Bee Hive	
M. May 27	Columbus		The Bee Hive	
M. Jun 3	Every One Has His Fault		La Perouse	
W. Jun 5	Columbus		The Bee Hive	
F. Jun 7	The Castle Spectre	No Song, No Supper	Killing No Murder	Part of the Office-keepers
M. Jun 10	Deaf and Dumb		Raymond and Agnes	Mr and Mrs Vining
W. Jun 12	The Point of Honour		**Paul and Virginia**	Miss Mathews
F. Jun 14	Speed the Plough		A Budget of Blunders	Part of the Office-keepers
M. Jun 17	The Family Legend	**The Critic** (*Act 1*)	Trial by Jury	Abbott
W. Jun 19	The Way to Get Married	Songs and dances	La Perouse	Stanley
F. Jun 21	Lovers' Vows		A Tale of Mystery	Cozens (*Box-Book Keeper*) (£79)
M. Jun 24	The Grecian Daughter	The Mayor of Garratt; 'A Tailor's Goose can Never Fly' (*song*)	The Farmer	Miss Jameson (£129)
W. Jun 26	George Barnwell	Hob in the Well; 'Farmer Stump; or a Peep at Bristol Fashions', by Mr Evans; 'Irish Promotion', by Mr Gattie	**Don Juan** (*with the representation of a sea storm and shipwreck*)	Mr and Mrs Egan (£75)

Date	Mainpiece	Interlude	Afterpiece	Engagement / **Benefit** (House receipts/*Notes*)
F. Jun 28 1811	The Poor Gentleman		Love Laughs at Locksmiths	Gattie, Miss Summers, Miss Chapman
M. Jul 1	The Gazette Extraordinary	Songs	The Forest of Hermanstadt; or, Princess and No Princess	Charlton (*Acting Manager*)
M. Jul 8	Coriolanus; or, The Roman Matron	Songs (*including* **Graham and Glory; or, The Battle of Barrosa**, *by Mr Gattie*)	Tekeli	Bengough (£179 '*Under the Patronage of the Officers of the Oxford Regiment*')
W. Jul 10	John Bull		A Budget of Blunders	Remaining Part of Office-keepers
F. Jul 12	The West Indian		The Blind Boy	
M. Jul 15	**Pizarro**		The Forty Thieves	Evans
W. Jul 17	**Much Ado About Nothing**	A Trip to Scotland	Ella Rosenberg	Mr Cunningham
F. Jul 19	The Belle's Stratagem	[Entertainments by Richer]	Hit or Miss	Richer
M. Jul 22 1811 [End of 1810–1811 season]	Gazette Extraordinary		The Forest of Hermanstadt	Richer
M. Sep 30 1811 [Start of 1811–1812 season]	Love in a Village		The Prize	Miss Feron
W. Oct 2	The Cabinet		The Bee Hive	Miss Feron
F. Oct 4	**The Mountaineers**	Songs	Of Age To-morrow	Miss Feron
M. Oct 7	The Haunted Tower		No Song, No Supper	Miss Feron
W. Oct 9	The Exile		Rosina	Miss Feron
F. Oct 11	Gazette Extraordinary		The Young Hussar	Miss Feron
M. Oct 14	**The Duenna**		A Tale of Mystery	Miss Feron
W. Oct 16	The Haunted Tower		**The Padlock**	Miss Feron
F. Oct 18	Artaxerxes	A Tag in Tribulation	The Prize	Miss Feron
M. Oct 21	The Royal Oak		La Perouse	
W. Oct 23	The Royal Oak		Raymond and Agnes	
F. Oct 25	The Grecian Daughter		The Forty Thieves	
M. Oct 28	The Royal Oak		Edgar and Emmeline	
W. Oct 30	As You Like It		My Grandmother	
F. Nov 1	**Pizarro**		The Forty Thieves	

Date	Main piece	Entertainment	Afterpiece	Performer(s)
M. Nov 4 **1811**	The West Indian		The Three and the Deuce	Elliston
W. Nov 6	Romeo and Juliet		Love Laughs at Locksmiths	Elliston
M. Nov 11	The Iron Chest		The Spoil'd Child	Elliston
T. Nov 12	George Barnwell	Sylvester Daggerwood	La Perouse	Elliston
W. Nov 13	The Dramatist		The Three and the Deuce	Elliston
F. Nov 15	The Fair Penitent		The Deaf Lover	Elliston
M. Nov 18	The West Indian		Raising the Wind	Elliston
M. Nov 25	Hit or Miss	The Quaker	Killing No Murder	Mathews and Incledon
M. Dec 2	The Venetian Outlaw	Sylvester Daggerwood	The Doctor and the Apothecary	Elliston
M. Dec 9	The Royal Oak	The Rival Rustics	No Song, No Supper	
M. Dec 16	The Peasant Boy	Love's Artifice	The Wedding Day	
M. Dec 23	The Peasant Boy	Dancing	The Irish Widow	The Giroux and Flexmore
Th. Dec 26	George Barnwell	Dancing	The Sultan	The Giroux and Flexmore
M. Dec 30	The Peasant Boy	The Wrangling Lovers	The Devil to Pay	Richer
W. Jan 1 **1812**	The Point of Honour	[Entertainments by Richer]	Mother Ludlam	Richer, The Giroux, and Flexmore
M. Jan 6	Fontainebleau	[Entertainments by Richer]	**Paul and Virginia**	Richer
M. Jan 13	The Haunted Tower		Valentine and Orson	Braham
M. Jan 20	The Cabinet	[Entertainments by Richer]	Barnaby Buttle	Braham
M. Jan 27	**The Castle of Andalusia**		A Budget of Blunders	Braham
W. Jan 29	The Maniac		The Midnight Hour	Braham
M. Feb 3	The Siege of Belgrade		The Widow's Vow	Braham
Th. Feb 6	Abroad and at Home		Barnaby Buttle	Braham
M. Feb 10	The Cabinet (*last act*)	The Haunted Tower (*Act 2*)	High Life Below Stairs	Braham
M. Feb 17	The Earl of Essex	**The Castle of Andalusia** (*Act 2*)	Rosina	Betty
M. Feb 24	Barbarossa		Obi	Betty
M. Mar 2	Hamlet		**The Follies of a Day**	Betty
M. Mar 9	The Recruiting Officer		Blue Beard	Betty
M. Mar 16	**The Doubtful Son**		Blue Beard	
M. Mar 23				
M. Mar 30	The Lady of the Lake		Blue Beard	(*Holy Week*)

Date	Mainpiece	Interlude	Afterpiece	Engagement / **Benefit** (House receipts/*Notes*)
F. Apr 3 **1812**	Concert			
M. Apr 6	Tancred and Sigismunda		The Boarding House	Betty
M. Apr 13	Alexander the Great		The Boarding House	Betty
M. Apr 20	The Siege of Damascus		Turn Out	
M. Apr 27	The Lady of the Lake		Turn Out	
M. May 4	The Birth-Day	The Agreeable Surprise	The Review	Fawcett
M. May 11	Cato		Twenty Years Ago	
M. May 18	**The English Fleet 1342**		Comus	Incledon
M. May 25	The Lady of the Lake		Blue Beard	
M. Jun 1	The Castle of Montval		Cinderella; or, The Little Glass Slipper	
M. Jun 8	The Sons of Erin		Cinderella	
Th. Jun 11	'Grand Concert'	Personation	Rugantino	Loder
M. Jun 15	Inkle and Yarico **Pizarro**		Tekeli	Abbott
T. Jun 16	The Merchant of Venice	Fortune's Frolics	Captain Cook	Stanley
M. Jun 22	**The Honey Moon**		The Citizen	Miss Duncan
W. June 24	The Surrender of Calais		Cymon	Miss Matthews
M. Jun 29	Macbeth	Robin Hood	William Tell	Bengough
W. Jul 1	Cymbeline		Forty Thieves	Mr Woodhouse
M. Jul 6	Which is the Man?	Valentine and Orson	Phantasmagoria	Miss Jameson
W. Jul 8	The Country Girl	Richard Coeur de Lion	Bombastes Furioso	Miss Kelly
M. Jul 13	The Sons of Erin		Cinderella	Charlton
W. Jul 15	Any Thing New	The Irish Widow	The False Friend	Woulds and Chatterly
M. Jul 20	Cinderella	A Tag in Tribulation The Castle Spectre	Mother Hubbard	Mr and Mrs Vining (*'Under the Patronage of the Oxford Regiment'*)
W. Jul 22	**King Henry the Eighth**	The Mayor of Garratt	How to Die for Love	Evans
F. Jul 24	The Young Quaker	Bombastes Furioso	Blue Beard	Cunningham

Date	A Bold Stroke for a Wife	Sylvester Daggerwood	Peeping Tom of Coventry	Bannister
M. Jul 27, 1812 [End of 1811–1812 season]	A Bold Stroke for a Wife	Sylvester Daggerwood	Peeping Tom of Coventry	Bannister
M. Sep 28 1812 [Start of 1812–1813 season]	The Sons of Erin		Turn Out	Miss Duncan
W. Sep 30	The Country Girl		The Devil to Pay	Miss Duncan
F. Oct 2	The Kind Imposter		Cinderella	Miss Duncan
M. Oct 5	The Provoked Husband		No Song, No Supper	Miss Duncan
W. Oct 7	The Recruiting Officer		How to Die for Love	Braham and Mrs Childe
M. Oct 12	The Siege of Belgrade		A Budget of Blunders	Braham and Mrs Childe
W. Oct 14	The Haunted Tower		Barnaby Buttle	Braham and Mrs Childe
F. Oct 16	The Cabinet		The Poor Soldier	Braham and Mrs Childe
M. Oct 19	**The Castle of Andalusia**		Cinderella	Braham
W. Oct 21	The Devil's Bridge		How to Die for Love	Braham and Mrs Childe
F. Oct 23	The Devil's Bridge		**The Follies of a Day**	Braham and Mrs Childe
M. Oct 26	**The Duenna**		A Tale of Mystery	Braham and Mrs Childe
W. Oct 28	The Siege of Belgrade		High Life Below Stairs	Braham
F. Oct 30	The Haunted Tower (Act 2)	**The Castle of Andalusia** (Act 2)	The Widows Vow	Braham
M. Nov 2	The Grecian Daughter	The Cabinet (last act) [Vestris and Mme Didelot – Pas Seul dancing]	The Romp	Vestris and Mme Didelot
W. Nov 4	**Pizarro**	The Wooden Leg; or, The Sailor's Return [Vestris and Mme Didelot – dancing]	The Devil to Pay	Vestris and Mme Didelot
F. Nov 6	The Pilgrim	[Vestris and Mme Didelot – dancing]	The Rival Soldiers	Vestris and Mme Didelot
M. Nov 9	The Foundling of the Forest	[Vestris and Mme Didelot – dancing]	Miss in Her Teens	Vestris and Mme Didelot
M. Nov 16	Adrian and Orilla	[Vestris and Mme Didelot – dancing]	Any Thing New	Vestris and Mme Didelot
F. Nov 20	The Lady of the Lake	[Vestris and Mme Didelot – dancing]	Lovers' Quarrels	Vestris
M. Nov 23	Macbeth		The Wedding Day	J. P. Kemble
M. Nov 30	King John		Marian	J. P. Kemble

Date	Mainpiece	Interlude	Afterpiece	Engagement / **Benefit** (House receipts/*Notes*)
M. Dec 7 **1812**	King Lear		Marian	J. P. Kemble
M. Dec 14	The Peasant Boy	(Vestris and Miss Mori – dancing)	Matrimony	Vestris and Miss Mori
M. Dec 21	King Lear		The Spoil'd Child	J. P. Kemble
M. Dec 28	Coriolanus (*at the end of Act 2: 'A Grand Ovation, upon the return of Caius Marcius from the Conquest of Corioli*)		How to Die for Love	J. P. Kemble
M. Jan 4 **1813**	Rich and Poor	Robinson Crusoe	Love, Law and Physick	Mrs Jordan
M. Jan 11	The Country Girl	Robinson Crusoe	Love, Law and Physick	Mrs Jordan
M. Jan 18	City Wives' Confederacy		**The Pannel**	Mrs Jordan
M. Jan 25	As You Like It		The Devil to Pay	
M. Feb 1	Love for Love		Peter the Great; or Russian Laurels	
M. Feb 8	Douglas		Peter the Great	Betty
M. Feb 15	Alexander the Great		The Guardian	Betty
M. Feb 22	The Royal Oak		The Wedding Day	Betty
M. Mar 1	Romeo and Juliet		Harlequin and Mother Goose	Betty
Th. Mar 4	Adelgitha		The Weathercock	Betty
M. Mar 8	**The Students of Salamanca**		Harlequin and Mother Goose	
M. Mar 15	The Knight and the Wood Daemon; or, The Clock Strikes One		The Wedding Ring	
M. Mar 22	The Knight and the Wood Daemon		The Two Misers of Smyrna	
M. Mar 29	The Knight and the Wood Daemon	**Love in Spain; or, The French Marauders** (*'entirely new ballet dance'*)	The Day after the Wedding	

Date	Mainpiece	Second piece	Afterpiece	Performers / Notes
M. Apr 5 1813	Remorse		Selima and Azor	*(Last night of performances till the Easter holidays. REMORSE: Mr Coleridge's very popular new TRAGEDY... As now performing at the Theatre Royal Drury Lane, with the most distinguished Applause; with the original Music, and appropriate Scenery; Machinery; Dresses, and Decorations')* (Holy Week)
M. Apr 12				
M. Apr 19	The Provoked Husband		Harlequin and Mother Goose	Mrs Campbell (*née* Wallis) and Blisset
M. Apr 26	Measure for Measure		Timour the Tartar	Mrs Campbell
W. Apr 28	The Winter's Tale		Harlequin and Mother Goose	Mrs Campbell
M. May 3	**The Duenna**		Midas	Sinclair
W. May 5	**The Renegade**		Midas	Sinclair
M. May 10	M.F. Or, the Bluestocking!		Timour the Tartar	Sinclair
W. May 12	The Lord of the Manor		The Quaker	Incledon and Sinclair
M. May 17	The Lord of the Manor		Poor Vulcan	Incledon and Sinclair
W. May 19	Love in a Village		Midas	Sinclair, Blisset and Incledon
M. May 24	Education		Cinderella	
M. May 31	Education		The Forty Thieves	
M. Jun 7	**The Virgin of the Sun**	The Sleeping Beauty in the Wood	Koah and Zoah; or, The Wild Island Girl	Miss Simeon ('Under the patronage of Lieut General Gordon Cuming')
W. Jun 9	The Exile	The Day after the Wedding	The Mogul Tale	
F. Jun 11	Fatal Curiosity (*billed as 'The Cornish Shipwreck'*)		**The Virgin of the Sun**	Gattie
M. Jun 14	Bombastes Furioso	Zeluco	The Hunter of the Alps	Stanley
W. Jun 16	The Fall of Fair Rosamond	The Natural Son	Koah and Zoah	Miss Willis, Blissett
F. Jun 18	Love's Last Shift	Inkle and Yarico	The Devil to Pay	Viney (Pit Office Receiver), Knight

Date	Mainpiece	Interlude	Afterpiece	Engagement / **Benefit** (House receipts/*Notes*)
M. Jun 21 **1813**	The Africans	Bon Ton	The Ghost	Bengough
W. Jun 23	**The Honey Moon**	'A celebrated shawl dance'	**Paul and Virginia**	Cozens (Box-Book Keeper)
F. Jun 25	The Double Gallant		The Mogul Tale	Wayland, Underwood
M. Jun 28	Love Makes a Man		The Brazen Bust	Charlton (*Acting Manager*)
W. Jun 30	King Henry the Fourth		The Forty Thieves	Chatterley
F. Jul 2	George Barnwell		Obi	Ley and Comer
M. Jul 5	The Privateer	Songs	The Review; or, The Wags of Windsor	Fawcett
T. Jul 6	Five Miles Off; or, The Finger Post	The Brazen Bust Songs	Tom Thumb the Great	Fawcett, Woulds
M. Jul 12	The Knight and the Wood Daemon		Blue Beard	Mrs Weston
W. Jul 14	The Way to Get Married	The Rival Soldiers	The Lake of Lausanne	Miss Matthews
F. Jul 16	Love's Last Shift		The King and the Miller of Mansfield	Ash, Mrs Egan, and Miss Hudson Mr and Mrs Lodge
M. Jul 19	The [Knight and the] Wood Daemon		The Blood-Red Knights; or, The Chieftains of Ireland	Mr and Mrs Vining (*'The band of the Longford Regiment will attend, and in the course of the Evening, play several select pieces of music'*)
W. Jul 21	Hamlet Travestie	Blue Beard **'King Joey's flight; or, Wellington in Spain'** (*by Mr Evans*)	The Forty Thieves	Evans
F. Jul 23	The West Indian		Cinderella	Cunningham and Miss Summers
M. Jul 26	Timour the Tartar		The Midnight Hour	Equestrian Troop
F. Jul 30	Animal Magnetism		Timour the Tartar	
M. Aug 2	Timour the Tartar		The Recruiting Officer	
T. Aug 3	Cymon		[Timour the Tartar]	
W. Aug 4	Cymon		[Timour the Tartar]	

Date	Main piece		Afterpiece	Performers
[… Aug … 1813]	Cyron		[Timour the Tartar]	Mrs Campbell
F. Aug 6	Blue Beard		Timour the Tartar	Young and Mrs Campbell
M. Aug 9 1813 [End of 1812–1813 season]	Cyron		Timour the Tartar	Young and Mrs Campbell
M. Sep 27 1813 [Start of 1813–1814 season]	Measure for Measure	The Jovial Millers	The Wedding Day	Young
W. Sep 29	Venice Preserv'd	Watkin and Winney; or, Taffy's Disaster	The Devil to Pay	Young
F. Oct 1	The Gamester	The Jovial Millers	High Life Below Stairs	Young
M. Oct 4	Coriolanus		The King and the Miller of Mansfield	Young
W. Oct 6	Hamlet		Mother Goose	Young
F. Oct 8	Julius Caesar		The Maid of the Oaks	
M. Oct 11	The Honey Moon		The Prize	
W. Oct 13	The Stranger		The Maid of the Oaks	
F. Oct 15	The Castle Spectre		Mother Goose	
M. Oct 18	The Wonder		Llewellyn, Prince of Wales	
W. Oct 20	Lovers' Vows		Llewellyn, Prince of Wales	
F. Oct 22	The School for Scandal		Llewellyn, Prince of Wales	
M. Oct 25	The School for Greybeards		Llewellyn, Prince of Wales	
W. Oct 27	The School for Greybeards		Llewellyn, Prince of Wales	
F. Oct 29	Lovers' Vows		Harlequin and Mother Goose	
M. Nov 1	The Beggar's Opera		The Deuce is in Him	Phillips
W. Nov 3	The Devil's Bridge		The Prize	Phillips
F. Nov 5	The Siege of Belgrade		The Citizen	Phillips
M. Nov 8	The Beggar's Opera	[Entertainments by Richer]	The Deuce is in Him	Phillips, Richer
W. Nov 10	The Siege of Belgrade	[Entertainments by Richer]	Don Juan	Phillips, Richer
Th. Nov 11	Lionel and Clarissa	[Entertainments by Richer]	The Deserter of Naples	Phillips, Richer
F. Nov 12	The Cabinet	[Entertainments by Richer]	The Citizen	Phillips, Richer
M. Nov 15	Lionel and Clarissa		The Blind Boy	Phillips
W. Nov 17	Wives as they were and Maids as they are	[Entertainments by Richer]	Oscar and Malvina	Richer
M. Nov 22	First Impressions		Rosina	
M. Nov 29	The Winter's Tale	Orange Boven	Obi; or, Three-Finger'd Jack	
M. Dec 6	The Winter's Tale		Obi	
M. Dec 13	The Maid of the Mill		Ella Rosenberg	

Date	Mainpiece	Interlude	Afterpiece	Engagement / **Benefit** (House receipts/*Notes*)
M. Dec 20 **1813**	Sherwood Forest	**Orange Boven**	The Sultan	Equestrian Troop
M. Dec 27	Barbarossa		Timour the Tartar	Equestrian Troop
T. Dec 28	The Earl of Essex		Timour the Tartar	Equestrian Troop
W. Dec 29	George Barnwell		Timour the Tartar	Equestrian Troop
Th. Dec 30	Fatal Curiosity		Lodoiska (*with equestrian troop*)	Equestrian Troop
M. Jan 3 **1814**	Lovers' Vows		Lodoiska (*with equestrian troop*)	Equestrian Troop
W. Jan 5	The Country Lasses; or, The Custom of the Manner		Lodoiska (*with equestrian troop*)	Equestrian Troop
Th. Jan 6	**The Doubtful Son**		Lodoiska (*with equestrian troop*)	Equestrian Troop
M. Jan 10	The Suspicious Husband		The Children in the Wood	Mrs Jordan
M. Jan 17	The Trip to Scarborough		The Devil to Pay	Mrs Jordan
M. Jan 24	The Belle's Stratagem		**The Pannel**	Mrs Jordan
M. Jan 31	The Way to Keep Him		**The Pannel**	Mrs Jordan
M. Feb 7	Jane Shore		Ella Rosenberg	
M. Feb 14	The Miller and His Men	Oroonoko	Lilliput	
M. Feb 21	King Henry the Fourth		The Miller and His Men	
M. Feb 28	The Point of Honour	Lilliput	The Miller and His Men	
M. Mar 7	King Henry the Fifth; or, The Conquest of France		The Miller and His Men	
M. Mar 14	The Royal Oak	Songs	The Miller and His Men	
M. Mar 21	The Maid of the Mill	[Waltz]	For England Ho!	
M. Mar 28	The Orphan of the Castle; or, The Black Banner		For England Ho!	
M. Apr 4				(*Holy Week*)
M. Apr 11	King Lear and His Three Daughters		The Beggar's Opera	J. P. Kemble
M. Apr 18	Coriolanus		The Wandering Boys	J.P. Kemble
M. Apr 25	**Pizarro**		For England Ho!	J.P. Kemble
M. May 2	Macbeth		Tekeli	J. P. Kemble
M. May 9	Cato		How to Die for Love	J. P. Kemble

Date				Performer
W. May 18	The Hypocrite		Killing No Murder	Mathews
M. May 23	The Good Natured Man	The Wedding Day	The Sleep Walker	Mathews
			Imitations	
W. May 25	The Farmer's Wife	Recitation: 'A Dissertation on Hobby Horses'	The Dead Alive	Mathews
M. May 30	Who Wants a Guinea?	Songs	The Lying Valet	Mathews
		Love a-la Mode (*Act 1*)		
M. Jun 6	The Flitch of Bacon	The Bath Road; or, Intrigue	The Magic of Hope; or, Columbine Captive	
		The Miller and his Men		
M. Jun 13	Wild Oats		The Miller and His Men	Elliston
F. Jun 17	The School of Reform		Bombastes Furioso	
M. Jun 20	The Knight and the Wood Daemon	The Bath Road	The Devil to Pay	
M. Jun 27	Debtor and Creditor (*in which Mrs Dickons will introduce, by particular desire, 'The Soldier Tir'd of War's Alarms'*)			(*General Illuminations*)
T. Jun 28			The Children in the Wood	
M. Jul 4	The Exile		No Song, No Supper	Mrs Dickons
T. Jul 5	The Cabinet	Songs	Matrimony	Mrs Dickons
F. Jul 8	The West Indian		Animal Magnetism	Part of Office-keepers
M. Jul 11	Alexander the Great	Britain's Glory	The Miller and His Men	Mrs Vining
W. Jul 13	Adelgitha	'A Loyal and Congratulatory Address on the late Glorious Events (*written expressly for the occasion by a Gentleman of Bristol*) delivered by Mr Warde'	Inkle and Yarico	Ash and Warde
F. Jul 15	The Knight and the Wood Daemon	The Bath Road	The Prisoner at Large	Cozens

373

Date	Mainpiece	Interlude	Afterpiece	Engagement / Benefit (House receipts/Notes)
M. Jul 18 **1814**	King Richard the Third	Britain's Glory!; or, a Trip to Portsmouth	Who's to Have Her?	Bengough
W. Jul 20	Fontainebleau	Songs	Chrononhontanthologos	Woulds
F. Jul 22	**Pizarro**	The Purse	How to Die For Love	Part of the Office-keepers
M. Jul 25	The School of Shakespeare (*Anthology*)	Sprigs of Laurel	Bombastes Furioso	Mr and Mrs Chatterly
W. Jul 27	Next Door Neighbours; or, The Gamester Reclaimed	Lilliput / The Absent Man	A Trip to Dover; or, To and From Calais (*to conclude with a view of the British Squadron prior to embarkation*)	Cunningham
F. Jul 29	The Castle Spectre	The Theatrical Candidates / The Corn Thrashers (*ballet dance*)	The Hunter of the Alps	
M. Aug 1	**Remorse**	Britain's Glory; or a Trip to Portsmouth (*nautical interlude*)	For England Ho!	Mrs Weston
W. Aug 3	Edward the Black Prince	Harlequin Skelton	Valentine and Orson	Stanley (*Entertainments chosen 'in accordance with public feeling [...] and the glorious Triumphs won by Englishmen of other days, in their advance upon Bordeaux, upon the same spot lately consecrated to fame by the VICTORIES of LORD WELLINGTON'*)
F. Aug 5	The Foundling of the Forest	Songs / Garrick's Pageant of the Jubilee	The Miller and His Men	Miss Summers (*Order of procession for the pageant included on reverse of playbill*)
M. Aug 8 1814 [End of 1813–1814 season]	George Barnwell	The Purse	The Children in the Wood	

1814–1815 season]

Date		(… dances by Misses Giroux)		
W. Sep 28	**The Duenna**	The Frolic	The Wedding Day	Mr and Mrs T. Cooke
F. Sep 30	The Haunted Tower		The Miller and His Men	Mr and Mrs T. Cooke
M. Oct 3	The Siege of Belgrade		The Spoil'd Child	Mr and Mrs T. Cooke
W. Oct 5	The Clandestine Marriage		**Paul and Virginia**	
F. Oct 7	The Haunted Tower		The Miller and His Men	Mr and Mrs T. Cooke
M. Oct 10	The Foundling of the Forest		The Cabinet	Mr and Mrs T. Cooke
W. Oct 12	The Earl of Essex		Aladdin	Mr and Mrs T. Cooke
F. Oct 14	**The Castle of Andalusia**		Aladdin	Mr and Mrs T. Cooke
M. Oct 17	Love in a Village	The Agreeable Surprise	Aladdin	Mr and Mrs T. Cooke
W. Oct 19	Ella Rosenberg		Aladdin	
F. Oct 21	Frederick the Great		Aladdin	Mr and Mrs T. Cooke
M. Oct 24	Frederick the Great		Aladdin	Mr and Mrs T. Cooke
W. Oct 26	The Siege of Belgrade		Aladdin	Mr and Mrs T. Cooke
F. Oct 28	The Devil's Bridge	Henry and Emma; or, Two to One	The False Friend; or, The Assassin of the Rocks	Misses Giront
M. Oct 31	Frederick the Great		Lock and Key	Mr and Mrs T. Cooke
Th. Nov 3	Mahomet the Imposter		Harlequin and Padmanaba; or, The Golden Fish	Grimaldi
F. Nov 4	The School for Daughters		Harlequin and Padmanaba	Grimaldi
M. Nov 7	Adrian and Orilla		Harlequin and Padmanaba	Grimaldi
W. Nov 9	The Blind Boy	**Paul and Virginia**	Harlequin and Padmanaba	Grimaldi
Th. Nov 10	George Barnwell		**Don Juan**	Grimaldi
F. Nov 11	The Funeral; or, Grief a-la Mode		Harlequin and Padmanaba	Grimaldi
M. Nov 14	The Young Quaker		**The Wild Man**	Grimaldi
M. Nov 21	Fountainville Forest		**The Wild Man**	Grimaldi
M. Nov 28	**Rule a Wife and Have a Wife**	The Shipwreck	Harlequin and Mother Goose	Grimaldi
M. Dec 5	Mail Coach Adventures	The Bath Road	Harlequin and Mother Goose	Grimaldi
W. Dec 7	Policy; or, Thus Runs the World Away	The Ghost; or, The Dead Man Alive	How to Die for Love	Mathews
M. Dec 12			Aladdin	
M. Dec 19	**The Fair Penitent**	[Entertainments by the young Ducrow]	Aladdin	Ducrow

375

Date	Mainpiece	Interlude	Afterpiece	Engagement / **Benefit** (House receipts/*Notes*)
M. Dec 26 **1814**	The Forest of Bondy	[Entertainments by the young Ducrow]	Raymond and Agnes	Ducrow
W. Dec 28	John of Paris	[Entertainments by the young Ducrow]	The Shipwreck	Ducrow
M. Jan 2 **1815**	The Forest of Bondy	The King and the Duke	The King and the Duke	
M. Jan 9	The Knight and the Wood Daemon	John of Paris	John of Paris	
M. Jan 16	The Siege of Belgrade	**Leander and Leonora**	The King and the Duke	T. Cooke and Mrs Mountain
M. Jan 23	The Peasant Boy	**Leander and Leonora**	Midas	
W. Feb 1	The Distressed Mother		The Cabinet	Macready
M. Feb 6	Alexander the Great		John of Paris	Macready
M. Feb 13	Fontainebleau		The Miller and His Men	Macready
M. Feb 20	**The English Fleet in 1342**		John of Paris	
M. Feb 27	The Hero of the North		The Hunter of the Alps	T. Cooke
M. Mar 6	Riches!		The Miller and his Men	
M. Mar 13	The Surrender of Calais (*First time in five years. In Act 3 'the Procession of Patriots to the Place of Execution, And the Celebrated Glee of Peace to the Souls of the Heroes'*)		John of Paris (*by particular desire*)	
M. Mar 20				(*Holy Week*)
M. Mar 27	Othello		The Forest of Bondy	Betty
M. Apr 3	Zenobia		Past Ten O'Clock, And a Rainy Night	Betty
M. Apr 10	King Henry the Fourth; or, The Humours of Falstaff		Past Ten O'Clock	Betty
M. Apr 17	Barbarossa	The King and the Duke	The Weathercock; or, Where Will He Fix?	Betty
M. Apr 24	**Much Ado About Nothing**		Turn Out	Mrs Davison (*née* Duncan)
M. May 1	Romeo and Juliet		The Spoil'd Child	Miss Booth

	The Lane	The Romp		Miss Booth
M. May 15	Oroonoko	John of Paris	A West Wind	Mrs Weston
M. May 22	Pizarro	Aladdin		Warde (*Retiring Benefit*)
M. May 29	Town and Country	John of Paris	Dances	Mrs Vining
M. Jun 5	Narensky; or, The Road to Yaroslaf	La Perouse	**Paul and Virginia**	
W. Jun 7	The Mysteries of the Castle	The Travellers Benighted; or, The Woodman's Hut	Dances	Stanley
F. Jun 9	Jane Shore	Rosina	The Jew and the Doctor	
M. Jun 12	Laugh When You Can; or, The Two Philosophers	The Miller and His Men	Quarter Day; or, How to Pay Rent Without Money	Mr and Mrs Woulds
W. Jun 14	A Cure for the Heart-ache	Cinderella	Blue Devils	Mr and Mrs Cunningham and Family
F. Jun 16	The Fortune of War	Aladdin	Comus	Miss Summers (*The playbills for The Fortune of War note that this piece was 'commanded three times during the last month by her Royal Highness, the Princess Charlotte of Wales, who never had been attracted to any theatre previous to its performance'*)
M. Jun 19	The Battle of Hexham; or, Lays of Old	The Young Hussar; or, Love and Mercy	Fortune's Frolics	Mr and Mrs Chatterly
W. Jun 21	The Maid of the Mill	Hob in the Well	Donald and Jenny; or, The Highland Lovers	Comer and Miss Rennell
F. Jun 23	**A Bold Stroke for a Husband**	The Black Forest	Songs	Willmott (Prompter)
M. Jun 26	The Knight and the Wood Daemon	The Fortune of War	Comus	Miss Nash

377

Date	Mainpiece	Interlude	Afterpiece	Engagement / **Benefit** (House receipts/*Notes*)
W. Jun 28 **1815**	Edgar and Emmeline	My Grandmother / For England Ho!	The Grand Alliance	<u>Highman</u> (The Grand Alliance – *as performed at Covent Garden 'before the Allied Sovereigns'*)
F. Jun 30	The Recruiting Officer		The Devil to Pay	<u>Underwood</u> (Pit Check Taker)
M. Jul 3	**King Henry the Eighth**	Doldrum; or, The Year 1822	Blue Beard	<u>Bengough</u>
W. Jul 5	My Grandmother	Midas	Tom Thumb	<u>Miss Sheen and Hoddeson</u>
F. Jul 7	Speed the Plough	Songs (*Mr Woulds – to sing 'an entire new Comic Song (upon the late Glorious News) called Victory Boys, Huzza! And Wellington for Ever!!'*)	The Hunter of the Alps	<u>Cozen, Box-Book-Keeper</u>
M. Jul 10	The Merchant of Venice		Midas	Kean
T. Jul 11	King Richard the Third		Comus	Kean
W. Jul 12 1815 [End 1814–1815 of season]	Othello	The Young Hussar	The Doldrum	Kean

Bibliography

Primary Material

Databases

The Adelphi Theatre 1806–1900: A Calendar of Performances. General Editors
  Alfred L. Nelson and Gilbert B. Cross http://www.emich.edu/public/english/
  adelphi_calendar/acpmain.htm.
Old Bailey Proceedings Online. http://www.oldbaileyonline.org.
*Prints from the Curzon Collection: Images of Napoleon and British Fears of
  Invasion, 1789–1815*. http://www2.odl.ox.ac.uk/gsdl/cgi-bin/library?site=loc
  alhost&a=p&p=about&c=politi04&ct=0&l=en&w=iso-8859-1.

Manuscript Collections

Arquivo Nacional da Torre do Tombo, Lisbon
The Garrick Club, London
John Johnson Collection, Bodleian Library, Oxford
Kathleen Barker Archives, University of Bristol Theatre Collection, Bristol
London Metropolitan Archives, London
Theatre Collection, Victoria & Albert Museum, London

Newspapers and Periodical Reviews

Annual Review and History of Literature for 1808
The Anti-Jacobin; or, Weekly Examiner
The Anti-Jacobin Review and Magazine
The Bristol Gazette
The British Review, and London Critical Journal
The Edinburgh Review
The Examiner and the Theatrical Examiner
Felix Farley's Bristol Journal
The Gentleman's Magazine and Historical Chronicle
Lloyd's Evening Post and Packet
The Monthly Mirror: Reflecting Men and Manners; With Strictures on their Epitome
The Monthly Review; or, Literary Journal
The Morning Chronicle
The Morning Post and Gazeteer

The New London Review; or, Monthly Report of Authors and Books
The Poetical Register, and Repository of Fugitive Poetry for 1809
The Quarterly Review
The Scourge; or, Monthly Expositor of Imposture and Folly
The Times
The True Briton

Published Works

Anon. *An Account of the Central or Supreme Junta of Spain, its chief members, and most important proceedings*. London, 1809.
———. *An Abridgement of Geography. Adorned with cuts representing the dress of each country*. London, 1800.
———. *Catalonia, A Poem; With Notes Illustrative of the Present State of Affairs In the Peninsula*. Edinburgh, 1811.
———. *The Cottage Warbler; or, New Song Book. Containing all the fashionable Songs, now singing at the Theatre Royal, Nobility's and Private Concerts, Royal Circus, Sadler's Wells, Royalty Theatre, &c. With a collection of Toasts and Sentiments*. London, [1809].
———. *The Covent Garden Journal. Embellished with four views*. London, 1810.
———. *A Critique of the Tragedy of 'Pizarro' as represented at Drury-Lane Theatre with such uncommon applause. To which is added A New Prologue, that has not yet been spoken*. London, 1799.
———. *The Entertaining and Amusing Song Book. To which is added a collection of Toasts and Sentiments*. London, [1808].
———. *Fairburn's Comic Constellation, or Eccentric Repository for 1814, Embracing an Extensive, Eccentric, Curious, & Droll Collection of New Songs, Now singing and lately sung at the Theatres Royal, Sadler's Wells, &c … Embellished with a Comic Coloured Frontispiece*. London, 1814.
———. *Fatal Jealousy; or, Blood Will Have Blood! Containing the History of Count Almagro and Duke Alphonso…*. London, 1807.
———. *The First of Two Grand Concerts of Oratorial and Miscellaneous Music, at the Theatre Royal, Bristol. On Thursday and Friday Evening in Easter Week, March 30 and 31, 1815*. Bristol, 1815.
———. *A Garland of New Songs Containing 1) Yo Heave Ho, 2) Paddy's Description of Pizarro, 3) My Grandmother's Eye-Water, 4) The Thorn, 5) The Parson*. Newcastle-Upon-Tyne, 1800.
———. *A History of the Campaigns of the British Forces in Spain and Portugal: Undertaken to Relieve those countries from the French Usurpation; comprehending Memoirs of the Operations of this Interesting War, characteristic reports of the Spanish and Portuguese Troops, and Illustrative Anecdotes of the Distinguished Conduct in individuals, whatever their rank in the Army*. London, 1812.

————. *The Jubilee; or, John Bull in his Dotage. A Grand National Pantomime; As it was to have been acted By His Majesty's Subjects, on the twenty-fifth of October, 1809. By the Author of 'Operations of the British Army in Spain'*. London, 1809.

————. *Liberty, above all things; and Conflagrations on Theatre, Manufactories, &c prevented or greatly checked*. London, 1809.

————. *Manifesto of the Spanish Nation, to the Other Nations of Europe*. London, 1808.

————. *A Memoir of the Life of R.B. Sheridan, Esq; with a Concise Critique upon the New Tragedy Entitled Pizarro*. London, 1799.

————. *Mr Fox's Title to Patriot, and Man of the People, Disputed, and the Political Conduct of Mr. Sheridan and His Adherents Accurately Scrutinised; in a letter to His Grace the Duke of Norfolk*. London, 1806.

————. *The Muse's Bower for the Year 1814; Being A New Selection of Fashionable and Popular Songs. Now singing at Sadler's Wells, Theatres Royal Drury Lane and Covent Garden, Surrey Theatre, Astley's, &c &c. Together with those lately sung at Vauxhall*. London, 1814.

————. *The Music of 'Pizarro'. A Play, as now Performing at the Theatre Royal Drury Lane with unbounded applause. The Music composed and Selected by Michael Kelly*. London, [1799].

————. *The Musical Olio: or, The Songster's Summer Companion. Containing all the most approved Songs and Duetts now singing at the Lyceum, Sadler's Wells, Haymarket, and Royal Circus &c Including that celebrated song of 'The Mail Coach'*. London, [1811].

————. *The New Sadler's Wells Songster for 1809. Being a collection of the Newest Songs, Now singing at the above and other places of public amusement*. London, 1809.

————. *Pizarro. A New Song*. Lincoln, 1799.

————. *Pizarro and Alonzo; or, Industry Better than Gold: An Instructive Story*. York, [n.d.].

————. *The Pleasing Songster, or, Harmonic Companion, for the present year. Containing the most approved, popular, and favourite New Songs, that are now singing and lately sung at Vauxhall, Sadler's Wells, and Lyceum, the Theatres Royal, Polite Concerts, Harmonic Meetings, and Convival Parties*. London, [18—].

————. *The Political Dramatist of the House of Commons in 1795. A Satire*. London, 1796.

————. *The Rebellion; or, All in the Wrong: A Serio-Comic hurly-burly in scenes, as it was performed for two months at the New Theatre Royal, Covent Garden – to which is added A Poetical Divertissement, concluding with a panoramic view of the new theatre, in prose*. London, 1809.

————. *Recitatives, duets, trios, choruses &c, with a description of the scenery, and other decorations, also the fables and arguments of the various pieces now performing at the Aquatic Theatre, Sadler's Wells*. London, 1808.

————. *Recitatives, duets, trios, choruses &c, with a description of the scenery, and other decorations, also the fables and arguments of the various pieces now performing at the Aquatic Theatre, Sadler's Wells*. London, 1809.

————. *The Regency Collection. Containing the newest songs, now singing at Covent Garden Theatre, Sadler's Wells, Astley's, &c &c*. London, [1811–1815].

————. *The Sadler's Wells Harmonist for 1810, forming a Lyric Collection of English, Irish, and Scotch Songs, singing at the Theatres & other places of amusement*. London, [1810].

————. *A Select British Theatre; Containing All the Plays Formerly Adapted to the Stage by Mr. Kemble: Revised by Him, with additional alterations*. London, 1815.

————. *Smeeton's Selection of the Most Approved Songs for 1809. As Sung at Vauxhall, Hay-market, Sadler's Wells, Circus, Astley's, &c in 'The African'; 'Yes, or No'; 'Harlequin Highflyer'; 'Spanish Patriots'; 'England's Glory'; 'Elfrida'*. London, 1809.

————. *Some Documents Respecting the History of the Late Events in Spain: Being, 1-'A Plain exposition of the reasons which occasioned the journey of Ferdinand VII to Bayonne, in April, 1808', by Don Juan de Escoiquiz, formerly tutor to His Catholic Majesty, and then his Counsellor of State &c &c. 2-'Remarks on the Preceding Work', by the Counsellor of State, Don Pedro de Cevallos. 3-'A Full Abstract of A Petition Addressed to King Ferdinand VII by sixty-nine members of the Cortes of Madrid, requesting his Majesty to abolish the new Constitution of Spain, and to re-establish the Inquisition, with the old form of government, under certain amendments'*. London, 1815.

————. *Songs, Duets, Trios, Chorusses &c with a description of the scenery, and other decorations. Also fables and arguments, of the various pieces performing at the Aquatic Theatre, Sadler's Wells*. London, 1810.

————. *Songs, Duets, Trios, Chorusses &c with a description of the scenery &c also fables and arguments of the various pieces performed at the Aquatic Theatre, Sadler's Wells*. London, 1811.

————. *The Songster's Companion. A Choice Collection, of more than two hundred modern songs. To which is added, a selection of toasts & sentiments*. 12th ed. London, 1800.

————. *The Spirit of the Public Journals for 1799. Being an impartial selection of the most exquisite essays and jeux d'esprits…with explanatory notes*. London, 1800.

————. *The Struggles of Sheridan; or, The Ministry in Full Cry*. London, 1790.

————. *The Theatrical Song Book for 1810. Containing all the Comic and other Songs, sung at the Theatres, Astley's, Circus, and Sadler's Wells. Including the much-admired Song, 'The Mail-Coach', Sung by Mr Matthews, with unbounded applause, To which are added Toasts and Sentiments*. London, [1810].

————. *The Thespian Preceptor; or, A Full Display of The Scenic Art: including Ample and Easy Instructions for Treading the Stage, Using Proper Action,*

Modulating the Voice, and expressing the several dramatic positions. London, 1811.

———. *A Tour through the principal provinces of Spain and Portugal performed in the year 1803, with cursory observations on the manners of the inhabitants*. London, 1806.

———. *The Warbler for 1808: containing all the new songs sung at the Theatres Royal, Vauxhall, Astley's, Sadler's Wells, Royal Circus, &c. To which are added, those sung by Mr Incledon in his new entertainment called 'A Voyage to India'*. Lambeth, [1808].

———. *The Whim of the Day, (for 1800). Being an Entertaining Selection of the Choicest and Most approved Songs, Now Singing at the Theatres-Royal, Anacrontic Society, the Beef-Steak Club, And Other Convival and Polite Assemblies*. London, 1800.

[Adams, John]. *The History of Spain, from the First Settlement of the Colony of Gades, by the Phoenicians to the Establishment of the Independence of the United Provinces, and death of Philip II. Collected from the most authentic documents*. 2 vols. London, 1814.

Andrews, John. *Characteristical Views of the Past and of the Present State of the People of Spain and Italy. Addressed to an English Traveller*. London, 1808.

Anquetil, Louis-Pierre. *A Summary of Universal History ... Exhibiting the rise, decline, and revolutions of the different nations of the world, from the creation to the present time*. 9 vols. Vol. 7. London, 1800.

Aulnoy, Countess d' [Marie Catherine]. *The Lady's Travels into Spain: or, A genuine relation of the religion, laws, commerce, customs, and manners of that country ... in a series of letters to a Friend at Paris*. 2 vols. London, 1808.

Baillie, Joanna. 'Introductory Discourse'. In *A Series of Plays: In Which It Is Attempted to Delineate the Stronger Passions of the Mind, Each Passion Being the Subject of a Tragedy and a Comedy* [1798], introduced by Caroline Franklin. London: Routledge/Thoemmes Press, 1996.

———. *De Monfort* [1798]. In *Seven Gothic Dramas*, edited by Jeffrey Cox. Athens: Ohio University Press, 1992.

Bardsley, Samuel Argent. *Critical Remarks on 'Pizarro', a Tragedy, taken from the German drama of Kotzebue and adapted to the English stage by Richard Brinsley Sheridan. With incidental observations on the subject of the Drama*. London, 1800.

Barker, Henry Aston. *A Short Description of Badajoz, and the surrounding country; With Extracts from the London Gazette Explanatory of the Picture Exhibiting in the PANORAMA, Leicester Square, Representing the Siege in 1812. Taken from the Fort La Picurina*. London, 1813.

Beaumont, Andrew. *The History of Spain, from the earliest accounts to the present times; with a geographical view of the Peninsula*. London, 1809.

Benson, Robert. *Britain's Glory; or, A Trip to Portsmouth, a musical entertainment. As it is performed at the Theatre Royal in the Hay-Market*. London, 1794.

Blayney [Major-General]. *Narrative of a Forced Journey through Spain and France as a Prisoner of War, in the years 1810 to 1814*. 2 vols. London, 1814.

Boaden, James. *Cambro-Britons; An Historical Play in Three Acts*. London, 1798.

Boswell, James. *On the Profession of a Player: Three Essays*. 'Now reprinted from *The London Magazine*, for August, September, and October, 1770'. Suffolk: Elkin Mathews & Marrot Ltd, 1929.

Bourgoing, Jean François baron de. *Post Roads of Spain, with the Distance in Spanish leagues. Illustrated with A Map of the Roads, in which the Posts are marked with the greatest accuracy*. London, 1808.

Bourke, Thomas. *A Concise History of the Moors in Spain, from their invasion of that kingdom to their final expulsion from it*. London, 1811.

Bradford, Rev. William. *Sketches of the Country, Character, and Costume in Portugal and Spain, Made During the Campaign, and on the Route of the British Army in 1808 and 1809…*. London, 1809.

Brayley, Edward Wedlake. *Historical and Descriptive Accounts of the Theatres of London*. Drawn and Engraved by the Late Daniel Havell. London, 1826.

[Brewer, George]. *The Life of Rolla: A Peruvian Tale … By the author of 'The Siamese Twins'*. London, 1800.

[Briggs, James]. *The History of Don Francisco de Miranda's Attempt to Effect a Revolution in South America: In a Series of Letters. To which are annexed Sketches of the Life of Miranda, and Geographical Notices of Caracas*. Boston, 1808.

Britton, John. *Sheridan and Kotzebue: The Enterprising Adventures of Pizarro, Preceded by a Brief Sketch of the Voyages and Discoveries of Columbus and Cortez, To which are subjoined the Histories of Alonzo and Cora*. London, 1799.

Bromley, Walter. *Treatise on the Acknowledged Superiority of the French over the English Officer in the Field. Extract from an intended Publication called 'Campaigning Made Easy', Recommended to Officers going to Spain and Portugal. A Farewell Letter to the Officers of the Welch Fusiliers, and an Essay on Happiness*. London, 1812.

Broughton, Samuel Daniel. *Letters from Portugal, Spain, & France, written during the Campaigns of 1812, 1813, & 1814, Addressed to a Friend in England. Describing the Leading Features of the Provinces Passed Through, and the State of Society, Manners, Habits &c. of the People*. London, 1815.

Burke, A. *Spain! Her Patriots! And Old England! A Poem; Also An Address of Condolence*. London, 1808.

Burroughs, George Frederick. *A Narrative of the Retreat of the British Army from Burgos in a Series of Letters. With an Introductory Sketch of the Campaign of 1812; and Military Character of the Duke of Wellington*. Bristol, 1814.

Byron, George Gordon. *Childe Harold's Pilgrimage*. In *The Complete Poetical Works*, edited by Jerome J. McGann. 7 vols. Vol. 2. Oxford: Clarendon Press, 1980.

Camden, Theophilus. *The History of the War in Spain and Portugal from its Commencement to the Triumphal entry of Lord Wellington into the French Territory, illustrated with anecdotes, civil, military, and political, to which are added Memoirs of the Life of Lord Wellington, and Biographical sketches from imminent commanders....* London, 1813.

Campe, J.H. *Pizarro: or, The Conquest of Peru. Being a Continuation of The Discovery of America. For the Use of Children and Young Persons.* Translated by Elizabeth Helme. Birmingham, 1800.

Carleton, George. *Memoirs of George Carleton, an English Officer. Including Anecdotes of the War in Spain under the Earl of Peterborough, and many interesting particulars relating to the Manners of the Spaniards in the beginning of the last century. Written by Himself.* 4th ed. Edinburgh, 1809.

Carr, John. *Descriptive Travels in Spain and the Balearic Isles in the Year 1809.* London, 1811.

Cevallos, Don Pedro. *An Exposure of the Arts and Machinations which led to the usurpation of the Crown of Spain and the means pursued by Bonaparte to carry his views into effect.* London, 1808.

Clinton, Henry. *A Few Remarks Explanatory of the Motives which Guided the Operations of the British Army During the Late Short Campaign in Spain.* London, 1809.

Cobb, James. *The Siege of Belgrade; A Comic Opera in Three Acts. As it is performed at the Theatres-Royal in London and Dublin.* Dublin, [1791].

Cobbett, William. *The Political Proteus: A View of the Public Character and Conduct of R.B. Sheridan, Esq.* London, 1804.

Code, H.B. *The Songs, Duetts, Glees, &c in the Opera of The Spanish Patriots A Thousand Years Ago, set to music by Sir John Stevenson.* London, 1812.

———. *The Spanish Patriots 1000 Years Ago* [1812]. Huntington Library Larpent Collection 1733. British Library Microfiche F254/490/1 & 2.

Coleridge, Samuel Taylor. *The Collected Works of Samuel Taylor* Coleridge, edited by Kathleen Coburn, et al. Vol. 7: *Biographia Literaria; or, Biographical Sketches of my Literary Life & Opinions,* edited by James Engell and W. Jackson Bate. Princeton: Princeton University Press, 1983.

———. *The Collected Works of Samuel Taylor* Coleridge, edited by Kathleen Coburn, et al. Vol. 3: *Essays On His Own Times in 'The Morning Post' and 'The Courier',* edited by David V. Erdman. 3 vols. Princeton: Princeton University Press, 1978.

———. *The Collected Works of Samuel Taylor Coleridge,* edited by Kathleen Coburn, et al. Vol. 5: *The Friend,* edited by Barbara E. Rooke. 2 vols. London: Routledge & Kegan Paul, 1969.

———. *The Collected Works of Samuel Taylor Coleridge,* edited by Kathleen Coburn, et al. Vol. 8: *Lectures 1808–1819 on Literature,* edited by R.A. Foakes. 2 vols. London: Routledge & Kegan Paul, 1987.

————. *The Collected Works of Samuel Taylor Coleridge*, edited by Kathleen Coburn, et al. Vol. 16: *Osorio*, in *Poetical Works: Plays III.1*, edited by J.C.C. Mays. Princeton: Princeton University Press, 1978; 2001.

————. *The Collected Works of Samuel Taylor Coleridge*, edited by Kathleen Coburn, et al. Vol. 16: *Remorse*, in *Poetical Works: Plays III.2*, edited by J.C.C. Mays. Princeton: Princeton University Press, 1978; 2001.

————. *Collected Letters of Samuel Taylor Coleridge*, edited by Earl Leslie Griggs. 6 vols. Oxford: Clarendon Press, 1956–1971.

————. *Coleridge's Criticism of Shakespeare: A Selection*, edited by Richard A. Foakes. London: The Athlone Press, 1989.

————. *The Notebooks of Samuel Taylor Coleridge*, edited by Kathleen Coburn. 5 vols in 10 books. Vol. 3. London: Routledge, 1957; 2002.

Collins, Francis. *Voyages to Portugal, Spain, Sicily, Malta, Asia Minor, Egypt, &c, &c, from 1706 to 1801. With Historical Sketches and Occasional Reflections, both Moral and Religious*. Philadelphia, 1809.

Colman, George (the Younger). *Inkle and Yarico*. London, 1787.

————. *The Mountaineers; A play ... first performed at the Theatre Royal, Haymarket, on Saturday, August 3 1793*. London, 1795.

————. *The Surrender of Calais ... as performed at the Little Theatre Hay-Market*. Dublin, 1792.

Cottle, Joseph. *Reminiscences of Samuel Taylor Coleridge and Robert Southey*. London, 1847.

Cowley, Hannah. *A Bold Stroke for a Husband* [1783]. In *The Broadview Anthology of Romantic Drama*, edited by Jeffrey N. Cox and Michael Gamer. Lancashire: Broadview Press, 2003.

————. *The Maid of Arragon: A Tale*. London, 1780.

Coxe, William. *Memoirs of the Kings of Spain of the House of Bourbon: From the Accession of Philip V to the death of Charles III. 1700 ... to ... 1788, drawn from original and unpublished documents*. 2nd ed. 5 vols. Vol. 1. London, 1815.

Crocker, John Wilson. *The Battles of Talavera: A Poem*. 6th ed. Corrected with some additions. London, 1810.

Cross, J.C. *Circusiana; or, A Collection of the most favourite Ballets, Spectacles, Melo-Drames, &c Performed at the Royal Circus, St George's Fields*. London, 1809.

————. *The History, Murders, Life, and Death of Macbeth: And a Full Description of the Scenery, Action, Chorusses, and Characters of the Ballet of Music and Action of that Name*. 1809. Reprinted by A.C. Sprague. In *All These to Teach: Essays in Honor of C.A. Robertson*, edited by Robert A. Bryan, Alton C. Morris, A.A. Murphee, and Aubrey L. Williams, 80–101. Gainesville: University of Florida Press, 1965.

D'Yriarte, Don Thomas. *An Abridgement of the History of Spain, from the earliest accounts of that country to the present time. With a Geographical Description of Spain and Portugal, by the same author*. London, 1808.

Dacre, Barbarina Brand. *Gonzalvo of Cordoba* [wr. 1810]. In *Dramas, Translations, and Occasional Poems*. London, 1821.

———. *Pedrarias* [wr. 1811]. In *Dramas, Translations, and Occasional Poems*. London, 1821.

De Pons, François Raymond. *Travels in South America, during the years 1801, 1802, 1803, and 1804. Containing a Description of the Captain Generalship of Caraccas [sic], and an Account of the Discovery, Conquest, Topography, Legislature, Commerce, Finance, and National Productions of the Country. With a View of the Manners and Customs of the Spaniards and the Native Indians*. Translated from the French. 2 vols. London, 1807.

Dibdin, Charles (the Younger). *History and Illustrations of the London Theatres: Comprising An Account of the Origin and Progress of the Drama in England; with historical and descriptive accounts of the Theatres Royal, Covent Garden, Drury Lane, Haymarket, English Opera House, and Royal Amphitheatre*. London, 1826.

———. *The Battle of Salamanca; and the Fall of Madrid. A Comic Song Sung by Mr Rees Junior at Sadler's Wells*. London, 1813.

———. *Grand Aqua-Drame, Vive le Roi; or, The White Cockade*. London, 1814.

———. *Memoirs of Charles Dibdin the Younger*, edited by George Speaight. London: Society for Theatre Research, 1956.

———. *Recitatives, Duets, Trios, Chorusses etc with a description of the scenery and other decorations, also the fables and arguments of the Various pieces now performing at the Aquatic Theatre, Sadler's Wells*. London, 1809.

———. *Songs, Duets, Recitatives, Chorusses, &c and other vocal compositions; and a description of the scenery, in the New Grand Aquatic Melo-Dramatic Spectacle, called 'The White Witch; or, The Cataract of Amazonia', with the argument of the piece*. London, 1808.

———. *Songs, Glees, Duettos, &c in 'The Rent Day; or, The Yeoman's Friend'*. London, 1808.

———. *Songs, and Other Vocal Compositions, with a description of the scenery, in the New Comic Pantomime called 'Dulce Domum; or, England, Land of Freedom!'*. London, 1811.

———. *Songs and Other Vocal Compositions in the New Pantomime called 'London; or, Harlequin & Time'*. London, 1813.

——— *Songs, and Other Vocal Compositions in the New Splendid Aqua-drame, called 'Johnnie Armstrong; or, the Caledonian Outlaw'*. London, 1812.

———. *Songs and Other Vocal Compositions in the New Aquatic Romance, 'The Wild Man; or, Water Pageant' Performing at the Aquatic Theatre, Sadler's Wells*. London, 1809.

———. *Vittoria; or, Wellington's Laurels*. London, 1813.

———. *Vocal Compositions in the New Grand Aquatic Romance 'The Council of Ten; or, The Lake of the Grotto'*. London, 1811.

Dibdin, Thomas. *The Cabinet: A Comic Opera in Three Acts*. London, 1805.

————. *The English Fleet in 1342; An Historical Comic Opera, in Three Acts. As performed at the Theatre Royal, Covent Garden*. London, 1805.

————. *The Reminiscences of Thomas Dibdin, of the Theatres Royal, Covent-Garden, Drury-Lane, Haymarket, &c.* 2 vols. London, 1834.

————. *Songs, Duets, Chorusses &c in the New Divertissement called 'Orange Boven; or, More Good News'. Medley Overture and Selected Airs from the works of Dibdin, Storace, Linley, Shield, Reeve, &c &c*. London, 1813.

Dodd, William. *The Beauties of Shakespeare. Selected from Each Play: with General Index, Digesting them under proper heads*. Chiswick, 1818.

Douce, Francis. *Illustrations of Shakespeare, and of Ancient Manners: with Dissertations of the Clowns and Fools of Shakespeare; on the Collection of Popular Tales entitled Gesta Romanorum; and on the English Morris Dance*. 2 vols. London, 1807.

Dougall, John. *España maritima, or Spanish coasting pilot; containing directions for navigating the coasts and harbours of Spain, in the Atlantic and Mediterranean, with the Balearic islands and coast of Portugal. Illustrated with twenty-eight charts and plans, drawn from the Spanish surveys of Brigadier Don Vicente Tofino de San Miguel, Director of the Spanish naval Academies, &c &c &c*. Translated from the Spanish by John Dougall. London, 1812.

Dutton, Thomas. *Pizarro in Peru; or, The Death of Rolla. Being the original of the new tragedy now performing at the Theatre-Royal, Drury-Lane. Translated from the last German edition of Augustus von Kotzebue, with notes, &c. by Thomas Dutton*. 2nd ed. London, 1799.

Erskine Baker, David, Isaac Reed and Stephen Jones. *Biographia Dramatica; or, A Companion to the Playhouse*. 3 vols. Vol. 3. London, 1812.

Estrada, Alvaro Flórez. *An impartial examination of the dispute between Spain and her American colonies*. Translated by William Burdon. London, 1812.

Fenwick, John. *The Indian: A Farce*. London, 1800.

Foote, Samuel. *The Mayor of Garratt; A Comedy in Two Acts. As performed at the Theatres Royal*. London: 1797.

Genest, John. *Some Account of the English Stage from the Restoration in 1660 to 1830*. 10 vols. Vol. 2. Bath: 1832.

[Gillray, James]. *James Gillray 1756–1815: Drawings and Caricatures*. London: The Arts Council, 1967.

Glanville, John. *Iberia: with an Invocation to the Patriots of Spain, A Poem. To which is added War; an Ode*. London, 1812.

Godwin, William. *Don Antonio; A Tragedy in Five Acts*. London, 1800.

Gough, James. *Bristol Theatre; A Poem*. Bristol, 1766.

Guthrie, William. *A New Geographical, Historical, and Commercial Grammar: And Present State of the Several Kingdoms of the World ... To which are added, A Geographical Index*. 15th ed. Glasgow, 1799.

Hamel, Nicholas. *The World in Miniature; containing a curious and faithful account of the different countries of the world, compiled from the best authorities*. London, 1800.

Hansard, T.C., ed. *The Parliamentary History of England, from the Earliest Period to the Year 1803*. Vol. 33: *3 March 1797–30 November 1798*, Vol. 34: *December 1798–21 March 1800*, Vol. 36: *29 October 1801–12 August 1803*. London, 1818; 1819; 1820.

———. *The Parliamentary Debates from the Year 1803 to the Present Time: Forming a Continuation of the Work entitled 'The Parliamentary History of England from the Earliest Period to the Year 1803'*. Vol. 11: *April–July 1808*. London, 1812.

[Hawker, Peter]. *Journal of a Regimental Officer During the Recent Campaign in Portugal and Spain Under Lord Viscount Wellington: With a Correct Plan of the Battle of Talavera*. London, 1810.

[Hayley, William]. *The Stanzas of an English Friend to the Patriots of Spain*. London, 1808.

Hazlitt, William. *The Fight and Other Writings*, edited by Tom Paulin and David Chandler. London: Penguin Books, 2000.

———. *Lectures on the Dramatic Literature of the Age of Elizabeth*. 2nd ed. London, 1821.

Hemans, Felicia. *England and Spain; or, Valour and Patriotism*. London: 1808.

Heron, Richard. *Pizarro, or The Death of Rolla; A Tragedy in Five Acts*. London, 1799.

Hill, Mary. *The Forest of Comalva; A Novel, containing sketches of Portugal and Spain, and Part of France*. 3 vols. London, 1809.

Hobhouse, John Cam. *The Journals of John Cam Hobhouse*, edited by Peter Cochran. http://petercochran.wordpress.com/hobhouses-diary/.

Holland, Lady Elizabeth V. Fox. *The Spanish Journal of Elizabeth, Lady Holland*. London, 1910.

Hook, Theodore. *The Siege of St Quintin; or, Spanish Heroism* [1808]. Huntington Library Larpent Collection 1559. British Library Microfiche F245/700/1 & 2.

Howard, Earl Carl Frederick. *Thoughts upon the Present Condition of the Stage and upon the Construction of a New Theatre*. London, 1808.

Humboldt, Alexander von. *Political Essay in the Kingdom of New Spain: With Physical Selections and Maps Founded on Astronomical Observations, and Trigonometrical and Barometrical Measurements*. Translated from the original French by John Black. 4 vols. London, 1811.

Inchbald, Elizabeth. *The British Theatre; or, A Collection of Plays, which are acted by The Theatres Royal, Drury-Lane, Covent-Garden, and Haymarket*. 25 vols. London, 1808.

Jacob, William. *Travels in the South of Spain, in Letters Written A.D. 1809 and 1810*. London, 1811.

Jephson, Robert. *Two Strings to Your Bow; A Farce in Two Acts*. London, 1791.

Joveallanos, Don Gaspar. *Bread and Bulls, An Apologetic Oration, on the flourishing state of Spain, in the reign of King Charles IV. Delivered in the Plaza de Toros, Madrid.* Mediterranean: Printed on board His Majesty's Ship Caledonia, Off Toulon, 1813.

Juan, Don George and Ulloa, Don Antonio. *Voyage to South America: Describing at Large the Spanish Cities, Towns, Provinces, &c. on that Extensive Continent. Undertaken, by Command of the King of Spain. With notes and observations, and an account of the Brazils.* Translated by John Adams. Illustrated with Plates. 5th ed. London, 1807.

Kelly, Michael. *Reminiscences*, edited by Roger Fiske. London: Oxford University Press, 1975.

Kemble, John Philip. *John Philip Kemble Promptbooks*, edited by Charles H. Shattuck. 11 vols. Charlottesville: Published for the Folger Shakespeare Library by the University Press of Virginia, 1974.

————. *Lodoiska; An Opera, in Three Acts ... The music composed, and selected from Cherubini, Kreutzer, and Andreozzi, by Mr Storace.* 2nd ed. London, [1794].

————. *The Pannel. As altered by J. P. Kemble. From Bickerstaff's translation of Calderón's 'El escondido y la tapada'; and first acted at the Theatre Royal in Drury Lane, November 28th, 1788.* London, [1789].

————. *The Portrait of Cervantes* [1808]. Huntington Library Larpent Collection. British Library Microfiche F254/666.

Knox, Vicesimus. *Elegant Extracts: Being a Copious Selection of Instructive, Moral, and Entertaining Passages from the Most Eminent British Poets.* 6 vols. London, 1810.

Lamb, Charles. 'On The Tragedies of Shakespeare, Considered with Reference to their Fitness for Stage Representation' [1811]. In *English Critical Essays: Nineteenth Century*, edited by Edmund D. Jones. Oxford: Oxford University Press, 1916.

Lamb, George. *Whistle For It! A Comic Opera in Two Acts, as performed at the Theatre-Royal, Covent-Garden.* London, 1807.

Landor, Walter Savage. *Count Julian; A Tragedy.* London, 1812.

Lee, Sophia. *Almeyda, Queen of Granada; A Tragedy in Five Acts.* London, 1796.

Lewis, Matthew. *Alfonso; King of Castile; A Tragedy in Five Acts.* London, 1801.

————. *The Castle Spectre; A Drama in Five Acts* [1797]. In *Seven Gothic Dramas 1798–1825*, edited by Jeffrey N. Cox. Athens: Ohio University Press, 1992.

————. *The Monk* [1796], edited by Howard Anderson. Oxford: Oxford University Press, 1995.

————. *Rolla; or, The Peruvian Hero. A Tragedy in Five Acts.* 2nd ed. London, 1799.

Lillie, John. *A Narrative of the Campaigns of the Loyal Lusitanian Legion, under Brigadier General Sir Robert Wilson, Aide-de-Camp to His Majesty, and Knight of the Order of Maria Theresa, and of the Tower and Sword. With some* account of the Military Operations in Spain and Portugal during the years 1809, 1810, and 1811. London, 1812.

Lillo, George. *The Fatal Curiosity; A Tragedy. By Mr. George Lillo. Adapted for theatrical representation, as originally performed at the Theatre-Royal, Hay-Market. Regulated from the prompt-book.* London, 1796.

Livingstone, Robert R. *Essay on Sheep: Their Varieties – Account of the Merinoes of Spain, France, &c. Reflections on the Best Method of Treating Them, and Raising a Flock in the United States; Together with Miscellaneous Remarks on Sheep and Woolen Manufactures.* [n.p.], 1813.

McQueen, James. *A Narrative of the Political and Military Events, of 1815; intended to complete The Narrative of the Campaigns of 1812, 1813, and 1814.* Glasgow, 1816.

Mackinnon, Henry. *A Journal of the Campaign in Portugal and Spain, Containing Remarks on the Inhabitants, Customs, Trade, and Cultivation, of Those Countries, from the Year 1809 to 1812.* Bath, 1812.

Malcolm, J.P. *An Historical Sketch of the Art of Caricaturing. With Graphic Illustrations.* London, 1813.

Marmontel, Jean-François. *The Incas; or, The Destruction of the Empire of Peru.* 2 vols. London, 1777.

Merdant, Daniel. *The Abdication of Ferdinand; or, Napoleon at Bayonne: An Historical Play in Five Acts.* 3rd ed. London, 1811.

Montaigne, Michel de. 'On the Cannibals'. In *The Essays: A Selection.* Translated and edited with an introduction and notes by M.A. Screech. London: Penguin, 1993.

Montagu, Elizabeth. *An Essay on the Writings and Genius of Shakespeare, compared with the Greek and French Dramatic Poets. With some remarks on the misrepresentations of Mons. de Voltaire. To which are added, Three Dialogues of the Dead.* 6th ed. Corrected. London, 1810.

Moore, George. *Lives of Cardinal Alberoni, the Duke of Ripperda, and Marquis of Pombal: Three Distinguished Political Adventurers of the Last Century: Exhibiting a View of the Kingdoms of Spain and Portugal, During a Considerable Portion of that Period.* 2nd ed. London, 1814.

Moore, James. *A Narrative of the Campaign of the British Army in Spain Commanded by his Excellency Lieutenant-General Sir John Moore, &c &c &c. Authenticated by Official Papers and Original Letters.* 4th ed. London, 1809.

Murphy, James Cavanah. *The Arabian Antiquities of Spain.* London, 1815.

Neale, Adam. *Letters from Portugal and Spain: An Account of the Operations of the Armies Under Sir Arthur Wellesley and Sir John Moore from the Landing of the Troops in Mondego Bay to the Battle at Corunna. Illustrated with Engravings by Heath, Fittler, Warren, from the drawings made on the spot.* London, 1809.

Nightingale, Rev. Joseph. *London and Middlesex; or, An Historical, Commercial, & Descriptive Survey of the Metropolis of Great-Britain, including Sketches of its Environs, and a Topographical Account of the most remarkable places in the above county.* Vol. 3. London, 1815.

O'Keefe, John. *The Castle of Andalusia; A Comic Opera in Three Acts. As performed at the Theatre-Royal, Covent-Garden.* London, 1794.

———. *The Poor Soldier; A Comic Opera, in Two Acts. As performed at the Theatre-Royal, Covent-Garden.* London, 1800.

[Officer of the Staff]. *Operations of the British Army in Spain: Involving Broad Hints to the Commissariat, and Board of Transports: with Anecdotes Illustrative of the Spanish Character.* London, 1809.

Oldys, William, ed. *The Harleian Miscellany: A Collection of Scarce, Curious, and Entertaining Pamphlets and Tracts, as well in manuscript as in print. Selected from the library of Edward Harley, Second Earl of Oxford. Interspersed with Historical, Political, and Critical Annotations, by the late William Oldys, Esq. and Some Additional Notes, by Thomas Park, FSA.* 10 vols. Vols. 2 & 3. London, 1809; 1811.

Ormsby, Rev. James Wilmont. *An Account of the Operations of the British Army and the state and sentiments of the people of Portugal and Spain, during the campaigns of the years 1808 & 1809. In a Series of Letters.* 2 vols. London, 1809.

Oulton, Walley Chamberlain. *The Beauties of Kotzebue; Containing the most interesting Scenes, Sentiments, Speeches, &c in all his Admired Dramas Freely Translated. Corrected and Digested Under Appropriate Heads, Alphabetically Arranged, with Biographical Anecdotes of the Author, a Summary of his Dramatic Fables and Cursory Remarks.* London, 1800.

———. *A History of the Theatres of London, Containing an Annual Register Of new pieces, revivals, pantomimes, &c. With Occasional Notes and Anecdotes. Being a Continuation of Victor's & Oulton's Histories from the year 1795 to 1817 inclusive.* 3 vols. London, 1818.

Padron, Antonio. *The Tribunal of the Inquisition; and Bread and Bulls. The Speech of Doctor D. Antonio Joseph Ruiz de Padron, Deputy to the Cortes, from the Canary Islands, Spoken in the sitting of January 18th, 1813, relative to the Inquisition.* Mediterranean: Printed on board His Majesty's Ship Caledonia, Off Toulon, 1813.

[Parliament of Great Britain]. *A Collection of Correspondence Relative to Spain and Portugal, Presented to Parliament in 1810.* London, 1811.

Pasley, Charles William. *Essay on the Military Policy and Institutions of the British Empire.* London, 1811.

Philipi [pseud]. *A Peep into the Theatre-Royal, Manchester; With Some Remarks on the Merits and Demerits of the Performers.* Manchester, 1800.

Phlippus Philaretes [Comber, Thomas]. *Adultery Analyzed; An Inquiry into the Causes of the Prevalence of that Vice in These Kingdoms, at the Present Day.* London, 1810.

Pinkerton, John, *A general collection of the best and most interesting voyages and travels in all parts of the world; many of which are now first translated into English. Digested on a new plan, by John Pinkerton, Author of Modern Geography, &c &c. Illustrated with Plates*. London, 1814.

Plumptre, Anne. *Pizarro. The Spaniards in Peru; or, The Death of Rolla*. London, 1799.

Plumptre, James. *Discourses on the Stage. Four Discourses on Subjects Relating to the Amusement of the Stage*. London, 1808.

Pocock, Isaac. *John of Paris; A Comic Opera, in Two Acts….* London, 1814.

———. *The Miller and His Men, A Melo-Drama in Two Acts….* London, 1813.

Poole, John. *Hamlet Travestie: In Three Acts. With Burlesque Notes, in the manner of the most celebrated commentators; And other Curious Appendices*. London, 1811.

———. *Intrigue; or, The Bath Road. A Comic Interlude in One Act*. London, [1857–1867].

———. *Othello Travestie: In Three Acts. With Burlesque Notes, in the manner of the most celebrated commentators; And other Curious Appendices*. London, 1813.

[Porter, Robert Ker]. *Letters from Portugal and Spain: Written During the March of the British Troops Under Sir John Moore. With a Map of the route and appropriate engravings*. London, 1809.

Power, George. *The History of the Empire of the Musulmans in Spain and Portugal, from the First Invasion of the Moors, to their Ultimate Expulsion from the Peninsula*. London, 1815.

Preston, Thomas. *The Jubilee of George the Third. Jubilee Jottings*. London, 1887.

Pugin, A. and Thomas Rowlandson. *The Microcosm of London; or, London in Miniature*. 3 vols. London: Methuen & Co., 1904.

Puigblanch, Antonio. *The Inquisition Unmasked. Being an Historical and Philosophical Account of that Tremendous Tribunal, Founded on Authentic Documents and Exhibiting The Necessity of its Suppression, as a means of reform and regeneration. Written and published at a time when the National Congress of Spain was about to deliberate on this important measure*. Translated by William Walton. London, 1816.

Raymond, George. *The Life and Enterprises of R.W. Elliston, Comedian*. Illustrated by George Cruikshank and 'Phiz'. London, 1857.

Rede, Leman Thomas. *The Road to the Stage. Contains clear and ample instructions for obtaining theatrical engagements To which is added a list of the London Theatres; Copies of their Rules and Articles of Engagement; An Account of the Dramatic Author's Society; The Members; Scale of Prices; and A Copy of the Dramatic Copyright Act*. New Edition: Revised and Improved. London, 1836.

Robinson, Henry Crabb. *Diary, Reminiscences, And Correspondence of Henry Crabb Robinson*, selected and edited by Thomas Sadler. 3 vols. Vol. 1. London, 1869.

————. *The London Theatre 1811–1866: Selections form the Diary of Henry Crabb Robinson*, edited by Eluned Brown. London: The Society for Theatre Research, 1966.

Rocca, M. de. *Memoirs of the War of the French in Spain*. Translated from the French by Maria Graham. London, 1815.

Ryan, Richard. *Dramatic Table-Talk: or, Scenes, Situations and Adventures, Serious & Comic, in Theatrical History & Biography*. 3 vols. London, 1825.

Sarrazin, Jean. *History of the War in Spain and Portugal, from 1807 to 1814. By General Sarrazin, one of the Commanders of the Legion of Honour; and formerly Chief of the Staff in the Corps of the Prince Royal of Sweden. Illustrated with a Map of Spain and Portugal, exhibiting the routes of the various armies*. London, 1815.

Schiller, Friedrich. *Don Carlos*. Translated by Georg Noehden and John Stoddart. London, 1798.

Scot, Elizabeth. *Alonzo and Cora, with other Original Poems, principally Elegiac*. London, 1801.

Scott, Honoria [Fraser, Susan]. *Amatory Tales of Spain, France, Switzerland, and the Mediterranean. Containing 'The Fair Andalusian'; 'Rosolia of Palermo'; and 'The Maltese Portrait'. Interspersed with pieces of original poetry*. 3 vols. London, 1810.

Scott, Jane. *Eccentricities; or, Mistakes at Madrid; or, The Witch of the Village: A Burletta* [1814]. Huntington Library Larpent Collection 1836. British Library Microfiche F 254/90/1 & 2.

————. *Songs, Chorusses, Duetts, Trios, &c in 'The Bashaw; or, Midnight Adventures of Three Spaniards'. From a Spanish Tale. A Melo-Dramatic Spectacle*. London, 1809.

————. *Songs, Duets, and Chorusses in the New Serio-Comic Burletta, entitled 'Disappointments; or, Love in Castille'*. London, 1810.

Scott, Walter, ed. *A Collection of Scarce and Valuable Tracts, on the Most Interesting and Entertaining Subjects. But Chiefly such as relate to the History and Constitution of These Kingdoms. Selected from an Infinite Number in Print and Manuscript, in the Royal, Cotton, Sion, and other Public, as well as Private, Libraries; Particularly that of the Late Lord Somers*. 2nd ed. 13 vols. Vols. 2 & 13. London, 1809; 1815.

————. *The Letters of Sir Walter Scott*, edited by H.J.C. Grierson. 12 vols. Vol 2: 1808–1811 & Vol. 3: *1811–1814*. London: Constable, 1932–1937.

————. *The Vision of Don Roderick: A Poem*. Edinburgh: James Ballantyne; London, 1811.

Semple, Robert. *Observations on a Journey through Spain and Italy to Naples*. 2nd ed. 2 vols. London, 1808.

————. *A Second Journey in Spain in the Spring of 1809…*. 2nd ed. London, 1812.

————. *Sketch of the present state of Caracas; including a journey from Caracas through La Victoria and Valencia to Puerto Cabello*. London, 1812.

Shakespeare, William. *King Richard II.* In *The Plays of William Shakspeare* [*sic*]. *In fifteen volumes. With the corrections and illustrations of various commentators. To which are added, notes by Samuel Johnson and George Steevens.* 4th ed. Revised and augmented (with a glossarial index) by the editor of Dodsley's collection of Old Plays. 15 vols. Vol. 8. London, 1793.

Sheridan, Richard Brinsley. *The Dramatic Works of Richard Brinsley Sheridan*, edited by Cecil Price. 2 vols. Oxford: Clarendon Press, 1973.

Smith, Adam. *The Theory of Moral Sentiments* [1759; 1790]. The Library of Economics and Liberty. http://www.econlib.org/Library/Smith/smMS1.html.

Sotheby, William. *The Siege of Cuzco: A Tragedy, in Five Acts.* London, 1800.

———. *Song of Triumph.* London, 1814.

Southey, Robert. *Carmen Triumphale, for the Commencement of the Year 1814*, edited by Lynda Pratt, Daniel E. White, Ian Packer, Tim Fulford and Carol Bolton. In Vol. 3 of *Robert Southey: Later Poetical Works 1811–1838*, edited by Tim Fulford and Lynda Pratt. London: Pickering & Chatto, 2012.

———. *The Collected Letters of Robert Southey*, edited by Carol Bolton and Tim Fulford, 'Part 3: 1804–1809'. http://www.rc.umd.edu/editions/southey_letters/ Part_Three/index.html

———. *Letters from England: By Don Manuel Alvarez Espriella. Translated from the Spanish.* 3rd ed. 3 vols. London, 1814.

———. *Letters Written During a Short Residence in Spain and Portugal, with some Account of Spanish and Portugueze Poetry.* 2 vols. London, 1797.

———. *Letters Written During a Journey in Spain and a Short Residence in Portugal.* 3rd ed. 2 vols. London, 1808.

Stockwell, Joseph. *The History of the Inquisitions; including the Secret Transactions of those Horrific Tribunals.* London, 1810.

Stothert, William. *A Narrative of the Principal Events of the Campaigns of 1809, 1810, & 1811, in Spain and Portugal. Interspersed with Remarks on Local Scenery and Manners. In a Series of Letters.* London, 1812.

Thelwall, John. *Mr Thelwall's Ode Addressed to the Energies of Britain in behalf of the Spanish Patriots.* London, 1808.

[Thriepland, Stuart Moncrieff]. *Letters Respecting the Performances at the Theatre Royal, Edinburgh, Originally Addressed to the Editor of the Scots Chronicle, Under the Signature of Timothy Plain.* Edinburgh, 1800.

Ticken, William. *Santos de Montenos; or, Annals of a Patriot Family. Founded on Recent Facts.* 3 vols. London, 1811.

Vaughan, Charles Richard. *Narrative of the Siege of Zaragoza.* 4th ed. London, 1809.

Vyse, Charles. *A New Geographical Grammar. Containing A Comprehensive System of Modern Geography, After a New and Compendious Method, to which is added an Appendix.* London, 1800.

Waldie, John. *The Journal of John Waldie: Theatre Commentaries, 1799–1830*, edited by Frederick Burwick. e-Scholarship Repository, California Digital Library. http://repositories.cdlib.org/uclalib/dsc/waldie/.

Walton, William. *An Exposé on the Dissentions of Spanish America: Containing an Account of the origin and progress of those fatal differences, which have bathed that country, in blood and anarchy….* London, 1814.

Weston, Stephen. *Remains of Arabic in the Spanish and Portuguese Languages. With a Sketch by Way of Introduction of the History of Spain, from the Invasion to the Expulsion of the Moors ... Appendix, containing a Specimen of the Introduction to the Hitpodesa Translated into three languages, the principal metre of which is that of the Sanscrit.* London, 1810.

Whittington, George Downing. *Travels, Through Spain and Part of Portugal: With Commercial, Statistical, and Geographical Details.* First American Edition. Boston, 1808.

[Wife of an Officer]. *Poems Founded on the Events of the War in the Peninsula.* London, [1819].

Williams, Helen Maria. *Peru, A Poem: in Six Cantos.* London, 1784.

Wilson, C.H. *The Myrtle and Vine; or, Complete Vocal Library. To which are added, biographical anecdotes of the most celebrated song writers.* 4 vols. Vol. 1. London, 1800.

Winston, James. *The Theatric Tourist, a facsimile of the first and only edition of 1805 preceded by a facsimile of the original prospectus.* London: The Society for Theatre Research and the British Library, 2008.

Woodley, Henry. *Portugal Delivered, A Poem. In Five Books, dedicated by permission to His Royal Highness the Duke of York.* London, 1812.

Wordsworth, William. *Concerning the Convention of Cintra: A Bicentennial Critical Edition*, edited by Richard Gravil and W.J.B. Owen. Tirril: Humanities – Ebooks, 2009.

Wright, F.B. *A History of Religious Persecutions From the Apostolic Age to the Present Time: And of the Inquisition of Spain, Portugal, and Goa.* Liverpool, 1816.

Secondary Material

Alexander, Catherine M. 'Shakespeare in the Eighteenth Century: Criticism and Research', *Shakespeare Survey* 51 (1998): 1–16.

Alford, W.E. 'The Economic Development of Bristol in the Nineteenth Century: An Enigma?'. In *Essays in Bristol and Gloucestershire History*, edited by Patrick McGrath & John Cannon, 217–51. Bristol: Bristol and Gloucestershire Archaeological Society, 1976.

Almeida, Joselyn M. 'Conquest and Slavery in Robert Southey's *Madoc* and James Montgomery's *The West Indies*'. In *Robert Southey and the Contexts of English Romanticism*, edited by Lynda Pratt, 151–65. Hampshire: Ashgate, 2006.

———. ed. *Romanticism and the Anglo-Hispanic Imaginary.* New York: Rodopi, 2010.

Altree, Ann. 'The Georgian Theatre'. In *Treasures of the Morrab: A Penzance Library that has more than Books*, edited by June Palmer. Penzance: Penwith Local History Group, 2005.

Anderson, Benedict. *Imagined Communities: Reflections on the Origin and Spread of Nationalism*. London: Verso, 1983: 2006.

Armitage, David. *Ideological Origins of the British Empire*. Cambridge: Cambridge University Press, 2000.

Arundell, Dennis. *The Story of Sadler's Wells, 1683–1964*. London: Hamish Hamilton, 1965.

Aspinall, Arthur. *Politics and the Press c.1780–1850*. Brighton, Sussex: The Harvester Press Ltd, 1949; 1973.

Atkin, Nicholas. *Priests, Prelates and People: A History of European Catholicism Since 1750*. Oxford: Oxford University Press, 2003.

Avery, Emmet, Charles Beecher Hogan, William Van Lennep, Arhur Hawley Scouten and George Winchester Stone, eds. *The London Stage 1660–1800: A Calendar of Plays, Entertainments & Afterpieces, together with Casts, Box-Receipts, and Contemporary Comment*. 11 vols. Part 1: *1660–1700* edited by William Van Leenep & Part 5: *1776–1800*, edited by C.B. Hogan. Carbondale: Southern Illinois University Press, 1960–68.

Backscheider, Paula. *Spectacular Politics: Theatrical Power and Mass Culture in Early Modern England*. London: Johns Hopkins University Press, 1993.

Baer, Marc. 'Burdett, Sir Francis, fifth baronet (1770–1844)'. In *Oxford Dictionary of National Biography*, edited by H.C.G. Matthew and Brian Harrison. Oxford: Oxford University Press, 2004. Online Edition, edited by Lawrence Goldman. http://www.oxforddnb.com/view/article/3962.

———. *Theatre and Disorder in Late Georgian London*. Oxford: Clarendon Press, 1992.

Bainbridge, Simon. *British Poetry and the Revolutionary and Napoleonic Wars*. Oxford: Oxford University Press, 2003.

———. *Napoleon and English Romanticism*. Cambridge: Cambridge University Press, 1995.

Banerji, Christine, and Diana Donald. *Gillray Observed: The Earliest Account of His Caricatures in 'London und Paris'*. Cambridge: Cambridge University Press, 1999.

Bann, Stephen. *Romanticism and the Rise of History*. New York: Twayne Publishers, 1995.

Barker, Hannah *Newspapers, Politics and Public Opinion in Late Eighteenth-Century England*. Oxford: Clarendon Press, 1998.

Barker, Kathleen. *Bristol at Play: Five Centuries of Live Entertainment*. Wiltshire: Moonraker Press, 1976.

———. *The Theatre Royal, Bristol 1766–1966: Two Centuries of Stage History*. London: The Society for Theatre Research, 1974.

Barrell, John. *'Exhibition Extraordinary!!' Radical Broadsides of the mid-1790s*. Nottingham: Trent Editions, 2001.

————. *Poetry, Language and Politics*. Manchester: Manchester University Press, 1988.

————. *The Spirit of Despotism: Invasions of Privacy in the 1790s*. Oxford: Oxford University Press, 2006.

Barrell, John and Jon Mee, eds. *Trials for Treason and Sedition 1792–1794*. 8 vols. London: Pickering & Chatto, 2006.

Bate, Jonathan. *The Genius of Shakespeare*. London: Picador, 1997.

————. *The Romantics on Shakespeare*. London: Penguin, 1992.

————. *Shakespearean Constitutions: Politics, Theatre, Criticism, 1730–1830*. Oxford: Clarendon Press, 1989.

————. *Shakespeare and the English Romantic Imagination*. Oxford: Clarendon Press, 1986.

Belaunde, Víctor Andrés. *Bolivar and the Political Thought of the Spanish American Revolution*. Baltimore: Johns Hopkins University Press, 1938.

Bell, David. *The First Total War: Napoleon's Europe and the Birth of Modern Warfare*. London: Bloomsbury, 2007.

Benítez, Rubén. Introduction to *José María Blanco White: Vargas: Novela Española*, edited by Rubén Benítez and María Elena Francés, 9–66. Alicante: Instituto de Cultura Juan Gil-Albert, 1995.

Bindman, David. *The Shadow of the Guillotine: Britain and the French Revolution*. [London]: British Museum Publications, 1989.

Black, Jeremy. *Britain as a Military Power 1688–1815*. London: USL Press, 1999.

————. *The British Grand Tour*. London: Croom Helm, 1985.

————. *The English Press in the Eighteenth Century*. London: Croom Helm, 1987.

Bloomfield, B.C., ed. *A Directory of Rare Book and Special Collections in the United Kingdom and the Republic of Ireland*. With the assistance of Karen Potts. 2nd ed. London: Library Association Publishing, 1985; 1997.

Borsay, Peter, ed. *The Eighteenth Century Town: A Reader in English Urban History 1688–1820*. London: Longman, 1990.

————. *The English Urban Renaissance: Culture and Society in the Provincial Town 1660–1770*. Oxford: Clarendon Press, 1989.

Borsay, Peter, and Lindsay Proudfoot, eds. *Provincial Towns in Early Modern England and Ireland. Change, Convergence and Diversion*. Oxford: Published for the British Academy by Oxford University Press, 2002.

Bratton, Jacky. 'Jane Scott the writer-manager'. In *Women and Playwriting in Nineteenth-Century Britain*, edited by Tracy C. Davis and Ellen Donkin, 77–98. Cambridge: Cambridge University Press, 1999.

————. *New Readings in Theatre History*. Cambridge, Cambridge University Press, 2003.

Bratton, Jacky, Richard Allen Cave, Breandan Gregory, Heidi J. Holder, and Michael Pickering, eds. *Acts of Supremacy: The British Empire and the Stage, 1790–1930*. Manchester: Manchester University Press, 1991.

Brett-James, Antony. *Life in Wellington's Army*. London: Allen and Unwin, 1972.

Brewer, John. *The Common People and Politics, 1750–1790s*. Cambridge: Chadwyck-Healey, 1986.

———. *The Pleasures of the Imagination: English Culture in the Eighteenth Century*. London: Harper Collins, 1997.

Broers, Michael. *Europe Under Napoleon 1799–1815*. London: Holder Headline Group, 1996.

Bromwich, David. *Hazlitt: The Mind of a Critic*. Oxford: Oxford University Press, 1983.

Bruhm, Steven. *Gothic Bodies: The Politics of Pain in Romance Fiction*. Philadelphia: University of Pennsylvania Press, 1994.

Burling, William J. *Summer Theatre in London, 1661–1820, and the Rise of the Haymarket Theatre*. London: Associated University Presses, 2000.

Burroughs, Catherine. *Closet Stages: Joanna Baillie and the Theater Theory of British Romantic Women Writers*. Philadelphia: University of Pennsylvania Press, 1997.

Burwick, Frederick. *Illusion and the Drama: Critical Theory of the Enlightenment and the Romantic Era*. Philadelphia: Pennsylvania State University Press, 1991.

———. *Playing to the Crowd: London Popular Theatre, 1780–1830*. New York: Palgrave Macmillan, 2011.

———. *Romantic Drama; Acting and Reacting*. Cambridge: Cambridge University Press, 2009.

Carey, John. 'Did the Irish come from Spain? The Legend of the Milesians', *History of Ireland* 9, no. 3 'Ireland and Spain through the Ages' (Autumn 2011): 8–11.

Carlisle, Carol Jones. *Shakespeare from the Greenroom: Actors' Criticisms from Four Major Tragedies*. Chapel Hill: University of North Carolina Press, 1969.

Carlson, Julie. *In the Theatre of Romanticism: Coleridge, Nationalism, Women*. Cambridge: Cambridge University Press, 1994.

———. 'Trying Sheridan's *Pizarro*', *Texas Studies in Literature and Language* 38, no. 3/4, (Fall/Winter 1996): 359–78.

Carlson, Marvin. 'Theatre Audiences and the Reading of Performance'. In *Interpreting the Theatrical Past: Essays in the Historiography of Performance*, edited by Thomas Postlewait and Bruce A. McConachie, 82–98. Iowa City: University of Iowa Press, 1989.

Carr, Raymond. *Spain 1808–1975*. 2nd ed. Oxford: Clarendon Press, 1982.

Cass, Jeffrey. '"The Race of the Cid": Blood, Darkness, and the Captivity Narrative in Felicia Hemans's *The Siege of Valencia*', *European Romantic Review* 17, no. 3, (2006): 315–326. doi: 10.1080/10509580600816751.

Cassin-Scott, Jack. *Costumes and Settings for Historical Plays*. 5 vols. Vol. 4: *The Georgian Period*. London: The Anchor Press, 1979.

Cavanagh, Dermot, Stuart Hampton Reeves, and Stephen Longstaffe, eds. *Shakespeare's Histories and Counter-Histories*. Manchester: Manchester University Press, 2006.

Chalklin, C.W. *The Provincial Towns of Georgian England: A Study of the Building Process 1740–1820*. London: Edward Arnold, 1974.

Chancellor, E. Beresford. *The Pleasure Haunts of London during four centuries*. London: Constable & Company, 1925.

David Chandler. *Dictionary of the Napoleonic Wars*. Hertfordshire: Wordsworth Editions, 1993; 1999.

Chandler, David John. 'Norwich Literature 1788–1797: A Critical Survey'. DPhil diss., University of Oxford, 1997.

Chappell, Mike. *Wellington's Peninsula Regiments (2): The Light Infantry*. Oxford: Osprey Publishing, 2004.

Chandler, James. 'History'. In *The Oxford Companion to the Romantic Age: British Culture, 1776–1832,* edited by Iain McCalman, 355–61. Oxford: Oxford University Press, 1999.

Chandler, James and Kevin Gilmartin. 'Introduction: engaging the eidometropolis'. In *Romantic Metropolis: The Urban Scene of British Culture 1780–1840,* edited by James Chandler and Kevin Gilmartin, 1–41. Cambridge: Cambridge University Press, 2005.

Chase, Malcolm. 'From Millennium to Anniversary: The Concept of the Jubilee in Late Eighteenth- and Nineteenth-Century England', *Past & Present*, no. 129 (November 1990): 132–47.

Child, Harold Hannyngton. *The Shakespearean Productions of John Philip Kemble*. London: Published for the Shakespeare Association by Oxford University Press, 1935.

Choudhury, Mita S. 'Imperial Licenses, Borderless Topographies, and the Eighteenth-Century British Theatre'. In *Of Borders and Thresholds: Theatre History, Practice, and Theory*, edited by Michael Kobialka, 70–105. Minneapolis: University of Minnesota Press, 1999.

Christie, Ian R. *Wars and Revolutions: Britain 1760–1815*. London: Edward Arnold, 1982.

Clark, Peter. *The Transformation of English Provincial Towns 1600–1800*. London: Hutchinson, 1984.

Coffman, Ralph J. *Coleridge's Library: A Bibliography of Books Owned or Read by Samuel Taylor Coleridge*. Boston, Mass: G.K. Hall & Co., 1987.

Colley, Linda. 'The Apotheosis of George III: Loyalty, Royalty and the British Nation 1760–1820', *Past & Present*, no. 102 (February 1984): 94–129.

———. *Britons: Forging the Nation, 1707–1837*. London: Yale, 1992; 2005.

Colmer, John. *Coleridge: Critic of Society*. Oxford: Clarendon Press, 1959.

Conolly, Leonard W. *The Censorship of English Drama 1737–1824*. San Marino: The Huntington Library, 1976.

Cox, Jeffrey. 'The Death of Tragedy; or, the Birth of Melodrama'. In *The Performing Century: Nineteenth-Century Theatre's History*, edited by Tracy C. Davis and Peter Holland, 161–81. Basingtoke: Palgrave Macmillan, 2007.

————. 'The French Revolution in the English Theatre'. In *History & Myth: Essays on English Romantic Literature*, edited by Stephen Behrendt, 33–53. Detroit: Wayne State University Press, 1990.

————. 'Ideology and Genre in the British Revolutionary Drama of the 1790s', *English Literary History* 58, no. 3 (Autumn 1991): 579–610.

————. 'Spots of Time: The Structure of the Dramatic Evening in the Theater of Romanticism', *Texas Studies in Literature and Language* 41, no. 4, (Winter 1999): 403–25.

Cox, Philip. *Reading Adaptations: Novels and Verse Narratives on the Stage 1790–1840*. Manchester: Manchester University Press, 2000.

Crane, Harvey. *Playbills: A History of the Theatre in the West Country*. Plymouth: Macdonald & Evans Ltd, 1980.

Cranmer, David. 'A Batalha do Bussaco: Um retrato musical'. In *Coloquio: A Guerra Peninsular, perspectivas multidisciplinarias*, edited by Maria Leonor Machado de Sousa. 2 vols. 2: 239–44. Lisbon: Comissão Portuguesa de História Militar/Centro de Estudos Anglo-Portugueses, 2008.

————. 'Opera in Portugal or Portuguese Opera? Is there Such a Thing as Portuguese Opera?', *The Musical Times* 135, no. 1821 (November 1994): 692–6.

Crawford, Robert. *Devolving English Literature*. Oxford: Clarendon Press, 1992.

Cruz, Manuel Ivo. *O Teatro Nacional de São Carlos*. Porto: Lello & Irmão Editores, 1992.

Cunningham, John E. *Theatre Royal: The History of the Theatre Royal, Birmingham*. Oxford: George Arnold, 1950.

Daniels, Barry. *Revolution in the Theatre: French Romantic Theories of Drama*. London: Greenwood Press, 1983.

Davies, Godfrey. 'The Whigs and the Peninsular Wars', *Transactions of the Royal Historical Society*, 4th ser., no. 2 (1919): 113–31.

Davis, Leith, Ian Duncan, and Janet Sorensen. *Scotland and the Borders of Romanticism*. Cambridge: Cambridge University Press, 2004.

Davis, Tracy C. and Peter Holland, eds. *The Performing Century: Nineteenth-Century Theatre's History*. Basingstoke: Palgrave Macmillan, 2007.

Demata, Massimiliano and Duncan Wu, eds. *British Romanticism and the Edinburgh Review: Bicentenary Essays*. Basingstoke: Palgrave Macmillan, 2002.

DeRochi, Jack. 'Removing the Romantic Rubric: The Dramatic Sameness of Sheridan and Coleridge', *Restoration and Eighteenth-Century Theatre Research*, 17 (Summer–Winter 2002): 51–70.

De Man, Paul. 'The Rhetoric of Temporality'. In *Blindness and Insight: Essays in Rhetoric of Contemporary Criticism*, with an Introduction by Wlad Godzich, 187–228. 2nd ed; rev. Minneapolis: University of Minnesota, 1971; 1983.

Dobson, Michael. *The Making of the National Poet: Shakespeare, Adaptation and Authorship 1660–1769*. Oxford: Clarendon Press, 1992.

Donohue, Joseph. 'Burletta and the Early Nineteenth-Century English Theatre', *Nineteenth Century Theatre Research* 1 (Spring 1973): 29–51.

———. *Dramatic Character in the English Romantic Age*. Princeton: Princeton University Press, 1970.

Duffy, Michael. *The Englishman and the Foreigner*. Cambridge: Chadwyck-Healey, 1986.

Eagleton, Terry. *The Function of Criticism: From the Spectator to Poststructuralism*. London: Verson, 1984: rpt 1990.

Earle, Rebecca. *The Return of the Native: Indians and Myth-making in Spanish America, 1810–1930*. Durham: Duke University Press, 2007.

Eberle-Sinatra, Michael. *Leigh Hunt and the London Literary Scene: A Reception History of his Major Works, 1805–1828*. Oxon: Routledge, 2005.

Ellingson, Ter. *The Myth of the Noble Savage*. London: University of California Press, 2001.

Elliott, John. *Spain and its World 1500–1700*. London: Yale University Press, 1989.

Epstein Nord, Deborah. 'The City as Theatre: From Georgian to Early Victorian London', *Victorian Studies* 31, no. 2 (Winter 1988): 159–88.

Erdman, David. 'Coleridge as Editorial Writer'. In *Power & Consciousness*, edited by Conor Cruise O'Brien, and William Dean Vanech, 183–202. London: University of London Press Ltd, 1969.

Esdaile, Charles. *Napoleon's Wars: An International History, 1803–1815*. London: Penguin, 2007.

———. *The Peninsular War: A New History*. London: Penguin, 2002.

Everett, Barbara. 'Spanish Othello: The Making of Shakespeare's Moor', *Shakespeare Survey* 35 (1982): 101–12.

Fairclough, Mary. *The Romantic Crowd: Sympathy, Controversy and Print Culture*. Cambridge: Cambridge University Press, 2013.

Favret, Mary. *War at a Distance: Romanticism and the Making of Modern Warfare*. Princeton: Princeton University Press, 2010.

Fergus, Jan. *Provincial Readers in Eighteenth-Century England*. Oxford: Oxford University Press, 2006.

Findlay, Bill, ed. *A History of Scottish Theatre*. Edinburgh: Edinburgh University Press, 1998.

[Finsbury Central Library]. *Britain's Literary Heritage: Records of the Great Playhouses. Series One: The Sadler's Wells Archives ... A listing and guide to the Harvester Microform Collection*. Brighton: Harvester Microform, 1988.

Foulkes, Richard, ed. *Scenes from Provincial Stages: Essays in Honour of Kathleen Barker*. Essex: The Society for Theatre Research, 1994.

Franklin, Alexandra, and Mark Philp. *Napoleon and the Invasion of Britain*. Oxford: Bodleian Library, 2003.

Freeman, Lisa. *Character's Theater: Gender and Identity on the Eighteenth-Century English Stage*. Philadelphia: University of Pennsylvania Press, 2002.

Fremont-Barnes, Gregory. *The Napoleonic Wars: The Peninsular Wars 1807–1814*. Oxford: Osprey Publishing, 2002.

Fulford, Tim. *Romantic Indians: Native Americans, British Literature, & Transatlantic Culture 1756–1830*. Oxford: Oxford University Press, 2006.

Gamer, Michael. *Romanticism and the Gothic: Genre, Reception, and Canon Formation*. New York: Cambridge University Press, 2000.

Gates, David. *The Spanish Ulcer: A History of the Peninsular War*. Cambridge, MA: Da Capo Press, 1986.

Gatrell, Vic. *City of Laughter: Sex and Satire in Eighteenth-Century London*. London: Atlantic Books, 2006.

George, Mary Dorothy. *Catalogue of Political and Personal Satires Preserved in the Department of Prints and Drawings in the British Museum*. 11 vols. Vol. 6: *1784–1792*. London: Printed by Order of the Trustees, 1938.

Gibson, Jeremy and Mervyn Medlycott. *Militia Lists and Musters, 1757–1876*. Birmingham: Federation of Family History Societies, 1989; 1990.

Gikandi, Simon. *Maps of Englishness, Writing Identity in the Culture of Colonialism*. New York: Columbia University Press, 1996.

Gilmartin, Kevin. *Writing Against Revolution: Literary Conservatism in Britain 1790–1832*. Cambridge: Cambridge University Press, 2007.

Gill, Stephen. *William Wordsworth: A Life*. Oxford: Clarendon Press, 1989.

Gowen, David Robert. 'Studies in the History and Function of the British Theatre Playbill and Programme, 1564–1914'. DPhil diss., University of Oxford, 1998.

Grieve, Patricia. *The Eve of Spain: Myths of Origin in the History of Christian, Muslim, and Jewish Conflict*, Baltimore: Johns Hopkins University Press, 2009.

Hadley, Elaine. *Melodramatic Tactics: Theatricalized Dissent in the English Marketplace, 1800–1885*. Stanford: Stanford University Press, 1995.

Hall-Witt, Jennifer. *Fashionable Acts: Opera and Elite Culture in London, 1780–1880*. Durham, NH: University of New Hampshire Press, 2007.

Hartnoll, Phyllis. *The Oxford Companion to the Theatre*. 3rd ed. London: Oxford University Press, 1967.

Haslett, Moyra. *Byron's 'Don Juan' and the Don Juan Legend*. Oxford: Clarendon Press, 1997.

Hattaway, Michael, ed. *The Cambridge Companion to Shakespeare's History Plays*. Cambridge: Cambridge University Press, 2002.

Heinowitz, Rebecca Cole. *Spanish America and British Romanticism, 1777–1826: Rewriting Conquest*. Edinburgh: Edinburgh University Press, 2010.

———. '"Thy World, Columbus, Shall Be Free": British Romantic Deviance and Spanish American Revolution', *European Romantic Review* 17, no. 2, (2006): 151–9. doi: 10.1080/10509580600687723.

Heller, Janeth Ruth. *Coleridge, Lamb, Hazlitt, and the Reader of Drama*. London: University of Missouri Press, 1990.

Hembry, Phyllis. *The English Spa 1560–1815: A Social History*. London: The Athlone Press, 1990.

Highfill Jr, Philip H., Kalman A. Burnim, and Edward A. Langhans. *A Biographical Dictionary of Actors, Actresses, Musicians, Dancers, Managers, and Other Stage Personnel in London, 1660–1800*. 16 vols. Carbondale: Southern Illinois University Press, 1973–1993.

Higgins, David. *Romantic Genius and the Literary Magazine: Bibliography, Celebrity, Politics*. Oxon: Routledge, 2005.

Hobsbawm, Eric, and Terence Ranger. *The Invention of Tradition*. Cambridge: Cambridge University Press, 1983; 2004.

Holmes, Richard. *Redcoat: The British Soldier in the Age of Horse and Musket*. London: HarperCollins, 2001.

Humphreys, R.A. *Tradition and Revolt in Latin America, and Other Essays*. London: Weidenfeld and Nicholson, 1969.

Iglesias Rogers, Graciela. 'Soldiering Abroad: The Experience of Living and Fighting among Aliens during the Napoleonic Wars'. In *Britain's Soldiers: Rethinking War and Society 1715–1815*, edited by Kevin Linch and Matthew McCormack, 39–54. Liverpool: Liverpool University Press, 2014.

Jackson, Russell. 'Before the Shakespeare Revolution: Developments in the Study of Nineteenth-Century Shakespearean Productions', *Shakespeare Survey* 35, 'Shakespeare in the Nineteenth Century' (1982): 1–12.

Jones, Robert W. 'Sheridan and the Theatre of Patriotism: Staging Dissent during the War for America', *Eighteenth-Century Life* 26, no. 1 (Winter 2002): 24–45.

Kamen, Henry. *The Disinherited: The Exiles Who Created Spanish Culture*. London: Penguin Books, 2008.

Keymer, Thomas, and Jon Mee, eds. *The Cambridge Companion to English Literature 1740–1830.* Cambridge: Cambridge University Press, 2004.

Knight, William G. *A Major London 'Minor': The Surrey Theatre 1805–1865*. [London:] The Society for Theatre Research, 1997.

Kooy, Michael John. 'Coleridge's Francophobia', *The Modern Language Review* 95, no. 4 (October 2000): 924–41.

Kruger, Loren. 'History Plays (in) Britain: Dramas, Nations and Inventing the Present'. In *TheorizingPractice: Redefining Theatre History*, edited by W.B. Worthen with Peter Holland, 151–76. Hampshire: Palgrave Macmillan, 2003.

Krumbhaar, E.B. *Isaac Cruikshank: A Catalogue Raisonné, With a Sketch of His Life and Work*. Philadelphia: University of Pennsylvania Press, 1966.

Leask, Nigel. *Curiosity and the Aesthetics of Travel Writing 1770–1840*. Oxford: Oxford University Press, 2002.

———. 'Southey's *Madoc*: Reimagining the Conquest of America'. In *Robert Southey and the Contexts of English Romanticism*, edited by Lynda Pratt, 133–50. Hampshire: Ashgate, 2006.

Lee, Nicholas. Introduction to *The Tryal* [sic] *of the Roman Catholicks* [sic] by Henry Brooke. In *The Catholic Question in Ireland, 1762– 1829*, edited by Nicholas Lee, v–xvii. 8 vols. Vol. 1. Bristol: Thoemmes Press and Edition Synapse, 2000.

Leech, Clifford, and Thomas W. Craik. *The Revels History of Drama in English*, edited by Michael Booth, Richard Southern, Frederick and Lise-Lone Marker, and Robertson Davies. 8 vols. Vol. 6: *1750–1880*. London: Methuen, 1975–1983.

Leerssen, Joep. *Remembrance and Imagination: Patterns in the Historical and Literary Representation of Ireland in the Nineteenth Century*. Cork: Cork University Press, 1996.

Leitão, Maria do Rosario Sampaio Soares de Sousa. 'Wellington na Poesia Portuguesa'. MA diss., University Nova de Lisboa, 1990.

Lieder, Frederick. 'Bayard Taylor's Adaptation of Schiller's *Don Carlos*', *The Journal of English and German Philology* 16, no. 1 (January 1971): 27–52.

Lindsay, David W. 'Kotzebue in Scotland, 1792–1813', *Publications of the English Goethe Society*, n.s., 33 (1963): 56–74.

Loftis, John. *The Spanish Plays of Neoclassical England*. London: Yale University Press, 1973.

———. 'Whig Oratory on Stage: Sheridan's *Pizarro*', *Eighteenth Century Studies* 8, no. 4 (Summer 1975): 454–72.

Lopez, John-David. 'Recovered Voices: The Sources of *The Siege of Valencia*', *European Romantic Review* 17, no. 1 (2006): 69–87. http://dx.doi.org/10.1080/10509580500520842.

López Ocampo, Javier. 'Juan García del Río'. In *Biblioteca Virtual del Banco de la Republica*. http://www.lablaa.org/blaavirtual/biografias/garcjuan.htm.

McCann, Andrew. *Cultural Politics in the 1790s: Literature, Radicalism, and the Public Sphere*. Basingstoke: Macmillan Press Ltd, 1999.

McGann, Jerome. *Don Juan in Context*. London: John Murray, 1976.

McPherson, Heather. 'Caricature, Cultural Politics, and the Stage: The Case of *Pizarro*', *Huntington Library Quarterly* 70, no. 4 (December 2007): 607–31.

MacMillan, Dougald. *Catalogue of the Larpent Plays in the Huntington Library*. San Marino, CA: San Pasqual Press, 1939.

Macaulay, Neil. *Dom Pedro: The Struggle for Liberty in Brazil and Portugal 1798–1834*. Durham: Duke University Press, 1986.

Macy, Laura. *The Grove Book of Opera Singers*. Oxford: Oxford University Press, 2008.

Macy, Peter T. *Eighteenth-Century Views of Bristol and Bristolians*. Bristol: Bristol Branch of the Historical Association, 1966.

Mahoney, Charles. 'Chapter 26: Coleridge and Shakespeare'. In *The Oxford Handbook of Samuel Taylor Coleridge*, edited by Frederick Burwick, 499–514. Oxford: Oxford University Press, 2009.

Mander, Raymond and Joe Mitchenson. *Lost Theatres of London*. London: New English Library, 1968; 1976

Matlaw, Myron. 'English versions of *Die Spanier in Peru*', *Modern Language Quarterly* 16, no. 16 (1995): 63–9.

———. '"This is Tragedy!!!": The History of *Pizarro*', *The Quarterly Journal of Speech* 43 (1957): 288–94.

Maxted, Ian. *The London Book-Trades 1775–1800: A Preliminary Checklist of Members*. Surrey: Unwin Brothers Ltd, 1977.

Mayer, David. *Annotated Bibliography of Pantomime and Guide to Study Sources*. London: Commission for a British Theatre Institute, 1975.

Meagher, Shelley. 'Islam in Irish Poetry: Thomas Moore and the Early Union Years'. DPhil diss., University of Oxford, 2006.

Melvin, Peter. 'Burke on Theatricality and Revolution', *Journal of the History of Ideas* 36, no. 3 (July–September 1975): 447–68.

Messenger, Charles. *Unbroken Service: The History of Lloyd's Patriotic Fund 1803–2003*. London: Redgate Press, 2003.

Miller, Jonathan. *Subsequent Performances*. London: Faber and Faber, 1986.

Mole, Tom, ed. *Romanticism and Celebrity Culture, 1750–1850*. Cambridge: Cambridge University Press, 2009.

Moody, Jane. 'Dictating to the Empire: Performance and Theatrical Geography in Eighteenth Century Britain'. In *The Cambridge Companion to British Theatre, 1730–1830*, edited by Jane Moody and Daniel O'Quinn, 21–41. Cambridge: Cambridge University Press, 2007.

———. *Illegitimate Theatre in London 1770–1840*. Cambridge: Cambridge University Press, 2000.

———. 'Romantic Shakespeares'. In *The Cambridge Companion to Shakespeare on Stage*, edited by Sarah Stanton and Stanley Wells, 37–57. Cambridge: Cambridge University Press, 2002.

Moore-Scott, Terry. 'Cheltenham's Theatre Royal (1782–1839), Cheltenham Art Gallery and Museum's Playbill Collection', *Cheltenham Local History Society Journal* 20 (2004): 10–17.

Mori, Jennifer. *William Pitt and the French Revolution, 1785–1795*. Edinburgh: Keele University Press, 1997.

Moro, Peter. *The Story of the Theatre Royal, Bristol, opened 1766*. Bristol: Published by the Trustees of the Theatre Royal, 1971.

Muir, Rory. *Britain and the Defeat of Napoleon 1807–1815*. London: Yale University Press, 1996.

Murray, Christopher. *Robert William Elliston: Manager*. London: The Society for Theatre Research, 1975.

Nattrass, Leonora. *William Cobbett: The Politics of Style*. Cambridge: Cambridge University Press, 1995.

Nettleton, George. 'Sheridan's Introduction to the American Stage', *PMLA* 65, no. 2 (March 1950): 163–82.

Nicoll, Allardyce. *A History of English Drama 1660–1900*. 6 vols. Vol. 4: *Early Nineteenth Century Drama: 1800–1850*. 4th ed. Cambridge: Cambridge University Press, 1955–1959.

O'Brien, Conor Cruise. 'Politics as Drama as Politics'. In *Power & Consciousness*, edited by Conor Cruise O'Brien & William Dean Vanech, 215–28. London: University of London Press Ltd, 1969.

O'Hayden, John. *The Romantic Reviewers: 1802–1824*. London: Routledge & Kegan Paul, 1969.

O'Quinn, Daniel. *Staging Governance: Theatrical Imperialism in London 1770–1800*. Baltimore: Johns Hopkins University Press, 2005.

O'Shaughnessy, David. *William Godwin and the Theatre*. London: Pickering & Chatto, 2010.

O'Toole, Fintan. *A Traitor's Kiss: The Life of Richard Brinsley Sheridan*. London: Granta Publications, 1997.

Oliver, Anthony, and Saunders, John. 'De Loutherbourg and *Pizarro*', *Theatre Notebook: A Quarterly Journal of the History and Technique of the British Theatre* 20, no. 1 (Autumn, 1965): 30–32.

Pagden, Anthony. *European Encounters with the New World, From Renaissance to Romanticism*. London: Yale University Press, 1993.

Palliser, D.M., Martin Daunton, and Peter Clark, eds. *The Cambridge Urban History of Britain*. 3 vols. Vol. 2: *1540–1840*. Cambridge: Cambridge University Press, 2000.

Park, Roy. 'Lamb, Shakespeare, and the Stage', *Shakespeare Quarterly* 33, no. 2 (Summer, 1982): 164–77.

Parker, Mark. *Literary Magazines and British Romanticism*. Cambridge: Cambridge University Press, 2000.

Paulson, Ronald. *Don Quixote in England: The Aesthetics of Laughter*. London: Johns Hopkins University Press, 1998.

———. *Representations of Revolution (1789–1820)*. London: Yale University Press, 1983.

Peck, Louis. *A Life of Matthew G. Lewis*. Cambridge, Massachusetts: Harvard University Press, 1961.

Peers, E. Allison. *The Romantic Movement in Spain: A Short History*. Liverpool: Liverpool University Press, 1949: rpt 1968.

Pellis, Valeria. 'The Fluctuating Shape of Authority: Some Reflections on *Pizarro*, from Kotzebue's Original Text to Sheridan's Great National Drama', *Textus* 20 (February 2006): 403–17.

Pemberton, Thomas Edgar. *The Theatre Royal, Birmingham 1774–1901: A Record and Some Recollections*. Birmingham: Cond Brothers, 1901.

Penny, John. 'Is the Economic History of the Bristol Region between 1780 and 1850 a Story of Relative Decline?' In *Bristol Past*, produced by Paul Johnson. http://fishponds.org.uk/brisecon.html.

[Penwith Local History Group]. *In and Around Penzance During Napoleonic Times*. Penwith: Penwith Local History Group, 2000.

Perojo Arronte, M. Eugenio. 'Imaginative Romanticism and the Search for a Transcendental Art: Coleridge's Poetry and Poetics in Nineteenth-Century Spain'. In *The Reception of S.T. Coleridge in Europe*, edited by Elinor Shaffer and Edoardo Zuccato, 135–66. London: Continuum Press, 2007.

Pratt, Mary Louise. *Imperial Eyes: Travel Writing and Transculturation*. London: Routledge, 1992.

Ramsey, Neil. *The Military Memoir and Romantic Literary Culture, 1780–1835*. Farnham: Ashgate, 2011.

Ranger, Paul. 'A Matter of Choice: A Comparison of Locations and Repertoire in Some English Provincial Theatres', *Nineteenth-Century Theatre Research* 10, no. 2 (Winter 1982): 61–84.

———. 'Thornton , Henry (bap. 1750, d. 1818)'. In *Oxford Dictionary of National Biography*, edited by H.C.G. Matthew and Brian Harrison. Oxford: Oxford University Press, 2004. Online Edition, edited by Lawrence Goldman. http://www.oxforddnb.com/view/article/38064.

Reid, Christopher. 'Patriotism and Rhetorical Contest in the 1790s: The Context of Sheridan's *Pizarro*'. In *Essays in Honour of Peter Dixon by Friends and Colleagues*, edited by Elizabeth Maslen, 232–49. London: Queen Mary and Westfield College, University of London, 1993.

Reiman, Donald, ed. *The Romantics Reviewed: Contemporary Reviews of British Romantic Writers*. 9 vols. Volumes 1 & 2: *Part A: The Lake Poets*. London: Garland, 1972.

Rhodes, R. Crompton. *Harlequin Sheridan: The Man and the Legends*. Oxford: Basil Blackwell, 1933.

Richards, Kenneth, and Peter Thomson. *Nineteenth-Century British Theatre: The proceedings of a Symposium sponsored by the Manchester University Department of Drama*. London: Methuen & Co., 1971.

Ritchie, Fiona, and Peter Sabor, eds. *Shakespeare in the Eighteenth Century*. Cambridge: Cambridge University Press, 2012.

Robertson, Ben P. 'Chapter 4: Literary Criticism and the Stage'. In *Elizabeth Inchbald's Reputation: A Publishing and Reception History*, 147–74. London: Pickering & Chatto, 2013.

Robertson, Fiona. 'British Romantic Columbiads'. In *Romanticism: Cultural Concepts in Literary and Cultural Studies*, edited by Michael O'Neill and Mark Sandy, 238–52. 4 vols. Vol. 2: Romanticism and History. Abingdon: Routledge, 2006.

Rogers, Nicholas. *Crowds, Culture, and Politics in Georgian Britain*. Oxford: Clarendon Press, 1998.

Rosenfeld, Sybil. *Georgian Scene Painters and Scene Painting*. Cambridge: Cambridge University Press, 1981.

———. *The York Theatre*. London: The Society for Theatre Research, 2001.

Roswell, George and Anthony Jackson. *The Repertory Movement: A History of Regional Theatre in Britain*. Cambridge: Cambridge University Press, 1984.

Roy, Donald, ed. *Romantic and Revolutionary Theatre, 1789–1860*. Cambridge: Cambridge University Press, 2003.

Russell, Gillian. *The Theatres of War: Performance, Politics and Society, 1793–1815*. Oxford: Clarendon Press, 1995.

———. 'Theatrical Culture'. In *The Cambridge Companion to English Literature 1740–1830*, edited by Thomas Rymer and Jon Mee, 100–18. Cambridge: Cambridge University Press, 2004.

Sachs, Jonathan. *Romantic Antiquity: Rome in the British Imagination 1789–1832*. Oxford: Oxford University Press, 2009.

Saglia, Diego. 'Borderline Engagements: The Crusades in Romantic Drama'. In *Romanticism's Debatable Lands*, edited by Claire Lamont and Michael Rossington, 186–96. Basingstoke, Hampshire: Palgrave Macmillan, 2007.

———. '"The Illegitimate Assistance of Political Allusion": Politics and the Hybridization of Romantic Tragedy in the Drama of Richard Lalor Sheil', *Theatre Journal* 58 (2006): 249–67.

———. 'Imag(in)ing Iberia: *Landscape Annuals* and Multimedia Narratives of the Spanish Journey in British Romanticism', *Journal of Iberian and Latin American Studies* 12, nos. 2 & 3 (August 2006): 123–46.

———. '"O My Mother Spain!": The Peninsular War, Family Matters, and the Practice of Romantic Nation-Writing', *English Literary History* 65, no. 2 (Summer 1998): 363–93.

———. *Poetic Castles in Spain: British Romanticism and Figurations of Iberia*. Atlanta: Amsterdam, 2000.

———. '"The true essence of romanticism": Romantic theories of Spain and the question of Spanish Romanticism', *Journal of Iberian and Latin American Studies* 3, no. 2 (December 1997): 127–45.

Salgádo, Gámini. *Eyewitnesses of Shakespeare: First hand accounts of Performances 1590–1890*. London: Sussex University Press, 1975.

Sánchez, Juan. 'Helen Maria Williams's *Peru* and the Spanish Legacy of the British Empire'. In *Romanticism's Debatable Lands*, edited by Claire Lamont and Michael Rossington, 172–83. Basingstoke, Hampshire: Palgrave Macmillan, 2007.

Scott, Matthew. 'Chapter 10: Coleridge's Lectures 1808–1819: On Literature'. In *The Oxford Handbook of Samuel Taylor Coleridge*, edited by Frederick Burwick, 190–202. Oxford: Oxford University Press, 2009.

Scrivener, Michael. 'Romanticism and the Law: The Discourse of Treason, Sedition, and Blasphemy in the Political Trials, 1794–1820'. *Romantic Circles Praxis Series*. http://www.rc.umd.edu/praxis/law/scrivener/mscrv.htm.

Semmel, Stuart. 'Radicals, Loyalists, and the Royal Jubilee of 1809', *Journal of British Studies* 46 No. 3 (July 2007): 543–69.

Sepúlveda, Christovam Ayres de Malhães. *Diccionario Bibliográfico da Guerra Peninsular: contendo a indicação de obras impressas e manuscritas em português, inglês, italiano, alemão, latim, etc.* 4 vols. Coimbra: Imprensa da Universidade, 1924–1930.

Shaffer, Elinor. 'Plumptre, Anne (1760–1818)'. In *Oxford Dictionary of National Biography*, edited by H.C.G. Matthew and Brian Harrison. Oxford: Oxford University Press, 2004. Online Edition, edited by Lawrence Goldman. http://www.oxforddnb.com/view/article/22399.

Shaw, Philip, ed. *Romantic Wars: Studies in Culture and Conflict 1793–1822*. Aldershot: Ashgate Publishing Ltd, 2000.

Staging the Peninsular War

Sherson, Erroll. *London's Lost Theatres of the Nineteenth Century: With Notes on Plays and Players seen there*. London: John Lane the Bodley Head Limited, 1925.

Shipsides, Frank, and Robert Wall. *Bristol: Maritime City*. Bristol: The Redcliffe Press, 1981.

[Society for Theatre Research]. *Studies in English Theatre History – In Memory of Gabrielle Enthoven, O.B.E. First President of the Society for Theatre Research, 1948–1950*. London: Society for Theatre Research, 1952.

Speaight, George. *The History of the English Toy Theatre*. London: Studio Vista, 1946: rpt 1969.

Steiner, George. *After Babel: Aspects of Language and Translation*. 3rd ed. Oxford: Oxford University Press, 1998.

Spencer, Jane. 'Inchbald, Elizabeth (1753–1821)'. In *Oxford Dictionary of National Biography*, edited by H.C.G. Matthew and Brian Harrison. Oxford: Oxford University Press, 2004. http://ezproxy.ouls.ox.ac.uk:2117/view/article/14374.

Spencer, William. *Records of the Militia & Volunteer Forces 1757–1945: Including Records of the Volunteers, Rifle Volunteers, Yeomanry, Imperial Yeomanry, Fencibles, Territorials and the Home Guard*. Kew, Richmond: PRO Publications, 1997.

Stallybrass, Peter, and Allon White. *The Politics and Poetics of Transgression*. London: Methuen, 1986.

Stern, Tiffany. *Rehearsal from Shakespeare to Sheridan*. Oxford: Oxford University Press, 2000.

Stockwell, La Tourette. *Dublin Theatres and Theatre Customs (1637–1820)*. Kingston, Tennessee: Kingsport Press, 1938.

Stratman, Carl Joseph. *Britain's Theatrical Periodicals 1720–1967: A Bibliography*. New York: The New York Public Library, 1972.

Suleri, Sara. *The Rhetoric of English India*. London: The University of Chicago Press, 1992.

Swindells, Julia and David Francis Taylor, eds. *The Oxford Handbook of the Georgian Theatre, 1737–1832*. Oxford: Oxford University Press, 2014.

Taylor, David Francis. '"A Vacant Space, An Empty Stage": *Prometheus Unbound, The Last Man*, and the Problem of Dramatic (Re)Form', *Keats-Shelley Review* 20 (2006): 18–31.

———. *Theatres of Opposition: Empire, Revolution, & Richard Brinsley Sheridan*. Oxford: Oxford University Press, 2012.

Taylor, George. *The French Revolution and the London Stage 1789–1805*. Cambridge: Cambridge University Press, 2000.

Thomas, Gordon Kent. *Wordsworth's Dirge and Promise: Napoleon, Wellington and the Convention of Cintra*. Lincoln: University of Nebraska Press, 1971.

———. 'Wordsworth's Iberian Sonnets: Turncoat's Creed?' *The Wordsworth Circle* 13, no. 1 (Winter 1982): 31–34.

Thomas, H. 'Shakespeare and Spain: the Taylorian lecture, 1922'. In *Studies in European Literature: The Taylorian Lectures Second Series 1920–1930*. Oxford: Clarendon Press, 1920–1930.

Thomson, Peter. *The Cambridge Introduction to English Theatre, 1660–1900*. Cambridge: Cambridge University Press, 2006.

Troubridge, St Vincent. *The Benefit System in the British Theatre*. London: The Society for Theatre Research, 1967.

Vaughan, Virginia Mason. 'Race Mattered: *Othello* in late Eighteenth-Century England', *Shakespeare Survey* 51, 'Shakespeare in the Eighteenth Century' (1998): 57–66.

Wahrman, Dror. *The Making of the Modern Self: Identity and Culture in Eighteenth-Century England*. New Haven: Yale University Press, 2004.

Waller, Philip. *The English Urban Landscape*. Oxford: Oxford University Press, 2000.

Walsh, T.J. *Opera in Dublin: 1798–1820: Frederick Jones and the Crow Street Theatre*. Oxford: Oxford University Press, 1993.

Ward, William S. *Literary Reviews in British Periodicals 1798–1820: A Bibliography with a Supplementary List of General (Non-Review) Articles on Literary Subjects, in two volumes*. 2 vols. London: Garland Publishing, 1972.

Watkins, Daniel. *A Materialist Critique of English Romantic Drama*. Florida: University of Florida Press, 1993.

Watson, J.R. *Romanticism and War: A Study of British Romanticism Period Writers and the Napoleonic Wars*. Basingstoke, Hampshire; Palgrave Macmillan, 2003.

Watson, J.S. *The Reign of George III: 1760–1815*. Oxford: Clarendon Press, 1960.

Wearing, J.P. *The London Stage: A Calendar of Plays and Players 1890–1959*. New Jersey: Scarecrow Press, 1976–1991.

Wells, Stanley. 'Shakespeare in Leigh Hunt's Theatre Criticism', *Essays and Studies* 33 (1980): 119–38.

West, Shearer. *The Image of the Actor: Verbal and Visual Representation in the Age of Garrick and Kemble*. New York: St Martin's Press, 1991.

Wheatley, Kim. *Romantic Periodicals and Print Culture*. London: Frank Class, 2003.

Wiesenthal, Christine S. 'Representation and Experimentation in the Major Comedies of Richard Brinsley Sheridan', *Eighteenth-Century Studies* 25, no. 3 (Spring, 1992): 309–30

Wiles, R.M. *Freshest Advices: Early Provincial Newspapers in England*. Ohio: Ohio State University Press, 1965.

Williams, Raymond. *Culture*. Fontana Press, Glasgow, 1981.

Wilmeth, Don B. *George Frederick Cooke: Machiavel of the Stage*. London: Greenwood Press, 1980.

Wilson, Kathleen. *The Island Race: Englishness, Empire, and Gender in the Eighteenth Century*. London: Routledge, 2002.

———. *The Sense of the People: Politics, Culture, and Imperialism in England, 1715–1785*. Cambridge: Cambridge University Press, 1995.

Wind, Astrid. 'American Indians in National Contexts: The Politics of Literary Encounter'. DPhil diss., University of Oxford, 2002.

―――. 'Irish Legislative Independence and the Politics of Staging American Indians in the 1790s', *Symbiosis: A Journal of Anglo-American Literary Relations*, 5 (2011): 1–16.

Winegarten, Renee. *Writers and Revolution: The Fatal Lure of Action*. New York, Franklin Watts Inc, 1974.

Woolf, Virginia. 'Sheridan'. In *The Essays of Virginia Woolf*, edited by Andrew McNeillie, 303–14. 3 vols. Vol. 1. London: The Hogarth Press, 1986.

Worrall, David. *The Politics of Romantic Theatricality 1787–1832: The Road to the Stage*. Basingstoke: Palgrave Macmillan, 2007.

―――. *Theatric Revolution: Drama, Censorship, and Romantic Subcultures 1773–1832*. Oxford: Oxford University Press, 2006.

Wyndham, Henry Saxe. *The Annals of Covent Garden Theatre From 1732 to 1897*. 2 vols. London: Chatto & Windus, 1906.

Subject Index

Page numbers in italics refer to figures and their captions.

Appendices Index